356 PORSCHE

Technical and Restoration Guide

ISBN 0-929758-10-2

Published by Beeman Jorgensen, Inc.
7510 Allisonville Road, Suite 126, Indianapolis, IN 46250
U.S.A.

Printed and bound in the United States of America
Cover design by Llew Kinst, Cupertino, California
Cover photography by Llew Kinst, Cupertino, California

First Printing, September 1994

Contents

Chapter 3 – Brakes, continued

Chapter 6 – Electrical, continued

Chapter 7 – Engine

Chapter 7 – Engine, continued

Chapter 10 – Fuel System, continued

Chapter 11 – Gearbox

Chapter 12 – Hardware

Chapter 13 – Interior

Chapter 19 – Suspension, continued

Foreword

The contents of this book represent nearly two decades of technical writing from the pages of *356 Registry* magazine, and behind all of the words and diagrams is a great deal of accumulated automotive wisdom. The members who contributed these articles over the years have done so with one basic motive – a deep and abiding fascination with the little bathtub-shaped car from Stuttgart. We are indebted to them for sharing the knowledge that was often earned through the "school of hard knocks", trial and error, experimentation, diligent research, perseverance and a determination to "do it well, do it properly." Why? Because these cars deserve it.

Although repair and parts manuals have existed since the first VW-based Porsche 356s rolled down the mountain roads of Austria, there were always conspicuous voids in certain areas of maintenance and "enhancement." These were addressed by American racers and later, restorers who have often led the way in making the most of the 356's performance and appearance. Along with assistance from the Porsche factory, enthusiasts in this country and around the world have filled in many blanks in the technical history of the cars. At the same time, racers have continued to put 356s in the winner's circle and restorers have set a standard of excellence in concours competition. A good deal of this activity has revolved around the 356 Registry organization for the last twenty years, and much of it is chronicled here.

The first Porsche was built nearly a half-century ago. The last 356 left the factory three decades ago and it has now been twenty years since the 356 Registry was formed. All of us who have owned, driven and loved these first Porsche models are determined that "driving in its purest form" should be preserved for future generations. We hope that this book is helpful to all who share that conviction.

Joe Johnson, Jr.

President
356 Registry, Inc.

User's Guide

As the Foreword states, the contents of this book are from the first seventeen volumes of the *356 Registry* magazine. The magazine has been published roughly every other month since October 1974. The *volume* and *number* in which each of the articles originally appeared along with the the the author's name is listed at the beginning of each article. Chapters are arranged alphabetically by major category and the Contents has detailed listings of topics in each chapter.

A technical committee has reviewed the text for accuracy. Some material was edited prior to publication to bring it up to date. Those who participated in this exercise were: Dick Koenig, Richard Miller, Ron Roland, David Seeland, Vic Skirmants and Duane Spencer. Text input and preliminary editing credit goes to Peggi Rafferty and final grammatical editing was done by William Fishback.

A number of things have changed since 1974 and the *Registry* did not always have consistency in its publishing schedule. As, such, the following list may help put those *volume* and *number* listings in perspective:

Volume 1, Number 1	October 1974
Volume 2, Number 1	October 1975
Volume 3, Number 1	October 1976
Volume 4, Number 1	October 1977
Volume 5, Number 1	October 1978
Volume 6, Number 1	October 1979
Volume 7, Number 1	October 1980
Volume 8, Number 1	October 1981
Volume 9, Number 1	October 1982
Volume 10, Number 1	November 1983
Volume 11, Number 1	May 1985
Volume 12, Number 1	December 1986
Volume 13, Number 1	June 1988
Volume 14, Number 1	October 1989
Volume 15, Number 1	October 1990
Volume 16, Number 1	January 1992
Volume 17, Number 1	May 1993

The 356 Registry, Inc. is an organization oriented exclusively to the interests, needs and unique problems of the 1948 - 1966 356 Porsche automobile owner and enthusiast. Its mission is the perpetuation of these unique vehicles via the *356 Registry* magazine, a central forum for exchange of ideas, experiences and information. Membership information, additional details, activities and list of regional 356 Porsche clubs may be obtained by writing to:

The 356 Registry
27244 Ryan Road
Warren, MI 48092

Chapter 1

Background/History

Model Changes

Vol. 1, No. 1 Vic Skirmants

1948 - 1951

The first car to use the Porsche name was a tube-framed aluminum-bodied roadster built in Gmünd, Austria, in 1948. As many of the mechanical components as possible were stock Volkswagen, except that the engine was slightly modified for more power and placed in a mid-ship location, behind the driver and in front of the rear axle. Tests of the car, including a couple of competitive hill climbs and trials, encouraged the displaced Porsche organization to go into "production" with a car, although not the roadster.

In order to offer a car with wider appeal, it was decided to build a closed coupe, with the engine behind the axle as in the VW. This resulted in some more room in the car behind the two main occupants. This space could be used for luggage or stuffing-in another younger, or smaller, or more limber passenger. The coupe also eliminated the tube frame in favor of a cheaper, more easily fabricated sheet-steel chassis.The body was still aluminum, although the doors and bumpers were steel (at least as of #37).The windshield was a simple, two-flat-piece of glass affair, with all the other "glass" in the car being plastic.Curved front quarter windows were a feature of the alloy coupes, with at least the first example having one that could be opened; subsequent cars used a fixed pane. There is no agreement on how many of these cars were built. The factory supposedly has the last one, #55; however, #57 definitely exists. If #57 is not the last one, how many more were there?

In 1950 Porsche moved back to Stuttgart, West Germany and proceeded to go into real production of a steel-bodied car. Although the "new" car looked basically like the "original 356" alloy cars, in detail examination it can be seen that not a single line or detail of construction of the chassis or body is the same. Mechanical components were, of course, still stock VW. The complete suspension, including lever-type rear shock absorbers, and non-synchromesh, or "crashbox", transmission were straight from Volkswagen. Even the engine retained the VW case, crank, connecting rods, and camshaft. The pistons and cast-iron cylinders were slightly smaller than VW to meet the rules for the 1100cc racing class. The pistons were high-compression types for more power. The heads were strictly Porsche's own design for better breathing. Two Solex 32 mm carburetors were used for the induction. Even the air cleaners were standard VW.

These early cars did not even have a tachometer, the only instruments being a speedometer and clock. Gas was checked through the large filler-cap with a scribed wooden stick. Three small "idiot" lights were for the oil pressure, generator, and turn signals. The turn signals were controlled by a small toggle switch on top of the center of the dashboard. The high-beam warning light was in the headlight switch. Seats were non-reclining and wooden trim was used on top of the doors and under the rear quarter windows, which were non-opening. The windshield was still a two-piece item, but was not as tall as the alloy cars, as well as being wider and having curved ends. All other "glass" in the cars finally became real glass.

The taillights consisted of a single round light per side for the turn signals, with a rectangular light above for the rear running lights. The single brake light was in the license light unit in the center. There was no back-up light.

The bumpers appeared to be almost part of the body, hung directly beneath the front and rear sheet metal and wrapping around to the wheel openings.

The changes for 1951 were quite minor, with the VW cast iron brake drums getting shrunk-on aluminum cooling fins during 1950. A 1300cc engine was added to the lineup with the standard 1100cc. The 1300 used larger pistons in aluminum cylinders, but kept the VW cam and crank. An oil temperature gauge and tachometer were added to the dash. The only visible outside change was the availability of swing-out rear quarter windows in place of the fixed ones.

Vol. 1, No. 4 Vic Skirmants

1951 - 1955
1951 also saw the addition of telescopic rear shock absorbers in place of

the VW lever-action type, as well as the introduction to the Porsche line of the 1500cc engine late in the year. A longer-stroke (roller bearing, made by Hirth) crank was substituted for the VW crank, different connecting rods were designed, and 40 mm Solex PICB carburetors showed up on some of these engines. The Porsche 16 in. slotted wheels, 3.25 in. wide, debuted to replace the standard VW 16 in. non-slotted wheels, which were 3.0 in. wide.

1952 was the year of drastic change. An early-1952 car is significantly different from a late-1952. The most obvious changes were: one-piece windshield replacing the two-piece, addition of aluminum trim strip in windshield and rear window rubber; different bumpers, set out from the body and higher from the ground; bumper guards added; front turn signals moved to directly beneath the headlights; rectangular rear lights made way for another set of round taillights incorporating the turn signal and brake lights. Rear reflectors were also added. The round lights front and rear grew to the familiar "bee-hive" type. A backup light replaced the early single brake light in the license-light unit, which was moved higher up to make room for the license plate, which in turn was forced higher by the new bumpers. The hood handle was slightly enlarged, and gained an opening through it.

The engine range lost the early 527 type 1500, which was replaced by the 528 1500 "Super" with hotter cam, higher compression, and the Solex 40 mm carbs; and the 546 1500 "Normal", still with stock VW cam, milder compression ratio, and 32 mm Solex carbs. The rocker arms on all engines were changed from the modified VW to Porsche's own design. The "crash-box" transmission was replaced by Porsche's famed 519 fully synchronized unit. The brakes became huge 11 in. aluminum and steel drums in place

2

of the 9 in. VW cast iron ones.

Inside the car, the wooden door sills and rear quarter window trim were changed to painted steel, and the gear shift mechanism was altered. The turn signal switch was moved to the steering column, with the flashing light inside the end of the handle. The idiot lights were enlarged, and the seats were changed somewhat in contour and seatback frame trim.

Many of the changes were found in conjunction with the older trademarks on many of the cars. I don't believe there were too many identical Porsches made during the middle six months of 1952. The cabriolets have even more complex combinations! With all the 1953 changes incorporated by the end of 1952, the only change in 1953 was the addition of the partial-flow oil filter to all the models as well as an increase of .010" in the main bearing bore in the crankcase to improve bearing retention.

1954 brought some more changes, the most obvious being the addition of horn-grill openings, the large trunk lid handle with Porsche emblem, and gold-plated "PORSCHE" insignias instead of the cast aluminum ones. Inside, the driver's seat finally got a recliner as standard equipment, a fuel gage was added, and the single cheap-looking dome light above the rearview mirror was replaced by a cheaper-looking one.

Mechanically, the transmission received a different front mount of sandwich construction in addition to the earlier "gumball" mount. 1954 was also the year of introduction for the type 540 (also known by some obscure term like "Speedster").

1955 was not a year of visual changes, but there were some nevertheless. Inside, the clutch and brake pedal shape changed from rectangular to the type used until the end of the 356 series (also used on 911, 912, and VW 914). The fuel gauge was changed from pneumatic to electrical.

Underneath, the big improvement was the addition of a sway bar up front to reduce the "dreaded oversteer". The big change, however, was the engine. Bore, stroke, and power all remained the same, but Porsche finally brought out their "own" engine. In place of the slightly-modified VW 2-piece magnesium case, Porsche introduced their own design aluminum case with detachable timing-gear cover; this was the "3-piece" case. The cam was changed slightly, the lifters were changed from VW curved-end models to the flat-faced mushroom tappets. Crankshaft, connecting rods and pistons didn't change, but the aluminum cylinders did match the different size holes in the case and heads and the different case stud spacing. The rocker arms and stands were changed further from the 2-piece case design. Carburetors, manifolds, and linkage remained the same. Finally, the crankshaft and generator pulleys were decreased in size.

Vol. 11, No. 6 Brett Johnson

Basic Model Descriptions
356

The steel bodied 356 came in two basic body styles: the coupe and the cabriolet. Both had two doors, rear-mounted air cooled engines, and sixteen inch wheels. The painted steel dash board was reminiscent of many American cars of the forties and fifties. Bodies were built by Reutter, a Stuttgart coach builder, which was eventually absorbed by the Porsche factory.

Both styles had a distinct aerodynamic appearance. Their narrow wheels, rear VW lever shocks, low horsepower engines, and non-synchronized gearboxes made them challenging to drive . . . challenging enough that with the exception of the wheels, all of these areas received major changes within the first three years of production.

3

Major changes affecting the outward appearance of the 356 model included the modification from two-piece to one-piece windshield, changes in bumpers from integrated to wrap around, and changes in tail light configuration. Other trim changes included two changes in hood handles and the appearance of horn grilles.

In 1954 (1955 model year) the low priced Speedster was introduced. It was produced for the American market and featured a low chrome framed windshield, light weight, removable soft top, and side curtains.

356A

Coupe, cabriolet, and Speedster models were continued from the 356. Major external changes were minor. A curved windshield for the coupe and cabriolet replaced the "bent" version used on the 356. 4 $1/2$ x 15 in. wheels replaced the 3 $1/4$ x 16 in. Other major changes were a more modern dashboard with a padded vinyl top and a larger displacement (1600 cc) engine.

The T-2 body change came mid-year 1957. All three models featured a lower positioned striker plate mounted by three screws (earlier cars were mounted by five). Cabriolets also featured a modified rear cowling which allowed a new optional hardtop to be fitted. Front vent windows were also featured for the first time on cabriolets. Prior to the T-2 change two other outward modifications occurred: tear-drop taillights replaced beehive units and U.S. market cars had chromed tubular overrider bars on the bumpers.

During the 1958 model year, the Speedster was replaced by the Convertible D. The "D" stood for Drauz, the coach builder. The Convertible D had a taller chrome framed windshield and roll-up side windows replacing the side curtains of the Speedster.

356B

Coupe and cabriolet body styles remained and the convertible D was replaced by the Roadster. The 356B T-5 body was totally new. While it closely resembled its predecessor, both front and rear end sheet metal was totally redesigned. The main visible change consisted of larger, higher bumpers. The headlights were also raised, and a larger chromed hood handle was present. Coupes received front vent windows. The interior was also face lifted with a new steering wheel and column. The rear seating area was modified. Mechanically, there were many changes, including new transversly finned brake drums and upgraded gearbox.

In 1961 another model was introduced: the Karmann Hardtop. It was basically a cabriolet body with a hard-top welded in place. It was built by Karmann, a German coach builder. Roadster production was changed from Drauz to D'Ieteren in Belgium:

The 1962 model year brought with it the final body change. The front lid was squared off and the fuel filler moved to the top of the right front fender. Windshield and back glass were enlarged on the coupe. From the rear, the there was an addition of a second vent grille on the rear lid.

The Roadster and Karmann Hardtop were discontinued during 1962. Karmann began producing coupes, sharing this task with Reutter.

356C

Coupe and cabriolet models were the only body styles available. The only visible change externally, aside from the model designation on the rear, was the slightly different wheel and hubcap necessitated by the new four wheel disc brakes.

The interior featured a slightly redesigned dashboard, but was otherwise similar to earlier models. The major mechanical improvement was the disc brakes, however, other improvements were made, including the most powerful pushrod engine ever produced: the SC at 95 hp.

Spotter's Guide

Front

Model	Year	Description
356	1950	Small hood handle without hole. Turn signals below and slightly inboard of the headlights. Integrated bumpers. Split windshield.
	Early 1952	Hood handle with hole. Bent windshield. Aluminum windshield trim. Interim bumpers. Pressed steel bumper guards.
	Late 1952	"A" style bumpers. Pressed steel bumper guards.
	1953	Turn signals directly below headlights.
	Early 1954	Horn grilles added. Low aluminum bumper guards.
	1955	"A" style crested front hood handle. Low chrome windshield frame on Speedster.
356A	1956	Curved windshield.
	Mid-1956	Overrider tubes added on U.S. cars.
	1958	Turn signal mounted on wedge-shaped base. Taller windshield frame on Conv. D than Speedster.
	1959	Higher overrider tube.
356B	1960	Flattened hood. Larger chrome-plated hood handle. Larger/higher bumpers with large chrome-plated bumper guard. Horn grilles above and below the bumper. Last year of front Porsche script.
	1962	Squared-off front hood. Vents on front cowl, except roadster. Gas filler on right front fender, except some RHD cars. Taller windshield on coupe.

Side

Model	Year	Description
356	1950	No trim decos. Coach builder badge on right front fender. Non-hinged rear quarter windows on coupes. No front vent windows. Solid 16" x 3" wheels. Moon hubcaps.
	Mid-1951	Hinged rear quarter windows on coupes. Slotted 16" x 3 1/4" wheels on 1500 cars.
	1954	Speedster features "beltline" aluminum trim. Speedster script on both front fenders. Speedster has aluminum and rubber rocker panel trim.
	1955	"Continental" fender scripts on U.S. spec. coupes and cabriolets.
356A	1956	"European" fender scripts on early coupes and cabriolets. Flattened rocker panels. Rocker panel deco trim on all models. 15" x 4 1/2" wheels.
	Mid-1957	Rear of door handle changed from square to rounded.
	1958 (T-2)	Vent window present on cabriolet. Removable hardtop option on cabriolet. High bow top on Speedster. Roll up windows on Conv. D. Crested "Super" hubcaps optional.
356B	1960	Revised front and rear fender contours. Thinner rocker panel deco trim. Front vent windows on coupes.
	1962 (T-6)	Pop-out rear quarter windows on Karmann Hardtop and removable hardtop.
	1963	Coach builder badges deleted.
356C	1964	Disc brake wheels and flat hubcap.

Rear

Model	Year	Description
356	1950	Vertical taillight placement: rectangular above, round below. Integral bumper. Shine-down license light with brake light in center. Single aluminum grille on rear lid.
	Early 1952	Interim bumper. Aluminum rear window trim.
	Late 1952	"A" style bumpers. Pressed steel bumper guards. Engine designation script added.
	1953	Two round beehive taillights side by side. Center lens on license light clear backup light.
	Early 1954	Low aluminum bumper guards.
356A	Mid-1956	Single overrider tube on U.S. spec. cars.
	Mid-1957	Teardrop taillights. Shine-up license light. Split overrider tube.
	1958 (T-2)	Altered rear cowling on cabriolet. Exhaust routed through bumper guards, except on Carreras.
356B	1960	Larger/higher bumper. Reflectors made by ULO and located either above lights on chrome pods or below bumper. License lights on bumper.
	1962 (T-6)	Larger rear window, coupe. Zip-out rear window, cabriolet. Two vent grilles on rear lid. Larger rear lid, coupe.

Interior

356 1950
Banjo steering wheel.
Turn signal switch on dashboard.
Ivory colored VW knobs and escutcheons.
Two main instruments: black/white speedo and tach or speedo and clock.
Small oil temperature gauge.
3 or more small idiot lights.
Ash tray in dashboard.
Black rubber floor mats
Non-reclining front bucket seats.
Rear seat area has various configurations.
Napped cloth headliner.
Green plastic sun visors.
Wood door tops.

1952
Black/green deep faced instruments.
Turn signal switch moved to steering column.
Reclining front seats.
Rear seat area standardized with folding back.

1953
Steering wheel with crest in center.
Larger idiot lights.
Metal door tops.
Most cars have corduroy interiors (1953 only).

1954
Knobs and steering wheel, ivory, grey or beige.
Unique dashboard for Speedster with vinyl covered top.
Larger interior light on coupe.
Speedster seats.
Speedster rear seat consists of cushion only.

Mid-1954
Fuel gauge added.

356A 1956
Redesigned dashboard, all models.
Padded vinyl top on coupe/cabriolet dashboard.
Three large shallow faced VDO instruments.
Smaller interior light mounted on dashboard.
Turn signal switch with chrome stalk.
Twist release handbrake.
Perforated vinyl headliner.

1957
Padded vinyl sun visors.

1958 (T-2)
Ashtray under dashboard.
Interior lights in coupe mounted in headliner.
Beige floor mats used occasionally, 1958-1959.
Thinner seat back with different pleating pattern.
No rear seat on Convertible D.
Window crank and inside door handle repositioned.
Locking pockets on Convertible D door panel.

356B 1960
Black plastic knobs, steering wheel and escutcheons.
Chrome shift lever with black plastic "mushroom" knob.
Rear seats with left and right cushions and separate folding backs.
No rear seats on roadster.

356C 1964
Lock on far right of glove box.
Padded vinyl grab handle.
Extension below ash tray.

Model Changes

356

Bent or split windshield, two large instruments, 1950-1955
Black/white instruments, 1950-1951.
Black/green instruments, 1952-1955.
Horn grilles present, 1954-1955.
Hood handle with crest, 1955.

356A

Curved windshield; three large instruments; grey, beige or ivory steering wheel, 1956-1959.
Striker plate with 5 screws, 1956-1957.
Striker plate with 3 screws, 1958-1959.
Ash tray in dash, 1956-1957.
Ash tray under dash, 1958-1959.

356B

Black steering wheel, finned brake drums, 1960-1963.
Gas filler under front hood, 1960-1961.
Gas filler on right front fender, 1962-1963.
One rear grille, 1960-1961.
Two rear grilles, 1962-1963.

356C

Disc brakes, padded grab handle, metal extension under ashtray on dashboard, 1964-1965.

Differentiating Models

Open Cars	Cab	Spd	Conv D	Roa
356	*	*		
356A	*	*	*	
356B	*			*
Back seat	*	*		
Roll-up windows	*		*	*
Front vent window	*			
Chrome removable windshield frame		*	*	*

	356	356A	356A T-2	356B T-5	356B T-6	35
Bent/split windshield	*					
Dual rear grille					*	*
External gas filler					*	*
Disc brakes						*
Vent window, coupe				*	*	
Vent window, cab			*	*	*	
16" wheels	*					
Exhaust through bumper guards			*	*	*	*

6

Literature

Vol. 3, No. 5 Jim Perrin

Overview

There has been a substantial increase in interest in Porsche literature, especially literature relating to the 356 series. Every issue of the *356 Registry* has a number of ads by individuals looking for literature pertaining either to a specific model or to the 356 series in general. Literature can be used to help restore a specific car, or to increase one's knowledge of 356s and the changes from model to model. This article is the first of what I plan to be a series on various phases of literature and literature collecting. In this article I plan to present an overview of the subject, discussing some of the various phases of 356 Porsche literature.

Literature in the sense I am using the term includes printed material relating to the 356 series. The major categories are as follows:

Porsche Factory Publications
    Owner's Manuals
    Shop Manuals
    Technical Bulletins to Dealers
    Parts Manuals
    Sales Literature
    Calendars Posters
Periodicals
    Christophorus
    Panorama
    356 Registry
Books

Owner's manuals were issued for 356, 356A, 356B, and 356C models. These factory publications are more complete, especially the A, B, and C ones, than most owners manuals put out by other manufacturers. When the 356 Speedster was introduced, the regular owner's manual was not changed to include it. Instead, a supplementary manual was supplied to early Speedster owners. The factory followed a similar practice for the various Carrera models, and did the same when the Super 90 was introduced.

Shop manuals and parts manuals have also been issued by Porsche for each of the 356, 356A, 356B, and 356C models. These are really invaluable to the restorer or the person interested in serious maintenance of his car. The parts manual has exploded views of some assemblies that are especially useful the first time you disassemble and reassemble a complicated assembly. Technical service bulletins were periodically sent to dealers, and contain information not in the shop manuals.

The Porsche Factory has released quite a variety of sales literature related to various models of Porsches. A few pieces of literature have also been issued by distributors such as Hoffman and Porsche of America Corporation. Sales literature includes items such as price lists, color charts, post cards, accessory folders. sales folders, sales catalogs, and tourist delivery folders. The number of these items on the 356 series is quite large, perhaps 100 or more.

The Porsche Factory has issued calendars continuously for 21 years, starting in 1957. There may have been earlier calendars, but if so, I have not heard of them. Starting in the early 1960s, Porsche issued a commemorative coin. referred to as a calendar coin, with each calendar. Calendars typically have 12 to 24 pictures. The first five calendars are spiral bound. Later calendars have loose pictures, with the picture size increasing over the years.

The Porsche Factory has been more active than most auto factories in issuing promotional posters to dealers for use in showrooms. This practice was apparently started in the early 1950s. Many of the posters were issued to commemorate specific racing victories. As a result, most posters have pictures of racing models such as

Spyders, 904s etc.

Periodicals relating to the Porsche 356 series include the *356 Registry, Panorama,* and *Christophorus.* You are all familiar with the *356 Registry,* but may not all be familiar with *Panorama. Panorama* is the monthly publication of the Porsche Club of America, and has been published since December, 1955. The earlier issues have many informative articles and pictures relating to 356s. PCA has compiled the technical articles from *Panorama* into a number of volumes called *Up Fixin der Porsche. Volume 1* and *Volume 2* of the series are of greatest interest to 356 enthusiasts. *Christophorus* magazine has been published for over twenty years, starting in the early 1950s. It is issued six times a year by the factory and is one of the finest factory publications of its type in the world. Early issues contain a wealth of information and pictures showing the development of Porsches over the years. The first English edition, designated No. 1, was issued in January/February. 1956.

Several books relating to Porsches have been issued by the factory. A number of others, perhaps approaching twenty or so, have also been published. These range from technical manuals to books on the history of Porsche.

Vol. 3, No. 6 Jim Perrin

Sales Literature

In this second article on literature pertaining to the 356 series Porsche, I plan to discuss sales literature. The most commonly known item of this type is the sales folder and the sales catalog, describing the various models available for sale.

The first several sales items issued by Porsche were sales folders. These are printed on a single large sheet of paper, both sides, and then folded into a smaller size convenient for displaying in a showroom, for passing out at an auto show, or for mailing.

The very first piece was issued on the Gmünd aluminum coupe and cabriolet. It was issued, as were many of the later sales folders. and catalogs, in both German and English. No actual pictures of cars were used. The artist's illustrations may have been made from actual cars or perhaps only from photographs. In either case, the illustrations are exaggerated, showing a more streamlined body than the actual car. At the PCA Parade in San Diego, I had the opportunity to discuss this piece of literature with Ferry Porsche. When I showed it to him, he told me it was their first piece of literature. He said that it had been prepared for the first showing of the Porsche at an auto show, which he told me was in Switzerland.

A slightly more elaborate type of sales literature than the sales folder is the sales catalog. This is composed of a number of sheets of paper, usually in color, and printed on both sides. The sheets are stapled together and folded once in the manner of this newsletter. Numerous sales catalogs have been issued on the 356 series at various times.

Porsche issued very few "prestige" catalogs. A prestige catalog is a deluxe edition, in color, using extra high quality paper, usually having a relatively large number of pages, frequently having a relatively large page size, and covering the full line of models. I know of no 356 catalogs that are what I would regard as a prestige catalog. However, there is a prestige catalog for the 356A, the 356B, and the 356C. These catalogs are relatively scarce, since they cost appreciably more to produce. They were probably reserved for only the more-promising customers.

Most of the sales folders and sales catalogs cover the full line of models. However, Porsche has also issued sales literature on specific models. The earliest example is apparently the

Speedster, for which the factory issued two folders. This was done to give extra publicity to a new model, and probably to avoid reprinting existing folders and catalogs which did not show the new models. Another new model for which Porsche issued a specific model folder was the Convertible D roadster. It is quite colorful and has some very good photographs.

The two Speedster and one Convertible D folders are the only single model folders of which I'm aware, with the exception of the "356 SL." I have seen a copy of a small folder on this model, which appears to be a Gmünd aluminum coupe with special racing accessories. I don't know if this really was a legitimate model, or if it was a phony new model introduced by Porsche so they could race a few special updated factory versions of the original Gmünd coupe instead of the regular production steel-bodied cars. Perhaps there was a sales folder on the 1952/1953 America roadster; do any of you readers know of such an item?

Another series of Porsche literature was a set of four single page handouts. These were on the four 356 models in production at the time: the coupe, cabriolet, Speedster, and 550 Spyder.

They included pictures and technical specifications for each model. There also were slogans for each model, as follows:

Coupe: "The World's most talked about car" and "The car not only for today, but for the day after tomorrow."

Cabriolet: "Drive it and be envied" and "The car women sigh over."

Speedster: "Yesterday's knowledge brings tomorrow's pleasure" and "The Porsche Speedster answers the call of the open road."

Spyder: "One look at the Spyder will start you dreaming."

The evolution of a model is sometimes reflected in the sales literature. For example, there is a 356A folder

that changed in the 1958 - 1959 period by deleting the Speedster and adding the Convertible D. In other respects the two folders were essentially the same, except for colors used.

The addition of a new model is sometimes incorporated into an existing catalog by the addition of an extra page in the middle. An example that comes to mind is the Carrera 2. There are two versions of one of the 356B catalogs. They are identical, except that the later version has a new page added to the center with a picture and description of the 356B Carrera 2. (For some reason, none of the 356C catalogs show the 356C version of the Carrera 2.)

In the next article of the series, I will continue the discussion of sales literature, covering some of the other varieties such as color charts, price lists, post cards, and accessory folders.

Vol. 4, No. 2 Jim Perrin

Other Dealer Literature

The last article in this series covered sales folders and sales catalogs on the 356 models. In addition to these items which describe the models available, there are a number of other related items which will be covered in the present article. The related items include color charts, price lists, postcards, accessory folders, and road test folders.

Price lists were used in an earlier article I wrote for the *356 Registry* on comparisons of the original prices of new 356 series Porsches. These were issued both by the factory and by importers or distributors. The factory price lists usually cover the ex-factory or tourist delivery prices. Sometimes major accessories are included in these price lists. Importers such as Hoffman in the U.S. also issued price lists.

Several types of postcards were issued. One type was simply an individual card with a picture of a car or cars on it. A second type was a set of postcards. There are three sets which I have seen, one on the 356, one on the 356A, and the third on the 356B. The 356 set is the nicest, and is composed of three postcards (actually not postcards, but pictures the size of postcards). The folder is white with the word PORSCHE embossed on the front. It opens up to show a display of three framed pictures, one showing a tan cabriolet, one shows a blue cabriolet, and the third shows a red coupe with two 356s in the background. The third type of postcard is a service reminder post-card. A picture of a car is on the front, and on the rear is a reminder to bring your car in for periodic service at the local Porsche dealership.

Color charts with color chips were issued for the 356A (1956 and 1957 - 1959), the 356B (1960 - 1961 and 1962 - 1963) and the 356C (1964 - 1965). These contain a list of colors available for each model, the paint number, and which colors were standard or optional colors. In addition, some information is listed on top and interior colors. I have a color list for 1954, but have no other pre-1956 color information, although lists of some type must have been available to prospective customers.

Accessory folders or booklets were issued by the factory for the 356, 356A, 356B, and 356C. These are fascinating to read, and list some virtually unknown accessories. For example, when was the last time you saw a right hand drive, a bench front seat, or driving/fog lights mounted directly onto the body below the front hood opening? Another rare accessory, which I've never seen, is a separate cushion for the Speedster bucket seats.

My best experience with the accessory catalogs was on steering wheels. I had been looking for an original accessory wood-rimmed steering wheel for my 356A for some time with no success. These were manufac-

tured by the Italian company Nardi. All I had was an after-market wood-rimmed steering wheel from a 356A Carrera GS Speedster owned several years earlier. Even though it was not a correct steering wheel, it was a little too nice to get rid of, so it was hanging on my garage wall on a nail. One day I was leafing through a newly-acquired

356A accessory booklet, which listed a "VDM" steering wheel as a factory accessory. I ran down to the garage and looked at the steering wheel on the wall. The first thing I saw on one of the spokes was the name "VDM"! Another type of sales literature Porsche has issued are road test booklets. There are three that I've seen, issued in 1961, 1962, and 1964. They are compilations of road tests written by journalists and published in various periodicals. Porsche apparently thought compilations of these road tests in booklet form would be good sales promotional pieces.

Vol. 4, No. 4 Jim Perrin

Porsche Periodicals

The three primary periodicals relating to the 356 series Porsche are the *356 Registry, Porsche Panorama*, and *Christophorus*. I do not plan to discuss the *Registry*, but will discuss *Panorama* and *Christophorus*.

Panorama is the monthly periodical put out by the Porsche Club of America. It has been put out almost every month since December, 1955. It has been edited since 1969 by Betty Jo Turner, who is producing the best monthly periodical put out by any sports car club.

The issues of *Panorama* of primary interest to us are the ones put out in the period from 1955 to the late 1960s. These are the issues containing most of the 356 information. The *Panorama* of today covers all models including the 356, 911, 912, 914, 924, 928 and racing models.

Most of the early *Panorama* issues of interest were edited by Charlie Beidler, and later by Paul Heinmiller. These were put out in a manner similar to how our *Registry* is now being put out, that is, the editor did it on a spare time basis and with the assistance of volunteer writers and photographers.

The articles of greatest interest in the early *Panoramas* are probably the technical articles. These have been periodically compiled and published in a book called *Up Fixin der Porsche, Volume I* covers technical articles from December, 1955, through 1960. *Volume II*, covering the technical articles from 1961 to 1966 also has much material of interest to the 356 enthusiast.

In addition to the technical articles, the articles on racing in early *Panoramas* are fun to read. They include articles on both the production cars and the early racing cars such as Spyders, Abarths and 904s being raced. In these issues you can find pictures of coupes and Speedsters that were driven to the track, a few items such as bumpers and hubcaps removed, lights taped, and numbers painted on. At this point, you had a race car.

"The Mart", which lists articles for sale and wanted, shows the types of items available. The one aspect that is discouraging in looking at The Mart in early *Panoramas* is the low prices for parts and cars. The commercial ads in early issues of *Panorama* show how few parts and accessories were available from sources other than the factory as compared to now. A few of these advertisers are still in the business, but most have long since disappeared or gone in other business directions. An early advertiser was Competition Chemicals from Iowa; one of their products was the now well-known Simichrome paste, available then at 69 cents a tube.

The stories of club activities show a club that was in a much more informal state than the present state of PCA. For example, the comments on concours activities in the late 1950s show a very casual approach, as our first few Holiday concours were.

There is relatively little factory-supplied material in early *Panoramas*. However, there is some material that appears to have come from factory press releases. It includes information on the introduction of the Convertible D, the 1960 T-5 356B, the 1962 T-6 356B, and the 1964 356C.

If you have ever had the opportunity to visit Germany and the Porsche factory, there is a series of articles that are great fun to read. They appear each year as a report on the annual Porsche Treffen sponsored by PCA in the late 1950s up until the mid-1960s. Many of the participants picked up their new 356 series cars on these trips.

The present day *Panorama* is a vastly-improved magazine as compared to the early issues. Unfortunately, the present issues do not have an extensive amount of 356 material.

Vol. 5, No. 1 Jim Perrin

Porsche Periodicals, II

In the last article in this series Porsche *Panorama* was described as one of the periodicals which contains much information of interest to 356 enthusiasts in early issues. The only other periodical which contains substantial information from the same period is *Christophorus*, which will be discussed in this article.

Christophorus magazine is a Porsche factory publication. It has been published six times a year since approximately 1952. Richard von Frankenberg was editor for many years; he was also simultaneously a racing driver for Porsche during the earlier years he was editor. In recent years Rico Steinemann, formerly racing director for Porsche, has been editor of *Christophorus*. Steinemann pro-

11

duces an exceptionally high quality magazine. However, the issues of greatest interest to 356 enthusiasts are the issues published from the 1950s to the mid 1960s, and this article will concentrate on these earlier issues.

The first 17 issues had German for the main text, with multilingual subtitles for the pictures. The German and English issues are published on alternate months with the German issue preceding the English issue. The following part of this article will be on the English edition, although most of the comments apply to the German edition also.

The first 37 English edition issues have a smaller format than the later issues, being approximately 8 1/4 in. by 11 5/8 in., instead of the larger 9 3/4 in. by 11 in. used for subsequent issues. There is one unnumbered issue of *Christophorus*. It is a special edition commemorating the introduction of the 356B. It not only introduces the new model, but also presents many pictures and comments on earlier models and significant milestones in the history of Porsche. Other commemorative issues include No. 2 (approximately, March, 1957) and No. 77 (September, 1968).

As a source of information, the early *Christophorus* have no equal. There are articles on such subjects as new models, early Porsche designs, race victories, racing drivers and other notable individuals associated with the Porsche factory, and technical developments. Of course, most of the information came directly from factory sources, tending to make it more reliable than other sources.

Pictures are used extensively in *Christophorus*, and are in general of high quality. These show good details on many models. In some cases they show cars in the process of being assembled at the factory. In other pictures you can occasionally spot unusual variation or rare optional equipment. One picture of this type is a front view of a 356B roadster. However, if you look at it carefully you discover it is set up with a Speedster windshield! As far as strange pictures, it is hard to match a few 356s in the early *Christophoruses* with wide whitewall tires!

A few of the *Christophoruses* published in the 1950s have what is titled "Special Supplement". These are typically four page loose inserts describing a major race victory which has occurred too late to be included in the regular issue. For example, English edition No. 4 (July, 1956) had a Special Supplement on an overall victory by Porsche in the Targa Florio, a race first run over Sicilian roads in 1906. In 1956 the race was run for 10 laps, each lap being 45 miles long. Maglioli was entered by the factory in what apparently was a 550A 1500 cc Spyder. The Spyder ran against other makes which included Ferrari, Maserati, OSCA, and Mercedes. Maglioli won first overall, in what the supplement describes as "Our most impressive victory".

Current issues of *Christophorus* periodically contain a feature titled "Hommage à la 356s". which describes restorations of 356s. Several cars of Registry members have been shown in this feature. If you would like to subscribe to Christophorus, the publisher is Dr. Ing. h.c.f. Porsche Aktiengesellschaft. 7000 Stuttgart-Zuffenhausen. West Germany.

Part Numbers

Vol. 3, No. 6 Bud West

Everything You Always Wanted to Know, But Were Afraid to Ask is an appropriate title for a book about sex; and it may be equally appropriate for the information following.

Most (but not all) Porsche part numbers are a series of eleven digits, separated in three groups of three and one group of two, by points, the German equivalent to commas, e.g., 644.559.011.00 (356A rocker panel trim). The first three digits or prefix, indicate the project for which the part was originally designed. The 644 in the 356A rocker panel trim part number means that the part was first designed for a 356A body, or chassis, or the first tunnel type transaxle.

The last two digits in the complete part number generally indicate a modification to the originally designed part. For example, the part number for the 356B rocker panel trim is 644.559.011.07. I understand, but cannot document, that a change in the last two digits may also signify a change in the manufacturer, even though the part itself may be identical to a part having a number with a lower pair of final digits.

It is important to remember that even though the three digit prefix indicates the project for which the part was originally designed, the part may fit later cars. A good example is part number 519.20.216. The 519 indicates that the part was originally designed as the spacer between first and second gears in the split case transaxle used for all type 356 cars through model year 1955. However, that same part was also used in the tunnel type transaxle first introduced in the 356A in 1956, and was also used in the 356B and C transaxles, even though the 356B and C transaxles were changed in many ways from the tunnel types first used in the 356A and were totally different from the split case transaxles used in the type 356.

In the very last section of all Porsche parts catalogues is a part number list. The purpose of the list is to indicate the part of the catalogue in which a part number in question may be found, so that a part can be identified. Unfortunately, with changes in part numbers, it is not always possible to identify every part. But it is important to know that in the part number list at the end of the parts catalogues, as well

as in parts price lists, the parts are listed in numerical order beginning with the second group of digits, regardless of the first three digits in the prefix. An example of this is part number 644.559.302.06 which follows right after 930.559.301.01 in the retail parts price list published for the period effective June 1, 1977.

There is, in addition to the parts catalogues, a "Spare Parts Interpretation List", more commonly referred to as the "Superseded List". If you ask your dealer's parts man for "two of those washers that go under the screws that hold the cover on the end of the tunnel on my 1961 coupe", he will look in the parts catalogue and find that this is part number 644.025.142.00. Then, looking in the "Spare Parts Interpretation List", he will find that this part is no longer available. (It is, if you ask the advertisers in the *Registry*). Or, if you ask for the four rubber buffers under the engine lid in your 356A (or B or C), he will find part number 644.025.635.00, and then find that it has been superseded by part number 999.703.086.40.

What does that 999 prefix mean that the part was designed for? Here is a list of all of the prefixes:

356 356 Chassis or body
369 1100 engine
506 1300 engine
519 2-piece transaxle
527 Early 1500 engine – 2-piece crankcase
528 1500 super engine – 2-piece crankcase
539 1500 engine – 3-piece crankcase
540 Speedster
546 Late 1500 engine – 3-piece crankcase
547 Carrera engine – roller bearing crankshaft
550 Spyder
587 2 Litre Carrera engine
597 1300 super engine – 3-piece crankcase
616 1600 engine – 3-piece crankcase

644 356 A chassis, body and tunnel type transaxle
690 4-speed transaxle for Spyder
691 5-speed transaxle for Spyder – split crankcase
692 1600 Carrera engine – plain bearing crankshaft
695 356 B and C chassis or body
716 Transaxle when new type synchronization was introduced
718 RSK Spyder and 5-speed transaxle, tunnel-type
719 RSK Spyder engine
741 Transaxle for 356 B and C
753 2 Litre engine installed in Carrera 2
771 2 Litre engine installed in Carrera 2
900 Standard hardware (previous DIN-numbers)
901 911 chassis, body and engine, model years 1965-1969
902 912 engine and body
904 904 body, chassis and gear box
905 Sportomatic transmission
906 906 body and chassis
907 907 body and chassis
910 910 body and chassis
911 911 chassis, body and engine, model years 1970 & 1971
912 911 chassis, body and engine, model year 1972
914 914 and 914/6
916 Fuel injection
923 912 E/1976
930 Turbo Carrera
999 Standard hardware (previous P-numbers)

Type 60

Vol. 8, No. 3 Gene Babow

The Pre-356

The Berlin-Rom Wagen or Berlin-Rome Car, also known as the Type 60K10 is more important than just being the forerunner of the Type 356. The concept involves constant improvement in design, competition to prove the design and streamlining. Dr.

Ing. h.c. Ferdinand Porsche lived these concepts from the Lohner-Porsche in 1900. He took the electric-motored Lohner-Porsche, increased the power, added a measure of streamlining and drove the car in a hill climb in record time.

When the time came for the Porsche design team to plan the people's car – the KdF-Wagen or Type 60 or Volkswagen; the concept didn't change. Among the next 60 designs, almost half involved improvements in the original design. Among the designs was the Type 64, a paper design for a sports car. It didn't get beyond a small model stage because of politics.

With the completion of the Berlin-Munich autobahn, a race was planned from Berlin to Rome. Several German auto firms made plans to enter the race. The good professor managed to talk ranking German officials into constructing and entering three cars based on the Type 60. Remember that the KdF-Wagen was a state project, not a private concern. Under state laws, parts could not be obtained in the private sector.

The Type 60 was not a race vehicle. It was a utility vehicle meant to be low-cost transportation. The flat windshield, separate fenders and fast-sloping back were compromises for function. A race car needed no such compromises; yet the Berlin-Rome car must resemble the Type 60.

Backtracking to 1922, we will introduce Paul Jaray. He was an engineer for the Zeppelin Company in Freidrichshafen. Germany. He worked out the critical 6:1 ratio of length to height so the Zeppelin could fly. As a result of the First World War, Germany was not allowed to have aircraft. Jaray turned to auto streamlining. He patented his findings. "A motor car comprising a chassis, a motor, seat and wheels and an envelope having the form of one symmetric half a drop and entirely surrounding said chassis, motor, and seat and the upper half of said wheels."

A simple graph showed that with his described streamlining, a 50 hp car would increase it top speed from 58 to 80 mph. Given the confines of the Type 60 and its engine, there is no doubt that the House of Porsche listened. Streamlining was tried on the Pierce-Arrow, Maybach and the Chrysler Airflow. It wasn't accepted.

A quick look at the Jaray drawing of 1922 and the resulting Type 60K10 shows amazing similarities. Dr. Erwin Kommenda, part of the House of Porsche, did the design work on the 60K10. The rear engine with the proper front slope, the small cabin with proper rear slope, and the flat floor pan were just what Jaray would have ordered.

Aerodynamics include protuberances such as bumpers, windows, door handles and anything that sticks out in the wind stream. Note the pictures of the car now owned by Otto Mathé of Innsbruk, Austria. Nothing sticks out; it is smooth, even to the elongated tail coming to a point.

It wouldn't be till much later that a Dr. Kamm would say that a sudden drop off would do better than the point. Even the wheels were covered as far as possible by fender skirts. The windows are mounted flush and open by sliding. Even the door handle is flush. The body, produced by Reutter, has tight seams, necessary for clean airflow.

It is obvious that a bird, a fish, a raindrop and the 60K10 are streamlined. It has been said that Professor Porsche drove the car from the KdF factory to Berlin at an average speed of 85 mph. Streamlining works; a small engine could produce speed.

The resulting Type 356, again a Kommenda design, just developed the theme–One of the first production streamlined cars. In just the last few years, the rest of the auto world has caught on to the idea of streamlining.

Mention has to be made of another Porsche design, the Type 114. It was also known as the F-Wagen, "F" for Ferdinand. The design was similar to the 60K10 and it may have been the good professor's idea for his first car to bear his name. It had a ladder-type tube frame and an engine of 1.5 liters mounted midship. By the way, the configuration of the engine was a V-10. A V-10? It is elementary, a straight 10 cylinder engine really wouldn't fit, would it?

Otto Mathé

Vol. 8, No. 3 Gene Babow

Biographical Sketch
(Note: With the distinct possibility of Otto Mathé coming to the 6th West Coast Holiday, I would like to present a thumbnail sketch of him, as the result of a visit with him last year. In spite of the language barrier – he speaks very little English, we spoke autos and got along quite well.)
Otto Mathé is at once a pleasant, likable man; one that you never guess to be so involved with autos. He was born in Innsbruck, Austria in 1907. He still lives there.

In 1926, he was a bicycle racer and hillclimb champion in Austria. In 1934, he switched to motorcycles. As an amateur, he could beat some of the finest European drivers. He became interested in oil additives for motors of all kinds. In 1934, he had an accident while competing on a dirt track in Graz, Austria. He lost his right arm. After the accident, he became a mechanic. He also patented ski bindings that are still being used. He started his own business selling oil and additives.

After the war, he opened a crankshaft rebuilding shop in the Tyrolian province. He also did work on the Wankel engine. He got the racing bug again. He bought the Type 60K10 from Professor Porsche, along with two right hand drive Gmünd coupes. He still has all three cars, along with a small collection of other cars.

He built a single seater racing car for ice racing, as well as a racer similar to a Spyder. He would drive in Austrian races and had many victories. He won the 1951 Austrian Alpine Trial outright. With his own four-cam Spyder-type racer he beat the Porsche factory team. The factory team included Huschke von Hanstein and Richard von Frankenberg.

In 1952, he won the Austrian championship and received a gold ring. He had 22 national and international victories. From Porsche, he received a porcelain and a silver model Porsche.

After the racing, he settled down to the oil additive business. He has a small collection of autos besides the 60K10, two Gmünd coupes and the two racers. He has a Lancia convertible owned by Mussolini's son-in-law, Graf Ciano, a Cisitalia racer once owned by Hans Stuck and an airplane owned by World War I fighter pilot General Udet. Mathé flew in the plane with Udet.

Besides autos, Mathé likes to ski, both water and snow. He is an ardent bird watcher. Recently, he joined in the era of historic racing. He has had the 60K10 out several times, including the August, 1981 races at Nurburgring honoring the 50th year of Porsche in Stuttgart.

Chapter 2

Body

Body Numbers

Vol. 7, No. 1 Richard Miller

Hood Hinge Alignment Holes and Identification Numbers

The alignment holes in the hinge and their counterparts in the hood itself are 5 mm in diameter. They were drilled following body assembly and prior to painting. As these holes vary from car to car it is a simple matter to see if the original hood is still in place. Of course, another way to tell this is to look at the left hinge bracket on the hood where the last two or three digits will be found. These digits also appear on the doors and deck lid. A number of other locations were also noted by Richard in his 1954 coupe: Dashboard, backside, middle at bottom; stamped aluminum side trim for dash, scribed left and right; aluminum hinge cover plate, stamped on back at bottom; door panels, crayon on backside; shift selector cover plate, crayon on backside. Finally he notes that the front hoods on pre-A cars are reinforced via spot welds on the inner perimeters, later cars do not have this.

Vol. 17, No. 6 Paul Goldzung

Body Part Identification Numbers

While in the process of restoring Convertible D #85643 (Drauz, October, 1958) I began to notice a large number of parts that were marked with the last two or three numbers of the car's I.D. number. I kept an ongoing list of these parts throughout the restoration process. To the best of my knowledge, all the numbers are authentic. They are listed in the accompanying chart.

PART	LOCATION	NUMBER
Chassis I.D. Plate	usual	85643
Bulk Head	usual	85643
Door Hinge I.D. plate	usual	85643
Door Hinge cover plate	bottom	43
Doors	usual	643
Doors	inside skin (yellow crayon)	643
Front Deck	hinge strap	643
Front Deck Latch	finger tongue	43
Front Bumper	inside lower lip	643
Front Bumper over tube	base at bumper	43
Rear Bumper	inside lower lip	643
Rear Bumper over tubes	Base at bumper	43
Windshield Frame	beneath top left latch	643
Windshield posts	base to car	43
Rear deck lid	bottom of weather shield	643
Rear Deck locking tongue	on face	43
Top bow	Front top brace	643
Eye brow wood	base to dash (pencil)	43
Gas Tank	lower left lip	43
Door Panel	inside (white chalk)	643
Seats	bottom (yellow crayon)	643
Seat backs	beneath hinge (yellow crayon)	43
Top Hinge cover plates	center inboard (yellow crayon)	D643
Door Garnish	inside of steel (chalk)	43
Window regulator	center (white chalk)	43
Rear Cowl cover Alum.	center each (stamped)	643
Dash trim Alum.	left side (stamped)	643
Dash Vinyl	inside (white chalk)	643
Drivers Pedal Board	backside (yellow crayon)	43
Windshield seal rails	backside	43

Sunroof

Vol. 6, No. 6 Mark Turczyn

Installing a Sunroof via Top Grafting

Let me say straight out that at this point in my life I prefer my 356s to have some sort of opening roof. Yes I want it all, the sun. the wind, the rain, the rust. For this singular reason I kept only my 1951 cab and my 1955 Speedster when I was forced to liquidate my collection of 356s or lose all the grass in my back yard. The coupes went first. Please do not get me wrong, I love old coupes, especially 356 A coupes. For me, here in the snowy east, a sun roof coupe represented the best of all possible worlds, wet feet only in heavy rains. On sunny days–read no snow or rain–you could gently slide the sunroof back, often under its own power. Of course I do recall now that I often had to drive with my chin and one knee while my left hand manipulated the switch and my right hand tugged back on the sliding roof to prevent motor burnout. Great fun on left-hand corners!

I never could find an original sunroof coupe I felt was restorable. Of course my idea of what is restorable has changed a great deal over the last ten years. Whatever, this situation dictated the need for a sunroof transplant. After one not-so-great attempt, I reviewed my methodology with a friend. After pointing out the obvious errors of my method, he quickly outlined a "simple" method of performing this delicate transplant in which the recipient was assured of a long and useful life. I performed several transplants and even assisted on the surgery of a BMW. The feasibility and the survival rate of the recipients of this operation are now well established.

One point that might be made here is to be sure the donor is a terminal case. Many cars are being restored today that would have been hopeless derelicts a few years ago. Don't remove the roof from a car that might be restored.

I confess that over four years have elapsed since my last roof transplant, so you should understand that there may be some unmentioned bits and pieces that upon discovery may drive the first-time surgeon to hair-pulling frustration until true Porsche patience or plain dumb luck bails him out.

First you need a donor from which you can extract the sunroof. It should be the same body type out of fear of tissue rejection. You want the entire roof down to the front posts and to the bottom of the rear window. Remember to take the switch located on the underside of the dash on the left if you are installing an electric rather than a manual sunroof. Make sure the roof is complete and works. If it does not, either make it work or find another. I swear to God, for such a simple apparatus-two wires driven by a gear – you can spend a whole afternoon making that baby work right. I must emphasize that you had best start with a healthy unit, so when you screw it up installing it, you have some hope of making it work again.

Remove the sliding roof liner next. Look at all them tiny clips – save them! When you get to the opening, the headliner is glued under the tracks the wires ride in. Loosen the screws that hold down the tops of the tracks and knock the tracks loose. Slip in a putty knife and work the liner loose. Notice that you just messed up the whole system early on and it may never work smoothly again. At this point resist any urge you may have to remove the tracks, gears and wires. Unless you are some sort of compulsive plastic baggy freak, you will immediately lose all the critical parts.

With the headliner out, all the guts are exposed. You will notice four or five stamped metal braces spot welded to the sunroof frame and the roof's inner sheet metal. Break the spot welds at the roof's inner sheet metal and bend them up. At the rear edge of the sliding roof opening, you will see a large steel band that is welded to the sides of the roof near the side window posts. The sheet metal at the opening is crimped around this steel band. One glance indicates how critical this member is. The length of this main brace controls the curvature of the roof allowing the sliding panel to move back and down without scraping. Therefore, when removing, cut the roof inner sheetmetal, not the brace. Disconnect the plastic drain tubes and also the motor control wires running up the left front window post. Remove the motor at the front.

Remove the front and rear glass from the transplant recipient. Now remove the headliner along with its hoops. More tiny metal clips. I cannot remember exactly but I believe the inside sheet metal that runs along the roof edges which holds your wires and courtesy lights is about 3 in. wide. Assuming this, use a scriber connected to a square and make a line 3.5 inches in on the recipients roof using the rain gutters and window top edges as guides (Fig. 1). Cut the roof panel out with an electric saber saw (a variable speed saber saw is the best $25 investment a Porsche restorer could make!) and take off all the remaining paint. Shiny metal helps better your welding by a factor of ten! Turning to the donor's sunroof, repeat this procedure but trace a line only 3.0 inches inward from the edge. This should just clear the inner sheet-metal so as not to break a saber saw blade. Remove and dress the edges of the main brace and after maneuvering it in first, the sunroof roof should plop right down on your recipient coupe's roof edges.

Scribe a mark around the edges of the donor roof. Remove the donor roof and cut a series of slots around the perimeter of your newly cut roof to this line. They will be about 0.5 inches deep. Bend each tab of metal to allow the insert to lie level with the remainder of your old roof. The tabs should be narrowest where the roof has the most curvature. If you do not like 0.5 inches of overlapped metal, you may use less. I like a lot of metal to play with.

At this point I usually have a beer and figure it is all downhill from here on. Well, not quite. You must now set the main brace. The success of the operation depends on doing this properly. I reinstall the sliding panel of the sunroof and using two large c-clamps, I clamp down the main brace to each side of the roof. Electrically, or manually, using either a screwdriver or by removing the cable drive gear, I open the sunroof. If it scrapes on the back lip of the opening, reposition the ends of the main brace by using shims or bending sheet metal. This affects the curvature of the brace and the roof. You should have no real trouble if you did everything else correctly. If you did mess up you will figure some way out! Once in position you must weld that main brace. Fasten the roofs together with six to ten pop-rivets before welding. The rest involves welding the roofs together and affixing the minor braces. The amount of

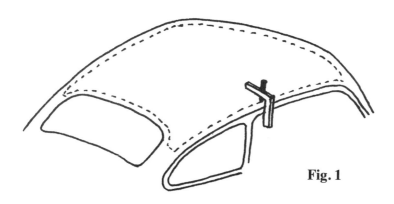

Fig. 1

final body work all depends on your welding skills.

Install the plastic drain tubes: the front go down the front pillars and into the hinge area or into the wheel wells and the rear go out the side of your roof, into the rear wheel wells or along the outside edges of the engine compartment and into the cavity between the inner and outer tail panels. I think they look real slick coming out the sides. "What are dem holes for anyway?"

Now install the motor and wiring. The wiring is a real knuckle-skinner. Install the headliner. Remember those clips? Having twice as many as the factory had will allow you to come close to the factory look. Replace your windows using the well-known powder and string method. Then spend an afternoon adjusting the sunroof so that it works under its own power. You may lose patience and practice my two hand (and knee and chin) approach and go out and drive your new creation so that everyone can marvel at your skill. No reason to hide your light under a bushel basket!

Editor's note: There are two other ways of installing a sunroof. The first is to cut both roofs off at the window posts and rejoin them there. Measure a lot before you weld because you don't want to mess up the shape of the window openings. Weld carefully so as not to weaken the roof structure.

At the time of this printing the method mentioned above was considered the preferred way to accomplish this proceedure – September 1994

I am now trying another way which I assume more or less duplicates the factory's installation method. This involves cutting a slightly smaller than sunroof-sized hole in the roof and bending the edges down into the sunroof "tray" and folding the rear edge around the cross-roof main brace. Accurate measurements are critical using this method. A jig must be fabricated to form the roof opening

because forming the right-angle bend in the roof edge tends to flatten the roof curvature, resulting in a roof with a different curvature than the sunroof panel, and probably an inoperative sunroof. Also, the jig makes it possible to put a properly sharp, straight bend in the edge of the sunroof opening. I'll repeat more fully on this method if I'm successful.- David Seeland

Vol. 8, No. 3 David Seeland

Installing a Sunroof the Hard Way

In the introduction to Mark Turczyn's article on his method of sunroof installation, I promised to report on my attempt at a "factory type" installation of a factory sunroof. At that time I had progressed as far as making a firm commitment to the project by saber-sawing a hole in the roof of Warren, our 1967 912. Now, only two years after sawing the hole, the installation is nearing a successful completion. Warren has been paintless since 1975, so two years is a mere moment – but what can you expect from an inveterate do-it-yourselfer overdosed on 11 cars (and a friend is trying to sell me his 1967 912! – I guess to try to keep it off the street). For those of you to whom sullying the pages of the *Registry* with words like 912 is blasphemy, please consider the fact that inflicting such a cruel, irreversible, untried surgical procedure on a 356 wouldn't be ethical. Therefore, I have in *Planet of the Apes* fashion used the 356s descendant (a 900 series car) for a trial operation, a reverse guinea-pig set up. The process is exactly the same if you are installing a sunroof in a 356. Be sure, however, that the organ donor is not reparable or there will be one less 356 in the world.

The installation procedure is detailed later, but briefly, it involves the following: 1) removal of the sunroof tray from the donor roof (the tracks and motor or crank are mounted on the tray), 2) cutting a slightly smaller than sunroof-sized hole in the recipients roof, 3) bending the edges down into the tray opening and welding the edges to the tray, 4) folding the rear flange of the opening around the cross brace at the rear of the opening using a pliers and a hammer, 5) installation and adjustment of the sunroof panel, actuating cables and motor or crank.

Jigs were made for the bends because forming the right-angle bend in the roof edge tends to flatten the roof curvature resulting in a roof with a different curvature than the sunroof panel (most undesirable). Also, the jig makes it possible to put a properly sharp, straight bend in the edge of the sunroof opening.

1) Drill out each of the spotwelds holding the roof to the sun-roof tray. Unroll the sheetmetal from the roof cross brace at the rear of the sunroof opening (do not remove arched cross-brace from the tray). Remove the braces from the roof structure at the front, sides, and rear, leaving them attached to the tray. Weld up the spotweld holes in the tray.

2) Carefully mark the centerline of the recipients roof.

3) Make a thin cardboard template of the opening in the sunroof tray - not of the sunroof panel. Mark the outline on the roof. Make another line in about $1/2$ in. (use the old spot-welded flange for exact measurements).

4) Gather up your courage and saber-saw around on the inside line.

5) Make jigs from two pairs of $1/2$ in. square steel stock from the hardware store. Curve one 36 inch pair to match the curvature of the front of the opening and one 14 in. pair to match the side curvature. The longer pair should be arched about $1/16$ in. more than the roof curvature to allow for flattening of the curve when forming the tip. It will take a while, but get the curve perfect. Check the arch at the front of the tray with one of the jig

pieces. Welding the spot weld holes shut flattens the curve.

6) Make a pair of corner templates, one is $1/4$ in. steel, the other is $1/8$ in. thick aluminum.

7) Bend front tip after clamping roof sheet metal between the two pieces of $1/2$ inch square stock. Use 12 C-clamps.

8) Bend a corner lip followed by the adjacent side.

9) Insert tray and check and remark other side and rear bending lines.

10) Re-arch long jigs to match rear roof curvature and check arched cross-brace for proper curvature, adjust if necessary.

11) Bend opposite side and rear.- Insert sunroof panel and check gaps: 4 mm front and side, 6 mm rear.

12) Cut away baffle inside of rear window vents (900 series only) to allow clearance for motor and cable tubes. Use a saber saw, chisels and lots of persistence for this.

13) Drill holes for drain tubes at upper corners of trunk opening. Solder in 4 inch lengths of copper tubing. Use plastic tubing up rear pillar to tray. Drill holes in body near front corners of tray and near base of windshield posts in hinge area.

14) Fold rear of opening around cross brace with one of the upper $1/2$ inch square guides clamped in place on top of the roof. Use a hammer to start the bend and a slip-joint pliers to continue the bend and a vise-grip pliers to crimp it tight. Be sure everything is okay before you do this because the tray is more or less permanently installed now.

15) Braze in side and front tray braces, pop-rivet rear-center brace so as not to distort window sealing area.

16) Pop rivet flange. Then gas weld carefully using lots of wet rags.

17) Install and adjust sunroof panel as detailed in the appropriate service manual.

18) Put in new sunroof headliner (with zipper). reinstall windows.

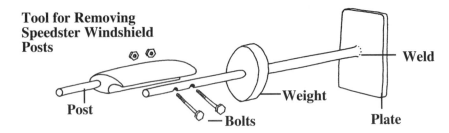

Tool for Removing Speedster Windshield Posts

Weld

Weight

Post

Bolts

Plate

19) Fuzzy seals installed and you have a completed sunroof

Windshield

Vol. 7, No. 1 Richard Miller

Removing Speedster Windshield Posts

I've devised a way of persuading obstinate Speedster windshield posts to become non-integral parts of the body as they seem to rust in place. Remove the 10 mm - 1.25 cap screw and bolt a slap hammer tool to the post. While you use the slap hammer you can carefully twist the post back and forth to break the rust loose. I made my own hammer out of a 3/4 in. diameter steel bar and an old diving belt weight. Weld a stop plate to the end of the bar, drill a hole in the weight, slide it onto the bar and bolt the bar to the post.

Vol. 10, No. 3 David Seeland

Speedster Windshield Installation

Now for a real can of worms – Speedster windshields. I have broken three of the silly things – and wouldn't you know it but the survivor is a Mexican windshield. All the broken ones were German Siglas. How did I manage to break so many? First, by removing the chrome frame from the posts and trying to slide the windshield out of the posts. The posts are just a bit too close together to do this which bends it and then the windshield cracks along a line parallel to the mirror rod. Second, I broke two

windshields across the lower corners.

One broke a few minutes after tightening a post down on the gasket that goes between the body and the post. The second broke in my great-uncle's garage in Louisville, Kentucky on the way back to Denver from the Reston Parade.

I had installed it about two weeks prior to this and driven about 2,000 miles since then. This was getting ridiculous so for the next try I made 1/8 in. aluminum spacers to fit beneath the posts, had the edges of the windshield ground smooth to eliminate stress risers, and used lots of silicone spray on the rubber and frame. I think I was successful because it has been nearly two years since I installed the last windshield. Someone suggested my problem might have been the frame which could have been bent during chroming. Check that the contour of the frame matches the contour of the windshield before attempting to install a Speedster windshield.

Vol. 8, No. 6 Don Rolph

Convertible D Windshield Installation

In restoring our Convertible D, we have had some problems with the top frame and windshield assembly. This may not be news to you old hands, but may be of interest to those just starting.

The top frame which came with the car was not the original. I suspect that it is a later B Roadster frame. The previous owner had also found a replacement windshield top bow, probably also from a later B, for the original

22

which was pretty beat up. When we tried to install the assembly, nothing fit. In checking measurements carefully, the revelation came; Convertible D and B Roadster top frames, windshields and windshield top bows are different sizes! Further searching turned up an old (1964 I think) Sigla catalog at a local glass shop which shows different part numbers for Convertible D and Roadster windshields. The D top bow and windshield is almost $7/8$ in. shorter than the Roadster along the top.

Also, the latches on the Roadster top frame will not match the original D lugs on the windshield top bow. The lugs have to be moved by redrilling and rethreading holes in the top bow (be careful, threads strip out easily in the thin brass top bow).

Another problem presented itself when we tried to remove the windshield posts for re-chroming. The tapered pins were rusted solid in the chassis holes. With a lot of heating, beating and more than a few choice words, the pins came out. Of course, because of the sophisticated removal technique and the rust, the pins were trashed. New pins had to be made. Since the fit between the pin and hole is of primary importance, we decided not to make new pins using the old metric taper. Metric tapered reamers to clean the hole are almost impossible to find (at least in my area). Instead, my machine shop and I decided to use Standard American Pin Taper, which is very close to the metric taper. But, for the American taper, reamers are readily available. I found them used at a local machine shop supplier. In making the pins, you should oversize slightly to allow for reaming out the rust in the holes. We made the new pins out of stainless steel (the cost was about $65 each), and used Never-seize so that some other poor slob can get them out again in the future. You will need a No. 8 and a No. 9 tapered reamer for the

hole, and can be mounted in a wood working brace or a T-handle for use. Go easy on the reaming and try the pin for fit often. Stop when the windshield post base is $3/16$ to $1/4$ in. above the body for the rubber gasket and a tight fit; drawing down the bottom bolt. We got a nice fit, but the job took a lot more (work and money) than we thought it would be. As far as I know, this method should work for any Convertible D or Roadster.

Vol. 4, No. 3 Tony Standen

Roadster Windshield Installation
    Tony Standen a Roadster owner in London, England listed the following reasons for cracked windshields:
    1. Side screws too tight
    2. Mirror support rod too tight
    3. Curve of windshield frame not bent to suit curvature of glass. See workshop manual.

Vol. 14, No. 3 Bruce Baker

Roadster Windshield Installation
    A Convertible D or Roadster is having the windshield replaced and the new glass has a l - 2 in. gap between the center of the glass and the cowl. The original glass (usually cracked or pitted) fits just fine. Measuring the two yields little satisfaction. They aren't exact but there is less than $1/2$ in. difference. In the long version of this story, the "We have broken one (or two or three) windshields already and the glass company says they won't do it now" addendum is added.
    The following bulletin affirms the factory's acknowledgment of nuances in windshields and the problems encountered. The windshield parts are numbered to match the car to which they were originally fit. When a "mix and match" situation is encountered, extra care is needed. "Time is money" is only part of this statement of caution. I, for one, hope to never break another glass upon installation

because I now adhere to the saying "if it looks right, it is right" (if only concerning Roadster windshields).

Most important is to match the glass. There are many areas in the whole assembly where the compound curves can trip you up, but the glass must be at least close to the original or the degree of difficulty goes up in geometrical progression. Then see item #2 of the factory bulletin.

Next, I take item #3 one more step by not only cutting the fins, but since repro rubber is usually thicker, I make two strips, to be trimmed and glued in where they look correct. This can be done outside or inside first, but relieve the curves with cuts at the radius.

I have also found that post-restoration installations can be the most time consuming after cowl rework and frame chroming distortion. Therefore, if after careful checking there is still a discrepancy, be prepared to shim, gently bend or relocate the various positions of the components.

It may appear on first trial fit that the posts are all the way down and the glass is still too short. This generally is fine after complete tightening and setting of the rubber base in the correctly positioned angle strip and the string-installed aluminum outer trim is complete (see item 5).

It has been so extreme a situation that I have, on occasion, had to eliminate the angular footing altogether and modify the base rubber and use sealer to locate (and retain water sealing). Several cases have required recontouring the glass by a local glass shop, but this was on cars which had improperly reworked cowls, either from roll over or other collision damage or from the hood-blow-up-at-speed syndrome (worn out latch adjustment could be another dissertation).

One last caution. Don't be married to the positioning of the aluminum strip retainers in relation to the wiper bases. They usually need a remake or

modification to sit just right. Patience and good luck!

SERVICE BULLETIN - All Dealers
No.. F 5/61 abroad
Subject: Changing the Windshield on Roadster Cars
Vehicle Type 356 B
Model: Roadster
Effective: Immediately

The following instructions for changing windshield on Type 356 B Roadster contain hints which are important especially in cases where the installation of the windshield is difficult due to deformation of the windshield frame through accident or distortion, or if the angle of inclination is not correct.

1. Lift out windshield with frame and remove windshield (see 356 B Workshop Manual, Section B, pages B 28 and 29).

2. Compare the shape of the glass and the frame. In case of differences the frame must be carefully straightened.

3. Cut the inner fins at the upper and lateral rubber strips (section rubber) which end left and right at the frame edges (see Fig. A below). This method prevents strains which occur with the modified installation angle of the windshield to the frame.

4. Install new windshield complete with upper and lateral rubber strips in the frame and fasten at two points.

5. Put windshield with frame without the bottom rubber strip on the body, align and bolt in the correct angle of the door windows (see 356 B

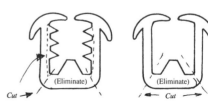

Fig. A

24

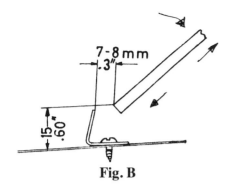

Fig. B

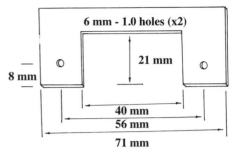

Hood Catch Retainer Plate

Workshop Manual, Section B, page B 30, item 8.)

6. The correct gap between the angular plate and front edge of the windshield must be 7 to 8 mm (see Fig. B above). If necessary, the angular plate has to be moved to obtain this gap.

7. Remove rivets of the angle.

8. Shape angular plate according to the contour of the windshield edge with an 8 mm gap and tighten on the windshield center with countersunk head screws.

9. Further instructions for installation of the windshield are given in the 356 B Workshop Manual, section B, pages 29 and 30.

Bumper

Vol. 10, No. 1 Richard Miller

Do-it-Yourself Bracket Retainers

This is the bumper bracket retaining piece (4 required) and can be made from $1/4$ in. x $3/4$ in. bar stock as shown.

Hood Catch

Vol. 10, No. 1 Richard Miller

Do-it-Yourself Retainers

This is the retainer plate for the hood catch (if you saw this in a junk box at a swapmeet, would you recognize it?) It is basically $3/16$ in. x 1 $1/8$ in. strap, drilled and tapped, but you can use $1/8$ in. material and weld nuts on the back side if you don't have a tap.

Speedster Top

Vol. 10, No. 1 Richard Miller

Rear Bow Hold Down Bracket

Judging from the number of parts that I have made for others I think a brief note on "pieces commonly lost during restoration" is in order. These are simple flat brackets with holes (threaded and not), the identity of which is often forgotten until you get to the point of needing them two years later. I'll describe them – you can give

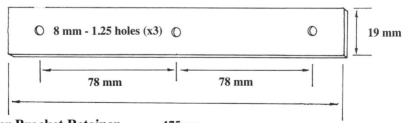

Bumper Bracket Retainer   175 mm

25

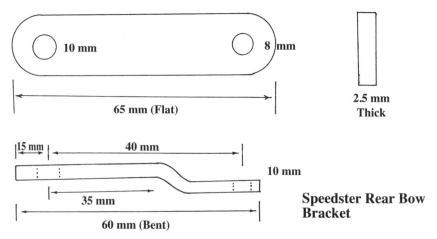

10 mm   **8 mm**

65 mm (Flat)

2.5 mm Thick

15 mm   **40 mm**

10 mm

35 mm

60 mm (Bent)

Speedster Rear Bow Bracket

them part numbers. The first is the little hold down bracket for the rear bow on a Speedster top (2 required). You can make these out of $1/8$ in. x $3/4$ in. strap. The only trick is the little jog near the middle which I hot bend (torch and hammer).

Jack Spur

Vol. 9, No. 5 David Seeland

A Cure for Mashed Jack Points
This is for western 356 owners – if you live in Maine or elsewhere in the salt belt, you probably have new jack points. I just got an axle tube from Maine and the nut on the brake line holder had pits nearly $1/8$ inch deep on each flat of the nut. Well, you say, what can you expect after 200,000 miles of salt spray? I doubt if the car had 50,000 miles – it still had the original one piece axle boots – a sure sign of low mileage. I wonder what the rest of the rust looked like.
Someone had used a floor jack under my Speedster's jack points and the inner portions were mashed up against the longitudinals. It is impossible to do much straightening from inside the jack point but it can be pulled down. Unbend the flange (pre-A, A, T-5 and early T-6 (mid-1963) 356Bs have flanges. Late T-6 cars

have no flange) with a chisel and pliers. Clamp Vise-Grip pliers firmly on the highest part of the flange. Next put a bolt through the jaw area, attach a chain to the bolt and run the chain around the front axle of your floor jack. The floor jack's front wheels should be about one inch off the floor when the chain is tight. Raise the floor jack's front end to the bottom of the car and drop repeatedly. If this isn't enough, push it down with your foot (block the handle so you can raise the front of the jack by levering the handle down). Repeat as necessary along the flange. Work out as many of the remaining dents as possible, fill, body schutz, and paint with black enamel. Not only do your jack points look better but they are less likely to rust-out from trapped water, salt and dirt.

Door Hinges

Vol. 9, No. 2 Dick Pike

Repairing Worn Out Door Hinges
Some of the vilest curses and most uninhibited screams of rage ever to be visited upon a hapless 356 are directed at the comparatively few hinges to be found in this vehicle. I'm not all that concerned about small-timers such as those on the glove-box door, the add-oil can, the folding top, the heater sys-

tem, and such. The hinges of real consequence reside on doors, the hood and Speedster seats (deck-lid hinges, though similar to those on the hood, rarely seem to be a serious problem). The remedial measures increase in complexity in just that order.

Door hinges on the Porsche 356 are no big deal provided both the doors and the outer skin just fore 'n' aft are straight (haw! haw!) and the car is not sagging amidships (oh, well!). Aside from redrilling them for oversized hinge pins, an uncommon repair, and rewelding rusted hinge mounts to the body (alright, Pike, that makes *four* qualifications!), misaligned doors yield to only two areas of tinkering (recall that latch problems can be dealt with satisfactorily only after things are kosher at the other end of the door). These are essentially side-to-side and up-and-down and fore-n'-aft adjustments. The former involves changing thickness of the shim packs between hinge and hinge-mounts to bring the door flush with the front and (to a lesser extent) rear edges of the outer skin.

The other adjustment really shouldn't require any extraordinary insight, but for cars that have gone through one or more bend-and-straighten cycles, there is a subtle tweak that may assist "problem" cases where correct clearance cannot be achieved otherwise. The latter involves routing out the oval holes in the hinge mounts and/or shaving metal from the 4-nut retainer plate behind them. Go easy with that file; it may not take much to get the clearance you seek. Other than that, door alignment is pretty much a lot of boring, cut-and-try grunt work (lucky Speedster people; your doors are so much lighter than the others!)

Hood Hinges

Vol. 9, No. 2 Dick Pike

Repairing Worn Out Hood Hinges

Porsche 356 hood hinges are of a simple but very clever design that works perfectly until the hinges (1) wear, (2) rust, (3) clog with oily dirt, (4) jam as the result of an accident that has deformed them, or (5) any combination of the above. The immediate symptom, as we all know, is that the hood won't close simply by lifting and letting go. Often the eventual result is an attempt – enter the mythic gas-station attendant – to force it shut. Only God knows (but he can't publish because his data are classified) how many ruined 356 hoods got that way because of faulty hinges.

This would be bad enough in and of itself, but if ignored long enough the damage propagates to the inner body panel, behind the fuel tank, where the hinges are attached (go on, take a look at yours). The first step in rehabilitating hood hinges is to straighten this panel and the shrouds around the hinge mounting holes, welding up any cracks you might find. I was surprised at the great improvement in rigidity this repair made to the hinge-mount area in my 1958 Speedster. But what about the hinges themselves, you say, those ~*&%¢$~ hinges.

Take heart, friends. They're a snap, even if you must hire out the minor welding involved. Like so much else, all the job takes is some patience, a good eye, and a little time. Assuming you have managed to extract both hinges from their recesses, step one is to remove the rust and oily grunge that may be clogging them. Still not moving nice and free?

Step One: Look the hinges over carefully, for almost certainly they are bent, possibly into some highly creative configurations.

Step Two: Straighten the hinges. The required work will be pretty much self-evident. Often the perforated parallel (well, they should be) arms of a hinge will be squeezed together or otherwise badly out of spec. Insert the

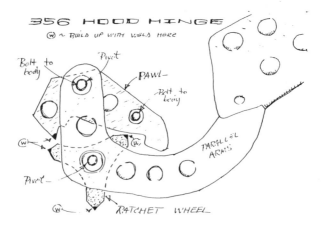

356 HOOD HINGE
(W) ~ BUILD UP WITH WELD HERE
Bolt to body
Pivot
PAWL—
Bolt to body
(W)
(W)
PARALLEL ARMS
Pivot—
(W)
RATCHET WHEEL

handle of a small square punch (Sears) between these arms as a spacer, using a large screwdriver or other device, as a pry-bar, and then squeeze the whole works in the bench vise with the punch handle serving as an anvil.

Work the punch handle back and forth in the slot until it is all the same width. This technique should restore parallelism and the correct clearance. Once you have bent and beat on the hinge sufficiently so that all parts move freely, operate the hinge (still out of the car) and see if the Good Doctor's ingenious ratchet-and-pawl mechanism functions correctly, every time. It does? Good. Isn't it an elegant device? This system is remarkably simple for the sequence of operations it must perform. Carefully watch the hinge function as you work it through several cycles; the mechanism is a lot more impressive than it seems at first blush. I'd like to have been the engineer that thought this one up. However, you certainly won't share my enthusiasm if your hinges no longer work as they should, especially after all that cleaning and straightening.

What has happened is that the pawl and the three-pointed ratchet wheel have worn and need to be restored.

Step Three: The only way to do this is to build up the worn areas by welding and then file them to the correct

contour. Don't get discouraged and throw the hinges away. The restorative process is much less intimidating than it sounds. The three tips on the ratchet wheel should be pointed, not rounded, and it takes very little welding to extend them sufficiently so that they will function as new. Likewise, by watching the mechanism work (or not work) you will see the tip of the pawl (where it contacts the ratchet points) that needs to be built up slightly as well. Once you've done this, there is no way your hood hinges will refuse to operate correctly. If you really want to get carried away, you can heat each of the three ratchet points cherry-red with the torch and then quench them in oil. This hardening should reduce the rate of wear sufficiently to allow trouble-free operation of your hood hinges well into the twenty-first century.

Vol. 11, No. 6 Bill Heidbreder

Repairing Worn Out Hood Hinges, II
Using the illustration attached, Dick suggested to "build up the worn areas on the three pointed ratchet wheel and the pawl by welding and then filing to the correct contour." While I really appreciated Dick's instructions on how to build a motor dolly, this solution sounded like too much work; and

besides, my welder would probably refuse to do anything "the way it's done in California."

Using a different approach, I fixed both hinges in less than ten minutes! Tools required? A bench vise and a flat file.

I filed the "trailing" edge of each point on the ratchet wheel so as to form a point on the tip. Then, I deepened the tip of the pawl.

Window Regulator

Vol. 11, No. 1 Vic Skirmants

Repairing Window Regulators

Window regulator falling apart. The culprit is usually the aluminum hinge pin that holds the end of the spring. The pin is just staked into the regulator and when it works loose, it falls out, letting the regulator fall apart. There are replacement steel pins available, but they are rather expensive. If the aluminum pin is broken, then there is no alternative but to get the steel one. But if it has only fallen out, it can be drilled and tapped for a 6 mm bolt. The bolt, with a washer, will hold the pin perfectly. Don't overtighten, use Loctite, and maybe grind the bolt head down a bit to ensure clearance to the window frame.

Chapter 3

Brakes

Brake Lines

Vol. 1, No. 3 Jim Lamb/ Vic Skirmants

Flexible Lines

When replacing the flexible brake lines, cut the old lines in two first to avoid twisting and putting undue strain on the solid tube, non-flexing lines. Also, it's a good idea to drain, flush and replace brake fluid about every two years. (Speaking of flexible lines, there seems to be an epidemic around here, probably from old age, of these lines rotting inside. What happens is, that the inside rubber swells up, blocking most if not all of the fluid flow. If you have problems of the brakes pulling to one side, and have fixed your leaking and frozen brake cylinders, put identical linings side-to-side, and have the correct return springs in the correct holes, check those lines!)

Vol. 13, No. 3 Vic Skirmants

Flexible Lines Revisited

One problem I have run across on 356s is the internal swelling of the brake hoses. Practically every 356 that comes in for brake work now-a-days needs new brake hoses. The hoses can look perfectly good on the outside. However, if they're the originals, chances are that they are swollen inside to the point where fluid flow is severely compromised if not completely shut off. It's very easy to tell if the hoses are bad. When bleeding the brakes, if the fluid comes out very slowly, you either have a bad hose or a restriction in the bleeder valve. Pull the bleeder valve, check it, and if it's clean, then the hose needs to be replaced. One bad hose will give you a bad pull to one side when braking. Two bad hoses at either the front or rear will give you poor braking ability, as well as the possibility of causing brake fade of the overworked functioning brakes.

Vol. 14, No. 5 Ed Hyman

Flexible Lines – Interference with Accelerator Linkage

Every year or two, I try to climb under each of my 356s – whether it needs it or not. (Really, at least twice a month in season.)

And guess what?

I found another stupid error that I had made in my inexperience . . . it seems that I adjusted the throttle at the same time as I replaced every hose in the brake system, including the little brass junction box in the back. As a slightly singed Harry Pellow might say, the Porsche gods have decided to play a little trick on me.

I had allowed the brake hose to the rear driver's side to stray into the path of the throttle ball socket where it exits the rear floor panel. It doesn't take a degree from a Large Eastern Technical School to figure out what happens when a rubber hose is allowed to rub constantly with a metal throttle part for... Oh, say ... nine or ten thousand miles. Luckily I caught my mistake in time.

After replacement of the hose, clearance was easy to adjust by changing the position of the brass junction box ever so slightly.

When inspecting or replacing any of the various cables, wires, hoses and or ball sockets, try to imagine whether or not the piece will be in the way of another system when the car is back on the ground.

Vol. 2, No. 3 William Steen, Jr

Making Your Own Brake Lines
Dr. William Steen Jr., Shreveport, LA, has added comments on brake lines. In making his own lines for his 904, he used $3/16$ in. tubing, fittings removed from other lines, a bending tool that is "...available from J.C. Whitney, gives nice smooth radius bends without kinks, ...(and is) relatively inexpensive", and a "Black Hawk double flaring tool... (from) ...a local supply house." On flaring the tubing, first be sure the fittings are on and facing the right way! An "American" brake line double flare looks like Fig. 1 in cross-section. A "metric" brake line double flare looks like Fig. 2 in cross-section. Using the double flaring tool results in the "metric" flare just before the final operation of squashing the tubing back in on itself, so stop there.

Vol. 7, No. 5 David Seeland

Restoring Copper Plated Lines
The crossover line between the wheel cylinders had only remnants of its original copper plating. I bought a bottle of Testors PLA copper enamel at a hobby shop and painted the lines and I'm very pleased with the results.

Trouble Shooting

Vol. 5, No. 1 Vic Skirmants

Brake Pulling
More hints and tips. Does your car pull one way when braking, and then the other way when you get off the brakes? Doesn't make any sense, does it. You've checked all the obvious things; adjustment, frozen wheel cylinder pistons, tire pressures (that's right, tire pressures), brake shoe return springs, leaking wheel cylinders. Even a small amount of brake fluid coating the brake shoe will cause a terrible pull. But that's not the problem. Why does the car pull the other way when you release the brakes? Swollen brake hoses! Those old rubber brake hoses can swell almost shut or even completely closed. You hit the brakes, the swollen hose doesn't pass enough fluid to actuate that brake cylinder as quickly as the other side, and the car pulls toward the other side. You correct with the steering wheel, you're going straight, enough fluid has finally passed through the restricted hose to actuate the cylinder. Now you release the brakes, the good hose releases the fluid, that wheel cylinder relaxes, and the car heads for the ditch

Fig. 1   **Fig. 2**

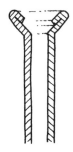   

on the side of the bad hose. Try removing the hose. If you can't blow through it easily, it's restricted. Once you have a replacement, cut that old hose open and marvel at how it closed off.

Master Cylinder

Vol. 5, No. 1 Vic Skirmants

Rebuilding the Master Cylinder in the Car

While on the subject of brakes, if you have to rebuild the master cylinder, it can be done in the car. This saves breaking off all the brake line ends when trying to remove them from the cylinder. Pull the floorboards, shorten the adjustment on the brake pushrod, and remove. Pull apart the master cylinder as usual. When putting the brake pushrod back in, be sure to adjust it so there is about one millimeter of free play before the master cylinder plunger is activated, or you'll have your brakes on all the time.

Vol. 5, No. 4 Dale Lucas

Using VW Rebuild Kits

The VW master cylinder rebuild kit, #111.698.183, is suitable for a 1958 356A. I don't believe this will work on 356C models, so if you get one of these kits, check out the similarity in the rubber parts.

Vol. 13, No. 3 Steve Proctor

Brake Pressure Switch Failure

While driving my 1967 Porsche 912 to work one morning, I applied the brakes and at once. the passenger compartment filled with smoke and I encountered a total and complete brake failure. Luckily, I was slowing for a stop sign at the top of a hill in my residential area and was traveling at low speed. Upon arriving home

(driving slowly and using the emergency brake), I noted that there was a massive brake fluid leak from the front-bottom of the car. Suspecting a master cylinder failure, I placed the car on jack stands, pulled off the protection plate and noted that the fluid was leaking from the brake light pressure switch on the master cylinder. I reached up to retract the somewhat degenerated boot over the switch and the switch crumbled in my hand.

Apparently, in the 21 years of this unit's life, the phenolic plastic insert in the pressure switch had degenerated and eventually suffered a traumatic failure. The smoke was caused by burning insulation when the two wires on the pressure switch shorted out. The brake failure was caused by the pressure loss when the fluid squirted out of the failed switch. I don't know whether to be amazed that the original switch had functioned for all of these years (my foot is most often on the pedal to the right) or upset that the unit failed.

I checked my catalogs and determined by the drawings, change in part numbers and price that Porsche went to a dual (left front/right rear, right front/left rear) configuration master cylinder in 1968. With this in mind, I would recommend that all owners of 1967 and older Porsches immediately (if not done in the recent past) replace the brake light pressure switches on their cars with a Porsche replacement unit. Volkswagens of the same vintage used interchangeable units at about the same price (approximately $20) and that some Volkswagen parts houses sell non-OEM units for about half the price. However, one must keep in mind that this configuration presents the potential for a single point failure which could result in failure of the hydraulic brake system. Saving $10 in this instance seems like false economy.

Incidently, I used this opportunity to purge the system of all old fluid, replace with new and bleed the system. I was embarrassed at the appearance of the old brake fluid and resolved to replace it at more frequent intervals.

Vol. 10, No. 3 Bob Heacox

Dual Master Cylinder Update
The 1967 VW type I master cylinder is a 19 mm dual circuit type. The part number is 113.611.015.BD.

Vol. 14, No. 3 David Seeland

Conversion to Dual Master Cylinder
A few years ago Larry Skoglund ran his Carrera 2 cabriolet hard in high speed track events. One day as he pulled up to a gas pump, his brake pedal suddenly went completely to the floor. No. brakes! A steel brake line had fractured. He could have been at the end of the straight at Brainerd at the car's terminal velocity of 125 mph. Not much to do but pray if brake failure occurred in that sort of situation. Brake failure could even be worse on the street. A neighbor rebuilt (?) his bug brakes. He did something wrong because they soon completely failed at a red light at the busiest intersection in town. He made the sharpest turn he could but went across the center island and ended up coasting the wrong way in three lanes of heavy oncoming traffic. It was sheer luck that he didn't hit anything.

If you have confidence in your ability to miraculously avoid near certain catastrophe, or if you are 18 years old and as Garrison Keillor describes it, "at the peak of your immortality," then skip the rest of this. Being far past 18 and most assuredly mortal, and having no guardian angel in constant attendance, I decided that I would install a dual master cylinder in my disc-braked 1959 356A sunroof coupe that I'm slowly restoring for a "driver." Federal safety regulations required that cars made in the U.S. or officially imported after 1967 have dual master cylinders, so that in case of failure of, say, a single front wheel cylinder, both rear wheel brakes will continue to operate. In some cars a "dual diagonal" system is used so one front brake and the diagonally opposite rear brake will continue to operate. Braking ability is much impaired, but you can stop.

All drum or disc braked 356s have an ATE (Alfred Teves) single master cylinder. Early master cylinders have a bolt-on aluminum reservoir. Disc brake cars (356C) have a special internal valve to relieve brake line pressure. This is attested to by the "spezial bodenventil" inscription on an aluminum band. For single-circuit disc brake conversions, it is possible to rebuild the drum-brake master-cylinder with a disc brake rebuild kit. (Concours note: currently available ATE replacements have plastic reservoirs instead of the original aluminum.)

Disc-brake master cylinders for 356s have a remote, in-the-luggage compartment reservoir attached via hose and tubing to a rubber plug in the top of the reservoir. The single reservoir indicates they are also single-circuit brakes. From 1968 on, Porsche 911/912s had dual cylinders). The 356 master cylinder extends only a few mm rearward from the mounting flange, but the 911 master cylinder extends 30 mm farther towards the rear because it is mounted on a double bulkhead.

As on the disc-braked 356, the 911 dual-circuit brake master cylinder has a reservoir mounted in the luggage compartment, but it is a dual compartment reservoir. If one circuit goes bad and loses its fluid, then the other circuit still has a fluid supply. Another widget is a brake failure warning sensor that provides a ground circuit when excessive piston movement occurs on brake failure. This causes a "brake failure" light to come on. It is not a brake light switch although they are similar in appearance.

The longer (early 911) 19 mm dual master cylinder can be made to work in a 356 providing fail-safe braking. The brake operating pushrod must be shortened 20 mm and the threaded area extended about 15 mm with a 10 mm x 1.5 die.

The outlet lines on the dual cylinder are both on the left side and there is only one front outlet. This forced me to use the arrangement pictured in figure 5 because I was unable to make new left and right front steel lines or extend the rear line. I bought a Snap-on metric double-flaring tool, but VW and Porsche steel brake-lines are not double-flared. They have mushroom-shaped ends.

Ron Redden is proprietor of Renn-werk, a Porsche-only wrecking yard here in Denver (303) 936-9192. He is the ultimate "tool junkie" and when I told him my problem he whipped out a Hazet VAG 1356/1 flaring tool and showed me how easily it made the proper 356 flares. (Another concours note: buy one of these and make your own plastic-tubing covered rear lines, but you'd better do a lot because it's an $80 tool. However, by making them an inch longer, you can replace the $17 356 rear brake hose with a one inch shorter $6 VW hose.)

The front lines are taken off the dual-circuit master-cylinder outlet via a 150 mm (about) piece of VW? steel brake line and a brass "T" (part number 914.355.667.00) from the brake tubes near the transaxle area of all 356s. Another short length of steel line and another "T" (not shown) provides a place to attach the long steel line for the rear brakes that comes through the tunnel, and a brake-light switch. The object of all this is to get the outlets from the dual cylinder to a place where the stock lines would attach on a stock master cylinder. A bolt was run through both mounting holes in the brass tees and wired to the cylinder body to reduce vibration.

Were I to do this again, I would use drum brake banjo ring (914.355.531 .00) and "banjo bolt with hose brace" (914.355.534.00) at each cylinder outlet and make a new longer right front line. The front banjo and bolt would be used for the two front lines and the rear banjo and bolt would be used for the lengthened rear line and the brake light switch. Use a "connecting piece" (914.355.661.00) and a short piece of brake line to extend the rear line. I used a VW bug dual reservoir (113.611.131) mounted just at the front of the gas tank of the 356A. I also used VW lines from the reservoir to the cylinder. These are blue cloth covered hoses specifically made to be brake fluid resistant. Do *not* use the cloth covered fuel hose. A single flare at the bottom end of each steel line was used to help retain them in the rubber inlet fittings in the master-cylinder.

For a dual master cylinder in a drum-brake car, use a Super Beetle (about $30) master cylinder (Fig. 7) or replace the dual disc brake cylinder ($90) check valve with a drum brake valve from a 356 master cylinder rebuild kit.

Work carefully, check for leaks, road test at slow speeds and check for leaks again before trusting your brakes. You don't need the excitement that my neighbor had in his bug and you might not be so lucky either. Brake pads have to be broken in before track use. Volatile components are released from new pads as they heat up resulting in a much decreased coefficient of friction until all the volatiles escape. Use them gently on the street for a while before track events.

Handbrake

Vol. 5, No. 5 Vic Skirmants

Frozen Handbrake Repair

Has your parking brake ever frozen up on your 1956 - 1965? I don't mean that it wouldn't work, I mean that it wouldn't release. Don't bother greasing the cable housings at the rear; that's usually not the problem. The problem generally is the parking brake cross-shaft up front. That's the large bellcrank-like piece that the cable from the brake handle pulls, then it in turn pulls on the cable that enters the forward part of the tunnel. There is a pivot at each end of the cross-shaft. These pivots are greased at the factory, have an O-ring, but no further provision for lubricating. You'll have to get underneath and loosen the two 10 mm head nuts on the left side clamp so you can move it and the cross-shaft to the left. Clean up the right side pivot, grease it, slide the cross-shaft back on and clean the left side pivot, grease it, and slide it back to the right. Tighten up the two nuts and you're all set. Don't worry, it's really much harder than it sounds. But if that's the problem, that's the only way to fix it properly.

Drum Brakes

Vol. 6, No. 6 Pat Ertel

Wheel Cylinder Rebuilding

I knew I shouldn't have done it. I should have ignored the pulling to the left and the earsplitting screech and left the brakes alone. I mean, they did slow the car down pretty fast if you kept a firm grip on the steering wheel and leaned on the pedal hard enough. But, I threw caution to the wind and, ignoring the tried and true "Sleeping Dog" theory of automechanics, I ripped the coupe's brakes apart for a complete rebuild. What started out to be a simple weekend project turned into a three weekend project and came frighteningly close to costing a lot of money. This is how I managed to get brakes without going broke.

The first thing I did was send the drums and shoes to a reputable local brake shop. They made the drums round again and re-arched the new shoes to fit the diameter of the drums. This was the only easy part.

Next I disassembled the front wheel cylinders and discovered that each one had rust pits down in the depths where the brake fluid lives. It is strictly verboten to rebuild rusty brake cylinders. The rubber cup inside will contact the rough, rusty surface which will soon wear out the sealing edge on the cup. Before long the brake fluid will have leaked out and your car will be reduced to a "parts car for sale" and in the back of the *Registry*. I found three ways to deal with the problem.

1. Buy new cylinders. A very expensive way to get the job done. It costs at least $170 for the front wheels alone.

2. Sleeve the old cylinders. Ed Statkus, of Chicago, brought this to my attention. Ed sent me an ad from White Post Restorations, PO Drawer D, White Post, Virginia 22663, (703) 837-1140. W.P.R. will bore the cylinder and press in a brass sleeve for $18 each. I have spoken with one of W.P.R.'s customers who was well pleased with the service and workmanship.

3. Use shorter cups. I discovered this by accident. This only works if the rust damage is confined to the brake fluid pool and has not progressed out toward the mouth of the cylinder.

ATE and Schaefer brake cups are very long as brake cups go and extend very far into the cylinder. American made United brake cups (sold at NAPA stores, use $3/4$ in. cups, which is only .002 in. larger than 19 mm) are about $3/32$ in. shorter than the German ones and don't extend into the rust damaged area. The total cost of rebuilding my front wheel cylinders using this method was $2.00.

Next came the master cylinder.

There were some rust pits in it so I pitched it and bought a new one. The short cup trick won't work and the cost of having a sleeve installed and buying a rebuild kit is almost as great as the cost of a new cylinder. New master cylinders are readily available and relatively cheap.

I replaced all the rubber brake lines on principle. The car had VW lines on it and they were not the right length anyway. The proper lines are available from *Registry* advertisers so you may as well get the right ones. I inspected the steel lines and replaced the ones with any rust spots, again the right length lines are available so I got those instead of fooling around making loops and all the mickey mouse stuff that had been on my car. The long line that goes from front to rear was perfect except for $1/4$ in. at the grommet where it goes through the front bulkhead. The rust here was severe, which goes to show that rust can be wily and treacherous.

Once I got to the rear wheel cylinders I thought I had it made. I honed them a little and they cleaned up perfectly. I stuck the new $3/4$ in. cups in and... they fell right through. The rear wheel cylinders were 20 mm! All the literature I consulted was emphatic, "Use only 19 mm cylinders". I checked my junk transaxles for some 19s, but they both had 20s. Bud West checked his parts stash and his spares were 20 mm too. I couldn't wait any longer to drive my car so I decided to use the 20s temporarily. Theoretically the rear wheels would get too much braking action and lock up under hard braking, but my car stops fine and shows no sign of premature locking at the rear. I suppose it would be better to have 19s but you can rest assured your car won't crash and burn on the way out of the garage just because the wheel cylinders have a big "20" cast on them no matter what the repair manuals say. But there are two questions raised by these wheel cylinders

that might have interesting answers. Why are there so many apparently incorrect wheel cylinders in use and why is the bore of a "20 mm" cylinder .813 in. ($13/16$ in.) instead of .787 in. (20 mm)?

Finally, I buttoned everything back up and poured in the silicone brake fluid. Ordinary glycol based fluid absorbs water which produces all the rust that caused all that trouble back in paragraph three. Silicone fluid doesn't absorb moisture and it doesn't eat holes in your paint either. It costs about twice as much as glycol fluid, but it's approved by an agency of the federal government (DOT) which makes it worth it. My coupe was full on 17 oz.

As soon as I made the car stop I took it down to the gas station and filled it up with gasohol. I've been running gasohol through my 1600 Normal all season. I've noticed no increase or decrease in performance and no change in mileage with the 10% corn juice mixture.

Vol. 10, No. 3 Vic Skirmants

Full Contact Brake Shoes
Dan Pelelovich, Monroeville PA, asks about getting full contact on the brake shoes. To accomplish this, the shoes have to be arc-ground to the diameter of the brake drums. Any fully equipped auto machine shop should be able to do this. The machine that does this is set to the diameter of the drum, and then merely grinds the friction material off the brake shoe to match the drum. Dan asked if there was a way to do it himself. Has anyone home-made something of this nature?

Vol. 12, No. 1 Vic Skirmants

Drum vs. Disc Brakes
First off, some questions from Bud Osbourne on 356 drum brakes. Bud's first request was for a comparison of

Porsche drums vs. discs in terms of performance. I don't have any specific figures as far as stopping distances and such, but from a seat-of-the-pants standpoint, both systems feel about the same when everything is working as it should. The drum brakes are more sensitive to adjustment, the discs don't have any adjustment to worry about. When it comes to hard use and fade, there is no comparison. The drums are totally inadequate for racing use, while the discs perform admirably.

To get maximum efficiency from the drum brakes, the shoes should be arc-ground to the exact radius of the drum. It might be difficult to find an auto shop that can still do this operation.

If a brake drum is worn beyond the maximum limit, it could theoretically be reconditioned by installing a new iron liner. If anyone finds a shop that could do this, please let us know. In reconditioning the hydraulic system, the only real problem is the breaking off of the bleeder screws if they are very rusted. If you suspect the screws might be stuck, remove and disassemble the cylinder, then heat the area around the base of the screw with an oxyacetylene torch. This should break the rust bond. Then hone and rebuild as normal.

Annular Disc Brakes

Vol. 7, No. 1 David Seeland

Rebuilding Annular Disc Brakes

The 356B Carrera 2 Type 695 disc brakes are unique. The disc is bolted at five points on its outer edge to a "hub spider". The hub appears to be similar to a finless aluminum brake drum, without the steel liner and cut away along the rim between the disc mounting points for pad access. The four-piston iron calipers (not aluminum as stated by Ludwigsen) grip

the disc from the inside rather than from the outside as on all the other disc brakes I've seen. Drum-brake wheels are used and until a wheel is removed it is not obvious that a 356 B Carrera 2 has disc brakes.

A booklet titled "Porsche disc brake" was published in June of 1962 and included with the owners manual, perhaps because the Carrera 2 was planned for production with drum brakes?

Returning to my leaky caliper piston seals, it is obvious the fix is seal replacement. These "square-cut" or "lathe-cut" o-rings have a square cross-section and are not available from Stoddard or Polak or anyone else that I tried. They are still listed as available parts by Porsche, but Ron Anthony wrote the factory and was told to replace his brakes with 356C discs because they had no parts.

I found that a friend had successfully replaced the square-cut caliper seals on a Simca 1100 coupe with the common round cross-section o-rings. Normally, in a disc brake, the square-cut o-ring deforms into a parallelogram when the piston moves toward the disc, and then as the hydraulic pressure is removed returns to a square cross-section pulling the piston back with it eliminating pad drag. I was worried that the round cross-section o-rings would not have this spring action but the trial assembly of a caliper indicated a similar spring effect. The o-rings are ethylene propylene rubber, Parker Seal Company numbers 2-213 (rear) and 2-218 (rear).

Before trying the "round" o-rings, I thought I had found a better solution: "Quad-Rings", o-rings that look like four smaller o-rings fused together into a near-square cross-section. Those available locally were nitrile (buna-N) rubber that have a brake-fluid compatibility rating of 3 (doubtful, sometimes OK for static seal). So, in spite of the geometric desirability of the Quad-Ring, I thought I was going to have to use the "1" compatibility ethylene propylene round cross-section o-rings.

Paul Rettig to the rescue – he had found Quad-Rings with a "1" brake fluid compatibility and bought the minimum quantity of 100 of each of the two sizes necessary. If you have a need for other sizes contact Minnesota Rubber, 3630 Woodale, St. Louis Park, Minnesota 55416, (612) 927-1400) the manufacturer of Quad-Rings (minimum order $250).

Two problems remain: dust seals and pistons. Porsche 911 rear dust seals are the same as Carrera 2 fronts. Although I haven't seen them yet, I think 1969 - 1972 Saab 99 and 99E rear dust covers might fit. The pistons are chrome plated and corrosion or wear can render them unusable. If the caliper body could be bored, then 35 mm 911 rear pistons might be used in place of the 33 mm Carrera 2 pistons, and 27 mm 1969 - 1972 Saab 99 rear pistons could be used in the 25 mm Carrera 2 calipers. This should decrease necessary pedal pressures but raises the problem of adequate master cylinder volume. If the stock $3/4$ in. master cylinder is too small, ATE makes $13/16$, $7/8$, $15/16$, 1 and 1 $1/16$ in. master cylinders.

White Post Restorations, Drawer D, White Post, VA 22663, (703) 837-1140, can bore brake cylinder or calipers and put in brass sleeves. I don't know if they can put the necessary 2 to 3 microinch finish on an un-sleeved bored caliper. One other outfit puts stainless steel sleeves in Corvette calipers. Ed Jarett, my machinist friend, says that the boring would have to be done with an internal grinder because the bore can't be honed smooth.

One other reported problem is cracking of the annular disc around the mounting holes. Check them occasionally.

A final word of caution, treat brake modifications with respect. Engine problems are expensive but rarely

cause injuries. Brake failure can cause severe trauma to both the vehicle and its occupants, so be careful!

If you would like to know more about o-rings than any of your friends, Parker Seals Company, (800) 272-7537, puts out an o-ring handbook for a nominal sum. I was given one at the local dealer.

Disc Brake Conversion

Vol. 8, No. 5 David Seeland

Putting Disc Brakes on a Drum Brake Car

First, although I've had excellent luck with drum brakes in 15 minute periods of $10/10$ths driving on tracks with the Speedster, it appears that disc brakes may offer some performance advantages (even cost advantages – drum brake parts are very expensive once you get past buying the rubber parts). Anyway, I had a set of C disc brakes and some 6 in. steel wheels so I thought I might as well use them.

Necessary parts for conversion

Front: Everything from the trailing arms out. The trailing arms are the same, as are the links, but the spindles are absolutely necessary.

Rear: Castings at the outer ends of the axle tubes and everything outboard (or the complete axle tube plus casting) If you are converting a 356A, you will need all the metal lines in the vicinity of the transaxle. Drum-brake 356B's have the same lines as the C from the torsion bar tube "downstream" to the axle-tube brakeline brackets. Be sure to get the emergency brake cables and sheaths.

Miscellaneous: Get the piece of bent sheet steel in the center tunnel that connects the single cable from the emergency brake handle to the dual rear cables (and the nuts at the cable ends). Also needed are either the entire disc brake master cylinder or a disc brake master cylinder rebuild kit. Except for the fact that the drum brake master cylinder has an integral reservoir, it is exactly the same casting as a disc brake cylinder. The difference is in the internal parts, specifically a small hole in one of the pieces. Put the disc brake cylinder indentifying band on your modified cylinder to help the next guy. You should get new pads and caliper rebuild kits. Buy ATE and you will get new pad-pin clips. New pistons are available.

Disassembly

A note on brake line removal. If you will inquire of Stoddard, you will find the outer rear plastic covered steel lines are $18 each. Remove them and the other lines very carefully. There will almost always be one of the fittings that will come loose so a whole section of line-hose-bracket or whatever can be removed. Once you have it out it can be disassembled rather easily by applying heat with a propane torch to the 11 mm ATF fittings and then penetrating oil after breaking the 11 mm end fitting loose from the steel line. If you try to force the fittings without applying heat you've just thrown away $18 because the steel brake line will twist off. If the steel lines are not usable because of excessive rust, or just too grubby looking to suit you, either buy new ones or make your own using your old (11 mm ATF) line ends (get them cadmium plated if they're rusty looking) and a piece of reclaimed steel line from inside the shift tunnel of a VW or Porsche. Flare one end with a Hazet metric double flaring tool, slide on plastic tubing from the hardware store, slide on the other fitting, flare, and bend to match your old line. Don't bend the line first or you won't be able to put the plastic tubing on.

The C shop manual supplement says not to use more than 40 PSI to remove the caliper pistons. I found that if I squeezed the piston inward

with a vise to loosen it up, sprayed WD-40 around it after removing the dust seal and used 100 PSI, I could just manage to get them out. I also discovered that I could screw a brake line fitting into my blow gun after unscrewing the tip, which made it easier to get full pressure behind the piston. Use a block of wood between the pistons and wrap the whole caliper in a rag because when the piston does break loose, it does so with a lot of vigor.

If you would like to install one piece boots for concours reasons or for the much better sealing they provide, you have to remove the castings from the axle. This is easy to do. First remove the casting locating pin with a drift. Then get a large angle iron (3 in. wide or so) several inches longer than the axle and place it vertically on the floor with the inside of the casting in the angle at the top and the transaxle end of the axle toward the floor. Drop a VW or Porsche rear axle bearing spacer into the casting because this spacer is just the right size to rest on the axle tube itself. Put a large socket against the sleeve and whack away with a large hammer or small sledgehammer.

To reassemble (don't forget the boot and the steel side-plate), place a steel plate over the casting and hammer it back on and re-install the locating pin. Be very careful that the casting slides on so the pin lines up exactly with the groove in the axle tube. If it doesn't, start over and be more careful. *Note: I haven't done this myself, but I have been told it is possible to work a well-lubricated boot over the bearing housing/shock mount casting with two large screwdrivers.*

Installation

The master cylinder is a direct bolt in replacement, but you will have to provide a mount for the brake fluid reservoir if you use the disc brake master cylinder. I used a large stainless steel clamp around the gas tank trap. If you have an unpitted drum brake master cylinder (I didn't) and rebuild it with a disc brake kit, you will avoid this problem, but it will be harder to check the fluid level.

Since this is a performance set-up, leave the dust/water shields off when you install the new brakes. This will provide somewhat better brake cooling.

Ventilated rotors from a 911 can be used by cutting off a bit of their outer diameter on a lathe. They are thicker, and I would suspect that the associated calipers would have to be used.

I used early 911 rear calipers on my conversion because the attachment ears were broken off both rear calipers in a wreck.

The ears on one axle casting were bent so I heated them and bent them back into alignment with a hammer. The eye-ball alignment was perfected by cutting a few thousandths off the mating surface with a mill. An ear was broken off the other casting and I arc-welded it after heating the casting; however, I didn't trust the repaired ears and used a different set of axle tubes and castings. Better safe than sorry when it comes to brake parts. Be very careful!

The only part of the installation that requires any fabrication is that the disc brake emergency cable end at the body is different. Remove the threaded adjusters at the body and braze on a $3/8$ in. long steel tube that just fits inside the disc brake cable housing. The carburetor idle (?) crossover tube from a 1973 (?) VW type 4 engine is perfect for this. The cables will flop around if you don't do this.

You will also have to grind down the area just behind the threads at the forward ends of the emergency brake cables or you won't be able to get them through the tubes in the tunnel. Other than that, installation is pretty much the reverse of removal. If you don't have to install the brakes right now, I would wait until all the sections of this series have been run because it will make some of the other suspension modifications easier if they were done first.

Drum Brake Wheels on a Disc Brake Car

It is also obvious that one of the possibilities for a disc-brake conversion is to use the Porsche-designed annular ring Carrera 2 disc brakes. The primary advantage being original wheels and hub caps. In fact I recently got a letter asking what I thought of such a conversion. In a nutshell, my answer is the Carrera 2 brakes are too expensive, it is hard to find parts, and they should be saved for Carrera 2s. There is another solution to the problem thanks to Keith Ingram of Clovis, New Mexico. He uses 5 1/2 in. drum brake wheels and hub caps with 165 x 15 tires on his ATE disc-braked Speedster! His trick is simple and practical. Cut the centers out of the drum brake wheels about at the center of the lug bolt holes with a lathe and weld in a quarter inch steel plate with an outside diameter equal to the inside diameter of the hole just cut. Cut a hub hole and drill lug-bolt holes in the plate after tack-welding the plate. It is not possible to use 185/70 tires at the rear. Keith uses 165 tires on the street with his modified 5 1/2 in. drum-brake wheels and 185/70 tires (XWX) on Fuchs 5 1/2 x 15 in. forged alloys for racing.

The 165 tires on the modified rims are a very close fit at the rear (on the outside against the body) because the shape of the drum brake wheels doesn't allow the wheel rim to be moved as far inward as with a disc brake wheel that has a flatter center section. As it is, a small amount of metal must be removed from the caliper. If you didn't mind having unique front and rear wheels a little more positive (toward the outside) offset could be used at the front. Or if you have a coupe, where you are not limited at the outside of the rear wheel, you could build the wheels with a little more positive offset (and probably use 185/70 tires on the modified wheels). Keith built his wheels with the center of the $1/4$ in. plate at the center of the rim cut but you could put them together with about $1/8$ in. more positive offset. Tack-weld if you are going to experiment.

Disc Brakes

Vol. 10, No. 3 Mike Robbins

Adapting Early 911/912 Front Rotors for the 356C

Are your 356C front brake discs worn beyond the factory specified limit? Have you tried to buy new ones and found out that there aren't any? Do you have access to some worn discs from an early 911 or 912? Well bunky, we have an answer for you. How to adapt 911-912 front discs to a 356.

The thickness of a new 356C disc is .406" to .413". The thickness of the new 911-912 disc is .492" to .500". A 911-912 disc can therefore be worn considerably and still be thicker than a new 356 disc. There is a problem in that the centerline of the disc section in relation to the hub is different. Following is a means of handling this. Be sure to read the comments at the end.

1. The distance from the surface where the caliper mounts on the bracket section of the stub axle to the inboard face of a new 356C disc is .663". You can confirm this by measuring a caliper from the mounting surface to the split line and subtract .206". (.206" is half the thickness of a new disc.)
2. Remove the caliper and the hub-disc assembly from the 356 stub axle.
3. Separate the hub and the disc.
4. Assemble the 911-912 disc to the

hub and mount this assembly on the stub axle. If the disc is still assembled to the 911-912 hub, you can use that assembly but don't mix bearing races.

5. Measure the distance described in 1 above. It will be greater than .663" unless you're using a new disc. Subtract .5 663" from the dimension you have to determine error. If you are using a new disc there will be no error and you can skip the next step.
6. Bring the inboard side of the 911-912 disc to the correct distance (.663") by one of the following methods:
   a. Shim between hub and hat section of disc.
   b. Machine the mounting surface of the caliper and/or the stub axle bracket section to move the caliper in the outboard direction.
   c. Combination of "a" and "b".
   d. It may be possible to remove material from the bearing spacer on the stub axle. I haven't checked this for other complications.
7. Machine the outboard face of the disc to give .406" to .413" thick (thickness of new 356C disc). The new face has to go down to $7 \, 5/16$ in. diameter.
8. Turn the disc around in the lathe and face the inboard side of the disc to remove the small step where the pad has run. Face to $7 \, 5/16$ in. diameter. These cuts to $7 \, 5/16$ in. diameter are necessary because the pads run closer to the hub axis on a 356 than on a 911-912. Leave the disc in the lathe for the next step.
9. Cut a chamfer 30° x $3/16$ in. deep where the hat section meets the inboard side of the disc. The 30° is relative to the face of the disc.

This relief is to give clearance at the lower end of the suspension link and the head of the lower link pin. This will not be necessary if you changed the disc-to-caliper location by method 6b. Check by turning the steering to full lock and rotating the disc. Removal of too much metal here may have disastrous consequences.

10. The outside diameter of the disc must be turned down to 10.81".

11. Remount everything on the car and you should have a disc the thickness of a new one and centered in the caliper.

In order to retain flexibility for component interchange between my three cars, I did not want to alter hubs, calipers or spindles. Not to mention the work involved. However, if the used 911/912 discs you have are worn excessively on the inboard side you may have to go that route (6b above). By the same token, there is some reasonable limit as to how much you shim between the hubs and the disc without losing the spigot feature. I suppose you could make up an extension for the spigotting diameter of the hub and fasten it to the hub. But you also have the clearance problem mentioned in 9 above.

I'm sure there are other ways of solving the worn brake disc problem. A friend of mine machined the faces of the caliper halves so they would fit the thinner discs but I don't think I'd go that route. Of course if you don't let your pads get too thin and don't use your brakes too hard, maybe you can live with thin discs. Now the next project is to see what to do about the rear discs.

Calipers

Vol. 6, No. 1 Vic Skirmants

No Brake Pedal Pressure Following Caliper Rebuild

I will refer only to the 1964 - 1965 C model discs, not the weird Carrera "inside-out" discs.

I have found, after a complete rebuild of the wheel calipers, that there is no resistance to the brake pedal hitting the floor. Even after several attempts at bleeding the system, with no air coming out, just pure, clean brake fluid, there is still no pedal. A couple of quick pumps and the brakes will work somewhat, but that's not the way to drive off into the sunset. If you do try to drive it this way, and you don't hit anything, you will eventually get a good pedal.

It seems that after everything has been apart, and new piston seals put in the calipers, the combination of the seals not being all seated in place and the built-in brake adjuster in the piston being shoved all the way back because of new brake pads, results in the piston trying to return too much after releasing the brake pedal. When you then apply the brakes, all the fluid being pumped by the master cylinder is used up pushing the pistons closer to the discs, and about the time they're ready to squeeze the pads, you're out of pedal travel. After a little use everything settles in a bit, and you have good brakes.

The solution is to rebuild and bleed the brakes as usual, then pull one brake pad at a time, put in a thinner used one or some type of spacer to keep the piston from coming out too far. Pump the brakes a couple of times, then remove the old pad or spacer, push back the piston and reinstall the new pad. Keep an eye on the fluid level in the reservoir.

Vol. 10, No. 4 Vic Skirmants

Stuck Caliper Pistons

The calipers usually stick after several years and/or very little use. Unless a piston is really badly stuck, it can be freed up by pulling out the brake pad and gently pushing on the

42

brake pedal. Put an old worn out pad in to keep the piston from coming out too far. Then push the piston back with a large screwdriver. Work it back and forth a few times and it should be fine. Silicone fluid will not hurt the rubber in the system, but I did not find it satisfactory for racing use. It will not hurt braided steel brake lines either. If the piston is very badly stuck, the caliper has to be removed. If the piston is stuck badly enough not to break free using the break pedal pressure, I can guarantee it won't pop out with air pressure. The way to get it out then, is to gently screw a grease fitting into one of the holes, remove the cross-over brake fluid line, put a bleeder screw in the hole to seal it, and use your grease gun to force out the piston; this will always work.

Vol. 10, No. 6 Vic Skirmants

Stuck Caliper Pistons, II

Two comments from Rick Veneski, New Britian, CT. Referring to an earlier column of mine about frozen disc brake pistons, Rick recommends using a 2250 psi scuba tank as a pressure source to blow out the stuck pistons. He says this will work. I say it will probably kill somebody! That's what's nice about using a grease gun; it's steady, controllable pressure. If you can't find the correct rear wheel seal for your disc-braked car, Rick says the "Vera" brand seal 65-2023 will fit. He thinks it's listed for some type of BMW.

This could not be verified – September 1994

Vol. 17, No. 4 Geof Fleming

Stuck Caliper Pistons and Other Disc Brake Troubleshooting

Whenever Porsche enthusiasts talk about brakes, the old disc versus drum question inevitably comes up. It should be noted at the start that both systems are excellent, assuming maintenance has been adhered to. The main ingredient that tips the scale in favor of the disc brake is consistency. It is the ability to provide repeated sure, straight stops that give the disc brake its edge over the older drum setup. Having said that, I'll now back track and reveal that I personally prefer drums and for a very good reason. I strongly dislike brake work, and have found that discs require much more work than the old drums.

One of our members had a semiserious disc brake incident while enroute to the Mystic Spring Fling. The entire caliper (rear) was engulfed in flames! No, this was not a case of "burning-in-the brakes" but simply burning brakes! While disaster was avoided and the car ultimately repaired, the weekend was diminished for the unlucky couple who had expected to have use of the car for the event.

I've had some similar experiences in the normal course of driving and can tell you how unpleasant it is. Disc brakes develop a tendency for the pistons to seize in the caliper bores. When such a seizure occurs, the piston is forced against the disc, as it should; however, when the pressure is released, instead of retracting back into its bore, the piston remains engaged. Driving the car in this condition will usually not give any adverse symptoms until the brake seizure is pretty far advanced; in which case you might notice that the car won't roll when on a steep grade, even with the handbrake off. Another sure sign that there is less than full release is to drive the car casually for a few miles, trying to minimize braking. Park the vehicle, and touch the rim of each wheel. You might also touch the wheel nearer the center. Under normal conditions, the wheel should be slightly warm, at best. If it is too hot to touch, you need those brakes looked after!

I have seen this situation happen with drum braked cars, but in those cases, it is usually caused by failure of the old rubber brake hoses not allowing the fluid to travel back from whence it came. The drum brakes at least have springs which aid the brake shoe retraction, unlike the discs.

In order to avoid becoming a victim of the old sticking brake system, an owner would be wise to periodically jack up the car and spin each wheel; first when the car is jacked, then after entering the cockpit, step on the brake pedal a few times. Now go back to the same wheel and see if it spins as easily as before.

To isolate whether or not it is brake hose failure or seized pistons, simply open a bleeder valve on the caliper in question. If, with the bleeder open a few turns you find there is no fluid pumping out when you apply pressure to the pedal, or if you find that the pedal pressure is still firm with the valve open, then you have brake hose blockage.

The cure for sticking pistons is not hard nor should it be expensive. A useful "tool" would be an old master brake cylinder with two of the three outlets plugged. You will then have only to remove a caliper from the car, use a large hose clamp to tie down one of the pistons (your choice), and connect the master cylinder to the caliper on your workbench or garage floor.

Now by pumping the master, the untied piston will eventually pop out of its bore, revealing plenty of rust or corrosion, usually from the internal rubber seal up to the outermost rim of the caliper. Remove the seal with a bit of wire or a dental pick and discard it.

The bore can be cleaned by honing gently with a fine stone, or even sanded with emery cloth. Reassemble with a new seal, switch the hose clamp to the piston that was just cleaned and repeat the procedure for the remaining piston.

Some people use compressed air to force out a piston, but I wouldn't. When they do pop out, they really

shoot forward. You could easily end up with smashed fingers or worse.

Compressed air also won't free a piston that is really stuck, but the old master cylinder trick will always work. Of course, I should have mentioned that the master should be filled with brake fluid to provide pressure. There will be some waste, but what can you do?

– Reprinted with permission from the *Nutmeg News*.

Fluid

Vol. 7, No. 1 David Seeland

Why to Change Your Brake Fluid
Apparently, after only seventeen years, the seals had given up. I suspect that a couple of days on the Aspen track, shortly before the brake pulling set in, contributed to the demise of my brakes. At Aspen the brakes got hot enough to lose all their squeeze. I noticed that they were fading so I decided to take a few slow laps. After about a quarter of a lap, I had no brakes and had to toss the car sideways to negotiate the next hairpin turn.

Just because your brake system is full of fluid doesn't mean it's adequate for racing use. Change the old fluid once a year, and before any racing use. Brake fluid, except silicone, is hygroscopic, absorbing water from the air. Heavy brake use turns this water to compressible steam resulting in no brakes. The water in the brake fluid also corrodes the master and wheel cylinders.

Vol. 10, No. 5 Vic Skirmants

Silicone Brake Fluid
Regarding brake systems and silicone brake fluid. Because of the nature of the silicone fluid, the complete brake system has to be disassembled and cleaned to prevent contamination by the old brake fluid. I used

44

silicone fluid in my old drum-brake Speedster during the last few years I ran it; no problem. I then tried it in my disc-braked roadster, and would lose my brakes completely after seven laps. I tried several different brands and viscosities; no luck. I currently use Castrol LMA brake fluid and have no difficulties. Under all-out racing conditions, the disc brakes on our cars work hard enough that some air bubbles are always present when bleeding the brakes. I don't know if the bubbles are from heating of the water vapor in the fluid, or possibly because some air gets drawn in upon piston retraction. This last item could explain the problem with silicone fluid; its higher viscosity possibly causes more air to be drawn in. Anyway, all of us E Production racers know the problem, no one has a solution, except to bleed the brakes regularly and often.

Competition Drum Brakes

Vol. 17, No. 6 Dick Koenig/David Seeland

Factory Supplied Competition Drum Brake Systems
Brake drums were all similar in that they were made of cast aluminum with an embedded, ring-shaped steel liner. While the aluminum was lighter, it was softer. Brake shoes pressed against the more durable steel surface when stopping. The inside diameter of all drums was 280 mm and all had the wide, five bolt lug pattern. Visible distinctions can be made between the various drums in terms of liner width, cooling fins and outside diameter, lightening devices, and track dimensions.

Width refers to an important dimension of the liner that is directly related to the size of the braking surface. Wider liners mean higher potential stopping capability.

The earliest competition drums all had 40 mm, (1 $9/16$ in.) wide liners. Sometime during the 1955 racing season, 60 mm (2 $3/8$ in.) drums were developed for the front wheels of Spyders. For the 356, however, these "big brakes" were made available after the introduction of the 356A model, and became readily available for the 1957 racing season. Rear drums remained 40 mm throughout the drum brake era.

Competition pressures generate enormous heat on the braking surfaces. Higher temperatures lessen braking efficiency while increasing stress on component parts. To help mitigate these effects, cooling fins were cast into the outer edge of drums. On all 40 mm drums prior to 356B, two circumferential fins were cast. While drums from different years look generally similar, the shape of the fins actually changed. Fins became shorter while the groove between them grew wider. Measurement of sample drums revealed that the outside diameter had been lessened by $3/16$ in. from 1955 to 1957. This change reflected the shift from 16 in. to 15 in. rims and tires. There is not enough clearance for the smaller rim with the pre-A drum. The big 60 mm front drums had 6 finned grooves cut into the outer edge reflecting the increased need for cooling. For 1960, the rear drum was the same as on 356B production cars. The fins no longer spanned the circumference but were perpendicular. They totaled 70 in number.

Lightening was another design objective, especially for racing. This could be accomplished by removing excess metal in areas where strength would not be compromised. This was most evident on the 356 SL (Gmünd coupes modified for racing) and RS (early 4 cam production cars) cars and was accomplished in three ways. First, holes were drilled laterally through the fins. Also, another set of 15 holes was drilled through the surface inside the fins. The location was ideal for inspecting the thickness of brake shoes as well. Finally, recesses were milled into the surfaces between the wheel lugs.

Track dimensions posed another problem. Increasing the width of front brake drums by 20mm on the 356A cars necessitated offsetting the wheel rims 20 mm inward in relation to the centers. The standard rear drums now required 20 mm spacers to bring the modified wheels out to the correct track dimension and prevent rubbing of the rear trailing arms.

Backing Plates

Backing plates used for competition were derived from whatever was in general use on production cars at the time. Standard "discs" were strengthened where necessary and also modified to create a flow-through ventilation/cooling system.

In the early 1950s backing plates were stamped from 1.3 mm steel, as opposed to 1.6 mm for the 356RS and later cars. Apparently, the use of metal this thin allowed for too much flex and a strengthening plate (4.1 mm thick) was needed. These reinforcements were no longer required when thicker metal was used. Small indentations, or pads, that raised brake shoes away from the disc allowed them to move more easily.

These elevated points meant less surface contact between shoes and backing plates. The earliest evidence of these pads was on the Spyder-style backing plate used on the 356RS. Indentations about 1 in. round were pressed into the disc stamping. For the early 356A, a 3/4 in. square metal piece replaced the indentation. The final step in this evolution was a larger and thicker metal platform (3/4 x 2 1/8 in.) which was found on the later 356A front discs and became standard on B models.

The front drums, which used the bigger brakes, had the greater need for strength. Reinforcing "ribs", or cir-

cumferential beads were pressed into the steel. There were two concentric partial circles located just inside the shoe pads. Ribs first appeared during the 1958 racing season and then were incorporated into all 356B race and production backing plates, both front and rear.

Another important set of modifications to the backing plates helped cool brakes from the heat of competition. Cool air entered at the front of the disc through an attached scoop and exited at the rear through vent holes. Over time, scoops were made larger so they might handle more air. For protection against the intrusion of stones and other debris, all air passages were covered with fine mesh wire screen.

There is an apparent logic to the changes in backing plate construction. Reducing assembly costs while improving strength and reliability were clearly in mind. The earliest examples were made with many peened rivets and spot welded straps. Both procedures required considerable skill and were still time consuming. Later on, scoops were attached completely by spot welds and all screens were soldered. The outer perimeter edges of scoops now had a 1/8 in. or wider flange surface that eased soldering the screen on.

We believe that, as standard procedure, scoops were present on both front and rear brakes. This statement contradicts an observation made in our prior article that early 356A discs might have been vented but not scooped. Very careful study of 1957 GT coupe #101385, upon which this initial observation was made, coupled with comments by some of our readers lead us to conclude that there were no "non-scooped" but vented discs sold by the factory.

Related Parts

Forty millimeter drums all used shoes drawn from stock parts. There were no special shoes developed for racing. However, modifications to the webs which resulted in faster reaction times occurred during 1958, and these are shown in our last article.

The most unique pieces were inside the 60 mm front brakes. Shoes obviously were 60 mm wide and were of two types: single-rib steel and double-rib aluminum. The single-rib variety was used during the 356A era and required special, elongated holding nails to mount these shoes, and special holes were required in the scoop.

When the dual-rib aluminum shoe was introduced in late 1959 (356B), no special accommodations were required because return springs held them in place.

Front Brakes

	1951-3	1954-5	1956-7	1958-9	1960-3
Approx. Dates	356SL	356RS	356A	356A	356B
Examples					
Drums					
Liner width	40mm	40mm	60mm	60mm	60mm
Outside Diameter	13-1/8"	13-1/8"	13"	13"	13"
Fin type	Circumferential	Circumferential	Circumferential	Circumferential	Circumferential
No of fins	2	2	6	6	6
Fin vent holes	82	82	none	none	none
Shoe Inspect. holes	15	15	5	5	5
Recessed grooves	no-yes	yes	no	no	no
Backing Plate Disc					
Basic stamping	early 356	late 356	356A	Hybrid 356A/B	Hybrid 356A/B
Stamp.thickness	1.3 mm	1.6 mm	1.6 mm	1.6 mm	1.6 mm
Outside diameter	12-1/2"	12-1/2"	12-1/2"	12-1/2"	12-1/2"
Shoe "pads"	none	pressed circle	3/4" welded	3/4 x 2-1/8" welded	3/4 x 2-1/8" welded
Reinforcements	4 - 1mm plate	none	none	2 circular "ribs"	2 circular "ribs"
Air hole no.	30	30	30	30	30
Air hole diamter	5/16" - 7/16"	7/16" all	7/16" all	7/16" all	7/16" all
Screen attachment	spot weld straps	riveted straps	solder	solder	solder
Backing Plate Scoop					
Inlet size	9-3/4" x 1-1/4"	9-3/4" x 1-3/4"	9-3/4" x 1-3/4"	9-3/4" x 1-3/4"	9-3/4" x 2"
Inlet shape	rectangle	rectangle	rectangle	rectangle	rectangle
Scoop attach. to disc	spot welds	rivets	spot welds	spot welds	spot welds
Reinforcing brace	no	yes	no	no	no
Side flange to attach screen	none	1/8"	3/16"	3/16"	3/16"
Screen attach to scoop	solder/straps	solder/straps	solder	solder	solder
Related Parts					
Shoe width	40mm	40mm	60 mm	60 mm	60 mm
Shoe type	standard 356	standard 356	steel single rib	steel single rib	alum. double rib
Lining	Energit	Energit	Energit	Fren-do T	Fren-do T

Rear Brakes

	1951-3	1954-5	1956-7	1958-9	1960-3
Approx. Dates	356SL	356RS	356A	356A	356B
Examples					
Drums					
Liner width	40mm	40mm	40mm	40mm	40mm
Outside Diameter	13-1/8	13-1/8	12-15/16	12-15/16	13-7/8
Fin type	Circumferential	Circumferential	Circumferential	Circumferential	Perpendicular
No of fins	2	2	2	2	70
Fin vent holes	82	82	none	none	none
Shoe Inspect. holes	15	15	0,5	5	5
Recessed grooves	no-yes	yes	no	no	no
Elong. studs/spacers	no	no	yes	yes	yes
Backing Plate Disc					
Basic stamping	early 356	late 356	356A	356A	356B
Stamp.thickness	1.3 mm	1.6 mm	1.6 mm	1.6 mm	1.6 mm
OUtside diameter	12-1/2"	12-1/2"	12-1/2"	12-1/2"	13-1/2"
Shoe "pads"	none	pressed circle	3/4" welded	3/4 x 2-1/8" welded	3/4 x 2-1/8" welded
Reinforcements	4 - 1mm plate	none	none	none	2 ribs, rain ring
Air hole no.	30	30	30	30	16
Air hole diamter	5/16" - 7/16"	7/16"	7/16"	7/16"	1/2", 1-3/16"
Screen attachment	spot weld straps	riveted straps	solder	solder	solder
Backing Plate Scoop					
Inlet size	10-3/4" x 15/16"	8-7/8" x 2"	8-7/8" x 2"	8-7/8" x 2"	9-1/4 x8-1/4 x1-3/4"
Inlet shape	rectangle	rectangle	rectangle	rectangle	non-rectangle
Scoop attach. to disc	spot welds	rivets	spot welds	spot welds	spot welds
Reinforcing brace	no	yes	no	no	no
Side flange to attach screen	none	1/8"	3/16"	3/16"	3/16"
Screen attach to scoop	solder/straps	solder/straps	solder	solder	solder
Related Parts					
Shoe width	40mm	40mm	40 mm	40 mm	40 mm
Shoe type	standard 356	standard 356	standard 356A	standard 356A	standard 356B
Lining	Energit	Energit	Energit	Fren-do T	Fren-do T

Chapter 4

Detailing

Factory Recommendations 1955

Vol. 6, No. 3

The following is reprinted from a pamphlet that was provided by the coachbuilder Reutter with new 356s. This one is circa 1955, since it deals with lacquer paint, which was discontinued with the introduction of the 356A model. It is presented as originally written with no attempt to source products recommended – September 1994

Reutter Recommended Preparations for Car Care
1. Lacquer Finish

In the wear and tear of everyday service, the lacquer finish on your car is affected by a number of mechanical, chemical and physical influences. Furthermore, even the very best of lacquers inevitably goes through a certain aging process. Nevertheless, the beauty of a high quality lacquer finish can be preserved over a long period of time, by regularly giving the body of your car the necessary care and attention at regular intervals.

To this end, we recommend observing the following fundamental instructions. For the proper treatment and selection of car care agents, it is essential that you know whether the body of your car is finished with nitro or synthetic resin lacquer. On the Porsche automobile bodies we manufacture, the information whether the body is finished with "nitro lacquer" or "synthetic resin" will be found below the small name plate bearing the body number. This name plate becomes visible on the hinge column when opening the left hand door.

Parking: If possible, never park the car in glaring sunshine.

Cleaning: Never dust the body off dry. Always wash it off with clear, cold water. Do not spray off the body while it is still hot from exposure to the sun or from engine heat, or treat it with cleaning preparations. Dirt adhering to the finish must be softened by a water spray. It should not be removed by a hard thin, high pressure stream of water. With a soft sponge and abundant water, especially after shampooing, flush off the body well and then chamois.

Preserving: Due to the exposure to the weather and especially as a result of the intensive effect of chemical cleaning agents, certain fatty substances are leached out of the lacquer. Consequently, the finish becomes rough and brittle. It is the duty of body treating preparations to provide new nourishment for such finishes and thus to restore their luster and elasticity. Simultaneously, they provide a protective film that keeps for some time.

Polishing: Do not apply polishing fluid to a finish until it gradually becomes dull and preservatives no longer suffice to restore a high gloss.

To avoid premature drying up of a finish, only apply polishing fluid by sections, rubbing it on with a soft rag or polishing wool, exerting light pressure and making straight strokes. Do not rub in circular fashion. Then give the finishing rub with clean cotton wool, until high gloss is obtained. This is followed by an application of preservative. Recommended every 6 to 8 weeks, not more.

To remove signs of lacquer aging, use polishing paste containing a higher degree of abrasive. Apply with care. If necessary, have the work done by a qualified body finisher. End up this treatment by applying a preservative.

Tar Splashes: Remove as soon as possible, or else discoloring of the lacquer finish may result. Such discoloring is difficult to remedy. First soften up the tar with a tar remover, then wipe off carefully. This is followed by an application of a preservative agent.

Spraying Rust Inhibitor on the Chassis: When spraying the bottom of the car and the chassis, take care that none of the inhibitor is sprayed on the lacquer.

Metallic Effect Lacquering
A modern specialty in lacquer finishing is the metallic effect lacquering that enjoys great popularity today, because of its subdued shades and soft silken gloss. It is a pronounced deluxe finish, demanding special care. In addition to our general instructions, we recommend:

During the First 6 Weeks: Only wash the car off with clean water. Do not shampoo or apply lacquer treating agents.

Special Precaution: Only apply polishes at intervals of 6 to 8 weeks, not more. Beware of abrasive pastes marketed as "Cleaners" because they are too sharp for metallic effect lacquer finishes.

For More Involved Lacquer Maintenance: We recommend entrusting work of this kind to an experienced lacquering specialist. Especially the repair of lacquer finishes should be exclusively done by an expert, because such repair jobs are by no means easy to perform, even if the original lacquer is available. Be careful when placing orders for body maintenance jobs with service stations and garages.

2. Windows
The windshield is made of compound glass, i.e., two plates of ordinary glass glued together by a transparent layer. If the windshield is damaged, the cracks will be localized and broken glass will adhere to the intermediate layer of gum. Uncracked window sections will retain their former unimpaired transparency. All other window panes, with the exception of the plastic rear window in the Convertible, are of hardened glass (Sekurit), a single layer safety glass with hardened surface capable of withstanding considerable shock, such as slamming doors shut. On a pane of this type, a heavy blow releases the internal stresses developed in the hardening process, so that the entire window is covered with crystalline cracks which render the pane practically translucent. In extreme cases such a glass will break down completely into harmless cuboid particles. Once fitted in place, hardened glass can no longer be worked upon; grinding or cutting the edges will destroy the pane immediately, as if subjected to a blow. If the doors jam in an accident, so that an exit through the windows becomes necessary, smash the windows in the doors by a short, hard blow. The tough compounding layer in the windshield would render such an exit impossible, unless the entire windshield could be pushed out of its frame.

It thus becomes apparent that both types of glass have their unique advantages. The combined use of both types in one car represents a far-reaching safety measure in the interest of our clientele.

Clean all windows with lukewarm water containing some fuel alcohol or a mild soap solution. It is best to use a sponge or chamois. Rub bright with a soft cloth.

Never put the windshield wiper into operation as long as the windshield is not adequately wetted by rain or otherwise. Dry dust and roadway dirt will act like emery on the unmoistened glass and soon scratch the same so that clear visibility is sure to be prejudiced.

3. The Interior

In general, the ceiling, walls and seats in the interior of a car are upholstered with textile fabric or imitation leather. Leather is standard equipment in cabriolets and it is also used on other cars too, on special request. Present day vogue favors deep, full colors.

But even if based on technically first class basic materials, these colors are often subject to abrasion when moist. In addition, convertible tops consist of top and bottom sheets with an intermediate rubberized layer. Glaring sunshine will scorch any textile and affect the fastness to light of colors. In addition, the intermediate sheet of rubberized fabric also deteriorates under such conditions.

We recommend:

Textile Fabric: Remove spots with a good spot remover by lightly rubbing until completely dry. Use a piece of the same cloth, or at least one of a not darker color. If the same cloth is not available, use an undyed cloth, to eliminate any danger of rubbing off color. From time to time beat the upholstery and brush out or vacuum clean.

Leather and Imitation Leather:

Clean with lukewarm soap water and a soft brush. If possible use rain water, boiled water or other soft water, with a mild laundry bar soap. Do not use much water and avoid the formation of small puddles on the upholstery. Rub every bit of upholstery dry with a soft rag after washing. Take care to clean and dry the crevices in the upholstery. Never use coarse sand soaps or hard brushes. When dry treat with Karneol (see list of cleaning and polishing preparations).

4. Convertible and Speedster Tops

Clean tops of dirt and dust with a not too hard brush, brushing lengthwise along the fabric. Then apply "Frischdienst" solution and waterproof the top with "Viktoria-Impregnating Preparation" (see list of cleaning preparations page 9). Wet or frozen tops must be dried before they are folded back.

5. Rubber

Rubber is applied at numerous spots on the body for sealing, sound damping, etc. In the course of time this rubber will loose its original elasticity, it becomes brittle and cracks. This aging process can be counteracted or postponed as follows:

Rubber Treatment: From time to time give all rubber pars a light coating of glycerin. Protect rubber against glaring sunshine. Replace worn parts in due time, especially the rubber bumpers on the doors.

6. Lubrication Points

Door Hinges are equipped with grease nipples which must be given some commercial grease, from time to time.

Cover Locks Lubricate with commercial grease

Cover Hinges: Lubricate with a resin-Ires Oil

Window Cranking Mechanisms are shop lubricated and require no routine maintenance. After a long time it is advisable to replenish the grease, for which purpose the door trimmings must be removed.

Door Locks are precision mechanisms and liable to develop trouble if not properly cared for. At regular intervals lubricate with a thin, acid-free oil. Lubricate with glycerin in the winter.

7. Bright Parts

Chrome Parts must first be cleaned with water and a sponge, then rubbed dry. Remove any tar spots with tar remover (do not use a knife or other sharp tool). A mirror polish gloss that will keep for a considerable period can then be obtained by treating with Brillant- Chrompflege.

Chromschutzpaste gives a reliable corrosion protective coating during the winter months. It also renders good service in regions along salt water coasts, where the salt-seasoned air is especially aggressive to chrome plating.

Light Alloy Parts: Revitalize, polish and preserve with Simichrompoli.

8. Sealing

Flooring and chassis are carefully sealed and subjected to a stringent water test at the factory. Should small leaks nevertheless occur, they can, in general, easily be remedied with sealing compound. If drops of water permeate through the seal of a window, fill the groove of the rubber profile with rubber cement (see list of recommended body treating preparations 9). In case of more serious trouble it is. however, advisable, to apply to the factory or our next licensed shop.

Exterior Finish

Vol. 14, No. 1 David Seeland

Post Paint Polishing

After color-sanding using 2000 paper, the finish will look shiny, but it can look a lot better and application of various magical potions with a power buffer or by hand will vastly increase the gloss of the surface.

Pat Scanlan at one time used some kind of stove polish (!) on his concours winning Speedster and other paint jobs. I have a small can of Classic Car "finish restorer, car cleaner and chrome cleaner" that is truly magical in its ability to bring up a blinding gloss by hand rubbing. But, I have never been able to replace it. Does anybody out there know where to buy it? If you do, please let me know. In the last couple of weeks I have spent about $150 on polishing supplies including buffing pads, rubbing compounds, swirl remover/polish and wax. I tried various combinations on the A coupe's Deltron (polyurethane) paint. One product was so outstanding, a true 10 on the magical potion rating scale, that I hesitate to let the secret out. Run, don't walk, to your nearest automotive paint supply store and buy a lifetime supply of Glasso 562-1602 polishing compound before Germany's Green Party decides it contributes to global warming or ozone depletion or some other environmental catastrophe. One $15 can should do three cars.

Apply the Glasso compound using terry cloth wadded up to baseball size with a single layer pulled smoothly over the outside surface. I hand applied it on paint that had only been sanded with 2000 grade Nikken sanding paper, and to paint that had been power buffed with a Mequiar's foam pad and "professional Hi-Tech Cleaner No. 2". The results were equal and outstanding.

I tried to power buff with Glasso compound using a 3M wool (?) pad, but it didn't seem to work as well. Although the label doesn't say, I assume that the Glasso is for hand application. With the exception of the Classic finish restorer, I have never found a hand rubbing compound that produced results nearly as glossy as power buffing. Hand application of the Glasso produces better results than power buffing. Bill Jones (Autowerkes, San Antonio, TX) criticizes power buffing saying he can always tell if a paint job had ever had a power-buffing wheel applied to it.

With hand application the Glasso compound first smears over the surface but with continued rubbing the compound is redeposited on the rag and forms a shiny(!) surface there. The oils or whatever liquid is in the compound are left on the paint surface and the process is similar to wet sanding with an abrasive coated rag. I'm not sure what is happening, but the results are outstanding. Here's what the Glasso 562-1602 can says: "For industrial use only, photochemically reactive. Glasso Polishing Compound 1602 is a white, silicone free water mixable compound for fine polishing. It is recommended for the fine removal of sanding lines, for losing the edge on border areas (for blending in spot repairs??), and for removal of overspray dust particles. 562-1602 is particularly recommended for the Urethane Line 21. "To get more shine use Glasurit-Universal Liquid Polish 560-1502 after polishing with Glasso Compound 562-1602." I'd sure like to see what "more shine" looks like. Al West Paint Co. in Denver sells most Glasso products, but didn't have any 560-1502. I'm going to see if they will order it, but I can't really imagine anything that will improve on the shine produced with 562-1602.

At the Parade in Michigan, I was awestruck by the roadster that Tim Goodrich had done. I tried to weasel some hints on polishing products and techniques out of him but ... and I understand because concours-winning cars are his livelihood. Bill Edwards, proprietor of Restoration Services here in Denver was also at the Parade and had another stunning roadster. Bill uses a trick polish which he sells

(actually Mothers Mag Wheel Polish). I tried some on "Ruff's rusty roadster" – its paint is a candidate for "most oxidized" honors. I wet sanded with 2000 paper and polished one area with Glasso compound and the other with Bill's trick polish. Bill's seemed to be slightly more abrasive based on the polishing-rag color change, although Bill finds it less abrasive than the Glasso, but the results were approximately the same. Bill color-sands with 1500 paper, power buffs with his trick polish, and then hand polishes with the same compound, finishing up with a cornstarch power-buff. AH-CHOO! Bill also uses the Glasso compound, and dozens of pads- rows of them everywhere! He emphasizes the use of clean pads. They can be washed and dried.

Here are some buffing tips for those of you who would rather power buff than hand rub. Synthetic fiber pads cut faster and make more obvious swirl marks than wool pads. Don't ever use a lace-on pad unless you would like to repaint your car. The cloth back works around and will groove the paint instantly. Use only screw-on pads, either one-sided (many manufacturers), or two sided pads (3M). Both of these types have curved edges and are less likely to burn or groove the paint. 3M makes two pads, one for fast cutting (-05701), the other (-05705) for polishing. Both look like synthetic fiber pads.

The newest type of pad is the foam pad by Mequiar's (5 $1/2$ in. for concave areas, 8 in. for flat or convex surfaces). Claimed advantages include "the elimination of swirl marks and superior reflection with greater clarity". I have three of them but I'm not sure if they are significantly better than fiber pads. Catch one on a sharp edge and instant shredded foam is the result. This is better than marred paint and they can be reshaped with a wire brush while rotating. Both the 3M pads and the Mequiar's should be used at a low angle, almost flat. Mequiar's suggests 1750-3000 RPM for conventional (non-catalyzed) finishes and 1200-1750 RPM for clear coat and urethane (catalyzed). 3M suggests 1500-2500 RPM.

Tom Conway, owner of Karosserie Fabrik (and a *Registry* advertiser Carquip) a Boulder, Colorado restoration body shop (303) 443-0298, is leaving for Guatemala in 10 days with a chromemoly roll-caged, oil-cooler-ed, disc-braked 1955 coupe to participate in the Carrera Panamericana. He took time away from assembling his 1955 to call me to give me some more polishing tips. He reminded me to emphasize cleanliness and concentration. Don't talk to your kids, watch TV, or eat while you are polishing. The polishing process is critical and mistakes can spoil untold hours of previous work.

Cleanliness, Tom says, cannot be overemphasized. Use clean pads, a different one for each type of polishing compound. Clean the pad at intervals while you work, paint buildup on the pad can mar the paint. Don't touch the floor or anything but the car with the pad. Don't use a pad that's been lying around gathering dust for two years since you last painted a car. Tom also suggested that you wear clean clothes and dust yourself off with the air hose before polishing.

Wash the car, dry it and then blow it off. Squirt the compound on the surface and with the pad slightly tilted, figure out which side pulls the material into the pad as you spread the material around on the surface with the buffer. The wrong pad to surface relationship just flings the (expensive) compound off onto you or the wall.

Keep the paint surface temperature down. Warm is OK, hot can warp the metal and burn the paint. Electrically, grounding the car (to a water pipe or a rod driven into damp ground) is helpful in eliminating static electricity that can cause cleaners and polishes to be attracted to the paint and can attract dirt particles.

Tom sees better results from power buffing because the abrasive particles gradually round and the polish gets better and better.

To go back to color sanding, clean your bucket before sanding, or maybe even get a new one. Be alert for dirt between the paper and the car. The tiniest piece of dirt will make scratches in the paint that won't show up until the polishing stage. Stop and clean the paint surface and the sanding paper as soon as you hear and feel a dirt particle. Tom describes it as a "zipper sound".

Another aside that should be mentioned is that 3M "microfine" paper is now available in 1200, 1500 and 2000 grades. I saw the ad in *WoodenBoat*, a magazine for REAL masochists. You passed on that rusty 1951 Cabriolet project because it was too much work? *WoodenBoat* talks about real restoration projects like a wooden 108 foot sail-powered cruising yacht first launched 60 years ago!

If you are going to have someone else do the polishing, Tom points out the value of isolation. Production shops have many stages of bodywork going on simultaneously in a limited area and dust from a silicon carbide grinding wheel flying through the air and landing on your Manhattan trophy candidate doesn't help the polishing process. Another room, a paint booth, another time (10:00 p.m.?) will all help. Outside is not adequate either, too much dust fallout. Be sure your painter understands this or find another painter.

Go get some Glasso compound 562-1602, a couple of sheets of Nikken (Mequiar's) or 3M 2000 paper and spend an hour on a lock post or the underside of your deck lid. You'll be ready to paint something or have it painted just so you can work the Glasso magic on something bigger.

How to Wax your 356 Porsche

Let's face it – most of us don't wax our cars often enough because it really is a lot of work. This article is not intended to describe a "quick and dirty" way to make your car look like new. Forget the one hour Simonize job. I do not believe in these polymer sealants or any other gimmick which promises quick and enduring results. It will take considerable work and frequent attention if you want to keep the paint in good condition. This article will show you how to do that.

First let's start with a little paint theory: Paint is a living skin somewhat similar to our own human skin. Like human skin, paint contains lubricants and emollients which keep it somewhat pliable, shiny, and protected from the elements. Over time these lubricants and emollients tend to evaporate and dry up. That's when a car's paint gets into trouble. It dries out, cracks, or oxidizes. Your goal as a responsible Porsche owner should be to delay this process. A proper wax job will restore these lubricants and emollients and at least delay the paint aging process. It will also reduce small scratches and swirl marks. If done properly and often enough, I believe you can delay this process indefinitely.

My procedure is a three stage process that will take about 5 hours all together. I do not recommend doing it nonstop unless you are awfully energetic. Maybe do part Saturday and part Sunday. Admittedly, it is hard work, but after the first time you do it, successive treatments will be much easier, if done about every 6 to 8 months. Successive treatments will only take about 2 hours. I think you will find that even though it is hard work, the payoff is worth it. Before you begin work, I suggest you read through this entire article and get a feel for what is involved. Good luck!

Stage 1: The first thing you need to do is to wash your car thoroughly with soap and water. Don't use strong detergents – you don't need them, plus over time they can be pretty harsh on paint. I prefer Ivory liquid. After you've finished washing the car, wipe it down with a soft damp terry-cloth towel to get most of the residual moisture off. Then take it for a short ride to get the water out of cracks and crevasses you can't get to. This will also dry off the brake shoes/pads. After you get back take a damp, clean terry-cloth towel and wipe the entire car down to get any remaining dust and dirt off. Total time is about 1 hour. The last thing you want to do is to wax a car that has any dirt on it – the dirt will act as an abrasive and you'll have scratches which you do not want. Now at this point you've got to make an evaluation about the condition of your car's paint. This will determine what course of action you take next. If it's heavily oxidized (shame on you!) then you will need a wax with cleaners (mild abrasives) or polishing compound to get rid of the oxidation. Notice that I said polishing compound not rubbing compound which is considerably more abrasive. I do not recommend the use of rubbing compound for normal car waxing. It is used for new car finishes to buff out imperfections or on small areas of the paint which need special attention. If you use polishing compound, use it only where you need it. I don't recommend using it over the entire car. Most Porsches do not need polishing compound.

Stage 2: O.K., let's assume your car's paint is in decent shape – meaning you wax it yearly or so. You do not need polishing compound – most Porsches I've seen don't. Next you should choose a good quality wax. I've had very good luck with Meguiar's which you should be able to get from any reputable auto body supply store or failing that from Imparts (*Panorama*). Cost is about $6-8 a bottle. After you've washed and dried your car off, you want to use Meguiar's #3 Professional machine glaze which has some very fine abrasives. Now the label on the bottle says that it is intended for machine application. Well, it can be put on by hand just as well. Meguiar's #7 resealer is wonderful stuff. It has no abrasives and lots of emollients for your paint. Ladies – it's like Oil of Olay, except you don't have to put it on at night. Use #7 if your paint is in really good shape (i.e., no fine scratches or oxidation) but it must be put on by hand. If you start with Meguiar's #3 by hand, then you should follow with an application of Meguiar's #7. This will be easier to do than the initial step with #3. After finishing with #7 you will have a finish that is as smooth and soft as a baby's rear.

Machine Application: I'm going to digress here for a moment because we have the option of applying #3 by hand or by machine buffer. If you have a machine buffer you can use that but a word of warning here. If you have a buffer, you can use it, but you better know what you are doing. *I do not recommend the use of buffers for beginners.* If you use a buffer, you should have a good idea how thick the paint is over every surface of the car. It is easy to burn through the entire layer of paint if you are not very careful. If you don't have a buffer or are a beginner, skip this paragraph and go to the next one on hand application. If you know how to use a buffer, then go ahead with a soft, clean, slightly damp (water) buffing pad. Add approximately 1 tablespoon (no you don't have to measure it with a tablespoon) of #3 to the buffing pad. I suggest starting on an area of the car that is flat and not very conspicuous. You can be the judge of that. Use the buffer on low speed only.

Try to get the feel of what the buffer is capable of and how it works. At high speeds this thing can get away

from you real fast. Start out on planar surfaces on the car first and then move to compound (curved) surfaces. You will have to be careful on compound surfaces because of pressure variations caused by the interaction of your flat buffer with a curved surface. Be conservative – you can always go back and re-buff an area but you can't go back and repaint it. Also be careful around areas where body parts join each other, i.e., doors to body, hood to body. The paint is thinner here and is easy to rub off. Do not put much pressure on the buffer and keep it moving constantly, preferably in a circular motion. Done properly this is an excellent way to get rid of swirl marks. If the buffer stays in one place too long, you can "burn" the paint or seriously thin the paint. After a while you will see that the buffing pad is actually removing the wax, leaving you with a nice bright shine. You will notice that small scratches and swirl marks are either reduced or no longer there at all.

After doing 25 square feet or two body panels, wash your pad off with water. You will have picked up microscopic bits of dirt along the way. You don't want to grind that stuff into the paint. *Note:* Do not make a regular habit of buffing your Porsche – you really shouldn't need to buff more than every couple of years. If used too often, you will eventually burn through the paint. When you have finished with the machine application of Meguiar's #3, then put on an application of Meguiar's #7 by hand as above. Total time is about 2 hrs.

Hand Application: Use a clean terry-cloth hand towel folded to approx. 4 by 4 inches slightly moistened with water. Add about a tablespoon of Meguiar's #3. As an alternative you can use #7 which doesn't contain any abrasives at all. Do this only if your paint is in really good shape (read new paint or new car).

Work in circular pattern of approximately 2 square feet at a time. You may need a clean dry soft terry-cloth towel to take off some of the wax. After doing this you will start to see a nice shiny, smooth surface. After doing each major surface of the car, wash the cloth applicator to get rid of dead paint and dirt. You do not want to rub that in to unwaxed surfaces. If you still see scratches or swirl marks you may want to do a second treatment. It gets better each time. Don't overdo it – wax can build up on the paint. After you've done the #3 then do the same thing with #7 but with a very thin coat. Yes, it takes work, but it'll be worth it – trust me! As with #3 you may need to use a towel to get the excess wax off. After you finish, notice how smooth and soft the paint feels – almost like new paint, isn't it? Total time about 2.5 hours.

At this point you've done most of the hard part, so relax for a bit. Have a cold one. Talk to your wife or dog (not necessarily in that order) for a while. Maybe finish the next step the following day. Put your baby (the car) in the garage for the night.

Stage 3: This part will be considerably easier than the previous two steps. Up to this point what you've been doing is prepping the paint by 1) removing old paint; 2) add emollients to the paint; 3) removing small scratches from the paint's surface. Already, you feel a rushing sense of pride as you admire your cherished Porsche. Now your mission (should you decide to accept it, Jim) is to seal and protect with a special type of wax called carnuba. This stuff is pure wax and comes from the carnuba tree in Brazil. Little men in the forests there take each individual leaf from these magnificent trees and carefully scrape the waxy surface off of them. The wax is then sent on to America for sale to Porsche maniacs like us.

You see, this wax protects the leaves from desiccation much in the same way it will protect your car's paint from drying out. And it does

bead water! Before you start on this step, take your faithful soft clean and damp towel and wipe your car down to remove any dust, pollen that has accumulated over the night. By the way, have you ever seen pollen under a microscope? It's really nasty looking stuff. It resembles one of those old WWII water mines – you know the big old fat things with all the spikes sticking out. With this analogy in mind, imagine what pollen can do to paint. By the way – do not ever wipe a dry car down with a dry towel. Always make sure the towel is slightly damp. Moisture adds a certain amount of lubrication (read microscopic ball bearings) between the towel and the paint, thereby protecting it from scratches caused by dust, it also helps remove dust better than a dry towel.

I have used a pure carnuba wax called Pro-Wax. It comes in a yellow metal can and can be bought from auto body supply houses. As an alternative, I would recommend Mother's. Make sure you get the Mother's that is pure carnuba. The cost is about $10. Do not get the kind that is a blend of carnuba and other waxes. They usually contain some cleaners (you've already done that in stage 2). Carnuba is about the consistency of Johnson's Paste Wax. Remember, it's like the stuff your mother used to use on the old wooden floors in your house when you were a kid. Apply it with a damp towel in a circular motion. You don't need much. Do two square feet at a time. See how easily it goes on. Use a dry soft towel to remove the wax. What a nice shine you have! Notice how soft the paint feels. Keep going until you've done the entire car. Time is about 1 to 1.5 hours.

Epilogue: Well, I hope this article has been informative, especially to those of you who simply put on a coat of generic car wax once a year. For you naysayers out there – I think you'll find this process far superior and more enduring that what you're presently doing. Give it a try! Good luck.

Vol. 16, No. 1 Tom Shea

Carnauba Wax

It is in the "Stage 3: section" that some of the information presented deserves some comment in the interest of authenticity.

That special type of wax called carnuba, or carnauba, does in fact come from a palm – Copernicia prunifera (this species was previously known as Copernicia cerifera) commonly referred to as the Carnauba Wax palm. It is native to Northeastern Brazil. The wax covers the upper surface of the leaves or fronds and is known to be the hardest of all commercial waxes with a very high melting point. The mature leaves are collected from both wild and cultivated palms (with 20,000 tons a year produced on carnauba plantations), then allowed to dry and the wax collected by flattening these leaves mechanically with a threshing device. The wax flakes off rather freely and is termed caducous (dropping off or shedding).

Of course, there are other palms that produce wax, such as Syagrus coronata, however, it is not caducous and the wax must be scraped from the leaves. Another palm, the so-called Wax Palm of the Andes (Ceroxylon alpinum) does produce wax which is used in candles.

Regrettably, I do not have a photograph of the great Carnauba Palm to show it in all its glory. However, it normally reaches a height of about 10 meters or 30 some feet and has a large round shaped crown with deeply divided fan-shaped fronds. For those interested, a specimen might be found growing in a greenhouse environment at a local botanical garden, or for the car care nut, a real conversation piece in the yard if the climate allows.

Chapter 5

Driving

Shift Points

Vol. 3, No. 1 Vic Skirmants

How, When and Why to Shift Your 356

As long as I'm rambling on about driving styles, I'd like to answer a question on shift points and rev limits. First the easy one, rev limits. Your Porsche has a tachometer and there's that terrible huge red area on the right of the dial. The factory said 5000 RPM for a Normal, 5500 for a Super, and 5800 for a S-90, with the red area starting 500 RPM sooner.The limitation on revs is determined by your engine condition, type of connecting rods, type of crank and type of valve springs. Remember also that engine longevity will decrease with higher revs. If you want the engine to last forever, stick with the factory specs; but there is more power available if you are willing to wind it up a little. If your connecting rod bearings have a ton of miles on them or are just plain worn regardless of mileage, your rev limit is not even going to be as high as the factory's quite conservative specs.

Assuming good bearings, let's proceed. The rods were improved during 1960 to 1961, and again in late 1962-63. How's that for a precise statement? Porsche may design a new, improved part on a certain afternoon, but by the time stocks of the old parts are used up, not to mention already assembled engines sitting on the shelf, a half-year or more could pass before all the cars leaving the factory have that part. The late rods are good for 7000 RPM plus. The old rods I wouldn't rev past 5500. The intermediates I would trust all the way to 5505 RPM. The older rods are weaker and when subjected to high loads will become oval at the bearing end.

The type of crankshaft determines your oil supply, The cranks through the 1962 "B" series had one oil supply hole per rod journal. The 1963 B, C, SC had two holes. The more oil getting to the rod bearing, the higher revs it can take. I use the C or SC cranks in my race cars, and they're good for 7500 RPM plus. The counterbalancing has nothing to do with the rev limit. I actually prefer the C to the heavier SC. But getting back to street driving, any of the cranks are good for 6000 RPM from the standpoint of oil supply. Your valve springs will probably determine your actual rev limit. Through 1959 Porsche used a fairly weak dual-spring set-up which won't let you get much past 5500 RPM before the valves float. The later single springs, especially from about 1962 on, are good for 6000 if shimmed to factory specs. Of course if the springs are very old and have become weak, that's another story.

To summarize, a Normal is as good as a Super for rev limit purposes. The Normal used the same crank, rods, and valve springs as the Super. The 1961 and older engines can be taken to 5500 without much need for concern. – *If they are in good condition!!* The 1962 and 63 engines are good for 5500, while the 1964 - 1965 C & SC are good for 6000 if that's what turns you on. – *If they are in good condition!!* I don't want a bunch of letters complaining about bum advice when someone blows up his 1958 Normal engine with 300,000 miles on it and a funny noise when you put a load on it.

Shift points can be anything you want. In slow driving, I'll shift around 3500 as a minimum. Depending on gearing, this will drop the revs to around 2000 in the next gear which is as low as you should go. For a little more oomph, just raise your shift point. For instance, I generally run my 1963 stock Super engine to 4000 or 4500, with occasional flat-out bursts to 5500. Speaking of 2000 RPM, let's discuss lugging. Lugging is worse than revving high. If you're in second, third, or fourth gear at less than 2000 RPM and mash on the throttle, not much will happen as far as acceleration until the revs come up. The S-90 and SC don't do much til 3000 and up. When you hit the gas at less than 2000 RPM, the oil film between the rod bearings and crank is not strong enough to support the loads put on it by the combustion pressures, and you get metal-to-metal contact or even localized flat-spotting. At higher revs the oil film is stronger due to higher crank speed and higher oil pressure and consequently it can support the loads imposed on it.

To finish the RPM discussion, be sure your tach is calibrated if you're going to use the upper end of the scale. The mechanical tachs have a tendency to read low at the top end after a considerable amount of usage.

Driving Perception

Vol. 3, No. 4 Phil Reese

Quantifying Sensory and Emotional Feelings about Your 356

For most 356 owners, the driving pleasure of the car results from the driver's perception of light, easy, free-running manner of the car. For years, 356 owners have been trying to define the reasons for this perception, partly just to be able to explain to non-owners why we like the cars so much. Well, careful thought has brought to light several very small aspects that have a very large influence on my driving perception.

First, the free-revving, no-drag response of the engine is perceived by the driver largely through two things: the pressure of his throttle foot, and the rapid climb of the tachometer around the dial. Over the years, there's a good chance that the throttle linkage of your 356 has gotten dust filled and gummed up. The links and hinges in the vicinity of the pedal itself are prime catchers of dust and dirt, as are the various links in the engine compartment. The bell crank mounted on the forward side of the fan shrouding is a real culprit for sticking. A gradual increase in the 'stiction' and resistance of each moving joint will dull the feel of the engine's response, when in fact the engine has nothing to do with it. Simply having to push harder on the gas pedal will drastically change your entire "feel" as to how eagerly the car is responding to your urges. A couple of hours spent in cleaning and greasing the various hinges and joints in your throttle linkage, systematically working through the entire system from front to back, may do wonders toward improving your perception of your 356s response. With the now-free linkage you might even experiment carefully with lightening the return spring tension slightly, taking care that the carbs are always returned to the closed position by the springs.

As for the tachometer and its effect, there have been some instances with both the mechanical tachs and the electrical ones in the C models of age leading to a certain amount of lag in the tach's response. This lag translates into your perception that the engine isn't responding as eagerly as it once did. Really, it works on your mind without you even realizing it! This can be checked out pretty well by a simple test. On a reasonably straight smooth road accelerate slowly in fourth gear upward through some specific speed like 50 mph. Carefully observe the tach reading as you pass through the speed. Next speed up to 10 mph above your chosen test speed and *decelerate* slowly, again noting the tach reading as you pass through the test speed. If your tach is suffering from lag, the reading at the test speed will be higher on the deceleration leg than while speeding up. A good tach will show no difference; a seriously ill one will show a difference of 100 to 300 rpm. The only cure is a cleaning/calibration by a capable VDO (or Veigel) agent. A small lag at low acceleration rates can spell a large lag at high acceleration rates, such as when you approach the red line all out in first. This could be disastrous. If you have a tach lag problem, fixing it will restore a measure of the engine's rapid response without the engine being touched.

The third area of perception is possibly of greater impact than the two above, depending on a simple bit of geometry on your own 356. The perception here is of how much power and engine response you get from how much depression of the gas pedal. As opposed to the first item above, how *far* you have to move the pedal to get the response is as important as how *hard* you have to push on it. Well, all 356s have a built-in adjustment on the amount of carb opening you get for a certain amount of gas pedal travel

over about the first half of the pedal movement. On the transmission is mounted a bell crank (the one with the well-known bushings that fail). The relative position of the bell crank with the carbs closed has a significant effect on the amount of carb opening off idle and through the first half of opening that results from a given amount of gas pedal travel. The whole thing is related to the geometry of the pulling and the pulled throttle rods. A little study of the sketch below will reveal the difference.

You can change the starting position of this bell crank by some easy shortening and lengthening of the appropriate rods in the linkage system. If you have a situation as shown on the left and adjust it to that shown on the left, you will be astonished at how much more power and responsiveness your 356 *appears* to have. A mere touch of the gas pedal will result in more acceleration with less effort than you ever had before. It's all a matter of perception.

Emergency Spares

Vol. 3, No. 2 Mike Robbins

What to Bring When You Travel
At the 2nd 356 Holiday, there was some discussion as to what spare parts should be carried on long trips. Back when many 356 Porsche items were readily available at VW dealers, emergency situations could be handled much easier. (Have you tried to buy parts for a 36 HP VW engine lately?) Following are lists of items I carry. I'm sure other items could be added and perhaps some people might think some of my items are superfluous. My lists might seem long but l like to be as self-sufficient as possible. I also recognize that you can't protect against every contingency.

The following are carried in a fishing tackle box of approximately $1/4$ cu.

ft. capacity.
Generator bearings
Assorted copper seal rings
Oil pressure switch
Oil filter fittings
Idle bleed screw
Assorted plain & lock washers
Assorted nuts & caps screws
Assorted bulbs
Starter brushes
Steering column contacts
Assorted Loctite
Spark plugs
Points & condenser
Fan belt
Rear axle bearing
Inner fr. wheel bearings
Outer fr. wheel bearings
Tach cable core
Coil of steel wire - 18 gauge
Distributor clamp
Assorted fuses
Generator key
Accelerator pump hardware
Rear axle cotter pin
Small O ring-rear axle
Large O ring-rear axle
Washer - rear axle
Assorted electrical terminals
Generator brushes
Rotor
Carb gasket kits
Clutch cable
Rear wheel bearing seals
Front wheel bearing seals
Throw out bearing
Speedo cable

In another box of approximately 1/4 cu. ft. volume I carry engine gasket set, voltage regulator, oil cooler, electric fuel pump and diaphragm for Hausermann pressure plate.

Based on the specific car, you can temper the above lists to suit your own needs. Of course, being able to do anything with some of the above parts depends on what tools are available. On long trips, I carry everything to disassemble the engine assuming I have access to floor jack, etc. to pull the engine.

Clutch

Vol. 7, No. 1 Richard Miller

What Not to do at Traffic Signals
Your recent article on transmissions was right on. I'd like to add that sitting at a stop light with the clutch in also wipes out thrust surfaces on flywheel and #1 main bearing. All that clutch release pressure is being applied to the crank and is trying to push it out the back of the car.

Hot Weather Driving

Vol. 12, No. 45 Jim Keller

Improving Ventilation
Driving a 356, especially T-5 and earlier coupes in hot weather can be miserable due to the lack of fresh air ventilation. Add to that the usual hot air leakage from the heater boxes and the "greenhouse" effect of the windshields and you have a proverbial sweatbox.

In the warm months (May to November here in Southern California) I remove the cardboard heater tubes and replace them with 18 to 24 in. lengths of new heater tubes. The cheap stuff is OK where there is little rainfall and humidity. One end is reattached to the heater can; the other end is looped back to face the airstream and wired in place to the forward clamp of the heater can. When installing, just make sure that the flapper in the can is open. The figure below shows the setup.

In two years of doing this, I have never had to cap off the hot air outlets of the heater boxes since my engine oil runs fairly cool. However, if you plan a high speed run through the desert or if your oil cooler has seen cleaner days, you'd be better off to tape off the outlets.

With this setup the cabin runs 15-20 degrees cooler, especially down around your legs and feet.

Refueling

Vol. 13, No. 1 Ron LaDow

Protecting your Exterior Finish from the Evil Fuel Hose

For those pre-T-6 owners who want to keep the gas hose off the front fender, the flap shown in the sketch sure helps.

I used "bubble-pack" (an industrial packaging material) and a headless $3/8$ in. bolt, masking taped together, but I'm sure it would be possible to substitute hide and plated hardware.

Anyhow, the weight stays between the gas tank and the fender panel and keeps the flap in place. After fueling, the flap stuffs back into the same "pocket". You can also move it side-to-side.

Vol. 15, No 1. Vic Skirmants

Why You Should Turn Off Your Fuel Cock When Your 356 is Not in Use

Have had several instances in the past year of people contacting me about finding excess gasoline in their oil. A leaking fuel pump diaphragm is a likely culprit, but a rather rare failure. The usual cause is too high a carburetor float level, or a weak needle valve. I'm beginning to think that today's gasolines have a different specific gravity than what we used to get.

Whether they are different or not, more people do seem to be getting their oil diluted. My favorite advice, regardless of what, if anything, may be wrong, is to simply turn off the fuel cock when parking the car. All of our cars have them, and if yours doesn't work, fix it! The consequences can be rather dramatic; wiping out the bearings due to poor lubrication capabilities, hydraulic lock and bent or broken internal engine parts, or even a fire that could destroy your car, garage, butt, etc.

The Refueling Fender Flap

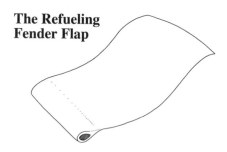

Heater Hose

Vol. 6, No. 6 Lew Larkin

Quick and Easy Heater Hose

The ravages of age as well as forgetting to disconnect them when pulling an engine, causes heater hoses to need replacement. There are probably other reasons but the reader really doesn't want to know about them! Everyone knows that heater hoses are readily available through many of the advertisers in the *Registry*. However, not everyone has the foresight to stock them for a future need.

Most "Detroit Iron" has used a piece of corrugated aluminum ducting leading heat from an exhaust manifold to the air cleaner. It comes in several diameters and is available in most auto parts and discount stores.

I have used one brand very successfully for several years. In fact, one pair are going on three years old and appear new. I bought them at Pep Boys, a discount auto parts chain on the East Coast. About $1.98 on sale. The ducting is 2 in. diameter and 18 in. long. It bends well, flexes and can be cut with a knife. It is made by G.M. Industries, Chicago, IL 60622. The package also says that it can be used for VW Heat Duct Hose.

The 2 in. diameter is slightly larger than the heat exchangers but this is an advantage because it makes installation so much easier. They should be cut a little longer than the original hose. This way the little extra pressure holds them securely in place. For those who are more comfortable with a positive attachment, ends can be secured with screw clamp or duct tape.

Jack Points

Vol. 4, No. 4 Richard Miller

An Opinion

There are four convenient, safe places to jack up a 356; the jack sockets, if they're still there, the front sway bar chassis clamp area, beneath the end of the torsion bars at the rear, and the transmission cradle, which is bolted to the chassis. Anywhere else invites bending or breaking something. If you must jack somewhere else, use a 2 x 4 between the jack and car to spread the load and remove point contacts.

That maddening "thunk-thunk" you hear as you drive down an uneven road could be a dented belly pan "oil canning" or popping in and out as the car flexes.

Vol. 8, No. 2 Vic Skirmants

A Second Opinion

How to jack up a 356. The factory jack points are ideal for jacking the car up from the side; if they're in good condition! You can raise one or the other front corner by jacking under the sway bar clamps, raise the complete rear end by jacking under the transmission cradle; don't jack by the engine or the transmission; you would be lifting the car by the rubber transmission mounts! After raising the rear and then putting jackstands under the torsion bar tubes, you can raise the whole front end by jacking under one of the sway bar clamps.

There is no safe way to raise just one side of the car without the factory jack points. There are other places on a 356 that one can, very carefully, jack

by, but it can be dangerous to your car and you, especially if the underside is getting a little "crunchy".

Vol. 8, No. 3 Ron Roland

A Dissenting Opinion

I am surprised! You should never jack up a Porsche with the factory jack points (race cars excepted). I have seen new (and especially used) 356s slip off the jack, crunching the rocker panel; the jack twists and breaks the socket; the owner slips with the jack tool, while letting down, installing a huge gouge in the door; etc., in no particular order. Factory jack points are ornamental only; use a scissors or hydraulic jack under one or the other positions mentioned. In fact, part of a 356 "travel kit" should always be a scissors jack!

Cold Starting

Vol. 4, No. 3 Vic Skirmants

Starting Without a Choke

Now for a little note on cold weather starting. As you know, Porsche didn't put chokes on the 356 after about 1954. The purpose of a choke is to richen the charge of air and fuel entering the cylinder. You do that on a 356 by pumping the accelerator several times to let the accelerator pump dump some gas down the carburetor throat. If your battery and starter are good, if your engine has decent compression and fairly good tune, it will start. Remember, you're not driving a slow-revving American V-8. Re-gap the spark plugs at least every 3000 miles. If a V-8 loses two or three cylinders to bad plugs, who cares? If your Porsche has a weak spark in one or two cylinders and it's cold outside, you're going to have problems.

Chapter 6
Electrical

Lights

Vol. 1, No. 2 Paul Allen

Corroded Tail Light Sockets
Corroded tail light sockets? Don't buy new tail lights. Pound out the old sockets and get new ones at any parts store.

Vol. 1, No. 3 Vic Skirmants

The Return of Corroded Tail Light Sockets
Corroded tail light sockets – you can't punch out the whole socket without first melting the exterior solder joint, although you can take out and replace just the interior portions by uncrimping and recrimping the lower part of the socket. Spring corrosion is usually the cause of socket failure. A kit consisting of a spring and fiber discs is available at auto parts stores.

Vol. 8, No. 3 Vic. Skirmants

Corroded Tail Light Sockets, Yet Again
If you have ever had trouble with the electrical contact in your taillights, here's a funky fix. There is a small, weak spring that pushes the contact up against the base of the bulb. When this spring rusts, it no longer pushes. You can either replace the whole taillight unit, knock out the socket part and replace with a universal bulb holder, or you can take a ballpoint pen spring, cut it in half, and solder it to the bulb contact.

Vol. 3, No. 6 Stuart Tucker

Dim Headlights
If your 356 has a long history of dim headlights and all contacts and connections have been checked and double-checked to no avail, check the wiring at the back of the headlight bulb against a wiring diagram. On my 356 C, even though I had *bona fide* low beams and high beams, the wires at the headlight bulb plug were not appropriately connected. Once the connections as tabulated below were made, I was rewarded by a tremendous improvement in headlight illumination.

Wire Color	Function	Contact Number	Bulb Prong Position
white	high beam	56a	right
yellow	low beam	56b	top
brown	ground	35	left

Vol. 4, No. 4 Richard Miller

Dim Headlights Revisited
Other than a 12 v. sealed beam in your 6 v. Porsche (they do fit), I have

found some common causes for the dim headlight malady. The problem is usually due to poor connections someplace. Typically, bad grounds, deteriorated connections, or loose wires at the bulb connectors, light switch, dimmer switch or fuse block are the cause. In what follows, I would like to give you my solutions to these problems.

Poor ground connections are easy to correct. The ground wire goes through the tube at the bottom of the headlight bucket and comes out in the trunk where it is bolted to the wall of the spare tire compartment. (Usually by a 6 mm x 1.0 cheesehead screw with a 6 mm nut). Undo the connection, check the wire in the crimp terminal to see if it's corroded or loose, clean all metal bare and bright and retighten securely. You can protect against further corrosion by applying *grease,* paint, undercoat or bubblegum.

Bad connections at the headlight bulb can result from frayed (i.e. partly broken) wires at the connector or if the car has been repainted there may be a lot of overspray in the connector contacts or just a lot of dirt or corrosion on the terminals. The remedy is to clean all contacts or if necessary cut back the wires and resolder them. This involves removing the terminals from the connector body. To disassemble I use two X-Acto knife blades or other thin, stiff pieces of metal. The terminals are locked into the plastic body by the two small tabs (see drawing).

From the backside of the connector, the knife blades can be used to unseat the lock tabs and the terminal can be pulled out as in the drawing. I don't know why but all of the connectors I have ever seen as original equipment say "COLE, BOSTON" on them - same with early VW, which is where you can get replacements. Also, note that the backside is labeled "GRD" (ground], *"LO* BEAM" and *"H. BEAM"* – no excuse for incorrect assembly. I have seen these miswired -

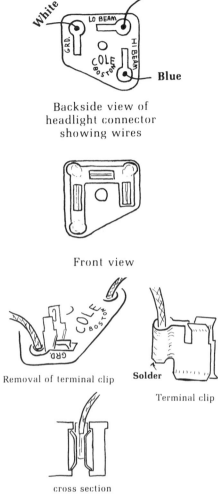

Backside view of headlight connector showing wires

Front view

Removal of terminal clip

Solder

Terminal clip

cross section

getting the ground in the wrong place can cause dimness on one setting - the diagram shows the correct connections. The wire is soldered in the bottom of the round part of the terminal. To reassemble just push the terminal back in until it clicks in place.

Often a loose or corroded connection can be located by touch while the lights are on – it gets hot – sometimes so hot you'll burn your finger or see discolored insulation. What happens is that looseness or corrosion causes resistance in the connection. This does two things, it reduces voltage available to the rest of the circuit and it makes heat. If the resistance is only $1/4$

ohm and the headlight is 48 watts, the current would be about 8 amps. This 8 amps flowing through the $1/4$ ohm resistance causes a voltage drop of about 2 v. and there is only 4 v. across the bulb to make light. In addition the power lost in the connection resistance is proportional to the current squared – so the *more* current, the more heat. The heat promotes further corrosion and the whole thing goes unstable. This can happen anywhere in the circuit but is often found at the light switch or the fuse block.

The flat, push-on connectors and the screw type terminals are prone to this while the round, push-in barrel connectors are relatively trouble free, The flat connectors can be slid off, cleaned and squeezed slightly to make better contact. The screw terminals, if you are lucky, will respond to tightening and cleaning. If you are not lucky the whole terminal turns and the loose connection is inside the switch or behind the fuse block. If the problem area is the light switch you can replace it or you can repair it. To repair, drill out the two rivets holding the switch together and gently open the switch case from the bakelite body. Note the orientation of the sliding contact block for when you reassemble the switch. If you blow it you'll have headlights in park position or worse.

The terminal extends through the switch housing and is riveted to the spring contact in the switch. The riveted connection is where the looseness is. Clean the metal around this connection and solder the two together thus making good electrical contact. This technique also works well on the back of the fuse block where the connecting links have become corroded and the connections are bad. After repair, reassemble the switch using two 3 mm - 0.5 x 15 mm screws with nuts and lock washers, and new rivets if you can find any. When reassembling the switch, check that the spring fingers touch the sliding contact block firmly

and be careful not to bend the wiper for the instrument light rheostat.

Vol. 4, No. 4 Steve Strahm

Electrical Problems, Especially Dim Lights
On the fuse block, each fuse clip is fastened to its screw block by a rivet method (unfortunately). Any looseness in this junction causes more resistance in junction. The current flowing in (any) resistance causes heat. The heat deteriorates the metal, causing more looseness and resistance. Repair by soldering around the *periphery* of the junction, but first brighten the metal by scrapping with the tip of the x-acto knife, then apply (electrical type) solder flux. Use only electrical type solder (rosin multicore or kester). Remove flux residue using isopropyl alcohol and Q-tips.

Vol. 4, No. 5 Pete Healy

The Origin of Headlight Sockets
The 356s were shipped to the states without headlights as the European bulbs are not approved for use here. We purchased the connectors plain or as pigtails from Cole-Hersee Co. in Boston and sold them to dealers in California, Las Vegas & Arizona for installation on new Porsches & VWs, since the cars arrived in the states with only the wires in the headlight bucket.

Vol. 8, No. 3 Lew Larkin

Use of Relays to Improve Headlight Brightness
Probably every 356 owner, except those who have a 356 that came with the 12 v. electrical option or has been converted to 12 v., has one major complaint – the lights or the lack thereof. When darkness comes, the low beams produce enough light to qualify as decent parking lights and the high beams permit seeing large objects about 75 feet ahead. The illumi-

nation at either setting would satisfy Military regulations for combat zone travel.

One obvious solution is to convert to 12 v. but that is a significant and expensive undertaking. There are other advantages to going to 12 v., such as being able to use modern radio, cassette players and CB units. But they can be used with the installation of a 6 v. to 12 v. converter. (maybe someone will write an article on their installation)

One reasonably simple and inexpensive solution is the installation of headlight relays. They will increase the brightness of your headlights by at least 80%. You'll really be able to see! The low beams will easily produce as much light as your present high beams, and the high beams will be at least twice as bright as your current high beams. Sight will be yours and the mere flash of your high beams will induce those oncoming turkeys to quickly lower their lights.

Another advantage is the significant drop in amperes required to operate your lights. On my Convertible D, which has an ammeter, sitting at rest, about 2500 RPMs were needed to stop discharging the battery with the high beams on. After installing the relays, only about 1800 RPMs were needed. So for about $22, you can correct your major complaint and see! (I haven't installed relays in my 1968 912 but I am confident that comparable improvements will be secured.)

The equipment and material you will need for this 30 to 45 minute job are as follows:

1) Two light relays. I used 2 Marchal 514 relays. One is needed for high beams and one for the lows. (Code 915 00002 is for 6 v. and Code 915 00012 for 12 v.) I also suggest you buy a couple of spare fuses (915 10033 6 v.-25 amp or 12 v.-25 amp)

2) Drill, bit and two large metal screws with hex heads for using a socket wrench for installing.

Fig. 1

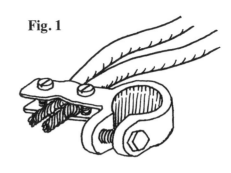

3) Approximately 15 feet of No. 12 electrical wire. For easier and a professional looking installation two colors are preferable. I suggest white and yellow to match the original colors for the headlights. A third color, red, would be nice for wiring the relays to the battery.

4) Six crimp line joiners for No. 12 wire. Nine crimp slide on connectors-female, and one crimp connector eye type, to attach to the positive battery terminal. If you have the standard Porsche positive wire connector, you will not need this eye type connector as you can insert the end of the wire and screw it down tight. (See Fig. 1)

5) A crimper and wire stripper tool.

Installation Steps

1) Disconnect the battery. (Sounds like Der Shop Manual, doesn't it?)

2) Locate, drill holes and install the relays. Fig. 2 shows where I installed the relays in my Convertible D (356 A) and a friend's 356 B. The main thing is to place them out of the way so the spare tire and other items usually stowed in the battery box area won't disturb them.

The relays are installed with the wire terminals facing up. See Fig. 3. I also separated the relays by about 1/2 inch.

3) Carefully cut into the wire bundles on each side of the car in the area before the wire bundle exits the battery box. See Fig. 2. Peel back the harness covering about 2 1/2 to 3 inches.

Fig. 2

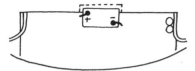

Relay Placement through 1961

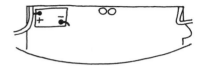

Relay Placement from 1962

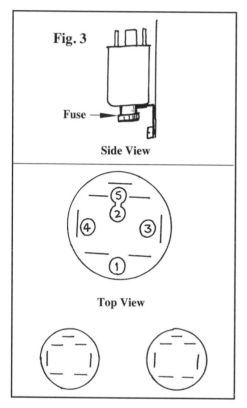

Fig. 3

Fuse →

Side View

Top View

Locate the two power wires to the headlights. It has been my experience that there are three wires to the headlights; a white one, a yellow one and a brown one which is ground. There are often two other wires in the hurdle; one for the horn, I think, and one for the parking light that is in the light bucket.

4) Pull the white and yellow wires away from the other wires as much as reasonably possible. Then cut them in half.

5) Strip off about 1/4 in. of covering on each wire on the driver's side.

6) Strip off about 1/4 in. of covering on the wires leading to the headlights on the Passenger side. Tape the ends of the wires coming from the body on the passenger side. See Fig. 4.

7) Install the wire clips that come with the relays on No. 4 and No. 5 terminal. See Fig. 4.

8) Using the crimp & stripper tool, connect wires as shown in Fig. 4.

Route wire along with the wire harness that runs under the lip of the

Fig. 4

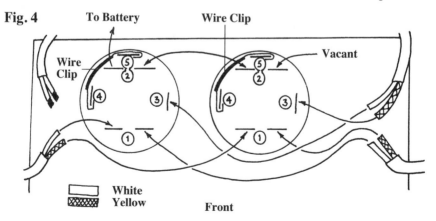

To Battery   Wire Clip

Wire Clip   Vacant

White
Yellow

Front

trunk above the battery box opening. There are 3 or 4 wire clips that will need to be bent out to accommodate the relays wires from a neat installation. Measure wire needed to connect to the relay, then cut, strip about 1/4 inch of covering from the wire, crimp on the slide connector and install as shown in Fig. 4.

9) Follow Step 8 for each of the connections required. Do the connection to the battery last. I suggest you tape this wire to the long positive battery wire; as it will permit movement of the battery without having to disconnect it from the battery.

10) Reconnect the battery. Try the lights and be amazed! Take a test drive at night. Now, there's safety and vision.

Now you can go one step further as I did. I installed a pair of Cibie Z Beams wilh H-4 bulbs in my Convertible D. What a difference over the conventional lights with the relays. Now I can haul with safety and can see the Bears in hiding.

Vol. 8, No. 6 Mike O'Meara

Even More About Dim Headlights

Concerning headlights and the lack thereof: I have found the following to be most helpful in securing better lighting.

1) Clean everything! This includes the three-pronged headlight terminals and sockets, battery terminals, ground strap mount, fuse block terminals, and wires at the fuse block. This could be done on a regular basis, as the grime that builds on these surfaces cuts into the power going to the lights, thereby limiting their effectiveness.

2) Clean the inside contacts of the light switch itself. The switch can be disassembled by carefully drilling out the rivets. I found an amazing amount of grime on the contact area. No wonder no lights! Cleaning this alone accounted for an immense improvement. To reassemble, use new rivets and a

pair of pliers to finish crimping them, as the rivet tool interferes with the sides of the switch and does not allow a complete crimp.

3) A strange, elusive problem occurred in the electrical systems of both 356As I have owned, so this may be common to others, also. On the back of the fuse block there are metal strips which act as connections between various fuse terminals (see Fig. 1). These are between terminals 2, 3, and 4: also between 5-6, 7-8, 9-10, and 11-12. The connective strip between 2 and 3 supplies power to the car, which of course includes the lights. At some point in my car's "previous life" this connection burned partially, leaving just enough juice to run the car, but as soon as greater demand was made, such as headlights, the power running through the strip caused it to burn more, and all power was lost. This happened to me when I switched to the high beams one night on a dark, deserted Wisconsin highway, late at night, 300 miles from home, with two sleeping kids in the back seat. Everything shut down, including the brake lights, tail lights and engine. After coasting to the side of the road by feel (it was that dark) a temporary fix was made by wrapping wire around the two small screws on #2 and #3 fuse terminals.

Fig. 1 – Rear View Fuse Block

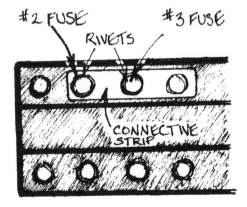

Fig. 2

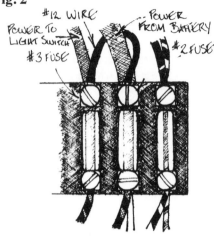

The permanent solution is to replace this connection, either in back by soldering in a new piece, or as I did, using a short piece of #12 wire, connecting the fuse terminals in front (see Fig. 2). If you use this method, however, be patient and work the wire into the terminal with the main wire, as wrapping the wire around the screws does not provide good conduction. I am wary of using solder on these connections for fear the heat buildup might melt the solder during greater demand. The Factory used some kind of rivet, but as I recall it's not easy to replace the connection in this manner.

These hints have greatly improved the lighting both inside and outside the car, and provide a good starting point for further improvement, such as light relays as described in the 8/3 issue.

Vol. 9, No. 2 Ron Koster

Another Reason for Dim Headlights

After reading the article about installing headlamp relays to increase brightness of the lamps in your Feb/March 1982 issue, I thought that you might like to publish an alternate method which is much more simple and accomplishes the same result.

A major cause of headlight dimness is resistance in the light switch from oxidation. When driving with the lights on, feel the knob shaft and bezel. If they are warm or hot, you have found the problem. I have taken the switch apart many times and cleaned the contacts but soon the problem returned.

Now, I have outstanding 6 v. illumination by installing a conventional 6 v. headlight relay mounted on the left side of the steering column brace. This position allows connection of the main current carrying wires without splicing or rewiring. All that is needed is about 10 in. of light 16 gauge wire and about 8 in. of heavy wire the same diameter as the main current wires, or solid copper 12 gauge house wire (red color), press fit terminals and solder. Solder all terminals on the main current wires. Solder the rivet connections on the relay bars or they will come loose and add resistance to the system.

When mounting the relay, give the horn and headlight flasher connections enough clearance. They protrude up through the steering column brace. I also have 7 in. halogen headlamps. You can buy 12 v. headlamps and get 6 v. bulbs for them. When changing the bulbs, be careful not to touch the quartz glass. Oil from your fingers will create a hot spot and the bulb will burn out faster.

Note: Solder all connections marked s and all main wire terminals.

Vol. 9, No. 4 Richard Miller

Dim Headlights, a Final Look

Ron Koster's article on correcting dim headlight problems sounds like the best approach to redesigning the system that I've heard of. It certainly reduces the current through the switch, which is part of the problem. If cleaning and retensioning the switch contacts doesn't help, the real problem is in the terminals on the base of the switch – either the screws are loose, the wires oxidized, or the rivet connecting the outside terminal to the inside contact is loose. The "burnt finger" test works well here as it does for the same problem at the dimmer switch or fuse panel. The cure that I've used is to clean the rivet and surrounding metal parts with metal prep, rinse in clean water and use a big soldering iron to sweat-solder the whole thing together (including the wires if you want to). This works particularly well on the bridge pieces on the back of the fuse panel. A quick way of curing the problem there is to add jumper wires on the hot side to take the place of the connecting straps if you can fit the wires in.

Vol. 16, No. 4 Cole Scrogham

Adjusting Headlights

In light of this point, I came across a rather unique diagram (below) that allows any 356 owner to adjust his own headlights. Isn't it frustrating to go down the road and see cars approaching with lights askew? I wonder how many fresh restorations have had their lights adjusted? Well, anyway, even if you have the desire to

Dimensions for Screen (European Standard)

a	Distance from lens to screen	5m (16 ft. 6 in.)
b	Distance between crosses	1170 mm (3 ft. 10 in.)
c	Distance between upper limit of low beam and center of cross	50mm (2 in.)

	Bosch	Hella
Vertical	Turn upper screw to right = beam down to left = beam up	Turn left screw to right = beam up to left = beam down
Horizontal	Turn right screw to right = beam left to left = beam right	Turn right screw to right = beam right to left = beam left

drive at night in a 356, and on top of that want to see where you are going, how in the world do you figure out which way to turn those screws?

Please note that when using this diagram, left and right are always in the driving direction, looking straight ahead. This can be confusing, and to add to the confusion, I know of at least one other variation of headlight assembly. Later Hella assemblies have adjustment screws at about 2 o'clock and 7 o'clock. This is probably just another case of opening a can of worms. There is certainly some 356 out there somewhere that came with "original" Lucas headlights and a special headlight switch for "on," "off" and "flicker." If you do have some wild creation, please drop me a line and let me know. Hopefully, this will help somebody that cannot find an old timer's headlight adjusting machine and is driven to tears over misadjusted headlights. If this is you, send me the next installment due your analyst and go enjoy driving your car.

Vol. 8, No. 3 Lew Larkin

Chrome Paint for Tail Light Restoration

While I was restoring my Convertible D, I stumbled on a product that is just great and should be on every restorers shelf.

The chrome reflecting interior surfaces of my tail lights were in rough shape; most of the chrome had flaked off. I cleaned them with sandpaper and steel wool, stuffed the bulb inserts with kleenex, then primed them. Then I gave them three light coats of chrome spray. This was then followed with a coat of high gloss clear polyurethane.

They looked like new. The painted surfaces looked like chrome. Only close inspection could detect they had been painted. Assembled, these produced light as good as new units. The successful technique is to spray two or three very light coats 12 to 16 inches away. A little goes a long way. A couple friends have used my paint and technique with the same excellent results.

I've tried several chrome sprays but this one is far superior to any I've tried. The product is NYBCO Chrome Spray. The 8 ounce can advertises "The Nearest Thing to Chrome" and "The Finest Chrome Aluminum Spray Enamel" and you'd better believe it! The manufacturer is the New York Bronze Powder Company. I bought the spray at Pep Boys, an automotive parts chain, for $2.49.

This brand could not be located at the time of publication, but similar products are available – September 1994

Vol. 14, No. 5 Phil Planck

Blown Backup Light Fuses

Everything electrical on my 1955 356 worked but the backup light. Every time I shifted into reverse, the fuse would burn. I have not found any manuals that tell or show where the backup light switch is. While working on a gear shifting problem I finally located this switch. Page R 39 of the factory manual describes how to remove and install the shift rod. The "removing" portion tells you to remove the tunnel cover. You must do this to find the switch. This cover is directly behind the gearshift lever assembly. The "installing" portion tells you to test the backup light switch. Looking down into the tunnel you will see this switch on the passenger side.

This switch is very similar to the starter switch. It has a button that is depressed by the shift rod when the

gear lever is in the reverse position. The shift rod connects the gearshift lever assembly to the rear of the tunnel where the transaxle inner shift lever enters. With an ohm meter, it was determined that the switch was grounded when the transaxle was shifted into reverse but not when in any other gear positions. The electrically grounded switch was the cause of the burned fuse.

Next the switch was removed, which is a bugger of a job almost deserving its own article. The switch did work but not well. It was easy to disassemble and clean up the contacts. After this was done it worked well.

After reinstalling the switch it still was grounding when shifted into reverse. The ground was caused by the dreaded bent bracket aging disease. The cause is shown in illustration A. This disease allowed the switch bracket to bend over the years. As it bent the switch terminals got closer and closer to a metal tube that runs along the passenger side of the tunnel. Eventually one of the terminals touched the tube when the transaxle was shifted into reverse.

Two things were done to fix the problem. First the bent bracket was re-bent to what I assume was it's original vertical position. I notice that the later 356 backup light switch had a rubber boot over the wire terminals. This switch had no boot and I do not know

In Neutral

Terminal That Shorts out on Conduit

Back-Up Light Switch

— **Tunnel**

Shift Rod

Floor Pan

Diseased Switch Bracket →

Conduit

Illustration A

In Reverse

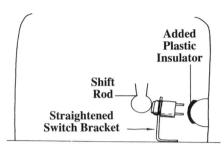

Added
Plastic
Insulator

Shift
Rod

Straightened
Switch Bracket

Illustration B

if it is supposed to. To get a similar effect of a boot the second thing I did was to glue a piece of plastic to the metal tube that the switch contacted when the bracket bent. This plastic was cut from a plastic container and was about 1 in. long and 3/4 in. wide. I used contact cement to attach it. The fix is shown in illustration B. Now, as the dreaded bent bracket aging disease does its thing, the bent bracket can come to its final resting position without burning a fuse.

Turn Signal

Vol. 5, No. 1 Richard Miller

1953 - 1955 Turn signal Circuit

This is another circuit which is not explained by the wiring diagram in the Porsche manual. The circuit shown here is for early cars having the non-self-cancelling type SWF turn signal switch with the red indicator light in the end of the handle. The trick here is the blinker unit. The heater circuit is controlled by the power circuit relay which is controlled by the heater circuit. Make sense? What happens is that nothing happens until you move the lever. Then current flows through the normally closed (NC) contacts and relay coil connecting terminal +49 to 49as. This current lights the turn signals selected by the switch and also pulls in the contact for the heater circuit. The heater then warms up a bi-metallic strip which bends and opens the normally closed contacts. This turns out the lights and also opens the heater circuit. The bimetal strip cools off and the normally closed contacts in the power circuit close again starting the whole procedure over again (i.e., it flashes). Also notice that the little light bulb in the handle is connected across terminals +49 and 49as. This means that when the normally closed power contacts are open, the light is on and vice versa. Have you ever noticed that the indicator light is on when the turn signal lights are off? They work in opposition. When the

Turn Signal Circuit

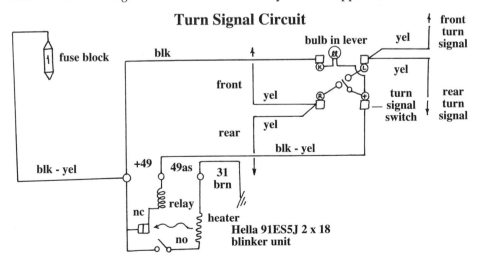

blinker unit is in the off state, current flows from terminal +49 through the indicator bulb, through the turn signal switch contacts and to ground through both turn signal bulbs. They don't light up when this happens because the small bulb takes so little current to light up, that is, the amount of current it lets through is not enough to light the turn signals. Then, when the power contacts in the blinker close, both terminals +49 and 49as are at the same voltage and the indicator light is, in effect, shorted out and goes off.

Vol. 10, No. 1 Richard Miller

Flash Rate Adjustment
   Another arcane, obscure adjustment provided on early cars was the turn signal flasher rate. On the big can flasher (with screw terminals of course) there was a hole (usually, covered by a tin label) in the end between the four terminals. Peel the paper off and a small set screw inside can be used to set the flash rate (if you're very careful.)

Battery

Vol. 12, No. 5 K. L. Martin

Prolonging the Useful Life of a Car Battery with EDTA
Very few car batteries are replaced because they stop working. In almost every case the battery is replaced because it doesn't work *well enough* any more. What is not generally realized is that something can be done at this stage which may well prolong the useful life of the battery – quite often by many years, and that the same treatment carried out earlier in the battery's life may well have stopped the symptoms from occurring in the first place.
   The reason for a battery failing to work properly any more is due to the chemical processes which take place within each cell when the battery is not fully charged. Even the slightest of discharged conditions allows both plates to react slowly with the sulfuric acid electrolyte to form lead ions. It is these lead ions which cause problems. They combine with sulfate ions in sulfuric acid to form highly insoluble lead sulfate. When this coats the plates of the battery, it fails to deliver enough power to be of use. The battery may well be thoroughly serviceable in every other way – only the "sulfating" stops the battery delivering enough power to start the car.
   The sulfating can effectively be removed, or prevented, by adding to each cell a chemical called tetrasodium ethylenediaminetetra-acetate (often abbreviated to tetrasodium EDTA). This chemical forms coordination compounds with many metal ions, including the lead ions formed in the discharge cycle of a battery. The compound formed by lead ions and the EDTA ion is not particularly stable in the acid medium of a battery, but when it breaks down again any lead sulfate generated tends to drop to the bottom of the cell where it lays harmlessly since it doesn't conduct electricity. Any regenerated EDTA ions are free to continue their work. As can be seen from above, treating a battery with tetrasodium EDTA is likely to be most effective when the battery, for one reason or another, spends periods when it is not fully charged, and so contains too many lead ions. This is likely to occur if the car is used for just short trips, is infrequently used, or has at any time suffered from an inefficient generator/ alternator. Treating with the chemical can also help in bringing back into use a stored battery.
   To treat a battery with tetrasodium EDTA you simply take a fully heaped tablespoon full of the powder, divide it up and add to each cell. This assumes an average size battery but the exact amount is in no way critical.

What you should then do is to use the car normally for a few days, or agitate the battery frequently for a few days, and then give it a thorough charge to build up on the cleaned plate areas. On the assumption that sulfating has been affecting the performance of your battery, an increased performance will be noted from here on. Over the past few years, many thousands of European car enthusiasts have used tetrasodium EDTA with great success on their batteries. You may wish to do the same by purchasing some of the chemical and giving it a try.

Vol. 12, No. 6 Robert Laepple

Prolonging the Useful Life of a Car Battery with EDTA, II

It seems Mr. Martin had sent the same article to many U.S. car clubs. *NINES* (SAAB club newsletter) quotes from the July issue of *Skinned Knuckles*, an auto restoration magazine: "the hypothesis put forth to explain the action of this additive is based on a very poor understanding of the electrochemistry involved in lead-acid batteries." Their recommendation is to regard Mr. Martin's claim with "considerable skepticism."

Well, there's the other side of the argument. Has anyone further information one way or the other? If Mr. Martin is correct, it would: be an interesting technical advance; if he's selling "snake oil," we'd like to know that as soon as possible. I have not decided for either side yet, but am awaiting further input from our membership.

Vol. 12, No. 6 Bill Block

Sources for EDTA

Vic mentioned in the last issue that tetrasodium EDTA might be useful for prolonging battery life but was not sure how difficult it would be to acquire. Here we find a happy and serendipitous intersection between my two

lives: the 5 ml purple top vacuum tubes, used to draw blood for hematology studies at your doctor's office or hospital pathology department contain 7.5 mg of either Sodium or Potassium EDTA as an anticoagulant. They are not particularly expensive and even better are dated. You may be able to pick up some outdated tubes for free! Potassium EDTA is in liquid form and Sodium is a freeze dried powder.

Vol. 17, No. 5 Daniel Pelecovich

Battery Safety

For as long as I can remember - whenever removing the battery of any negatively grounded car as our Porsches, I always disconnect the negative battery terminal first. If you disconnect the positive terminal first, you stand a chance if you contact any metal (ground) with your wrench of causing a direct short circuit. This is easier to do than you might think, especially in some of the tight quarters in our cars. Of course, whenever installing a battery the positive terminal is connected first for the same reason.

Also, several years ago I had an electrical fire in my coupe caused by the heater box coming in contact with the B+ terminal on the starter solenoid, causing a short circuit to ground. Since the smoke and flames were concentrated in the starter vicinity, I was sure the problem was electrical and immediately attempted to disconnect one of the battery terminals. The terminals were both tightly bolted and time did not permit hunting for a wrench. Although it was scary for awhile with flames licking up under the right Solex, a water hose was fortunately nearby and was used to extinguish the fire with only cable and wire damage.

Some time later Tom Oerther told me that he just snugs up one of the battery terminal so that it can be disconnected by hand in case of an emergency. This is very good advice and I have been doing it ever since – and you should too.

Vol. 17, No. 6 Mick Michelsen

Battery Safety, Use of a Master Switch
I tried to figure out how to write this without appearing self-serving, but couldn't-so I said what the hell, I'll write anyway. Daniel Pelecovich wrote in the last *Registry* about battery safety. We have just the ticket for a quick disconnect which beats leaving a cable loose (we've had a couple of cars where the cables were all that held the battery in!) The master switch we sell is $10, all brass and a no-brainer to use.

Fuse Block

Vol. 7, No. 4 Dale Lucas

SAAB Fuse Box Swap
For fuse boxes up to the early 356B's, the cover from a SAAB 96 or 95 looks and fits properly. However, more notches need to be filed into the sides to clear all the Porsche wires.

Vol. 17, No. 5 John Jenkins

Electrical Resistance and the Fuse Box
The fuse block of the 356 is not a perfect device and is prone to development of internal resistance which lowers the voltage to the wires leaving said block. If your lights are not re-

ceiving the full 6 volts due to them, you can make a quick check on your fuse block to see if it is the culprit.
The new information for me was the insidious construction of the terminals in the fuse block and how they can mess you up when you're looking for problems. What you see when you examine the rear of the fuse block are jumpers that are mechanically fastened by the riveting of the terminal to the brass jumper. One would think that by soldering the jumpers you could decrease the resistance caused by the corrosion between these two brass pieces. Simple. Put the fuse block in some diluted acid, clean off the corrosion on the brass parts, re-tin (solder) the ends of the wires, solder the jumpers on the back, and presto-a new fuse block. Well, almost. If you were to break apart the fuse block, you would find that the fuse holder is not an integral part of the wire terminal. It is a clip that is held behind the terminal by nothing but the pressure of the riveting of the terminal to the jumper. Simply stated, it's a piece of brass stuck behind the terminal.
So why is this a problem? Well, if you didn't know this you would measure the resistance of the terminals (about 0.2 ohm) and think you had the problem solved. You need to measure at the point where the fuse resides. If there is corrosion behind that fuse clip/holder, you will miss it if you don't measure there. If you still have some resistance after soldering the jumpers, then you need to solder that clip/holder to the terminal. Note: small tip needed for this.
Want to do a quick check? Pull the fuses on two, three and four. In A cars (are there others?) fuse three is the third one from the right. It is the one that has the big red wire coming from your battery connected to it. Guess what happens if the terminals on this wire are corroded? Measure the resistance between terminals three and four. Use the top terminals. The ones

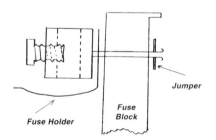

Jumper

Fuse
Block

Fuse Holder

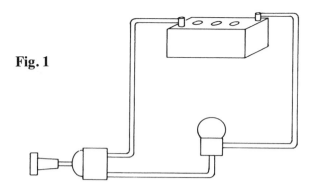

Fig. 1

on the bottom are not jumpered. Now measure three and two. They should both be 0.1 to 0.2 ohm. Move your probes to the fuse clip/holder now. Same reading? Good. If not, that may be your problem. This test is further complicated by the movement of the clip/holder. Marginal pressure from a corroded rivet can make the continuity between the clip and terminal intermittent or variable in terms of resistance if there is some corrosion between them. Check the resistance whilst moving the clip the same distance the fuse would cause it to move. You might be surprised.

Trouble Shooting

Vol. 4, No. 2 Brett Johnson

Basic Trouble Shooting I

How many of you have reinstalled lights, horns and the like on your semi-restored vehicle and had everything work correctly without additional complications? All answering in the affirmative are obviously compulsive liars and likely to spend the majority of their free time telling people that their 356 has 200,000 miles, the original pan, original paint, and original tires.

I have never had a car that much more than half of the electrical components have functioned normally after reassembly.

To troubleshoot your electrical sys-

tem, you need only a few simple tools:
1. A wiring diagram. Color coded if possible.
2. A voltmeter or test light.
3. Wire strippers, a knife will do.
4. Solderless connectors (not for purists).
5. Electrical tape (see #4).
6. Wire of similar gauge to that used in car.
7. Sandpaper.
8. Spare fuses.
9. Soldering iron and rosin core solder.

There is one other thing you need... time. (on occasion, days, weeks, years.)

First let me dispel all those nasty rumors about wiring. It is not difficult and only on rare occasions does your wiring harness ignite and your car burn to a smoldering heap before your very eyes.

At this point I will make a brave assumption. I assume that you are more concerned with functioning electricals than pretty electricals. While normally these two are synonymous, on occasion there are instances when splicing and such are considerably less time consuming than inserting a new wire of the correct color into the harness. Without going into complex circuit theory, the electrical circuit for any part on the car must be complete from the positive terminal of the battery to the negative terminal in order to have a functional light or horn. (Fig. 1).

If something is not working, there

Fig. 2

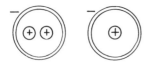

are two immediate avenues to investigate the light, horn, motor (whatever) and the wiring to and from the battery.

The first of these two is the easier. Lights are the easiest to repair. Burned out bulbs may be replaced with little effort and expense. Horns and windshield wiper motors, however, may be quite costly and if replacement does not cure the problem, can be very frustrating. To avoid potential money wasting, you should have a voltmeter. Most of these are part of some multipurpose analyzer, have multiple scales, and more knobs than a computer terminal. Find the scale for voltage which has 6 volts nearest the top. In other words, a 0-12 v. scale is better than a 0-110 v. scale.

Next, disconnect the wires from the offending piece. In the case of lights, removal of the bulb is sufficient. If you do remove wires, remember where they came from. If a goodly number of wires are involved, a diagram is in order.

Most things have only two wires: 1) a hot lead, which may be any of a number of bright springtime colors, and 2) a ground, which on 356A - 356C cars is brown. Converts from British cars (to which voltmeters were fitted as standard equipment, I believe) probably think ground wires are black. Black wires in the wiring harness of late 356 Porsches have totally different functions, and should not be confused with grounds. On 356s built prior to 1956 ground wires may be black... now I'm confused!

However, I digress, your voltmeter should have two leads; a positive and negative, usually red and black. These leads end in metal probes or alligator clips. Now a very important step, turn the voltmeter on! To determine whether or not something is getting power, hook or touch the leads to the loose wires. In a light socket, place one probe, the ground, against the side and the other on the hot lead which is usually mounted on a fiber washer. A single filament bulb has a single hot lead while a dual has two (Fig. 2). Choosing the correct one is not always apparent, so trial and error is the best way to approach this.

If you are one of the fortunate few with a voltmeter sprouting gigantic alligator clips which will not fit inside the light socket, cut a piece of wire from your spare wire supply and insert it in the alligator clip. (Fig. 3) Easy, huh?

Now what you have done is demonstrated in Fig 4. If everything is functioning properly, by activation of the proper switch on the dashboard the meter will deflect: hooking up the meter backwards will oddly enough cause a backwards deflection, but this is readily corrected by reversing the leads.

If the meter deflects, you should suspect a bad light, horn, etc., or bad connections. Lightly sand all connections and try again. If there is still nothing, replace the offending item. If deflection is appreciably less than the full six volts, again clean the connections and recheck the voltage. If it remains low, the ground may be bad.

If, on the other hand, you got no reading on your voltmeter, assuming it works, a bad ground is still a possibility. Determining this is quite simple. Remove the negative lead from the

Fig. 3

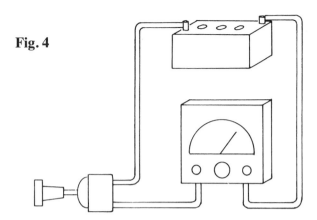

Fig. 4

ground wire and place it anywhere on the car that is metal, clean, unpainted, and free from rust. (ha! ha!) In the front or back of the car – try suspension parts or bumper brackets. In the interior – gearshift lever, dashboard supports, or pedal assembly are good. If you doubt the quality of your chosen ground, connect the voltmeter's positive lead to the battery's positive terminal. If the meter deflects, the ground is good.

If the meter now deflects when the switch is activated, you have solved your problem... bad ground. Usually it is due to poor connections either where it leaves the light, etc., or where it attaches to the body. This of course brings up the time worn problem of where the attachments to the body are. Items such as early beehive tail lights and turn signals ground themselves directly without wires. If they are not firmly tightened on clean metal they won't work. The teardrop tail lights have a small metal strap which assists in grounding.

The horn, on the other hand, grounds within the luggage compartment and dashboard electrics have at least one common ground terminal in the general vicinity of the back of the gauges. (It's the bolt which radiates brown wires). The latter is rarely at fault, however, which is fortunate. If cleaning the connections and reat-

taching the wires does no good, the wire must be broken. Finding the break and repairing it with a solderless connector is certainly the easiest fix. Solderless connectors are readily obtainable at the old local hardware store. There are several varieties. A weather proof version is probably best for most applications.

If you are looking for concours appearance this will not do however. The only solution is to replace the wire. This may be difficult, but patience and ingenuity have always been the hallmark of the American people and I'm sure those who have the inclination will be able to fix just about anything.

Soldered butt splicing of wiring is a superior way of accomplishing the same goal. The resulting splice may be covered with shrink tubing – September 1994

If you need connectors which also have original appearance, take your wire cutter with you next time you go to the junk yard. Any German car of approximately the same vintage will have connectors identical to the ones on your 356. Junk dealers have been known to get very testy if you go around cutting things off their prized relics. So either be very straightforward and honest and explain your desires, or be very sneaky and devious and don't get caught. If you do, don't

Fig. 5

say I told you to do it.

Those push-in connectors (Fig. 5) are soldered on. Removing them from an old wire requires the heat supplied from a soldering iron. Resoldering it onto the new wire is not terribly complicated just be sure to use rosin-core solder.

Vol. 4, No. 3 Brett Johnson

Basic Trouble Shooting II

Now what happens if our hot lead is not hot? Now comes the time to unfold the dreaded wiring diagram. Porsche, in their infinite wisdom decided it would be best to print these in black and white with no color coding in factory workshop manuals. If you do not have the financial means to procure a copy of the official good book you may take solace in the fact that your after market cheapo workshop manual is every bit as good as the real thing in this respect.

While full color is a definite benefit, it is possible to use a black and white version without too much difficulty. Now comes another problem – your aftermarket manual has only one wiring diagram which is usually for a different model. Those of you who are PCA members have, over the past year (1977), been fortunate enough to see nearly all wiring diagrams revealed within the pages of *Panorama*.

Reading the wiring diagram is often confusing especially when all those little lines cross over each other resembling lunch at Pasquales'. It is often helpful to have an enlarged copy made, one which you can draw on to help trace the path of that illusive taillight wire.

The first thing to do is trace the path of the wire to where it enters the fuse block. Now check the fuse. If burned, out replace it. If not, don't ignore it. Take it out and lightly sand the ends. Check for corrosion on the fuse block and sand it. If necessary, replace the fuse.

By hooking your voltmeter's black lead to an appropriate ground, test current on each side of the fuse. If this circuit goes through the ignition, it will be necessary to turn the key on and activate the appropriate switch. If hot on only one side, the fuse is bad. If hot on both sides, the problem lies between the fuse and offending item. If not hot on either side, it is between the battery, and the fuse block.

A fourth situation is that the circuit is hot on both sides and the fuse blows out. In this case the problem again lies between the fuse block and offending item.

From this point on it is all a matter of following the path of the circuit testing voltage at each point where a switch or plug occurs. If hot at one point and dead at the next point along the circuit where it arises, try disconnecting both ends and running a piece of wire to the two ends. If successful, you will have found your problem. You have done what is shown in Fig. 1.

If you wish to preserve original appearance you may at this point follow the wiring harness and trace the actual path of the wire. Chances are there will be a break in the wire or a spot where the insulation is rubbed off, or most likely a bad connection at the switch or plug. In any case, these problems are easily rectified.

If inserting the wire as in Fig. 1 (next page) doesn't do anything, don't remove it. It is possible and indeed likely that there are multiple problems with the circuit. Go back to the fuse block and try again or check the ground. Essentially what you do is trouble shoot the entire circuit again.

Fig. 1

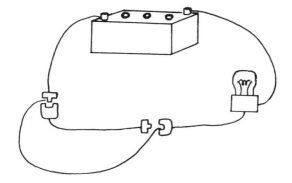

That's really all there is to it. Simple right? Well, there is one other thing, righting the wrongs which prior owners have inflicted. If you have been inspired by the utter simplicity of wiring as previously extoled, the best policy is remove all wiring which doesn't look like it belongs. Reconnect all original wires in their correct locations as depicted in your wiring diagram and trouble shoot. One of the most frustrating problems is brought on by improperly wired switches, fuse blocks, and relays. These can be quite frustrating as they look just fine but don't work. Unauthorized switches have a similar effect.

Your best bet here is to look up one of your local 356 buddies. Find one whose car runs and electricals function and look at the wiring. Try hooking yours up in the same manner. Usually the results are staggering.

Vol. 4, No. 4 Tony Standen

Electrical Connections
In my experience 40% of Porsche electrical problems stem from fuse block, 40% from poor grounds and the rest are gremlins. On the subject of poor grounds, I don't remember if Brother Brett mentioned battery ground strap connection. This is a vital one – keep it clean and vaselined and many minor problems disappear. Procedure: unbolt strap from floor of battery box. Mount wire brush in electric drill and clean strap, nut, bolt and

area around bolt hole scrupulously. Everything must *shine!* Reassemble, smearing liberally with vaseline.

Back to the fuse box. Remove all fuses, noting which sizes went where. Shine end of each fuse with fine sand or emery paper. Shine dimples which receive fuse ends with ditto – this is a nuisance, but these dimples do get corroded, and must be clean. Make sure every screw is tight on the wires it holds in place and that every wire is fully inserted into its hole. Give fuse ends a little coat of vaseline, and replace fuses.

If you are a perfectionist, clean and grease every connection made by plug and socket on the car in the same way – especially relay connections and under the steering column.

If you still have serious problems, God help you! Try having a 6x blow up made of the wiring diagram of the car. Then follow each circuit with a colored pen until you understand it.

Vol. 4, No. 4 Joe Diviney

Homemade Circuit Tester
While, maybe for some, the remaining task would have been an obvious exercise of "this one goes here and that one goes there," such was not the case for me. Except for the body in one piece, I bought the rest of my car packaged in paper bags including the fuse block and all electrics, relatively few as they are. All the wires had been left in the body for me to figure out, I

think? Since the car now had its new engine, tires, and fresh paint, etc., the last thing I wanted to do, even if only a remote possibility, was to begin re-connecting wires off a hot lead from the battery and run the risk of burning out the car not to mention the garage and house.

About this time, another friend, Ralph Meaney, professional Porsche mechanic extraordinaire and genuine Porsche enthusiast, recommended to me a three-dollar homemade circuit tester which not only eliminated such potential hazards but greatly assisted in tracing wires after they disappeared behind the fuse block. The device it-self is quite simple, consisting of a small buzzer (found in most hardware stores), four 1.5 volt batteries (C size), twenty feet of rubber coated braided copper wire (regular extension cord is also fine), one foot of $1/16$ in. solid copper wire, a 3" x 6" x $1/2$" block of wood, two rubber bands and a few small wood screws. *See diagram.*

When the circuit being checked is completed the buzzer will be activated, or if there is a short circuit the buzzer will make a slightly different sound. If, for example, you do not know which wire running *from* the fuse block is connected to the left brake light, connect one lead of the tester to the wire at the left brake light and with the other lead test connections to each wire under the dashboard or to the fuse terminals if the wires are still connected, until the buzzer is activated. Since some fuses service more than one device, it is best to check the disconnected wire to be sure you have the right one.

The real value of this type of tester is that it allows you to trace wires from under the dashboard where they will connect directly to the fuse block to their point of use, i.e. headlights, taillights, etc., without the need for a hot lead from the battery. In fact, the battery doesn't need to be in the car at all. Switches can also be checked for

proper functioning before or after in-stalling simply by connecting both leads of the tester to the terminals on the switch and then moving from "on" to "off" positions. Three-position switches, i.e. headlight switch, can be checked in similar manner to *determine* which terminal is for parking lights and which is for headlights. If your car is like mine, the color cod-ing of various wires is virtually use-less after 20 years of accumulated dirt and numerous coats of paint. In many cases, patch wiring by the well-intended previous owner has added additional confusion to an already mysterious problem-solving exercise.

My own experiences, however, in finally getting all the electricals in good working order was made possi-ble through continual reference to a wiring diagram.

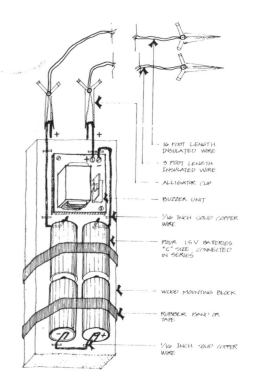

- 16 FOOT LENGTH INSULATED WIRE
- 3 FOOT LENGTH INSULATED WIRE
- ALLIGATOR CLIP
- BUZZER UNIT
- 1/16 INCH SOLID COPPER WIRE
- FOUR 1.5 V BATTERIES "C" SIZE CONNECTED IN SERIES
- WOOD MOUNTING BLOCK
- RUBBER BAND OR TAPE
- 1/16 INCH SOLID COPPER WIRE

Homemade Circuit Tester

82

Voltage Regulator Adjustment

Hot starting problems have plagued my 1960 Roadster for the past year. It got so bad at the last autocross I left my engine running between my last two runs. Doing so brought my fuel level down to the point I suffered from fuel starvation during the final run. I decided I had to solve the problem before another event.

I asked everyone who would listen what the problem might be. I got all kinds of advice. Everything was suggested from incorrect timing to a bad ground to a corroded primary battery lead. Each time I heard a new hypothesis, I checked it out. I removed, cleaned, and retightened each connection. I reset the timing. (I did not replace the primary battery lead as the car has a new harness.) Someone suggested an 8 volt battery. Someone else suggested a 6/12 volt battery, apparently a battery designed to produce 12 volts during starting and 6 volts during operation. I didn't try any of these "alterations" because I felt the problem had to be one of condition, not design. I also know there are thousands of six volt systems operating without such difficulties.

I finally solicited the help of Tom, neighbor, ex-VW mechanic, and antique American car restorer. Tom restores cars as a hobby, but unlike me, he does everything (except paint) himself. As such, his understanding of and experiences with electrical systems runs much deeper than mine.

On the pre-arranged Saturday morning I drove over to Tom's garage (an 1800 square foot structure devoted to pre-1950s Detroit technology.) I had charged the battery during the previous 24 hours, (For the record, the car has a 1964 356C engine with a "big bore" kit and somewhat fly cut heads.) I had observed that the battery lost capacity slowly over time and suspected the root of the problem was low volt-

age. I further suspected the voltage regulator because it was one of the few components that had not been replaced when I restored the car. First thing we did was reset the timing to be sure we were on spec. After only a couple of starts, the car began to exhibit its cranking lethargy. We disconnected the lead from the generator back to the battery and ran a (short) test to see that the generator was functioning. It pegged the meter immediately. Next we checked the voltage regulator output at the regulator under load (3000 rpm's) and got a reading of about 7 volts.

We performed the same test at the battery. This test entails simply connecting a multimeter across the battery terminals while someone holds the engine at speed. You must hold the speed for a half minute or so until the voltage reading stabilizes. With the engine under load we measured 6.5 v. The specification calls for 7 to 7.5 v. I had never taken the time to study the specs and did not appreciate how critical half a volt can be.

Having determined the voltage regulator to be the weak link, we investigated (I use the pronoun loosely, my participation consisted of pointing Tom to the relevant page in the workshop manual) how one adjusts the Bosch regulator. Unfortunately, the book suggests it be returned for service by the manufacturer. Determined not to be stymied by such a caution, Tom proceeded to study the diagram and decide which contact points regulated current flow (see Fig. 1). The

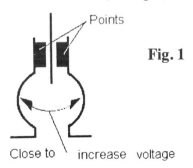

Fig. 1

Points

Close to increase voltage

question was whether the points needed to be spread or closed to increase the level. We experimented a bit with the cover off and the engine running and determined the points must be brought closer together. Their layout in the regulator does not make this easy. Had a new regulator been available, I would have installed it. As it was, Tom was able to close the points enough to get a reading of nearly 7 v. at the battery under load. It took some trial and error because you must try to bend the point arms, then replace the cover and start the car before you can see if you've made a difference.

After we finished we thought we had solved the problem but had no immediate way to know. I've been driving the car for three weeks now and it's started each time without difficulty. It still occasionally turns over slowly for an instant before it really kicks in; but it has always started and has pretty good cranking speed after that initial revolution. The initial slowness may be due to an elevated compression ratio or a worn out starter bushing (another part I didn't replace); but I can live with it.

The big test comes this Sunday when we go back to autocrossing. If I can get through the day without a jump start, I'll consider the problem solved.'

P.S. Everything worked okay on Sunday. The starting is reliable although not perfect. But then we didn't get quite the specified voltage. I might have to break down and install a new regulator. If your car cranks too slowly, add the voltage regulator to the list of suspects.

Zeke didn't mention which regulator points; the far right, or BAT +.

Horn

Vol. 14, No. 5 Ed Hyman

356 B/C Horn Contact Repair

A few days ago while driving my SC in the "wilds" of the North Shore of Long Island, I had an uncomfortable occurrence. As I turned the wheel (stock & original) the horn went off. At first just a peep, but later, quite convincingly. I was able to simply twist off the stock horn button. It seems that the spring device to keep the horn button contact open is a piece of rubber that is designed to crush when you need to sound the alarm. Well, 26 years is enough for this piece of rubber and mine wasn't gonna push no mo'. Of course the trip back from Long island to Connecticut (over the bridge from Queens to the Bronx) is not a safe one without a horn.

Luckily my car was delivered in France and has what seems to be an early edition of an air horn, with its own switch that protrudes from the dash to meet your fingers right next to the turn signal – pretty convenient!

Back to the stock horn. When I got home a quick perusal of various catalogs confirmed that the special piece of rubber (between the horn button and the steering wheel nut) was either NLA or darn hard to find. Also as this area is the 'hot contact' area for the horn – no metal spring need apply to help bolster up the horn button. A quick glance at my workbench and I had the answer. At least a temporary one... I had some tie rod end boots (seals) left over from the front end overhaul on the Speedster and by placing one on the steering wheel nut, and replacing the horn button (with the old piece on it) over it. I once again have a firm button that will not flop around and set off the horn until I need it too.

Vol. 16, No. 6 Brad Ripley

Horn Restoration

No doubt, during your Porsche restorations, you've had to deal with the two signal horns up under the headlights. They're usually oversprayed with body color and/ or primer and probably well undercoated too. And, maybe they work, maybe they don't. From my experience, here's what I've learned about which horns go where, how they work and how to restore them.

Motor vehicles are required by law to have an "acoustical signaling device", better known as a horn. In the case of Porsches, two horns are used, each with different tonal frequencies, to give sufficient loudness and a pleasing combined tone. The frequency (Hz) is called out on the data plate on the front of the horn, a "3" (300 Hz) or a "4" (400 Hz), and on later 12 volt units as 290, 335, 345, 390, 400, 520 and 590 Hz. The "high tone" (numerically higher Hz number) is installed on the left and the "low tone" on the right side of the car. In parts catalogs the high toned horn is identified as the "road horn" and the lower toned horn as the "deep toned" horn.

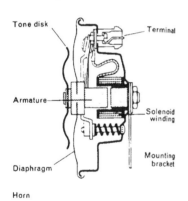

Horn

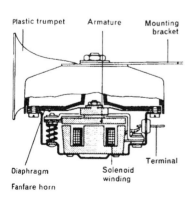

Fanfare horn

There are two basic types of horns, the Impact Horn and the Fanfare Horn. Both types have been used on 356s and 911s, but the Impact type is the most prevalent. These horns are the Bosch "Supertone" brand which were also used on Mercedes and other German cars. As you can see from the diagram, the horn is a simple device: an electromagnet attached to a diaphragm which oscillates very rapidly, controlled by a set of breaker points. The sound is caused by the armature impacting against the magnetic core and the diaphragm/tone disc together radiate harmonic waves at the specified frequency. The mounting bracket, made up of three leaves, is part of the unit and helps determine the final sound.

Rebuilding and Detailing the Horn

Although the horn is a simple device, take care on disassembly as each washer and spacer has a function and the horn won't honk afterwards unless you've put it back together the correct way. The exploded view photo shows a typical assembly (356B/C) but there are some differences among early and late horns, so disassemble carefully and make notes. If the horn actually worked and you're doing a cosmetic restoration, note the position of the threaded insert in the adjusting block under the diaphragm. The insert should be replaced in about the same position so you'll have a head start on the tuning process described below. In case somebody before you switched data plates on your horns, you can easily check the tones by hanging the diaphragm plates from a thin wire and hitting them lightly with a metal object; one will be a lower tone than the other, although they will appear to be the same shape and thickness. The base housing is easiest restored by leaving the magnet/ point assembly intact. However, unsolder the two leads to the plastic terminal block so it can be removed for cleaning and replacement of the screws. Then, tape off the large opening and bead blast the housing and the other painted parts. For painting, apply liberal coats of primer to fill in any rust craters, especially on the outer rim. Use glossy black for the finish coats.

For reassembly, use the hardware/ data plate sets and the paper gaskets available from *Registry* advertisers. Check the various screws against the originals; you may want to replate your original screws for complete authenticity.

To "tune up" the horn, you'll need a battery and a pair of leads. Into one lead, wire in a switch so that you can securely hook up both wires to the battery and to the horn. Hold the horn in a vice by the mounting strap so you'll get the true sound of the horn. Find the slotted oval adjusting screw on the back of the housing (it should be covered with a drop of wax) and a screwdriver that fits correctly. You might also find some ear plugs and warn the neighbors! Throw or press the switch and turn the screw until you get a solid sound, although the tone might not be quite right. To get that distinctive 356 tone, turn the center spindle on the front side of the horn in or out slightly until you get the right sound. Good luck on all your future horn tune ups.

Vol. 17, No. 3 Cole Scrogham

Horn Adjustment for Optimum Tone
There has been a great deal written about the Bosch horns used on most 356s, usually centering on how to best restore them. Harvey Smith has some good ideas on restoring horns and I believe that Volume 16, #6 also includes excellent information. It is interesting to note, however, that I have seen some NOS 6V horns that have the face screws painted and only the badge with screw(s) in a bright finish, so there may be some leeway in what is considered to be "original."

The focus of this issue is not to rehash the restoration topic, but to move on to another aspect of the Bosch horn; how to adjust them. Generally, the horns stay in good adjustment, with only some minor tweaking as the breaker points wear. Where they become a problem is when they are disassembled (read "restored") and then put back together. Some magical force then decides that this horn will never blow right again, kind of like a cyanide pill so you can not find out a captured pilot's secrets.

The low and high tone horns are easily distinguished from each other, even when way out of adjustment, so there is not much fear of having two of the same type (you will either get the foghorn effect or angry LeCar sound). The difficulty arises in getting a crisp combination of the two. I have heard of people who try to test both horns at the same time to get the right pitch, but this is mostly, well, it is a waste of time. Without getting into a discussion of wave mechanics, suffice it to say that when both horns are adjusted to their "peak" note, they will interact well together. The Bosch engineers have already done their job, so we need not be worried about more than is necessary.

The first step to tuning the horn(s) is to examine the face plate to make sure there are no obstructions in the grill, or extra amounts of undercoating or dirt (or bondo) on the surface of the face plate. The horn has a resonance plate that vibrates when activated, so anything that serves to deaden the vibration is fighting you. The most common problems are a small rock wedged against the plate or extra undercoating sprayed through the face of the horn.

Next, you should put the horn in a vise so that it is supported by its mounting bracket (as it would be when bolted to the car), so that the note will not change when you "deaden" the horn by bolting it to the car.

Next, run two test leads to the battery matching the horns voltage (no, do not try a 6 volt horn with a 12 volt battery), and give it a shot. On the lower right rear of the horn is an adjusting screw that you may turn in either direction to achieve the highest and clearest pitch. Take care to lubricate this screw well, if forced, it will break and leave you in trouble. Bosch places a small amount of wax over the screw to hold it in place; you will want to replace it with a drip of candle wax for that same reason and also to reduce the chances of corrosion. When you have completed tuning both horns, mount them on the car and give them a try. You should be greeted with a crisp horn note that is very characteristic of the 356.

Radio

Vol. 17, No. 2 Wilford Wilkes

Period German Radios

Shown here is the installation guide for Becker's push-button Europe model ($189.95 AM-FM or $129.95 AM only) dated July 1, 1959. The Becker Mexico, with signal-seeking, touch-bar tuning listed for $259.95 in a Porsche. It was installed exactly the same way, with the separate power supply mounted near the top board and connected via an extension cable. The Blaupunkt used a similar extension cable for its installation.

The Europe had a variety of frequency band options: M, I.M, LMU, MU. Push buttons came in black, brown and ivory with pushbutton designations M, U, L and plain face. The later Europas used the AM, FM, M, and L pushbutton designations.

Another drawing below shows the Becker Monte Carlo, a manually-tuned unit that was relatively inexpensive at $89.95. There were early and late versions of this radio, which differed from the Europa and Mexico in that it had no separate power supply.

The first Monte Carlos were AM only, and about 1958 the model was updated to receive both AM and Long Wave. A Becker "Reimo" shortwave adapter was listed at $39.95.

Band designations:

European	American
M	AM
U	FM
K	Short Wave
L	Long Wave

On American-style pushbuttons M is for Marine band

Longwave is a band of frequencies below the standard AM frequencies on the radio. This band was mostly used in Europe in the 40s and 50s. It was rarely used in the U.S. There is almost nothing on that band now.

Shortwave covers a broad band of frequencies above the standard AM band. LW, AM, and SW are for the most part AM (Amplitude Modulation) signals. The commercial FM band on our radios started in the late 1940s and is an improved way of communication over the AM method.

This page shows items from a 1957 Blaupunkt advertising handout which was supplied to their dealers. Using the headline seen above, it was a colorful and informative sales promo, but did not show or mention the large power supply unit that went with these radios.

Starting in 1957, Blaupunkt made other models that ended up occasionally in Porsche 356s that were dealer installed in Europe, such as Wiesbaden, Stuttgart, Hannover and Berlin. These radios, along with Beckers, were certainly "state of the art", none finer for this era.

On the next page are diagrams showing the parts and procedures for interference elimination in RF-stage and FM-equipped cars. Figs. 1 and 2a apply to Europe AM radios. Figs. 1, 2b and 3 apply to AM-FM Mexico radios. Suppressors were installed at the ends of the spark plug leads.

RF stage (Radio Frequency) is a

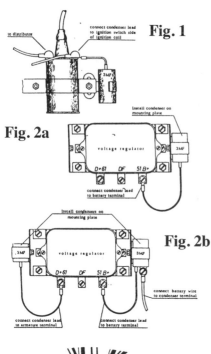

Fig. 1

Fig. 2a

Fig. 2b

Fig. 3

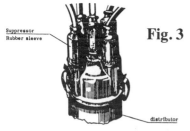

section which provides amplification of the signal to improve reception (more stations) and to obtain more volume from a weak station.

The Becker Monte Carlo and the Blaupunkt Bremen did not use an RF stage but the majority of the other models did.

Security System

Vol. 14, No. 4 Steve Thein

DIY Security System
How to build a small inexpensive security system for your 6 volt Porsche

It's dedicated to all you 356 people clammering for more "how-to projects" in the *Registry*! For under $20, you can build an electronic security system that will protect your "tub" from one "moore" tampering thief and/or "Camouflaged Brown Shevroley Pick-up Truck Driving Maestro" who braille parks!!

A Radio Shack motion detector is modified to operate on 6 v. and trigger your car's horn in the event your car is bumped or tampered with. A hidden toggle switch, mounted outside the car, turns the alarm system on or off, and an optional blinking red L.E.D. warns the potential thief that the car is equipped with an alarm system.

Parts List
1 Radio Shack electronic motion and shock sensor (Cat #49- 630A)
1 Radio Shack 5 v DC PC SPDT relay (Cat. #275-243) 13 1/4 in. piece of 4 conductor computer ribbon cable
1 SPDT toggle switch (small, see article)
Optional
1 blinking red L.E.D. (Radio Shack Cat. #276-036)
1 500-1000 ohm 1/4 or 1/2 watt resistor
You will also need:
a small 25 watt pencil point soldering iron and solder
super glue
a few inches of bare #22 copper wire (or reasonable facsimile)
10-20 ft. of stranded 2 conductor wire

Construction
1. With the Radio Shack motion detector before you, remove the 4 screws from the bottom plate and carefully lift the top, being careful not to break the wires connecting the top to the internal circuit board.
2. Slide the circuit board out of the cube, using the three heavy leads that protrude through the case, to assist you.

3. Orient the printed circuit board so that the component side is face up and you can read the part numbers which are silk-screened on the board. "LED 1," the small red light, should now occupy the upper left hand corner of the board. Now locate "Dl" (a black diode) and "Rl" (a 3.3k resistor with four stripes: orange, orange, red, gold). These components lie horizontally on the lower portion of the board and will be removed. (Note: "Dl" and "Rl" serve as polarity guard and current limiting devices. Removal of these parts will allow the sensor to operate on a lower voltage, but you will now have to be careful not to reverse polarity to your completed sensor.)

Now, using a low wattage soldering iron, unsolder and remove "Dl" and "Rl." Take care not to lift the foil from the printed circuit side of the board. Also, unsolder the brown (fused) lead from the board, leaving the cable tie in place.

4. Take a short (about 3/4 in. long) piece of bare copper wire and insert one end in the hole closest to the "R" of "Rl" and the other end into the hole nearest the "1" of "Dl." Before soldering this wire bridge into place, bend this last ("Dl") end over to jump the hold left by the "1" end of "Rl" (see illustration #1). Carefully solder all

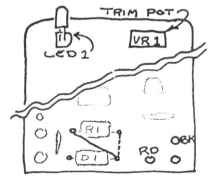

Location of R1 and D1 (removed) and wire jumper. Dotted line shows jumper on foil side of PC board.

Illustration #1

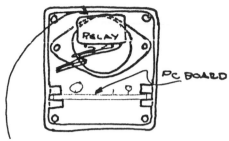

Insure that relay is centered, but does not overhang this edge.

Illustration #2

three points taking care not to bridge other traces on the circuit board.

5. Drill a 1/6 in. or smaller hole on the "B" of "BK," where the black (ground) lead is connected to the circuit board. You may now set this circuit board aside.

6. Cut a piece of 4 conductor computer ribbon wire 3/4 in. long, strip the insulation back 3/16 in. from all four wires of both ends and tin (apply a light coating of solder) each wire. Orient the relay so that the single protruding pin facing you is in the lower left hand corner and the remaining six pins are across the top (see illustration #2 for assigned pin numbers). Using one end of the ribbon cable, solder one wire to pin numbers 1, 3, 4 and 5. Now bend these pins down against the relay bottom and cut off pin

7. You are now ready to solder the relay wires to the circuit board. Double check to make sure that the correct wire is used; it may be helpful to color code the ribbon with a felt tip marker. Solder the other end of the wire connected to pin 4 to the hole remaining from "Dl." Solder the wire from pin 1 to the hole you drilled through the "B" of "BK" (adjacent to the black or ground lead). Now solder the wire from pin 3 on the relay to the hole where the brown lead (n/o output) used to go. It is marked "BN" on the P.C. board. Slide a long piece of shrink tubing over the brown wire,

that used to be soldered in the hole marked BN, and connect it to the remaining wire from the relay (pin 5). Make a small neat joint, slide the shrink tubing over joint and shrink it in place. Note: you can use a piece of electrical tape, wrapped carefully around this joint, if you don't have any shrink tubing. Be careful to keep this joint small and wrapped tightly. Leave the small plastic wire tie wrap in place. Nurse the brown wire down, and then back, to maintain a compact and strong feed through. Upon reassembly, this tie wrap serves as strain relief, keeping you from pulling these wires loose.

8. Now, carefully slide the P.C. board into its case, L.E.D. end first. Ensure that the L.E.D. slides into its lens and that the red, black and brown wire bundle protrudes through the case with the tie wrap inside. Make adjustments as necessary and then remove the P.C. board from the case. Before final assembly, you may now wish to bench test the sensor by applying 6 v + to the red lead and 6 v - to the black lead. Using a voltmeter or a 6 v timing light probe (like that used to set the points), connect one end of the probe or voltmeter to 6 v + and the other to the brown (n/o output) lead. A slight bump to the sensor should start the L.E.D. blinking and the bulb (voltmeter) should light (indicate 6 v.) until the L.E.D. stops blinking. It may be necessary to make a slight adjustments to the trim pot, located next to the

L.E.D.

Final assembly requires that you glue the relay to the top of the black cylindrical motion switch (see illustration #3). This must be done carefully to ensure that the entire assembly will fit within the original case. With the bottom cover sitting on the workbench, orient the black cylindrical motion switch toward the back of the bench and then insert the P.C board into the slots beneath the cylinder. The L.E.D. and black trim "pot" face up. With a small dab of super glue, glue the relay to the top of the cylinder with the bottoms facing the P.C. board. The relay must be centered but mounted as close to the outer edge as possible. Hold it steady while the glue dries.

Slide the assembly into the housing, fit the cover piece with the relay attached, and secure with the original four screws. Finally, remove the mobile alert and arrow stickers on the case so that a would-be thief can't identify the alarm components. This completes construction of the sensor module.

Installation

Mount the sensor in a convenient yet unobtrusive location. In considering a location, remember that you will need to connect the brown wire to the horn relay or to the connector on the steering column that connects the horn button to the lay. This connection, when grounded, sounds the horn. Replace the 250 ma. fuse, in the inline holder with a 5 amp fuse. Locate a switch outside the car in a hidden, weather protected location. A bracket that bolts to the inside of the front bumper and holds the switch tucked inside the bumper works well. A fused lead from the battery (or other 6 v source) is connected to one switch terminal. The other terminal is connected to the red wire on the alarm module. If you wish to add a visual reminder, a small blinking L.E.D. may be connected to this same red wire. Be sure to

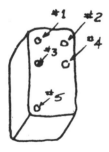

Illustration #3

connect a 500 to 1,000 ohm resistor in series with one lead of the L.E.D. and observe the polarity as described on the package. Several locations are available that require no drilling or modification to the car. On my Speedster, I installed the light on top of the defogger slot, driver's side. "B" cars accept the light by pulling the leads through the often unused upper heater/fan control slot. Using a small dab of easily removed silicon, you can attach the L.E.D. to the space between the padded dash and the windshield. Other ideas are welcome.

Final Adjustment

After installation is complete, test the alarm's sensitivity by opening and closing your car's door. Such movement should trigger the alarm and sound the horn. The package that came with the sensor describes how to adjust the sensitivity via the trim pot. I have found, however, that the vibration from the car's horn and relay can provide sufficient movement to keep the alarm triggered or continually retrigger it. If this is the case, and the alarm does not shut itself off, it will be necessary to reduce the alarm's sensitivity. A little experimentation will provide the optimum setting. Also, it is normal for the car's horn to honk briefly when the alarm is turned on.

More Security

On my cars, I have used a DPDT toggle switch instead of the SPDT suggested in the parts list. The other "pole" of this switch is used to ground the coil when the alarm is set. Connect one lead of the switch to the wire that goes between the points and the coil, and the other to ground. This required a little more effort and wire but adds another level of protection.

Future Additions

This alarm requires a relay to trigger your car's horn. If a siren could be modified to operate on 6 v., both your car's horn and the added relay, would not be necessary. I will work on developing one, as well as a remote arming

device. Currently, all marketed receivers that receive a code from small hand held "key chain transmitter" operate only on 12 v. A converter is too inefficient and would drain your car's battery quickly. A 6 v. receiver that draws little current would be a nice clean alternative to the remote toggle switch. All ideas and thoughts are welcome.

Starter

Vol. 1, No. 4 Jon Ramer/Vic Skirmants

Hard Starting

In case of hard starting, Jon recommends installing an American-size 6 v. battery rated at 135 amp/hours. My comment is that a larger battery will give *longer* cranking ability, not *more* cranking ability. All 6 v. batteries put out equal voltage, but the larger ones put it out longer. If you have hard starting, make sure your battery is good, check all the wire connections for corrosion, especially the ground wires. Don't forget there has to be a *good* ground strap between the transmission and the chassis. Check your starter. A big problem here is often that the starter bushing mounted in the transmission is worn. The starter armature is supported by one bearing in the housing, and then by this bushing in the transmission. If the bushing is worn excessively, the armature drags. The bushing is a VW part, 1966 and older.

Electrical metering should preferably be done with a volt meter. If you must use an ampmeter, use wire as big or bigger than the original generator/battery wire.

Vol. 4, No. 3 Richard Miller

Hard Starting, Revisited

Poor starter operation, like dim headlights, can most often be traced to excessive voltage drop due to poor electrical connections, both ground and power. Of the many Porsche electrical problems I have cured, few are as insidious as the weak starter. In most instances of this problem, especially where experts (dealers and independents) had recommended replacement of entire wiring harness, conversion to 12V or addition of a starter relay (a common VW problem also), I have found the solution to invariably be one or more of the following.

* Clean and tighten connections to ignition switch or replace switch if internal contacts are faulty.
* Clean and tighten connections to and on starter motor and solenoid (this includes starter mount bolts and transmission ground strap).
* Clean and tighten battery connections or replace battery, if it fails a load test.
* The power contacts in the solenoid do erode – check for voltage drop across these and replace If necessary.
*Check for wear in starter shaft bushing in bell housing – wear here causes binding of shaft and armature in starter and binding of gear teeth on flywheel. This is more common than one might think.
* Rebuild or replace starter – they do wear out eventually.

In my opinion the design and engineering of the 356 Porsche (and early VW) is a superlative example of teutonic thoroughness. The addition of a starter relay is an attempt to redesign the electrics and while it may appear to solve the problem in some cases, it avoids the basic issue of proper maintenance. If the system functioned well for 15 to 20 years, which is more reasonable to assume; that the wiring has worn out, or that some component or connection needs servicing? Wiring does not wear out – it may become cut, damaged or corroded, in which case it may be spliced or replaced.

Vol. 8, No. 4 Lew Larkin

Hard Starting, Yet Again

Recently, I attempted to start my Convertible D after it had been sitting for a couple of weeks. I pumped the accelerator several times, then turned the key. The starter cranked the engine over but not with the usual vigor of a 6 v. system. (A bit of humor here) I released the key and made a couple more attempts, then nothing. I could hear the solenoid click lightly. The ammeter showed discharge when I turned the key but not the usual amount it normally showed when cranking the engine.

I assumed that the battery was weak. It was, after all, one item I had not replaced in the restoration. As best as I could tell, the battery was at least 18 months beyond its 36 month guarantee. Fortunately, 356s start very easily with a slight push. I went for about a 45 minute drive, figuring that would charge the battery back to an acceptable level. While driving, I noticed that the generator was not charging very much. I reasoned then that the battery was probably OK, particularly since both the generator and the voltage regulator had been checked during the restoration process.

I drove home and parked the car. A couple hours later, I went to start the car to move it into the garage and nothing! I did notice that the ammeter would show different rates of discharge each time I turned the key. Well, I again started the car by pushing it and resigned myself to changing the starter since I assumed that it or its solenoid was bad.

Since changing a starter is not my idea of a fun project, I decided to approach this situation scientifically. First, I checked and cleaned the battery terminals. The next step was to crawl under the car. I checked the ground cables since I have experienced how sensitive Porsches are to having good grounds. Then the obvious. I checked the starter electrical connections. The two cable connections fastened by nuts were tight and secure. I didn't bother to remove them for cleaning as they had been thoroughly sanded and cleaned within the past year. As I removed my hand, the slip-on electrical connection wire to the solenoid came off. Ah Ha! There's my trouble! I took a pair of pliers and carefully squeezed the clip and inserted it.

I got in the car and turned the key and the starter worked fine. After repeated tries, the starter continued to work fine. I was quite proud of myself. I had solved the problem and didn't have to change the starter.

Several days later when I tried to start the car, the starter wouldn't turn over. Uttering the usual words reflecting on this frustrating situation, I resigned myself to the prospect of having to change the starter.

I started the car again by pushing it. I drove it for about 15 minutes and returned home. In the garage, I noticed that the generator and oil pressure warning lights glowed at idle and increased in intensity as I increased the engine speed. Now I was stumped. I turned off the engine and attempted to restart it. Nothing! I did notice that the ammeter showed little discharge when I turned the key to the start position.

Then I got to thinking, as much as it hurt. The power to the instrument cluster (generator and oil pressure lights) is transmitted through the ignition switch. In short, I diagnosed that the ignition switch had gone bad. I went down into my Porsche parts bin, got another switch and installed it. Voilà! I turned the key and the starter turned over immediately. I have had no trouble since. So the next time your starter won't turn over, don't jump to the conclusion that the starter is at fault. Check out your ignition switch!

Vol. 13, No. 5 Vic Skirmants

Even More Hard Starting

Just finished fixing a hard-starting 1963 coupe. Nope, not another 6 v. to 12 v. conversion. I fixed his transmission mounts! Huh?!

The car came in for an engine overhaul. After reinstalling the engine, it was very difficult to crank, even given the ultimate test, zapping it with a 12 v. battery. A new starter and bushing made no change whatsoever.

When the car had arrived, the bottom engine nuts were not tight. Before I pulled the engine a second time, I loosened the lower nuts and tried the starter; perfect cranking! Obviously something was keeping the engine from seating flush to the transmission housing. Initial inspection showed that no washers, nuts, mice, or whatever had been jammed between the engine and transmission. Up-close inspection did reveal that the top of the right rear transmission mount was shifted rearward and extended past the face of the transmission. It didn't project more than maybe .020 of an inch, but the shiny spot on it and the corresponding mark on the engine case proved that this was the culprit! It seems that some previous owner had been fiddling with the front transmission mounts and had the shims in wrong. This moved the transmission forward but the rear mount stayed where it wanted to be in relation to the transmission hoop. Upon reshimming the front mounts properly, the rear mounts then settled down nicely, and everything worked perfectly. Here was a situation where a sloppy starter bushing probably would have worked just great.

Vol. 11, No. 1 Mike Robbins

High Torque Starter

Recent J.C. Whitney catalogs list a "factory rebuilt high torque starter for 59-66 Volkswagen." (catalog no. 72-0870R, $49.95 less 10%). I decided to get one of these to see if it would fit in

93

a 356A. If it didn't fit there, I could use it on my Beetle. Lo and behold, this turns out to be a starter for type 3 VW (the Fastback and Squareback) of 1965 & 1966. It was also used on VW transporters at about that time. The VW part no. is 311.911.021 and the Bosch no. is 001.310.007. This is a .6 hp starter whereas regular 356A starters are .5 hp. The outside diameter is larger than the Beetle or Porsche unit but it went into my 1958 coupe with hardly any more difficulty than the normal starter.

Vol. 13, No. 2 "Name Withheld"

Starter Short Circuit Fireworks

After some clutch work on my 1958 coupe, the engine was routinely installed with no apparent problem. After installation, while fitting the ground terminal to the battery, a small spark was drawn, indicating a small current draw. The current draw was what you would expect from the interior lights or ignition being left on and no further thought was given. The engine started right up and while testing the clutch action by going forward and backward a few feet, a small amount of smoke was seen rising out of the open engine compartment. This small amount of smoke was attributed to oil spilled on the exhaust manifolds, as valves were adjusted when the engine was out.

After some additional clutch testing, smoke intensity increased and the engine was shut down. Running to the rear of the coupe, flames could be seen licking out in the vicinity of the starter, just forward and under the right hand Solex 40 P II-4. During the panic situation that followed, I elected to flood the flames with water, as a garden hose was conveniently hooked up and within reach, instead of disconnecting the battery first. The flames were extinguished in short order, but then heavy dense smoke was seen issuing from under the closed front

hood. The hood was quickly opened and the battery cables were smoldering due to an apparent short circuit to ground. The battery ground terminal was disconnected as quickly as possible with foolishly no regard to personal safety. After things settled down a bit, I momentarily touched the disconnected lead to the battery terminal in order to determine if the ground still existed. A shower of sparks confirmed the ground did not burn itself free.

The rear of the coupe was raised next and the right rear wheel removed in order to get a better look so that cause of the short circuit and the subsequent fire could be determined. What happened was the right heater junction box was out of position and was making contact with the starter solenoid B + terminal. So much heat was generated at this terminal that the end of the stud was melted off and it will probably be very difficult to remove the nut in order to disconnect the cables if the need should occur in the future.

Please be careful the next time you install an engine to be sure that you have clearance between the right hand heater junction box and the B + starter solenoid terminal. I taped a piece of insulation on the solenoid side of the heater junction box, as the factory does not provide very much clearance and just one bottom cap screw is used to secure the box, allowing the box to swivel out of position if not tight.

I consider myself very lucky not to have lost the coupe, the only damage being the burnt B + stud and other burnt and melted cable insulation, which doesn't seem to have affected operation.

Also, it was fortunate that the battery did not explode. I have seen batteries explode for far less reason and believe me, you don't want to be around one when it blows- I'm still finding bits and pieces of a battery that exploded in a thousand pieces in my barn when I hit the starter on my

94

Ford pickup truck and that was two years ago.

I have a healthy respect for the power in a storage battery and so should you.

Wiring

Vol. 4, No. 4 Brett Johnson

1956 - 1965 Wiring Colors

Paul Rettig sent a beautiful color coded diagram which yielded the following information:

Left parking light - Gray/Black
Right parking light - Gray
Left front turnsignal - Black/White
Right front turnsignal - Black/Green
Left rear turnsignal brakelight - Black/Yellow
Right rear turnsignal brakelight - Black/Red Taillight/License light - Grey/Red
Horn, Relay to horn - Black/Yellow
Foglight - White/Yellow

Vol. 8, No. 3 Skip Montanaro

Pre-1956 Wiring Colors

In several of the past *Registry* magazines there have been color lists for wiring. Maybe this is a big can of worms (pun intended), but I have the harness from my 1955 Speedster (80511) out of the car and pretty well dissected and it appears that very few of the major circuits listed in the *Registry* previously match my car.
To wit:

The wires in my harness have plastic (not braided cloth) insulation and there do not appear to be any wires for a windshield wiper circuit (suggesting that perhaps mine came originally with a Bowden tube). However, my dash has an authentic looking windshield wiper switch and a wiper motor with three terminals (+, -, and S). This treatise sets the vintage (I hope).

The major wire colors are:
Headlights:
Low Beam - Blue
High Beam - Black
Turn Signals:
(all wires to lights) - Yellow
(other wires) - Black/Yellow
Horn - Gray
Front Parking Lights - Black
Brake Lights - Black/Red
Tail Lights - Green/Black
Back-up Lights - Black/White
License Plate Light - Black/Green/White

These matches were made based on the switches and/or fuse block terminals to which the wires lead.

Vol. 9, No. 5 Richard Miller

Installing a New Wiring Harness

Wrestling with the black octopus– there is probably less wire in a 356 than there is in a 928 (what's that) air conditioning system – but the 356, being older and probably modified and butchered by more incompetent idiots may need replacement. I've repaired, spliced and restored a few 356 wiring harnesses but I recently came across one which was terminal. Some one had welded the shift tunnel and forgotten that the wires also run through there (along with too many other things). In addition our electrical handyman had produced his version of how the good doctor would have done things if he had access to a war surplus store. The only solution was to replace the whole mess. (Especially those parts which had dragged on the highway between LA and San Diego).

I have yet to see a reproduction part that reproduces the original as well as YnZ's wiring harness. It was actually fun to put in, and it really was made to fit. The color codes are right–the vinyl tubing is where it should be and the woven cloth part is just right. And it fits just like it came out of the car.

To do the installation, take out your frustrations on the original harness –

cut it, burn it, wrap it around a stick or do a Pat Ertel on it. Next, lay out the new harness on the ground and visualize what goes where in the car. Decide which end is which and vinyl tape the loose ends of the rear part into one smooth bundle along with a pull wire (an old brake or tach cable works.)

Check the conduit through the shift tunnel for dents, cuts, rust, etc. and correct as necessary. Feed the pull wire through from the front to rear and gently work the bundle through with liberal doses of silicone or teflon lubricant. Once through, all of the arms of the octopus fall into place and you simply route and clamp them with those little strips of sheet metal conveniently spot welded in all the right places. Connect the numbered terminals according to the instructions and you're done. In the harness I installed, there was one underdash wire labeled "unknown" which is no problem identifying if you've seen a few unbutchered cars – it goes to the accessory plug on the left-hand underside of the dash. What is really unknown is what happened to all the accessories which are supposed to plug into this little goodie.

There are also instructions for those who want to do away with the starter push button and extra wires for a later style windshield wiper circuit. The harnesses I installed (in a Speedster) also had interior light circuits which can be cut off flush or hidden. I removed the number tags as I went along so it didn't look like a paint by the numbers job (leave the little pieces of tape on some of the wires which is original). Or you can leave the on the wire numbers for trouble shooting at a later date.

Before starting, it helps to study your wiring diagram and to be familiar with the color codes and wiring of the fuse block. I think the high and low beam feeder wires were reversed or the hi beam indicator went to the wrong terminal, but that's a small

thing to correct. For the record, the attached figures show wire connectors to fuse block and some switches which may be of some help.

Vol. 10, No. 1 Ron Roland

356A Green Trunk Wire
The lone green wire in the trunk of a 1959 coupe is for the electric fuel pumps if the car were to have been built as a Carrera. All the 1956 - 1959 cars had the wire, whether they were Carreras or not; it was part of the wiring harness as was a second coil wire for the dual ignition. The other end of the green wire is to be found wrapped up behind the driver's side defroster duct, and should reach far enough to plug into a black wire from the ignition switch.

Wipers

Vol. 4, No. 5 Richard Miller

Windshield Wiper Electrical Circuit
While the wiring diagrams in the Porsche maintenance manual do help to understand the system and assist trouble shooting, they leave a lot to be desired when it comes to details. For instance, wires are shown going to the windshield wiper switch, but which terminals do they go to and what are the internal connections of the switch and the motor? There are very few Porsche fixers who really understand how this circuit works and the diagram in the manual is no help. The detailed schematic of this circuit is given here and shows how the wires are connected as well as what the internal connections are in the switch and motor. The subsequent schematics show how the circuit works.

Power is applied to the motor via connection 54d by pulling the switch ON to start the sequence. The same circuit supplies power while running but note the internal switch contacts

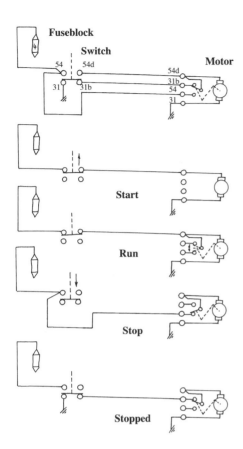

of the motor are short-circuited; sort of like short-circuiting a generator; the load slows it down rapidly. Clever, no?!

Early 356 cars had a push-pull cable from the dash "switch" which opened or closed a single power contact in the motor to run or stop it. In addition, there was a brake band around the motor armature which tightened to stop the motor when the panel button was pushed. With this setup you had to wait until the wipers were where you wanted them to stop and push the button quickly or wait for the next chance.

Vol. 7, No. 1 Richard Miller

Early Wipers, Part Deux

I want to add a comment to the windshield wiper circuit article. If you look at the schematic you can see that the odds are against hooking up the wires at random until it works (the same is true of other circuits like generator-voltage regulator, etc.), without smoking something. In the case of the wiper, you usually demonstrate the second corollary to Murphy's Law. "When something goes wrong it does so in such a way as to cause maximum damage to other components". Incorrectly connecting certain wires can torch the internal contacts in the wiper motor. Since it should draw only $1/2$ to one amp unloaded, it might be wise to use a 1 or 2 amp fuse for testing.

Vol. 7, No. 2 Lew Larkin

Installation of 'C' Wipers in an 'A'

Being a realist, I know that in spite of my best efforts there will be a time when my Convertible D will be caught in the rain and good dependable windshield wipers will be necessary. In fact, with my luck, I know that I'll get caught in a deluge on an interstate.

The wipers on 356As and early Bs are really kinda Mickey Mouse. With

operated by the motor itself while running. This is the park circuit which comes into action when the switch is turned off. With the wipers at some position other than parked, power is supplied to the motor directly by the wire to terminal 54. This means that with the switch off, the motor continues to run until the switch in the motor transfers over, thereby opening the power circuit. At this point the motor would coast down if it were not for the circuit from the motor terminal 31b through the panel switch to ground. This circuit causes dynamic braking and assures a prompt stop in the park position. If it were not for this circuit, the motor could coast until the internal switch reconnected terminal 54 and started the motor again. Dynamic braking is an electrical phenomenon which occurs when the windings their single slow speed, assuming that they haven't spun on their shafts, they aren't too capable of handling more than a heavy mist at best. Further, it is questionable how long they can handle that. All of those damaged aluminum lower windshield strips on Roadsters and Convertible Ds attest to the problem!

The answer to me at least was to substitute a 356C wiper assembly for the 356A's. Very simple. The 356A wiper arms on the motor are similar to the adjustable rods used on the carburetors. They pop right off. If not, everyone knows the secret to pop them off – right? Simply wedge a 10 mm wrench between the ball and the socket and gently pry. Off it comes! (Aren't you glad you read this far? Now removing the accelerator rod from the ball socket on the engine shroud will be a snap, won't it?)

There are four bolts holding the motor to the body. Remove them and the wires. Mark the wires or immediately insert them into the 356C assembly. Remove the wiper blade arms, the serrated round washer affair on each wiper shaft. (There are two small hex head screws that must be loosened.) Remove the washers and the nuts. Pull off the outer rubber grommets and the assembly is ready to be removed.

Use the inner rubber grommets from the 356A's assembly, assuming they're still usable – most are. The 356C assembly slides right into place. However, only three bolts are used to hold it in place. Connect the wiper motor arms.

Now remember that ground wire you cut. It appears that all that is required is to solder or tie the two ends together since the brown wire coming from the wire harness being joined to the one on the wiper motor which is bolted to the body should ground the system, right? Wrong! The wire is not grounded. The joined wires should have a round electrical fitting on it. Simply remove one of the mounting

bolts, insert it through the fitting and tighten. Now you're grounded. If by chance the electrical fitting is not present, tie a wire from the ground one and ground.

Now you will need to substitute the 356C wiper switch for the A switch. Now don't get excited. While the 356C switch is considerably larger than the 356A, there is room for it. A little tight, but it'll fit! However, the hole in the instrument panel must be enlarged to accommodate the larger shaft. I used the chrome face nut from the 356C as well as the larger knob. A purist might try to cut down the diameter of the shaft with a die to accommodate the original small knob.

Use the outer grommet from the 356A (if it's usable, if not get a replacement.) Put a small dab of GE silicone sealant around the wiper posts and reassemble as you would if the assembly were on a 356C.

The 356C coupe's wiper arms fit perfectly. *Up-Fixin, Volume II,* I believe, reported that the wiper arms would have to be shortened because the wiper blade would go off the windshield. I'm pleased to report that 356C cabriolet wiper blades (Bosch 3 398 110 422) fit perfectly and make a large sweep of the windshield at just about any speed you want or need. Further, with the proper positioning of the wiper arms, the blades will not strike those valuable aluminum strips at the base of your windshield.

Vol. 12, No. 1 Richard Miller

The Evolution of 356 Wiper Systems
From parts manual research, my experience, inputs from other Registry members and some logical deductions (guesses) I get the following as an evolutionary sequence for the 356 windshield wiper system.

Coupe #5001 - 11778 and cabriolet #5015 - 15072, 1950 - 1952, used a Bosch system à la VW with handed arms and blades (i.e., blades fixed to

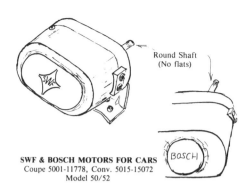

SWF & BOSCH MOTORS FOR CARS
Coupe 5001-11778, Conv. 5015-15072
Model 50/52

left and right hand arms as in early VW – some of these appear to have been chromed rather than the usual fine grained metallic silver paint.) The blades were flat and rigid and were riveted to the arms. Given that these appeared many years ago, it is not surprising there are not many around and what are presently on what few cars are left are probably not original.

Also, in some cases, parts were su-

perseded or obsoleted. Control was by a dash mounted switch (356.61.045) with a small ivory knob, wire terminals (g, +, -) and had internal self-parking provisions. A direct power connection to the motor activated the parking provision and the dash switch controlled power to turn the system on. Some motors may have been SWF as I have one which may have been a replacement. The actuation mechanism was through simple linkages of pressed sheet metal arms, similar to VW at the time, and there were no gear boxes. The linkage shown in the parts book will produce opposite motions of the blades and the motor was mounted to a body bracket (see sketch of motor).

1953: As a result of intensive marketing by SWF, Bosch was dropped in favor of a complete bolt-in assembly, SWF 53, Motor, rods, and gearboxes were mounted on a plate which installed under the dash with the wiper box shaft housings sticking through the cowl. The mounting plate was a flat formed sheet metal "boomerang" with upturned edges for stiffness.

Control was by means of the same dash mounted push-pull switch. There were three wires to the motor: positive, ground, and switched power. The motor had an internal cam operated self parking circuit and a solenoid operated mechanical band brake around the armature. The motor cover was similar to later units in appearance having the deep drawn aluminum cover retained by a wire bail clip. The height of these covers varies with the model of motor. This system, at first, also retained the opposite motion early blades. After 1954 you could retrofit SWF 53 to "sprung" blades (same LF and RH) and change the linkage to get parallel motion. The wiper portion of the wiring harness would be the same as in 1950 - 1952, but the body mounting brackets would be different. This configuration was used on coupes #11779 to #52029, cabriolets #15073

SWF WIPER SYSTEM LINKAGE ARMS

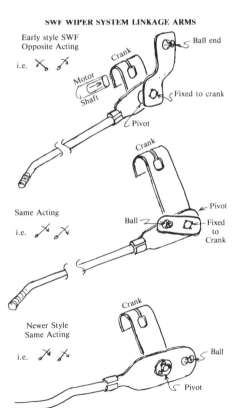

to #60549 (see sketches of different linkages for SWF systems).

In 1954 (for coupes #52030-on, cabriolets #60550-on) there were profound changes in the philosophy of how to go about wiping windscreens (these would later be forgotten in the schism that divided the true believers and produced the first semi-Porsche, the 356A).

While from the driver's seat things looked almost the same (there was now a fuel gauge instead of a wooden dip stick), the wiper switch was replaced by a dash mounted mechanical push-pull control (Bowden wire) which connected to internal contacts in the new SWF 54 motor assembly (I have nothing but contempt for those pseudo 356 owners who don't know this). The ivory knob was replaced by a complementary grey or beige one of a different shape. The bowden wire now also actuated the mechanical brake band which stopped the motion when park position of the now parallel arms was reached. The arms could now be identical and the blades were "sprung" for flexibility on the contoured windshield (although they never quite flexed around the peak in the middle).

The wiper motor cover appeared the same but was 5 mm taller to accommodate the additional internal hardware. Also, the gear boxes were different. The variety of these over the years, with different length and diameter shafts and shanks, has made restoration full of surprises.

Somewhere in 1954 or 1955 the mounting plate for the motor was changed to a flat aluminum gull wing boomerang, possibly with the body changes to the curved windshield.

The wiring harness was still the same but the wires to the old switch were tucked back into the bundle. This electro-mechanical system, like the pneumatic Beck fuel gauge, disappeared with the change over to the 'A', with dynamic braking and a new

wiring harness for it and the electrical fuel gauge among other things. However, since these are all aspects of the first in a long line of progressively non-Porsche cars, they will not be covered here.

In outline then, the evolution was, Bosch driven opposite motion system on the split window cars using simple flat blades on RH and LH arms controlled by a dash mounted switch. The change to bent windshields and SWF systems in 1953 at first retained the opposite motion and had RH and LH arms with detachable blades - also control by the dash mounted switch. The similarities to 50/52 can be viewed as an update which retained many features of the split window cars. For 1954 the effects of cost cutting and modernization set in. Parallel motion meant the same wiper parts for both sides and this also would work better with the soon to be introduced curved (but not bent) windshield. The bowden wire eliminated the solenoid in the motor and the dash switch at the same time. Supplies of these war surplus Panzertank gunsight adjusters soon ran out and these in turn were replaced by a switch and four wires for the electrically braked motor introduced as the original Porsche was phased out near the end of 1955.

12 Volt Conversion

Vol. 5, No. 4 Pat Ertel

12 Volt Conversion, I
In late 1977 I vowed to put my 1956 coupe on the road as a viable daily transportation/long distance travel automobile. One of the high priority items on the agenda was a conversion of the electrical system. In the true spirit of the "If some is good, then more is better, and too much is just enough" school of thought, I figured that if six volts worked, then twelve of

those little rascals running around in my wires ought to be just super. I was right. My reasons for wanting more voltage were sloth, cowardice, and a desire for modern amenities that Porsche hadn't thought of in 1956. I wanted to spend my Sunday afternoons driving my car, not hunting around for that bad ground or slightly loose connection that kept the starter from working, and I have an abiding fear that a matron wearing a blond wig and driving a pink Eldorado is going to rear end me because she can't see my brake lights. Also I wanted to install a tape player and maybe a C.B. radio, both of which require lots of 12 v. current. Though things are no longer "original" everything electrical works *much* better than in my 6 v. Speedster. In accomplishing the task of converting to 12 v. I took some expediencies which may not be available to everyone. I will try to provide alternatives at the end but first here is how my car was converted.

My first concern was a generator. Though I researched a way to make a 6 v. generator produce 12 v. I didn't get a chance to put it into practice because a '66 912 generator almost literally fell out of heaven and into my hands. So I went looking for a regulator. A 912 has the same specifications but costs more than a 1968 VW voltage regulator so I opted for the VW unit at a cost of $17.69. The 912 generator bolted right in but I had to fabricate a bracket to mount the 2 bolt VW reg. in place of the 3 bolt Porsche unit. Easy.

The lights were no problem as there is a 12 v. bulb that is an exact replacement for every 6 v. bulb in the car. I suggest stopping at a VW store for the instrument lights and the long bulbs in the interior and license light units. The parts store I went to had the bulbs listed in candle power rather than watts. I simply chose the highest candlepower for the stop/turn bulbs and the second highest for tail/parking lights.

The most difficult problem I faced was the wiper motor. I tried using the original motor with a Zener diode in the ground wire and I suspect this method would work well for one of the newer cars with variable speed wipers. I took the motor apart and insulated the wire from the ground brush. I ran this insulated ground wire through a Sylvania ECG 5245 50 w. 6.0 v. Zener diode to ground. (Zener cost $6.80) With my single speed wipers this method was not satisfactory. At first the wipers went a little too fast. I added a 1 ohm resistor between the motor and the switch and they were perfect from 1500RPM up but slowed and sometimes stopped at idle.

I gave up, went to the junkyard, and bought a 1968 VW wiper motor and switch for $18. This gave me strong, dependable 2 speed wipers and I have been very happy with them. The switch knob doesn't fit the decor of the interior but a little imagination and one of the new knobs being reproduced will fix that. The VW motor doesn't bolt right into the Porsche bracket. Some drilling and cutting is required and the VW arm must be ground off of the motor and the Porsche arm must be silver soldered onto the armature shaft. Silver soldering is necessary to prevent overheating the tiny wires on the armature. Get a VW wiring diagram and hook up the motor and operate it. Pay close attention to where it stops in the park position and drill the bracket and mount the motor on it so the wipers park as far to the left as possible. The drilling and cutting took about 30 minutes and it cost $3 to have the silver soldering done so the operation is not prohibitive. The installation of the 2 speed VW wipers was a major improvement over the old Porsche system and reason enough itself to change to 12 v.

The next step was to make the gauges work. I used the same Zener diode I had tried in the wipers to drop the voltage to the Oil and Fuel gages

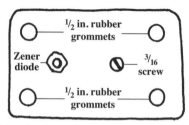

$\frac{1}{8}$ in. aluminum plate

to 6 v. This required construction of a heat sink for the diode and a method of isolating it from ground. The heat sink/isolator I made was a 2 in. x 3 in. aluminum plate, $\frac{1}{8}$ in. thick, with four $\frac{1}{2}$ in. holes near the corners, one $\frac{9}{23}$ in. hole to the left of the center of the plate and a hole drilled and tapped for a $\frac{3}{16}$ in. screw to the right of the center.

The $\frac{1}{2}$ in. holes near the corners take rubber grommets for mounting the plate without it touching the car, the $\frac{9}{32}$ in. hole is for the diode, and the hole with the $\frac{3}{16}$ in. screw is for attaching the wires for the 6 v. power supply. I attached the plate to the firewall behind the dash board using self tapping screws through the rubber grommets. *It is imperative that no part of this plate come into electrical contact with the body of the car!*

Once the diode is bolted to the plate and its lead is connected to a 12 v. power supply you have an aluminum plate that carries a 6 v. 50watt poten-

tial capable of operation the gauges and a radio or other 6 v. appliance. I picked up the 12 v. for the diode at a convenient place on the fuse block that was only hot when the switch was on. The back of the combo gauge is a mess of wires and most of them are blue with yellow tracers. You must separate the bl/yel wires that go to the indicator bulbs from the two bl/yel wires that go to the gauges. The wires to the gauges get connected to the $\frac{3}{16}$ screw on the 6 v. plate and the others are reconnected to the original supply wire.

For the horns I simply wired them in series instead of parallel and left the relay as is (illustration next page).

I installed a 12 v. heavy duty flasher unit of the type used in trailer towing vehicles. This flasher has its own timing device so the turn signals flash properly regardless of the bulbs being used. Cost about $5.

I reasoned that just about any 12 v. battery would be powerful enough for my Porsche so I measured the battery compartment and went to Sears and bought a battery of the proper physical dimensions. (this is the part that hurt) Cost $39.95.

I left the starter as it was and I've had no sign of trouble from it. It spins the motor over very fast, much more reassuringly than in the past. If you crank the starter over for a long period of time, it would theoretically over-

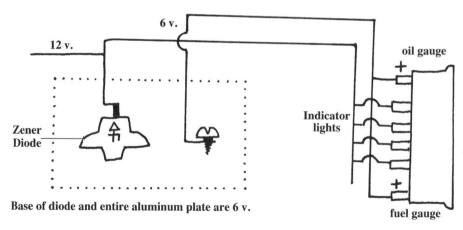

Base of diode and entire aluminum plate are 6 v.

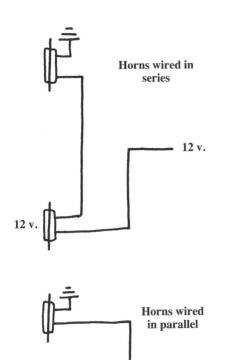

Horns wired in series

12 v.

12 v.

Horns wired in parallel

6 v.

6 v.

heat so keep the car in tune so it starts easily. I cranked the starter for a full minute, raced back and put my hand around it, and found that it was not hot to touch. My car usually starts in about 10 seconds so I don't think the starter is being abused.

The ignition coil I used was one of unknown origin that I found lying in the dirt behind the garage. I have intended to replace it with a Bosch unit but Brand X is working well and I haven't taken the time to make the switch. The coil must be a 12 v. specification and it helps if it's not the type that uses a ballast resistor.

No changes are needed in the distributor. The original condensor is the same one listed for a 912 and the points, of course, are just another switch.

As you may know, the 6 v. wires and switches are all heavier than what is commonly found on 12 v. cars so don't worry about overheating any wires. The fuses should all be changed to 15 amp. (according to a book I consulted) actually, I haven't changed any of the fuses in my coupe and I've had absolutely no problem.

That is the way my car was converted. It seems a somewhat haphazard approach, I'll admit, but that is the result of many hours of trial and error mechanics and financial bone picking. Every item was smoke tested months ago and has been in use for over 10,000 miles. (The "Smoke Test" is when you plug it in and see if it starts to smoke.) We are fortunate that 356's are very simple electrically and that many cheap VW components are similar enough to be adapted to our cars.

The entire conversion of my coupe cost about $90.00, easily a bargain. Add another $100.00 for a new 912 generator and it's still worth the money. I have been more than satisfied with my car since converting it and I heartily recommend such a conversion to anyone planning to *drive* their 356. The key advantage is confidence. When I hop into my car, I'm confident that the starter is going to start, the headlights are going to let me see where I'm going, and the brake lights are going to give that old bat in the pink Eldo plenty of warning that *I am stopping*.

As to making a 6 v. generator produce 12 v., after digging through many books and manuals, I theorized that using a later model 200 watt generator (1960 and later) and adding a 1 $1/2$ ohm resistor to the field circuit would give me a generator with specifications close to those of an early 12 v. VW. By using a 12 v. VW regulator I should have a reliable 12 v. generating system. This method hasn't been

103

tested so be careful. Also, if your car is one of the late ones with a headlight relay, I suggest replacing it with a 12 v. relay. Since I haven't had to deal with this problem, I can't suggest a specific relay to use.

There are as many ways of converting these cars as there are people willing to try the project. I have approached the problem with emphasis on low cost and simplicity. Whatever your goals are in converting your car to 12 v. I hope you will find something useful in my experience.

Vol. 8, No. 5 Don Rosa

12 Volt Conversion, II

My solutions may seem unorthodox at times, but a limited budget and a strong desire to drive my car before age 50 (mine and the car's) helps one to become quite creative.

Problem: How does one talk to other Porsche drivers from, a 356? Or, how does one use his Snooper (Escort or whatever) in a 356? No wisecracks-even a Subaru can top the double nickel.

The problem, really, is that funny looking battery up front with the three missing filler caps. The one that eats up trunk floors and only gives 6 v. in return.

The simplest solution is to convert the car to 12 v. Simple, yes – expensive, yes. Plus, the concours judges will not accept any reason for this change.

This type of conversion used to be the envy of 356 owners. Rather than power for accessories, the main reason for this conversion was that the car would start in the winter. Now, who in his right mind is going to drive a 356 in the winter? – outside anyway. Scratch simple solution!

The second most common solution is to run an auxiliary battery – the kind with six filler caps (actually the kind with NO filler caps is best, but then you can't figure out the voltage).

With this solution, the cure is as bad as the disease. Do you keep the battery in the trunk so it will spill sulfuric acid up there;or in the luggage area so it can spill there? How about venting the fumes? Then, you have to recharge the battery.

The costs can run up quickly for this fix. And even if you have a spare battery and charger, the cost of an acid spill on wool carpet is unreal!

How about buying separate 6 v. accessories and CB for the car? Have any of you tried to buy a 6 v. anything for a car? Most clerks at the local NAPA or Bargain Biggie think 6 v. power is for flashlights.

Harry Mershimer has a unique solution on his 1953 convertible. A 6 v. to 110 converter and a 110 v. tube type CB. That remedy, also, has many drawbacks. First, the size of all that 1950s electronic gear practically eliminates the passenger's leg room. Secondly, that gear is as scarce as 6 v. batteries. Third, the concours judges go nuts when they see all that stuff. *But* – We're close!

The simplest, least expensive solution is a $6.95 "Tenna" converter that changes 6 v. (negative ground) to 12 v. (negative ground). This contraption is only 1" x 3" x 3" and fits in or under the glove box almost invisibly.

To be very clever (and to also allow transfer of my accessories from car to car) I changed the 6 v. cigar lighter socket in my 356 to a 12 v. type. Rather than connecting the converter to my accessories with a maze of wires, I have it powering the cigar lighter. There it is – 12 v. accessory power from a standard 12 v. plug socket. Just plug in the CB, Snooper, utility light, coffee pot, air compressor...

Ah, a super cheap conversion that is practically undetectable by concours judges! But, there is one minor problem. If you smoke, carry matches. The converter is only good for 3 amps – if you use the lighter, fuses go "poof"!

If you can't find one of these gems

at your local Radio Shack, try our friends at J.C. Whitney.

Vol. 9, No. 6 Wade Douglas

Wiper Motors for 12 v. Conversions

I've seen several 12-volt conversion articles over the past several years in the *Registry* and the biggest problem as anybody who has tried one knows, is what to do about the wiper motor. There is a very simple, relatively inexpensive perfect solution that avoids mickey mouse resistors or soldering a 356 arm on a VW shaft, etc.

For As and Bs up to the advent of the round wiper motor, simply pick up a 2-speed 12 v. VW motor. Turn it over and remove the screws retaining the gearbox. Do the same with your original 6 v. motor. Swap them, but before you do, remove the VW cover and note that next to the head of the retaining stud, is a boss. Drive out the 4 mm VW stud, and then drill the boss, next to it for the Porsche style 5 mm stud. Plug the removed stud hole with whatever suits you and then note that the second Porsche style stud came with the Porsche gearbox. Voilà! The VW assembly bolts right up. The only remaining modifications are to swap your bullet connectors or bare wire tips (early cars) for spade lug females, and then wire in a concealed mini-SPST switch to enable the utilization of the two-speed capability, unless the installer is one of those who dig unoriginal appearance and like the VW switch in place of the original.

Now the solution for late Bs and Cs with the round motor. A 1967 912 works perfectly if you relocate the mounting holes. The original mounting hole positions would place the end of the motor through the dash and into the passenger compartment. I have done both conversions with complete success as a subcontractor to a local professional restoration works... and they both work.

Vol. 7, No. 3 Harry Kurrie

Use of a 12 v. Battery Pack

Rather than convert the whole system, install a rechargeable 12 v. battery pack. It is called a Porta Pac and available from General Electric. Of course one could install a small 12 v. battery in the trunk instead.

Vol. 7, No. 4 James Teunier

Use of an 8 v. Battery

I purchased an 8-volt battery, then had the regulator adjusted by a competent shop to charge according to the requirements that came with the battery. My 1962 hardtop now always starts on the first try and the 6-12 volt converter now has the amperage necessary to run the 12 v. tape player even while parked. No bulbs to change, no wiper motor worries. Very simple and effective.

Vol. 7, No. 6 Frank Richard

Use of a 6 v. to 12 v. Inverter

From Frank Richard, Caen, France, comes another solution for a 12 v. power supply for a 6 v. Porsche. He bought a 6 v. to 12 v. inverter, delivering 3 amps of power. He got it from Radio Shack, catalog 80, part #22.129 ($25). He put a switch with idiot light under the dash, so that he uses it only when he needs 12 v. for his CB radio. He installed the inverter in the trunk near the relays and fuse box; the unit is compact, easy to remove, and comes with its own fuse.

Generator

Vol. 7, No. 3 Lew Larkin

Troubleshooting – Non-Charging

Just two weeks prior to East Coast Holiday VI, I was in the final stages of completing the total restoration of my Convertible D. I had rebuilt the 1600

S engine and with some friends, it was installed. The electricals were connected and gas was added to the carburetors. Then the moment of truth.

I turned the ignition key and after a few cranks to build up oil pressure, we reconnected the coil wire, turned the ignition key again and with a few barfs, she started!

What a beautiful sound! Clean, crisp and willing to rev. A symphony to the engine rebuilder! A round of beers!

Then I noticed that the generator light did not go off and the ammeter did not show a charge. A simple problem, we thought as we opened a second beer. Someone must have misconnected something. We discovered that the D- and the D+ wires at the generator were reversed. No big deal, we just reversed them and restarted the engine. Still no charge. Most perplexing.

Another beer is always part of the solution. Some one said (the one who admits he knows nothing about the electricals) "Ya got a bad ground." We proceeded to trace the wiring. All the grounds were good as was the ignition switch. Then the same guy says, "Then, it's gotta be the voltage regulator." That seemed reasonable. So down to the parts bin. We swapped voltage regulators and got another beer to bolster our hopes.

The engine fired but still no charge. At this time, it was getting near the supper hour and the crew departed, vowing to think about the problem. It had to be simple.

The next day, I consulted with an electrical engineer friend at work about the problem. About an hour later, after a lecture on elemental electrics complete with diagrams and all types of electrical symbols, 1 was armed with several simple tests to try. The following weekend, the crew assembled, confident that we'd solve the problem.

Frustrated, we decided to suspend the garage rule of no beer before 10

AM. The beer was working. Someone decided that all the tests pointed to a bad ground in the generator and besides, we'd changed everything else. So, back down to the parts bin for another generator.

While it's installation wasn't done as fast as a Richard Petty pit stop, it was pretty speedy. This had to be the solution! I fired the engine and big zero – nothing! Revving the engine, however, we noticed that the ammeter showed a higher rate of discharge as the revs increased.

The beer we'd opened to celebrate was quickly dispatched and a successor opened. C'mon guys, the "red witch" can't defeat us. Someone opened the shop manual. We'd read the sections on the generator 15 times but this time, we read on to Section 6 LI "Removing and Installing Regulator." Step 3 of installation read, "polarize generator (See 8 LI note)". "Of course," said Dave (who professed no knowledge of electricals and continued to try to prove it) the generator is running in reverse, that's why the ammeter shows discharge commensurate with engine revs!

Naturally, it was with a great deal of skepticism that we turned to 8 LI to find out how to polarize the generator. Simply remove the V belt, connect the heavy red battery cable (DF) to terminal D+ of the regulator. The generator then runs as a motor in the direction of the engine rotation (clockwise).

Sure enough, we got the generator to run in the direction of the engine. Then we reconnected the V belt and fired the engine. Hooray, the idiot light went off and the ammeter showed charge.

Vol. 17, No. 4 Geoff Fleming

Troubleshooting – Non-Charging, II

How many of us have had the displeasure of anxiously awaiting that first nice day to finally use the 356, only to find, after start-up, that the red generator light is reluctant to go out, or blinks? Pretty upsetting, eh?

Not to panic my friends – this is really not all that serious, so don't call the tow truck. If your generator light stays on, first, open the rear lid,and see if there is a broken fan belt. If the fan belt is intact, and reasonably tight you should give each of the three wires atop the generator a little pull, maybe one is loose enough to prevent current from being conducted. When doing the loose wire exam, check at both generator *and* where the wires end at the regulator.

Suppose you've run through the checks and everything checked out - now what? We now shift into phase two. With the engine off, take a screwdriver and remove the two side screws which hold the cover on your regulator. This will give you access to the inner sanctum of this black box. If you look at the right hand coil, there is a set of breaker points mounted somewhere on the side. Start the engine, then, give the points a push or two. If you are like the average person, the red dash light probably went out, since these points sometimes stick in the wrong position due to atmospheric conditions. If, however, you are like me, and that doesn't do the trick, then replace the regulator cover (engine off during replacement), and remove the fan belt and pulley shims and actual pulley halves.

If you have a set of metal-handled pliers, open them and utilizing the handle ends, touch the tab under the regulator at the extreme right, (marked B 51 +), and now touch the other handle end to the left tab (marked 61 +). The generator should spin like a motor, and quite fast at that. You need to hold this position for a few seconds. With everything reconnected, restart the car. If the red light *still* comes on, let the car run, but open the trunk and remove the ground strap from the battery. If, after removing the ground, the engine dies, you most probably have a

bad generator. I personally doubt that you'll have to go this far, as polarizing the generator usually gets the electrons flowing along the way we want them to.

Something quite important to remember is to maintain the water supply in the battery-in each chamber. A friend swore he always filled his battery with enough water, but only opened one filler cap, thinking it fed each chamber with water. Open each cap and fill as needed.

Vol. 17, No. 4 Larry Wapnik

Generator Removal and Replacement

For those of us familiar with the functions of a generator, we would have to admit that this device housed in a 356 is very unique. To be even stronger you could say that it is the heart of the engine power plant. If the generator breaks down physically, if the bearings freeze, the engine will not work properly, and if you continue to run it you will most definitely suffer major engine damage.

Through a multitude of events that happened over the last two weeks, I gained a lot of respect for this device. I realized after I installed the new generator that it was responsible for the following: better mileage; more horsepower; less noise; more smoothness; better idle; better cooling.

To understand the above a little easier one must first have an idea of how a 356 generator functions, and why.

It is obvious that this engine component is multi-functional. In addition to charging the battery electrically, the mainshaft of the generator also serves as the axle for the cooling fan, as well as the axle shaft of the fan belt pulley. If you think about this for a little while, you realize that this device has to be exceptionally strong and well balanced. Just imagine the torque exerted on the generator shaft. The shaft is concentric to the commutator which creates electricity and also turns the rather large cooling fan in the engine shroud. Imagine the strength of the bearings supporting this shaft, as well as the strain from the tension of the fan belt. These bearings are mostly responsible for the six improvements previously listed. Attention must be paid to their lubrication and wear. To concur, my gas mileage was almost 18 mpg average city and highway, it is now 24 mpg. The engine was noisier, the oil temp gauge was slightly higher when warm, and the engine was not smooth.

If for any reason your generator is suspect; weak battery, fan noise, bearing wobble, shaft rotation not smooth, etc., I might suggest the following. First remove the fan belt. Of course lay out the pulley shims in proper order so that the fan belt has the same tension when you put it back. Factory specs call for approx. 15-20 mm of inward play, this is accurate! Less than this is looking for horsepower loss and strain on the generator and more means belt slippage. Two, gently turn the shaft and listen and feel for smoothness. Too smooth means the brushes might be worn. You should be able to feel the rotation of the commutator against the brushes. Now is the time for the decision to proceed, or stop.

Going further means the removal of the oil filter, and then the generator stand (be careful not to damage the thin gasket underneath the generator stand). The two rear bolts, even though they secure the slotted rear part of the stand, should be completely removed as well as the fronts to make it easier to remove and reinstall that gasket without damage. Next remove the wiring, label them if you are not sure, remove the right support bolt of the oil filter bracket (careful to hold the bolt on the rear of the fan shroud, sometimes synthetic clay or gum type of cement in the end of a box wrench does a good job in becoming another hand.) Remove the generator clamp.

Now remove the four bolts securing the generator to the fan shroud. Gently with slight lateral left and right pressure remove the generator and fan from the engine. If you are lucky, your shroud gasket will still be intact. Even if it is, and it is made out of cork, I would still replace it. This new gasket is the secret for a quieter engine. It also provides for a better fit and easier alignment of the generator to the fan shroud housing.

Do not over tighten these four screws on reassembly. Make them snug and if in doubt, use some Locktite. Now check the inside of the fan shroud, vacuum the inside, and check for leaves and other debris in the fan itself. If you have to remove the fan, carefully secure the front of the shaft in a vise and use a 36 mm socket to remove the rear gland nut securing the fan.

(Here Vic disagrees.) If you clamp one end of the generator in a vise and try to loosen or tighten the 36 mm nut, I guarantee you will shear the tiny key between the shaft and pulley hub before the 36 mm nut loosens. The only successful way is to use an impact wrench while holding the fan by hand; don't just stick a big screwdriver in the vanes! When reinstalling the 36 mm nut, a drop of blue Loctite and some medium impact wrench application will take care of it.

Carefully make note of the order of removal of the shims and fan washers as well as the fan plate and fan itself. Once again make note of this order! It is now time to remove the press-fit hubs of the fan and fan belt pulleys. They are press fit over keys in the shaft and are rather tricky to remove. Patience and good tools are essential in completing this task.

As stated in the manuals, reassembly follows in the reverse order. However, since I did not write the book, I will guide you backwards! After assembling the fan to the generator, check for smoothness, tightness and cleanliness. Gently slip a new gasket over the fan. A spot of gasket cement here and there might make the installation easier for you. Remember, don't overdo it, the gasket is the seal to the shroud, not the glue. Secure the generator to the fan housing by installing the four bolts and tighten them. Not too tight. Spin the axle just to make sure the fan is freely rotating and clear of the shroud.

If you installed the fan, its shims and the rest of the parts properly, you will be on target and the fan should spin freely. Now slip the generator stand under the generator. Now with a little upward pressure on the generator, gently slide in the stand's gasket, properly referencing the contour of the stand to the gasket. Replace the stands bolts, do not tighten. Now, spin the axle again. If it is still smooth, then tighten the bolts. If not, move the stand slightly until you can spin the axle smoothly. Install the generator clamp. Again turn the axle and feel and listen for roughness or noise. If smoothness still prevails, complete the installation by securing the coil and oil can brackets. Spin the axle again. You cannot be too cautious! Then finish up by putting back the fan belt and its pulley halves. Check the belt once again for proper tension.

During this procedure I would check the oil sending unit, gas lines and other components for leaks, wear and looseness. The removal of the generator stand and oil filter enables us to perform good preventative maintenance to our cars.

– Reprinted with permission from the *Nutmeg News*.

Ignition System

Vol. 4, No. 3 Richard Miller

"Flat" Distributor Caps
If you own an early pre-A 356 and are looking for an original style dis-

tributor cap, the one where the wires come out of the side, try a car parts store that sells Niehoff electrical parts. The cap and rotor are American made but are identical to the original except for the Bosch logo. The part numbers are WA70 for the cap and WA45 for the rotor (or by Niehoffs new numbering scheme WA424 and WA 316).

These were not available at the time of publication – September 1994

Vol. 4, No. 4 Vic Skirmants

Repairing Worn Out Distributor Clamps
You say your distributor keeps moving around because someone overtightened the hold-down clamp and now it's squished together at the bolt and still won't hold the distributor tightly enough anymore; is that what's troubling you? Re-bending the clamp seldom does enough good. Grab your (t)rusty hacksaw and whack off about one-eighth inch of warped metal as illustrated. Either side will do. Or get fancy and take off one-sixteenth inch on both sides. And then don't you overtighten it !

While on the subject of distributors, don't forget to put a drop of oil on the felt pad in the distributor shaft under the rotor. Grab the dipstick and let a drop drip on it. You should do this every time you tune it up. The oil in the pad lubricates the space between the rotor shaft (which is controlled by

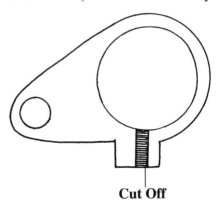

Cut Off

the advance mechanism) and the drive shaft (which drives the advance mechanism).

Vol. 8, No. 1 Vernon Crotts

Reconditioning Distributor Caps
The following brief note is an addition to the "Shade-Tree Supplement" of the Four-Cam Forum. After having great difficulty finding new distributor caps for my four cam, not to mention the incredible price, I decided that there had to be a better way! Why not recondition my old caps? The process described here can be applied to any hard to find cap or rotor, the only prerequisite being that they be physically sound, i.e., no breaks or missing parts.

The process is fairly simple. I used a glass bead cleaner with the air pressure at 30 to 40 PSI so as not to erode the cap material. The glass bead cleaner can be anything from an expensive industrial machine to an inexpensive Sears siphon-feed "sandblaster" gun.

A typical candidate for the reconditioning process is a well aged, dirty, carbon-tracked cap. By the way, in order to prevent a recurrence of the carbon tracking you should correct the cause. Usually it is caused by dirt, moisture, an open secondary lead to a spark plug, or a combination of some or all of these.

Remove the hold-down screws, the center carbon button and spring from the cap. The glass-beading of the cap is done after removal of these parts. Be brief except on the carbon-tracked areas. Do not clean the plug terminals excessively because erosion of the brass can cause a decrease of spark at the plug.

To finish the cap spray it with a clear epoxy. A little lacquer thinner applied to the plug terminals inside the cap will remove the insulation between the rotor and cap.

After the cap is thoroughly dry, install as usual. Not only does it work,
but it looks good, about $91 good!

Vol. 8, No. 4 Lew Larkin

Why to Make Sure You Have the Right Spark Plugs
In the process of restoring his 356, a friend decided to investigate the innards of an SC engine. By the time he removed the cylinders and discovered several broken piston rings, a common situation with SC and 912 engines, he decided that a proper restoration should include an engine rebuild; particularly since I could teach him how to do it.

The rebuilding went as uneventful as engine rebuilds go. It was loaded on to the back of his pick-up truck and taken to his house for later installation. He had forgotten to buy new spark plugs, so the previous ones were temporarily installed. Several weeks passed and then came time to install the engine. His mother went to the local parts store to pick up a set of Bosch plugs he had ordered for the SC engine. He removed the old plugs and installed the new set.

I went over to his house that evening to help install the engine. The engine was jacked up and with some pushing and shoving, it slid home and we buttoned it up. As I began to set the ignition, I found the engine would only turn about a quarter of a revolution and could not be moved further. Moving it back and forth merely produced a heavy metallic "clunk". Most mystifying I knew that when we finished rebuilding the engine, it rotated reasonably freely 360 degrees.

Hopefully, we thought that something may have fallen into the bell housing and was jamming the flywheel. We proceeded to remove the engine and as you'd expect, there was nothing in the bell housing.

The next logical step was to remove one of the heads. When we did, we could see that the top of one of the pistons had a beautiful round mark on it

110

and some white pieces and powder on it. The material wasn't there when the heads were assembled. Looking then at the head, the problem became eminently clear. The spark plugs had been struck by the pistons and had been mashed. The white powder and pieces were ceramic from the plugs. How could that be? Well, I tell ya.

The parts store had given him plugs for a Porsche alright; – for a 911T (W200T30) instead of W225T35. A simple mistake – haw. The physical difference between the two plugs is very significant. The correct plug has a reach of about $5/8$ of an inch whereas the length of the incorrect plug was $7/8$ of an inch. That $1/4$ inch difference was too much. The piston did not have sufficient room to come to the top of its stroke.

We had to remove the heads, and the cylinders, then reassemble them after cleaning everything. Then the valves had to be set, sheetmetal added and the engine installed. Not something planned or desired.

So the moral of this story is: *Don't take anything for granted.* Check the parts you buy to be sure they are right. Incidentally, the parts store steadfastly maintained that they gave his mother the exact plugs he had ordered and gave no indication of being sorry. My friend had not ordered the plugs by number, he had ordered plugs to fit his 1965 SC engine. The parts store was clearly at fault. You can bet that they don't get any more of our business.

Vol. 15, No. 1 Vic Skirmants

Why to Make Sure You Have the Right Spark Plugs, II

Another one of my rebuilt customer street engines "developed" a knock. It seems the engine was running a little rich and had fouled a spark plug. After his local mechanic replaced the plug, the customer's engine had a knock and a loss of power. Apparently the parts store gave him a Bosch W6DC

plug, when he had asked for a W6BC. The W6DC is only another $3/8$ in. longer than the W6BC! Yes, the piston had hit the plug, closing the electrode (therefore no spark), and furthermore, it was hitting the threaded body of the plug, hence the knock.

Vol. 16, No. 5 Vic Skirmants

Why to Make Sure You Have the Right Spark Plugs, III

Dave Butcher, Ft. Worth, TX, sends some current Champion spark plug numbers. The old L-85 has become L82C, and the extended tip UL-82Y is now L82YC. Dave says he has used both and is satisfied with them. Whatever spark plugs you use, be sure they have the proper reach. Compare the new ones to the old if you are changing types. If the new ones have an extended tip and the old ones didn't, put one in, rotate the engine with a wrench, pull it back out, and check that the electrode hasn't been closed by the piston. In 99% of the plug changes, especially with fairly standard pistons, you should have no problems. If the new plugs have a noticeably longer threaded body, don't put them in. You probably got the wrong plugs. I seem to recall writing about a car that had one spark plug replaced, and then it only ran on three cylinders and had a knock. The plug had a $3/4$ in. threaded body versus the standard, which is less than $1/2$ in., and the piston had closed the electrode and was hitting the end of the plug body that was now sticking well into the combustion chamber.

If you have a race engine, don't even think about extended tip plugs.

Vol. 14, No. 3 Vic Skirmants

Comparison of Distributor Types

I personally have never encountered a worn-out Porsche distributor. Of course here in the rustbelt all of our mechanical parts are low mileage, but that old cast iron Bosch distributor is still one viable piece of equipment. I find that most distributors simply need a slight disassembly for lubing the advance mechanism, and then proper reassembly.

The Bosch 050 distributor is good and has the same 15 degree total advance as the original. We have used these on our race cars, but the total advance requires setting the static advance so low that the starting and idle performance suffer. Also, parts availability is sometimes spotty. The Bosch 009 distributor only puts 10 degrees of advance (20 degrees at the crank), so has been preferred for an all-out race engine. Unfortunately, some 009s have a retarded #3 lobe for the VW boys, and the points supplied with the 009 were not always heavy-duty enough to preclude point-bounce at high RPM. Substituting 050 points solved that, but the problem remained of not knowing if you were getting a good-lobe or retarded-lobe distributor. No one seemed to have a definitive answer, some people even claimed there was never a non-retarded-lobe 009!

My personal preference is a stock cast iron body Bosch distributor. There are plenty of them out there, the points, the condenser, cap and rotor are all readily available and the advance curve is right for a street-driven car. For a race engine, I disassemble the distributor, add some weld material to limit the advance to 10 degrees, then rebuild with the early 911 points, part number 901.602.960.03, Bosch number 1 237 013 60. These have a heavier spring and won't float at any RPM the engine is capable of.

Vol. 14, No. 5 Dick Weiss

Comparison of Distributor Types II
Bosch VJR 4 BR 18, 0 231 129 022 are cast iron bodied; 0 231 129 031 & 0 231 129 061 are aluminum bodied. All are mechanical advanced includ-

ing the 061 (1968 - 1969 912). Even though the Bosch catalog says the 061 has a vacuum advance diaphragm, it actually retards the timing at idle only to pass the 1968 regulations. If you wish, the diaphragm unit can be removed and the hole plugged. The mechanical advance curve is virtually the same. Oh yes; retarded #3 lobe on a Bosch distributor is only found on a VW type III pancake engine. Any discrepancy on point lobes is "wear". Distributor point spring 1 237 013 60 is .5 mm thick vs. .45 mm.

Timing

Vol. 3, No. 6 Stuart Tucker

Everything You Wanted to Know...
For those mechanics interested in the engine timing of their 356 model cars, the proper procedure is amply described in any of a host of sources. The sources, however, all seem to disagree on how far the 30/5° BTDC timing mark would be placed from the OT (i.e., top dead center or TDC) notch on the crankshaft fan belt pulley. Furthermore, the sources rarely mention dynamically timing the 356 Porsche engines, completely disregarding this valuable check on distributor function.

Porsche parts catalogs for the 356A, 356B, 356C, and 912 indicate that the crankshaft fan belt pulley for the many engine variants fitted during the evolution of the 1600 engine has a single part number 539.02.113. On the basis of the information culled from the parts catalogs, it can be surmised that part number 539.02.113 fits at least the following models: 356A: 1300, 1300S, 1600, 1600S 356B: 1600, 1600S, 1600S90 356C: 1600C, 1600SC 912. The 356A catalog shows a pulley with no holes in the radial body of the pulley; the other three catalogs show pulleys with four holes; my own 1965 356C has a pulley with

112

two holes. This pulley has a measured diameter of approximately 145 mm (5.70"), corroborating the diagram on page L53 of the 356 B/C Shop Manual which indicates that the radius of the pulley is 72.5 mm.

Since the same pulley fits so many engines, one would expect to find consistent values given for the placement of the 3° and 5° BTDC timing marks, which the Porsche works neglected to permanently inscribe into the pulley. However, the expected consistency has hardly been forthcoming, as evidenced by the table below.

Although the disparities are certainly not great and are probably not significant, they are annoying. More annoying, however, is the absence of worthwhile information on dynamic timing. How can one believe even the 356 B/C Shop Manual when, on page L54, 35° BTDC is indicated to be 47.3 mm from the OT timing mark and on page L53 the diagram indicates 37° BTDC is 45.5 mm from the OT timing mark? This is clearly a geometric impossibility if both measurements are chords across the "circle" of the pulley.

By using the timing chord in all timing mark measurements, all ambiguity is eliminated from possible confusion with circumferential measurements. Further, the timing chord is easily measured out on the pulley in situ. I have found that an inexpensive vernier caliper from Sears is the easiest device to use to lay out the chords; I use a wax pencil to mark the chord length, i.e., mark the timing mark, onto the pulley, clockwise from the

OT mark in the usual manner. The crankcase seam is used for both statically and dynamically aligning the appropriate timing marks.

The above formula has universal application in that if a non-stock power pulley (e.g., from Electrodyne, Inc., Alexandria, Virginia) is fitted, timing can be determined without difficulty once the diameter of the non-stock pulley is measured. Based on the above formula and on a stock pulley diameter of 145 mm, the following chart was generated for use in statically and dynamically timing Porsche 1600 engines:

crankshaft degrees advance	timing chord mm
1	1.3
2	2.5
3	3.8
4	5.1
5	6.3
6	7.6
25	31.4
26	32.6
27	33.8
28	35.1
29	36.3
30	37.5
31	38.7
32	40.0
33	41.2
34	42.4
35	43.6
36	44.8
37	46.0
38	47.2
39	48.4
40	49.6
90	102.5

Source	mm 3°	mm 5°	Notes
Porsche Spec's, p. 96		6	2-piece crankcase: 1100, 1300, 1500
		6	3-piece crankcase: 1300, 1500, 1600, 1600S, 1600C
	3.6		1600S90, 1600SC
356C Driver's Manual, p. 92	3.6	6	1600SC, 1600C
356 B/C Shop Manual, p. L51		6.3	1600, 1600S
Up-Fixin der Porsche, vol. III, p. 88		7.5	2-piece crankcase: 356A
		6.5	3-piece crankcase: 356A
		6.3	356 B & C: N, S, and C
	3.8		S90, SC
			912 not specified

When measuring the above timing chords from the OT mark on the pulley, an assumption is made that the OT mark, when aligned with the seam in the crankcase, accurately indicates that piston number one (or three) is at TDC. This assumption may be only approximately correct within a few degrees of crankshaft rotation, as it has been reported to me that a separate determination of TDC by measuring piston motion may yield a true TDC position slightly deviated from the OT crankcase seam alignment position.

To find the true TDC point of crankshaft rotation for any piston, a dial micrometer must be used to measure the piston travel directly. Only then can the true TDC position be known to its greatest precision.

Tune Up

Vol. 3, No. 1 Vic Skirmants

Tune-Up Information

Re-gap the plugs to .026 - .028", or throw them away if they have reached 12,000 miles. I can't keep track of Champion plug nomenclature changes; I've been sticking to Bosch plugs for quite some time. Bosch W6BC are good, reliable plugs for our cars. NGK and Champion also make good plugs, but I don't have much experience with their different numbers.

If your engine is basically healthy and you keep them properly gapped, they will not foul up unless you drive like a little old lady; in which case what are you doing in a Porsche? However, the warmer, WR7BP platinum plugs might be a safer bet for less fouling.

Getting back to maintenance, while gapping the plugs you should also check the ignition dwell and timing, and lubricate the distributor cam; also pull off the rotor and put one drop of oil on the felt pad in the center of the distributor shaft; that's for the advance mechanism. I set the point dwell with a static dwell meter; if you use a feeler gauge, you will have to file the points smooth first for a proper adjustment. Replacement of points depends on how they look. If they are very pitted or if they have over 12,000 miles on them, they should be replaced. I don't have a regular schedule for replacing the condenser, rotor, or distributor cap. I do check the spark plug wires and plug connectors with an ohmmeter. If the resistance is too high, the trouble is usually in the connectors; they have a resistor in them for radio interference suppression. This resistor deteriorates with age. Never use graphite-center wire; it's useless.

Vol. 3, No. 6 Stuart Tucker

Point Gap

Too little point gap may promote sparking between the points, which may result in misfiring and in rapid point wear.

Too much point gap may decrease dwell angle to such an extent that the coil charging time at high rpm is inadequate, resulting in misfiring.

Chapter 7

Engine

2-Piece Case Engines

Vol. 6, No. 2 Vic Skirmants

Two-Piece Case 356 Engines With Oil Filter

The oil line from the filter back to the case is different from any of the ones for a three-piece case engine, and I haven't seen any source for them. One end of the line is straight, one has a right-angle bend, and they both use a compression fitting. Cutting the banjo fitting off of an early inlet line would work, but these lines, used up to 1957, are also hard to find. There is a way to come up with at least the outlet line. Take one of the 1958-69 inlet lines, cut off the banjo fitting, and use a tubing bender to make the 90 degree bend. There isn't much length to work with, but it can be done.

Vol. 7, No. 1 Richard Miller

Cam and Tappet Wear

There might be some pre-A freaks like me who could use the following information on 2-piece case motors. These motors, 369, 506, 527, 528, and 589, derive from the 36 HP VW and share the same weakness in the tappets and camshaft. They seem to run forever – until the cam lobes wear off. You can measure the lift at the rocker arms (it should be about 7 to 8 mm) or

you can remove the strainer and look at the cam. If the lobes are badly worn the cam must be replaced –you can use a 36 HP VW cam (for better performance have it reground – I use Schneider Cams 43-R or 135-F) VW part #111.109.021. If the cam is not worn badly you can extend its life by using good oil, changed frequently and inspecting the tappets each tune up. The tappets usually begin to wear first and if you catch one going you can resurface it. Pull the two bolts retaining the rocker arm assembly and withdraw the pushrods – the tappets come out with them – they snap onto the other end – no, 36 HP VW pushrods with integral tappets will not work, they are too short. The tappets have an asymmetrical radius profile and should show no signs of excessive wear or galling.

If tappets are not worn more than 1 mm, they may be resurfaced. The cam end is curved as in the sketch and is ground to shape the way rocker arms are resurfaced. It is important that the radius of the curve is 22 mm and that its center is offset from the tappet centerline, as shown. The reground end must be straight and square to the cam.

I made a jig which holds them 22 mm away from the grinding surface and with an offset pivot point to get the right curvature. A sketch of the jig

Radiused Tappet Grinding Jig

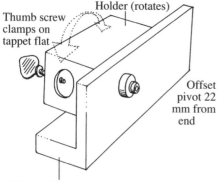

Thumb screw clamps on tappet flat

Holder (rotates)

Offset pivot 22 mm from end

Mount this end towards grinder

is shown. It can be used with a valve grinding machine or a high quality belt sander and 120 grit paper. I've never tried it but you might be able to pull the pushrods out of 36 HP VW tappets and press in your old pushrod sockets from old Porsche tappets if your tappets are worn too badly.

At this point your only remaining problem is how to reinstall the tappets. The flat surface has to align with the tappet guide and twisting the pushrod doesn't help. The factory manual says to use Porsche tool P-6 which is probably unavailable. I made a tool which works from a steel rod and a piece of sheet metal. Saw a slot in one end of the rod and press or braze a piece of sheet metal to make keys to fit the slots in the tappet. Put the tappet on the end of the tool, push down pushrod tube, and turn until tappet can be felt to slide into place. Withdraw tool, insert pushrod (clicks into place), and reassemble. Reset clearances and all is fine until next time.

Vol. 7, No. 1 Gene Lents & Don Zingg

Early Speedster Engine Details
Initial deliveries of Speedsters were equipped with two piece "VW" case engines of either 1500N or 1500S construction. Except for the cast iron barrelled 1100, all two piece engines were now delivered with aluminum pushrods. The side exit distributor caps were fitted with a brass plate stamped with the new valve clearance specs. A year earlier Porsche had moved the voltage regulator with its script-form *Bosch* logo to the firewall (1954 workshop manual page L23a). Mufflers with those flattened "crevice tool" tail pipes had been modified to round exhaust pipes. Chrome tail pipe extensions were added. A big removable oil breather, held in place by a battery cover clip and spring, was another feature of two piece engines in 1954.

Vol. 9, No. 4 Richard Miller

Reducing Oil Leaks
One other bit of trivia for anybody who would like to reduce the number of oil leaks in an old two piece case motor to less than its age. Oil leakage from under the generator and around the plug-in type breather – oil filler assembly can be stopped by the modifications shown in the attached sketch.

First, the pedestal under the generator is wide open to the crankcase and the thick gasket usually screws up the generator mounting so I cut a close fitting, tapered, wooden plug and hammered it into the opening until it came

Tappet Detail

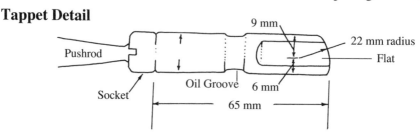

Pushrod

Socket

Oil Groove

9 mm

22 mm radius

Flat

6 mm

65 mm

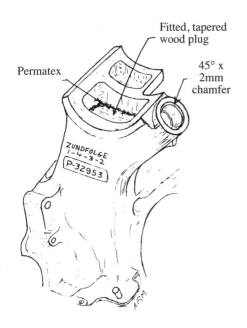

Fitted, tapered wood plug

45° x 2mm chamfer

Permatex

ZUNDFOLGE 1-4-3-2
P-32953

to the top of the hole in the side where the oil goes in and caulked it in place with Permatex No.1B hardening sealant. Next I chamfered (or countersunk) the lip of the hole where the breather plugs in to provide a wider sealing surface for the O-ring (part number 111.115.475.A at the VW agency). No more dribbles from under the generator and no more oil mist in the engine compartment at high revs (other than blow-by past the old type oil slinger and spiral seal on the crank pulley).

Vol. 9, No. 5 Richard Miller

Cylinder Recycling
For those who are having trouble finding barrels and pistons for 2-piece case motors and also believe the only substitute for cubic centimeters is more cubic inches – Ray Litz of Competition Engineering, Lake Isabella, CA, (619) 379-3879, will punch out and resleeve your old aluminum barrels. He has done a lot of R & D and knows what he is doing. You have to supply the pistons – he will fit the new sleeves.

Compression Testing

Vol. 1, No. 4 Vic Zeller

Accurate Readings
For accurate compression readings, the gas pedal be held to floor while cranking the engine. (I agree wholeheartedly).

Vol. 10, No. 1 Vic Skirmants

Leak-Down Compression Testing
Several months ago Dan Pelecovich, Monroeville, PA, asked about compression readings. I answered him directly, but also kept his letter to remind me to write something in the column. Dan asked what should the numbers be for the various engines.

Basically, I really don't know. I've been using a leak-down tester for so many years I'm not even sure where my compression gauge is. A leak-down test is a static test of how much each cylinder "leaks down". In other words, you apply compressed air to a cylinder, with the engine at top-dead-center for that cylinder and a wrench on the pulley bolt to keep the engine from turning, and the gauge tells you how much pressure that cylinder holds. If you apply 100 PSI and the gauge reads 95-100, that's fine.

The lower the number, obviously the worse condition the cylinder is in. If there is leakage, you know where the problem lies; put your ear to the exhaust pipe and you can hear if it's an exhaust valve; open the throttle and listen at the carburetor for a bad intake valve. Pop open the oil filler and find out if the bad rings are pressurizing the crankcase. You have a bad reading and none of the above sound bad? I'll bet you can hear a general escaping air noise around the heads; yes, the head-to-cylinder sealing is bad. A compression test only tells you it's bad, but not where. The leak-down tests is much more sensitive also. A difference of five or ten PSI on a compression test can sometimes (depending on the source of the leak) show up as twenty to forty PSI on a leak-down. The compression test is too dependent on a good battery and starter, having all the spark plugs out and the throttles wide open, and the cam overlap and compression ratio.

Valve Adjustment & Valve Covers

Vol. 1, No. 4 Vic Skirmants

Fitting New Valve Cover Gaskets

While on adjusting valves, if you have to replace the valve cover gasket, and the new one is usually too small, rather than soaking in hot water to expand it, I've been using a quicker method. If the gasket is not ridiculously under-size, lay it on the floor and beat it gently with a hammer all the way around. This will expand it, without diminishing the thickness appreciably. Don't hit it too hard, or too much in one spot; it will split. Also, the gasket *has* to be glued to the cover firmly, otherwise it will work itself inward.

Vol. 3, No. 1 Vic Skirmants

Valve Adjustment

Judging by some of the questions I receive, now would be a good time to cover some of the general maintenance procedures to keep the 356 running. I won't rehash the factory recommendations because it's been so long since I've looked at them I honestly don't remember; and I'm too lazy to look it up. I'm going to express my opinions on the frequency of doing, changing, or adjusting whatever needs to be done, changed, or adjusted.

The valves should be adjusted every 3000 miles unless the engine has just been overhauled, in which case they should be adjusted after the first 300 miles, then another 1000, then another 2000, then every 3000. Of course, they have to be set cold.

Vol. 4, No. 4 Vic Skirmants

Ball-Check Valve Covers

For those of you with the ball-check valve covers (S-90 and later Supers), something to check if you have a persistent valve cover leak. The ball-check housing on some of these can actually interfere with the cylinder head, keeping that area of the cover from seating properly. With the hold-down clip off, check to see if the cover rocks back and forth. If there is interference, file the end of the ball-check housing. Usually just the top part interferes.

Vol. 5, No. 4 Vic Skirmants

Do Your Valve Cover Gaskets Slip?

First of all, you have to use a good glue between the gasket and cover, not a sealer, such as silicone. Clean the cover, fit the gasket. Many gaskets have shrunk while in storage, so they don't fit. I have seen many old-time articles about soaking the gaskets in warm water, then drying them, etc, etc. Sounds great if you have two days to replace a lousy gasket. I'm usually in a hurry, so I get out my hammer...

That's right, lay that gasket on a cold concrete floor and gently tap on it with a hammer. This will make it grow. Check the fit and tap some more if necessary. Don't hit it real

illustration

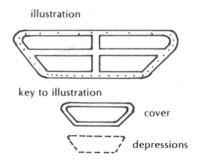

key to illustration

cover

depressions

hard, or it will split. Now apply a contact cement on the cover and on the gasket; make sure you get the glue on the right side of the gasket. Wait 7.36 seconds and put them together. Install the cover, being careful not to slide it before you pop the clip in place.

Vol. 10, No. 5 Vic Skirmants

Installing Valve Cover Gaskets

Bob has problems with his valve cover gaskets "growing". It sounds as if they're not properly glued in place.

The gasket has to be firmly attached to the cover. The best way to do this is to use a good contact cement. 3M yellow weatherstrip cement is very good for this. Apply a bead of glue to the gasket, a bead to the cover, wait a minute, and press together.

Vol. 1, No. 6 Vic Skirmants

Valve Adjustment

Porsche used to recommend adjusting the valves on the 356 series every 1500 miles. Unless you drive like an animal, every 2500 - 3000 miles is alright. After an engine rebuild and valve grind, I usually adjust the valves with .002" extra clearance to permit the valves to seat without closing up the lash excessively. I then readjust after 300 miles to the recommended setting, then again in 1000 miles, and then 1500 miles. If the valve clearances haven't changed much, I then go on the 2500 - 3000 mile interval.

I will outline the procedure I use, while emphasizing the fact that different people use different methods, all of which are correct, as long as the basic idea is adhered to: make sure you are at Top Dead Center (or near it) for the cylinder you are trying to adjust. Remember that you do not have to set the crank pulley with a dial indicator; one inch either side of the mark will still ensure you are on the base circle of the cam, and not beginning or ending a lift cycle. Various

procedures are used by people from personal preference; here's mine: (Remember that the valves must be set cold.) Remove the distributor cap and look at the rotor.

On the top edge of the distributor body is a very light scribed line in the 4 - 5 o'clock position. The rotor should point to this line or near it when cylinder #1 is at Top Dead Center. *Note!* It is possible, if your engine was ever rebuilt, that the distributor drive gear may not have been installed in the correct orientation, in which case check to see where the ignition wire for #1 is located in the distributor cap. Assuming you've found the approximate point where #1 should fire, look at the crank pulley. It should be close to the "OT" mark. Now rotate the crankshaft clockwise to the point on the pulley that is 180 degrees opposite "OT".

You are now hopefully on #4, which is the left rearward cylinder, and your distributor rotor has rotated 90 degrees clockwise from #1. (rearward and forward on a Porsche are always referenced to the direction of travel; the flywheel is the forward end of the engine, the crank pulley is the rear of the engine). Some people jack up the car to get to the valves; it is not necessary, but does make the job easier. Lay some newspaper under the left valve cover, pry off the wire clip holding the cover, gently pull the cover off, and wipe the oil off your elbows. Check the gasket in the cover; if at all loose, replace it. As I mentioned in an earlier column, be sure to glue it in place (in the valve cover only). Permatex #3 and 3M contact adhesives do a good job. While checking the old gasket, look at the oil in the valve cover. If anything of a wearing nature is going wrong with your engine, the particles will flow up the pushrods and some will settle in the bottom of the cover.

Take the necessary feeler gauge (see table for clearances) and slide it between the valve stem and rocker arm. Some people now loosen the adjusting screw locknut, rotate the adjuster until the clearance feels "right", and then tighten the locknut. As soon as you tighten the locknut, your clearance changes, no matter how tight you hold the screw with a screwdriver. My procedure is to determine if the clearance is too loose or too tight, then: unlock locknut, loosen or tighten screw very slightly, lock locknut, then check again. Repeat as necessary. This may sound tedious, but it isn't any more difficult than adjusting, then tightening, and then re-doing because it changed on you. Because, if you have to rotate the screw more than one-half turn, you're probably on the wrong cylinder, or something is wearing too rapidly in your engine. The exhaust valves are toward the outside, the intakes toward the center of the head. Adjust exhaust and intake, then rotate pulley 180 degrees clockwise to the "OT" mark; you're now on what is the left forward cylinder. Adjust #3. Wipe off cylinder head mating surface, and install valve cover. Make sure the cover is seated. Rotate the crank another 180 degrees clockwise, pull the right valve cover, adjust #2. Rotate crank one last time (yes, 180 degrees clockwise), and adjust #1. If you've stayed awake during all this, you may have noticed that I merely followed the firing order; 1-4-3-2, I just start at 4-3-2-1.

If your engine has been rebuilt and has different cylinders or pushrods

Valve Clearance Table

Engine Type	Valve	2-Piece Case Steel Pushrods	2-Piece Case Aluminum Pushrods	3-Piece Case "Short" Aluminum Pushrods	3-Piece Case "Long" Aluminum Pushrods
1100	Int.	.008			
	Exh.	.006			
1300	Int.	.004	.008	.004	
	Exh.	.004	.006	.006	
1300A	Int.		.008		
	Exh.		.006		
1300S	Int.		.008	.004	
	Exh.		.008	.004	
1500	Int.	.004	.008	.004	
	Exh.	.004	.006	.006	
1500S	Int.	.006	.008	.004	
	Exh.	.004	.006	.006	
1600N, 1956 - 1963	Int.			.004	
	Exh.			.006	
1600S, 1956 - 1959	Int.			.004	
	Exh.			.006	
1600S, 1960 - 1961	Int.				.006
	Exh.				.004
1600S, 1962 - 1963	Int.			.004	
	Exh.			.006	
1600 S-90, 1960 - 1963 "Ferral"	Int.				.006
	Exh.				.004
1600 C, 1964 - 1965	Int.			.004	
	Exh.			.006	
1600 SC, 1964 - 1965 " Biral"	Int.			.004	
	Exh.			.006	

than originally supplied, stick to the following:

Basically, for the engines with the aluminum rocker arm pedestals, aluminum cylinders, and long aluminum pushrods, set to .006" in. and .004" ex. The pushrods with the short aluminum center (long steel ends) had the same expansion rate as the steel pushrods.

The S-90 "Ferral" cylinders (thin steel coating in aluminum cylinder) are to be treated like the "Super" aluminum cylinders with chrome lining (as far as expansion rate is concerned). The SC and 912 "Biral" (thick iron liner in aluminum cylinder) cylinders are to be treated like cast iron cylinders. For engines with cast iron or "Biral" cylinders and steel pushrods, set to .004" in. and .006" ex. If you have cast iron cylinders with long aluminum pushrods, change the pushrods.

Valve Train

Vol. 8, No. 3 Dick Monahan

Broken Valve Spring

I encountered the broken valve spring in the following manner:

1) Thinking my generator fan was hitting the shroud, I disconnected the generator belt but the noise persisted.

2) Removed right valve cover to check the springs. Manually turned the engine to check all the springs. Found #2 intake spring broken. Cause – rust-stress point (presence of brown powder on cylinder head wall.)

Remedy

1) Removed rocker stand completely.

2) Took a spare engine-mounting bolt -the one for the starter - it's long and has an extended thread.

3) Ran a nut and large fender washer up the thread and inserted the bolt into a cylinder head bolt-snug but not tightened.

4) Placed a set of valve spring compressor jaws on the bolt below the washer and nut.

5) Placed a block of wood on the bottom lip of the cylinder head to spread the load when applying pressure.

6) Turned the engine so the rotor pointed to #2 wire, thereby extending the piston out to prevent the valve from falling into the head. (Also to ensure both valves were closed, or the next step won't work-Vic).

7) Then, having the luck to have an air compressor. I removed #2 spark plug, inserted my hose attachment from my engine compression tester and connected the air hose (air pressure would keep the valve closed after removing the spring).

8) Keeping the bolt from turning. I tightened down the nut to compress the spring and remove the keepers.

9) Reversed the nut to release the pressure and remove the old spring, etc.

Vol. 11, No. 3 Vic Skirmants

Using Valve Seals on 356A and 356B

In an attempt to control oil consumption, Porsche finally added valve-stem oil seals on the intake valves of the C, SC, and 912 engines. The valve stem of these engines has a longer straight section so that part of the stem is always in contact with the oil seal. The earlier valves neck-down too soon toward the valve keeper end of the valve, so that when the valve is fully open the stem is no longer in contact with the seal. I have installed seals on the older valves with mixed success. First, the type of seal is critical. Some of them immediately pop off the valve guide when the valve opens, others seem to stay on fairly well. The ones that stay on do help the oil consumption somewhat, although not as well as on a C-type valve. On the 1960- 63 engines using the Super rocker arms, the exhaust rocker arm originally came with a small oil hole to provide extra oil to the guides during break-in. This oil hole was supposed to be closed up after the first 1500 miles. This was published in some special bulletin long ago. Does anyone know if the factory still recommended closing these holes on the 1964 and later engines? Anyway, the earlier engines will use more oil than the later ones for the above reason alone. One solution is to replace the A or B intake valves with the C valves. The head diameter is the same, the oil seals will now work, and all you need is a set of C retainers and keepers. By the way, don't put seals on the exhaust valves! They work hard and hot enough normally, don't starve them of their required lubrication.

Cylinder Heads

Vol. 6, No. 3 Vic Skirmants

Machining Concerns
    Many engines have heads that develop combustion leaks between the head and the top of the cylinder. The remedy is to have the sealing surface in the head remachined to bring it back to the proper flatness, smoothness, etc. However, an equal amount of material must be removed from the surface of the head, in order to keep from bottoming the head on the top fins of the cylinders. If that happens, the heads aren't going to seal very well.
    While on cylinder heads, here's a third engine tip. Sometimes the heads get machined often enough through the years that when the rocker arms are bolted in place, they cannot be adjusted out far enough to have any clearance. This same condition can occur if the washers that go under the cylinder head nuts are left out on the 1960 - 1965 engines; 912s also. I have seen engines of this type where some flaming moron has then proceeded to

grind down the hardened ends of the rocker arms for clearance! The solution is to put spacers under the rocker arm stands. Front suspension link pin shims are absolutely perfect for this application.

Pistons/Cylinders

Vol. 2, No. 3 Dick Coyne

Aftermarket Piston/Cylinder Cautions
    From Dick Coyne, Santa Anna, CA, added precautions on the Japanese-made 1750cc piston & cylinder sets. If these sets are to be used with 1963 and older style cylinder heads, check the clearance between piston and head; chances are you will have interference. Either have the pistons machined, or modify the heads. No recommendations on specs for machining. I would suggest removing metal from the heads and keep checking the clearance with clay or round solder strips. You want a minimum of .040" with a plain-bearing crank and .050" with a roller-bearing crank. If driven hard, the upper piston ring grooves will wear out by 30,000 miles.

Vol. 3, No. 6 Mike Robbins

Aftermarket Piston/Cylinder Cautions, II
    A few months ago someone inquired about the NPR piston and cylinder sets sold by J.C. Whitney and others. These are advertised as fitting 356 and 912 engines. About a year and a half ago, I used a set of these pistons and cylinders on an engine using an S cam and C heads and they worked okay. In fact. that was one of the smoothest running engines I've seen. However, let me relate a more recent experience. I was building what was basically a Super 90 engine but with an Isky 107 cam. I found inadequate clearance between the exhaust

valves and pistons and had to remove .060" in the valve pockets. Also, the bevel on the crown of the piston is 30° which is compatible with C, SC and 912 heads but interfere with the older style heads that have a 22° bevel. I had to have the bevel on the piston crown machined .020" at 22° to provide clearance between the piston and the combustion chamber. To go back to the valve clearance problem – the Isky cam has the same lift as the S-S90 cam but its increased duration apparently caused the problem. The moral of the story – be sure to clay your pistons – particularly if using any non-standard combination of parts.

Vol. 7, No. 4 Vic Skirmants

Aftermarket Piston/Cylinder Cautions, III – Check Those Pushrods
Now for some tips from me. There are more and more 356 engines being converted to big-bore kits. That's fine; you can't beat the cost. However, if you have a 1960 - 1963 S-90 engine or a 1960 - 1961 Super with alloy barrels, you'd better change the pushrods also. Those engines used aluminum cylinders; the S-90 with a sprayed-on ferrous coating, the Super with a dimpled chrome plating. They both used pushrods with long aluminum center sections with short steel end caps. This was done so that the expansion rates of the cylinders and the pushrods would be compatible. Engines with cast iron cylinders or biral cylinders used pushrods with:
1) long steel center section with short steel end caps (Normals, 1962 - 1963 Supers, C & SC)
2) short aluminum center section with long, skinny steel end caps (Normals, 1962 - 1963 Supers, C & SC)
3) long stainless steel center section with short steel end caps (912)
The long steel and short aluminum center pushrods were found in all iron and pre-912 biral cylinder engines, indicating that the factory believed

them to have comparable expansion rates. Therefore, if one puts iron or biral cylinders in an engine with long aluminum center pushrods, the pushrods will expand to a greater degree than the iron or biral cylinders, causing the valve clearances to be too tight when hot, no matter how carefully you adjust them when cold. The other thing one could do would be to check hot clearances on an engine with the proper combination of cylinders and pushrods, then adjust yours accordingly. If anyone does try that, let me know. I don't feel like doing it myself; I don't like hot oil burns.

Flywheel

Vol. 4, No. 5 Vic Skirmants

Repairing Elongated Dowel Holes
I've been asked about the feasibility of welding and re-drilling elongated flywheel or crankshaft dowel holes. Don't do it! You'd get too much warpage. Have the flywheel and crank re-drilled for a larger dowel. Many VW shops can do this. I know Ray Litz's Competition Engineering, Lake Isabella, CA, does an excellent job.

Vol. 6, No. 4 Vic Skimants

Tightening Gland Nuts
I'll start with the prejudices. A couple of years back I wrote about how to tighten the flywheel gland nut. I mentioned using a four-foot pipe and $3/4$ in. drive handle and putting most of one's weight on it. I have used this technique for 16 years and never had a problem; never lost a flywheel, and only two very used old gland nuts started to yield. You can feel this as you tighten. Simply unscrew that one and install another one. I was glad to hear from others who agreed with my method. As far as replacements go, the only gland nut to use is an original Porsche replacement. There are others

123

on the market, but I wouldn't recommend them. They might work fine if you use the torque specs for an old Normal, but they will stretch if you over-torque them as I do; I personally wouldn't use the Normal torque specs on a Volkswagen, let alone a Porsche.

Connecting Rods

Vol. 8, No. 1 Vic Skirmants

Rod Failure

In the previous column I mentioned a rod failure I had at the beginning of this racing season on my race car. First a little background on Porsche connecting rod piston pin oiling holes. The early rods all had three oiling holes one directly at the top of the rod, one on each side 120 degrees apart. Sometime, maybe the early 912s?, they went to a hole at the bottom of the piston pin end, drilled in at an angle through the main column of the rod; again, with two more holes 120 degrees apart. On later 912s only these last two holes remain; no more hole through the center of the rod. Now I know why not ! Somewhere along the line Porsche must have discovered what a neat little stress-riser that hole was, and just stopped drilling it.

That's what happened to my main engine in qualifying at IRP on April 25. A crack started at the hole of number one rod, proceeded down the center of the rod, then took off for the side, at which point it came apart; at 7200 RPM! The flying pieces took the nuts off of number three rod, permitting it to do its own liberation dance. End result: one 356 engine case totally opened up from one side to the other, and from #1 main bearing web to #2 web; biggest hole possible.

Vol. 13, No. 1 Vic Skirmants

Carillo Connecting Rods

Two issues ago I mentioned two

engine failures I had experienced last year caused by Carillo connecting rod bolt problems. I'd like to explain further, but first some background on Carillo rods as applicable to Porsche 356s.

The stock late-style 01 Porsche rods are great. Don't use the 1966 912 ones with the piston pin oil hole in the rod beam, and you've got one heck-of-a strong connecting rod. Extended use in the 7600 to 8000 RPM range will sometimes cause failures, so some people like to go to something stronger yet. Carillo makes some of the strongest rods available. For quite a few years they have had a rod that is the correct length and uses the same bearing and piston pin dimensions; theoretically they should fit. They do fit VWs, but not the 356. Because of the closeness of the camshaft lobes, these rods cannot be used in two of the cylinder positions on our engines.

Several years ago John O'Steen and others convinced Carillo to make a rod to fit all the holes in the 356. Even these rods sometimes need grinding for clearance on #4, depending on the cam profile and cam timing. Due to the size restrictions on the rod, Carillo had to use a special $1/4$ in. aircraft bolt. This $1/4$ in. bolt has to be torqued to a very specific stretch. Remember, anytime you torque something, you are actually stretching the fastener, which is what holds the assembly together.

The information sheet that Carillo supplies with the rods specifies a bolt stretch of .0045 - .0050", or a recommended torque of 275 - 300 in-lbs. When we first received these rods and checked the bolt stretch, it seemed that 275 - 300 in-lbs. gave a stretch of .008 - .009". Deciding to go with the higher value, we used the torque spec and ran the bolts at 275 in-lbs. Nothing failed, but after several uses, the rods started showing a "fretting" at the mating surfaces, indicating a movement of the rod cap in relation to the rod. A couple of times, I even found some of the locating tabs broken off the rod bearing! When I finally had a used bolt yield before the 275 in-lb. torque, I decided the stretch was too great. Testing some bolts by torquing them in a rod seemed to show that 200 in-lbs. was the figure required to get about .005" stretch. I started using the 200 in-lb. torque and had no problems for about three years. No more fretting, no more broken tabs, no more yielded bolts.

Then last year, having done nothing differently in assembly, I had a brand new engine come apart on the second lap of practice. Inspection indicated that a rod bolt had probably loosened up. Trying to figure out how not to have a repeat of the problem, I decided to finally get a special bolt-stretch gauge. This gauge fits onto the ends of the bolt and you can watch the actual stretching as you tighten the bolt with a regular wrench.

The gauge had not arrived when I had to finish the engine, so I went with the torque wrench again. It's not that easy to measure the bolt stretch with anything but the gauge. Guess what? Yep, another scrap engine, same problem. Part of my difficulties may have been the age and previous over-stretching of some of the bolts. Carillo, for some reason, doesn't like to sell the bolts separately. They say that they should last forever. Well, maybe if they're never overstretched (due to someone recommending 275-300 in-lbs.) they will last forever.

Anyway, I didn't have eight new bolts, and did not know which ones had been overdone.

I received the gauge right after the last failure, have used it on three engines since, and am happy to report all three have been raced and are still together!

Vol. 14, No. 4 Vic Skirmants

The Need to Check Over New Porsche Factory Connecting Rods

Tim Berardelli mentions another problem with new parts, namely connecting rods. I know Harry Pellow had mentioned them before, but it wouldn't hurt to repeat the info. The new replacement connecting rods currently available really aren't machined very well. The big-end bores aren't held very closely to the specified size, usually being over-size, as well as somewhat tapered. Yes, these new rods usually need to be re-built. The weight differences in a set can be quite extreme as well. Makes you wonder if these were the ones Porsche rejected.

Vol. 17, No. 1 Vic Skirmants

912 Rod Clearance Problem in Earlier Engines

Thirty years with these cars (March 6, 1963; chassis # 103614, engine # 69666, Fjord green 1958 coupe), now after 429 engines built, 186 transmissions built, and I'm still learning! Just put a set of 912 connecting rods in a 1959 case; no problem, I've done it before! *Wrong!* #1 con rod wanted to hit the head stud bosses inside the case. Luckily, it hit the bosses very obviously when rotating the crank and checking the cam gear backlash. I can imagine if it had barely cleared, and only hit later on at medium to high engine revs. This might explain some people's newly rebuilt, but knocking engines! The solution of course was to cut down the bosses with a rotary carbide cutter. Harry, if you've mentioned this in your books, I apologize for missing it. If not, here's a new one for your data base.

Exhaust

Vol. 4, No. 2 Vic Skirmants

T-6 European Heater System

Now that winter is here some people who still drive their 356s in cold

125

weather have become concerned about heat. As most of us know, the standard "export" heating arrangement is none too good in really cold climates. There are two alternatives, the first being a gas heater; either an original Porsche one, unobtainable as far as I know, or an old 6 volt VW one modified to work in the 356; also getting hard to find. The second, and to me more desirable one, is the "European" heater set-up as used on the later non-American B and C models. If you can get the heat exchangers, fan shroud, etc. that go on the engine, you still need the heater control valve boxes that attach to the chassis underneath.

The C models have larger heater duct ends than the older models, so you will have to make an adapter to fit the heater control boxes to an older model. If you can't get the control boxes, I have used the standard heater system forward boxes with a pulley arrangement for the heater cables to open them in the proper direction.

Is the effort worth it? You bet! In my own personal experience, the European heater is as good as a gas heater, and four times better than the American heater.

Vol. 4, No. 5 Vic Skirmants

Muffler/J-Pipe Junction Leaks
Tired of exhaust leaks where the exhaust #1 and #3 pipes slide over the J-pipe ends? Assuming the pipes are in some semblance of proper condition and that you've been using the factory-type clamps and all they do is bend when you tighten the nut and bolt, go to an auto parts store and get some regular 1 1/2 in. exhaust pipe "U" clamps. Tighten them just enough to stop the leak. Over-tightening these will either break them or deform your pipes so that you'll have a heck of a time getting them apart when you need to.

Vol. 8, No. 6 Vic Skirmants

What System to Use?
The following information is based solely on my own personal experience, prejudice, and general orneriness. There are no dyno results to back up my claims; any member input on exhaust systems is really welcome.

The stock system is a good, long-lasting medium price system that fits well. For a stock engine, it's about as good as any tuned exhaust, and it's quiet. There are the cheap "tuned" exhausts that are cheap, who-knows-how "tuned", cheap, noisier than hell, cheap, having mediocre to fair longevity, cheap, atrocious to semi-decent fit, and best of all they're cheap. One step up from these "no-name" generic exhausts are the ones that substitute a "turbo" muffler for the straight-through fiberglass packed bullet "muffler". These are a little more expensive because of the muffler, and they are actually about as quiet as a stock exhaust.

Then there are the premium priced systems that have chrome pipes sticking out all over the back of your car. These things are expensive; have who-knows-what-kind of "tuning"; are expensive, mellow sounding, $$, *heavy*, $$, long lasting (something that heavy has to last long!), $$; have mediocre to good fit (of course they are so rigid and strong that when they don't fit properly, you have a problem). One system in particular has several mufflers, and connecting pipes that are smaller than the stock 1 1/2 in.! This is high-performance?

Yes, I will now name an exhaust system that works. An honest-to-goodness tuned exhaust is the Bursch. I believe Bursch was the first actual tuned exhaust. It still is the best you can buy for a hopped-up engine. It is medium-priced, long-lasting, and fits well. You can get the noisy one with the fiberglass-packed "bullet", or you can get the turbo muffled version. In summary: stock engine, stock exhaust: high-performance engine,

Bursch exhaust. If you want chrome pipes all over your car, do what I saw on one car at last year's East Coast 356 Holiday. Cut the chrome tips off one of the high-dollar exhausts and clamp them to the outlets on your stock muffler.

Vol. 9, No. 3 Craig Richter

Building Your Own Custom Exhaust

The old reliable Bursch exhaust offers superior quality and fit at a reasonable price. And great performance for stock to semi-hot 356/912s. Awfully hard to beat. But if you are running a really hot 1720 or 1840, a few more horsepower can be found in a proper custom exhaust system. You will have to build it yourself (or hire a proper professional), but if you feel like a challenging project to fill a few free afternoons, it will be worth your time.

Gene Berg carries tubing kits for VW's, even complete with the fully-welded merged collector. Get some rectangular Porsche exhaust flanges (old mufflers?), break out the welding tanks and tubing snips, and let's see how to make things work:

When the exhaust valve is starting to open, the piston has not even come near the bottom of the power stroke. High energy in the cylinder literally blasts by the opening exhaust valve in the form of a pressure wave. As the piston rounds the bottom and starts back up, it pushes the remaining exhaust gas out; but the intake valve starts to open well before the exhaust closes. Unless the intake velocity (RPM) is high enough to overpower whatever piston push remains, the exhaust will be pushed right up *both* open valves. One look at the carbon stains inside a used intake manifold will verify that this happens even with a stock cam.

Little intake flow will happen until the piston creates a vacuum by going down on the intake stroke when the intake velocity is low and no ram effect has yet started. If the exhaust system can somehow contribute to pulling the exhaust gas out of the combustion chamber, a neutral or even low pressure could exist as the intake is starting to open, greatly enhancing cylinder filling at low RPM's.

Picture that high-pressure pulse that just escaped by the exhaust valve as a solid slug. As it moves down the exhaust pipe a low pressure is created in it's wake, pulling less motivated air behind it. That slug extracts or scavenges whatever exhaust is left in the cylinder like a bullet pulling its propelling blast with it out the barrel. Of course this scavenge effect can be overdone and pull a lot of new mixture out the exhaust valve; but the point is that the higher the velocity of the exhaust gas, the more efficient the extractor action. The perfect extractor effect has just enough pull to get the exhaust out and the intake flow in, but not so much that lots of fresh mixture is pulled out the exhaust. And all this over a wide range of pumping speed, because the backpressure cannot increase as rapidly as the volume increases or top end power suffers. A certain volume of exhaust gas will be produced at full throttle at a given RPM. Start increasing the volume (RPM) and the flow speed will increase until the pipe finally fills up and becomes a restriction to flow. Tremendous pressure increases would then be necessary to move more exhaust once this "filled" condition is reached. Racing VW's use $1 \frac{5}{8}$ in., even $1 \frac{3}{4}$ in. header tubing; but a $1 \frac{1}{2}$ in. tube can handle up to 500cc, and is perfect for motors in our displacement range. The fact that $1 \frac{1}{2}$ in. fits the heater boxes is irrelevant, because the primary tube length is the first thing to get changed.

Long pipes measuring 44 - 46 in. from the port flange to the collector will accelerate smaller flow volumes quickly and scavenge well from 3000 to 5000 RPM. This is the *shortest* pipe that can be fitted with stock heater boxes, and governs the design of the rest of the system. Going up in volume, whether through increased displacement or RPM, requires shorter primary lengths or the induced back-pressure will be too much at high RPM. 40 in. is probably the shortest you can fit, although 36 -38 in. would give better extraction at 7000+ RPM. This certainly eliminates the heater boxes, and is a very tight fit for the forward facing cylinders; but never resort to restrictive bends coming out of the ports. Some extra bends must be used to extend the length of the rear cylinders so each pipe comes out the same length, important that the extractor effect be the same for each cylinder. This can be accomplished in several ways, so look to the Bursch or ads in the VW cult magazines to find a shape you like, but remember the pipes must be equal length.

The collector is not just where all the runners merge, but where they interact. It should not be a restriction, but a nice smooth-flowing device for making the header more efficient by making each slug of speeding exhaust help scavenge the slug following. The merged collector is about 7 in. long to really smooth the transitioning flow, and an interior cone has been fabricated to avoid a pressure drop into the collector.

With the shorter primaries, the collector exit does not need to be larger than the primary tube! The flat-four design fires each cylinder 180-degrees apart, so the collector is only handling one cylinder volume at a time. When the exit is much larger than the primary pipe diameter, the flow expands and slows, losing some drafting action. Shorter primary lengths are especially sensitive to losing any draft, hurting torque or low-speed velocity, and a 1 $5/8$ in. exit works great.

When using the four-into-one merged collector, the pipes should fit into the collector in their firing order sequence. The most drafting action is achieved by firing adjacent tubes in succession, rather than tubes across from each other.

The Bursch systems shows several differences from all this theory. No, exhaust engineering knowledge has not really outstripped the design, but the heater boxes have! Those long primary tubes necessary to retain the stock heater boxes keep the flow quite high at lower RPM, and the large 2 $1/2$ in. collector/stinger releases pressure at higher RPM. The merged collector with 1 $5/8$ in. exit becomes most useful with the short primary pipes necessary to really extend the RPM range. It restores mid-range lost because of the short primaries without limiting the high-range. Hard to have your cake and heaters too!

Stinger length really fine-tunes the back-pressure induced by the whole system. And luckily so, because whatever collector and primary tube length was fit is awfully hard to change! A shorter stinger releases some overall back-pressure, just like shorter primaries, and will extend high-RPM capabilities at the expense of some low-speed torque. 16 -18 in. will be close, smaller motors liking longer stingers. An interesting effect of varying the stinger length is the height of the fuel standoff seen materializing above the carburetors. That cloud of fuel spray seen hovering above the air intake (under load on the dyno) will expand and contract. Usually about 4 in. must be maintained above the carburetor entry, or fuel spray will condense into big drops on the air cleaner cover and fall back through causing mixture problems.

A little time on the dyno with a slip-tube should zero-in on the best stinger length for your particular motor, for both power and minimum fuel fog. Too long a stinger won't hurt much, unless you trip over it, but horsepower will definitely drop when it gets too short.

Why the long tapered stinger? Well, the greatest exhaust volume per cycle happens at the peak torque point. Each cycle above that RPM contains a progressively smaller volume, although more and more cycles are happening so the total exhaust volume continues to increase. The larger slugs of peak torque exhaust must travel farther up the tapered tube to be fully released to atmospheric pressure, making the tapered stinger seem longer to the motor, and inducing some needed back-pressure. As the revs go up, the flow is released earlier and earlier, and the motor believes the stinger is getting shorter and shorter.

The exhaust gas is also cooling rapidly as it flows through the exhaust system. Cooling makes it contract and become more dense again, occupying less and less volume. Which makes the venturi action through the merged collector, followed by the gradual expansion into the "variable-length" stinger even more critical. Proper orchestration of the various parts will greatly extend the power range of your new tubing exhaust system.

Wave Entrapment

Remember that the high-energy exhaust rushing by the exhaust valve was described as a pressure wave? Well, in addition to making a bunch of hot exhaust gases, the combustion process produces sound waves that are tuned to the opening and closing of the exhaust valve. Just stand beside any running engine and the frequency can be both heard and felt. Low frequency sound waves produce the deep throaty growl at idle, and the higher frequencies produce the high-pitched scream of a motor "on the pipe".

These pressure pulses travel the length of the exhaust system, and then reverberate right back up the whole exhaust system again! In fact, they'll sneak right on up the intake manifolds and are responsible for that odd phenomenon known as "fuel standoff".

These pulses have their own pressure, in this case back-pressure, associated with them. If the waves are timed to arrive back through the open exhaust valve on the next cycle, their pressure interferes with the extractor effect. When their return to the exhaust valve coincides with the end of the valve overlap period, a little extra pressure will actually keep the incoming mixture from being over-scavenged out the closing exhaust valve. The big problem when trying to play with pressure waves is that they spend most of their time messing up the extractor effect, only during a relatively narrow range can they actually help out. So it may be worth investigating a way to get rid of them altogether.

A few VW exhaust systems have tried to do this by using small reverse cones right at the exhaust port flanges to catch these returning pressure pulses. Strictly speaking, these cones were not meant to actually improve performance at any RPM; but they were supposed to keep the system from being terribly inefficient, especially at lower engine speeds where the low-velocity intake cannot overcome much interference from the pressure waves. If the cones can stop the pulsing, it may be at the expense of top end flow. One company that produced such a system (now belly-up) only advertised dyno tests (which were fairly impressive) with little 1200cc off-road race motors, nothing larger.

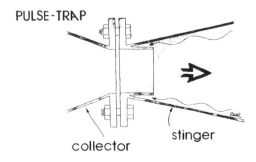

PULSE-TRAP

collector   stinger

Since the return of the waves (isn't that an old movie title?) is somewhat timed by the stinger length, they should be catchable anywhere along the system, not just at the port which is a critical velocity point. A pulse-trap can be created by extending the collector exit into the stinger. Only $3/4$ in. or so is needed to capture some waves, and the little velocity lost by expansion into the stinger should be less critical than dampening some of those pulses. The idea of wave entrapment is controversial, but at least a whole exhaust system need not be sacrificed to try it.

Street Exhaust

After all this explanation about pipe size, merged collectors and stinger length, here's a little curve ball: the stock muffler works awfully well! Well enough for almost all applications except all-out racing. Those German engineers knew about all sorts of weird things, and one of them is called the Expansion Chamber or Air Elasticity phenomenon.

Trap the exhaust in a big can and it will pack-up until the can is full, and then begin to search for the exit. By restricting the outlet (the two exit pipes) somewhat, a little backpressure can be induced at even low revs to help control over-scavenging. As the revs increase, the trapped exhaust is compressed more and more; and if the can is large enough, a "pillowing" effect will keep the back-pressure from increasing as fast as the flow volume. Air elasticity is even partly responsible for the effects of primary tube and stinger lengths.

In other words, each rate of flow will have an ideal back-pressure. But no matter how you match pipe lengths, tubing systems can only be effective over a fairly narrow range. A large can will permit the engine to come in tune earlier and stay in tune longer. (Which is exactly the reason the dual-quiet mufflers have become so popular on hot street VW's lately.

Two mufflers increase the expansion chamber size over one muffler, or the stock VW can which is also just too small to be effective.)

The stock Porsche can is also very effective in cancelling those pulses or pressure waves. Once in the can, they can't find where they came in and get lost!

Now if you had been told all this at the start, you probably wouldn't have paid nearly as much attention. Boy, some people will try any tricks to keep you reading...

Exhaust Finish

Tubing exhaust systems don't last very long. Rust, caused by the cooling metal absorbing moisture every time the motor is turned off, eats through tubing and even stock exhaust cans in no time. Chroming is expensive and doesn't last that well on an exhaust system anyway, because the tubing will rust away below the chrome plate. High-temperature paint won't stick unless the system is completely sandblasted first, and even then has a marginal life expectancy. But combine the sandblasting with Aluminizing (spraying molten aluminum), then a few cans of VHT (the rough aluminized finish absorbs paint like crazy), and you'll get a long-lasting finish. One drawback is a tendency to stain, especially with hot oil.

Powder-coating gives a beautifully smooth and glossy finish, much more aesthetic than rough aluminizing, much more durable than any spray paint, and easy to clean. But the heat-resistance is not yet quite up to peak exhaust temperatures. Only an inch or two up from the head flange gets hot enough to burn the powder-coating away; and since this area is usually out of view under the rear sheet metal, you can decide if powder-coating qualifies as a good exhaust system finish.

Whichever you choose, the extra money is well spent here, as rusty pipes and cans are really ugly and a travesty on an other-wise clean act. Now you know more than you probably ever wanted to about cans, pipes and powder – consider the subject exhausted.

Vol. 10, No. 4 Vic Skirmants

Stock Mufflers and S-Pipes

First item: mufflers. I still prefer the stock muffler for a stock or fairly mild engine. The Bursch tuned exhaust is the only one to put on a modified engine. Of course it also works just fine on a stock engine. All the other fancy, multi-chromed-pipe systems are, in my opinion, expensive junk. The cheapo "tuned exhausts" are good value for the money, and work well on stock or mild engines. They don't last very long, but for the price, what do you expect? One comment on the stock muffler. There are currently elbow pipe kits on the market that, unfortunately, don't work quite right. The first elbow coming off the muffler is bent at a 90 degree angle; the correct, original pipe is bent at more than 90 degrees. This makes a big difference in trying to fit the elbows without rubbing on the bodywork or the bumper guards. Secondly, the clamps generally do not tighten enough. I don't know if the correct factory parts are still available, but I strongly recommend staying away from the current elbow kits until they are redesigned properly.

Vol. 11, No. 5 Vic Skirmants

Exhaust Leaks

Rick Veneski, Norfolk, MA, has a problem and a tip. His 356 has started backfiring through the exhaust on rapid deceleration. The loudness of the bang increases proportionally to the engine speed. This problem is almost always indicative of a leak somewhere in the exhaust system. Even a pinhole can permit fresh air to be drawn in to mix with the excess hydrocarbons,

resulting in an "external" combustion engine.

Vol. 14, No. 4 Vic Skirmants

Why Torches and Exhaust Pipes Don't Mix

Occasionally hearing about people having garage fires makes me somewhat cautious in making certain no hot parts lie around without supervision after welding. Recently I was repairing a set of J-pipes by welding on a new pipe to the old curved section. After welding, I kept getting a burning smell from the pipes long after a reasonable time for cooling had passed. What was happening was that the thirty years' accumulation of carbon in the original curved section of pipe was slowly smoldering away. I finally realized what was happening when the "fire-line" finally advanced to the port-end of the pipe and I could see the thin red line of advancing combustion. So, be careful when welding on used exhaust pipes.

Another exhaust story. I had a customer tow his car in with a rather loud knocking noise. Having rebuilt the engine last year, and having a big-enough ego to not expect failure this early, I did not expect a bottom end problem. I did check the dipstick for oil and looked inside the oil filter for signs of "gold" on top of the filter element. The customer did mention that the knock developed immediately after being taken to a muffler shop for custom modification of a perfectly good Bursch system to look like a twin-exhaust special. Suspecting abuse at the hands of the muffler shop personnel, I began looking for bent exhaust valves by checking for excess valve lash. I didn't find any, but did notice a definite resistance to number two cylinder's upward travel. The engine became very difficult to turn past top-dead-center for either #2 or #4 cylinder. Since the noise came from the right side, it seemed that something had gotten inside #2 cylinder and was being squashed between the piston and cylinder head. The spark plug showed no damage, so whatever was in there was stuck to the piston or head, and not bouncing around. Of course, the engine had to come out, and the right head had to come off. Inside the cylinder were a couple of strange pieces of metal that I couldn't identify at first. Closer inspection showed them to be pieces of slag created when an oxy-acetylene torch is used to cut off metal; the pieces matched perfectly with the larger piece I had found in the carb pre-heater opening of the heater flapper box! The air cleaner had not been off the engine; how did these pieces get in there? Very simple. At the muffler shop, instead of simply unbolting the old muffler, they torched it off at the pipes, then unbolted the pipes. While torching the pipes, the exhaust valve for #2 cylinder was open. The flying slag went into the cylinder, and voila! Bad knock! Luckily the piston and cylinder head were only slightly marked, and inspection of the rod bearing showed no damage.

For many years I have used shop towels or other suitable materials to plug the intake ports in the heads, intake manifolds, and finally the carbs when assembling an engine. I don't want to take any chances of something falling into the cylinder. Very few things upset me more than seeing an engine sitting around with naked carbs or heads, just waiting for a stray metal object to fall in undetected. As a result of the above episode, I will now make more of an effort at plugging up the exhaust ports as well.

Oil System

Vol. 3, No. 3 Vic Skirmants

Rapid Cool Oil Cooler
I have had no experience with the "Rapid-Cool" on a Porsche. I have one on my VW camper, and according to the oil temperature gauge, it seems to help. Of course the latest factory oil cooler for 356s is a lot more effective than a VW cooler. Does anyone have any first-hand experience with this?

Vol. 5, No. 6 Vic Skirmants

Oil Pressure Relief Valve
When rebuilding an engine, you should always pull the oil pressure relief valve plunger and oil by-pass valve plunger in the timing cover to clean them. If either one is stuck, take a $1/4$ in. pipe tap and screw it into the open end of the plunger. Turn the tap until the plunger breaks loose, and then use the tap to pull out the plunger.

Vol. 6, No. 1 Vic Skirmants

Crank Pulley Oil Leaks
Do you ever get a slight trace of oil leakage from under the crankshaft pulley bolt and washer? I don't mean an oil drip, but a definite radial seepage caused by centrifugal force when the engine is running. Yes, that's what those little radial tracks of oil are on your pulley. The oil is escaping between the nose of the crankshaft and the pulley, then coming out under the pulley bolt washer. This is not a very common problem, and hardly that terrible when it does occur, but it can be annoying to someone whose engine is dry and spotless otherwise (someone must have one of those).

The fix is extremely simple. After removing the pulley bolt, (that's the hardest part), run a bead of silicone rubber sealant around the end of the crank, between it and the pulley. While on pulleys, be sure to check yours when rebuilding the engine.

Aside from the usual check of the pulley seal surface for excessive grooving, look very carefully for cracks. The most common area is at one of the corners of the keyway slot, at the seal end. This can happen on the two-hole or four-hole pulleys. Also on the four-hole pulley, check for cracks between adjacent holes. Not very common, but it can be unnerving if it breaks.

Vol. 6, No. 3 Vic Skirmants

Oil Pump
First, the oil pump cover. The oil pump cover is located to the timing cover by two diagonally opposed dowel pins, and held down by three 6 mm nuts and one 6 mm bolt. The dowels ensure that the pump cover is lined up properly with the timing cover so there is no side load on the oil pump gear shafts. Changing one of the components, such as the timing cover or the oil pump cover could cause a binding on the gears. The way to check for this is to assemble the oil pump gears, gasket and pump cover on the timing cover before it is installed on the engine case. After assembly, rotate the oil pump gear from the inside using only your fingers. If it rotates freely, you're all set. If it is hard to turn, disassemble, pull the two dowel pins out of the cover. Now reassemble with only finger pressure on the holddown nuts. Rotate the gear and tap the pump cover in different directions with a soft hammer or screw-driver handle until the gears rotate freely. Now torque down the nuts. This procedure was first suggested to me by John O'Steen of Cincinnati. When installing a timing cover with the oil pump pre-assembled, be sure the cam drive slot lines up with the pump drive tang.

Vol. 8, No. 3 Vic Skirmants

Installing Later-Style Oil Pressure/ Temperature Senders on a 1955 - 1957 3-Piece Case Engine
If you have a 1955 - 1957 engine case and would like it to look like a later one in the area of the oil pressure

sender, or if you can't find a replacement oil line to the filter and would like to convert to a later one, have I got a mod for you! First off, however, this might not work unless you've converted to Zenith, 40 P II Solex or Weber carburetors and no longer have the sideways carburetor linkage necessary for the single-barrel Solexes. I haven't checked, but I'm not sure if there is room for the single-barrel Solex carburetor linkage and the later-style oil temperature and oil pressure sender block. Anyway, if you do want to convert and have all the pieces, you've already discovered that the hollow bolt that screws into the case on the 1958 - 1969 engines is much larger than the hole in the 1955 - 1957 case. Big deal! Drill and tap to a 12 x 1.5 mm and install everything as if it were a later case. Now you even have a second oil temperature sender!

Vol. 11, No. 6 David Seeland

Enhanced Oil System, I
The stock system is elegantly simple and reliable and does an admirable job in most circumstances. So, why mess with a good thing? There are three problems with the stock oil system in pushrod engines: 1) oil surge and the attendant oil pressure problem; 2) incomplete oil filtering by a bypass oil filter; 3) high oil temperature under full load at high ambient temperatures. All of these problems were solved by the factory with the introduction of the four-cam engine in 1955. There were only 1317 four-cam cars built so I won't suggest an engine swap, but there are some not-too-expensive fixes for the pushrod engine oil system problems.
First, let's look at the oil surge problem in the pushrod 356 engine because dirty oil or hot oil are secondary problems compared to no oil. Although Ludvigsen said that the factory determined that a 356 could corner at 0.83 g, probably on rock-hard

stop-tread Michelin X's, "street" tire technology has advanced much of late Yokohama now has dry/intermediate/wet DOT legal "street" tires available! Today's high performance tires result in high forces that create an oil surge problem, laterally under cornering forces, and longitudinally under braking forces. Flat opposed engines are prone to oil surge because if the crank is to be at axle height the oil "pan" must be broad and shallow because the engine is short and because of the need for adequate ground clearance. Porsche realized this and dry sumped (a narrow, deep external oil tank, pressure and scavenge pumps) the four-cam 356 and the 911 engines.

An even earlier factory solution to oil surge problems was the deep-sump found on 1500-S two-piece case engines in 1952 on both the 356 SL (aluminum body Gmünd coupes raced by the factory) and the America Roadster. This sump was the size and shape of a finned Carrera GT 60 mm brake drum. The deep sump bolted to the bottom of the engine at the oil screen access hole. Two types were made. The 356SL sump had the oil screen at the bottom. The America Roadster type left the oil screen in its original position on the engine case and had a single drain plug in the bottom.

Two types of after market deep sumps are (or were) available for 3-piece-case engines. Performance Products sold the first type that was the size of the sump plate (3 x 6 inches), a couple of inches deep, and used a piece of hose to extend the oil pick-up tube. I had one made at a local machine shop for about $30. I supplied the aluminum block and made long studs from metric threaded rod. The second type is the "VW" type which is a large finned casting about the size of the case in plan view and maybe 2 1/2 or 3 inches deep. Automotion and J.C. Whitney sell these. Keith Ingram of Clovis, New Mexico found that his Speedster's oil pressure was

dropping to zero on corners in track driving. He added a VW type deep sump and no longer has oil pressure problems. He doesn't run a lot of negative camber and hasn't had ground clearance problems yet.

Deep sumps have a serious ground clearance problem (unless the 356 engine is in a VW bus). At the 1986 Down East Porsche Parade in Portland, "Fast Eddie's" 356A coupe had a deep sump and probably 3° of negative rear camber. He said it touched the pavement occasionally on the bumpy asphalt of the rally route (he also beat me by 3 seconds in the auto-cross–so either my car needs Yokohama 001R's or more negative camber, or most likely, a better driver). A local driver tore a Performance Products style deep sump loose in an off-track excursion. I also have a recollection of reading about a factory rally car that lost its oil at a railroad crossing – a deep sump wasn't mentioned but I suspect it had one. Both type of deep sumps have a clearance problem and I think the smaller one has a capacity problem. I worry about how long $1/16$ of a gallon can supply oil to a pump that is pumping many (?) gallons per minute. Maybe a second or two, maybe less. Sixty miles per hour is 88 ft/sec. What happens in a 300 foot (3 second) curve? I worried enough about this problem that I never used my small deep sump.

Mark Eskuche of Ecurie Engineering, (414) 271-2929, now makes an $1/8$ in. steel plate sump guard that is nearly bomb-proof. It is used by many vintage racers. Its only drawback seems to be expense – September 1994

A "no-cost" improvement (but not fix) is to overfill the crankcase by about two-thirds of the distance between the two marks on the dip stick. This has to help some and seems to be what most autocrossers do. But, Keith Ingram, who is a good enough driver to watch his oil pressure gauge in corners, found his oil pressure dropped to zero in spite of an extra quart of oil.

Warren Holcomb of Evergreen, CO who went to the Runoffs at Road Atlanta this year has a dry-sump set up on his Speedster that he had a machinist make and which has been very effective. Leo Droughton explains his method of dry-sumping a 356 on p. 8-10 of *Upfixing Vol.. V.* Dry sumping a 912 was explained in a two-part series in *Hot VW's.* All of these setups involve substantial machining, complexity and cost. A fourth dry-sump set up is possible only if you have an early 1955-1957.5 engine with the removable pump. Steve Ruddock of German Precision in Boulder, CO adapted a VW dry sump pump (look through old *Hot VW's* magazines for a pump source) to one of these engines with a removable VW type pump.

If not a deep sump or a dry sump what then? After reading Craig Richter's *How to Make an Old Porsche Fly* I decided I had to have an Accusump. An Accusump is a 4 inch diameter, 2 foot long cylindrical tank with an "O"-ringed piston, air on one side that acts as a spring and oil on the engine side. Engine oil pressure pushes the piston against the air. If the engine loses oil pressure the oil, routed in the proper direction by a one-way valve, supplies oil to the bearings (Fig. 1).

I have a 3 quart Accusump which will put out about 2 quarts of oil depending on how much the Accusump is pre-pressurized with air. If the Accusump is pre-pressurized to 8 psi on the air side of the piston, then the minimum pressure as the last of the 2 quarts of oil flows to the bearings is 8 psi.

I bought a used Accusump, but new ones are available for about $150. It will need a shut off valve which can be electrically or manually operated. The valve is used to keep the extra 2 quarts of oil in the Accusump from going back into the engine when the engine is shut off. If the valve is opened on the pressurized Accusump on starting, start-up wear is minimized. Opening the valve is most easily accomplished electrically, but a cable might be rigged up to operate the mechanical valve. Racers have it easier, most mount the Accusump in the passenger seat area. In a street-driven car the shelf behind the engine is the best place for the Accusump. If you find a used Accusump, beware

Normal, No-Surge Situation

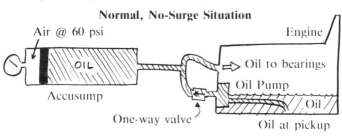

Oil-Surge Situation, Cornering or Braking

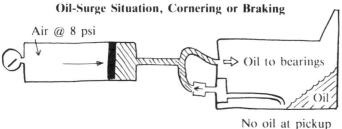

Figure 1. Accusump operation.

of the earlier ones (without the cast aluminum ends) because they had a strength problem and in some cases would fail.

Access to pressurized oil is through the oil pump cover (easier if you have an electric tach). Ray Litz (Competition Engineering) modifies both types of Covers. I had a friend heliarc a block of aluminum on mine which I then drilled and tapped. I used a 45° "elbow" AN10 (0.47 inch i.d.) out of the pump cover to clear the collector on my extractor exhaust. A stock muffler might require a 90° elbow or a bit of muffler modification for clearance. If you can, avoid the cast elbows that lack a smoothly radiused tube because they restrict the flow of oil. My friend with the heliarc said that he would have bought an aluminum elbow and heliarced that directly into the pump cover. I tapped the cover because I wanted to be able to plug the cover and return to a stock configuration.

Modified covers are available from Competition Engineering. Although you may be tempted to install the modified cover without removing the third member of the case, don't. You must be able to fiddle with the cover position (remove the locating pins) until free movement of the pump gears is obtained. Heliarcing the cover will distort it and it must be flattened. I used 80 grit wet-or-dry paper lubricated with WD-40 on my tablesaw table to flatten the cover.

Mike Forster used a modified oil pump cover to add an external cooler and had intermittent oil pressure failure. My guess is that his gears were binding and that the drive gear spun occasionally on its shaft. Some gears are keyed to the shaft – the shaft slides out easily. Others, and I'm guessing here, don't slide off the shaft and appear to be an interference fit. I used keyed gears because after flattening the cover, the recess in the cover that the outboard end of the shaft turns in was too shallow and the gear was held

away from the inside of the cover. End clearances on the gears must be minimal for good oil pressure. Just be sure to check and if you have the same problem and don't have an oil pump gear collection, grind down the end of the shaft.

The oil gallery in the timing gear cover on the outlet side of the pump must be plugged if all the oil is to flow out through the modified cover. A $3/8$ inch pipe plug is too big. The walls of the oil gallery are thin and could break using a $3/8$ inch pipe plug. Use a $1/2$ inch long section of a $9/16$ inch x 18 pitch bolt. Slot the end for a large screwdriver blade. Carefully tap the case and insert the plug using Loctite.

The oil returns on the left side of the timing gear cover at a $1/2$ inch diameter boss having an aluminum plug in a horizontal gallery. Drill and tap the plug for a 6 mm x 1.0 pitch threaded rod. Take a one foot section of the rod with a couple of nuts and washers at one end, then remove the sliding weight from a slide hammer, slide it on the rod, thread it into the plug and extract with a few taps against the washers and nuts. Drill ($9/16$ in.) and tap ($3/8$ in. pipe) the gallery. If you drill and tap it at the slightest upward angle, the fitting and hose will clear the top of the left heater box and you will avoid having to recess the top of the heater box. Do not seal the fitting into the case with teflon tape. you will increase your chances of cracking the case. Pipe threads seal by mechanical deformation. The fitting is trying to expand the aluminum case and what you want is flow, not failure, so take it easy. Better to have to retighten or reseal the joint than break the third member of the case.

I used Parker reusable fittings and hose because of Warren Holcomb's generosity (SCCA rules now require steel reinforced hose and the steel braid must be external). Similar fittings in steel or aluminum are available from Aeroquip. Steel is stronger, cheaper, heavier, and doesn't come in blue or red. Hose covered by braided steel is good to use near exhaust systems. Elsewhere rubber covered, steel reinforced hose is adequate. I'm using Parker 231 hose which is reinforced only with fabric because it was a gift and trouble-free on Warren's E Production Speedster. Use nothing smaller than dash 10 hose, 0.56 inches i.d.

Don't use barbed fittings and hose clamps, they are cheap but don't flow as much oil and are failure prone. Do everything you can to make oil system modification reliable or stick with the stock system. Several information bulletins, numbers 5942, 5978, and 5872 are available from Aeroquip Corporation, Jackson, Michigan 49203. Phone (517) 787-8121. Your local hot-rod shop will stock or have access to an Accusump and installation kits, including the one-way valve.

Vol. 12, No. 1 David Seeland

Enhanced Oil System, II

In "Part 1" some of the cures for the no oil pressure problem that can result from oil surge induced by acceleration (maybe), deceleration, or cornering were discussed and I concluded that an Accusump (oil accumulator) was the best solution. William Gordon of San Antonio wrote questioning the complications of the Accusump. He is right of course. Parts you don't have won't fail (and don't cost anything), but complications can be entertaining and beneficial. A 100 horsepower 1500 four-cam engine is certainly more complex, and less reliable than a 100 horsepower pushrod engine, but the four-cam engine is more entertaining. An Accusump is definitely overkill (but entertaining overkill) for the street and provides instant oil pressure which greatly reduces cold-start scuffing, the cause of much, or even most, engine wear. If you drive your 356 on a track or in autocrosses, its engine

will definitely be more reliable and last longer with the Accusump. Other questions in the letter referred to "longer pushrod tubes," the S-90 oil pickup and ball-check valve covers.

Pushrod Porsche engines have long had pushrod tubes that extended an inch or so past the crankcase wall into the engine. The idea being that during hard cornering, more of the oil would remain in the case in the vicinity of the oil pick-up instead of going up the tubes into the valve covers.

These have recently become available for VWs which normally have pushrod tubes that ended at the crankcase wall. The Super-90 oil pickup was designed to move the oil pickup point toward the sloshed oil. A good idea, but they often stuck. If you have one, it is best kept in a cardboard box, *not* in your engine.

Ball-check valve covers were designed to keep more of the oil inside the engine. They may help some, but they are not a lot less leaky than the early covers with the screen "sock" over the breather hole.

Larry Skoglund called to explain some of the oil system modifications he makes to 356s that are vintage raced. His tips have been incorporated in the remainder of this series of articles.

To get down to business, what about filters? Does your pushrod 356 have both full flow and by-pass filters? If this were a tech quiz you'd probably answer "false" and you'd have made a mistake. The bypass filter is on the fan shroud, the full-flow filter is the window screen around the oil pickup. This illustrates the importance of the design of the filter. It must filter out very small particles to be effective. Because the sump screen filters out only large rocks it is not very effective even though it really is a full flow filter.

Is the bypass filter enough? Bill Fisher in the book *How to Hotrod Volkswagen Engines* published by

H.P. Books (Buy one, you'll learn a lot) quotes a Ford Motor Company study on oil filtering published as an SAE paper: in a comparison of bypass versus full flow filtering, the following wear reductions were observed when a full flow filter was used: 50 percent, crankshaft; 66 percent, wristpin; 19 percent cylinder wall; and 52 percent, rings. Considering these, can you really afford not to have a full-flow filter? I've seen 356 engines where each indentation on the top of the rocker stand had its own sand accumulation. I suppose it originated from the road dirt that collected at the valve cover-head joint and fell into the engine each time the valves were adjusted. How much more fell into the head and was circulated through the engine before it went into the bypass filter and was trapped? What about dirt or metal particles introduced by a rebuild that was not quite meticulous enough? Did you clean the passages in the rocker arms of all the bearing particles that last time you rebuilt your engine after that rod bearing went out?

Did you wash those new barrels with hot soapy water until they were completely clean? Was there any dust in your oil can spout? I doubt if any rebuilt or new engine was ever completely clean on assembly. The engine as it runs and wears produces its own abrasive particles: carbon, brass from the distributor drive gear, camshaft, and lifter pieces. All this circulating garbage produces even more abrasive particles.

Enough of the scare tactics, you say, I've heard of 356s that went 200,000 miles before they were rebuilt. That's true, but maybe that engine would have gone 300,000 miles with a full flow filter (if the crank didn't break first). The crank in my Corvair engine (in my VW bus) has more than 175,000 miles and probably does not need grinding (it was perfect at 100,000 miles). VW type four-914 engines with more than 100,000 miles commonly have unworn cranks. All these engines have full flow filters. Cranks in full-flow filtered 911 engines also show little wear at high mileages. Most 356 cranks that I've seen have needed regrinding at the first overhaul.

Filter choices are restricted because oil pressure at the pump outlet are very high. My engine pegs a 160 psi gauge at the pump outlet on a 60°F morning start with 20-50 oil! Vic Skirmants said that he heard of someone with a VW-engined dune buggy who put a gauge at the pump outlet and found that the oil pressure pegged a 700 psi gauge! Larry suggests the use of 10-30 for better oil flow unless the engine is over 140 hp or the ambient temperature is over 80°F.

Mecca makes an expensive canister-type filter for race cars (Larry suggests that you get their informative oil-system catalog: Mecca Development, Route 41, Sharon, CT). A Fram HP-1 filter is O.K. but costs seven or eight dollars. I recommend the Oberg filter with a reusable filter screen, about $60 from Oberg USA, 4840 Mill Street, #1, Reno, NV 89502, (800) 992-2202, and other suppliers. It has a sensor and a dash light that tells you when oil is being bypassed and therefore when it should be cleaned. It filters out smaller particles and has a lower pressure drop than the HP-1 according to Craig Richter (*How to Make an Old Porsche Fly*). To my mind, one of the major benefits appears to be the ability to inspect the debris on the screen for both quantity and source. This may be the reason Porsche never used a throw-away filter cartridge on the four-cam engine and a point to consider if you are thinking of converting your four-cam to a spin-on filter. I'm going to use an Oberg on my 2-liter.

Vic has noticed that even the Oberg filter halves start to bulge on his "G" car, for some reason). He said that he just keeps his race cars running ("idles") and warms them up until he can rev them to 3000 without the Oberg by-pass light coming on. Then they can be driven.

Richter says the Oberg filter bypass valve "will never bypass the oil with reasonable maintenance." The movement of the bypass valve closes the contact for the dash light, so if the dash light comes on, some of the oil is bypassing the filter screen. The light will also come on with cold oil on start up, even with a clean filter. Maybe not in sunny California, but for the rest of us unfortunates it will come on, showing that oil is being bypassed. However, this occurs in all "full-flow" filters but we just don't have any way to tell when it occurs. The Oberg probably bypasses less oil under similar conditions.

Now for the plumbing. The $9/16$ inch bolt plug for the original oil pump outlet is present (see part 1 for details, Vol. 11, No. 6). The pump outlet for a transistor-tach car has no tach drive. If you want to use a mechanical tach drive, Ray Litz at Competition Engineering can modify your oil pump cover.

The oil returns to the case at the boss on the left side of the timing gear cover of the case. Do not use barbed fittings (50 psi max working pressure according to an Aeroquip catalog). Use Aeroquip fittings and dash ten (10/16 I.D.) hose. Although I am currently using fabric reinforced hose (maximum burst pressure is 1000 psi, working pressure is 250 psi), Vic's 700 psi figure has me worried and I'm going to convert to a steel reinforced hose (5000 psi burst pressure and 1250 psi working pressure). No oil pressure is a lot worse than dirty oil so be sure any modification of the stock oil system is as reliable as you can make it or stick with the stock system.

Although it may be appealing to mount the Oberg filter in a vertical position, don't do it. Larry says the oil screen will slide down out of position

on reassembly after cleaning and not only will it leak, but you'll need a new screen. Mount the latter horizontally to avoid this problem. Mount the filter on a vertical aluminum plate attached to the body by the left rear bumper bracket bolts, and be sure it is in a position so that the screen can be easily removed for cleaning. If you are just adding a filter, the line from the filter outlet goes to the left side of the timing gear cover. This hole is tapped ($3/8$ in. pipe, again, see part 1 for details) for the oil return line.

Vol. 12, No. 2 David Seeland

Enhanced Oil System, III
First, some "oil" comments from Registry members. Bart Bartholomew called from California. The engine in his 1960 cabriolet has 330,000 total miles on an unground crank and about 205,000 miles since its "C" engine was rebuilt (NPR 1720, Isky cam). The "C" engine had 125,000 miles on it when he rebuilt it 14 years ago. It was balanced very carefully and assembled using standard rod and main bearings. He has changed the 10 W-40 Valvoline oil every 5000 miles – whenever the second digit on the odometer is five or zero – a handy way to keep track of oil changes. He also has used a Frantz oil filter in series with the original filter. You do know about the space-age material that the Franz uses for a filter element don't you? Toilet paper! His cab gets a new roll every 5000 miles (and hang the expense!) and the downstream stock filter gets changed every 10,000 miles. Of course, this is still a bypass system, and a full flow system would theoretically be superior.

I also received a letter from Harlan Halsey, a long time 356 owner who successfully follows the adage that "oil is cheap." He changed the oil in his 1600S engine every 1000 miles during the 60s and every 2000 miles during the 70s. The engine was disas-

139

sembled at 96,000 miles (accident) and the crank measured on the high side of standard. It now has 150,000 miles. He changed oil every 2000 miles in his SC and at 148,000 miles the crank was still within specs. He points out that with care the original oil filter system is okay for a street machine.

Leo Droughton who built a successful dry-sump system and was mentioned in my October 1986 column in the *Registry* wrote: "The oil pump gears, yes, some are keyed, some are pressed onto a knurled section of the shaft (which I theorized might slip under heavy loads – i.e. cold oil). The knurl is approximately 11 mm in length. An often overlooked component is the bearing diameter of the drive gear shaft, mechanical tach gears can be pushed apart, sleeved with stainless steel, sized, and the gear pushed back on the shaft."

"Machining on my dry-sump system is nil, cost was for the Ford oil pump, heliarc and for hose and fittings. Your comment about not using barbed fittings and clamps is well taken. On the dry-sump system -10 (10/ 16 in.) hose is used for the by-pass relief valve and for the scavenge and supply lines, -12 hose. For the oil cooler, which is picked off under the stock oil cooler, - 6 is used. After the *Panorama* article on the dry-sump system was written, a thermostat was added."

"The system that I wrote about eons ago was duplicated on a 356C used for autocrossing. Both systems are still in operation on the street car with a 7200 rpm redline, and on the race car with a 7600 rpm redline. Under no circumstances has there been a failure of the oil system or its components. Even the hex to square coupling shaft that I thought could cause problems because of loading due to RPM changes has been trouble-free; polished yes, broken or twisted, no."

"People that overfill with engine oil to help alleviate oil pick-up problems are doing incredible things to internal engine stresses. *Windage!* At the RPM and velocities involved with the rotating/reciprocating masses and the mass of the oil, we are talking about trying to move solid steel through concrete. The horsepower losses are phenomenal. Deep sumpers out here (west coast SCCA) underfill by one quart and have external coolers and Accusumps."

Oil Coolers

The final step after oil pressure and cleanliness are assured (covered in parts one and two of this series), is oil temperature control. Why would it be necessary to modify and complicate the oiling system that is now so neatly contained within your 356s fan shroud and crankcase? Only if your type of driving and climate result in oil temperatures that lie far enough outside the ideal 176°F to 220°F range that it causes you concern. If the oil temperature remains less than 176°F, friction losses are higher and moisture builds up in the oil. If oil temperatures rise above 220°F, oxidation degrades the oil, the viscosity of the oil decreases resulting in decreased load bearing ability with possible metal-to-metal contact. Larry Skoglund says Hank Godfredson's vintage racer, a push-rod-engined right-hand-drive 356A Carrera coupe, puts out 114 horsepower on a "conservative" dyno and doesn't need auxiliary cooling (1720 NPR, Elgin cam, headwork). My stock 1600SC engine runs the temperature gauge nearly to the peg on 90 plus days on the track. Larry suggests that I check the sender/gauge combination by immersing the sender in boiling (212°F at sea level) water. He pointed out that the original sender/ gauge combination was calibrated but that nobody has the original pair in their car any more.

The racing experience of Bill Randle suggests that a stock 1600S engine can't be run hard enough to hurt it.

After a dozen races in the 1956 Speedster that he bought new and raced in nearly stock form in SCCA events in the late fifties, he tore down the engine only to find no appreciable wear anywhere. The oil temperature gauge read "very high" during races but was ignored.

Richard von Frankenberg in a *Christophorus/Panorama* (Vol.. 6, No. 1, Jan. 1961) exposition on 356 oil says the following about oil temperatures: "In summer when the car is being pushed, eventual temperatures rising to between 110°C (225°F) and 130°C (266°F) no damage can be done. Probably not up to 140°C (248°F) either. What bothers me far more are the too low temperatures in fall and winter. Under 40 C (104°F) I get very careful. There, I principally don't turn over 3500 rpm. On the other hand, not under 2000."

Remote coolers, even if not necessary for temperature control, can help alleviate problems with cooler breakage or cracking of the case in the cooler mount area. Bill Fisher *(How to Hotrod VW Engines)* says that if a VW engine/transmission has solid mounts (as mine has), the vibration will eventually break off the oil cooler mounting ears. My cooler hasn't failed yet, but I'm worrying. But, if the stock cooler is removed, and you rely on a front mounted pair of coolers, what happens to the oil temperature if you're stuck in a slow moving traffic jam? More worry. This is the set up with a 4-cam engine, but it has a dry-oil (more mass to heat) so the oil-temperature rise time is slower.

The high-mileage engines and the oil-temperature anecdotes will probably cause all but the most die-hard tinkerers (or worriers) to say "Why worry?" and turn the page. For the tinkerer/worrier contingent let's take a look at temperature control methods and hardware. We need two devices: a heat exchanger (oil cooler), and a thermostat, plus the plumbing to connect them and the engine.

According to the Maestro, the early oil cooler has a surface area of about 144 square inches and the late cooler has an area of 560 square inches. I don't know how to equate coolers of different designs but cooler size (area) adequate for a Carrera 2 should be adequate for almost all pushrod 356 engines. These are 9 in. by 3 in. by 3.25 in. and constructed like a late 356 cooler and the pair of coolers have a volume (which should be proportional to area because of the similar construction) of 175.5 cubic inches compared to the stock cooler's 49.5 cubic inches. A local 356 with a high-compression racing-piston 1720 set-up and no stock cooler uses a "flat-plate" 72 plate 132 cubic inch cooler (8" x 11" x $1/2$", no. 35-6018, $62.95 from Small Car Specialities) mounted in the horn location in the left front fender. Larry Skoglund recommends a pair of 914/VW type 4 coolers to which fittings have been welded in the front fenders. They should be plumbed in parallel (as in a Carrera 2) because the rate of heat transfer from oil to air is greater with a larger temperature differential. There are other high quality filters, such as the Harrison, available. Talk to your local SCCA racer or write for some race oil system catalogs – Mecca, Earls.

I now have a single Carrera 2 cooler behind the left rear wheel that is plumbed in series with an Oberg and an Accusump. The result is some lowering of the oil temperature (2/3 scale max) but this setup needs an oil thermostat for street use in the winter and could use more air-flow. Ron LaDow is using a similar set up, but he has cut air exit holes in the fender for more air flow. Some Carrera GT Speedsters have a pair of "early" stock 356 coolers mounted on aluminum manifold blocks behind the horn grilles, others have a pair in the right rear fender well behind the wheel.

Thermostat

The coolers must be sized to cool the engine in the most severe conditions, which means that under less severe conditions the oil would be overcooled. This means we must control the flow rate through the coolers with a thermostat. Larry pointed out that the desired oil temperature is 180°F and an engine is down 10 percent on horsepower at both 200° and 150°F. Even if you don't fiddle with your oil system at all, find out where 180° is on your unmarked gauge and try to keep it near there next time you autocross and have about 10 free, legal, horsepower that you wouldn't have had if the oil temperature was 150°F or less.

I bought a "Perma-cool" remote oil thermostat (about $25) but ran out of time and didn't install it (Fig. 1). El and C1 are always connected. When the oil is below 170°F all four ports are connected internally. As the temperature rises, El - C1 and E2 - C2 become separated and oil flows through the cooler. This is typical of all thermostats and it is important to note that a thermostat does not reduce cooler pressure (160 psi plus in this set-up). This is not good and I wish I knew why the pressure relief valve doesn't relieve this pressure. I suspect resistance to flow in the cooler and filter. Larry Skoglund had a far superior thermostat housing, which is unfortu-

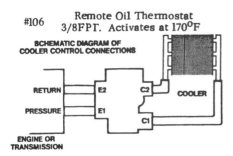

#106   Remote Oil Thermostat
3/8FPT. Activates at 170°F

SCHEMATIC DIAGRAM OF
COOLER CONTROL CONNECTIONS

RETURN   E2   C2   COOLER
PRESSURE   E1
   C1
ENGINE OR
TRANSMISSION

Figure 1 — Perma-cool oil thermostat. Four port design appears to block off cooler from high-pressure (cold) oil, but doesn't. Same internally as 3-port thermostats.

nately no longer available. It was a machined block of aluminum that could be mounted right on top of an Oberg filter with a 1 in. piece of pipe (or elsewhere) and took the reliable trouble-free 911 thermostat. The threaded oil line holes were much bigger than those in the Perma-cool thermostat.

Plumbing

The major plumbing decision is where to pick up and return the oil. Because of the high pressures that seem to occur in the filter circuit fed directly from the oil pump, I tend to favor the use of the stock oil cooler inlet and outlet on top of the case for the auxiliary cooler(s).

There is a newly available aftermarket VW adapter that fits between the stock cooler and the case and allows another cooler to be plumbed in series (I think, but it could be a parallel outlet) with the stock cooler. (Available from Johnny's Speed and Chrome, a hot VW supplier). Fan shroud clearance problems at the top of the cooler will occur because it is about an inch thick, but the interfering vane can be cut away.

Other types of aftermarket VW cooler replacement adapters that replace the stock cooler come in two port (remote cooler and/or filter), no port (cooler after an added external oil pump outlet) or one port (an alternative inlet for oil that left the pump cover). Any of these adapters will have to be modified slightly to fit the 356 because the VW bolt pattern is slightly different.

Don't be tempted to use a VW outlet block under the stock cooler for a filter. This would be ideal, but its not quite a full flow system. Why? Because the cooler bypass valve would become a filter bypass valve when the oil is cold or filter is clogged.

Vic Skirmants said he uses a 2-port VW adapter and puts a bolt under the oil cooler by-pass piston so that "all the oil goes through the cooler and filter." I assume this meant he had the filter on the same circuit as the cooler. The filter should be upstream from the cooler – hot oil, less pressure drop – so that shouldn't be the cause of the ruptured cooler in his 'G' car but may not have been part of the problem. I'd try larger hoses for less flow resistance before I'd make the cooler bypass valve inoperative.

Leo Droughton in a December 1980 *Panorama* article (also *Up - fixin, Vol.. 5,* p. 17) details the installation of a pair of front-fender mounted 912 coolers. The oil comes out from a drilled aluminum block that fits between the stock cooler and crankcase. The extra pair of coolers are in series with each other and are in parallel with respect to the stock cooler. This arrangement allows the front coolers to have a shut-off valve for use in cold weather. Droughton protected the oil lines by running them through the gearshift tunnel, an excel-

lent idea. Any oil system additions must be 100 percent reliable or you may end up facing an engine rebuild.

Droughton uses dash six hose (about $3/8$ in. i.d.) which I think is much too small. I would use dash ten (about $5/8$ in.) hose. The front coolers should also be in parallel rather than in series for maximum effectiveness – the efficiency of a given cooler being a function of the air-oil temperature difference. I also think that the parallel relationship between the front coolers and the stock cooler would favor flow through the stock cooler and limit the contribution of the auxiliary coolers (particularly if dash six hose is used). One final point, Larry Skoglund suggests not bolting the coolers down as Leo does, but allowing them to "float", decreasing the possibility of cooler failure by fracture.

The "ideal" oil system

I think an ideal oil cooling system (Fig. 2) which I intend to install in my "new" Roadster, would be the "series

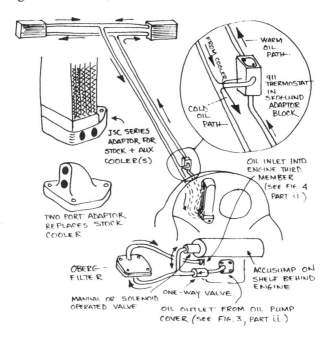

Figure 2 — A vintage race-time trial-drivers school oil system (or maximum complexity for the street!).

type" VW adapter between the stock cooler and the block with a fender mounted parallel-plumbed pair of coolers (or a single cooler) controlled by a 911 thermostat in a "Skoglund" housing. If traffic jams are no problem, the "two port" VW adapter replacing the stock cooler would simplify the system slightly and allow the use of solid engine mounts (use an air restrictor in place of the stock cooler as shown by Craig Richter in *How to Make an Old Porsche Fly*). A full-flow Oberg filter and a solenoid-valve electrically controlled Accusump would complete the oil system (see parts one and two of this series).

Plumb everything with metal braid reinforced Aeroquip hose using as few right angle fittings as possible and you'll have a system that will provide your engine with a continuous supply of clean oil at the ideal temperature. It won't be cheap, but your engine will love it!

Vol. 12, No. 3 Vic Skirmants

Windage!

Dave Seeland's column on oil systems has a comment that always raises my hackles; whatever they are. I just have to challenge Leo Droughton's claim of high oil level in a 356 engine causing terrible windage losses. That statement is true for an engine where the crankshaft is on the "bottom" and the crank journals can "hit" the oil when the level is too high.

Since our engines are "upside-down," crank on top cam on the bottom, just take a look inside the engine case and see where the oil level is in relation to the camshaft. Even if the cam does hit the oil, it's only going half as fast as the crankshaft and those little lobes aren't going to cause much "windage." I don't recommend going way over the mark, but I do believe in checking the oil level in a competition-bound engine when it's running and keeping the level at the top mark.

I have seen engines blown up because someone thought they'd gain some horsepower by running a lower level; *Bunk!* Anyway, I just couldn't resist re-stating Leo's claim that the California boys are a quart low (yuk, yuk!).

I ran an S-90 pickup and Accusump for years and had no oil problems *except* under hard braking at two corners at Road America and Blackhawk Farms. Putting on a deep sump (the large one) finally cured that last problem. With a large deep-sump, there really isn't a need anymore for the Accusump. I do run a skid-plate under my deep-sump.

Also, the oil should go to the filter before it passes through anything else, especially the Accusump.

Vol. 13, No. 4 Vic Skirmants

Accusump Disclaimers

In spite of what the Accusump ads claim, it will not save a 356 engine that experiences more than a couple of seconds of oil pressure loss while under load. The other problem when using an Accusump is that the proper oil level can be elusive. If the oil is hot and the engine is idling, the pressure will be low. Shutting off the Accusump at this point will leave very little oil in the Accusump, therefore more will show up on the engine dipstick. You could be low on oil, and the dipstick says you're okay! I always tell racers to check their oil level with the engine running and fill it to the full mark. This is especially important if you're using an Accusump. In the hot engine example above, if the oil level is checked when cooled off, it will read full. Start the engine, open the Accusump, and the higher cold-oil pressure will fill the Accusump, thereby leaving less in the engine case. Now go out on the track and immediately wipe out your bearings. However, if you check the oil level with the engine running, you notice the need for more oil, and add same. No, there are no "windage" losses to worry about in a 356 engine! The crank is up high, not splashing around in the oil like on other engines.

Vol. 14, No. 3 Vic Skirmants

Replacement Oil Coolers
News flash! Oil coolers! I just ran into some interesting details on the replacement coolers. The ones I will discuss are all stamped 10/86 on the mounting flange by the 6 mm stud. What I have noticed, at least on the four in my possession, is that the mounting flange extends lower than the base of the cooler. This seems to be because the soft-mount cooler has a lower flange so someone has decided to make all the coolers with that flange, even though the hard mount cooler should have an even flange.

When this cooler is bolted down, the mismatched flange forces the cooler to tilt slightly toward the left. This actually caused one of the coolers to wear a hole in the top of one of the tubes where it had contacted the fan shroud. The flange is not easily bendable, so my solution is to space the left side of the cooler with a couple of washers over the 8 mm studs, between the cooler and the case. The stock oil seals seem to be fully capable of accommodating the slightly taller cooler mounting. Don't use the taller brown seals that come in the gasket kit! I haven't used these since I had one blow out on a month-old rebuild on a 912 with soft cooler mounts. I also do not soft-mount the coolers anymore! The soft cooler gets bolted down firmly with appropriate spacing. You also need to put washers over the bottom of the studs so that the cooler can be bolted down firmly.

Vol. 17, No. 5 Vic Skirmants

Why Not to Sandblast Your Oil Filler
I came across an interesting engine recently. Fresh rebuild, only several hundred miles, rod knock. Tear down revealed rod bearings worn to the copper and a crank that was worn about .015" under-size and oval. This engine started out with proper parts, as did another one I saw several years ago. Both engines were horribly worn, and both engines had one thing in common; pretty, shiny, powder-painted oil-filler cans. No, not oil filter, *oil-filler!* My theory: preparing oil-filler cans for painting, many people would sand-blast or bead-blast, then prep and paint. The problem here is that the sand- or glass-grit gets inside the can, sticking in the oily corners. This grit eventually comes loose and forms a grinding compound with the oil. Once the grinding starts, unless the oil is changed often, the partial-flow oil filtration system guarantees a geometric increase in wear as the additional particles join with the original grit and just grind away. Another pretty-it-up-item that scares the hell out of me is bead-blasting the case itself. Just picture all those little oil-system holes with grit in them!

Vol. 14, No. 3 Harry Kurrie

Temperature Switch Repair
Here's a fix for those of you with broken off electrical connector tangs on your oil temperature senders. I filed away the insulator, thereby exposing enough of the tang to reattach a wire. It's been working for over two years. I want to emphasize that you need to do it gently.

Vol. 10, No. 1 Richard Miller

Adjusting Early Pressure Switches
Transition from more costly screw type terminals to push ons or push ins, was probably part of plot to increase agency repair shop revenues. A recent article pointed out that early oil pressure switches had screw terminals for connecting indicator lamp wire. I'd

like to point out that real early oil pressure switches (like the "Messmer" unit alongside the Bosch in picture) were adjustable. Remove the terminal screw, which can be used to set the level at which the switch turns off. No fair buggering it to compensate for zilch oil pressure.

Vol. 3, No. 1 Vic Skirmants

Oil Change Interval
3000 miles is also my favorite time for an oil change. Drain it when warm, use a suction gun to draw the old oil out of the filter can, don't change the filter unless it has at least 6000 miles on it; it's a partial flow, so that means it doesn't do much anyway. Pull the plugs at 3000, check the compression if you have a gauge; the readings will be lower than you thought they should be, so don't worry about it unless one or two are way different than the others.

Vol. 3, No. 3 Vic Skirmants

Leaky Oil Strainer
If you have a leaky oil strainer plate, the next time you pull it out, take a good look at the metal around the stud holes. After years of over-tightening by previous owners, chances are the metal has been pulled up, resulting in bumps around all the holes, which keep the rest of the plate from "squashing" the gaskets sufficiently to prevent leaks. A simple fix for this is to put the plate on the floor, magnet up, place the round end of a ball-peen hammer on the bump, and strike it with another hammer. Done properly, this will flatten the bump to the level of the rest of the plate border. Of course you should put on new gaskets. I also like to spray mine with Permatex Spray-a-Gasket. I only pull the plate and screen every 6000 miles or more. There's really no way to sludge up or otherwise block the screen.

Vol. 10, No. 3 Vic Skirmants

Oil Sump Leak Prevention/Cure
What is the best way to torque the nuts on the oil sump plate to minimize leaks? First off, make sure the flange on the plate is straight. The area around the bolt holes is usually warped from over-tightening; place the plate on the garage floor, place the ball end of a ball-peen hammer on the warped bolt hole area, and smack it with another hammer. Put your preferred sealant on the gaskets; I use Permatex silicone sealant. Just snug the nuts, don't over-tighten! I believe the listed torque is 3 lb-ft; try doing that while standing on your head! Just common sense and a 10 mm wrench are all you need. Check occasionally and re-tighten; they will loosen slightly as the gaskets take a set.

Vol. 11, No. 1 Vic Skirmants

Stripped Oil Sump Studs
Of course if the stud is stripped, just pull it and replace. If the hole in the case is stripped, sometimes there might be a thread or two left at the top of the hole, which permits installing a long bolt from inside the case.

Vol. 15, No. 1 Vic Skirmants

Oil Capacity
The first fill for a freshly rebuilt engine is indeed 5 1/2 quarts. Some of that oil is used in filling up the nooks, crannies, and pockets inside the engine that are dry and can never be drained on a standard oil change. Subsequent oil fill-ups will require only 4 to 4 1/2 quarts, depending on how well you drain the sump and wipe out the oil filter can.

Oil

Vol. 3, No. 3 Vic Skirmants/Chris Ramel

Synthetic Oil

In the last *Registry* issue Col. Donald Zook asked if anyone had any experience with Mobil 1 synthetic oil. Chris Ramel, Denver, CO, has a partial answer. He tried a synthetic oil, Allproof, for 5000 miles in a rebuilt 1963 Super engine after a 3000 mile break-in on Valvoline. The manufacturer's claims for Allproof are:

1. Easier cold weather starting.
2. Better gas mileage.
3. Less friction, hence lower engine temperature.
4. No carbon buildup; oil stays cleaner. Retail price in Denver is $5 per quart.

Chris' results are as follows:

1. Incredible bills for oil changes!
2. No noticeable change in gas mileage.
3. No noticeable change in starting.
4. No lower engine temperature.
5. Better oil mileage.
6. Oil stayed cleaner, but still had to be changed regularly.

The better oil mileage was more than offset by the higher price. Chris is now back to using Valvoline. It remains to be seen if Mobil 1 is any different.

Vol. 9, No. 1 William E. Sovik, Jr.

Multigrade Oil, The Complete Story

Back in the early 1960s the Porsche factory conducted a series of engine endurance tests using both single and multi-grade engine oils. Multi-grades performed so poorly that Porsche would not approve their use in Porsche engines. But for someone to state that you shouldn't use multi-grades today because of what happened in the 1960s would be a real life exemplification of the automotive engineer in our Opening Story.

Quality multi-grades of today are, superior to single grade oils in many ways. But before we show why, let's look around at some of the other areas of automotive development.

Back in the late 1950s Porsche didn't feel it necessary to paint the pans of the 356s as they were factory undercoated. Today, aftermarket suppliers enjoy a nice replacement business for severely rusted pans. Drum brakes and manually operated sunroofs were then the state of the art for production Porsches.

When you compare a shock absorber from the mid-sixties with one of today, everything is different. For example, the seals used are made from a synthetic material that didn't even exist fifteen years ago.

Today, the street tires on your Porsche are better than the race tires of 10 - 12 years ago. And there are two primary reasons why: One is the advancement in tread design, the other is a vast improvement in rubber compounding chemistry.

And the superiority of today's multi-graded oil is also due to chemical compounding. Today's oil is simply the chemistry of compounding base stocks with additives that assist the oil in doing a better overall job.

But in order to understand what happened in the Porsche engine tests, we must understand what types of oils were available in the early sixties.

Prior to 1970, the API (American Petroleum Institute) Service Classifications were simply definitions. For example, an "MS" oil was suitable for use in any spark ignition engine under most severe conditions (if we don't ask it to perform very long). Therefore, nearly any oil could meet this requirement since any oil would work in a spark ignition engine (as opposed to a compression ignition engine, i.e., diesel).

Fortunately, the American Society for Testing and Materials (ASTM), the Society of Automotive Engineers

(SAE) and the API jointly established in 1970 a new API Engine Service Classification System – This system enabled engine oils to be defined and selected on the basis of their performance characteristics but remember, this occurred long after Porsche engine tests. There are now six classes that apply to spark ignition engine oils:

SA is the lowest grade and additive free. SB is typical of oils available since the thirties, is non-detergent and your lawn mower probably deserves better. However, this oil presented the state of the art when Porsche ran its engine tests.

SC was developed to meet the 1964 - 1967 engine warranties and their new problems such as the control of temperature deposits plus corrosion and rust deposits. SD grade oils are simply improved SC oil that meets the needs of 1968 - 1971 engines.

SE oil (1972 - 1980) has a complete additive package offering more protection than before. With shrinking crank-case capacities, smaller displacement engines that rev higher and develop more horsepower per liter, even greater demands were being placed on oils so the SF classification was developed from 1981 engines. And SF oils do everything the SE oils do, only better.

For an oil to carry any API classification on the top of its can, it must meet a series of very rigid qualification tests. Major oil companies develop engine oils to meet these performance characteristics, which is understandable considering the huge automotive lube oil market. This development and testing costs many thousands of dollars so oil companies formulate their products with a comfortable safety margin – no one wants their oil to squeak through. Incidentally, straight weights and multi-grades must meet identical performance standards to carry the appropriate API Service Classification.

What are the functions of an engine oil? Today's oils should lubricate, seal, minimize wear, cool, dampen shock loads, protect against rust and corrosion - while maintaining engine cleanliness. They should also permit engine cranking with up-front lubrication during start up to minimize fluid friction.

Multi-grades were first conceived as early as 1945 as a way to have the best characteristics of both a light weight oil for cold start ups and the protection of heavier oils at high temperatures. When multi-grades were being developed, what held true in the lab didn't always hold true in an engine's crankcase. Fortunately auto manufacturers recommended oil changes at 3,000 mile, sometimes even at 1,000 mile intervals and very few people drove their cars at 5,800 RPM for the equivalent of 16,000 to 17,000 miles as simulated in the Porsche tests, so engine failure clue to lube oil break-down was not a problem.

The most significant single change in multi-grades between then and now is the polymers, that chemical compounding we spoke of earlier. Twenty years ago, even ten years ago when the ASTM DS49 and DS49 S-1 reports came out (we will discuss these later) these polymers had what is referred to in the industry as a very low shear rate.

The shear rate on a long chain hydrocarbon is like slicing up a loaf of bread. And of course, you put in the full loaf of bread to a base stock 10 weight oil to obtain a 10W-40 multi-grade. You don't want that to change, at all, that 40 weight characteristic at 210F. But they did know that because of this low shear rate back then, that what started out as a 10W-40 would end up a 10W-30 or 10W-25. This shear would occur in the lube oil gear pump; that nice long hydrocarbon chain that was put in there to make it a 40 weight was cut in half and cut in quarters so it became a 30 or a 25 weight. Consequently, the oil became overly thin and two things happened when it was subjected to heavy loads as in the Porsche engine tests: its higher fractions evaporate (high oil consumption) and its lubricating film breaks down (engine failure). This degradation usually took place during the first 800 to 1,000 miles. These facts are supported in the Porsche tests by the number of hours running time converted to equivalent road miles.

But let's talk about what is going on today, not two decades ago. After all, in the early sixties, mankind was only on the threshold of space, but has since put men on the moon.

Today's high molecular weight polymers that are used in the SE and SF rated oils have extremely high shear rates. Imagine these polymers in a l0W-,10 weight oil as a shrimp. At 0°F (-18°C) the oil acts like a 10 weight and the polymer is curled up like a shrimp in cold water; while at 210°F where the 40 weight is needed, the polymer opens up like a shrimp in hot water.

Modern multi-grade oils meet the same API standards as their single weight counterparts while offering additional features and benefits.

All SE or SF rated oils, single or multi-grade, have a seven part additive package that accounts for 8 - 20% of their volume, depending upon the manufacturer. They start out with their base stock plus they contain oxidation inhibitors which prevent oxidation of metal parts which manifests itself as "black mayonnaise" or sludge.

The alkalinity additives neutralize the sulfur from the fuel (fuel dilution during start up under rich operating conditions) which prevents upper ring wear.

The detergents/dispersants prevent the agglomeration of molecules by bombarding them to knock down their size so they won't drop out of solution in slow moving areas like timing or rocker arm chambers.

The rust inhibitors provide demulsification of condensation and moisture while the EP package provides additional anti-wear protection in those extreme wear areas of the valve train.

The pour point depressants promote better flow at low temperatures while the anti-foam additives reduce bubbles when the oil comes in intimate contact with air at high RPM's.

But this is where the single grade oils stop and the multi-grades continue to provide additional benefits due to their synergistic ability to function over a broad temperature range.

A single grade oil like a 40 weight is rated only at 210°F (99°C) as it is very resistant to flow at lower temperatures. We have all patiently held onto a can of 40 weight on a cool autumn day while it is slowly poured from the can. This 40 weight might be fine at normal operating temperatures in the Porsche engine (180°F - 210°F) but during start up, those first 10 to 20 seconds where most engine wear takes place, that 40 weight simply takes a long time to move. But with a multigrade like a l0W-40 you get that immediate flow of oil out to those bearing surfaces and other critical areas. You gain by faster cold starts, less drain on the electrical system and most importantly better bearing wear protection.

Later, as the engine warms up, the polymer unfolds and the 40 weight characteristics of the multi-grade come to life; these are the viscosity improvers, those high shear, long chain polymers that make it act exactly like that straight 40 weight at 210°F.

A multi-grade will offer lower operating temperatures which translates into better efficiency, longer life, not to mention peace of mind. This is because multi-grades have a better specific heat (holds more heat without a temperature rise) and better thermal conductivity (permits heat dissipation). This is demonstrated by a 10° to 30°F drop in oil temperatures at the upper limit when you switch your Porsche from a single to a multi-grade.

Do we fool Mother Nature? Not really, we just improve upon her as we have in so many areas such as hybrid plants and livestock. After all even with the straight weight oils we don't take Mother Nature's product directly from the earth and pour it into our Porsche crankcase.

Two ASTM publications (144 pages total) DS49 and DS49 S-1 address the issue of the shear stability of multi-grade engine oils in both U.S. and European fleets. Ninety-two test vehicles were driven a total of 552,000 miles with thirteen different oils tested. Of the ten SAE 10W-40 grades tested, 53%, still met the 40 weight viscosity requirements at the end of the test, 26% fell only to the upper end of the 30 weight limit (i.e. missed the 40 weight by less than 10%) while the remaining 24% dropped to the middle of the 30 weight viscosity range. So in the early 1970s, when these tests were conducted, if you started out with a 10W-40, you had better than even odds of maintaining that 40 weight characteristic and at worst, dropping down to the mid 30 weight level.

Of course oils have improved a lot since then, especially with the introduction of both SE and SF service classifications. Which is probably why in 1977 Porsche approved the use of multi-grade oils in the Porsche 911 engines. In 1978 they extended its use to all air and water cooled engines and in 1980 includes even synthetic oils.

However, be it single grade, multi-grade or synthetic, the oil must be labeled for API/SE or API/SF service and the viscosity ratings must conform to those specified in the owner's manual for the vehicle.

Crankshaft

Vol. 13, No. 1 Vic Skirmants

Oil Choice for Roller Crank Engines

John Paterek has asked about the proper care and lubrication of an engine with roller-bearing crankshaft. There aren't too many of these around anymore, but for those who have them, I would say they should be treated like any other 356 engine. Use a good grade oil, preferably a straight 30-weight in the summer, and I assume no one would be driving it in the winter, but 20-weight if they do. For really hot summer days or high speed running, a straight 40-weight. No Porsche engine should be subjected to wide-open-throttle below 2000 RPM (that's called lugging, and it's really bad). Part-throttle up to 3000 RPM, and then you can floor it.

Vol. 16, No. 6 Vic Skirmants

How to Set Crankshaft End-Play

When setting the crankshaft end-play, be certain that you're not getting a false reading. If you install the #1 main bearing, bolt on the flywheel and check the gap with a feeler gauge while on the work bench, this won't affect you. If you check the end-play with a dial-indicator after assembling the case, be sure to install the old shim before attaching the flywheel, then check the end-play. If you try to determine the total play without a shim, you can have a condition where the crankshaft actually hits the edge of #2

PORSCHE		All	Group **17**
Product Circular			February 8, 1978
Reference to Rep. Manual Page: N/A			No. 78-01
Subject: Engine Oil		Key Points:	
Part Identifier N/A		Multi-grade oil can now be used (Supersedes P-Circular of Dec. 29, 1977)	

Besides the single grade oils which you have been allowed to use, Porsche now allows the use of multi-grade oils that also bear the API classification SE. These are:

Air and water cooled cars	Air cooled cars only	CAUTION
SAE viscosity	SAE viscosity	Do not use 20W-50 oil when prolonged ambient temperature is below +5°F (-15°C)
10 W-40 15 W-50 20 W-50	10 W-50	

VOLKSWAGEN OF AMERICA, INC.

main bearing. This will give you a false indication of the total clearance available. If you install a shim and then check, you will be measuring a smaller dimension and should get a good, repeatable reading. Obviously, if the shim is too thick and binds, you won't learn anything until you put in a thinner shim. If you get readings that don't make sense, such as putting in enough shims to bind the crank, and you still have end-play, you have a #1 main bearing that's loose in the case.

One condition that I've noticed in recent years is that the crank will occasionally wear the flywheel-side edge of #2 main bearing, even with the proper end-play shimming. I don't know if the bearing manufacturers have moved the locating tab, or what the cause is, but the solution is quite simple. When placing the crank into the case, check if the crank journal fillet gets into the edge of the bearing. If it looks close, simply chamfer the edge of the bearing with a bearing scraper or similar tool.

Camshaft

Vol. 14, No. 6 Tim Berardeli

Cracking Replacement Cams
Tim Berardelli brings up another new product problem. Replacement wide lobe cams marked R0200 have dowel pin holes that are a bit too small and tend to crack when the pin is installed. Tim also mentions a trick stainless steel racing exhaust system that doesn't fit for squat. Remember what I said about exhaust systems; the Bursch system fits, and it works; I can't say anything more.

Pushrod Tubes

Vol. 15, No. 6 Vic Skirmants

Proper Pushrod Tube Installation

One of the prime oil leak sources in a 356 engine are the pushrod tubes. The factory manual tells you to stretch the pushrod tube before installation. This advice is based on reusing the old tubes. Don't stretch new tubes! First of all, the new tubes are the correct length for proper seal "squeeze". Secondly, the new tubes are of a different material than older tubes, and are much more "brittle"! These tubes have been the only ones available for many years. They are a gold color, as compared to the silver or gray of the old tubes. The old tubes are made of a softer, more "flexible" metal and can be reused many times, especially if they're not over-stretched. My racing friend Dave Helmick told me he never stretched his old tubes and did not have a leakage problem. I tried it and sure enough, no problem. The new type pushrod tubes are brittle enough to break at the bellows after using on one or two rebuilds of our race engines. For street engine rebuilds you should use new tubes, even though they are expensive. If you like to do your own work, and don't mind replacing tubes if you get a leaker, you can certainly save money by re-using old tubes.

Some owners of 1962 - 1965 356s get concerned about worn-out transmission mounts when they see that the engine sealing rubber does not line up evenly with the rear sheet metal in the engine compartment. All the 356s, 356As, and 1960 - 1961 356Bs did have engine rubber that lined up flush with the engine compartment metal. For some reason, the T-6 cars (1962 - 1965) do not line up! I don't know the answer.

Sheet Metal

Vol. 2, No. 3 John Paterek

Detailing, Painting Shrouds, etc.
Be sure your disassembly is fol-

lowed by careful placement of small parts and fasteners. Plastic sandwich bags work well. It is a good practice to examine screw tops and replace if distorted before they are plated.

Also check your generator pulley for stress cracks. I had the misfortune of one coming apart at 5000 RPM; it sheared the belt and damaged surrounding sheet metal (Not to mention almost frying the engine!).

If your sheetmetal is full of rust or excess paint, glassbead or sand blasting is recommended, especially for heat exchangers. List all parts and a brief description for the plater or sandblaster. These pieces are not only rare but are very expensive to replace if lost.

A few helpful products. If you have no facilities for sandblasting, either strip the parts with Zip Strip or DuPont Remover or sand them with 380 or 400 grit paper. Treat rust with Metal Prep Conditioner and coat bare metal with Zinc Chromate. (Krylon and Rustoleum make an aerosol spray.) Use a mask to prevent breathing harmful vapors.

If you are lucky enough to have a compressor and exhaust system for spraying, use DuPont Zinc Chromate and Preparacote (which can also be brushed). Preparacote is the best primer surfacer for rust problems. It fills flaws without the use of spot putty. Sand all marks out with 320 and recoat if bare metal shows up again.

The best finish for the novice is made by a company called Parko. It is called Underhood paint and comes in flat black, an exact match to factory engine paint. It comes in a 16 oz. aerosol can and covers well. Be sure the room temperature is observed even for spray bombs. If you can spray with a gun, I recommend Masury Satin Black. It flows out nicely and is sprayed without the use of a reducer. Be sure all parts are free of oil and dust before spraying and beware of open flames and concentrated fumes.

Finish your job off with the proper decals for that concours accent.

If you don't have time to do the entire job, select a piece such as the air filter or valve covers and work your way up. I'm sure you will be pleased with the results.

Vol. 4, No. 5 Brett Johnson

Urethane Paint Problems
One last bit of miscellany, there seems to be a lot of painting of engine shrouding with polyurethane paints. Be warned, original style water transfer decals have a problem with non-adherence to these surfaces. Mylar decals will stick better, but of course are somewhat lacking in authenticity.

Vol. 17, No. 1 Mark Turczyn

Early Engine Sheet Metal
I thought some of you motor guys may want a short introduction to the changes in sheet metal for two-piece case motors. As you all know, the two-piece case was a VW item. It was bored out for the later 1300 cc and 1500 cc motors. The mains were also about .010 in. bigger than the stock VW so first-over VW mains should work for standard Porsche cranks. I have align bored my cases for second-over VW mains. The early type 1300 cc motor had a small bore and a long stroke. All cylinders were aluminum with chrome bores except for the 1100 cc cylinders which were cast iron. The spacing of the head studs were 66.96 mm so later three piece cylinders which had stud spacing of 70.71 mm would not fit, at least not easily. I have heard that people have creatively machined three piece case 1500 cc cylinders, so it is possible. The early chrome bores were smooth and the later cylinders were dimpled to retain oil. Both Supers and Normals had the dimple cylinders. The last changes the factory eventually made to the VW case to make it more reliable were to

use two through-bolts rather than the single one used on the early motors, and to weld a splash shield to the oil pickup pipe to help retain oil pressure when winging through quick corners.

As far as I can tell – Ken Daugherty could steer me right on this – the very early 1100 cc motors which had the valve adjustment on the valve stem end and four bolt manifolds used VW sheet metal with this exception: the "clamshell" type fan shroud was modified for the dual carb set up and the single flap heat exchangers were bigger due to the increased width of the heads with the angled valves. So what does this early sheet metal look like? Well the very early cylinder covers were one piece. You could only take them off by removing the cylinders or cutting the tin. I suspect that a lot of early mechanics trimmed them. In 1951 the factory did the trimming and the cylinder tin reflected the Porsche design influence. The major difference in this early Porsche tin and the Porsche tin that is common on the later two- and three-piece motors is the way the cylinder and the spark plug tin joined together. The early tin forms a "clamshell" around the exhaust headers-one "clam" half formed by the spark plug tin and the other half formed by the cylinder tin. The later cylinder tin went around both sides of the exhaust header. You have to look at the drawing to see what I am talking about. The early spark plug tin had "McDonald's" type

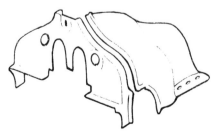

Early sheet metal had the famous double arches – Would you like fries with that?

double arch cutouts to clear the early intake manifolds. This double arch was retained for the early Super steel tube manifolds using 40 PBIC carburetors. About the time of the 3-piece case introduction, the normal manifolds received a cast baffle around the tin with the tin changed accordingly. The Super manifolds were now also cast aluminum in similar style.

The "clamshell" fan shroud (modified VW shroud to accommodate dual carb setup) was used until mid-1952, I guess (I do mean guess). The shroud was made from two pieces of metal with a lap joint along the top center line-thus a "clamshell." I think it is safe to say (yeh, right!) that it was used on the 502 1500 cc motors with the small carbs and also on the early 527s. For 527s with the 40 PBICs the clamshell linkage pivot was modified and notched to allow clearance for the accelerator pump linkage on the right carb. On the early 527s, Porsche used a 1 $^1/_2$ in. adapter plate to mate the 40 PBICs to the 32 type manifolds. The factory soon provided the neatly made tall tubular steel manifolds.

The new "square" shroud was introduced in 1952. The factory parts manual states that the first model shroud was used until motor# 30500 which puts it near the end of the production of the 527. This means the square shroud was used starting June/July of 1952. I just have not seen that many clam shell shrouds that have been modified for the bell crank type throttle linkage (introduced in May 1952) so I have my doubts. From factory pictures and other documentation I would guess that the clamshell shroud was dropped very early in 1952. Anyway, the new shroud provided the required clearance for the 40 BPICs with a notched-out section at the right rear and also had the bell crank support on the backside for use with the new rod-actuated throttle.

This shroud was used up to the early 1600 cc three-piece case motors

153

that had the bolt-on pulley seal plate. The first early square shrouds had only one pivot point and pivot mechanism for the carbs. You either got a set that worked for the 32 PBIs whose butterflies opened by pulling or pushing (cable actuated-pulling left, rod actuated-pushing right), or a set for the 40 PBICs whose butterflies opened by pulling right-cable or by pushing left-rod actuated. Later the shrouds had both pivot points welded to them. The parts manual states that there were 32 PBJs and 40 PBJCs. Small error? For you early, early (1950) freaks, the manifolds for the early 32s were secured with four studs and bolts to the head rather than the traditional combination of three studs or one long bolt and two studs.

Just to spark some talk, until late in 1951 the throttle cable was indeed just a pull cable running through a tube up over the transmission. In May 1952 the factory came up with the now common bell crank and rod that you see on all 356s. The factory says that the cable was used until motor number 20994, 1.3 liter; 30259, 1.5 liter. The motor found in cab #10202, registered in March 1952, was 30159. This would indicate that May 1952 was the time that the factory went to the bell crank and long accelerator rod. The pivot plate (near the pedal) was also modified from the boomerang-shaped unit used for the cable to the straight style used for the rod.

The most interesting and hardest to find piece of sheet metal is the back pulley tray. It obviously had no cut outs for pre heaters. What makes it a bit of a pain to duplicate, using an early A tray as a base, is that it has the dipstick sheet metal as part of the tray. Later trays use the common separate dipstick sheet metal.

The flip-up cover for the manual crank was always spot welded shut. There would be no way you could use a manual crank even if you did put the neat crank type VW pulley nut on

your motor unless you cut a hole in the body of the car. Some cars have this hole but I can only conclude that an owner would have done this.

Other early items that are bringing big bucks are the "star" ignition coils, the "D" type regulators, the early side-drain filter canisters with their bolt-on band clamp, the canister-type fuel filter, the 383 distributor, and the large crank pulley.

The "star" coils look like small juice cans with three "star-like" radiating ridges on the top. Unlike later coils, the bracket that holds the coil to the fan shroud is spot welded to the body of the star coil Be aware that there are two types of "star" coils, the normal diameter VW model and the early Mercedes type which is much larger in diameter-about 3" O.D. I have seen both types on "original" motors. Factory pictures show what I feel are the Mercedes size coils. I am not sure which is correct but I believe bigger is better when it comes to spark. Yeh right!

The "D" type voltage regulator (or cut out) fit on top of the generator and from the top is shaped like a black capital D lying on its back. It is usually mated to a 55 watt RED 130/6 generator.

The early filter canisters had a drain on the side so you could unscrew the bolt and drain the canister. Oddly enough, I have seen era pictures of the first 1100 and 1300 cc motors that were equipped with (optional?) oil canisters (1950 - early 1951). On these early motors the factory mounted the canisters on a slant like the coil (dealer installation?). This makes sense because it allows the oil to completely drain out of the canister. It would also make the filter a mess to put in if you did not drain the oil. I have no idea when they started mounting the canister in its common upright position but I would say mid-1951. Some early, early ones had a wing nut rather than just a bolt on the top to hold the lid on.

I have never seen one so I do not know if the wing-nuts are authentic, but I would not be surprised. Porsche used these drain type canisters until late 1955 on the early three-piece case 1500s. The factory probably figured out that the mechanics were not bothering to completely drain the oil out of the canister (especially once they started mounting them vertically) so they removed the drain plug. There must be at least 15 styles of oil canisters used on 356 motors since the first one. The first-style band clamp was bolted directly to the fan shroud with four bolts, two on each side of the canister.

The canister-type fuel filter was a two-piece unit. The bowl held the filter and screwed into the top section that had the special metal fuel lines. One line ran to the main fuel feed by the bell housing sheet metal and the other connected the filter to the fuel pump. The two-piece case fuel pumps (on some early three-piece motors) themselves are not real easy to find but if you go to enough VW swap meets, you will find them.

In the ignition department, what people are going after is the 383 distributor with the wire cap hold down clips. These distributors and the flat caps that go with them are not really hard to find since the 25 and 35 hp VWs used them. What is hard to find is the brass valve lash information plate that Porsche screwed onto later two piece motor distributor caps. I have only seen these on 383 distributors in 1954 and 1955, but this is not to say that they should not be on the earlier cars. The valve lash dimensions on that brass plate you may have in your possession will give some clue as to what motor it belongs on.

The last item that is frustrating to locate is the large diameter Porsche-only fan belt pulley. This is a cast iron item while the VW pulleys were built-up from steel stampings. You can put the whole motor together using: a two-piece case, heads, cylinders, valve train, cam followers with any steel pushrods, VW cam along with an A crank, rods, 1500 cc normal pistons, early three piece case sheet metal, Solex carbs and manifolds. A or later valves can be used provided you install larger 10 mm valve guides (requiring later 2-piece heads that have enough meat). Unfortunately, without this pulley, the motor will not look right and of course the fan will not run at its intended speed. I thought I would pass this tidbit along to those of you who have just bought a case, some heads, and the valve train (do not buy VW push rods and followers-they will not work) and need something else to worry about.

Clutch

Vol. 3, No. 6 Stuart Tucker

Clutch Cable Adjustment
Too little clutch pedal free play may result in increased wear of throw out bearing, diaphragm spring, pressure plate, clutch plate, and flywheel, even if the clutch pedal travel is correctly adjusted.

Too much clutch pedal free play results in no real deleterious effects, provided that the clutch pedal travel is correctly adjusted.

Too little clutch pedal travel results in increased wear of the pressure plate, clutch plate, flywheel, and transmission synchronizer mechanism because the clutch plate is not able to fully disengage from the flywheel. Too much clutch pedal travel results in unnecessary strain on the diaphragm spring fingers of the Haussermann pressure plate assembly.

Vol. 8, No. 5 Vic Skirmants

Adjusting Clutch and "Frozen Clutch Syndrome"
If you've ever had problems getting enough clutch adjustment, there are

some not so obvious reasons. First of all, you adjust the cable at either end or at the guide tube at the transmission such that you have 3/4 in. to 1 in. free play. Then adjust the stop plate under the clutch pedal so that the clutch starts to engage as soon as the pedal comes off the stop. If you've moved the stop all the way up and the trans-axle still grinds when you try to put it in gear, it means you're not getting enough movement at the clutch release lever for a given movement of the clutch pedal. If you have a some-what rusty car, the pedal cluster can move with the floor. Consequently part of the clutch travel is spent moving the floor. Okay, so you've got a California car with a perfect floor and you still can't get the clutch to release fully. Assuming no bent transmission input shaft causing a drag in the fly-wheel gland nut, or a warped or cracked pressure plate, there is a possibility of worn out clutch cross-shaft bushings in the transmission housing. I don't even know if these are available, but I did encounter one worn so badly that even the aluminum of the transaxle housing was worn. The solution was to ream the hole oversize to get rid of the ovality, then make a special bushing to fit.

If your car has been in storage for a while, and you just got it out, and the clutch is not even close to releasing, you have a clutch disc that is frozen (rusted) to the pressure plate or fly-wheel. You could pull the engine, remove the pressure plate, knock loose the clutch disc: and reinstall. Or, if you're brave, jack up the back of the car by the transaxle hoop, using a hydraulic jack, put it in first gear, start it up, keep the clutch pedal down, rev it up, have an even braver friend drop the jack fast, and hope for the best. If it doesn't break loose, turn the key off, brake hard, or pull it out of gear before you run out of driveway. If you don't want to try the above for what-ever reason (sanity, intelligence), you could try starting it in gear, and once you're rolling with the clutch pedal down, brake hard. If anyone tries the above methods, I take no responsibility for flattened cats, dogs. kids, or T-6 noses.

Vol. 10, No. 4 Vic Skirmants

Bad Aftermarket Throw Out Bearings
Many years ago a replacement throw out bearing appeared on the market. It came in a flimsy brown cor-rugated cardboard box with no name on it. The bearing was painted black, it had a cardboard dirt seal over the ball bearing, and sounded and felt as if it was full of sand. This little gem would promptly ruin a brand new pressure plate in just a few thousand miles. After a while this garbage dis-appeared and we received the good bearings again. Packed in a thin white cardboard box with no name, they were unpainted, just like the originals. They had a metal dirt seal over the bearing, and they felt just great when turned. All was right for a few years.

Unfortunately, the black-painted junk bearings are back! Sure, they're supposedly made in Germany, but they are still junk!

If you receive any of these junk bearings, send it back, raise hell, and maybe someone will listen and get the good ones back. In the meantime, if your old bearing is good, keep it. If it's getting shaky, remove the clip, and with a small punch, gently tapping first in one hole, then the other (on the back of the bearing), drive out the ball bearing, clean it, repack it with a molybdenum grease, and reassemble. If yours is totally shot, or you have one of the "black ones with cardboard seal", try and buy a used one from somebody. Just remember not to accept the bad throw out bearings.

Vol. 11, No. 1 Vic Skirmants

VW vs. Porsche Discs

Now for a comment on clutch discs. It seems the 180 mm Porsche-type clutch discs are getting scarce. Of course any VW 180 mm disc will fit, and they're a lot cheaper, so many people have been using them all along; no problem with that. However, there are many manufacturers of VW clutch discs, so there is quite a variation in the detail assembly. One disc I came across last year interfered with the gland nut. The only symptom was a squealing noise upon partial engagement, as the disc would rub against the gland nut just before full pressure was applied by the pressure plate. So, go ahead and use the VW parts, but check for interference to the gland nut and to the pressure plate if you are using the spring-center type disc.

VW discs are thinner and, as such, do not last as long – September 1994

Vol. 15, No. 2 Cole Scrogham

Haussermann Clutch Information
The Haussermann (hoy-zer-man) pressure plate was made famous as standard equipment in the 356 Carrera beginning with the Type 692/1 engine in 1958. It replaced the Fitchel and Sachs K12 and is used in vintage and club racing because of its durability. The second version of the Haussermann is referred to as the A-12 and can be used in any 356 with the correct flywheel and "guided" throw out bearing. The most common Haussermanns are part 616.116.014.01 for the pressure plate and 692.116.016.00 for the clutch disc. There are, of course, some variations in these numbers, notably the four cam's pressure plate number also begins with the prefix 692. This pressure plate is unique because it is not a captured design, but can be disassembled and reassembled when necessary. It also has a release pressure of 700kg compared to 560kg for the old K12.

Performance/Competition

Vol. 12, No. 6 Vic Skirmants

Competition Pistons and Head Work
I did hear that the Arias pistons were getting a bum rap. I use Venolia and Arias + .040" pistons in my race engines. I have built several street engines with the 86 mm Arias pistons. I have had no problems. I retire the race pistons when the top grooves become excessively worn; usually ten to fifteen race weekends. Never due to a scuffing or seizing problem. Our races may only last half an hour, but that's at peak oil and cylinder head temperatures; not something you'd experience on the street too easily. Certainly not for a solid 30 minutes. The people who do have seizing problems with these pistons are probably experiencing one or several of the following conditions: too much ignition advance, too lean a fuel mixture, insufficient octane gasoline, too high a compression ratio.

All of these will produce excess heat. Excess heat will over-expand the pistons and cause skirt scuffing and eventual seizing. Unfortunately, I guess most people just buy these pistons, bolt them on and proceed on their way. When we build a race engine with the +.040" pistons, we try to get the cylinder head cc around 64. When the heads are fully ported and the combustion chamber recontoured, the cc usually come out at 66-67. Further fly-cutting and 30° angle recutting gets it down to 64 cc. This gives us a compression ratio around 11.5:1. If you bolt an engine together with pistons that produce this much compression with 64 cc cylinder heads, then a set of stock heads around 61 to 60 cc will produce a compression ratio of 12.5 to 12.7:1! Find me any Porsche piston that will live at that compression! Couple this with the stock 115 Solex main jets (didn't think to change those?), 36° advance and 95 octane gasoline at best, and, yes, you have piston "failure" in a couple of thousand miles; or sooner. The stock heads used with the 86 mm Japanese pistons result in a 9.3 to 9.4:1 compression ratio.

Incidentally, you can't completely trust the factory-stamped cc number on the head. I "cc" every head on which I do a valve job; race or street. Only then can I know what compression ratio I'll end up with. This also tells me if I need to run an extra spacer under both cylinders on one head to match the cc more closely to the other head. One standard .010" copper shim changes the cc by 1.4. It's rare that the heads on an engine that's been apart before will come within 1.0 cc. Even uncut heads can vary 0.5 to 1.0 cc from one chamber to it's neighbor.

Vol. 16, No. 2 Vic Skirmants

More Racey Engine Stuff
Straight-cut camshaft gears are my current object of derision. Anything that produces that much noise can't possibly be saving any horsepower! A helical gear will always be stronger than an equal-size straight-cut gear.

There are also three different set-ups available. The aluminum gear combo will chew the aluminum gear up in about six races (I didn't try it, a customer did many years ago). Okay, then both gears should be steel. The problem is, one of the "steel" gears available is actually cast-iron! With the thin web necessary to attach the gear to the cam, this sucker will shatter after a number of races.

The real steel-to-steel set-up should last. It's also the absolutely noisiest. My theory is: if it makes that much noise it has to be costing power. Incidentally, don't cut a groove in your stock cam gear. You won't gain power, just a weaker gear.

Carbon-fiber pushrods; totally wrong coefficient of expansion. You'll end up with terribly loose

valve clearances at operating temperature. Besides, Smokey Yunick just said in *Circle Track* magazine that a higher RPM capability can only be gained by reducing the weight of components on the valve-side of the rocker arm. That man's smart; I tend to believe a lot of what he has to say.

Ceramic coatings for heads, pistons, and valves have not proven to gain anything yet. Anti-friction coatings may be beneficial on some piston skirts, but I have never had a scuffing problem with either MC, Arias, or Venolia pistons. The "secret" is simply to use adequate fuel, timing, and cooling.

One new item I am impressed by is the new TRW high-silicone alloy race piston that can run with a clearance of 0.0015", that's one-and-a-half thousandths of an inch! That's incredible, especially when all the other race pistons need a minimum of 0.007 to 0.009"; that's seven to nine thousandths, or over five times as much. The tighter clearance means better sealing, therefore more power. With less piston rock in the cylinder, the rings will work better and last longer. I have run the 83.5 mm version on the dyno, and they do work!

Vol. 16, No. 2 Vic Skirmants

Racing Clutch
There is available a replacement flywheel, clutch, and pressure-plate assembly that is very expensive, light, expensive, uses a thin metallic clutch disc, is expensive, doesn't fit correctly, is expensive, and will leave you stranded with a slipping clutch with no warning or gradual slippage increase. I use a lightened standard flywheel, (180 mm is totally adequate for any power we can generate), a 3-puck metallic clutch disc from Gene Berg and a Kennedy Engineered Products pressure plate, also from Berg. That clutch will take any abuse you can give it.

158

Chapter 8

Engine Lore from The Maestro

The following are excerpts from *The ABC's of Porsche Engines, Secrets of the Inner Circle, Murphy is My CoPilot,* and *Little Spec Book,* by Harry Pellow (the Maestro) – reprinted with permission.

Crankshaft Dimensions, all 1500/ 1600s, 1955 - 1969

Rod Journal Diameter

Millimeters	Inches
Standard	
53.000-52.987	2.0866-2.0861
First Undersize	
52.750-52.737	2.0768-2.0763
Second Undersize	
52.500-52.487	2.0669-2.0664
Third Undersize	
52.250-52.237	2.0571-2.0566

Note: Undersizes are 0.25, 0.50 and 0.75 mm; Not 0.010",0.020" or 0.030" If you grind a crank to 0.030", it will be at low limit on third undersize- which is not good... so watch out!!!

Note: Connecting rod bore is always the same @ 56.980-56.999 mm, (2.2433-2.2440 inches)

Crankshaft Main Bearing Journals – 50 mm mains (A/B cranks having 50 mm main bearings; and flywheel main

bearing journal on C/SC/912 cranks)

Millimeters	Inches
Standard	
49.991-49.975	1.9681-1.9675
First Undersize	
49.741-49.725	1.9583-1.9577
Second Undersize	
49.491-49.475	1.9485-1.9478
Third Undersize	
49.241-49.225	1.9386-1.9380

Crankshaft Main Bearing Journals – 55 mm mains (all 3 main bearings on S-90; middle two main bearings on C/ SC/912)

Millimeters	Inches
Standard	
54.990-54.971	2.1650-2.1642
First Undersize	
54.740-54.721	2.1551-2.1544
Second Undersize	
54.490-54.471	2.1453-2.1445
Third Undersize	
54.240-54.221	2.1354-2.1347

All Models, #4 Bearing Journal on Crankshaft – In third piece of the case

Standard	
39.982-39.971	1.5741-1.5747
First Undersize	
39.732-39.721	1.5643-1.5638
Second Undersize	
39.482-39.471	1.5544-1.5540

Third Undersize
39.232-39.221   1.5446-1.5441

Case Bore Diameters and Bearing Sizes

Standard case bore is: 60.24 ± 0.005 mm (2.37165 ± 0.0002") Allowable Range: (2.37145 - 2.37185")

Main Bearing Outside Diameter, Std.: 60.29 mm (2.3736")

First Over Align Bored 356/912 Porsche Case/Bearing Dimensions

First over case bore is: 60.49 ± 0.005 mm (2.3813-2.3817")

First Oversize Main Bearing Outside Diameter: 60.54 mm (2.3835")

Note 1: Generally, the third piece of the case is not align bored; thus, #4 main bearing will usually not be oversize.

Note 2: Main bearing outside diameter is about 0.002" larger than case bore. This is to provide the 0.002" crush on the bearing when installed!!

Standard 50 mm Crank and Case Tolerances
As Given in the 356B Factory Manual

Item	"Small" Limit		"Large" Limit	
	mm	in.	mm	in.
Case Inside Diameter (Case Bore)				
	60.235	2.3715	60.245	2.3719
Crank Main Bearing Journals				
	49.975	1.9675	49.991	1.96815
Main Bearing Thickness				
	5.085	0.2002	5.099	0.20075
Connecting Rod Bore				
	56.980	2.2433	56.999	2.2441
Crank Rod Journals				
	52.987	2.0861	53.000	2.0866
Rod Bearing Thickness				
	1.96	0.0772	1.97	0.07756

The factory also gives the range of "running clearances" as follows:

Rod Bearing Running Clearance

	mm	in.
Lower Limit (New)	0.040	0.00157
Upper Limit (New)	0.092	0.00362
Wear Limit	0.130	0.0051

Main Bearing Running Clearance

#1 Bearing (Flywheel Main)

Lower Limit (New)	0.028	0.0011
Upper Limit (New)	0.078	0.0031
Wear Limit	0.170	0.0067

#2 And #3 Main Bearing

Lower Limit (New)	0.046	0.0018
Upper Limit (New)	0.100	0.00394
Wear Limit	0.170	0.0067

#4 Main Bearing (In Timing Cover)

Lower Limit (New)	0.040	0.0016
Upper Limit (New)	0.104	0.0041
Wear Limit	0.170	0.0067

Main Bearing Dowel Pins Sizes

VW or Small Dowel Pin (Used with 50mm Cranks in 356 A/B Engines)

Number Needed: 4
Length: 0.312"
Diameter: 0.195"

912 or "Big" Dowel Pin (Used with

C/SC/912 cranks in C/SC or 912 Engines)

Number Needed: 1
Length: 0.428"
Diameter: 0.205"

Rod Bearing Thicknesses For All 356/912 Cranks

Rod Bearing Size – Allowable Range- Low to High Limit (All Models)

	mm	in.
Standard	1.960 - 1.970	0.0772 - 0.0776
First Under	2.085 - 2.095	0.0821 - 0.0825
Second Under	2.210 - 2.220	0.0870 - 0.0874
Third Under	2.335 - 2.345	0.0920 - 0.0923"

Note: The numbers given in the spec book appear to be wrong! The above dimensions are correct!!!

Note that the previous tables give what the factory says should be the allowable range of the main and rod bearing clearances. If one were to calculate the possible clearances from the dimensions of the three component parts, one would get interesting answers. The *Exactly Nominal Running Clearance* is that obtained if *all* the parts have dimensions that are *exactly* in the middle of the tolerance range.

Exactly Nominal Rod Bearing Clearance

Clearance = Big End i.d. - Crank Journal o.d. - 2x (Bearing Thickness)

Clearance = 56.9895 mm - 52.9935 - 2(1.965) = 0.066 mm = 0.0026"

Loose Rod Bearing Clearances:

For the loosest rod bearing clearances, we need the "largest" big end diameter, the smallest crankshaft rod journals and the "thinnest" rod bearings:

Clearance = Big End i.d. - Crank Journal o.d. - 2x (Bearing Thickness)

Clearance = 56.999 - 52.987 - 2(1.96) = 0.092 mm = 0.00362"

Tight Rod Bearing Clearances:

For the "tight" clearance, we will use the smallest allowable big end diameter, the largest diameter crankshaft rod journal diameter and the fattest rod bearing thickness:

Clearance = Big End i.d. - Crank Journal o.d. - 2x (Bearing Thickness)

Clearance = 56.980 - 53.000 - 2(1.97) = 0.04 mm = 0.00157"

Exactly Nominal Main Bearing Clearances For 50 mm Cranks

Case (Standard)	60.24 mm	2.37165"
Crank (Standard)	49.983 mm	1.96783"
Main Bearing Thickness	5.092 mm	0.20047"

The *Exactly Nominal* Main Bearing Running Clearance obtained with the above dimensions is:

"Nominal" Clearance = Case i.d. - Crank o.d. - 2x (Bearing Thickness)

"Nominal" Clearance = 60.24 - 49.983 - 2(5.092) = 0.073 mm = 0.00287"

But, suppose that your engine was on the *loose* side – with all the dimensions of the parts *making up the main bearing running clearance* being right on the *too loose* side – this means, a *Large* case, a *Small* crank and *Thin* bearings.

The "Loose" Main Bearing Running Clearance For 50 mm Crankshafts:

Clearance = Case i.d. - Crank o.d. - 2 (Bearing Thickness)

Clearance = 60.245 - 49.975 - 2 (5.085) = 0.10 Mm = 0.00394"

The "loose" clearances are not within the factory's tolerance range for a "new" engine (0.0011" - 0.0031") for #1 main bearing, but which is within the tolerance range for #2 and #3 main bearing!

The "Tight" Main Bearing Clearances For 50 mm Crankshafts

Clearance = Case i.d. - Crank o.d. - 2x (Bearing Thickness)

Clearance = 60.235 - 49.991 - 2 (5.099) = 0.046 mm = 0.00181"

This is exactly equal to the factory's low limit running clearance for new engines (on #2 and #3 main bearing).

We have learned that if you have a 50 mm crank (an A or a B Normal or Super), and if all three participants that determine the Main or Rod Bearing Running Clearance are between the Factory Specified Low and High Limits, your Running Clearance will be proper! *(except, possibly for #1 main bearing!)*

Running Clearances With 55 mm Crankshafts

Item	"Small" Limit		"Large" Limit	
	mm	in.	mm	in.
Case Inside Diameter (Case Bore)				
	60.235	2.3715	60.245	2.3719
Crankshaft Main Bearing Diameter				
	54.971	2.1642	54.990	2.1650
Main Bearing Thickness				
	2.603	0.1025	2.615	0.10295

So, if one were to calculate the *exactly nominal* main bearing clearance for the C/SC/912 engine, one would get:

"Nominal" Clearance = Case i.d. - Crank o.d. - 2x (Bearing Thickness)

"Nominal" Clearance = 60.24 - 54.9805 - 2(2.609) = 0.0415 mm = 0.00163"

If one were to calculate the "loose" main bearing running clearance, with the largest allowable case size, the smallest allowable crank size and the thinnest allowable bearing thickness, the running clearance would be:

"Loose" Main Bearing Clearance For 55 mm Mains

Clearance = Case i.d. - Crank o.d. - 2x (Bearing Thickness)

Clearance = 60.245 - 54.971 - 2 (2.603) = 0.068 mm = 0.00268"

"Tight" Main Bearing Clearances For 55 Mm Crankshafts:

Clearance = Case i.d. - Crank o.d. - 2x (Bearing Thickness)

Clearance = 60.235 - 54.990 - 2 (2.615) = 0.015 mm = 0.00059"

This is below the factory's low limit

of 0.0011"!!! Thus, it is possible to have all three components making up the running clearance of the #2 and #3 middle main bearings of the c/sc/912 engine be within factoy tolerance, but have the running clearance be too small!

Now, you'll probably never run into this problem, as it's unlikely you'll *ever* find a case that is at "low limit" in bore diameter. *But*, if you had the case Align Bored and the machine shop bored it to low limit, *and* ground the crank to high limit on an undersize, *and* you had "fat" main bearings, you *could* end up with *too little* clearance at the #2 and #3 Middle Main Bearings of the C/SC/912!

Sizes And Tolerance Range Of The 50 mm A/B Crank And Case

Case Size	Allowable Range (Low To High Limit)
mm	in.
Standard	
60.235 - 60.245	2.3715 - 2.3719
First Over	
60.485 - 60.495	2.3813 - 2.3817
Second Over	
60.735 - 60.745	2.3911 - 2.3915

Crankshaft Rod Bearing Journal Diameter For All 356/912 Engines

Standard	
52.987 - 53.000	2.0861 - 2.0866
First Under	
52.737 - 52.750	2.0763 - 2.0768
Second Under	
52.487 - 52.500	2.0664 - 2.0669
Third Under	
52.237 - 52.250	2.0566 - 2.0571

Crankshaft Main Bearing Journal Diameter (For #1, #2 And #3 Main Bearings Of 50 mm Cranks)

Standard	
49.975 - 49.991	1.9675 - 1.9681
mm	in.
First Under	
49.725 - 49.741	1.9577 - 1.9583
Second Under	
49.475 - 49.491	1.9478 - 1.9485
Third Under	
49.225 - 49.241	1.9380 - 1.9386

Crankshaft Main Bearing Journal Diameter For 55 mm Cranks (For #1, #2 And #3 Main Bearing Journal Of The Super-90 And For #2 And #3 Main Bearing Journal Of The C/SC/912)

Standard	
54.971 - 54.990	2.1642 - 2.1650
First Under	
54.721 - 54.740	2.1544 - 2.1551
Second Under	
54.471 - 54.490	2.1445 - 2.1453
Third Under	
54.221 - 54.240	2.1347 - 2.1354

Rod Bearing Thicknesses For All 356/912 Cranks Allowable Range Low To High Limit

Standard	
1.960 - 1.970	0.0772 - 0.0776
First Under	
2.085 - 2.095	0.0821 - 0.0825
Second Under	
2.210 - 2.220	0.0870 - 0.0874
Third Under	
2.335 - 2.345	0.0920 - 0.0923

Note: the numbers given in the spec book are wrong! The above dimensions are correct.

Main Bearing Thickness For 50 mm Cranks, Standard Case Bore Corrected Version Of Factory Specs! (Old Thickness In Parentheses)

163

Standard

5.096 - 5.108	0.2006 - 0.2011	
(5.087 - 5.099)	(0.2003 - 0.2007)	
mm	in.	

First Under

5.221 - 5.233	0.2056 - 0.2060
(5.212 - 5.224)	(0.2052 - 0.2057)

Second Under

5.346 - 5.358	0.2105 - 0.2109
(5.337 - 5.349)	(0.2101 - 0.2106)

Third Under

5.471 - 5.483	0.2154 - 0.2159
(5.462 - 5.474)	(0.2150 - 0.2155)

For First Over, Align Bored Cases, With A 50 mm Crank, The Main Bearing Thicknesses Are:

Standard

5.221 - 5.233	0.2056 - 0.2060
(5.212 - 5.224)	(0.2052 - 0.2057)

First Under

5.346 - 5.358	0.2105 - 0.2109
(5.337 - 5.349)	(0.2101 - 0.2106)

Second Under

5.471 - 5.483	0.2154 - 0.2159
(5.462 - 5.474)	(0.2150 - 0.2155)

Third Under

5.596 - 5.608	0.2203 - 0.2208
(5.587 - 5.599)	(0.2200 - 0.2204)

For Second Over, Align Bored Cases, With A 50 mm Crank, The Main Bearing Thicknesses Are:

Standard

5.346 - 5.358	0.2105 - 0.2109
(5.337 - 5.349)	(0.2101 - 0.2106)

First Under

5.471 - 5.483	0.2154 - 0.2159
(5.462 - 5.474)	(0.2150 - 0.2155)

Second Under

5.596 - 5.608	0.2203 - 0.2208
(5.587 - 5.599)	(0.2200 - 0.2204)

Third Under

5.721 - 5.733	0.2252 - 0.2257
(5.703 - 5.724)	(0.2245 - 0.2254)

For A Standard Case, With A 55 mm Crankshaft Main Bearing Journal:

Low To High Limit (mm)
Low To High Limit (in)

Standard Crank	
2.603 - 2.615	0.1025 - 0.1030
First Under Crank	
2.728 - 2.740	0.1074 - 0.1079
Second Under Crank	
2.853 - 2.865	0.1123 - 0.1128
Third Under Crank	
2.978 - 2.990	0.1172 - 0.1177

For A First Over Case, With A 55 mm Crankshaft, The Main Bearing Thicknesses Are:

Standard Crank	
2.728 - 2.740	0.1074 - 0.1079
First Under Crank	
2.853 - 2.865	0.1123 - 0.1128
Second Under Crank	
2.978 - 2.990	0.1172 - 0.1177
Third Under Crank	
3.103 - 3.115	0.1222 - 0.1226

For A Second Over Case With A 55 mm Crankshaft, The Main Bearing Thicknesses Are:

Standard Crank	
2.853 - 2.865	0.1123 - 0.1128
First Under Crank	
2.978 - 2.990	0.1172 - 0.1177
Second Under Crank	
3.103 - 3.115	0.1222 - 0.1226
Third Under Crank	
3.228 - 3.240	0.1271 - 0.1276

The Maestro's Equations For Cranks, Cases And Bearing Sizes:

50 mm Crankshaft Main Bearing Diameter: (mm)

Diameter: (High Limit) = 49.991 -

0.25* (Undersize Number:1,2 or 3)

Diameter: (Low Limit) = 49.975 -
0.25* (Undersize Number:1,2 or 3)

55 mm Crankshaft Main Bearing
Diameter: (mm)

Diameter: (High Limit) = 54.990 -
0.25* (Undersize Number:1,2 or 3)

Diameter: (Low Limit) = 54.971 -
0.25* (Undersize Number:1,2 or 3)

Case Bore Size: (Exactly Nominal,
mm)

Case Bore = 60.24 + 0.25* (Case
Oversize Number, 0,1 or 2)

Main Bearing Thicknesses

For 50 mm Cranks:
A. High Limit Bearing Thickness, 50
mm Crank: Bearing Thickness =
5.108 + 0.125* (Case Oversize Number + Crank Undersize Number)

B. Low Limit Bearing Thickness, 50
mm Crank: Bearing Thickness =
5.096 + 0.125* (Case Oversize Number + Crank Undersize Number)

C. "Exactly Nominal" Bearing Thickness, 50 mm Crank: Bearing Thickness = 5.102 + 0.125* (Case Oversize Number + Crank Undersize Number)

For 55 mm Cranks:
A. High Limit Bearing Thickness, 55
mm Crank: Bearing Thickness =
2.615 + 0.125* (Case Oversize Number + Crank Undersize Number)

B. Low Limit Bearing Thickness, 55
mm Crank: Bearing Thickness =
2.603 + 0.125* (Case Oversize Number + Crank Undersize Number)

C. "Exactly Nominal" Bearing Thickness For 55 mm Cranks: Bearing

Thickness = 2.609 + 0.125* (Case
Oversize Number + Crank Undersize
Number)

*Note: Cases Oversize Number = 0.0
For A Standard Case, = 1.0 For A
First Over Case, = 2.0 For A Second
Over Case Etc.*

*Crank Undersize Numbers = 0.0 For
A Standard Crank, = 1.0 For A First
Under Crank, = 2.0 For A Second
Under Crank, = 3.0 For A Third
Under Crank*

Plug the numbers into the above
equations, crank out the answers, and
you can calculate the bearing thicknesses you need for any case oversize
by any crank undersize.

Calculating Compression Ratio

The higher the thermodynamic efficiency of the engine and the higher
the gas mileage! But, how high is too
high?
In an engine having flat-top pistons,
there are three things, volumes actually, that determine the compression
ratio of your engine. They are:

1. Cylinder volume – the volume
swept out by the piston

2. Head Volume – the volume of the
combustion chamber in the cylinder
head.

3. Deck Height or *Clearance* Volume
– the volume of that area between the
top of the piston and the cylinder
head. (since the piston can't touch the
head, there must therefore be a clearance volume!)

Given the above Volumes, the
Compression Ratio is determined
by the following formula:

C.R. = {(Cylinder Volume) + (Head

Volume) + (Clearance Volume)} ÷ {(Head Volume) + (Clearance Volume)}

In Porsche's case, not so simple, because the Porsche piston has a dome on it that protrudes into the combustion chamber of the head. Thus, since the dome protrudes into the head, you must subtract the volume of the dome from both the top and the bottom of the above equation. (that is, from both the numerator and denominator!)

In addition, you need to know the clearance volume and the dome volume, if you want to get an accurate compression ratio calculation! Both are difficult to determine on a Porsche!

Simplify the equation, letting "x" equal the Clearance Volume minus the Dome Volume! That is:

X = (Clearance Volume) - (Dome Volume)

Then, we obtain the Correct Compression Ratio Equation:

C.R. = {(Cylinder Volume) + (Head Volume) + X} ÷ (Head Volume + X)

Now, all we have to do is get "X"! We know the Cylinder Volume, as it is merely the "piston displacement" of one cylinder – or the engine displacement divided by four. The Head Volume was determined at the factory and is stamped into the head between cylinder holes in cc – that's the little 58,5 or 60,0. (The *comma* is the German *decimal point*) and we know the Compression Ratio – the factory gives it in the Spec Book! Thus, we know everything in the Compression Ratio Equation *except* "X"".

X = {(Cylinder Volume) ÷ (C.R. - 1.0)} - (Head Volume)

The cylinder volume is 1582/4 = 395.5 cc; the Compression Ratio Varies – the Normal is 7.5:1:

X (Normal) = {395.5 ÷ (7.5 - 1.0)} - Head Volume
X = 60.846 - HEAD VOLUME

Since most cylinder heads have a head volume of around 60.0 cc, let's assume that the head volume equals the 60.846, and "X" then is 0 for the Normal (The Dome Volume = the Clearance Volume).

For the Super, with a compression ratio of 8.5:1, "X" is:

X (Super) = {395.5 ÷ (8.5 - 1.0)} - Head Volume

X (Super) = 52.73 - Head Volume

This time, 52.73 is obviously *not* the Head Volume, so we must make some assumptions about Head Volume. Head Volume on the A/B Normal, Super and Super 90 engines varies from 58.0 to 60.5 cc, with an average of 59.0 for the A/B Normal and Supers and 60.0 for the Super-90. For C/SC/912 engines, the head volumes go from 60.0 to 62.0 cc, with 61 cc as the 912 median. So, let's use 60.0 cc Then, "X" for the Super is 7.27 cc.

For the "Super-90" engine, with a Compression Ratio of 9.0, "X" becomes:

X (S-90) = {395.5 ÷ (9.0 - 1.0)} - Head Volume

X (S-90) = 49.44 - Head Volume

Since we're using 60 cc for Head Volume, "X" for the Super 90 is 10.56 cc.

C, (Compression Ratio 8.5:1), X for the C = 7.27 cc

SC (Compression Ratio 9.5:1), X for the SC = 13.47 cc

912 (Compression Ratio 9.3:1), X for the 912 = 12.35 cc

Now, since we have found "X" for all engines (to a first approximation, at least) lets us return to the definition of "X". Remember, "X" was defined as the clearance volume minus the dome volume! Since we don't really know exactly what the clearance volume, we must estimate it. A *clearance* between the top of the piston and the head must be of the order of 1 mm. Less than that, and the piston will hit the head. Much more that that and the compression ratio would be too low! Thus, using 1 mm (0.1 cm) as the deck height or clearance, the clearance volume is:

Clearance Volume = (3.14159) $(Clearance)$ $\{(Diameter\ Of\ Cylinder)^2\} \div 4$

Clearance Volume = (3.14159) $(8.25\ cm)^2$ $(0.1\ cm) \div 4$

Clearance Volume = 5.34 cc

Since "X" for the Normal was 0, the clearance volume must equal the "dome" of the Normal. But there is a very slight dome on a Normal – a mere 5.34 cc. – just about equal to the Clearance Volume.

And For The Others:

Dome Volume (Super) = 5.34 - (-7.27) = 12.6 cc
Dome Volume (Super-90) = 5.34 - (-10.56) = 15.9 cc
Dome Volume (C) = 5.34 - (-7.27) = 12.61 cc
Dome Volume (SC) = 5.34 - (-13.47) = 18.81 cc
Dome Volume 912 = 5.34 - (-12.35) = 17.69 cc

Note: Since we know that the SC and 912 pistons are the same, their domes should be the same. But, there is a slight difference according to the calculation. The difference lies in the assumption of the *same* Head Volume for our calculation of "X" and then Dome Volume. Actually, SCs and 912s have about one more cc in the head, and if we repeat the calculation using 61 cc for the 912 head, we would get a Dome Volume of 18.68 cc for the 912 close to the 18.81 cc of the SC.

Dome Volume (cc)		"X" Value (cc)
Normal	5.34	0.00
Super	2.6	-7.27
Super-90	15.9	-10.56
C	13.6	-7.27
SC	18.75	-13.41
912	18.75	-13.41

If you were to use stock factory pistons in your engine, along with stock, unflycut heads, you could calculate your Compression Ratio fairly closely. For Example, with 912 head of 62.0 cc and 912 pistons, we have a Compression Ratio of 9.14 (Since the Compression Ratio of the 912 with 61cc heads was Stock at 9.3:1, *the difference one cc makes can be significant*)

If you put a Normal piston into a 912 head, the compression ratio is 7.38. If, however, you replaced your 912 head with a B head having a Head Volume of 58.0 cc, and used the 912 pistons, your Compression Ratio would be 9.87!

What Happens When You Flycut The Head

If you flycut the head a bit – to *clean it up*, or to fix a warped or leaking head. When you flycut the head, you remove say, 0.010" off both the inside, sealing surface of the head and a like amount off the outside surface of the head. Thus, the depth that the cylinder protrudes into the head is the same and the cylinder shoulder won't hit the outside of the head! But,the piston will now *protrude* .010" further into the combustion chamber, since .010" of the combustion chamber just isn't there any more! Thus, flycutting the heads reduces the Head Volume. We can calculate this amount by the same technique used to determine Clearance Volume! In fact, if 1 mm (0.040") is surfaced from the head, we know from a previous calculation that that volume (82.5 mm diameter, 1 mm long cylinder) is 5.34 cc. Or, if just $1/4$ mm (0.010") were removed from the head, the head volume would be decreased by some 5.34 ÷ 4 = 1.33 cc. Not very much of a volume decrease, but the Compression Ratio of the 912 engine with the 912 pistons, a 912 head having a head volume of 62 cc, with the head having been flycut $1/4$ mm (0.010") is 9.37, Just a bit higher than a "stock" 912!

Installing additional cylinder base gaskets increases the Head Volume, by spacing the piston out from the head the thickness of the base gasket (s)! (i.e. it's equivalent to spacing the head out further... or increasing the Deck Height or Clearance Volume if you like.) And, if one makes the assumption that each cylinder base gasket (in addition to the one normally used) is $1/4$ mm thick (0.010"), then, we can calculate the Compression Ratio fairly easily!

So, in conclusion, the final formula for Compression Ratio, considering Cylinder Volume, Head Volume, Clearance Volume, Dome Volume, Flycut Volume and Shim Volume, (where "X" is the Clearance Volume minus the Dome Volume) is:

C.R. = {(Cyl. Volume) + (Head Vol-

ume) + (X) + (Flycut Volume) + (Shim Volume)} ÷ {(Head Volume) + (X) + (Flycut Volume) + (Shim Volume)}

Note: in the equation, both "X" and the flycut volume are negative.

If you want to use all positive numbers, and break down "X" into the clearance volume minus the dome volume, the formula is:

C.R. = {Cyl. Volume + Head Volume + Clearance Volume - Dome - Flycut + shim} ÷ {Head Volume + Clearance Volume - Dome - Flycut + Shim}

Compression Ratio Calculations For The "Big Bore" Kit

We'll confine the discussion to the 86 mm Big Bore Kit. The New Cylinder Volume of the Big Bore Kit is 429.85 cc. For all four cylinders, the engine displacement is some 1719.4 cc. The Clearance Volume for the Big Bore kit is 5.81 cc. X is -9.21. The Dome Volume is 15.02

Using an un-flycut, B Super head, with a Head Volume of 58.0 cc. The Compression Ratio would be 9.8! Most heads have a bigger Head Volume, so the 9.8:1 compression for an un-flycut, A/B/S-90 head with a Big Bore Kit is the *worst case* in this case!

Frequently the Big Bore piston will hit the head on A/B Normal/Super/ Super-90 engines, (especially the early As) and will necessitate additional cylinder base gaskets or cutting the head/piston.

If you flycut the B Super head $1/4$ mm (0.010"), then the Compression Ratio would be 10.08, which is getting *way* up there.

The Maestro's Interesting Data For Compression Ratio Calculations

Stock Pistons: 82.5 mm Diameter
Volumes in ccs

Engine Type	Dome Volumes	"X" Values	Head Volumes	Compression Ratio (Stock)
Normal	5.34	0.00	58-60	7.5
Super	12.6	- 7.27	58-60	8.5
Super-90	15.9	-10.56	59-61	9.0
C	13.6	- 7.27	60-62	8.5
SC	18.75	-13.41	60-62	9.5
912	18.75	-13.41	60-62	9.3

Note 1: Cylinder Volume, all 1600 cc 356/912 = 395.5 cc/cylinder
Note 2: Clearance Volume @ 1 mm (0.040") = 5.34 cc
Note 3: Flycut Volume @ 0.25 mm (0.010") = 1.335 cc
Note 4: Additional cylinder base gasket volume = 1.335 cc/gasket
Note 5: Additional cylinder base gaskets = (total number -1.0)
Note 6: Assumed thickness of cylinder base gasket = 0.010"

1720 Japanese Big Bore Kits – 86 mm Diameter
Volumes in ccs and Using Only One Cylinder Base Gasket
("Stock" Set Up, Except the Addition of the Big Bore Kit)

Engine Type	Big Bore Dome Volumes	Big Bore "X" Values	Approx. Head Volumes (Unflycut)	Calculated Compression Ratio (With Big Bore) And Head Volume
Normal	15.02	-9.21	58	9.83
Super	15.02	-9.21	59	9.63
Super-90	15.02	-9.21	60	9.46
C	15.02	-9.21	60.5	9.38
SC	15.02	-9.21	61	9.30
912	15.02	-9.21	62	9.14

Note 1: All above calculations are for the 86 mm Big Bore 1720 Kit:
Note 2: Cylinder Volume, with 1720 Kit 86 mm = 429.85 cc/cylinder
Note 3: Clearance Volume @ 1 mm (0.040") = 5.81 cc
Note 4: Flycut Volume @ 0.25 mm (0.010") = 1.45 cc
Note 5: Additional Cylinder Base Gasket Volume = 1.45 cc/gasket
Note 6: Additional Cylinder Base Gaskets = (Total Number -1.0)

Shim Table For Use With Japanese 1720 Kit

Head Type	Amt. Flycut Off Head	Shims Req. (Total #)
A/B	0.000"	2-5 (avg. 3-4)
Normal Or	0.010"	3-6 (avg. 4-5)
Super Or	0.020"	4-7 (avg. 5-6)
Super-90	0.030"	5-7 (avg. 6-7)
C/SC/912	0.000"	1-2 (avg. 1)
	0.010"	2-3 (avg. 2)
	0.020"	3-4 (avg. 3)
	0.030"	4-5 (avg. 4)

Case Acorn Nuts Torquing Sequence

```
6   2   4

5   1   3
```

First, torque all the nuts to 15 ft-lbs. Then, try turning the crank over by grabbing the nose of the crank and rotating (don't get your fingers caught in the cam gears!) If the crank turns over easily – wonderful – if it doesn't, stop! Find the reason – Usually the reason is that the main bearings are not seated properly on their dowel pins. But sometimes, the crank is ground incorrectly or the bearings are the wrong size! If the crank *does* turn over easily (as it should, since the case bore, crank and bearings *were* measured), continue to torque the case acorn nuts in the above order to 20, then 25 and finally 29 ft-lbs. Then, repeat *three* times the 29 ft-lbs torque setting. Note: during the torquing, you will have to hold the other end of the through bolt to keep the through bolt from turning. Use your 17 mm open end wrench or a 17 mm socket with another socket wrench to hold the through bolt head. If the through bolt is allowed to turn, (and it will turn, if allowed), it can screw up

the little O-ring and cause a leak. (A leak that's hard to find and *very* difficult to fix!)

The case perimeter bolts have 14 mm ATF heads and 14 mm ATF nuts if they're from a 356, 13 mm ATF nuts and bolts for a 912. The torque is 15 - 18 ft-lbs and the sequence is 3 - 1 - 2 - 4.

Head Bolt Installation For Cast Iron Rocker Stands

Now, take your two not-so-wide-brimmedhead bolt and place them into the two middle holes in the lower row of head stud holes. Just start them with your fingers, don't tighten them down yet. Then take the two wide-brimmed head bolts and install them in the two outer holes in the lower row of head holes! Then,take the four top, short ($^3/_4$") head bolts and install them on the top row of studs. Again, just start them (you will have to use your 10 mm allen head (internal hex) wrench to start the top row of head bolts!)

The Head Bolt Arrangement For Cast Iron Rocker Stands

```
S   SS   S

W   **   W
```

Where: S = short ($^3/_4$") head bolt used on top studs, W = wide brimmed head bolt used on outer, lower studs, * = not-so-wide brimmed head bolt used on middle, lower studs.

Head Bolt Installation For Aluminum Rocker Stands

Take your three wide-brimmed head bolts and install them in the lower row in every hole *except* the left-hand middle hole. The installation drawing for those of you using the aluminum rocker stands is:

S   SS S

W *W W

Okay, now get out your 10 mm internal hex wrench (Allen wrench) that's about 5" long (available from Snap-on and others), with the $3/_8$" drive and attach it to your regular socket wrench. Now, go around to the head bolts in the following order, tightening them *only* a turn or fraction thereof at a time, once the obvious slop or gap has been removed. The order is (according to the Factory):

6   2 4   8

7   3 1   5

Although I also use the pattern:

8   2   6

5   3 1   7

Torquing The Heads

Get out the torque wrench and attach the 10 mm metric Allen socket to it. Begin at one head and torque the head bolts, using your particular pattern, to 15 ft-lbs. Now go to the other head and torque to 15 ft-lbs. Return to the first head and torque to 20 ft-lbs. Then, repeat on the other head. Return again to the first head and torque to 25 ft-lbs. Repeat on the other head. Now you have a choice – the Factory Manual says to torque the head bolts to some 22 ft-lbs, but the Maestro likes a little more (if some is good, more is better), between 24 - 26.5 ft-lbs on the heads.

Repeat the final torque at least three times on each head – alternating heads between each torquing. This alternate torquing sequence was mentioned in the book *How to Hotrod VW Engines*. As you torque one head down, the head studs distort the case a bit. Then as you torque the other head, the head studs of the other head also distort. If you do the complete torquing of one head and move to the other, you may end up with one (or both) heads improperly torqued when you're finished. If you alternate the torquing procedure, going from one head to the other, as you build up the torque towards its final value, the distortion is neutralized (or minimized, at least) as you go back and forth between heads. Likewise, that is the reason for repeating the final torque at least three times, again alternating between heads. Using this procedure (and decent sealing surfaces), the probability of having a leaking head is reduced to less than 5%.

Oil Pressure Springs, Plungers and Caps

In an attempt to clarify the confusion concerning oil pressure relief springs, plungers and caps, here is a table.

Pre-1957.5 Engine Having Only One Relief Spring/Plunger

	Plunger	Spring	Cap
Length	0.607"	2.05"	0.918"
Diameter	0.470"	0.450"	0.625"
Thickness	0.077"	-	
Wire Thickness		0.050"	
Number Of Turns		5	

1957.5 - 1963 Engines Using Two Plunger/Springs (One Bypass + One Pressure Valve = Two Plunger/Springs)

	Bypass Plunger	Spring	Cap	Relief Spring
Length	0.713"	2.68"	0.840"	2.60"
Diameter	0.590"	0.485"	0.700"	0.485"
Thickness			0.040"	
Wire Thickness	0.050"			0.055"
Number Of Turns	17			13

For Engines Having The *Long* Plunger – Some 356 Bs, And All C/912s

Plunger

Length	0.875"
Diameter	0.590"
Thickness	0.040"

Now, for a bit of explanation. The 1955 - 1957.5 engines had only one plunger/spring in the form of a pressure relief valve. This valve was made up of a plunger that is the *smallest* in diameter of all the 356/912 plungers. In fact, it really is a 36 hp VW plunger! A shorter spring (actually, the *shortest* spring at 2.05") was also used with the *smallest* diameter plunger. This combination, making up the oil pressure relief valve, went into the timing cover from the lower left hand corner, pointing upwards towards the crankshaft at about a 45 degree angle.

Crank Type, Year, Distinguishing Characteristics

"A", 1955 - 1957, 50 mm main bearing journals; looks like a VW with 8 dowel pins; not counterbalanced, uses one piece main bearing in front of cam drive gears; won't roll if rotated around crank axis.

"B", 1958 - 1963, Same as "A" crank except that it has oval shaped flanges connecting each pair of rod journals; 50 mm main bearing journals; will roll if rotated around crank axis; not coun-

terbalanced

"S-90", 1960 - 1963, 2 types of s-90 cranks; both have 55 mm main bearing journals for all three main bearings, including the flywheel main bearing: one is counterbalanced; one is not; otherwise they are identical; both require special split flywheel (thrust) main bearing, special thick, larger diameter flywheel shims; both use the slightly different S-90 flywheel.

"C", 1964 - 1965, 55 mm center two main bearing journals; 50 mm flywheel main bearing journal; uses split main bearings held into case by tabs, not dowels; not counterbalanced.

"SC/912", 1964 - 1969, both SC and 912 cranks are identical; both have 55 mm center two main bearing journals; 50 mm flywheel main bearing journal; both *are* counterbalanced.

Connecting Rod Types And Part Numbers

Rod Part Number, Year, Approximate Type, Distinguishing Features

502.03.105, 1955 - 1959, "A", Rod bearing tab on left-hand side.

502.03.105, 1960 - 1961, "Early B", Similar to the "A" rod, but with rod bearing tab on right hand side.

616.103.101.00, 1961 - 1963, "B" Different part number from "A" or "Early B" rods, somewhat stronger; rod bearing tab on (with a triangle) right-hand side.

616.103.101.01, 1962 - 1969, "C/SC/ 912", Much thicker rod cap; rod centers on itself, not on crank; tab slot on right hand-side; The best and strongest rod

Flywheel Synopsis In Chronological Order

Type, Year, Description

356A, 1955 - 1959, 180 mm clutch diameter; 6 v. ring gear on flywheel heavy, unlightened flywheel; 180 mm VW style spring-type pressure plate; Late As got a special diaphragm pressure plate, still 180 mm, with a collar to mate with the "A"" style throw-out bearing of the "A" transmission. Clutch depth of 24 mm (0.945")

Early S-90, (1960), 180 mm clutch used; 6 v. ring gear teeth; flywheel was somewhat lighter; otherwise is similar to "A"; Factory spec book gives a clutch depth of 24 mm for the Super 90. (the distance between the top surface of the flywheel where the pressure plate mounts and the inner surface of the flywheel)

Later, S-90 (1960 - 1963) 200 mm clutch, 6 v. ring gear, somewhat lightened 25mm (0.984") clutch depth; hub of flywheel protrudes into crank 1 mm less than other non S-90 flywheels.

C/SC, (1964 - 1965), 200 mm clutch; 6 v. ring gear, similar to A/B flywheel, but takes a 200 mm (TYPE 200M) clutch. 25 mm (0.984") Clutch depth.

912, (1965 - 1969), Completely different flywheel than that used on 356s. Larger diameter, will not fit into 356 transmission case; 12 v. ring gear teeth; takes different, 200 MX pressure plate; early 912s had same clutch disc as "C/SC"; 1969 912 clutch disc with rubber center won't work with 356 C 200 mm pressure plate. 22.5 mm (0.886") Clutch depth.

Cams

Porsche camshafts are a little easier to do an anthropological study on, since the factory was nice enough to put pretty definitive part numbers on them. The Porsche part number will usually appear between the first and second cam lobe nearest the flywheel end of the cam. The last three digits of the part number will tell you what the cam really is assuming that it hasn't been ground in the interim. Then check the end of the cam where the drive gear bolts. If the cam has a part number on the gear end, it is most likely an early normal. In addition, there is, on some cams, a "15" or "16" on the nose of the cam, near the slot used to drive the oil pump gear. Depending upon what you find on the cam, here is the translation:

Last 3 Digits Of Part #	# on End Of Cam	Model
.103	None	Normal
.102	None	Super or S-90
.102	15	"C"
.102	16	"SC/912"
.105	16	Wide Lobe 912
None	Ro 200	Replacement Wide Lobe
None	None	

Interesting Characteristics Of Oil Pressure Senders

Manufacturer's Name or Identification, May Include Date Stamp	Pressure Rating	Color of Plastic	Type Of Nut Connector
SH/L010/1166	0.5 atu (+0.2-0.1)	Black	Screw
.10.3... Bosch	0.6 atu	Brown	Screw
0.6.0.3. 1 63		Black	Screw
6.72 M10x1	0.4	Black	Screw
		Black	Screw
		Black	Serrated Spade Nut
A Square Embossed Into Plastic Top, Near Connector		Black	Screw
Strange Double-Terminal Type		Black	Two Terminals (Both Nuts)
Messmer Radolfzell		Black	Spade
Messmer Radolfzell (West Germany)		Black	Spade
Messmer Radolfzell DPB			Spade
VDO 111/4/20 03.3	0.4 (+0.2-0.1)	Black	Screw

Interesting Characteristics Of Temperature Senders

Mfg.	Part Number	Max Temp	Voltage	Terminal Type	Date
VDO	-	250 C	6v	Nut (Long!)	1.55
VDO	-	250 C	6v	Nut	10/58
VDO	-	250 C	6v	Nut	2/59
VDO	-	250 C	6v	Nut	1/60
VDO	-	250 C	6v	Nut	5/60
VDO	-	250 C	6v	Nut	6/61
VDO	-	250 C	6v	Nut	12/61
VDO	-	250 C	6v	Nut	2/62
VDO	-	250 C	6v	Nut	11/62
VDO	-	250 C	6v	Nut	3/63
VDO	-	200 C	6v	Spade	10/63
VDO	-	250 C	6v	Spade	2/64
VDO	-	200 C	6v	Spade	5/65
VDO	-	200 C	12-24v	Spade	11/65
VDO	-	200 C	6v	Spade	9/66
VDO	901.741.632.00	200 C	12-24v	Spade	11/66
VDO	901.741.632.00	200 C	12-24v	Spade	4/67
VDO	901.741.632.00	200 C	12-24v	Spade	1.68
VDO	323 801/4/18	150 C	6-24v	Weird Spade	12/68

174

Bearing Part Numbers

Main Bearings – 356 A/B Normal and Super – With 50 mm Main Bearing Journals on Crank – 1955-1957.5

Part Number Of Bearing Set

Type: KS	Glyco	Porsche
STD X STD:Set# 87 985 600	H845/4-STD	546 101 901 00
STD X .25:Set# 87 985 610	H845/4-.25 mm	546 101 901 50
STD X .50:Set# 87 985 620	H845/4-.50 mm	546 101 901 55
STD X .75:Set# 87 985 630	H845/4-.75 mm	546 101 901 65

Part Number Of Individual Bearings Within Above Sets

KS	Glyco	Porsche
Flywheel Main Bearing		
85 035 600 (STD X STD)	02-2783 H	546 101 101 00
85 035 610 (STD X .25mm)	02-2783/.25	546 101 101 50
85 035 620 (STD X .50mm)	02-2783/.50	546 101 101 55
85 035 630 (STD X .75mm)	02-2783/.75	546 101 101 65
Middle Main		
78 019 600 (STD X STD)	02-2966	539 101 174 00
78 019 610 (STD X .25mm	02 2966/.25	539 101 174 50
78 019 620 (STD X .50mm)	02-2966/.50	539 101 174 55
78 019 630 (STD X .75mm)	02-2966/.75	539 101 174 65
#3 Main Bearing		
85 037 600 (STD X STD)	02-2967	546 101 103 00
85 037 610 (STD X .25mm)	02-2967/.25	546 101 103 50
85 037 620 (STD X .50mm)	02-2967/.50	546 101 103 55
85 037 630 (STD X .75mm)	02-2967/.75	546 101 103 65
#4 Main Bearing:		
85 038 600 (STD X STD)	02-2348	539 101 146 00
85 038 610 (STD X .25mm)	02-2348/.25	539 101 146 50
85 038 620 (STD X .50mm)	02-2348/.50	539 101 146 55
85 038 630 (STD X .75mm)	02-2348/.75	539 101 146 65

Note: For 1955-1957.5 Engines, #4 Main Bearing:

85 039 600 (STD X STD)	02-2968	
85 039 610 (STD X .25mm)	02-2968/.25	
85 039 620 (STD X .50mm)	02-2968/.50	
85 039 630 (STD X .75mm)	02-2968/.75	

Main Bearings 1955 - 1963 N/S With 50 mm A/B Cranks
Align Bore Bearings – First Over on the Case (60.49 Mm/2.3815")

Part Number of First Over (Align Bore) Main Bearing Set

KS	Glyco	Porsche
87 986 700 (FIRST OVER X STD)		546 101 901 60
87 986 710 (FIRST OVER X .25mm)		546 101 901 70
87 986 720 (FIRST OVER X .50mm)		546 101 901 75
87 986 730 (FIRST OVER X .75mm)		546 101 910 85

Part Numbers of Individual Bearings Within First Over Main Bearing Set
(50mm Crank)

Flywheel Main, First Over Size:

85 035 700 (FIRST OVER X STD)		546 101 101 60
85 035 710 (FIRST OVER X .25mm)		546 101 101 70
85 035 720 (FIRST OVER X .50mm)		546 101 101 75
85 035 730 (FIRST OVER X .75mm)		546 101 101 85

Middle Main, First Over Size:

78 019 700 (FIRST OVER X STD)		539 101 174 60
78 019 710 (FIRST OVER X .25mm)		539 101 174 70
78 019 720 (FIRST OVER X .50mm)		539 101 174 75
78 019 730 (FIRST OVER X .75mm)		539 101 174 85

3 Main, First Over Sizes:

85 037 700 (FIRST OVER X STD)		546 101 103 60
85 037 710 (FIRST OVER X .25mm)		546 101 103 70
85 037 720 (FIRST OVER X .50mm)		546 101 103 75
85 037 730 (FIRST OVER X .75mm)		546 101 103 85

#4 Main (Usually Standard, Timing Cover is Not Align Bored)

85 038 700 (STD X STD)		539 101 146 00
85 038 710 (STD X .25mm)		539 101 146 50
85 038 720 (STD X .50mm)		539 101 146 55
85 038 730 (STD X .75mm)		539 101 146 65

Main Bearings For Super 90 Engines- Having Three 55 Mm Main Journals

Part Number Of Bearing Set

KS	Glyco	Porsche
87 796 600 (STD X STD)	H534/4 STD	616 100 130 00
87 796 610 (STD X .25mm)	H534/4 .25	616 100 130 50
87 796 620 (STD X .50mm)	H534/4 .50	616 100 130 55
87 796 630 (STD X .75mm)	H534/4 .75	616 100 130 65

Part Numbers Of The Individual Bearings Within The Above Sets:

Flywheel Main Bearing (Split, Two-piece Flywheel Main Bearing

78 171 600 (STD X STD)	72-1972	616 100 131 00
85 499 600 (STD X STD) with elephant logo on back of bearing		
78 171 610 (STD X .25mm)	72-1972/.25	616 100 131 50
85 499 610 (STD X .25mm) (with elephant)		
78 171 620 (STD X .50mm)	72-1972/.50	616 100 131 55
85 499 620 (STD X .50mm) (with elephant)		
78 171 630 (STD X .75mm)	72-1972/.75	616 100 131 65
85 499 630 (STD X .75mm) (with elephant)		

The Two Middle Main Bearings (Both Middle Main Bearings Are The Same)

78 198 600 (STD X STD)	72-1973	616 100 132 00
85 384 600 (STD X STD) (with elephant)		
78 198 610 (STD X .25mm)	72-1973/.25	616 100 132 50
85 384 610 (STD X .25mm) (with elephant)		
78 198 620 (STD X .50mm)	72-1973/.50	616 100 132 55
85 384 620 (STD X .50mm) (with elephant)		
78 198 630 (STD X .75mm)	72-1973/.75	616 100 132 65
85 384 630 (STD X .75mm) (with elephant)		

#4 Main Bearing (In The Timing Cover)

85 038 600 (STD X STD)	02-2348	539 101 146 00
85 038 610 (STD X .25mm)	02-2348/.25	539 101 146 50
85 038 620 (STD X .50mm)	02-2348/.50	539 101 146 55
85 038 630 (STD X .75mm)	02-2348/.75	539 101 146 65

Align Bore Main Bearings For Super-90 Cranks (Only Porsche Number)

Bearing Set

616 100 130 60 (FIRST OVER X STD)
616 100 130 70 (FIRST OVER X .25mm)
616 100 130 75 (FIRST OVER X .50mm)
616 100 130 85 (FIRST OVER X .75mm)

Flywheel Main

616 100 131 60 (First Over X Std)
616 100 131 70 (FIRST OVER X .25mm)
616 100 131 75 (FIRST OVER X .50mm)
616 100 131 85 (FIRST OVER X .75mm)

#2 And #3 Middle Mains (Same)

616 100 132 60 (FIRST OVER X STD)
616 100 132 70 (FIRST OVER X .25mm)
616 100 132 75 (FIRST OVER X .50mm)
616 100 132 85 (FIRST OVER X .75mm)

#4 Main Case is Usually Not Align Bored

539 101 146 00 (STD X STD)
539 101 146 50 (STD X .25mm)
539 101 146 55 (STD X .50mm)
539 101 146 65 (STD X .75mm)

Main Bearings For C/SC/912 Cranks- 55 mm on Middle Two Mains 50 mm on Flywheel Main

KS	Glyco	Porsche
STD X STD	H799/4	616 100 138 00
STD X .25mm	H799/4 .25mm	616 100 138 50
STD X .50mm	H799/4 .50mm	616 100 138 55
STD X .75mm	H799/4 .75mm	616 100 138 65

Flywheel Main Bearing Part Number

STD X STD, 85 035 600	02-2783	546 101 101 00
STD X .25mm, 85 035 610	02-2783/.25mm	546 101 101 50
STD X .50mm, 85 035 620	02-2783/.50mm	546 101 101 55
STD X .75mm, 85 035 630	02-2783/.75mm	546 101 101 65

#2 And #3 Middle Main Bearing Part Number (Same)

STD X STD (See Super-90	72-1973	616 101 132 00
STD X .25mm middle main	72-1973/.25mm	616 101 132 50
STD X .50mm bearing numbers)	72-1973/.50mm	616 101 132 55
STD X .75mm	72-1973/.75mm	616 101 132 65

#4 Main Bearing

STD X STD 85 038 600	02-2348	539 101 146 00
STD X .25mm 85 038 610	02-2348/.25mm	539 101 146 50
STD X .50mm 85 038 620	02-2348/.50mm	539 101 146 55
STD X .75 85 038 630	02-2348/.75mm	539 101 146 65

Align Bore Main Bearings For C/SC/912 Cranks – 55 mm Middle Two

Mains, 50 mm Flywheel Main:

KS	Glyco	Porsche

Bearing Set

FIRST OVER X STD		616 100 138 60
FIRST OVER X .25mm		616 100 138 70
FIRST OVER X .50mm		616 100 138 75
FIRST OVER X .75mm		616 100 138 85

Flywheel Main

FIRST OVER X STD		546 101 101 60
FIRST OVER X .25mm		546 101 101 70
FIRST OVER X .50mm		546 101 101 75
FIRST OVER X .75mm		546 101 101 85

#2 And #3 Middle Mains

FIRST OVER X STD		616 101 132 60
FIRST OVER X .25mm		616 101 132 70
FIRST OVER X .50mm		616 101 132 75
FIRST OVER X .75mm		616 101 132 85

#4 Main Bearing

STD X STD		539 101 142 00
STD X .25mm		539 101 142 50
STD X .50mm		539 101 142 55
STD X .75mm		539 101 142 65

Rod Bearings "A" Style – Tab On Left

STD	71-1657	616 103 141 00
.25mm	71-1657/.25mm	616 103 141 50
.50mm	71 1657/.50mm	616 103 141 60
.75mm	71-1657/.75mm	616 103 141 70

Rod Bearings B/C/SC/912/Super-90 – Tab on Right

STD 87 797 600 78 170 600	71-1971	616 103 142 02
.25mm 87 797 610 78 170 610	71-1971/.25	616 103 142 52
.50mm 87 797 620 78 170 620	71-1971/.50	616 103 142 62
.75mm 87 797 630 78 170 630	71-1971/.75	616 103 142 72

Pin Bushings For Small End Of Connecting Rod

KS	Glyco	Porsche
85 892 690	55-3280	

Crankshaft Identification By Part Number

If you can find and read the Porsche Part Number on the crankshaft, this is what it was when it was new:

Part Number	What It Was/Is
616 102 013 00	A/B Normal and Super Crank – 50 mm Main Bearings
616 102 013 03	C Crank – 50 mm on Flywheel; 55 mm on 2 Middle Mains
616 102 101 00	Super-90 Non-Counterbalanced Crank – 55 mm on All Three Main Mains
616 102 015 00	Super-90 Counterbalanced Crank – 55 mm on All Three Main Mains
616 102 015 01	SC/912 Crank – 50 mm on Flywheel Main; 55 mm on Middle Two Mains

Distributors

Distributor Number – Points Adjustable With Off-Center Screw?

VJR4 BR18 – Yes
VL4 BRS 383 – Yes
VJ4 BR9 – Yes
VJR4 BR8 – Yes
VJU4BR8 – Yes
0 231 129 022 – No (Super-90)
0 231 129 031 – No (replacement type with aluminum case)
9 230 081 050 – No (replacement)

All Porsche distributors except the late 1968 - 1969 912 were of the all-mechanical advance type – meaning that no vacuum advance was used. Instead, as the RPM of the engine increased, weights underneath the point plate in the distributor moved outward as a result of the increased centrifugal force caused by the higher RPM. As the weights moved outward, they caused the shaft holding the rotor and the point activating cam to rotate slightly, thus advancing the timing with increasing RPM. The advance weights were brought back to the idle or stop position with two small, but fairly strong springs.

Normally, everything would work fine, and original distributors would go amazing distances with no difficulty or maintenance. However, they eventually wear out, sometimes in strange ways. Occasionally, the advance mechanism will stick in one position which means that no advance at all occurs. Then, you can static time the engine until you're blue in the face, and it still won't run properly.

Sometimes, the center shaft that opens the points and turns the rotor gets a wobble in it from excessive wear in the "bearings", and the timing wanders about 10 degrees or so, thereby causing erratic operation of the engine.

Chapter 9

Engine/Gearbox Conversions

Engine Swaps

Vol. 12, No. 3 David Seeland

356 Engine in a VW Bug

Of course, for a real "sleeper" an engine swap involves an exotic engine in a mundane body like the V-12 Ferrari in a Jeep Wagoneer body done at Harrah's some years ago. Or, a Porsche engine (push-rod or four cam) in a Bug. Maserati engined Bugatti's (exotic engine into exotic body) are relatively uncommon.

Steve Ruddock sent me a photo of a BMW motorcycle. Let's see, two cam covers on each side... four cams! Yes, you're right, a four-cam Carrera engine! An example close to the exotic engined exotic category. Too much power or weight or something because the front fork collapsed killing the owner.

I've put 356 engines in VW's twice for different reasons. While attending grad school at the University of Utah in Salt Lake City, I owned a black 1963 Karmann Ghia and it looked so much faster than it was that I first tried a Judson Supercharger ($5 from a laundromat bulletin board – missing the drive pulley and the "Marvel Mystery Oiler"). It helped some, but burned big notches in all the valves in the process. I sold the blower to someone else who hoped it would work bet-ter for him. Next I decided to try a 140 hp Corvair engine, but the junk yard had sold it in the period between talk-ing to them and arriving in Pocatello, Idaho – but, they knew of a wrecked 356 in Boise. The next trip was to Boise with the passenger seat re-moved. Success! A 1962 1600-S with 40,000 miles. After re-ringing it and ignoring advice to "rebuild the carbs", it went into the Ghia. One spin around the block with no muffler and I was ecstatic. Plenty of power!

The reason for the second swap was even simpler. I had just bought a very used and engine-less $150 1973 Super Beetle. My original intention had been to only buy the transaxle, but I found that for only 50 bucks more I could have the whole thing (the owner prob-ably thought I was nuts and would have paid me to haul the body away if I had bargained a little. What to do for motive power? Eureka! The ex-snowcat Porsche industrial engine that I had rebuilt using 1600S pistons and cylinders and Super dual carbs and used briefly in my Speedster was sit-ting in the corner waiting to be used. After installing the industrial engine, I was most definitely not ecstatic, more like puzzled. In stoplight drag races with stock VW's (whose owners never even suspected that they were being raced), I was left well behind watch-ing that pair of puny stock exhaust pipes fade into the distance.

So I had one successful swap and one that provided transport but no joy. The Super Beetle/Porsche got both of our daughters through high school. No tickets, either, possibly because it would hardly get over 30 mph in the two miles between our house and the high school. Especially before I got four consistent cylinders working (dirt in one carb). Imagine what a slow bug is like on three or three and one half cylinders.

Last fall our 1969 6.3 Mercedes decided that the full-rich diesel imitation mode was the only way to take advantage of the gas-glut. I spent many frustrating hours messing with (or up) the fuel injection to no avail. Both daughters were away at school so the Bug was available. It was slow on the flat, but a semi-mobile road block in the mountains. In fact, compared to the 6.3 (0-60 in 6.4 seconds) the Bug felt like it might be in reverse. Twenty-three hours of continuous thrashing later and the Bug had a new transmission and a 1720 cc "C" engine. Now it felt like the 1600S-engined Ghia.

Other reasons to put a Porsche engine in a VW? The roads may be too wet and salty in the winter for the continued health of your Porsche's body. So put the body away, but put the engine in a similarly constructed body and chassis and enjoy the Porsche sound and power all winter long. The handling and brakes can be upgraded if you feel the need (it might be wise to remember the BMW/four-cam). Bugs rust less than Porsches and are available in decent shape sans engine for less than $750, so even if it does get rusty, just buy another.

It is also just plain fun to have a "sleeper" that goes faster than it should. Moreover, the law probably will pay less attention to a stock looking bug than a red speedster if you have a tendency to push the speed limit.

Some interesting present or former VW-Porsche owners are Paul Newman and Miles Collier. Collier, the new owner of the Cunningham automobile collection and the owner of some very nice 356s, is having a flat-fan four-cam engine put in a Bug. Years ago, Paul Newman owned a Porsche engined Bug (also replacing doors and lids with aluminum copies). His mid-engined V-8 powered Bug is for sale in the latest *Autoweek*.

Enough "why?," now for the "how-to." Use the Porsche 6 v. flywheel and a 6 v. Porsche starter and solenoid in both 6 and 12 v. Bugs. If you don't want to have a voltage mismatch Malcolm Lindeman used a 22 foot length of #8 gauge multistrand vinyl insulated wire coiled up behind the engine compartment between the tail lights as a heavy duty resistor allowing only 7 volts to arrive at the starter. A 12 v. solenoid is used on the 6 v. starter. A more elegant fix is offered by Steve Ruddock of Rennwagen Motors in Boulder, Colorado (303/443-5686) who will put a 6 v. gear on a 12 v. starter. A thin-walled starter bushing will have to be used to allow the use of a 6 v. starter with a large shaft in a "12 volt" VW transaxle. These are available at any of the big aftermarket VW parts suppliers.

A more difficult problems is pressure plate-throw out bearing compatibility. A Porsche diaphragm pressure-plate from a B or C engine is a finger-type that requires a sleeve around the output shaft to guide the throw out bearing. The early "Carrera" 180 mm diaphragm-type pressure plate (still available) had a ring (about the size of the throw out bearing) attached to the inner ends of the fingers and can be used with an unguided VW or Porsche throw out bearing in the stock VW throw out bearing fork. However, there is no 200 mm pressure plate with the central ring for a Porsche flywheel and an unguided throw out bearing. A VW pressure plate of this description does exist but requires machine work to the Porsche flywheel to work (bolt surface-friction and surface depth must be machined to VW specs.).

Nevertheless, it is possible to easily modify a Porsche throw out bearing guide sleeve to fit either early or later VW transaxles. The "early" VW transaxle has no guide sleeve, the late transaxle (such as in a 1973 Super Beetle) has a VW (wrong diameter) sleeve. A little rat-tail file work on the three sleeve mounting bolt holes allows a Porsche guide-sleeve to fit the VW hole spacing on the "late" transaxle. It is more difficult, but still possible, to put a Porsche sleeve on an early swing axle VW transaxle. I did this when installing, consecutively, a 912 then a 911 engine in a Manx-type dune-buggy with a 1964 VW transaxle. This entails the welding of two ears to the sleeve base and the drilling and tapping of three holes in the transaxle. The sleeve centers itself on the main-shaft seal which helps get it concentric with the shaft. But what about the fingers that operate the throw out bearing? They aren't right for a 200 mm diaphragm clutch in either the early or late VW transaxle.

For the early transaxle case, one method is to hacksaw off the VW fork fingers, file the shaft smooth, and slide on a Porsche fork. Then drill appropriately for the four roll pins that hold the Porsche throw out bearing fork. Or, it is possible to make metal copies of the appropriate Porsche fork fingers and weld them onto the VW cross-shaft.

For the late transaxle, the stock fork fingers are not notched for the Porsche-type throw out bearing's mounting ears, and as I remember, the cross shaft is too large in diameter for the Porsche throw out bearing fork. Therefore, one solution is to make new fingers . Drill, file, and hacksaw the fingers and weld them to the VW cross-shaft. I used an arc-welder. It is also possible to change to an early

VW cross-shaft with notched fingers for use with a 180 center-ring clutch.

Throw out bearings are no problem. When using the industrial engine with a 180 mm flywheel and a Carrera ring-type diaphragm pressure plate, I used an earlier VW cross-shaft (1967, Fig. 5) and a 1967 VW throw out bearing. With the 200 mm flywheel C engine setup, I used a B throw out bearing with welded-on forks.

In the 1963 Ghia with the 1962 super engine, I may have mismatched the throw out-bearing and pressure-plate using an unguided stock VW throw out bearing with a Porsche finger-type diaphragm pressure-plate. Whatever I did worked fine for 40,000 miles.

If you want to put a 911 in your 356, use a 1965 911 flywheel and a stock 6 volt starter spaced forward about $3/16$ in. with aluminum spacer rings.

Miscellaneous problems include the accelerator cable where a carb heat ball joint-pinch bolt assembly can be attached to a shortened gas cable. Or just hook the cut-off cable through a small hole drilled in the rod end of a section of carb linkage. 912 rear sheet-metal can be cut to fit against the stock engine compartment rubber seal.

The carb heat will have to go. Cut VW 40 hp side sheet metal to fit. 356 or 912 (no rubber seal) sheet metal can be used at the front of the engine with little modification. Stock VW heater mufflers will fit the A, B, C heat exchanger outlets. Tomato can elbows allow the use of 912 heater boxes.

Stock gas lines work fine with 4-cylinder engines but do not have the flow capacity to supply a 2 liter 911. I had lots of trouble with a stiff throttle and a bending gas pedal in the Ghia and none in the Super Beetle. A gate hinge bolted into the Ghia stopped the bending, but not the heavy throttle pressure problem.

Finally, the muffler. I much prefer

the stock mufflers sound, so I'm willing to go to more trouble to use a 356 muffler. Jack Magrane's VW-Porsche conversion article (in Secrets of the Inner Circle, by the Maestro) points out that Fourtuned Exhaust Co. makes an extractor header system specifically for this engine swap. It is possible to fit a shortened and modified A, B, C or 912 muffler in a Bug or a full-length modified muffler in a Ghia. The engine will not go in, or come out, without removal of the muffler - which requires removal of the heater boxes. If this is too much trouble for the near-stock look and pleasing sound, skip the following and buy the Fourtuned extractor set-up.

For a Bug the muffler is cut off just outboard of the J-tube/head pipes and new end-plates welded on. Next shorten both J-tube pipes and the upper cylinder head pipes as much as possible bringing the muffler as close as possible to the engine. An A muffler might give fewer clearance problems. Weld up the stock outlets. Install the engine without the heater boxes, then install the muffler. Now the holes for the new outlets can be cut and the new pipes tack welded in place. On a Ghia the muffler does not have to be shortened, but the inlet pipes must be modified (mostly shortened) to get it to fit.

Two last hints, one carb and intake manifold must be removed to install the engine. When the oil cooler on the C engine began leaking, I found that by removing the lid and hinge supports I could just remove the fan shroud to replace the cooler.

Start looking for that $200 bug now so that next winter you can still be Porsche-powered. Life's too short for Chevettes, try a Porsche-powered Bug. That 356 purr and push in the back is there and if the sun is just right the shadow of the bug zipping along the roadside even looks remarkably Porsche-like.

Vol. 13, No. 1 David Seeland

911 Engine and 5-Speed Gearbox in a 356

A 5-speed 356? A 200 + horsepower 911 engined 356? No more prehistoric swing-axle suspension? Do adherents to the 356 faith find these thoughts sacrilegious? Some may, but judging from my mail, interest in this conversion runs far ahead of any other topic on which I've solicited comments.

My personal experience related to this is the conversion of a 1963 VW bus from swing axle to 4-joint (post 1967) bus suspension and a reverse ro-

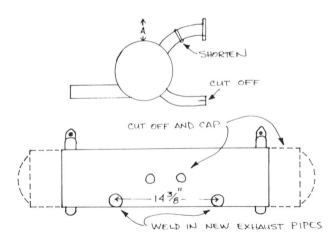

Modifications to the stock 356 muffler for placment in a VW Beetle

tation Corvair engine. I also put a 911 engine in a dune buggy with a shortened 1964 VW pan and swing axle transaxle. Jim Rinker and Ron LaDow have generously provided much of the 356-specified information. Jim's shop, Rinkertoys, converted a notch-back into a cabriolet powered by a 2.2 911S engine with a 911 transaxle and suspension. His car was written up in VW and Porsche magazine. Ron's Speedster is a bit different in that he utilized the 911 transaxle and suspension but retained the pushrod four.

Larry Chmura did a conversion similar to Jim's but started with a Roadster (*Porsche Panorama*, January, 1987).

But first, before leaping into the nuts and bolts aspects of the complete conversion, let's look at the pros and cons and some alternatives. Although everyone who has driven Ron's Speedster raved about its handling, Ron says, "I wouldn't do it again because I don't see another 2 + years of spare time soon." Jim says, "the conversion took a lot of time (2 $1/2$ years) and could be done wrong."

The 901 transaxles (early 911) first four gears translated into 356 equivalent ratios are BBAA (Carrera GT ratios for Europe), yet the "Y" 5th gear is the equivalent of a D 4th gear. This is "Having your cake and eating it, too"; better acceleration and low rpm cruising, even with the original 356 engine. Jim's car with its 2.2 911S has seen 6800 rpm in 5th, probably about 135 mph! Better handling? Well, maybe. I felt that my 1963 bus with 6 and 8 inch wheels handled better prior to its conversion to four-joint (IRS) rear suspension, although a simultaneous tire change may have affected this comparison. Stiffening the stock 356 suspension, 195-60 Yokohama 001R tires and/or using a camber compensator or Z-bar can be a simpler way to get all the handling you would ever need on the street (and probably the track). If you are going to compete, in

what class will you have to run with a modified suspension and 5-speed? Will you be allowed to run at all?

If you don't exceed the torque capacity of the 356 transaxle, and improve the suspension, and use disc brakes, then an engine swap only would be a far simpler and more easily reversible proposition, even if less technically interesting. Obviously a 2 liter 130 DIN hp 911 won't cause any more transaxle problems than a 2 liter 130 DIN hp 4-cam (its transaxle does have a steel intermediate plate, but ...). Used with some restraint, a stock 356 transaxle should be able to handle a 2.4 liter 911 engine. The lighter the car, the fewer the transaxle problems. A 2.7 liter Corvair pushed out the differential cover on my swing axle bus transaxle (but no problems in 75,000 miles with the 911-like 1975 transaxle). In the light dune buggy a swing axle transaxle gave no problems even though autocrossed with a 2.5 liter 911.

Other possible engine swaps that might result in less rearward weight bias than a 911 swap are a 2180 cc type 1 VW or a 2400 to 2800cc type 4 (914 too). The type 4 can be converted to an "upright" engine using either a 911 or VW fan and alternator. A long time ago I received a letter from a Carrera 2 owner whose 2180 VW engined car "was faster than the 2 liter 4-cam engine had ever thought of being."

Other possible engine choices are limited only by your imagination and range from reverse rotation Corvair to Mazda rotary to that extra 904 engine you have lying around. KEP (Kennedy Engineered Products, (805) 272-1147) probably makes adaptors for most swaps.

If you have serious horsepower in mind – Larry Chmura's 2.5 911 race engine (0-60 in 5.4 seconds) then a 901 or even a 915 (post 1971 911) transaxle might be necessary. Note: the 915 is physically larger and may be harder to install in a 356, so measure before you buy.

Are your welding and fabrication skills up to the level necessary? Suspension brackets are not floor pan patches. They are critical welds and must not fail. I watched the Indy 500 telecast and saw a car go into the wall because one front wheel was no longer connected to the steering wheel. Scary! Unwanted rear wheel steering in drastic amounts could result if a diagonal arm bracket failed, so if you aren't sure of your skills have an expert welder do the suspension welds.

Vol. 13, No. 3 David Seeland

911 Engine and 5-Speed Gearbox in a 356, II

This final installment will concentrate on the "how-to" aspects of the conversion to a 911 engine and rear suspension. Ron LaDow and Jim Rinker provided most of the "how-to" information and I'm most appreciative. If you have the necessary skills for the project you should be able to fill in the blanks left by this article.

Conversion to disc brakes is necessary both for safety and simplicity if you begin with a drum-brake 356. In order to get the wheels approximately centered in the 356s wheel openings, the short wheelbase 911 suspension (pre-1969) is used providing you with either solid or vented rotors from the donor 911. Vented 911 front rotors can be cut in a lathe to reduce the diameter and used with early vented-rotor calipers (the rotors are thicker) on C spindles. It is best to convert to a dual-circuit master cylinder although a 356 C single-circuit master cylinder will work. Spacers are necessary between the body and the emergency brake bowden tubes. The emergency cable-end anchor should be changed to a "C" piece if you are converting an A or B.

For an overall view of the 911 suspension in Ron LaDow's Speedster,

see the illustration in part 1. Ron suggests laying things out by dropping vertical lines from the car to a full-size plan. Because Ron was using a 356 engine he wanted it to fit in the stock position (although this necessitated difficult modifications to the torsion bar tube and transaxle front cover). The 911 engine is longer so the inner skin at the rear of the engine compartment must be moved rearward and the top edge of the 911 aluminum blower housing beveled slightly. The remainder of the sheet metal around the engine must be modified to fit and seal off hot air from the engine compartment.

The 911 exhaust system is critical, so Jim needed different jetting after switching to a two muffler unmerged system utilizing headers (no heat). He used two short glass-pack mufflers on each side, one oriented fore and aft and the other across the rear. The outlets exit through a Carrera 2 rear skirt available from Obsolete Parts for Porsches, McMinnville, OR. The stock 911 heat exchangers will probably run into the transaxle support hoop. The hoop also interferes with the under-engine oil tube. Jim still chose to utilize the hoop, probably because of the lack of major structural support at the rear of the engine. Nevertheless, he still made mounts at the rear of the 356 body which mate with the transverse rear 911 engine-support bar. Larry Chmura ("Six in a tub", Feb. 1985, *Panorama*) did not use the hoop, based on the photo of the underside of his 1956 356A Coupe. This explains the statement that "the roll cage was extended to the rear of the car to support the engine."

Because of minimal clearance at the rear of the 911 engine, the engine and transaxle can't be separated and removal must be done by lowering the entire transaxle-engine assembly. To allow this, the half-moon covers at the top of the hoop are not installed so the pair of bolts that attach the hoop to the body can be removed and the assembly lowered.

Installation of the 911 rear suspension is simplified if the rear seat area of the body is removed for access and then welded back in. Short wheelbase "early" or pre-1969 911 spring plates and diagonal arms (bananas) will work giving about a $1/2$ inch increase in both track and wheelbase. Jim Rinker was able to use 7-inch wheels and 195/50 x 15 tires with no fender modifications, Ron LaDow found that 185/70 x 15 tires cleared the stock fenders throughout the full range of suspension travel.

The front transaxle mount is widened by welding together two 911 mounts. The position of the banana arm pivots is a major determinant of the rear wheel toe and camber so extra care should be taken to install them precisely in the 911 position. A better method may be to position them by trial and error, checking wheel alignment as you go, and welding in place when the alignment is satisfactory (the technique I used on my swing axle to IRS VW bus conversion). Raising and lowering the mounts affects the camber while lateral movement affects the toe. The torsion bars can be left out to somewhat simplify this process.

Spring-plate spacing on a 356 and on an early 911 are about the same at 41 inches. This should mean that since each banana mount includes one of the front transaxle mounts (see the photo in part 1) the stock 911 front transaxle mount should work. The problem must be my "about measurement of spring-plate spacing. Aluminum plate spacers with longer bolts can be used between the wheel hubs and the trailing arms if a track increase is desired. VW bug axles and CV joints are compatible with the axle flanges and slightly shorter (or longer?) than 911 axles. Check them first if you find it necessary to change the axle lengths.

An interface problem exists be-tween the outer CV joints and the chassis side members near the base of the bump stops. Carefully notch and re-weld the chassis for clearance. Spring plates from an early (pre-1969) 911 that have removable grommets can be used with A, B or 911 torsion bars. The caps on the 911 spring plates must be removed so that the torsion bars can protrude. Incomplete spline engagement results, but seems to work. Alternatively the 356 spring plates could be shortened and cut to match 911 spring plate dimensions. Jim Rinker also mentions that he had to notch the spring plate at the lower rear torsion bar cover plate boss to allow greater spring plate inclination. This is because inclinations on a 356, depending on model, range from 10° to 21° but range from 33° to 39° on an early 911 or 912.

Larry Chmura used early 911 shocks after fabricating a new upper mount. Notes from my conversation with Jim Rinker are a bit cryptic but they say: "cut off shock mount and use heim joint." I don't know if this refers to the upper or lower mount.

The oil tank and filter assembly is mounted in the standard 911 position in the right wheel well. Brackets and holes should cause no problems. Low air cleaners fabricated by Jim for the Webers on his conversion used "ovalled" low Buick elements.

On Ron LaDow's conversion using a 356 engine but 911 suspension and transaxle he found the throttle, clutch, emergency brake, and shift (use 900 series shifter) linkages to be easy. Heater linkages and ducting weren't, as they are in the travel arcs of the new banana arms.

A couple of final points made by Ron LaDow are worth repeating. These modifications may result in unfavorable changes in the value of your 356. In 1971, when he modified his Speedster, they were much less valuable so the decision to modify it was far easier. It probably wouldn't be wise to convert your Carrera 2 even if it already has the rear skirt. Welded modification will be required in high stress locations. Know your welder and consider nondestructive test procedures.

References
Finsilver, E.J, 1985, "Six in a Tub: The Story of Dusty": *Panorama,* vol. 30, no. 2, p. 66-69. 901 transaxle, 911 suspension, and 2.71 carbureted 911 engine in Larry Chmura's 1956 356A coupe.

Finsilver, E.J, 1987, "First Child": *Panorama,* vol. 32, no. 1, p. 63-64.901 transaxle, 911 suspension, and 2.51 911 race engine in Larry Chmura's 1960 356B roadster.

Gilbert, Jim, 1986, "Rinker Toy": *VW and Porsche,* vol. 17, no. 1, p. 22-24. 901 transaxle, 911 suspension, and 2.21 911S carbureted engine in a 356B notchback that Jim Rinker converted to a cabriolet.

Gearbox Swaps

Vol. 3, No. 3   Vic Skirmants

Putting a 356B Transaxle in a 356A
If you're planning to put a 1960-65 transmission into a 1956-59 Porsche, chances are you have the 1956-59 transmission for parts. Only the 644-716 tunnel-type transmission can be used for parts; the 519 won't help you; you'll have to find someone with a 644 or 716.
First, have both transmissions next to each other. Pull the nose off the 644, then pull the intermediate plate with all the gears. Now pull the shifter shafts and detents out. Save the nose, shift finger in nose, and shifter shafts. Sell the rest for parts. Now, pull the nose off the 741, then pull the intermediate plate and gears, *being careful not to lose the gaskets between the*

plate and tunnel! You will have to measure these gaskets to know what thickness for new ones to put in later, or you can re-use the old ones after cleaning and spraying with Permatex. These gaskets determine the ring and pinion setup. Now pull the shifter shafts and detents out of this one. By now you should know how to put it back together. Put the 644 shafts into the 741 plate and shift forks. Be sure the shift forks are lined up properly, use some standard Loctite on the fork bolts, and torque to 18 lb-ft. For the detents, remember the one longer spring is for the reverse shifter shaft. Put the intermediate plate with gears back into the tunnel; don't forget those gaskets. Now put the 644 nose and shift finger on. If you don't have a gasket for the nose, a bead of G.E. or Dow Corning silicone sealant works great. The nose gasket means nothing as far as ring and pinion set-up. Two external details on a 741 that differ from a 644. The 716 and 741 boxes used a different clutch throw-out arm, so the 1956 to 58 clutch cable will not hook up as originally. Also, the 741 uses a guide tube and different throw-out bearing, which will *not* work with the 1956-59 type pressure plate, whether coil-spring or diaphragm. The easiest thing to do is put a later pressure plate on the engine you plan to use. If you have a choice of 644 or 716 nose pieces, use the 716, which has a shift finger seal on the inside, while the 644 uses no seal.

Vol. 10, No. 3   Vic Skirmants

VW Transaxle in a 356
Can any VW transaxle be fitted to a 356B, assuming no change to the mounts? No. There is no VW transaxle that would fit without major reworking.

Vol. 10, No. 4   Vic Skirmants

VW Transaxle in a 356, Long Version

Dan Somers, Ben Lomond, CA, asks about installing a VW transmission into his 1956 A coupe. I mentioned last issue that a VW transmission won't fit easily into a B or C; primarily because of the shifter location. While the VW shifter location is close enough to that of the A, I still don't think this is a worth-while modification. The VW first and second gears are too short and third and fourth are too tall; therefore, there's too big a gap between second and third. The VW transmission is totally unsatisfactory in a 356. I will now hear from all the guys who will inform me about the different gears available for the VW, their cheapness, etc. I'm not interested. Save your bucks for a real Porsche box, and do it right.

Chapter 10

Fuel System

Fuel

Vol. 3, No. 4 Carl Gerster & Vic Skirmants

Octane, Cheap Gas and Other Tales

Carl also had a couple things to say about gasoline. The first had to do with octane rating. If you're using a higher octane gas than your owners manual calls for, you're wasting money. Hi-test gas is no more energy producing than regular; it just has additives in it that enable it to operate in a higher compression ratio engine. If you have a late model Porsche and are using hi-test gas, you're wasting money for additives that you don't need. Have you ever wondered why off-brand gas is cheaper than the big name versions? The difference is the additives again. Not octane additives, but the type that prevent our carb or injection system from gumming up. Carl has personally seen the effects these cheap gases have on carburetors, and you don't want it to happen to your Porsche. Better to pay the extra 3 - 4 cents for a name brand product.

That's good advice on the gas. Of course by "later model" Carl is referring to the newer 911s. Our own 356 seems to like the following: Normals – Regular gas – Supers and Cs – good quality regular or premium – S-90s and SCs – premium.

As far as the gumming up of carburetors when using cheap gas, I can't report any problems after years of using the cheapest gas available locally. Injection systems might be a different story because of the super-critical tolerances involved.

Vol. 13, No. 1 Expert Forum

Unleaded Fuel and Gasohol

You may have read in the newspapers or in your favorite automotive magazine "Disappearance of leaded gas to cause problems for older cars" or "Lead is dead". In the early 1970s, the EPA banned the use of leaded fuel in new cars and ordered the gradual reduction of lead from the then common 3.0 grams/gallon to 0.1 grams/gallon by January of 1987. This amount is what an EPA study said was a level that would cause no harm to agricultural machinery. The 1987 mandated level (currently in effect) is only a quarterly average allowed at a given refinery: there is gasoline being sold today as leaded that has lead levels below 0.1 grams. And as pre-1975 vehicles wear out, the demand for leaded fuel is dropping, and as we know, corporate decisions are usually economically motivated. Sohio, the major gasoline retailer in Ohio, stopped marketing leaded fuel on March 1 of this year.

Jerry Keyser conducted a mail interview of the distinguished Messrs. Vic Skirmants, David Seeland, Harry Pellow, Chuck Stoddard, Bruce Anderson, Dick Weiss and Mike Robbins regarding fuel concerns and received very detailed and thorough information from them.

Q: What does tetraethyl lead do for an engine other than boost octane rating for anti-knock reasons?

Anderson: "... it acts as a shock absorber between the exhaust valves and valve seats. The concern is for the potential of excessive valve seat recession or 'pound-in' because of being run without leaded fuels. The reason lead is so important to older cars with 'soft' seats is that the lead acts as a lubricant... cushioning the valve each time it seats..."

Pellow: "... using no-lead in engines with cast iron cylinder heads produces iron oxide from the oxidation of the head. The iron oxide acts like an in-the-car valve grinder on the cast iron valve seats. Even heat treated cast iron heads suffer from this recession ...."

Seeland: "Creates combustion chamber deposits that (undesirably) raise the designed compression ratio." Bruce Anderson comments additionally that: "It is also interesting to note than when lead was introduced to gasoline in 1923 there was very similar concern about the effect on the engine's valves and valve seats because of the addition of lead to gasoline, as there is today with the removal of lead from the gasoline. At the time, the engine designers felt that the lead caused a serious service problem with the spark plugs and exhaust valve damage caused by the corrosive effect of lead oxide. The designers forged ahead and used lead as an additive because of lead's superiority over all other antiknock additives of that era. With higher octane gasoline, the engine-designers could use higher compression ratios to achieve major gains in both power and fuel econo-

my. During this period of automotive history, the designs and materials used in high-compression engines made tremendous improvements over a very short period of time. These included special alloy exhaust valves and seats, and sodium cooled valves – all to combat valve and valve seat erosion, caused not by the removal of lead, but the addition of lead to the gasoline. With the introduction of lead to gasoline, the octane number was increased from about 50 to today's 90 + for high octane unleaded gasolines making possible a boost in compression ratios from 4 to 1 up to the 9 + to 1 used by all of our modern Porsche engines.

Q: What about 356 engines?

Pellow: "All post-1960 Porsches have hardened steel seats pressed into the aluminum heads. Hardened steel seat inserts don't suffer from the valve recession. Post-1960 Porsches don't suffer from no lead!"

Skirmants: "In the really early cars, they had brass valve seats... we don't need lead for the valve seats."

Stoddard: "All 1600 cc 356 engines have hard steel (exhaust) valve seats and compatible valves; most of the early cars have bronze alloy seats (even with a fresh valve job, don't worry)."

Harry Pellow comments additionally that "It is a good idea to replace the brass seats at overhaul time with hardened steel seats."

Q: Are there negative consequences of driving 356s exclusively on unleaded fuel?

Skirmants: "No problems as long as the octane is adequate."

Weiss: "No problems, but check your valve adjustments every 3,000 miles."

Anderson: " ... the best way to keep track of what is happening until we are sure, will be more frequent checks of valve clearances. I suspect that we will find that our valves and seats will wear at a faster rate than they did with leaded fuels, but that the difference will not be drastic. Say that if it is 20% faster, a valve job wears out in 80,000 miles instead of 100,000 miles."

Q: Are there any advantages of using unleaded fuel, other than the well-established environmental benefits?

Robbins: "There are fewer spark plug deposits."

Stoddard: "... runs cleaner (fewer deposits in combustion chambers), so plugs generally last longer; carburetors don't care."

Pellow: "Less contamination of the oil, which means less crud in your bearings since the oil filter is of the bypass type and not a full flow filter."

Anderson: "Yes, the engines that are run on unleaded gasoline burn cleaner and will run much longer between tune-ups ... It also looks like engines that have been run on unleaded fuels will last longer – it is not uncommon for 911SC engines to run for 175,000-200,000 miles without requiring any major maintenance."

Q: What about the after-market add-to-your-tank lead additives?

Stoddard: "Save your money, it isn't necessary."

Seeland: "If you would add this stuff for lead's lubricating properties – forget it – it is too dangerous. If you add it for an octane booster, copper cylinder spacers cost less and are a lot less toxic."

Pellow: "Tetraethyl works best, but it's a controlled substance and you won't get your hands on it. Besides, you wouldn't want to: it's highly toxic and is absorbed through the skin."

Q: What about the octane requirements for 356s?

Stoddard: "No Porsche ever built by the factory (from a 962 on down) ever required more than 98 ROZ octane gas – this is equivalent to a Pump Rating of 94 octane. *But*, a 356 wouldn't benefit (nor any other car) from excess octane – so in reality this translates into a Pump Rating of 89 octane

Regular, which is plenty good for any 356, except a SC/912 or 4-cam which might benefit from Hi-Test rated at 92 octane – if you run it *hard* (who's dumb enough to do that?)."

Robbins: "The fuel octane requirements as specified in Porsche Driver's Manuals are: *ROZ octane rating is about 4 - 5 points higher than US pump octane rating."

Anderson: "Octane is a widely used, but not well-understood, term to describe gasoline's ability to deal with higher pressures and temperatures in the engine's combustion chamber without knocking (premature detonation). The higher the octane, the higher the temperature before knock occurs... higher octane gasoline can be... compressed more before the engine will knock. Generally, higher compression means higher power and better fuel economy. In a high performance engine the idea is to burn the gasoline at the highest compression possible without knock. The compression ratio versus required octane is not a linear function. The thermal efficiency of different engines will vary because of combustion chamber shapes, more efficient cam shaft designs, etc., which affects both the performance of the engine and how much compression can be used running a specified octane fuel.... The unleaded fuels available meet most of the octane requirements for various Porsche models ... The Super 90s, SCs and 912s all seem to be right on the ragged edge when it comes to accepting (currently available high test, 91-92 octane gasoline). This is because the combustion chamber design is not as efficient as some of the more modern designs. There is nothing we can do about this, so if we experience knocking, detonation or pinging in our 356/912 engines, then we should reduce the compression by using barrel spacers into the 8.0:1 to 8.5:1 range. Octane ratings enable an owner to buy the correct gasoline to prevent engine damage. You will not get better performance by using higher octane gasoline, you will just spend more money."

Pellow: "... it is impossible to calculate the proper octane requirement on rebuilt engines unless the engine was designed and built to a specific compression ratio... Flycut the cylinder head and you've increased the compression 0.2 compression ratio numbers. If the head has been flycut previously, you increase compression by 0.4. Stick a big bore kit into a twice flycut head and *boom!*, you're up to 9.8: 1, which from the Disaster Data Base has a life of 20,000 miles!

Always use the highest octane unleaded premium you can find! (even) in all "stock" Supers, Cs, SCs and ALL 912s!! Original Normals with 7.5:1 can run on Panther pee, maybe even kerosene."

Q: What about octane boosters?

Seeland: "Somewhat effective, very dangerous and toxic...(Either) buy racing gas, let it ping or shim the cylinders."

Pellow: "Aniline is the next best additive to tetraethyl lead, but it too is dangerous, a carcinogen and a protein solvent. It works, but at 20 times the dosage of lead. Everything else adds octane by volume percent mixed, which means you'll need *gallons* of benzene, tolulene, or xylene to up the octane significantly."

Anderson: "... not cost effective. Assuming that you purchased an additive that was 100% aniline (it's not) – it would take 3 pints, at about $12/pint, added to 20 gallons of gas to raise the octane about three points."

Q: What about alcohol/gasoline mixtures?

Weiss: "No, no! It will affect the plastic floats and small Zenith gaskets and it will suspend any water and debris in the fuel, which will end up in your fuel filter or carbs."

Pellow: "Gasohol dissolves the accelerator pump gaskets in Weber carbs."

Stoddard: ". . . *Avoid* alcohol in a 356. It tends to cause difficult running/stumbling, etc., because it is not as stable in a hot engine compartment as is gasoline (the gas available today is less stable than it was back in the days of 356, so adding alcohol is double trouble)."

Anderson: "... The major oil companies west of the Rockies do not use alcohols as octane boosters. Some of the independents use it extensively. In the San Francisco area, Beacon gasoline usually contains ethanol, and they have just recently started posting it on the pumps. Some gasohols contain ethanol, some contain methanol and others contain mixtures. Ethanol is less corrosive than methanol, but methanol is cheaper and contains more energy.

We originally thought that the oil companies would be required by state law to post that fact on their pumps, but only about 30 states require posting. The others don't care if it is posted or not, although some oil companies are posting in states where it is not required. Oil companies using alcohol vary from area to area. It is most common in the Midwest and is frequently found along the east coast from New Jersey to Georgia."

Q: When you gaze into your crystal ball, what do you see in store for 356 owners regarding fuel for the next 5, 10 and 20 years.

Skirmants: "I don't really see a future fuel problem."

Seeland: "I see increasing octane available to satisfy the performance car market. Supercharging is the high-performance wave of the future and it requires higher octane gas than turbos ... we might even be able to run higher-than-stock compression ratios on pump gas."

Pellow: "356s ought to be able to use unleaded fuel which other newer Porsches use, not to mention Corvettes, BMWs, Jaguars etc. etc."

Stoddard: "... my guess is no problems. The internal combustion engine will be around for many more years – and there'll be millions of them built, all needing fossil (gasoline) fuel. Anyhow, we can always burn garbage in them, as Porsche did after WWII, to keep the V-Dubs running."

Anderson: "I don't see any problems for 356s, the unleaded fuels of today are fine and it's doubtful that the quality will be degraded any more in the future."

Weiss: "Second and third world countries have always had lesser quality fuel and 356s got by – regular maintenance and checks are, and will continue to be, the key."

Robbins: "I see a misty fog – is that redundant?"

Q: Any other comments or observations?

Anderson: "... Before the removal of lead from gasoline, we were able to mix unleaded premium gasoline and leaded regular gasoline and boost the octane above that of the unleaded premium. The reason that this worked was that the gasoline producers were mixing more lead than was necessary in the leaded gasolines. Mixing unleaded and leaded gasolines doesn't do us any good anymore, now that the lead content has been cut to 0.10 gram per gallon in the leaded fuels. In fact, now it may actually lower the average octane rating in your tank."

Stoddard: "I don't know *anyone* who is driving a *good* 356 today hard enough to wear it out. If (your 356) is about shot, *now's the time* to rebuild it while parts are relatively easy to get – then it will go another 10 to 20 years, right? For any engine, if the distributor is not advancing/retarding properly and the timing is not set properly, it can self-destruct from detonation, but that is another story not caused by no-lead and/or the present general octane availability. Just think what a sheltered 356 – life the next 20 years will be, compared to the last 20!!"

Vol. 13, No. 1 Vic Skirmants

Unleaded Fuel and Gasohol, Condensed Version

More people are becoming concerned about the decrease in the amount of lead in today's gasolines. Let me state that: "We don't need lead for valve-seat lubrication!" Our valve seats are not cast iron, so they will not recess due to a lack of lead. As long as the gasoline is high enough in octane to not cause detonation, you will have no problems using unleaded fuel. I would stay away from gasohol because of alcohol's affinity for water. I see enough condensation in normal gasoline due to the infrequent usage some of our cars get.

Fuel Tank

Vol. 7, No. 4 Richard Miller

Repairing Corrosion Damage

The early tanks appear to have been lead covered steel with crimped and soldered seams. If you don't scratch through the lead or strip the gas tank in a caustic bath (hot tank), you should not have corrosion problems. I've fixed many tanks that did have corrosion holes that probably originated from thinness of the lead plate or scratches especially from outside where jute pads at bottom hold water (and promote corrosion) or where the tank has had water in it for a long time (the lead dissolves eventually). My method of repair is to flush the tank with water until the smell of gas is gone and then use a large (200 to 400 watt) soldering iron to fill holes with solder. The small holes up to a few mm in diameter can be filled, large ones I put a brass patch on. The area around the hole should be dimpled to provide a good bond, structural strength and thickness to the repair. You can pick out the holes by holding the tank up to strong light (sun) and looking through the fill hole. Then take a center punch and punch the hole in like the sketch.

If you try to solder the hole without dimpling it, you'll find the solder pulls away from the hole or is too thin to be strong. On tanks that are pretty bad, strip the paint and look closely at the surface. Any small indentations or what appear to be bubbles are probably holes in the making as the metal inside rusts away. Push on them gently but firmly with a punch or blunt ice pick. If they go through, or flex, punch and solder them. I spent 3 hours doing a Carrera tank this way which, to my knowledge, still holds gas. To do large areas, clean and tin the whole area, tin a brass patch (.005" shim stock) and sweat solder the whole thing. I've seen jobs done with brass screen which worked very well also. You can solder through the screen and it holds the solder. Don't use a torch – if the tank doesn't explode, you will still have difficulty controlling the heat.

Vol. 15, No. 2 Dick Koenig & David Seeland

Large Fuel Tanks

Large tanks were first used in Porsches in the Gmünd alloy bodied coupes modified for racing (356SL) by the factory. These 1951 and later 356SLs had through-the-hood fillers and the single cross-ways tank hold-down strap was stamped 78 (liters?), although the tank's actual capacity is 70.1 liters (18.5 U.S. gallons). These and the later large tanks (commencing in about 1956) were developed as a replacement for the standard 52-liter (13.7 U.S. gallon) tank (fig. 2) for use in long distance races and rallies, particularly in the thirstier four-cam cars, but were also used in the T-5 Super 90GT pushrod cars. In 1956 and later they were available in any car, however. An early 356A parts book lists (but does not illustrate) a 70-liter tank for

Carreras (644.56. 015). The May, 1957 and later 356A parts book lists (but again does not illustrate) an optional 80-liter (21 US gallon) tank (644.201.010.50).

The same 80-liter tank part number was used for the T-5 356B tank, but the external ribbing changed from A to B and the internal baffles were enlarged. The external changes may be improvements or may only reflect a change in suppliers. There are no manufacturers' names or dates on the 80-liter 356A (although senders are dated on all tanks), but the B tank has "Schmid" stamped just behind the breather vent at the center-rear of the top.

Identification of the "Schmid" tank as a 356B tank is a probable, but not an iron-clad conclusion. The evidence is as follows: 356A 52-liter tanks are not stamped "Schmid", a 3/60 52-liter tank is stamped "Schmid" as are all other 52-liter T-5 tanks that we have seen, two 80-liter non-Schmid tanks have 1957 senders, thought to be original, and are in early 1957 and early 1958 GT Speedsters, and the first parts book that illustrates an 80-liter tank (early 356B) has a Schmid tank. There may be a slight bit of overlap of Schmid tanks into the 356A models because Weldon Scrogham's "last (GT) Speedster" has a Schmid 80-liter tank (that is thought to be original). Do any other 1959 cars have 52 or 80-liter Schmid tanks?

The 80 liter 356A tanks are characterized by fewer reinforcing ribs embossed in the tank surface than the 80-liter T-5 356B Schmid tanks. On the 80-liter 356A tanks, the center section is fabricated from two sheets with horizontal seams at the front and rear. On the 80-liter 356B (T-5) tanks, the center section is fabricated from a single sheet wrapped around the sides with a horizontal seam at the back center. The sides of the 80-liter tanks are less strongly contoured than the stock 356A and T-5 356B 52 liter tanks. The embossed side of an 80 liter T-5 356Bis similar to an 80 liter 356A tank side, but lacks the embossed edge seen on the 356B tank.

Now for this column's puzzler. An interesting asymmetric (70 liter?) tank was found in an alloy-wheeled 1956 356A coupe by Jim Breazeale, proprietor of EASY (a salvage yard specializing in Porsches) in Emeryville, CA. This tank looks much like the B "Schmid" tank with about 75 mm amputated from the right-hand side. The right side of the tank is flat with a stiffening ridge in contrast to the "bulged" left-hand side. All other large tanks have "bulged" sides on both left and right. This asymmetric tank also had a small (25 mm(?)) factory-appearing plugged hole on the top right side (now patched shut). Does anybody know why?

In spite of the lack of a "Schmid" embossed into the tank top, the lack of the depressed groove forward of the filler hole, the sender-wire hold-down clips, and more baffle-attachment points, it is most likely that this is a retrofitted 356B tank that was specially constructed by Schmid to allow room for something mounted between its right side and the front compartment wall – police or rally electronics? – an oversized windshield washer fluid container? Are there any more tanks like this out there? Let us know

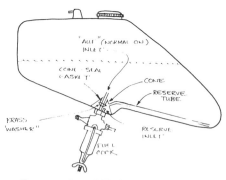

Cross section of 80-liter tank showing internal plumbing for reserve pickup (not to scale)

if you have one, or understand the origin of asymmetric large tanks.

Operation of the reserve pickup on the fuel cock is unique to these larger tanks. This is necessary because the bottom of the forward wedge-shaped portion of the tank slopes down the trunk floor and lies below the fuel-cock pick-up. Without some special provision, fuel below the reserve pick-up, about 3.7 U.S. gallons, would not be accessible. However, there is a metal tube running forward along the floor of the tank from a 60 mm diameter cone shaped compartment over the petcock area to the front of the tank. The cone acts as the "elbow" between the reserve pickup line in the tank and the short vertical reserve tube in the fuel cock.

The 356A parts book indicates that the fuel cock for the 80-liter tank is nearly the same as for the standard tank with two exceptions . First, the cylindrical wire mesh filter-screen that normally surrounds the pickup tubes is absent. Second, the normal (Auf-position) pickup tube is modified. It has a 13 mm diameter cupped washer-like brass piece soldered on 45 mm below the top to support a rubber gasket (644.201.231.50). This gasket seals the inside of the cone at the bottom of the tank to the outside of the auf-position gas pickup tube that protrudes into the tank through the apex of the cone. If the gasket is absent, the reserve pickup line will not function. This means that instead of an 80 liter tank, it will be a 60 liter tank (and no reserve). If the gasket is NLA, and it probably is, an appropriate length (about 15 mm) of fuel line can be used in its place.

Inside the 80 liter tanks (but not the 52 liter) are two vertical baffle operations extending from top to bottom, but not from end to end. The 32 cm long baffles in the 80 liter 356A tank are confined to the rear rectangular part of the tank and do not extend into the wedge-shaped part of the tank, as do the 46 cm long baffles in the 80 liter T-5 356B tanks. These baffles are attached by rivets visible on the outside of the tank. During sharp or frequent turns the baffles slow sideward movement of gasoline, improving the car's handling and stability. The longer baffles in the 356B tank result in less slosh than in the shorter-baffled 356 tanks. The 80-liter 356A tanks have a stiffening channel that is soldered to the inner surface of the tank about halfway down the sloping "front". It extends completely across the tank.

Changes in the size of the fuel tank dictated alterations elsewhere. The trunk compartment floor (644.501. 035.50) is unique. It has a 165 mm long x 10 mm x 50 mm "U"-shaped reinforcement is for the mount of the right tank-retaining strap. There are two holes through the trunk floor at this point. The two forward strap mounts for the 53-liter tank are absent.

The length of the forward tank retaining straps was increased from 570 mm to 735 mm. They attach to the floor and steering-box cover by two bolts (each) 5 mm in diameter. The forward end of the long straps are bent at right angles around reinforcing doublers. Light-brown felt is glued to the underside of each strap.

The steering gear cover was modified to provide a strap mount and provide access to the steering-box-filler plug and adjustment screw without tank removal (because the rearward pair of cover hold-down screws are under the 80-liter tank). The cover reinforcement for the strap mount was of exactly the same size as the floor reinforcement previously described. In addition, the "cover for oil filler screw" had patterned "tar-paper" on the underside, as did the upper 60 percent of the cover. The presence of the sound-deadening material on Speedsters is unusual and even more unusual on GT Speedsters that even lack undercoating!

Vol. 15, No. 3 Dick Koenig/David Seeland

Large Tanks Addendum

Gas Tanks: a 1960 S-90 GT coupe was found to have 3/60 alloy wheels, a 3/60 gas-tank sender and an "A" GT (80 liter) tank having all the appropriate internal baffle characteristics and external ribbing. There is some chance that this tank was added to a small-tank car at a later date, but it seems unlikely because of the car's history and the date on the sender. Any other B cars out there with original "A" GT tanks?

Additional comments on our gas-tank article would be appreciated. No one has figured out the origin of Jim Breazeale's asymmetric "B" tank. Weldon Scrogham has sent photos of another "weird" tank (356?) that he found while hunting an aluminum Porsche "being used as a doghouse"!

Fuel Cock

Vol. 9, No. 5 Pete Geiger

Everything You Always Wanted to Know About Fuel Cocks

We all at one time or another have had that smelly gassy odor in the passenger compartment due to a leaky fuel cock. And without thinking, we have removed the gas tank and all just to rebuild the fuel cock. I figured that there had to be a better way to do this, and I'm sure that some others have found one. Anyway, here is the simplest way I could think of to do it, and maybe it will help others.

First, remove as much fuel from the gas tank as possible from the trunk side of the car (through the gas cap opening that is). Shut off the fuel cock (ZU). Remove the fuel cock cup.

Hook up a funnel with a long hose to the outside of the car (right door side). Put the funnel under the fuel cock and turn the selector to Reserve

(RES). When the gas has drained as much as possible, turn to off (ZU). With the earlier models with the large gas caps you can get your hand right inside of the tank (if your hand is as small as mine) and wipe the little extra gas up with a rag. (During this whole procedure, please don't smoke). Now you can remove your fuel cock from inside the car and start your rebuild.

After rebuilding the fuel cock, but before reinstalling it, you should give it a good test to make sure that it doesn't leak. (Why go through all this trouble just to have a gassy smelly compartment again.) A good way I have found, and simple, is to attach about a two foot piece of plastic clear tubing to the tall inlet standpipe of the fuel cock. Put a small funnel into the other end of the tubing and hang the whole thing on a hook or some other device so the fuel cock dangles free. Turn the selector to off (ZU). Put some gas into the funnel. Holding your finger over the outlet, turn the selector to on (AUF). Remove your finger from the outlet and add more gas to the funnel just so the tubing is full. Let this set for a couple of days just to be sure. During that time, I maneuvered the selector to make sure the cork was setting correctly and continuously checked for leaks. If there are any leaks, of course you will have to correct them. Possibly a faulty cork, or you have some corrosion in the main body of the fuel cock itself or the selector. (If there is a lot of corrosion, you know what you will have to do). But this is better than putting it back in the car, having it leak, and removing it again.

When reinstalling the fuel cock back in the car, make sure you get it at the right angle so that there is no undue pressure or stress placed on the fuel cock selector by the selector rod, as this can create leaks by shifting the pressure on the selector.

Making your own Fuel Cock Corks

Rebuilding the earlier model fuel cock presented a problem for me because I could not seem to find the right cork of the right thickness. Although I ordered rebuild kits, they never had the right size corks. This was baffling because all of the corks seemed to be for the later model 356s, or maybe the real early ones. I finally gave up and found out that I could make my own, with a little ingenuity, that is.

First off, you have to obtain some good sheet cork, not the pressed stuff that you find at K-mart used for gaskets. The only place that I know of where you can obtain sheet cork is from a music supply house, or if you happen to know a friendly music instrument repair man. Sheet cork is sold in thicknesses at these places varying from $1/64$ in. to $1/4$ in. in sheets of 4 by 12 in. One sheet should last the Porsche owner the life of his car. Costs run from $2 to $10 per sheet.

The fuel cock in my 1959 coupe uses a thickness of around $1/16$ in. to $3/32$ in., with a diameter of 26 mm. That seemed to be the maximum thickness that it would take. The later models, and the kind that come in the kits, are $3/16$ in. thick by 26 mm diameter. There is a 22 mm listed for my car, which was too thick and too small in diameter. I don't know which car uses 22 mm corks. If the corks are too thin, you could score the movable gas transfer lever and then you will really have some leaks.

After removing the fuel cock from the tank (see my earlier dissertation on removing fuel cock without removing tank) I used an ordinary $1/2$ inch drive $1/2$ inch socket from my socket wrench set. I fit this over the little round projection that the gas handle goes on and put it in a vise. *Gently* and very carefully turn the vise in. This releases the pressure of the spring in the fuel cock and then you can remove the circlip. Undo the vise, and it comes apart.

Be sure to remember which way it comes apart because you will have trouble if you don't put it back together right. It can be reassembled wrong but appear to be right.

Now that we have it all apart, check to see if there is any scoring or if it is so badly corroded that it's unusable, in which case you will know what to do right away. If everything seems to be okay and the cork seems to be old and dried out, take your sheet cork (the good stuff), and with one of those little plastic circle cutters (using the old cork as a template), cut the new cork in the desired diameter. Once that is done, using the old cork as a template again, mark those little holes onto the new cork. Now here it gets a little tricky. I use a tool that I made from a short piece of thin rod steel. This has to be slightly smaller than the holes you marked. I drilled out one end of the rod so that the edges were quite thin. I then ground the edges sharp. (Once this is done you always have the tool) Once this is done heat up the tube quite hot and just press and turn at the same time, and you have a nice clean hole with no ragged edges. By cutting and burning the holes in, it seals off the cork and keeps it from crumbling and getting into the gas line. (It's a good idea to have a good filter anyway just to be sure) You have to have a smaller diameter tool because when you burn the holes they enlarge somewhat.

Now put all the parts back together the way you took them apart (with whatever new parts you want to add). Before you put the fuel cock back in the gas tank, be sure to test it for leaks.

Solex 40 P II-4

Vol. 3, No. 4 Vic Skirmants

Float Level Adjustment
   While on the subject of carburetors,
a hint on float-level adjustments on Solex 40 PII-4s. I've never had any luck with the method of setting the levels by removing the plug on the side of the bowl opposite the adjusting screw and adjusting til the fuel runs out the opening. If you really want your floats set accurately, get the expensive little screw-in sight-glass float level gauge. Now you can watch the float level as you adjust. Turn the screw in to lower, out to raise, and set the level at the low end for street use.

If the setting is hard to achieve, with the float sometimes staying too high or too low in spite of adjustments, and then suddenly dropping or rising, check the following: pull the top off the carb, lift off the gasket, pull out the float, pull the little brass holder that holds down the adjustment fulcrum and pin. Now pull out the fulcrum and pin and check to see that the fulcrum pivots easily on the pin. This sometimes gets bent in improper adjusting, and will then bind on the pin, causing the float to stay too high or too low for the adjustment. If your float level is too high or low after adjusting the screw all the way in or out, pull the carb top and add a shim under the needle valve to further lower the float, or put a thinner shim or gasket than the one already there to raise the float level. Then adjust as before.

Vol. 15, No. 5 Vic Skirmants

Float Level Adjustment, II
   Solex 40 P II float levels. Whether using these carbs on the street or in racing, to properly set the float levels, you need the factory-style float level gauge. Using the screw-out plug in the side of the carb to set the level just does not work properly! I'm sure some of you have used this method and have no problems. The rest of you need the sight gauge.

If the level does not adjust properly; staying high, or not coming up, or seeming to move up or down of its own accord, you will have to pull the carb top to investigate. First of all, don't use the Grose-jet needle valve; the two balls don't do the trick! I know one person who used them for ten years and never had a problem. I know twenty people who never could get a consistent float level with them. The standard needle valve works just fine. Be sure there is no dirt in it. Now check the brass bracket that the float pin sits on. If the bracket is bent in where the float adjusting screw contacts, then the bracket will drag on the sides of the carb and cause float level problems, or it will try to bend the thin brass rod it hinges on and cause float level problems. Straighten the bracket and the rod it pivots on and make sure the bracket swings freely. One of the causes of "bent-bracketitis" is the replacement of the float pin hold-down springs in the carb top. The standard springs are pretty soft and merely hold the float pin down on the bracket. These springs sometimes get lost or they get mangled when the carb top is installed; be sure the spring is through the hole in the gasket, and seated in the well on top of the float pin! These springs then get replaced by heavier springs that are readily available (ball-point pen springs are usually found).

When stiffer springs are installed, it seems the bracket becomes very prone to bending. Maybe the bracket bent even with the soft springs, for Porsche or Solex eventually installed a thicker bracket that even had a horizontal stiffening rib pressed into the long part. I don't know when this change occurred. Many of the later split-shaft carbs had then, but not always. Take care of these items and you should have no more float level problems.

Vol. 3, No. 4 Alex Finigan

Modifying Original Air Cleaners
For those of you who would like

better air filtration out of your Solex cage type air cleaners, yet wish to retain stock appearance, here's a tip. I drilled out the retaining rivets with an 8 mm drill and removed the top cover.

Once this is off you see that the screen is in three sections. Remove the two innermost screens and cut a piece of Filtron 440 mm by 80 mm. Take the Fiitron and wrap it around the five studs and glue the ends together with Loctite Super Bonder; be careful here as a little goes a long way. Now take the remaining screen and put it around the outside of the Filtron and simply bolt the top back on. The Filtron works best when it is lightly oiled.

Now you have a stock appearing air cleaner with a removable, cleanable filter element. Filtron should be available through local speed shops.

Vol. 4, No. 2 Vern Lyle

Solex 40 P II Flat Spot
Anybody else have this dead spot at 3000 - 4000 rpm on acceleration? I tinkered with almost everything to no avail. Finally, in frustration gave the problem to the dealer and said, "No matter what it costs, fix it." He kept it 2 days and admitted he didn't know the answer.

Then one day I was pouring over a diagram of fuel flow in the carb at various speeds. It dawned on me that the idling jet (pilot jet) way up at the top of the carb body was not an air jet as I assumed, but was a fuel jet. Fuel passes through here at idle and continues through here as the main jet circuit takes over. In other words, it acts to insure a smooth transition from the idle circuit (which works up to about 3000) to the main circuit. A flat spot here indicated that the jet was not passing enough fuel. The standard jet in my 912 carbs was a 57.5, and a change to a 60 eliminated the flat spot entirely.

The Carburetor/Distributor Connection

Solex 40 P II-4 Vindication! The parts columns are smattered by ads for Solex 40 P II carbs for sale at reasonable prices ($75 or so each). Most of these are being discarded by their owners because they (the carbs) are taking the rap for a crime they didn't commit; uneven idle.

The horror stories of Solex carbs and their bad throttle shafts and worn bodies are numerous, embodied deep in the literature of the Pellowian era. I won't pretend there is no problem; I can personally attest to the fact that there is. However, 75% of the Solex carbs I've looked at are in fact good and should not have been disgracefully fired from their job (usually to be replaced by Webers that, because of their smaller venturis, actually don't perform as well as the original Solexes).

In many cases, the carbs take the rap for a distributor problem. As a case in point, I recently rebuilt my Solexes, then replaced them, to no avail. The same problem persisted: the idle was uneven- proper RPMs one time, too high or too low the next time. After a series of time-consuming rebuilds, I decided the carbs were in fact innocent of charges against them, and found the real culprit in sticking distributor weights.

Apparently what happens here is that the Bakelite plate the factory provides in the distributor for the weights to slide on wears out and disintegrates over time (or is removed by some turkey). The weights slide on this plate to advance ignition at higher RPMs (they are forced outward by centrifugal force). As RPMs are reduced, the weights are supposed to be pulled back by springs to their original rest position. Unfortunately, a bad or missing sliding surface impedes their progress, thus resulting in bad timing

(too much advance) at idle. Of course, all cars (even those with Zenith carbs) are susceptible to this problem, but Zenith is usually exonerated (while Solex is immediately adjudged guilty). In addition, the problem is more noticeable with Solexes, because Solexes are capable of subjecting the distributor weights to more centrifugal force (more venturi – more air flow – more horsepower and torque).

I have had good success thus far with the Teflon sliding plates supplied by Stoddard's. They're not perfect, and will undoubtedly wear out long before the original Bakelite, but they do the job. More importantly, they are a relatively cheap fix of only a few dollars, as compared with the huge expense of rebuilding Solex carbs (that probably didn't need work to begin with). I've been buying up Solex carbs at reasonable prices and simply cleaning them in solvent and installing new seals and gaskets (a bead blasting makes them look nice, too). So far, three consecutive sets have performed nearly perfectly. One note of caution: if you decide to go this route yourself, be careful not to soak the plastic floats or idle-adjustment knobs in Hydroseal or other carb cleaner (they get eaten).

Also be sure to blow out the carbs carefully, in every nook and cranny after bead blasting.

Vol. 17, No. 1 Bruce Baker

Air Cleaner Restoration

Ron Zahuranec from Corona, CA wrote about his Solex mesh air cleaners that always look nasty. I called the nice folks at Auto Research to check progress on #10712 and posed the question to them. Their advice was to glass-bead them and then have them clear cad. plated. This leaves a nice dull silver color and acts as a barrier to oxidation. A light coat of silver paint will bring them back to original appearance.

Weber Carburetors

Vol. 8, No. 1 Vic Skirmants

Adaptor Plate Problems

A word of caution on Weber carb conversions. If you use the adapter plate that's bolted to the stock Solex intake manifold, don't use the gaskets supplied with the kit. These gaskets have too big an opening, permitting air leaks past the allen-head bolts that attach the adapter plates, through the lower passages of the carb base, and into the manifold. You will have to cut your own gaskets from standard gasket material.

Vol. 9, No. 6 Rick Veneski

Using a Uni-Syn on Webers

For those people who are converting from Zenith and Solex carburation to Weber and are wondering how to synchronize them without buying a special flow meter, it is possible to convert the Uni-Syn. The mouth of the Uni-Syn is a larger diameter than the intake of the Weber. Connection of the two can be accomplished by simply cutting an ordinary plastic funnel to fit: Some material, pliable in nature such as caulking, might be used to seal the funnel to the base (the mouth) of the Uni-Syn to assure minimum air leakage.

Base of Uni-Syn

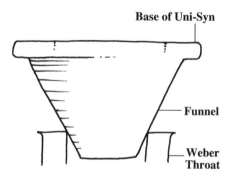

Funnel

Weber Throat

Vol. 14, No. 3 Vic Skirmants

The Trouble With Webers...

I just prepared a set of heads for someone using Weber carburetors. The heads were small-port "Bs," and the manifolds were the aftermarket ones supplied for the small-port heads. Some testing on the flowbench showed that these manifolds, with my 38 mm venturi flow test Solex, flowed less than a stock set of Zenith manifolds with my flow-test Zenith! This should be evident from the reverse-of-direction shape inside the manifold. Some reshaping of the Weber manifolds and the head ports resulted in some good flow figures, but I believe they could have been better with decent manifolds. These particular manifolds were mentioned as undesirable in Craig Richter's *How to Make an Old Porsche Fly,* copyright 1983. Speaking of Webers, I'm a big fan of the original Porsche carburetors, Zenith and Solex. I'm not very impressed with the Webers, with their flimsy linkage arms and usually unsatisfactory manifolds or adapters. Also, they come with several different venturi and jet combinations. In my type of racing the rules have mandated the original carbs, so I've had to work with them exclusively, and I've found in over twenty-five years, that they are very good carburetors indeed. The two biggest problems are when they are not set up properly, or when the Solexes wear out their throttle shaft holes. Bieker Engineering, Burbank, CA, (213) 849-2720, (818) 856-8704, does a great job of literally remanufacturing the Solex carb. It's not cheap, but it's a better solution than Webers. I don't have any experience with the Dellorto carbs, but have been told by a couple of people that they are better than the Webers.

Another problem with Webers is that most of the 40 mm Webers come with 28 mm venturis, the same size as Zenith Supers. The stock Solex 40 mm had 32 mm venturis. So, you rebuild your engine with a slightly hotter cam, big-bore pistons, maybe even some cylinder head porting. Then you bolt on brand new Webers and wonder why the performance isn't what you expected. Of course it isn't. You just put on a set of Zeniths! Of course you can change the venturis and jets, but they still seem to have a bit of a flat-spot on acceleration.

Zenith 32 NDIX

Vol. 1, No. 5 Bob Napier

Replacing Soft Plugs on Zenith 32s

For a number of years, the so-called "soft plugs" in Zenith 32 NDIX carburetors have been "no-longer available," at least from any sources known to me. For this reason a number of 356s are running around without either one or more of these soft-plugs. Each Zenith 32 NDIX originally utilized two of these plugs to fill the hollow opening (about a $1/4$ in. in diameter) that runs longitudinally, from front to back, through the carbs near the top. (See illustration.) If they are in place they are easily spotted, being made of a brass or bronze alloy and, therefore, having a characteristically dull yellow ochre hue, in contrast with the dull grey body of the carb.

If you are missing one or more of these soft-plugs, gas can spill from these openings, especially when cornering. The gas fumes used to be clearly evident in the cockpit of the "A" after a hard, left-hand corner, due to a missing plug.

Short of having plugs machined from a soft alloy, a good, permanent solution can be accomplished by using lead fishing sinkers, available from hardware, sporting goods, or discount stores.

I went looking for the pendant-shaped sinkers called "bank" sinkers, but I ended up with size 8 "Oval Egg

Sinkers" when I was unable to find the first kind. These are about the size of a filbert nut meat and have a small hole all the way through (for your fish line).

In that this metal is very soft (your thumbnail will easily mark it), it is quite simple to cut about 40% off one end of the oval sinker with a hacksaw blade, touch-up the rough edges with an emery board (avoid using a file because the soft lead will clog the teeth), fill the hole down the center with solder, and then gently tap the resulting soft plug into the opening in the carb.

If, like mine, the one you are missing is either of the ones which face the rear of the car, it is very simple to tap the plug into place, but if you are missing one of the ones which are in the side of the carb facing the front of the car, you'll need to remove the air filter and work in a slightly awkward situation. Of course, you could just pull the engine, or wait until the next time your engine is out of the car, to get one of these front plugs in.

Vol. 2, No. 3 Mike Robbins

Alternate Method for Mounting Zenith Carburetor Tops

There was mention in Vol. 2, No. 2 of the availability of Helicoil inserts for repairing Zenith carburetor bodies. Although purists may rebel at the idea, I've found what I feel is a better and easier solution. That is, to put studs in the carburetor body and use nuts to hold the cover. For each carburetor you should use (4) M5 x 21 and (1) M5 x 25 stud (overall length). The longer stud is used in the position for the bracket for the return spring. Loctite or epoxy the studs in place. If you want to get fancy, you can use Nylok type nuts, à la Weber. A distinct advantage to this method versus Helicoil is the elimination of the two pins normally used to hold the gasket to the cover. (due to the fact that the stud now locates the gasket) I also question if there is adequate wall thickness for Helicoils in most cases. Studs and nuts are available from Metric & Multistandard Components, 120 Old Saw Mill River Rd., Hawthorne, N.Y. 10532, (914) 769-5020. Incidentally, this is a very good source for all types of metric hardware, tools, etc.

Vol. 3, No. 4 Vic Skirmants

Float Level Adjustment

There is also a sight-glass fuel level gauge for the Zenith carbs. However, it is almost impossible to install or read the gauge on the left carb. The gauge reads at one end of the bowl so the carburetors have to be dead level, and you have to pull the top off to change anything anyway! In other words, don't bother getting one.

Simply pull the carb top, slide a 6 in. metal ruler with pocket clip down the side of the carb at one end and watch the light reflection on the fuel surface. As soon as the reflection jumps, you've hit the meniscus of the fuel (that part of a fluid that tends to climb up the side of its container). That's the dimension you want so read where the pocket clip stopped, repeat at the other end of the carb, average the readings, and you have your dimension. To change the level, add shims to lower, subtract to raise, or very carefully bend the float arm. Factory spec is about .77". Set it anywhere from .70 to .77", but be sure both carbs are within .02" of each other! After changing shims or bending the arm, put the tops on, run the engine, shut off, pull the tops, measure, repeat, etc., etc., til you get it. Theoretically, if you move the needle valve a certain amount, that will change the float level by a factor of four. I have found this not very accurate in practice. Just keep doing it over and over.

While your Zenith carb tops are off, take your six-inch ruler, place it along-side one of the floats, hold the float hinge down with the other hand, and push the scale and float toward the opposite end of the carb. Now try to move the float up and down with the scale. If either float sticks to the side of the carb, you will have fuel starvation in severe cornering. Check the floats in both directions, bend them very carefully whichever direction is necessary so that they do not touch the bowl sides. For best results, there should be fuel in the carb so the floats are at their normal working height. It is advisable to do this before setting the float levels, as it could have an effect on them. Wear in the hinge assembly makes this check necessary.

Vol. 5, No. 6 Vic Skirmants

Miscellaneous Zenith Lore

If you have a Zenith-equipped Porsche using the metal air filter cans, they are probably loose. If they are loose, they can actually wear a hole in the top of the carb or a gas line. Also, the right one can rotate and keep the throttle linkage from returning. OK, so you're aware of this, but you've tried tightening the slotted bolt for the clamp with a screwdriver, and the cleaner is still loose. Note that the bolt also has a hexagonal head. Snug it down with a socket. Don't overtighten! Previous overtightening is probably the cause of your problem in the first place. If you can't get the socket to grab the bolt head because the clamp is distorted enough to keep the socket from fully engaging the bolt, put a flat washer or two under the bolt head to space it out. If after all this you find the bolt head is rounded because of the ever-present problem of "previous owner abuse", grind or file the sides of the hex until you can get some kind of socket on it.

While on Zenith carbs, a tip on what to check if your accelerator pumps aren't delivering any fuel. If just one of the two per side is not

204

delivering, check the nozzle and jet for clogging. Usually if both are dry, the problem is elsewhere, although in a rare case maybe both are plugged.

Check the accelerator plunger for wear-through at the side, check the pump pressure valve beneath the plunger for sticking. Also check the pump suction valve next to it for sticking. This suction valve has the same thread size as the plug in the bottom side of the carb body and I have seen several carbs where these two items got switched. Lack of the suction valve of course permits the plunger to push the fuel back into the float bowl instead of through the accelerator pump circuit.

While still on Zenith carbs, I'd like to say a few words in their defense. To those who say toss them away and put on Solexes , have you ever had your Zeniths adjusted correctly? I don't mean only synchronization, but most importantly float levels and accelerator pump delivery.You won't find Zeniths idling terribly due to worn carb bodies and throttle shafts, like the Solexes do.

Vol. 11, No. 1 Vic Skirmants

More Zenith Lore

Rebuilding your carburetors? First off, you don't have to remove everything to do a good job. No reason to remove the venturis, for instance, and for heavens sake don't pull the butterflies and shafts! I've seen it done, so don't laugh. If you must remove the venturis, sometimes you will find they can be quite stuck; even with the setscrew backed out. Beating on them with a punch is not smart. On Zeniths, after removing the cast iron base, the venturis are in full view and a plastic or wooden screwdriver handle can be placed on them. A smack with a hammer on the blade end of the screwdriver should pop the venturis out. On the Solexes, there is no base to remove, so the throttle shafts obstruct the access. Placing a large washer on the venturi,

then tapping the washer, works fine. A king-pin thrust washer fits nicely.

Speaking of Zenith carbs, if you have ever had the thin brass plug fall out of the top by the accelerator pump lever, you should replace it. If the plug on the left carb falls out, fuel will slosh out of the hole on acceleration, especially in a right-hand turn. This gives a definite flat spot in performance as the float level on that carb drops, and it also dumps a bit of gas all over the #4 spark plug wire. I have used a small washer, piece of tape and five-minute epoxy to make a quick, satisfactory repair. The top of the carb should be removed, the washer is dropped in the open hole, the tape is put over the hole in the washer, and the epoxy is used to cover everything. I suppose one could do the same without removing the top by putting a piece of tape over the epoxy until it sets. I'm sure there are better/more elaborate ways to accomplish this, so let me know and I'll pass them along.

Still on the subject of fuel systems, I'm sure most of you understand how your reserve fuel system works. It's just a lower pipe in the fuel tank, and when the fuel cock is turned to reserve, the regular, taller pipe is blocked (so you don't draw air if the level is too low) and the lower pipe starts feeding the fuel line. Due to condensation, especially in cars not regularly used, there can get to be an appreciable amount of water in the bottom of the fuel tank. Short of disconnecting fuel lines, draining the tank, etc., one good, easy way to be sure you don't switch to water when you run out of gas on the standard setting, is to occasionally put it on reserve while driving. The best time is on the expressway, so that if there is more than just a touch of water and the car starts to stumble, you can switch back to "AUF" before everything stalls out. If you suspect there might be an accumulation of water, switch to reserve for about a half-

205

minute at a time, so you don't flame out completely.

Vol. 11, No. 4 Richard Miller

Carb Top Plugs

On Zenith carb tops: some car parts stores have a selection of ultra-small core plugs, one of which works to plug the hole in the top you mentioned in your last column. The same parts stores also carry helicoil kits – a 6 mm 1.0 for about $25 is a safer solution to stripped oil sump studs and you'll have enough coils left over to do your friends' or the stripped holes for the side cover plates in your heads.

Vol. 1, No. 3 Jim Lanb

Leaking Zenith Carburetors

Suffering the seemingly ever-present problem of gasoline seepage on my Zeniths, even after complete rebuild and replacement of worn screws, etc., I recently used General Motors' "Gasket Sealing Compound" on all the gaskets and washers. Now, after 3 months, the Zeniths look just as clean as when I put them in after the rebuild. This is a non-hardening sealer that comes in a spray can. GM 1 #1050805.

Vol. 2, No. 2 Paul Spurgas

More Leaking Zenith Carburetors

If your Zenith carbs are leaking at the top, a little bit of the new Perma-tex Form-a-Gasket works nicely. *(Don't use just any of the available silicone sealants, most of them swell up in contact with gasoline. Just ask me– Vic.)*

Paul also mentions that Helicoil has inserts available for the carburetor body in case the top hold-down screws have been stripped out.

Vol. 15, No. 6 David Grant

Even More Leaking Zenith Carburetors

While there are other carb options on 356 cars, the most common and troublefree is the 32 NDIX used on the 356 A, B, C. After hundreds of thousands of miles, the owner is likely to be faced with a cover gasket leak, and perhaps a worn float valve. These problems are easy and cheap to fix. You need not replace them. The following paragraphs can be applied to the repair of any Porsche carburetor, but they are directed to the lucky owners of Zeniths. If you succumb to the siren's call, and install *Italian* or *oriental* carbs, remember, most of us still have the OEM carbs, and we and the concours judges may snicker and point rudely!

30 years ago, someone wrote in *Up-fixin'* that the cure to leaking Zeniths was to install helicoils in the carb body for the 5 cover screws. In this way, more force could be applied, without stripping the (5 x 0.8 mm) 8 mm ATF cover screws. Unfortunately, even with stock arrangement, it is too easy to overtighten, and warp the cover, when the gasket hardens, and no longer seals. If one has a stripped thread, one can either use oversize bolts, with the original hexplus-slot head, or have helicoils installed. You should not need much torque to achieve a seal. An 8 mm socket will not damage cover bolts, the way a poorly used flat-bladed screwdriver will.

Taking Apart Your Carburetors

When you have had enough of leak-ing, gum-covered carburetors, you can remove them, and take them apart. I recommend that you read the repair manual, if you are not very familiar with your carbs, before you start. If the carb has not been used in years, keep in mind that some of the residues on it may be toxic. If it still has fuel in

206

it, drain it, and allow it to dry. Wash your hands when you are done, and if you must take it apart on the family's dinner table, do it on an open newspaper, so you don't get lead flakes in their dinner, or peanut butter on your check-valves. You may need a diagram to show where all the parts go. If there are only two carbs like yours in your town, do only one at a time. That way, if you can't figure where a part goes, you need only look at the other one. If you have several carbs to clean, and you "know-it-all" (i.e., you figure that the jet size list from the manual is all you need to *put Humpty together again!*), you can clean all the parts together. Use properly ground screwdrivers of the proper size. If someone has put burrs onto the carb hardware, you should repair each damaged piece. You can use a small hammer and a pin driver to push the larger burrs down, while the part is still in the carb. After the part is out, a fine file will nicely repair bolt heads and jets. Don't remove the stamped numbers. If any of the steel hardware is scratched, burred, or rusty, you may want to include it in your next cad or zinc plating order. If any steel part has a scratch, burr, or pitted area, file it off, and use fine wet sandpaper to shine the piece before you have it plated. This goes for any steel, copper or brass items you send for cadmium plating. About half of the plated engine parts were zinc; the balance were factory cadmium plated. While the factory and its suppliers only polished trim and interior pieces before plating, the surface finish of most hardware remains today almost bright enough to see your face in. Avoid the funny-colored washes which some platters use. You don't need extra corrosion protection, unless you still drive in winter slush and park outdoors in an industrial area. My Porsches did this in the 1960s; I believe that most 356s with replated parts now live in garages.

To do this job right, you will have to remove everything but the venturis and the 11 pressed-in plugs. If you are planning to have the zinc pieces electropolished, you might have to remove the large brass, and tiny aluminum plugs. The slotted 5 x 8 mm bolts which retain the venturis will have to be removed if their plating has been dulled. Try to thread a 5 x 8 mm nut on each one. If it won't start, you should chase the threads on each one with a suitable die, as their contact with the OD of the venturi usually folds over the first thread. You can do this after they are plated, but you increase the risk of damaging the plating. The venturis may come out with light tapping, on a solid aluminum cylinder 31.5 mm in OD. If they are stuck, leave them. You should carefully pry the fittings from the ends of the throttle shafts, without banging the throttle plates into their bores; if you need to apply force to their shaft, support its other end on your workbench. You should not use pliers to remove anything! You might need a small scraper or knife to remove traces of old gasket. You might need to hit some of the larger gasket pieces with a plastic mallet, or a screwdriver handle to loosen them.

The mixing tubes can be worked out with your fingers. Don't ruin them with pliers or prying tools. Leave the upper/outer injection lever in place, after you remove the carb cover. Slip a copper or steel tube over the outer lever, while you turn the inner nut with a thin 10 mm open end wrench. Don't damage the inner threads with the inner lever. If you find the surface damaged where the fuel line banjo attaches, or if these threads are stripped or damaged, find a new top. You could have it milled or filed, if you do it perpendicular to the threads.

Appearance
The discoloration can be removed from any brass parts (if you fear a

concours judge might see them) with a soft wire brush, or a fine abrasive pad, after you file off any burrs. The gums from old fuel (which are partially oxidized and polymerized hydrocarbons) can be removed by soaking (the parts!) in a mixture of equal parts methanol and toluene. (If you soak too long in these or any other solvents, you may lose interest in the whole project!) Do any solvent or paint work outside, or in a fume hood. Keep solvents out of your eyes and lungs; wear rubber gloves if you have to splash in solvents like these. You should soak and brush all the parts until they are free of everything but oxidation. The more aggressive chlorinated solvents are worse for your health and (according to some people) for the upper layers in the atmosphere. If your solvent cleaning leaves the die cast pieces a uniform light or medium gray color, you are done. If they are a dark gray, and you want a light, shiny zinc surface, you can try glass beading or electro-polishing. (Try to avoid beads larger than 0.050 mm, and definitely don't use old beads, which are so jagged they will leave the same dull finish you would get with sand.) Pickling the parts in hydrochloric acid will restore the original light gray color, leaving a dull surface, but leaving no grit for you to wash out of your carbs.

If you grit blast parts with a soft, soluble grit like NaCl crystals, a water soak will remove all residues from blasting. For my own cars, I prefer either leaving the parts dirty, or using solvent followed by microscopic glass beads. If you are worried about grit, you can plug most of the passages with tape or modeling clay, before you bead the carb parts. Use compressed air or soap and water and a brush to clean the beads from the parts before you remove clay and tape. Remember that the beads are so small that a few will not cause the kind of damage that sand can. They are soft enough that they will not jam a shaft, etc.

Your Cover is Warped: Here's how to fix it

When the cover is bare, mount it in a lathe, holding the 2.5" inlet tube by either the outside or the inside, in a 3-jaw chuck. Check that you have it straight with a dial indicator, so you do not cut the top in an amusing lop-sided shape. Use 300 to 400 rpm, with a sharp, round tool. The area, around each bolt hole may start out 0.005" + higher than the rest. You could use sandpaper or a milling machine if you have sufficient skill to ensure that it is flat when you are done. With a single cutting tool, you have assurance of flatness.

The 3 large, flat gasket surfaces of the body can be cleaned and checked for flatness with wet 200 - 400 grit sandpaper on a mirror or flat piece of glass. If the part is not flat, you can lathe turn it or use your glass plate and sandpaper. It is unlikely that the body will have warped as much as the typical cover. Only when the surface is flat, smooth and shiny, can you be assured that a new gasket will seal. It is unlikely, but you might find a zinc lump somewhere on the carb. I have seen them on the ID of venturis and on carb cover-gasket surfaces. These seem to result from gas bubbles near the surface. When the part came out of the mold, it was apparently near its melting point, and the pressure caused zinc above the bubble to rise. If you see such a bubble on a gasket surface,, it will have to be carefully machined (not sanded) off. Remember that there is likely a bubble under any suspicious lump. Don't file away a lump on the float bowl! You might turn a reliable carb into junk.

Further Cosmetic Improvements

In published period pictures, it is obvious that the cast iron base of the Zenith was quite black and the zinc parts were light in tone, and a little shiny. The black finish on the base did not extend to the area around the mixture screw, or the steel plug above it. These portions should be left bare, or hand painted with a clear varnish, if you are afraid they might rust. Some brands of urethane paints will resist the inevitable film of gasoline, to which these parts will be subjected. Virtually every steel part of the Zenith was originally bright zinc plated (The thin throttle shaft lock plate may have been yellow zinc plated on later cars. It is more likely that this part was frequently replaced with a 1970s part!) You can still see a reflection in the protected places on most hardware. A cad or zinc plating is a suitable replacement. If your cad plater has used organic or zinc salt brighteners, you need not dull the finish with abrasives. The dull finish on some plated hardware is due to decades of corrosion; period photos indicate rather bright components. While brass and copper parts can be cad plated to look just like the steel ones, the original brass parts (including the turnbuckle hex bars) in my collection of Zeniths have no zinc or cad on them. The metal analysis I use can measure plating thickness-below 0.003 microns. If an uninjured area has less than this thickness, it never was plated with the metal in question. The knurled brass idle air screws which are included with rebuild kits are pretty, but noticeably different in four areas. Polish your original ones, unless you banged them on the car body when the engine was halfway in the car, or unless someone put a ridge on the tapered tip by tightening them!

Reassembly

You may find that a factory-made gasket is a little too small to fit the bolt pattern of the parts it is to join. This is common, with many of the gaskets for the 356. It is the result of drying and shrinking of the vegetable fibre based paper gasket. After a few years a new gasket will shrink on your shelf. Even more drying will occur

during use, but by then, the gasket will be compressed in place. The equilibrium moisture of cellulose drops by 80% as its temperature goes from 20°C to 60°C. If your cover gasket is not very soft (a light tap with your fingernail should leave a mark in a soft gasket) you should either get a new one, or soften it. I have been successful with a few minutes soak in room temperature water. Five seconds under the tap is often enough. ASTM and SAE specifications allow such gaskets to swell, up to 30% after a day under water. Since you want the gasket to conform to the cover, you should install it between $1/2$ hour and two hours after you take it out of the water.

Don't overdo the amount of water or the length of soak, as you may leach some soluble compounds out of the material, leaving it a little less soft when it finally dries completely. A few seconds under the tap will not do a gasket any harm. Since you cannot get a seal with a very hard gasket under your carb cover, and it will not soften in use, this is a good compromise. If you are Mr. Goodwrench, and you gasket unprotected cast iron parts, you might want to let the parts dry for an hour or two, to prevent rust. In that case, your flanges will be many times as strong as the thin Zenith cover.

When you are trying to figure out which jet and bolt goes where, you may discover that the jet numbers in the book are not quite what you have. This indicates that the factory or a previous owner has tried a little "adjusting". I have found common deviations on Zeniths from different sources, so I have learned to ignore some of the numbers listed in the workshop manual, and Elfrink, preferring to use what was in the carb when I got it. If one has an example of both jets, one can measure them both, solder one type closed, and drill it out to the size one wants. Be sure to use a larger drill to chase the passageway, just like the factory did, so the narrow passage is no *longer* than the original. Note this in your logbook or memory, since you may not be able to change the number stamped on the jet. Remember, someone else might have done this years ago, so check for evidence of solder in all jets, before believing the numbers stamped in them! If you really want to *do things to excess*, you can check the ID of the various critical orifices in your Zeniths. While it could happen, I have not come across a jet which had been drilled but not soldered in 25 years. Checking IDs would be advisable if your carb shows other ominous signs of inexpert "souping up". The ID of a 0115 main jet is .045"; a 0130 main is .048". A 230 air correction jet ID is .093"; a 210 is .086".

When you have finished putting the carbs together, adjust the idle screws for an opening of about 1 mm, and install them. They should be close enough for you to start the car. They will still need a level adjustment (see the next chapter) as soon as it is running and you have fuel pressure. *After* you have finished a proper float level adjustment, *then* balance and adjust idle speed and mixture.

Zenith carb fuel level measurement
If you don't have the factory tool (P77), you can make one. If you drill and solder on a piece of copper tube to a spare drain bolt, you can attach a piece of clear vinyl tube, bent up, and over the carb body. Use a thin o-ring for a seal, so you will not have to wrench-tighten the fitting.

I prefer a custom made brass bolt. It attaches by 7 x 1 mm threads, like the drain bolt. I use a $^1/_4$ in. ID thickwall tube as a sightglass, curled over the carb. Using a smaller ID tube will introduce a great meniscus-effect error.

If you have neither a lathe nor a 7 mm die, you could drill out a 7 mm bolt from your industrial fastener store, to make such a tool, rather than drill out an original brass drain bolt.

It seems to be normal for the level to drop a little (2 to 5 mm) when the throttle is momentarily opened, to bring the engine from idle to 3000 rpm. The factory says the level should be within 1 mm of 18.5 below the carb-cover gasket.

Twenty years after I started doing levels this way, I got a copy of *Upfixin*. It turns out someone else thought of some of this before I did.

Vol. 16, No. 3 Vic Skirmants

A Correction and More Zenith Lore
I always welcome any correction of errors that appear in my column. Steve Bareis, Cordova, TN, points out that the Zenith carburetor top screws mentioned in Vol.. 15, # 6, are not 5 x 0.8 mm, but are 5 x 0.9 mm. Correct, Steve! Helicoil does not make this size repair coil. Steve fixed his carbs by using the available 5 x 0.8mm coil and new allen head bolts. Steve did not check with the "TIME-SERT" Company on availability of 5 X 0.9 mm coils. If anyone does find a source, let me know.

Still on Zenith carburetors, Alan Surgi points out the fact that the main jet thread size is the same as the carburetor bowl drain plug. So, if you want to make a site-level gauge that screws into the drain plug hole, you can use an extra main jet and slip-on plastic tubing, rather than drilling out a drain plug.

Carburetors, General

Vol. 7, No. 1 Richard Miller

Redrilling Carbuetor Jets
In regards to your comments on #60 idle jets a while back, the number 60 stands for 0.6mm or approximately 0.024" diameter. So get a number 73 drill and open up your old 45, 50, 57.5 or whatever. You can even solder

210

them up carefully and redrill to some smaller size (old Weber carburetor procedure).

Vol. 13, No. 6 Vic Skirmants

Plugged Jets

One of the more common complaints I hear concerns the engine "not running right". If the engine was running well previously, and then started performing poorly, many owners immediately start checking and changing electrical components. While they can certainly be culprits, 90% of the problems I have seen lately have all been fuel-related. Specifically, a plugged main jet or idle jet. The idle jets on Zenith and Solex carbs have some very small passages, and can get plugged up very easily. The main jets are quite a bit larger, but can still get plugged.

One recent example towed in was a vintage racer that hadn't been run for a couple of months. What had happened was that one of the main jets was totally plugged with some white deposit that I had to actually ream out! Maybe some fuel expert can send us a good explanation of what happens to gasoline that sits around for a while, but what I have seen are some pretty slimy deposits that seem to be a chemical combination of fuel, lead, water, or? These eventually dry out and become hard.

In addition to storage related jet-plugging, of course are the tiny bits of crud that sometimes seem to pop up in a fuel system no matter how many extra filters one might have added. If the engine idles fine, but feels like it's on three cylinders from mid-range on up, check the main jets.

If the idle is down, as well as the pulling power up to about 2500 RPM, (yes, the idle circuit is effective up to that range), then check the idle jets. Finding a plugged idle jet is very easy. Carefully pull the plug leads out of the distributor cap one at a time until you find the one that doesn't cause a change in the idle speed. First loosen up the leads by partially pulling them out of the cap before you start the engine. This way you lessen the chances of getting zapped when pulling the wires. Also don't touch the car while pulling them. Of course, replace each wire before you go on to the next one.

Vol. 16, No. 3 Vic Skirmants

Carburetor Return Springs

Are you aware of the correct placement for the throttle return spring on Zenith versus Solex 40 P II carbs? On the Zenith carb, the spring bracket is held by the screw furthest away from the throttle arm. On the Solex 40 P II, the bracket is held by the screw closest to the throttle arm! If put under the further screw, the spring can actually go over-center on some carburetors, thereby trying to hold the carburetor open at full throttle! (I don't care what they show in the Stoddard catalog; check the factory parts book).

Vol. 17, No. 2 Dick Weiss

Solex and Zenith Miscellany

Proper rebuilding of Solex 40 P II-4 carbs is cheaper than buying brand new (when Solex decides to run production on a whim) units which will have the same problem as the originals - throttle shaft spacing to prevent the butterfly plates wearing away the throat sides when your foot releases the pedal. This is where excess air is upsetting the idle and transition/ crossover tuning. Carbs manufactured earlier than the split-shaft 1968 version don't have bronze bushings in the body castings and thusly wear out prematurely. Finally, the engine must be in good condition with compression on all cylinders within specs. One can fudge only so much when one cylinder is up to 25% of power loss.

Proper Solex rebuilding takes time,

but the rewards are great and will still pass concours inspection. The work requires full disassembly to the shafts, then send to Bieker Engineering or Eurometrics for their hot-cook cleaning, broaching of tops and bottoms flat, R and R of shafts + plates, bore throats .5 mm oversize throttle plates, set the shaft end play, and add seals. Split-shaft versions cost more due to re-pinning the adjusting blocks and additional parts. They can do complete rebuilds for slightly extra cost. Final setting of float levels, injection quantity, balance bank-to-bank, and full throttle linkage operation can provide amazing results. Zenith carbs are less fussy if set up properly. They have 3-piece body assembly, unlike Solex, cast iron non-warping bases, and chrome plated throttle shafts, but also lack proper shaft spacing to prevent throttle throat plate wear.

Tips on assembly: Solex has eight top cover screws but one should be 2.5 mm longer (different part number) and is used for the return spring hook which is also 2.5 mm thick. Zenith has five top cover screws (all equal in length).

Now you know why some strange screws, bolts, etc. show up at the return spring hook location and thusly, the tapped hole is stripped! Moving the hook to another hole? Eventually, that hole will strip, too. Tapped holes can be repaired with special inserts, or Loctite thread repair. I undercut one screw 2.5 mm to accommodate the hook thickness – still looks the same with enough hex head showing. Solex injection nozzle – hold-down countersunk screw is 12 mm long vs. the two short similar screws used on the acceleration pump cover assembly.

Idle air and power enrichment jets look the same, so don't mix them up . The sizes may not the same as stamped, also. To be sure, use a jet gauge – .05 mm is a lot of difference overall. Use OEM thin gaskets for carb bases so they won't get re-

warped. The same for the top cover, especially if carb can't be set within specs for float level as a thick gasket will raise the float valve. Again, don't overtighten the top cover screws, or air and fuel leaks are *back!* Notes for Zenith: wet-look of carbs is due to "fuel standoff" syndrome, caused by cam overlap timing, especially during acceleration, or throttle blipping – can be seen with air cleaner removed. Way back in the early 1960s *Up-Fixin* shows aluminum extensions to raise the mesh air filters and gives a slight ramming effect. Later type canisters leaked around the clamp neck-to-carb body until a raised version with internal O-ring became available for the C series. Therefore, don't keep tightening the top cover screws hoping to stop the wet-look. Recheck injection quantity, or don't over-blip.

Today's fuels aren't the same as in the past when these carbs were designed. Use a good brand fuel, check plug readings, all around operation. Float levels may require lowering to prevent excessive "boil-over" from heat/fuel expansion after shutdown. OEM parts may cost more, but they're better in overall performance. Too bad Zenith float levels aren't easy to adjust.

Vol. 17, No. 5 Vic Skirmants

Carburetor Notes
I once tried to adjust a pair of Zenith carbs and could not get the idle speed down. Unlike the Solexes, the Zeniths have a chromed brass throttle shaft running in a cast-iron base. No real chance of wear there, so high idle speed is not a Zenith characteristic. Well, it seems the owner had rebuilt his carbs – took them all apart – all the way apart. He had removed the throttle butterflies; who knows why? Upon re-assembly, he just put them in and tightened the holding screws. Well, the butterflies were not well centered, so they could not close completely;

therefore the idle speed was high.

Similar problem, more recently, only this time with Solexes. The shafts were snug in the carb bodies, but one throat was pulling more air. The butterfly was centered, but something wasn't right. I finally noticed the holding screws had been removed and replaced. That's right; someone had pulled the butterflies! At least they tried to get them centered. So what was the problem? Well, the edges of carburetor butterflies are not square to the surface plane. The edge has an angle so that when closing, the edge seals to the throat when the butterfly is still at an angle short of horizontal. If you put the butterfly in upside-down, the edge goes the wrong way and keeps the shaft from closing all the way, which keeps the other butterfly more open. In short, don't pull the butterflies! There's no reason. Even if you get them in perfectly, you're taking a chance on the screws eventually falling out. Did you notice that the threaded ends are staked over after they're put in at the factory?

Throttle Linkage

Vol. 2, No. 1 Bill Walsh

Freeing Frozen Linkage and Routine Linkage Maintenance
Wintertime problems with a frozen accelerator linkage (gas pedal won't return after releasing) can be remedied easily by spraying the coupling behind the fan shroud with a liberal coat of CRC 5-56 lubricant.

A light coat of GE clear silicone under and around the windshield washer nozzles will stop the annoying drip down on your ankles in a rain storm.

As a safety measure to avoid fire, I heartily recommend replacement of the fuel line slip fittings behind the fan shroud with standard tubing and stainless hose clamps. Hopefully, everyone already carries a charged fire extinguisher. (Good idea!)

An occasional application of light lubricant or CRC 5-56, using a wand, into the cable release tubes for the hood, fuel lid (if applicable) and engine compartment will avoid excessive wear, cable rust and avoid troublesome cable replacement.

Vol. 9, No. 5 Francis Hunt

Linkage Adjustment
I own a 1959 Cabriolet which had always suffered from poor throttle response and a lot of sloppiness in the accelerator linkage. The engine and carburetors were rebuilt along the way but the problem was still there, and I just never did get around to proper trouble shooting until I installed the Webers that were my Christmas present. Then I just *had* to get things right.

The procedure below can be found in the Fuel System section of the B/C Workshop Manual p. SF 25 and SF 26 but I overlooked it and fumbled around trying to solve the problem by trial and error so maybe this will save someone that trouble.

Inspection of the throttle linkage on the fan housing turned up one problem to be solved before going into linkage adjustment. The "Top Linkage Cross Bar" rides on a ball that is swedged onto a support that is part of the left side of the fan shroud on later "A"s and "B"s with Zenith Carbs. (I highly recommend Harry Pellow's *ABCs* and *Secrets* books for excellent descriptions and pictures of this and everything else to help sort out the thousands of possible combinations of 356/912 engine pieces.) Anyhow, the ball had begun to work loose and was allowing the linkage to flop around so much that it was totally impossible to ever hope to balance the carbs. This was repaired by having it welded in place. If one is concerned about originality and the engine is out of the car, it should be possible to reswedge it. This done, linkage adjustment could be started.

Go to the bell crank on the front of the engine shroud. Disconnect the rod leading to the bell crank on the transmission. Adjust *that* ball joint so that it is 50 mm (approximately 2 in.) from the fan housing by shortening/ lengthening the rod that connects the crank to the "Top Linkage Cross Bar". Lubricate the sockets and bell crank shaft, secure the lock nuts and reinstall. The process would be easier with the engine out, but adequate measurements can be made with a ruler cut to 2 in. and using touch to set the distance.

Now jack the car up onto jack stands and go to the bell crank on the transmission. Remove the rod that leads on forward to the accelerator pedal. Adjust *this* ball so that it is about 20 - 21 mm ($3/4$ in.) to the rear of the centerline of the bellcrank by shortening/lengthening the rod that you removed from the fan housing bell crank previously. Now hook it up at both ends and adjust the rod going to the pedal so that it can be pressed on without moving the bell crank.

Now you adjust the accelerator pedal so that its upper edge is about 80 mm ($3^1/8$ in.) from the floor board and adjust the throttle stop – the bolt in the floorboard–until the carbs open to the stops on the carb bodies and the job is done. All sloppiness should be gone and throttle response should be progressive and smooth. If there is still too much play to suit you, check and replace any loose fitting sockets on the various rods for the final touch.

And if you *really* want to have fun, sell your old carbs and install 40 IDF Webers! Once you switch you'll never go back.

Vol. 12, No. 6 Vic Skirmants

Linkage Adjustment, II
Ever have trouble getting all of your throttle linkage adjusted for full throttle? The factory finally realized the A's and early B's had a problem (especially with the Solex 40 PIIs). The throttle bellcrank on the transmission was changed sometime in 1961 (?) I think. Anyway, the Cs definitely had it. On the later bellcrank, the arm for the throttle rod up to the engine is longer. This gives more travel for the same amount of gas pedal movement. If you have a problem getting full throttle, and can't get the later bellcrank, you can always cut the arm on your old one and lengthen it about $1/2$ in.

One could almost write a book about adjusting all the links and rods on a 356, but basically you just have to make sure that all the bellcranks are within the limits of their travel. If the transmission bellcrank or the bellcrank on the fan housing are fully extended, don't make adjustments that will require more movement; it won't happen. Check another point of adjustment. Eventually you should get full throttle without a 3000 RPM idle, because the linkage won't let the carbs close fully!

Fuel Pump

Vol. 9, No. 4 Richard Miller

Installing an Electric Fuel Pump
One final note on installing an electric fuel pump in a 356. If you're tired of cranking for a half hour every morning because the float bowls have leaked down overnight and you don't want to rebuild the carburetors again, try an electric fuel pump. There are two advantages to this modification. First, it starts pumping as soon as you turn the ignition on and when it stops "clucking", you can start immediately. Second, it gives you a brief warning of the "outa gas – hit reserve" syndrome by clucking rapidly moments before you flame out and have to look for the reserve selector under the dash

while you get out of everybody's way. The installation requires drilling two holes, some new fuel line, a piece of wire and a pump. J.C. Whitney sells a 6 v. electric pump with an adjustable pressure regulator for under $30 with all the required hardware. I mounted the pump directly under the tank, in front of the floor boards, as shown in the pictures.

This way it blows instead of sucks, and reduces the chance of vapor lock which might happen if it were mounted in the engine compartment. Actually there is very little extra space available in a 356 which is convenient. The pumps are supposedly preset at 3psi – mine wasn't. The pressure should be about 2.5 to 3psi. Higher pressures will force the float valves open and cause flooding or rich running. (Same thing can happen if mechanical pump is not mounted properly.)

Pull out the mats, floorboards, and foot panels. Move the wire bundles, tach cable and rats nests around so you can locate the pump neatly. Drill two holes from the passenger side through the shift tunnel wall, avoiding wires and brake lines. Install new fuel hoses from the petcock to the pump and from the pump to the metal fuel line. Route a 14 or 12 gauge wire from the pump to the fused side of the fuse panel terminal 1 and then decide what to do with the old mechanical pump.

You can take it off completely and blank off the opening with a gasket and plate made up to fit but then you have to modify the gas lines at the engine. I preserved the original appearance by disabling the pump without removing it from the car. Disconnect the fuel lines, remove the top of the pump, remove the little valve cover plate from inside the top, along with the valves and springs. Remove the diaphragm and spring assembly and make an aluminum disc replacement for the diaphragm out of sheet aluminum about $1/16$ in. thick. Reinstall this, with gaskets on both sides,

under the cover, hook up the fuel lines, check for leaks, and now the electric pump pumps straight through the old mechanical pump body. The only clue giving this modification away is the incessant cluck, cluck, cluck as you burn up the miles (and gas).

Vol. 15, No. 6 David Grant

Rebuilding hints for the 356B/C/912 fuel pump, type PE 15057

The most common reasons for disassembling the pump will be a failure to pump sufficient fuel (500 cc per minute at 4500 rpm). If the pump has been unused for a long time, it may have debris in it. This will keep the check valves from closing fully. Corrosion can occur even when the car is used daily in a dry climate. This has the effect of keeping the inlet valve (a thin steel sheet) from sealing against the pump head. If the pump is very old (i.e., original) its diaphragm will have hardened. This can keep the coil spring from returning the diaphragm to its starting position. If you cannot bend the edge of the diaphragm (which you can test without removing or taking apart the pump: dig your fingernail into the exposed edge) it is likely that the working portion is too hard for further use. Confirm this by checking for pliability when you have it apart. There are two sheets of fabric reinforced rubber in each diaphragm. If you are at the side of the road (i.e., desperate and without a repair kit), and have confirmed that the diaphragm is keeping the plunger from moving, you can check that the more flexible piece has no holes, and carefully cut the outer (harder) diaphragm sheet away. The remaining single layer will last for years, or at least until you buy a rebuild kit.

Taking the pump apart

With the pump out, check the large o-ring which keeps your crankcase oil

215

off the ground. If it is like a piece of hard plastic, get a new one, then cut away the old one. Don't gouge your fingers or the groove it seals against. If it feels like soft rubber, leave it in place, or set it aside. Set the heat insulating spacer aside. Remove the 5 mm bolt (mm hex). If the cover will not come off easily, put a steel rod about 5 mm into the hole, and lightly pry it off. If it still resists, you can thread the hole for a 6 x 1 mm bolt, and "slide-hammer" the cover off. Do not bend the cover, pry on its edges, or distort the flat annular surface around the hole.

Make a diagram of the original orientation, or you may have the brass tubes pointing wrong when you are done. If you never do as you are told, and have a spare pump, or pictures of one, skip the sketch. Remove the six slotted screws which hold the head to the pump. If the head does not slide off readily, try to hit a solid wooden object (the end of your workbench?) with the strongest part of the head (away from the brass tubes). When the head is off, you can remove the screw which holds on the inlet valve plate. The plate should be either very flat, or bent so that the seal portion is flat, but its waist is about 1 mm above a flat surface. Clean the part of the die-cast head which the inlet valve touches with fine (240 +) sandpaper until it is very flat and smooth.

If there is nothing wrong with the outlet valve, leave it alone. If you have a new one, and the valve has obvious damage, you could try threading the retainer's bore, and pulling it out.

Clean the plastic screen with a soft toothbrush, and some paint thinner. If it has shrunk over the years, and is too small to touch the lower "shelf" made for it, you will have to replace it, or dirt will get through to your check valves, and your car will annoy you some day, in some way.

Replacing the diaphragm – Taking apart the lower end

If the diaphragm is soft, and the inner parts are dirt free, you likely have no reason to take apart the rest of the pump. Carefully separate the diaphragm from the pump body. Push the (engine end) spring cap down, and remove the c-clip. The cap and spring can be removed. The rod, etc. will come out the head end of the body. The cross pin will soon fall out, allowing the diaphragm assembly to be removed. The oily parts can be solvent washed, if desired.

Flattening the diaphragm clamping surfaces

While the pump is likely to be warped less than the average carb cover, it is worth checking. Put a wet sheet of fine wet sandpaper on a flat surface (plate glass or a very flat area on a countertop). With light even downward force, move the diaphragm-clamping surface of the cover in a circular path, until shiny spots appear around the bolt holes, you are done, if you have not allowed the cover to rock as you moved it. Repeat with the pump body. Wash the grit from the two parts, using a small stream of water. Try to keep it out of the pump valve area. While the diaphragm surfaces must be flat, the surface which contacts the heat insulating plastic block need not be flat. It is often warped 0.020" or more. This will not cause problems.

External appearance

Typically 356 zinc die cast parts start off with a mottled light gray smooth, semi-gloss surface, much like newly hot-dipped galvanized steel. They will take on a much darker hue, unless they have corroded. This dark hue can be converted to a lighter, even gray, by careful soaking in diluted hydrochloric acid. It is not possible to re-create the "hot-dipped zinc" appearance which is found inside some die cast 356 parts. While the inside of the pump or curb body are a clue to what the outside would have looked like, before it darkened, a better clue is the appearance of the inside of the bubbles cast into the parts by mistake. This surface is the same uniform light gray which results from acid pickling treatments. With any solvent or acid, you should keep it off your skin, the pushrod seal, and any metals which are not die cast zinc. Do not sand, polish, or wire brush your zinc parts. They were not intended to be very shiny. If you want horribly unoriginal parts, just send them out to be plated with the metal of your choice. If you bead blast the pump, use fresh beads of about 20 microns diameter. Do it on an intact pump, after you plug all vent etc. holes with putty, and before you plate the steel parts.

Final Cleaning

If you want to use compressed air to remove dirt and solvent, you must take care that the outlet valve is not fluttered by such a stream. This can chip the plastic disk, whose pieces can cause untold trouble later. Reports of chipped valve disks are more likely from this than (as some repair facilities might claim) from natural aging. You could try to hold your finger over its 10 mm port, hold it open while you air-blast the area, or use only solvent and shaking instead of pressure.

When everything is clean, put in the inlet valve. It should be almost flat, with a slight bend near its mount, to pre-load it against the head. Its die cast retainer has a natural 3 mm bend, allowing the valve to bend elastically as it opens. Oil and put together the lower end, and line up the head and diaphragm holes. Refer to your sketch for tube orientation. Note that 1963 356B pumps had thickwall 8 mm brass tubes; C/912 pumps use thin wall 8 mm brass tube; the only other difference was the date stamp. Put all six screws in finger tight. Torque them all gradually. Put the valve cover on, with "perfect, used" or new gaskets. The 5 mm bolt gasket must be almost as soft as the perimeter gasket. Little torque is required; do not bend the cover. Install the plastic heat insulator, and a soft o-ring, to seal against the crankcase.

If someone before you has thrown out the original rubber hose and fittings, remember that the late B used short rings with four dimples; C/912 hoses used longer (20 mm metal ferrules, compressed with an 8 point swage. These are pictured in the workshop manuals. New steel lines can be made up, with 8 mm or $5/_{16}$ in. tube, after drilling out the old fittings. The factory brazed their lines; be sure that the solder/braze you use is copper plated before it ruins the cad or zinc of your final replating. You can easily make new fittings for the later lines on a lathe. It isn't much more work than salvaging originals. The same applies to the ferrules, if your local industrial hose shop can't find "originals".

Chapter 11

Gearbox

Gearbox Types

Vol. 16, No. 1 Vic Skirmants

A short history of transmissions.

The first transmissions used by Porsche were VW crashboxes, using the standard Volkswagen serial numbers. The numbers I have range from KD0244975 to 0359615. I only have four data points for these!

Sometime in 1952, Porsche introduced their all-synchro 519 transmission. The magnesium VW crashbox housing was still utilized with some internal re-machining and a change of all the internals, including a new nose to cover the reverse gear which had been in the main housing on the previous transmissions. The nose is aluminum, although I have seen one in magnesium. These first 519s had steel shift forks and slider sleeves that looked like the late 741-style, but were not interchangeable. Also, the ring and pinion was an 8:35 and the differential carrier was the very early VW style. The numbers in my file start at 454 H1 and go to 1885 H4. Six data points.

In 1953 VW changed transmission housings and Porsche used what was available. The housing was still magnesium, but no longer had the big bump for the oil filler. The internal parts were still the same. At some as yet undetermined point, numbers the shift forks were changed to brass (the steel ones wore themselves and the shift sleeves terribly) and the shift sleeves and spiders were changed to what I'll call the 644 style. Numbers KD 2899 to 7526 H5; 29 data points. H1, H4, H5? No H? Evidently a code for the gear ratios. The H5 quite often appears in Speedsters with BBAB gears and H1 has BBBC. However, this is not always consistent.

With the introduction of the 356 A, the 519 carried on, with a new dual mount nose and the addition of a second stud by the pinion rear bearing for better clamping. Numbers 8077 H5 to 10538 H3, fourteen data points. H5 now seems to indicate BBBC gearing, and only one of the numbers is from a speedster. Incidentally, three of the transmissions are from 550 Spyders, numbers 10014, 10063 and 10067.

In 1956, transmission information gets interesting. Porsche introduces its own aluminum tunnel-case for its transmissions, but the internals are 98% identical to the last 519 gearboxes. The housing now has the week and year of its creation cast directly into the left side near the part number. The housings were subsequently machined in batches, not necessarily in order of casting. The month and year of completion were now stamped on the front bottom cross-ridge, followed by the gear ratios. Example: serial #11404; on cross-ridge, 96 BBAB (completion in September of 1956). Casting number 32/56: case was cast in 32nd week of 1956 (end of August). This is getting exciting, isn't it? OK, I'm easily amused. Numbers on file, 11048 to 16634 (?); 33 data points. One change occurred in the casting of the 644 cases around that last number. The side-cover stud holes had more material added internally to make them "blind" holes, rather than "through-holes". The 644 case now remained unchanged until superseded by the 716 case. Numbers 17042 to 23599 (casting unknown) although #23118 was cast in 30/58, assembled Nov., 58; 25 data points.

The housing and synchronizers were changed with the introduction of the 716 transmission in December 1958. The synchronizers were re-designed to be much more effective. The housing had some material added for eventual installation of a throw-out bearing guide tube, although the tube didn't appear til late 1959 on the first 741 transmissions. The gear ratios were no longer stamped after the completion date, instead the transmission type (716) appeared, followed by a number code for the ratios; 0 for BBBC, 2 for BBAB. Numbers 25023 to 29627; 25 data points. Incidentally, #25023 is missing, and Ed Venegas would like to know its whereabouts. August of 59 seems to be the end of the 716, with the first 741s completed in September of 1959. Does anyone have a transmission numbered 30,000 to 31,999?

The first 741 transmissions still used the 716 case and 716 synchronizers. The only change was the "B" model throw out bearing guide tube and the ineffective single front mount (even Porsche can goof-up). The stamped transmission type was now 741, followed by 0 for BBBC gears, 2A for BBAB gears, 2 for BBBD gears, and 1 for BBAA. The 741 trans-

missions completed in 1959 of course carried a 9 after the month number. The 1960 transmissions did not carry a "0", for the year but instead a 6, which stood for 1960. For instance, 16 meant January 1960. These "6" numbers should not be confused with 1956, because as you have learned, the 1956 housings were 644, right? Serial numbers 32147 (Sept 1959) to 34503. (34473 completed Jan., 1960); 14 data points.

Next change, the re-introduction of a dual mount nose, of course with the low shifter as introduced with the first 741. Numbers 35044 (Jan. 1960) to 42274, (Dec 1960); 28 data points. I also have #42332 to 43273, type of housing (716 or 741) unknown; five data points.

Around the 49th week of 1960, the first 741 housing was cast, #741.301.101.00. Internally identical to the 716, externally differentiated by different ribbing and a cast-on pad for the S-90 camber compensator. Also, at an as-yet undetermined date the 3-4 shift fork was strengthened. The synchronizer blocks, bands, and clip were also improved, but that may not have occurred until later in 1961. First 741 housing, #43328 (Feb 1961) to 50596 (Sept 1961); 33 data points. 741/0 meant BBBC gearing, 741/2 BBBD gearing. The factory spec book differentiates transmissions after #50000 as 741A. This may be the synchro change referred to above. 741/0A, BBBC gears; 741/2A, BBBD gears, 741/20A, BBAB gears.

Around the 34th week of 1961, the 741.301.101.10 cases were first cast. Externally the same, but internally stronger. An iron insert was cast in place for the rear mainshaft and pinion bearings. It was also located slightly rearward to provide more space for the wider, stronger first gear that appeared around this time. Number 51074 (Oct 1961) to 70451 (July 1963). 53 data points.

The 741 transmission for the 356 C

debuted in August 1963. Identical to the 741 A, but having a 12 bolt ring & pinion. 741/2C, BBBD gears; 741/0C. BBBC gears. Numbers 70931 (Aug. 1963) to 86517 (March 1965); 77 data points.

In this last batch of transmissions is a group that shows once again that we're all human, even Porsche. During the casting weeks of 9 to 18, 1964, someone cast 741.301.101.00 on the housings. The ones examined internally so far all show that they really are 741.301.101.10.

Vol. 16, No. 6 Mark Turczyn

Early Gearboxes

The early cars used VW non-syncro "crash" boxes which employed sliding pins to engage third and fourth. They modified the VW bellhousing mount yoke by welding on a squarish looking hoop that attached to the car using two overhead bolts like all later 356s. This gearbox's most distinguishing feature was the neat little cuplike oil filler that was cast into the right side (facing the bell housing) of the box. Based upon the VW and Porsche spec sheets I have read, I believe that the gears were the same as the VW box. The only other transmission I have ever seen mentioned in the Porsche literature is the interim synchro box. This is a VW crash box with synchro gears inserted and a thick metal spacer plate added to the end of the box to hold the reverse gear which had been moved to the outside of the box because there was no room inside for it. This box can be considered an early version of the 519. It used the same modified hoop as in the earlier cars. The factory supposedly used this gearbox in the August-September 1952 time frame. I have seen it in earlier cars, but most earlier cars did have straight crash boxes. The August-September time frame makes sense because the synchro 519 box came out in about October 1952.

Let me tell you about a second style crash box that can be found lurking in old Porsches. This is 'ol 21015, first cousin of 'ol 21014, the crash box Porsche used. Well, sure as the sun comes up, VW decided that vertically pouring gear lube into the gearbox was a pain so they cast a new case for the crash box. This casing had two major changes. It had a horizontal side filler rather than the vertical top filler (sort of like a small one-inch high volcano coming out of the side of the case), and rather than using two cast lugs on each side of the bell housing to mount the transmission to the mounting yoke, this one used two rubber pads bolted to each side of the bottom of the bell housing. It had a smooth case (no external ribs) just like 21014 but the nose piece was given two additional ribs running 45 degrees to the shift rod. This nose/rubber doughnut mounting scheme was used until some time in 1952 when VW changed to a solid rubber bolt-on-block scheme. They of course changed the nose piece design to accommodate this block. The 21015 was used only on standard models while upscale bugs got the new three synchro gear boxes sometime in 1952/1953.

Now remember, VW attaches the transmission mounting yoke to the body under the transmission and Porsche attaches its mounting hoop above the transmission. Therefore, for the early crash boxes Porsche modified the VW yoke by welding on the familiar looking U bracket (actually more squarish than the later U shape) to the VW yoke. Oddly enough, for their 519 synchro box Porsche used the same two-pad mounting scheme that VW used for their newer crash boxes. One reason that the cradle type mounting system was probably dropped by VW was because the band running under the case would pack with dirt and the retained moisture would eat the magnesium case. If a crash box went bad, you could just pull a 21014 crash box out of VW. If he couldn't find a 21014, an enterprising fellow could take an early 21015 crash box out of a standard, put on a hoop from a Porsche gearbox and be back in business. Later on he would have to substitute a 21014 type nose piece to the newer style 21015 and of course reset the bearing pre-load with the right gasket. Why would someone stay with a crashbox if he could get a VW or Porsche synchro box? Crashboxes were cheaper and some drivers were traditional-minded enough to prefer them. If he did want a synchro box he had a few problems to contend with. Dropping in one of the early crash/synchro boxes would be the best solution. All he had to do is find one and that was not easy. If he was looking for a synchro box in late 1952 or later, he could buy a new 519 Porsche synchro gearbox. Unfortunately, to put it in his car, he had to pound up the sheet metal in the hump between the two rear jump seats to make it fit. This is why some humps have been savagely cut up. But his troubles did not stop there. He then had to hope that his simple crash-box gear shift mechanism had enough adjustment to accommodate the newer gearbox. Porsche added a ton of monkey motion on the gear shift mechanism in the back seat to make the 519 synchro boxes a shifting delight. For the record, I have talked to owners of late 1952 cars which have the new style shifting mechanisms that swear that the crash box they have in the car is original. If this is true, we know that the factory made this unlikely retro-combination work.

So as I said at the start of this discussion, the easy way out of having to mess with a new synchro box (especially if you were an early purist) was just to put in a plain old VW crash box which I believe was the same as the Porsche crash box, or to use a 21015 VW crash box and add a synchro

mounting hoop. Now I am going to stand out on a limb here, but I believe that when it came to straight crash boxes, Porsche just bought them from VW. They just added the square hoop and a clutch cable bracket with an additional clip for the throttle cable (a simple pull cable was used until May/June of 1952 the factory says until motor number 20994, 1.3 liter and 30259, 1.5 liter). After June the factory added the bell crank for the rod type throttle control. Of course, the center tunnels were modified to accommodate this change. The crashbox numbers (seven digits) were pure VW. I say this because every 21014 I have removed had a number that corresponded to the date the car was made-the later the car the higher the gearbox number. This cannot be coincidence, or could it? I have never seen a transmission number listed on any Kardex that had an unmodified 21014 gearbox. I have seen some early factory accounting sheets that give the serial number for each chassis number. There were six numbers, but since the first number on a VW box is 0, I can see they just skipped the first digit. Later, when the factory modified 21014 boxes to insert synchros to create the crash/ synchro box, the factory did identify the boxes with numbers such as 219/H5. They also added the mushroom breather. The bell crank was added in May.

A quick aside is that all early crash boxes and synchro boxes used these neat pressed-steel triangular lower shock mount brackets that were bolted to the end of the spring plate and axle. So if you see one of these guys at a swap meet, you will know who to buy it for.

Inspection

Vol. 10, No. 2 Vic Skirmants

What to Look For on an Aged

Transaxle

While on the subject of transmissions, I've been asked whether one should pull the transmission to check it over when the engine is out or the car is apart for other reasons. If the transmission has over 100,000 miles on it, or you have just bought the car and don't know the history of it, it's a good idea to check the differential housing to make sure it's not cracked, and that the ring gear bolts are tight.

Those are the two usual problems that could cause a catastrophic, disabling failure. While the transmission is apart, all the bearings can be checked, as well as the shift sleeves and forks. The 716 and 741-style synchronizers get a shiny, worn appearance when they are bad, as opposed to the very rough, cast finish with which they start. The 519 and 644 synchronizers are smoothly machined to begin with, so there's no easy way to determine if they are good or bad. The only way to really tell is to drive the car before disassembly and see if it crunches when shifting at a normal speed. Fast shifting will cause even good 644 synchros to crunch, so just shift moderately.

Rebuild Information

Vol. 3, No. 3 Vic Skirmants

Cracked Differential Carriers

Mike Robbins, Indianapolis, IN, brought up the subject of cracked differential carriers. The cracks always start at the cross-shaft pin hole and eventually spread to the point where the carrier can actually break in two; this last occurrence is pretty rare, but cracks at the pin hole are extremely common. I seriously suspect some of these came from the factory cracked!

If you have one of these broken beasts, head down to a VW dealer and order a differential carrier for a 1960 or older bug with the split-case trans-

mission. You'll notice your old Porsche carrier says VW and even has the VW number cast right on it. I have heard rumors that the carriers used on Porsches are heat-treated, but you couldn't prove it to me! So, get the VW carrier, measure and compare the appropriate dimensions, change the differential shims if needed, and you're back in business. If you don't know what I'm talking about in the previous sentence, you shouldn't be doing it without help anyway.

Vol. 6, No. 4 Vic Skirmants

Gearbox Installation

Moving right along, let's talk about transmission installation. For those of you who hadn't noticed yet, your transmission is part of your rear suspension. No, it doesn't move up and down; unless your mounts are really bad! In which case you'd better replace them soon. Anyway, the transmission position determines the location of the inner pivots of the swing axles. There are shims at the front mounts (only on dual-mount models) to move the transmission either forward or backward, depending on whether they are installed between the chassis mounts and the transmission mounts, or on the nut side of the chassis mounts. You will also notice a steel cup over the rubber transmission mounts from mid-1957 through 1965 (not counting those wild-and-crazy single front mounts on the first few hundred of the "B" models; whose stupid idea was that, Ferry?). This cup lends additional support to the rubber mounts in shear, thereby decreasing flex under acceleration without going to a stiffer rubber. This cup is at least as thick as the spacing shims; don't just throw these cups on your 1956-57 car and re-install the transmission as usual! By effectively moving the transmission back in this way, you have increased your rear wheel toe-in. A worst case is to leave these cups off of a car that once had them. Without compensating for the decreased thickness of the mount, you will thereby move the transmission forward; this will decrease the rear toe-in, maybe even putting the rear suspension into an actual toe-out situation. This is not very conducive to good handling!

All of the above is predicated on your having reinstalled the axle tubes in the trailing arms exactly where they originally were. You will notice three large bolts and nuts holding the axle tube to the trailing arm. There is a fourth identical bolt holding a large, thick washer. This is strictly a marker to tell you where to reinstall the axle tube. The tube should be pushed right up against the washer.

If your car is original and none of this has been altered, your rear alignment is probably all right. If things have been changed and your SC handles like a 1952, you will have to check the rear toe-in. If you can take it to a shop, fine. If not, you can check it pretty easily yourself. Borrow a friend, a piece of chalk, and a tape measure. Put the car on a fairly smooth surface. Put a chalk mark in the center of the tread of each tire forward of the ground contact patch, and as high up as you can get and still run the tape measure under the car without contacting something. Measure the distance between the two chalk marks. Now push the car forward until the chalk marks are to the rear, and about as high up as they were at the front. Take this measurement and compare to the first. You want the rear measurement to be about $1/16$ to $1/8$ in. more than the front measurement. A larger difference means too much toe-in, a smaller difference means not enough toe-in. If the rear measurement is smaller than the front, then you've got the dreaded toe-out! If you have toe-out, move the axle tubes forward in the trailing arms. If you have too much toe-in, move the tubes rearward.

How do you know if the rear wheels are symetrically toed-in in relation to the centerline of the car? The way to do this is to run a string parallel to a rear tire forward to the centerline of the front wheel and measure the string's distance from the front hub. Do this on both sides. If the dimensions are identical, you're all set. If one is larger, that side is toed-out in relation to the centerline of the car and the other is toed-in. You then have to move one axle tube one way and the other the opposite way. Fine. Now how do you run those parallel strings? You say there's a body in the way. I made an H-shaped bracket that fits against the edges of the wheel. The two arms of the H are equal length. The string is then run against the arms so as to clear the body. I said you could check the toe-in easily; I didn't say the complete operation was easy. It takes a lot of fiddling, adjusting, measuring, re-adjusting, and re-measuring.

Vol. 6, No. 5 Vic Skirmants

Heating Gears for Installation and Other Rebuild Tips

While on transmissions, a couple of comments on rebuilding same. When installing second, third, or fourth gears on the input shaft, the manual tells you to heat them in oil. This is good advice, because you won't over-heat the gear that way; there's only so much oil smoke one can stand. I have seen gears that someone evidently heated with a torch to install (or remove). The gears are hardened steel. Heating them too much, and then letting them cool slowly, will anneal them, and literally make them soft. They will not last very long after that.

On any of the tunnel case transmissions, after the shift rails have been installed in the intermediate plate, the shift forks have to be adjusted before they are tightened down. To help in lining things up, put a front suspension link pin through the reverse gear idler and into the intermediate plate. This is a perfect substitute diameter-wise for the reverse gear shaft that is part of the transmission nose. This will hold your reverse gear and shift rail in alignment while you adjust the other two rails.

Vol. 7, No. 3 Bill Uselmann

Ring and Pinion Code

The earlier Porsche ring and pinion sets had the dimension "R" (distance between the centerline of the differential and the face of the pinion gear) etched directly on one of the gears. Sometime in 1962. instead of a dimension of 59.xx (mm). a + or -number began to appear. The + or -number is the deviation. in hundredths of a millimeter, from a nominal "R" dimension of 59.22 mm. Therefore, if you find a +13, it means your "R" dimension is 59.35 mm. Bill thanks an unknown mechanic at Stoddard's for the information, and Charlie White of Phoenix, Arizona, for a copy of the service bulletin (No. H7/62).

Vol. 15, No. 3 Vic Skirmants

Rebuilding the Gearbox

Okay! You've asked for it before, but I've been reluctant to do it. Yes! I'm going to tell you how to rebuild your transaxle! First, two assumptions: 1) You know something about wrenches and have the brains to figure out which way to turn a nut (or bolt). 2) Your ring and pinion are in good condition, are not being replaced, and have not been set up improperly during a previous "rebuild". Like I said, four assumptions. Make that five; this will only cover the 644, 716, and 741 tunnel-type gearboxes. Maybe I'll cover the 519 in the future.

The only magical mystical part of a 356 gearbox is the adjustment of the ring & pinion. For that you do need some special tools or the ability to innovate and adapt other equipment to accomplish the same goal. The basic information on ring & pinion setup is covered in the workshop manual and is much too involved to be covered in a short column such as this.

First, pull the gearbox. I won't insult your intelligence by telling you which bolts to remove (see assumption #1). I will mention a couple of hints. On a B or C shifter set-up, don't pull the shift coupler out of the gearshift rod, unless you enjoy readjusting the shifter. Merely pull the 8 mm square-head set-screw out of the back end of the coupler. Don't forget to unbolt the ground-strap from the chassis.

Unbolt the front donut mounts from the ears on the torsion bar tube. Unbolting the trans ears from the donuts won't work. Note the arrangement of the shims between the donuts and torsion bar tube ears; you could end up with some strange rear toe-in or toe-out if you don't pay attention to this.

I'll assume you've disconnected the throttle rod, clutch cable, battery and starter wires. Not to mention the brake lines and however much of the rear brakes you've decided to pull off first. On B and C models, pull the back-up light switch wires.

The 1961 and later transmission can be balanced very nicely on the cast-in S-90 compensator mounting pad on the bottom of the differential bulge. The 644 to 1960-741 transmissions don't have the pad, so you'll have to figure out a way to hold the transmission based on your jack or removal method. I've made up a metal U shaped bracket that I bolt to my jack pad that holds the transmission by the drain plug area and forward of the differential bulge. You can probably make something up with 2 x 4s to accomplish the same thing.

Now that the transmission is out; you did drain the oil first; right? You should spread a week's worth of newspapers under the trans and axle tubes. This thing is going to be messier than you can imagine! When you pull off the axle tubes, you'll find that they can hold what seems like a quart of oil in the axle boot.

Tip the transmission up on its bell-housing, putting a 2 x 4 under the top end of the housing to keep from resting the input shaft on the ground; you won't hurt the input shaft by resting the transmission on it, but this way the housing won't go "clunk" onto the floor when you pull out the gear cluster.

Remove the eight through-bolts that hold on the front cover. Some light taps with a plastic mallet should remove the front cover. If the shift finger wants to come off with the cover, try cleaning up any burrs by carefully using a file. On B and C models, don't ever grab the shift finger with vise grips, channel locks, pliers or whatever to see how it's shifting! The rod part of the finger is mild steel and incredibly easy to gouge, resulting in a nice oil leak because the seal was not designed to seal a buggered-up shaft. Both 644 and 741 type shift fingers should be welded for longer life. The 644 finger is a one-piece forging, and a used one will always be slightly cracked on the inside fillet between the arm and the "finger". Have it welded up in that area. The 741 finger is a two-piece construction and cannot even be checked for cracks in the shaft because the machined-down part of the shaft (where the cracks start) is covered by the finger. Just have the finger welded to the shaft all the way around. Keep the weld small, and you won't have to worry about clearance to the inside of the nose-piece; otherwise you'll have to chamfer the nose-piece. The 644 does not have an interference problem.

After the cover is off, loosen up the intermediate plate by tapping with a plastic mallet. Now pull out the gear cluster, and measure the thickness of the gasket or gaskets between the intermediate plate and housing. This gasket is part of the pinion gear depth adjustment, so be sure you don't lose track of the proper thickness.

With the gear cluster lying on your workbench, the next step is to pull the shift rails and shift forks. Remove the three detent ball plugs from the intermediate plate and pull out the springs and balls, as well as the spacer from the bottom hole. Now remove the shift fork bolts and pull the third-fourth gear shift rail out. Remove the interlock plunger between the third-fourth gear shift rail and the first-second gear shift rail. Then pull out the first-second gear shift rail, remove the interlock plunger between that rail and the reverse gear shift rail, finally remove the reverse shift rail.

Pull the cotter pins from the input shaft nut and the pinion shaft nut. If you have a vise with soft jaw inserts or covers, clamp the intermediate plate in the vise. Now shift one shift sleeve into third or fourth gear, and the other shift sleeve into first or second gear. The shafts are now locked, and you can remove the input shaft and pinion shaft nuts. Then pull the upper and lower reverse gears off the two shafts, as well as the three keys from the shafts.

If you have the special tools, you next press the two shafts out of the intermediate plate. You are reading this because you don't have the special tools. You will need a good two-arm gear puller. By pushing each shaft just far enough before the gears start jamming each other, you can press the shafts out without damage. It's tedious, but it does work. Don't even think of bashing on the ends of the shafts to drive them out! Not even with a brass hammer. The shafts are quite hard, but that's a case hardness over a relatively soft inner material. The outer hard case will break up and the inner metal will then mushroom over.

There is no need to remove the other gears from the input shaft unless you're changing a gear. To remove a gear, use the gear puller or a press. A press can be used to reinstall a gear cold. Otherwise, support the shaft on a block of wood and use a piece of pipe to drive the gear on. If you choose to heat up the gear, don't overdo it! I have seen gears turned blue from over-zealous heating. If you change the color of the gear, you have just changed its hardness.

On the pinion shaft, you can remove the two spacers and then fourth gear by merely pulling them off. The fourth gear bearing race is pressed on. Adjust your gear puller to grab first gear and pull the entire assembly off the pinion shaft. The little roller bearings will now be falling all over the place. You might want to do this operation over a tray or something that would collect any stray rollers. The pinion adjustment shims are located between the first gear bearing thrust washer and the rear pinion bearing. Don't lose them. If you are replacing any of the bearings, they are made accurately enough that you can assume the ring and pinion setup will not be changed. When reassembling the pinion shaft, all the bearing races, washers, shift spiders should slide on. Only the fourth gear bearing race will have to be persuaded with a pipe and hammer; again, support the pinion gear on a piece of wood. Now you have to construct a support to hold the input and pinion shafts in the proper relationship while you carefully tap on the intermediate plate using a piece of pipe that drives against the inner bearing races.

Put the intermediate plate in the vise, install the reverse keys and gears, and shift into two gears again to lock the trans. Torque the input shaft nut to 25 lb.-ft.; check to see if the cotter pin holes line up with the castellated nut. If they don't, tighten the nut some more until one of the holes lines up and the cotter pin can be installed.

Don't back the nut off to line up the holes! Next torque the pinion shaft nut to 70 lb.-ft. Tighten some more if necessary to line up cotter pin holes; install cotter pin.

Put both shift sleeves into neutral. Install the shift rails, detents, and interlock plungers; you do remember how they went, don't you? The reverse gear detent spring is slightly longer than the other two. There is a factory tool for holding the ends of the shift rails while adjusting the shift forks; totally unnecessary! You do need to support the reverse idler gear; a link pin is perfect. Just slide it through the gear and into the hole in the intermediate plate. The shift forks need to be set equidistant between the two gears they engage. Also, the ends of the rails that the shift finger engages should be aligned so that their sides are a couple of millimeters apart. I use blue Loctite on the shift fork bolts and torque to 18 lb.-ft.

The gear cluster is now ready for reinstallation. I use sealer on the gaskets (Permatex Ultra-Blue). Slide the gear cluster carefully into the case, being sure not to damage the new input seal you've already installed. When putting on the nose-piece, be certain to keep the shift finger engaged properly in the shift rails. Torque the through-bolts to 18 lb. ft.

Vol. 15, No. 4 Vic Skirmants

Rebuilding the Gearbox Continued
Now let's review the disassembly of the differential. The one tool that will come in handy is a standard two-arm gear puller. After removing the six nuts that hold the left axle tube to the side-cover, use the puller to remove the axle tube. Of course if you have the special wheel bearing puller, you can remove the bearing and then just pull off the axle tube. I prefer to leave the right axle tube attached for now. Next, remove the eight nuts holding the left side-cover to the trans-

mission housing. You can now use the gear puller on the end of the right axle to push the axle and differential assembly out of the housing. You can tap the assembly out by using a brass mallet on the end of the right axle, but be careful of damaging the axle threads.

Remove the left side-cover from the differential carrier by using two large screwdrivers between the cover and carrier. Equal pressure on opposite sides of the carrier should remove the side-cover. Keep track of the differential shims at this point! There will be one thick shim on each side of the differential carrier; there may also be a .010" thick additional shim on either or both sides. The thick shims are obvious; the thin ones sometimes stick to the bearing in the side cover. Be sure you have all your shims, mark them in some manner (masking tape and ball point pen work just fine), and don't mix them up side-to-side!

The next step is to remove the ring-gear bolts. Early transmissions used safety wire through holes in the bolt heads. The next locking style was a metal lock plate that went under each pair of bolts, then had the ends bent up to lock the bolts. Despite the bad reputation of the six-bolt carriers, if the bolts are tight, they will not break. When they loosen up, then things get exciting. The bolts can break, or simply start backing out and machining the left side-cover. To prevent the backing out, Porsche developed their final locking method, the one where a special metal tab fits into slots in the periphery of the bolt heads, and is then bent over to lock the bolts. This technique is used on the late 6-bolt as well as 12-bolt carriers. Obviously the tabs are different lengths for the 6 and 12-bolt set-ups.

With the bolts removed, pull off the small end of the differential carrier and remove the left axle shaft, side-gear and fulcrum plates. Next, drive out the soft steel lock pin that holds

the spider gear cross-shaft to the carrier. Don't be alarmed just yet if you already see cracks in the carrier outside the lock pin. Once you have removed the cross-shaft, spider gears, and right side-gear and axle shaft, you can now examine the carrier for serious cracks. Look inside the carrier at the curved surface against which the spider gear nearest the lock pin bears. Any cracks are visible to the naked eye; you don't need to spend money magnafluxing. If there are no cracks between the lock pin hole and the spider gear surface, you're in luck. If there is a crack on the narrow side of the spider gear hole, but none on the opposite side, you could still re-use the carrier, depending on your planned driving style. If there is a crack on the opposite side as well, better get another carrier! You've already noticed the VW part number on your old carrier. Yes, it's the same part as the VW split-housing transaxle. It is not the same as the VW tunnel housing trans. Mike Robbins has information that the Porsche factory started hardening the spider gear area around 1958, but we've had no problems using the stock VW part.

If you have to change the carrier, you can carefully measure your old carrier and the replacement, and figure out if you need to change the differential shim arrangement.

When re-assembling, proceed in the reverse order, as the factory manuals always say. The factory also recommends using new ring gear bolts.

That's good advice, but those bolts are now priced at over $12 apiece! If the old bolts appear sound, they can be re-used. Be sure all traces of oil are gone from the ring gear bolt holes and the bolts. Use red Loctite and torque the bolts to 65 lb ft. Don't over-torque. The bolts are short and hard, therefore they will not accept excess torque without snapping.

When re-installing the differential assembly, don't forget to install the shims, and be sure you put the shim's chamfer against the carrier.

Front Seal Replacement

Vol. 4, No. 2 Ralph Garretson, Jr.

Seal Replacement Without Gearbox Removal

In reply to Major Frank's question in the August issue reference replacing the shift rod seal in the nose piece of the transmission, I have successfully done that without removing the transmission. As I recall, what was required was the following: Between the transmission and the chassis is a boot which covers a removable link in the shift rod. Push the boot back and remove the link and then the boot in order to make room to work. With a small chisel and a punch, destroy the seal – especially the outer casing – to the point where it can be levered out or pulled free with pliers. It is important to work carefully and with plenty of light in order to avoid scoring either the shift rod or the seal seat in the nose piece. (I didn't, but if I had, I would have filled it with epoxy and sanded it smooth with fine emery cloth.) With the old seal out, make sure the seat is clean, slide the new seal over the shift rod, and seat it with a small hammer and/or a short length of pipe. The job takes about two hours, not including all the things that usually go wrong in accordance with Murphy's Law.

Linkage

Vol. 9, No. 4 Vic Skirmants

Linkage Adjustment

As for adjusting the linkage, on a 1950 - 1959, the side-to-side adjustment can only be done at the nose of the transmission and the fore and aft adjustment is accomplished by mov-
ing the shift cup retainer and/or the base of the shifter. On a 1960 - 1965, the side-to-side and fore and aft adjusting is all done at the coupler at the transmission nose. The shifter base can also be moved a small amount, but shouldn't be necessary. The linkage should be set so that when the gearshift is against the reverse lockout plate, first and second can easily be engaged.

The fore and aft adjustment is correct when the travel of the gearshift from neutral to full engagement of first and from neutral to full engagement of second is equal. On B and C models this is no problem, but on the older ones, part of the Michael Rodent linkage at the transmission nose can sometimes bump into the torsion bar tube, preventing full engagement of first and third gears. If all the parts are up to snuff, this should not happen. However, with about thirty years of wear, things might be a little sloppy. One then has to inspect how all those parts interact and try to cure the slop problem. I'm sorry I can't be more specific, but you'll learn more just by looking at all that stuff than by me writing five pages about it.

Selector Rods

Vol. 5, No. 3 Vic Skirmants

Broken Shift Fingers, I

Have you ever been driving your 356 when you suddenly had no gears or ended up in one gear, the shifter having no noticeable effect? If you have checked the gearshift lever and shift coupler at the transmission, and found everything in order, you have a broken shift finger inside the nose of your transmission. Of course if you can select the gears, but the car won't move, then you've got some other problems. Fixing a broken shift finger on a B or C involves pulling the engine and dropping the transmission

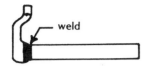

weld

down after pulling the front mounts and disconnecting the rear hoop; you do not have to pull the axle ends! On a B or C the shift finger usually breaks at the finger end of the shaft. If you have never had this problem and have the transmission apart for any reason, I would suggest reinforcing the shift finger by welding the finger to the shaft as shown in the illustration.

The bead of weld can interfere with the nose of the transmission, so you'll have to machine out some aluminum from the inside of the nose where the shaft enters. This can be done with a rotary file in a drill, or even with a sharp screwdriver as proven by Stan Adams at the racetrack.

In the 356 race cars around here we have had an equal number of failures between 644 and stock 741 shift fingers. I don't know of an easy way to reinforce a 644, but have never seen a reinforced 741 break. I have converted several of the 644s to 741 noses and shift fingers. This involves cutting a hole for the shifter in the rear of the car below the torsion bar tubes. One can then install a complete B or C shifter assembly after suitable modifications to the tunnel for mounting.

Bolting up a 741 nose directly to a 644 chassis raises the front of the transmission one-half inch. To put the transmission nose back down where it belongs I make up offset front transmission mounts. Since we use solid mounts on the race cars, this poses no problem.

Vol. 14, No. 4 Vic Skirmants

Broken Shift Fingers, II
Most of you have heard of broken shift fingers in our transmissions. The 741 shift finger cannot be checked for cracks because the crack usually starts in the stepped portion of the rod covered by the "finger". The best thing to do is weld around the juncture between the rod and finger. When it comes to 519 and 644 fingers, yours is cracked right now! Every 519-644 shift finger I have checked in the past two years had already developed a crack at the angle between the rod and finger. The piece is forged out of a single piece of metal and is quite strong, but the stresses are pretty severe in that area of the shift finger. The solution again is to weld the area to reinforce it.

Axle Boots

Vol. 4, No. 4 Richard Miller

Vinyl vs. Neoprene Axle Boots
If your transmission seems to be making more noise than usual, check the rubber boots at the inboard ends of the swing axles. These crack and let the oil out over a period of time during which the gear noise gets louder and louder.

When you replace them, make sure you use original equipment neoprene boots (part number 111 598 021A for VW work well) instead of the shiny black vinyl boots. The transmission oil leaches the plasticizer out of the vinyl and they get stiff and crack in a year or so. The neoprene boots last at least five times as long. It is easier to install one if you jack up the axle tube so it is perpendicular to the transaxle. In the normal drop-down state it's harder to get the axle boot on properly. Also, position the bolted seam horizontally; the tube moves up and down, and the seam will only flex properly in a horizontal position.

Vol. 6, No. 4 Vic Skirmants

Installation of Axle Boots

Also a while back I talked about the rear axle boots, mentioning that the split seam should be parallel to the ground, not vertical, because the seam was not designed to flex in that direction. Recently I found another reason for not putting the seam vertically, at least on the driver's side. A customer complained of a sticking throttle after he had reinstalled his transmission, with new axle boots. One of the problems I found was that the throttle rod from the transmission bellcrank to the engine was rubbing on the rubber seam of the axle boot. There was plenty of room when the car was on stands with the axles drooping, but when on the ground, there was interference. In this case, a very noticeable notch had started to wear in the seam.

Synchronizing Rings

Vol. 6, No. 5 Vic Skirmants

Types of Synchro Rings

I often have 356 drivers complain to me about their gears "crunching" when they shift. If nothing is wrong with the clutch or its adjustment, the synchronizers are usually to blame. The first 356s used a stock VW "crash-box" transmission. There were no synchronizers, and one had to be good at double-clutching to drive these early cars.

In late 1952, Porsche came out with their own gears and synchronizers, still installed in a VW housing. These early Porsche transmissions were highly praised by the road testers and magazine writers of the period. Compared to most other cars of the era, these transmissions were excellent, especially when the synchronizers were new. As anyone who owns a 519 - 644 style transmission can attest, however, these gearboxes aren't that great after any kind of mileage has been placed on them.

In 1959 Porsche introduced the 716

synchronizers, which, with slight modifications became the 741. These synchros were really excellent, and almost crunch-proof. After many hard miles, however, even these synchros will wear out, but usually only the first and second gear synchros are bad enough to worry about replacing: this is because these are the two most-used gears.

There is a problem with a 716 - 741 first gear that is not widely known. Even with a fairly new synchro on first gear, let alone a well worn one, you will get a crunch when pushing in the clutch and shifting into first with the car standing still. This is a common complaint. Well, there's not much you can do about it. First gear synchro is not designed for an upshift, which is what you are doing when engaging first from neutral, while standing still. It is designed for a downshift, and if you're not getting a crunch that way, I wouldn't worry about the synchro. To avoid the crunch, you can push in the clutch, wait a full second or two, then put it in gear. This allows all the gears time to stop spinning. This same problem occurs with reverse, which of course is not synchronized at all. The solution is the same; wait one to two seconds before putting it in gear. If it still crunches, your clutch isn't releasing completely.

If you're in a hurry and don't feel like waiting two seconds, push in the clutch, touch second gear, then put it in first or reverse. Touching second (or third or fourth if you feel like it) lets that gear's synchro slow down the gears, which have been spinning off the input shaft while the transmission was in neutral and the clutch was out. You will notice this more on a warm transmission when the fluid has thinned out, than on a cold one. Of course you can sit at a stop light with the clutch in, but I wouldn't recommend it. The throw-out bearing wears the pressure plate enough as it is.

644 Synchros With 741 Spiders

A gear with the 644-style synchronizers can be used with the later 741-style shift spiders and sleeves. There is a problem with interference between the face of the synchronizer hub and the shift spider. Do not grind down the shift spider! It's thin enough in the area in question. Simply grind down the face of the synchronizer hub.

Trouble Shooting

Vol. 7, No. 6 Vic Skirmants

519 Gearbox Popping Out of Gear

How about a transmission problem? Just got in a really nice, solid early 356 with a first gear problem; it not only jumped out of first gear on acceleration, you couldn't even hold it in gear! The transmission was an old 519, so of course the problem was worn shift forks and sleeves not permitting full engagement of first gear, resulting in the above problem. Upon disassembly, it was discovered that this was a really early 519; steel shift forks. Porsche learned very quickly after the first 519s came out; steel shift forks rubbing against steel shift sleeves wore both down at a dramatic rate. Making the forks out of brass to act as a bearing material resulted in no wearing down of either part in normal usage; and even in racing usage. Of course the driver who used the gearshift as a hand rest in fourth gear could still manage to wear the hell out of fork and sleeve.

Upon replacing sleeves, forks, and even first gear (due to the damage to the synchro teeth from all the popping out of gear), the transmission was reassembled, road-tested, and still popped out of gear; only under hard acceleration, and you could even hold it in, but still not quite right.

Upon finally deciding that it really did have to come out again, I pulled engine, transmission, split transmission, replaced first gear synchronizer and sleeve, reassembled, re-installed. and road-tested in five hours. That includes almost one hour of analyzing, measuring, and just plain staring at the first gear synchro and sleeve that were at fault. They were not new parts (anyone know of a source?), but had appeared to be good. I replaced with another sleeve and synchro that didn't really look any different, but obviously did the job. I have never run into this problem on a 716 or 741 box, and would like to ask if anyone can tell me a real good way to check old, used 519 or 644 sleeves and synchros so that I don't run into that again.

Ever fix a 644, 716 or 741 gearbox, then find you can't shift into third gear? No, you probably did it right. However, there is one stud on the left side of the differential cover area that goes into the hole that the 3rd-4th shift rod moves in. If the eight studs were on the face of a clock, it would be at about the eight-o-clock position. Normally, the stud does not protrude into the hole. If, however, the nut is hard to turn on the stud and ends up turning the stud a few times so that it enters the shift rod hole, then it will prevent the engagement of third gear. The solution of course is to turn the stud back out a bit.

Vol. 17, No. 3 Vic Skirmants

And a 356A That Pops Out of Gear

Just recently had in the shop a 1957 Speedster for the usual post-restoration adjustments. You know, minor stuff like front wheel cylinders in backwards, rear drums full of oil due to improper O-rings; etc. The car also liked to jump out of gear, so when the shift finger in the transmission broke on the second test drive, it seemed like a good idea to open up the transmission as long as it was out and the nose-piece was off. At first glance, nothing seemed amiss. The shift fork for the first and second gear was properly centered, and the synchro hub teeth didn't appear too badly battered.

Nothing to do but tear it all the way down. After extensive staring and pondering, I decided that the contact surfaces where the synchro hub is driven by the synchro spider had to be the culprits. No really horrible wear, but comparing both pieces to several other used but good condition ones, showed that there was apparently just enough wear on both pieces to cause at least one of the three contact areas slip out of engagement. When under full load, this was sufficient to cause one contact point to try and slip past, thereby popping the synchro sleeve out of engagement with the gear.

Installation of two good used parts cured the problem completely. Incidentally, the factory manual specifies installation of the first-second gear spider in a way with which I disagree. I believe both spiders should be installed in the same direction; the mark on one of the three arms should face away from the pinion gear. The very slightly longer contact length of the arms should be installed toward first and third gears. This gives a little more area when the thrust loads try and pull the gears toward the pinion. The transmission I had just described had the shift spider in per the manual.

Gears

Vol. 10, No. 6 Vic Skirmants

Racing Gear Sets
Airport gears. Back in the 1950s many road races were conducted on old airfields. Due to the nature of these tracks, i.e., short straights and tight corners, cars with good acceleration, not necessarily good top speed, were the most competitive. The best way to improve your acceleration is to put shorter gears in the transmission, or put in a shorter ring and pinion, or both. Porsche produced additional sets of optional gears for our cars in the late 1950s. Complete gearboxes were available set up with shorter gears, including a gearbox with "airport gears". This simply meant very short gear ratios. We E-Production racers have gone one step further. Since all our races use a rolling start, we've dispensed with first gear, moved second down, installed two different third gears, and voila! A "five speed" gearbox with no first gear, just four useable ratios. How about 2D, 3E, 3B, 4A; that translates to four gears covering a shorter span than even the speedster ratios of 2B, 3A, 4B. That equates to acceleration! And it's expensive.

Differential

Vol. 11, No. 1 Vic Skirmants

ZF Limited Slip
Care and repair of ZF limited-slip differentials. Not much to say here. The ZF is a high-friction limited-slip and usually wears out in 10,000 miles of street use due to the rubbing of the internal parts when going around slow corners. In racing use they almost last forever. I know of nothing that can be done under the "care" heading, and nowadays it's even getting difficult to "repair" them. This is due to scarcity of parts, not difficulty of working on the ZF.

Vol. 15, No. 2 Cole Scrogham

Competition Ring Gear and Other Toys
In the differential department, two parts of note are the 6:31 ring gear and pinion and the limited slip differential, both common in airport or racing gear sets. The part # for the 6:31 is 550. 302.921.00 (note 550 part number) and the # for the limited slip is 716.

332.055.00 for all gearbox types after 519. Underneath the gearbox, a compensating spring could be added with the part 69.333.901.00 until the introduction of the 356C, when the number changed to 695.330.002.04 (higher spring rate for a heavier car). Some believe that the spring changed from the "A" to the "B," but the spring remained the same but a different attachment was used. A heavy duty swaybar (16 mm) could round out the "performance" package, carrying the part number 644.41.603.1.

Vol. 16, No. 3 Vic Skirmants

Wear and Fulcrum Plates

A very serious problem in any racing 356 is the wearing of the fulcrum plates. The large amount of negative camber, combined with the torque and heat cause a literal friction welding of the side-gear, fulcrum plates, and axle shafts. When similar metals are forced together hard enough, they will weld to each other. The solution is to

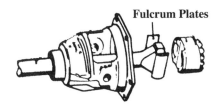

Fulcrum Plates

change one of the materials involved. Porsche produced a bronze fulcrum plate, with cross-hatch grooves for better oiling. My understanding is that this piece was developed for the Carrera 2, and maybe even the early Spyders. Anyway, when I bought my current E-Production roadster in late 1975, it came with the bronze fulcrum plates. I raced that combination for many years, with no problems. The old fulcrums finally started to fall apart, so we tried making replacement pieces from the best industrial bronzes we could find. Nothing was satisfactory. Finally, we returned to the steel fulcrums, cross-hatched them, and had a little better success. The fulcrums and axles would still fail, especially with the ZF limited slip. The ZF housing is very closed and doesn't permit much oil flow to get into the fulcrums.

Lately we've been experiencing a rash of failures, including my E-Production roadster at the June Sprints. Well, it seems vintage racer David Kopf has recently been advertising bronze fulcrums, so I called him. David had the factory material spectrographically analyzed, and determined that the material was not available in this country! So, he hired a foundry to cast up a mill-run of this specific bronze! I recently installed two sets of these fulcrums and will report later on how they're holding up.

Chapter 12

Hardware

Refinishing

Vol. 7, No. 5 David Seeland

Refinishing Using Metal Conditioner
Now for a couple of restoration tips. The fittings and bolts on my GT backing plates were rusty so I soaked them overnight in DuPont 5717 metal conditioner which turns them black, but if they are brushed lightly with a fine wire brush they look like new. However, they are ready to rust at the slightest hint of moisture. Some people get all the nuts and bolts cadmium plated which stops the rust and looks nice but is not original. I tried another attack on the rust problem. After assembly I took clear enamel and a small brush and went over all the steel bolts and fittings and the polished brass banjo fittings. This should stop the corrosion and preserve the original finishes.

Bolt Failure

Vol. 9, No. 4 Richard Miller

Bolt Testing at Home
Just for fun sometime take some 8G (or K) and 10K bolts, put them in some hole and overtighten them and notice how they fail. The modest strength bolt (8 or less) will generally stretch quite a bit before failing or stripping the threads. The 8 or 8.8 on the head tells you that the strength is about 120,000 pounds per square inch, and that the yield or plastic deformation point is about 80% of the ultimate strength, or breaking point. The 10K bolts, while they are stronger (about 150,000 pounds per square inch) have a plastic deformation strength closer to the breaking point and will snap more readily when overtorqued. The point of all this is that in any critical application you should use the right bolt and a torque wrench. That old, bent, rusty bolt out of your junk box may be the wrong strength rating. It may be fatigued, and it may be a likely candidate for stress corrosion cracking. The rust pits don't help at all. Ideally to select a bolt for any critical use, you should take a number of them, tighten them until they snap or stretch, note the failure torque and then select a torque level (for the new bolt) of about 60 to 70% of the maximum. This works provided additional loads in use don't push them over the edge.

Richard makes a lot of sense with his above comments. However, the average reader shouldn't get too concerned that his 356 is undrivable if he notices that the bolts are rusty. I have never seen a failure of an original bolt, whether in street use or racing.

General

Vol. 16, No. 6 Cole Scrogham

Bolt Brands and Other Trivia

The bulk of this column is from a letter received from Cleve Lickado in Richmond, VA. If there is anything you would like to add or expand on, write in a letter of your own. The first area to cover concerns hex head bolts. There are 6, 8, 10, and 12 mm bolts of various lengths found throughout the car. There are bolts from manufacturers such as KARRO, KAMAX, VERBUS, NSF and others. Which bolt manufacturer is correct, can you get them, and is it important to have them?

First off, it is important to remember that Porsche did not assemble all of the components of the 356 themselves until after the Reutter purchase, and even then used Reutter's supply network. The actual Porsche line installed the suspension, engine, brakes and other technical items. The car came to the Porsche line as a completed unit side-loaded on a hauler, and then went through several different stations to receive sub assemblies from different areas of the plant. So it is easy to assume that the same bolt manufacturer was not used for the whole car. For instance, engine bolts generally are from KARRO while you may find VERBUS bolts holding the front suspension together. Some bolts used by Reutter are again from another source. The one way to do the best that you can is to disassemble and catalog these bolts, making note of where they came from. Even if some have been replaced, you can develop a pretty good idea of which manufacturer supplied bolts for which area. These areas may well vary from year to year, but should follow a fairly close pattern. I do not know of any modern source for these fasteners. Our shop buys from Würth, but these bolts will not have the old "G8" grade marking

or original name. The original bolts in my estimation do make a difference, we make every attempt to save and replate the original where possible. If the original bolt is missing and/or not obvious, usually it will be replaced with a modern grade 8 metric bolt.

There are a number of 8 x 1.25 nuts on the car that are either 12 mm or 14mm across the flats. Can you buy these? The 12 mm nut is still available (and the 13 mm of course), but the 14 mm is not as far as I know. Würth offers the 12 mm wrench 8 x 1.25 nut. You have to save the 14 mm because the difference here is more than just replacing it with a modern fastener - they are different sizes and this is not correct. You see the 14 mm nut most often in the transmission area, on through-bolts and side covers. Up to 1960, I believe these bolts are black, then change on the through-bolts to bright cad. Again, your car will tell you this, then you have to back it up. The original plating used on fasteners is a point of contention, as is the plating on fuel lines, valve covers, etc.

Most suspension and gearbox fasteners, as a loose rule, are black, while the engine fasteners are usually bright cad. When I refer to bright cad, I am not referring to nickel plating, chrome plating or any true "bright" plating. Bright cad is only used to distinguish from black or chromate cad or gold chromate which is a rainbow effect gold coating used on later cars. I think a mistake is made when fasteners are nickel or chrome plated for a "show" look. Our goal is to re-create history, not change or "improve" it. Almost any good metal shop can perform all three of these procedures at a reasonable cost. All of the pieces for a car should not cost more than $300 or so.

Vol. 17, No. 1 Cole Scrogham

NLA 14 mm Nuts

In other news, in response to last issue's point that certain fasteners do

235

not exist, I have once again been proven wrong. Richard Troy has gone to the expense of having a batch of 8 x 1.25 mm nuts with a 14 mm wrench size made.

Now, when I refer to "batch" I am speaking of a paltry 5,000 pieces. He would like to have some help in ridding himself of these nuts to get them out of his dreams. I understand they are available in lots of 100 for about $15. If you would like them, they should be a good detail part, finished in "clear" or "bright" zinc, which incidentally is two ways of saying the same thing. Give him a call at 510-531-1320 or send a check to 1169 Wellington, Oakland, CA 94602.

Vol. 17, No. 5 Brad Ripley

Authenticity of Replacement Hardware

Many of the parts available today, 25 years after production of the 356, are *not exactly* original appearance, fit, finish or function. Fortunately, in most cases, a spare part being a little different really doesn't take away from driving enjoyment. But then this article is titled "trivia", so here's some *not exactly* comments on nuts and bolts hardware.

In the later 1960s, international hardware standards (DIN standards) changed. In some cases, only head dimensions changed and in other cases a DIN standard was dropped and replaced with another standard with an entirely different head design and/ or dimensions. Some examples follow. Striker Plate Screws – For the early 356-356A 5-hole strikers, the correct slotted flat head screw was DIN 87, 8 x 10 which had a 16 mm diameter head. That standard was replaced with the current DIN 963 which has a 14.5 mm head. For the B/C strikers, the phillips flat head screw was DIN 7987 with a 16 mm head; the new standard is 965 which has a 14.5 mm head. Obviously, the later DIN spec. screws

with smaller head diameters don't fit flush in the striker.

Seat Rail Screws – For 356 through 356B (T-5) seat rails the proper slotted flat head screw spec. was DIN 65 which had a 10 mm head. Now, the only spec. available is DIN 963 which has an 11 mm head which sticks up too far above the rail, which is another *not exactly*.

Hex Cap Screws – Two things changed with what we call normal DIN 933 bolts. First, tensile strength markings changed from "8G" to "8.8" for "normal" strength bolts and head sizes were changed: 5 mm threaded bolts went from a 9 mm head to an 8 mm head; 8 mm threaded bolts went from a 14 mm head to a 13 mm head. You should find the 14 mm-headed bolts on 356s right up through the 356C. Certainly, if you see a bolt with the modern "8.8" strength designation on next year's Manhattan winner, that's another *not exactly*.

Early Fuel Pump and Carrera Fan Shroud Screws – These screws are still designated DIN 85 but have a dramatically different head style. Figure 1 compares these two head styles. Incidentally, in the U.S. the head style on the left is called a "binding" head and the other (and now currently supplied metric version) is called a "pan" head.

There are a few other examples where the currently available metric hardware doesn't match what was used when the 356s were built. Tom Scott and Dick Koenig are working on a collateral project to further document hardware, especially with regard to plating and manufacturer's brand name; their report will be in future issues. Meanwhile, just because the

Fig. 1

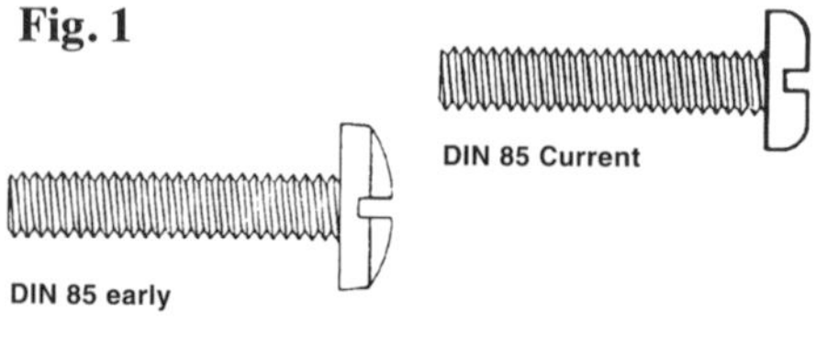

DIN 85 Current

DIN 85 early

236

parts sales guy says it's original, it may be *not exactly*.

Vol. 17, No 6 Dave Grant

Determining Original Finishes

All these parts were traceable to Porsche production from 1959 to 1962. None were replated, except as noted; none were repro parts. All sample areas were thoroughly solvent washed before being acid treated over the area noted to dissolve the plating in question. All water and acids were AAS quality; while the transmission plug had a very low level of cadmium, this did not come from lab materials, or from traces of hydrocarbon sludge. These sludges often incorporate metal ions, but they can be removed by aggressive organic solvents, and they are not dissolved by the acids used to remove Zn and Cd.

A microscopic examination of the surface to be sampled before acid is applied will determine that it is free of all but metal coatings. The lab work was done 1990-12-06. As has been noted since by others, the appearance of plated parts can be affected by post plating treatment. It may make less difference what metal is used than its *appearance characteristics*.

If you can see who is behind you in the glare of the black paint on an over-restored engine, does it matter if all the shiny bits are cadmium plated? I would hope that all those parts which were painted, those which were black-treated, and those which had no protection will all be documented by the *Registry*, for correct restorations.

Chapter 13

Interior

Seats

Vol. 7, No. 1 Richard Miller

Installing Recliner Springs
I've also made another tool to make installation of springs in seat recliners a lot easier. After a lot of bloodshed trying to do the job with screwdrivers, pliers, and three hands and a foot, I put two 5 mm diameter pins in the end of a piece of steel bar stock – load the spring into the pins – insert the spring tang into the slotted bolt and crank the spring around until it can be pushed into the retaining slot in the recliner.

The only thing to look out for is that you don't put the spring in back-

wards. On some recliners the slotted bolts are not interchangeable left to right, and must be properly aligned before installing the springs.

Vol. 8, No. 6 Bruce Baker

Quick Fix for Recliner Weld-Nut Failure
Here is what to do for those annoying little nuts that always drop off their work hardened tacks on seat backs (when they fall off themselves or when removed to change sides for wear, rechrome or reupholster). If you aren't tearing the seats apart so you can "do it right", here is a "fast fix":
1. Check the measure of metal (20

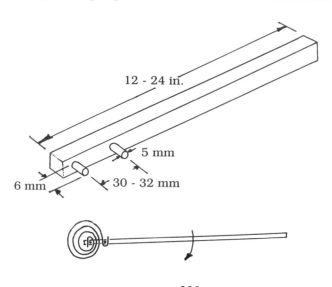

238

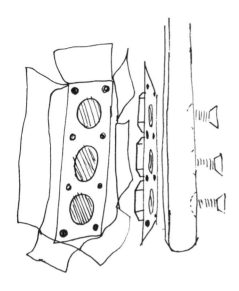

ga.) scrap needed to cover the holes on side of seat (one side-for both).

2. Trim to allow excess for fastening of $3/16$ in. pop rivets.

3. Drill appropriate number of 7 mm holes for the missing nuts, using chrome hinge piece for appropriate spacing.

4. Weld (braze, MIG, whatever) 6 mm nut(s) to sheet metal over 7 mm holes.

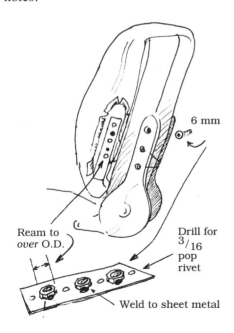

6 mm

Ream to over O.D.

Drill for $3/16$ pop rivet

Weld to sheet metal

5. Ream hole in side of seat back frame (after peeling back glued on vinyl (or leather) over size (hand ream or rat tail file) or (step drill) to allow nuts to insert.

6. Line up drill for rivets, fasten, reglue cover material, and – Voilà! No more see-saw seatback.

Vol. 16, No. 4 Brad Ripley

Headrests

All seat headrests weren't made in Germany! You'll see them at swap meets, the round ones with the two chrome attaching straps. Look carefully at how the vinyl or leather cover is attached; some are sewn on the bottom, others have a nice zipper. Would you believe that the ones with the zipper were made in the U.S.?

Before he passed away last year, I had the opportunity to talk with Bill Colgan of Colgan bra fame. He told me that in the early 1960s, he copied the factory headrests and sold them through Performance Products and Porsche Stuff. Later, some were also sold to the Porsche parts organization until about 1969.

Along with the headrests, Bill Colgan also manufactured the hardware pieces for the back of the seat. How can you tell Colgan's from the factory original? The original screw usually has a standard 6 x 10 thread 12 mm in length, the head is 5 mm thick and the knurl on the edge is fine; Colgan's has UNF $1/4$-28 thread $3/16$" in length, the head is .118" thick and the knurl is coarse. I recently found some of the Colgan screws with 6 mm thread, so the fine knurl is the obvious difference to look for. The plate screwed to the seat back is also slightly different in that the original has large, countersunk screw holes and is 2.5 mm thick. So, at the next swap meet, now you can tell the good from the not-so-good.

Speedster Seats

Vol. 9, No. 3 Dick Pike

Repairing Speedster Seats

Not above stooping to a little cheap drama and suspense, I've saved the best for last: the hinges on Speedster seats. Those of you cursed with badly deteriorated Speedster buckets really have your hands full. I'm not talking about upholstery, either. If there is rusted metal beneath, there's no way you are going to get out of this one without spending a whole lot of time or else a whole lot of money. As we all appreciate, Speedster seats are sexy-looking, lightweight, and supremely comfortable. (*if*, by chance your body happens to like them). They are also flimsy, in some ways poorly engineered, and (*if* your body happens to not like them) God's ultimate gift to chiropractors, osteopaths, neurologists, and other specialists in ailments of the lower back.

I will pass over significant non-hinge problems. These include those fiendish stress-risers so cleverly formed by the little triangular holes left in the seat frame after the upholstery hooks were punched out, the almost inevitable cracks along the sides of the frame where seat back meets seat bottom, and the cracked area around the rake-adjusting bolts. Should the seats have been stamped out of 18 ga. steel? The 20 ga. has not held up very well.

Nowhere is this flimsiness more evident than around the area where the hinges bolt to the seat bottoms. Much of the problem could have been alleviated if the seat designer had boxed in the front ends of the mounting channels welded to the bottom of the seat proper. The rear ends of these channels (where the rake-adjustment bolts are located) are boxed (although even this precaution does not prevent the weld-nuts for the rake-bolts from breaking loose and/or cracking the

surrounding channel).

Often the weld-nuts securing the hinge-mounting screws, and indeed much of the surrounding sheet metal, will be missing. Amateurs are known to have compounded the problem. One cute trick is welding the hinges to the seat channels (usually not straight enough to work properly). These butchers should be taken out and shot (Ah, but that's a good German response). You can undo their stupidity by carefully grinding the hinges free of (and at the expense of) the channels. But saving hinges is not the problem; fixing the channels poses the real challenge. If you like to weld and want to rescue your original seats, the rest of this is for you.

If new to this particular repair, please do one seat at a time. Furthermore, complete all other welding repairs (there may be plenty) on the seat before dealing with the sheet metal around the hinges. This means that you will not have to worry about possible subsequent distortion of your hard-won alignment of the hinges. This is important. If the hinges on each seat are not parallel, the wooden mounting frames will loosen and/or crack and split. I further recommend repairing one side of a seat at a time so that you can relocate the hinge-mounting holes in exactly the right place in one channel from their position in the opposite channel.

Step one is to cut away non-functioning weld-nuts and torn sheet metal from the front end of the seat-mount channel, and straighten this area with hammer and dolly. The bottoms of both channels should be parallel (vertically only). If you are really lucky, you may get away with simply welding up some cracks and/or installing new weld-nuts. Caution: if this is all you need, be sure to get the weld-nuts in now, before boxing in the channel. However, it can be difficult to remove a ruined weld-nut without taking a goodly part of the surrounding sheet metal (already weakened and rusted, right?) with it. Thus you may have to remove two inches or so of the channel bottom (where the hinge lies against it); in this case, new weld-nuts can wait until later.

Step two is boxing in the front of the channel. Obtain the requisite quadrilateral shape for the end piece by tracing the cross-section of the channel front on a piece of cardboard. Cut a good cardboard pattern before attempting the steel piece, which will need to be bent (it is not a planar surface). Try twisting it to fit in the bench vise with wide-nosed Vise-Grip pliers. Use 18 ga. steel, and refrain from making the piece so large that it lies too close to the seat (in which case you will have trouble refitting the upholstery later on). Take plenty of time to get the end-piece to fit evenly around the front of the channel. If some of the channel has been removed, use a straight-edge to ensure that the end-piece will correctly butt with the soon-to-be-patched channel bottom. Weld the new piece to the front end of the channel (pretty easy; edge-welds). Feel how much more rigid the area is now!

Step three is to fabricate a patch (again, do a cardboard pattern first) to cover any hole left in the channel bottom from removing the two weld-nuts and the surrounding torn metal. Try 18 ga. steel for this. I found it convenient to overlap on the inner side of the channel. Carefully fit this patch-piece, getting it to lie flat and parallel to both the bottom of the channel and to the bottom of the opposite channel. Lots of test-fitting and reworking with hammer and anvil. Carefully locate positions of the two holes for the hinge. Do not weld the patch on yet! Now for the tricky bit.

Step four involves attaching new weld-nuts to the patch you have just fabricated. What I did was to drill two holes in the patch, larger than the diameter of the machine screws to go into the weld-nuts. I chose coarse-thread SAE weld-nuts, a diameter larger than the stock fine-thread metric fitting they replaced, to insure strength and future ease of removal.

Now test-fit together your new machine screws (watch the length; if too long, they will contact the end-piece you just put in), the weld-nuts, the hinge, and the patch you just fabricated. With some persistence, and perhaps enlarging of the holes in the patch, you can get everything to line up the way it should be when the job

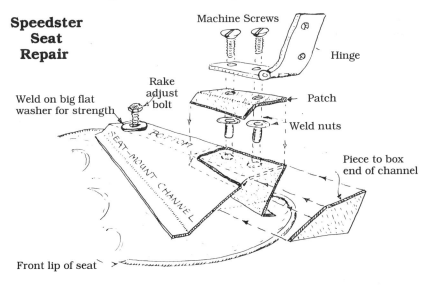

Speedster Seat Repair

Machine Screws

Hinge

Rake adjust bolt

Weld on big flat washer for strength

Patch

Weld nuts

SEAT-MOUNT CHANNEL

BOTTOM

Piece to box end of channel

Front lip of seat

241

is done. Move the hinge around in the enlarged holes until it parallels the one on the opposite channel (or where that hinge should lie). Watch for interference of weld-nuts with cut-back edges of the channel bottom. Test-fit the wooden seat-frame, or a facsimile, to ensure that the position of the hinges will allow the rake-adjustment bolts to engage both routed depressions in the wood. When satisfied that all is good and true, tighten the machine screws; recheck the hinge position. Remove the assembly from the channel, turn it over, and weld the weld-nuts to the patch. Dunk the assembly in water to ensure easy removal of the machine screws.

When cool, remove the screws and hinge and: Step Five, weld the patch to the channel. First relocate the patch and check the fit. Tack it and then go all the way around to get maximum strength. Boy, is that good work!

Repeat the whole agonizing exercise on the opposite channel, and then do it twice more on the other seat. You'll now have two of the best-hinged Speedster seats in All Creation, and they will be considerably more sturdy than the stock setup. You will also have killed better than two very full weekends, but then what is a little time between friends, especially if one of them is a Speedster, eh?

Dashboard

Vol. 5, No. 3 Bill Brown

Aluminum Trim Strips
As a Speedster owner, I have talked to many others who have need for the aluminum trim strips on the dash and door tops. I obtained some 1/4 in. o.d. aluminum tubing from McMaster-Carr in Chicago to make my own. The 12 ft. section cost $2-3. First, I cut the proper lengths, then, using a bench grinder fitted with a thin cutting wheel, cut the tubing lengthwise.

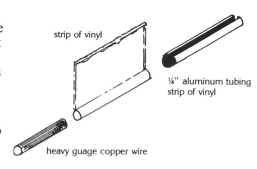

strip of vinyl

¼" aluminum tubing
strip of vinyl

heavy guage copper wire

I used a piece of vinyl left over from my dash top for the mounting piece, folded it around a piece of wire and slid it through the split aluminum tubing. Now the aluminum tubing is ready to be bent for the proper fit on the dash. 1/8 in. o.d. aluminum tubing is also available for the outside of the door top.

Vol. 12, No. 4 Jeff Gambel

Aluminum Trim Strips,II
The disappearance of dashboard beading and door reveal molding for Speedster, Conv. D's, and Roadsters, has owners and upholstery trim shops simply omitting this important detail.

The old solution was early Ford fender welting. This worked fine when it was made of aluminum, but now that source is NLA. Now available is welting made of stainless steel. The stainless is great on the outside reveal molding on a Speedster for durability but it is too rigid to make the contour and corner bends required around the dash ends. A trip to the local hobby shop revealed a good answer to the problem. Their 1/4 in. diameter aluminum tubing stock is very close to the original beading plus it can be polished to a high luster.

First step is to fill the tube with sand to make the curve and corner bends around the dash ends. The sand will prevent the tube from crimping. Once you have the exact shape, pour the sand out and polish. Now that you have an exact fit to the dash, you must

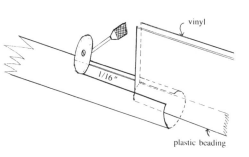

vinyl

1/16"

plastic beading

make a cut for the backing in order to hold the bead in place. Using eye protection, take your Dremel tool with cutting disc and carefully cut longwise down the top of the rear of the tube . A practice test here might be helpful! To complete the job, visit your upholstery supply to purchase a strip of plastic beading, then wrap the beading with vinyl to slide inside your finished dashboard beading!

Vol. 16, No. 5 Cole Scrogham

Aluminum Trim Strips,III

One job that can be most difficult in the last stages of restoration is making a Speedster's dash and door caps look right. Not only Speedsters actually, for Convertible D and Roadster owners have that dash trim to deal with as well. After many hours of screwing up, a recipe for this job becomes necessary. Yes, I do know the hard way that you can bend up your expensive trim kit into a pretzel or scratch the dash or door. Here is the best way that I can come up with.

First, you must purchase the trim kit, which comes in six pieces. These kits are readily available from many advertisers and are of relatively equal quality. They are not an exact duplicate, however, much to our surprise. The trim bead is larger on a reproduction and secured with cardboard instead of vinyl as originally. Due to the lack of original parts, these differences have been accepted, but make note that they are not identical. There should be four identical lengths, with

one slightly longer and one only 8 in. or so in your kit. They come with a plastic covering to avoid damage to the bright work, so do not forget to tear it off when the time comes.

The first step is to secure the door cap (Speedster only), find or make your holes and screw to the door. Leave the door cap loose. Next, bend the trim carefully (it will kink) every 4 - 6 inches or so until it perfectly fits the shape of the door cap. Measure the length and mark with a black magic marker so that you can take an equal length off of each end. Put the cardboard backing into a vise and use a hacksaw to cut each end. Do not crimp or crush the ends, and make sure that the hacksaw does not ride down the trim and scuff it up.

Next, you must remove the cardboard that is visible in each end by cutting it out about a half inch back from the edge. If you must open the trim to get the cardboard out, remember to lightly squeeze the end back into a round shape and lightly file the coarse edges from the hacksaw cut smooth. Then take about half of the cardboard's width off the entire length of the trim strip so that it will fit under the door cap (or dash piece) without running into anything. Before sliding the trim under the door cap, run the black marker along the cardboard at the trim strip edge to cover any tan cardboard that may be seen if you did not get the bend exactly right. Pull off the protective covering from the chrome and slide it under the outside door cap. It may be advisable to put masking tape on the door ends of the trim to avoid scratching the paint with a rough edge.

Next, slide the inside trim piece under the door cap. I do not recommend using glue to hold them in place because this is a remedy for disaster working close to paint and it usually takes a few tries to get the trim where you want it. Tighten the door cap screws, using finger pressure to hold the trim against the door cap as it tightens up. The trim will move along the door and door panel into position and should fit very well.

The procedure for a Speedster, Roadster of Convertible D dash is the same with one small exception. There is a rather acute bend at the corner for each trim strip. Use a 1 1/2 in. piece of brass stock or even a pipe to help you hand bend these corners without kinking the trim. Most people just cut the ends off there and do not worry about it, but it is not that bad. The dash trim must fit under the door seal on both outer edges, and under the instrument hood on the inside. For this reason, cut each length off with side cutters or something that will make a crimped or crushed edge and do not worry about the cardboard. This is opposite of the Speedster door cap trim. Again, follow all of the tips above in the same order and your dash will come out looking picture perfect.

Vol. 8, No. 2 Lew Larkin

Hand Throttle

When I was restoring my Convertible D, I had been told that to remove the hand throttle cable fromthe instrument panel, it had to be first removed where it connected to the tunnel support near the brake pedal and at the side of the accelerator. Then unscrew the backing nut holding the cable to the instrument panel and pull the whole unit from the instrument panel.

Now anybody who has ever disconnected the thin piano wire from the bulkhead connection, let alone where it attaches to the accelerator, has probably uttered those magic words – "Oh Pshaw!" as the wire ricochets from its fittings. There is virtually little possibility that a person with average sized hands can do it, even if he can see in that area. Factory elves, yes but not mere mortals!

I did remove the wire from the top connection, then in a fit of wisdom, assessed the likelihood of further disassembly and reassembly as being nil and stopped there. I did loosen the cable from the instrument panel, pulled it loose, then covered it in plastic and left it dangling. The painter was able to do his job with no real problem.

Upon reassembly, I replaced all of the switch knobs except the one on the Cold Start Idle Adjustment cable. (I had replaced the original wipers with one from a 356C and that switch required a standard sized knob instead of the very small diameter one.)

About a week before the 1981 East Coast Holiday, I mentioned to a knowledgeable friend that I wished I could replace the grungy Idle Adjustment Cable knob. "Dummy", he said, (I respond to that and to Hey, You) "It unscrews like the other knobs!"

Indeed it does! In fact, one can unscrew the knob, turn the cable and it'll slide out. Loosen the retainer nut holding the fixture on the instrument panel, and the fixture is free from the panel. No need to even think about disassembling the piano wire in the tunnel.

Using a thin pair of Vise-Grips, I clamped the cable and with an appropriate sized wrench, unscrewed the knob. (Leave the Vise-Grips attached or the cable will retract into the holding fixture and you'll spend another half hour trying to fish it back out.)

Now all I have to do is to screw on the new knob and everything will be great. Wrong! The threaded portion of the standard knobs is far too large. I had another problem. There was no time to see whether a replacement knob could be obtained. Since I sure didn't want to put the old one back on, here's what I did.

The idle adjustment cable knob differs from those on the light and windshield switches, even though it is the same size. It differs by the use of a threaded metal insert. There is a lot of tension required to pull the cable and

Fig. 1

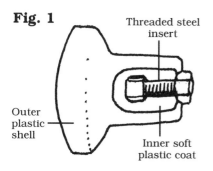

Threaded steel insert

Outer plastic shell

Inner soft plastic coat

screwing a metal cable directly into a plastic knob will not assure any durability.

This special threaded metal insert is hexagonal at each end. Apparently in the manufacture of the knob, the insert is bonded to a soft plastic and in turn, the standard sized knob is then cast around it. Outwardly, there is no discernible difference. See Fig. 1.

I took a hammer and smashed the knob. The outer shell disintegrated, leaving the soft inner shell surrounding the metal insert. That was cut and peeled away. See Fig. 2. Then, I ground down the hex on one end and ground away about half of the hex on the other end. This latter part is necessary to assure that the insert can be fitted deep into the knob with only about an eighth inch of the hex head showing; just enough so that a wrench can be used to tighten the knob securely to the cable.

See Fig. 3. The failure to do this will result in the knob appearing not to fit against the fixture on the instrument panel and will look funny. Then I selected a drill bit just slightly smaller than the insert, and carefully drilled out the new knob. Again, remember that the cable requires a fair amount of effort to be pulled out, so it is necessary to have the insert fit snugly but not too tight as to cause the new knob to split. The new knobs are pretty tough and won't split easily but remember the effect of the sun and the natural aging process of plastic. You may have to grind the metal insert to obtain a better fit to one of your existing drill bits.

I epoxied the insert, placed it in the new knob, and tapped it home. The finished product looked like this. See Fig. 4. I let it dry overnight, then screwed it on the cable and tighten it with a wrench.

Now, all of the instrument knobs are new and so far the cable has functioned well. I don't know whether replacement knobs are available or not, but if they are, they probably cost significantly more than the $1.50 or so for a replacement standard size knob.

This is not as complicated as it sounds. The total working time involved, excluding drying, was about 30 minutes.

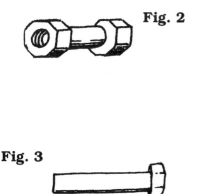

Fig. 2

Fig. 4

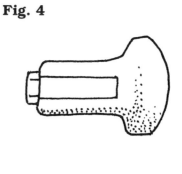

Fig. 3

Vol. 8, No. 3 Ron Roland

Knob Restoration

I have renewed the oldest, crazed, even slightly cracked white knobs with lacquer thinner. The plastic will dissolve in lacquer thinner, so: Mount the knob on the end of a bolt to avoid touching the soft plastic. Use a clean rag liberally dipped in lacquer thinner to smooth over all the crazed surfaces, even blending in small cracks, and removing all discoloration and "age". When the knob is smooth again and all "rag marks" are removed, dip the knob in lacquer thinner and twirl it.

Finally let it drip dry by clamping the bolt in a vise knob up. After a day or so, the knob can be polished if you wish. You now have an original knob that looks like new.

Vol. 10, No. 1 Richard Miller

Speedster/Roadster Dash Script

Minor point: Porsche script on right hand side of Speedster, etc. dash is plated gold and silver – not chrome.

Steering Column

Vol. 9, No. 5 Richard Miller

Rubber Bands

I've always been puzzled by air coming in through the slot near the top end of the steering column until I found two early cars in the junkyard (1954 and 1955 pre-A coupes) which had "rubber band" sleeves covering these holes. Tom Birch says the hole was for a steering column lock which engages the funny looking section of the steering shaft inside. If not used, the hole was covered by what looks like a piece of bicycle tire tube. In addition, the "wrap around and thread through the slot" type of sheet metal clamp holding the turn signal wires goes around the rubber band.

Re-upholstery

Vol. 3, No. 4 Jon Early

Basics, Material, Tools, Headliners

You have to be convinced you've got enough built-in talent to upholster your own car, because without it and a lot of self-confidence, it just ain't gonna happen. Not to mention patience ... that's a requisite too. It'll take you eleven times longer to do it than you ever expected.

Tools Of The Trade are what you need after you've decided you do have what-it-takes to even consider this endeavor, so here's whacha call your *Basic List:*
* A heavy-duty Industrial Sewing Machine that's got a walking foot and can handle nylon thread. (No, you can't hit up your sweetie-pie for her home-makers zig-zag deluxe; it's too lightweight) You can probably find one for as little as $300, or as much as $1,000 for a new one, but you get what you pay for. Sounds like a lot of bucks, I know, but you can always unload it later, probably for a profit. You can also rent one from one of the larger sewing machine shops, but however you get one, consider these brands; Pfaff, Singer, Juki & Consew. (The last two are excellent Japanese copies of Singer, with interchangeable parts throughout.) You'll also need a set of interchangeable feet for regular sewing, welting, and smooth bottom for leather top stitching.
* You'll need a decent Working Table, at least 4' x 8' and preferably the same height as the sewing machine table
* Sharp scissors (on the large side)
* A set of screwdrivers & wrench
* Disposable paint brushes & pot for glue

The following can be obtained from one or more upholstery supply wholesalers in any large city. (Check around

246

and see who supplies the auto uphol-
stery businesses.:)
* A Tack Puller
* Three rules – a 60 in., a 36 in. and a
carpenters square
* A packet of chalk
* Two staple guns – An Arrow T-50
w/$1/4$ in. & $3/8$ in. staples and an
Arrow P-22 w/$5/16$ in. staples
* A magnetic Tack Hammer and a box
each of #8 tacks, #4 tacks and #4 gimp
tacks
* A set of curved, diamond point nee-
dles
* A small box of hog rings & hog ring
pliers

You'll need initially, from the
upholstery supplier, to purchase:
* Small spools of #12 thread in the
colors you'll be needing. (Pre-wound
bobbins are available for most industrial machines if you don't want to
wind your own.)
* A spool of heavy-duty hand stitching thread called Consew
* A roll of carpet binding in the color
you need. (Original 356 cloth carpet
binding can sometimes be obtained
from old established carpet stores)
* A roll of welting cord
* A gallon of contact cement
* A quart of contact cement thinner
* 5 yards of $1/4$ in. foam
* 10 yards of $1/2$ in. foam scrim
(backed with cheese cloth)
* A bottle of aspirin
* A box of razor blades
* Three sheets of waterproof cardboard
The first step in upholstering an
entire Porsche, after tools and materials have been accumulated, is the
headliner. Needless to say, you'll want
the original for a pattern. This goes for
all the other upholstery components as
well. They not only provide you with
a nice pattern (sometimes), but they
also are a good reference for knowing
just how it was done originally. Therefore, don't damage anything on
removal, if you can help it.

Perforated vinyl can usually be
obtained from the local auto upholstery supplier. Don't get the stuff with
the dots painted(!!) on.

Headliner Installation
Remove all windows and door
seals, sun visors, mirror, etc. Pull the
glued edges of the headliner free from
the body after removing and saving
those nifty little clips along the edge
of the windshield and rear window.
Remove the bows (none in sunroof)
from their slots and extract the headliner in tact. Mark each bow before
sliding free from the headliner #1 - #4
from the front. (*very important!*) With
a razor, pop the stitching and flatten
the headliner out on a table. (Note the
little "Ear" sections sewn on the rear
that fill in the areas between the rear
window and quarter windows.
Remove these only after their original
location has been marked.) Draw a
center line (Front to rear) on the old
headliner backside for reference, and
do the same on the backside of the
new material, which if it's the perforated vinyl, should be 51 in. wide.
Allow yourself a few inches to play
with on either end and proceed to
copy *exactly* the old headliner. Bow
sleeves #1 and #4 both have tapers. #2
and #3 are straight $1/2$ in. (when folded) sleeves. Use the center line for
measuring distances between sleeves
and use a carpenters square to make
sure the sleeves are perpendicular to
the center line. I can't stress enough
how important it is to check, double
check and triple check all the measurements. All distances must be right-
on or you'll spin your wheels trying to
get the bugger to fit.
As for those tricky tapers, it's hard
to describe, so your intuition comes in
here. From the center line of the original, decide how far out the bow sleeve
taper starts, and mark it on the new
one. Here's the trick - I determine the
taper by the number of rows of dots in
the perforated cloth the stitch crosses

247

over a given distance. Got that? Wish I could explain it better, but keep in mind the new material is going to have a different dot pattern, so you must compensate. To check if the taper is correct, after you've marked it on the new material, measure, in the vehicle, the distance between bows where they join the body.

Finally, sew the "ears" on the back end, exactly like the original is, except much bigger so there's room to adjust it. Put the bows in the slots.
To Install: Glue a $1/2$ in. layer of foam to the inside roof of the car for sound and temperature insulation before installing your new creation. Cross your fingers, because chances are good it won't fit. But try it like this, and if it doesn't work, note why and repeat the procedure, with corrections, if you can't repair the first one.

In the vehicle place the bows in their respective slots and with chalk, mark on the vehicle the center of the windshield and rear window. With contact cement stretch and glue the headliner at these two points, aligning the center line (!) with these two marks. From inside the car, slide all slack material on the bows to the sides, making sure any and all wrinkles are from front to rear, not diagonal!

With about two dozen clothes pins or similar clips, clip the headliner, around its edges, to the car in its (approximate) correct location. Start at the front and rear and then the sides by tacking the headliner in place with the cement. When you've satisfied it's where you want it, glue it for good. Slide those nifty little clips on again, and you're done. Oh yeah, don't forget those pieces you must glue to the windshield & door posts, and under the back window.

Sunroof coupes have their own problems, but aren't as complex to make. (No bows). When you install it, again using the center line as a reference, glue the edges of the sunroof opening first, taking care to wrap the material well around the edge before you trim it so it tucks cleanly under the aluminium trim and doesn't show any cuts from the outside when all is assembled and the sunroof is open. The zipper is important, or you'll have a hard time getting to the motor mechanisms later on. Most upholstery shops carry zippers in any size.

Headliners for cabriolets are a real pain in the can. Don't bother trying to make one unless you're the hottest duplicator outside of Japan. No words of advice here. You're on your own. The herringbone material is available, but not always. Try Stoddard.

Vol. 3, No. 5 Jon Early

Carpet and Upholstery Installation
For those of you that didn't read the previous article, you'll have to do so in order for the following to make sense, at least in regards to materials and tools needed. After the headliner is properly installed, carpets are the next logical step in an entire upholstery job. You'll have to decide if you want something functional, like nylon or original wool.

Original carpet can be had in roll form from several suppliers; they also carry kits that are already cut and bound – a real time saver! If you buy yardage of original or acrylic, you'll need about 10 square yards.

Cutting the nylon carpet can be a real blistering experience. Use your large, sharp scissors and cut the pieces oversized to your original patterns. If you don't have originals for patterns, check out another car that does and get the basic pattern idea. Then make a basic set out of brown paper on your car and go from there. Fit the cut carpet and mark exactly where you want to trim it for binding.

Installation of carpet (not unlike a Chinese puzzle) should be in this general order, keeping in mind that different models vary:

1. Front pockets. (L & R)

2. Quarter sections (L & R), from door to rear panel. (cabriolet, Roadster, Speedster,; entire rear section next)

3. Hump between jump seats.

4. Rear lateral piece, (under rear panel from quarter to quarter straddling the hump).

5. Forward lateral piece (in front of jump seats straddling the tunnel).

6. L & R Longitudinals over the heater outlets.

7. Jump seat backs (must be removed). Be sure to replace cardboard stapled to jump seat backs; it keeps the carpet from sagging. After gluing, use the gimp tacks to secure these pieces to the wooden frames of the jump seats.

8. Center tunnel aft of shift linkage.

Use liberal amounts of contact cement in a thin film, but don't gob it. Secure in necessary places with screws as the original was.

Panels:

I'm assuming you have original (or reasonable facsimile thereof) components to work with as patterns. There's no way I can put down on paper an accurate detailed description of how to do it from scratch.

Door Panels are cut from the waterproof cardboard and the steel lip at the top (not in Speedsters) is removed from the old panel and pop riveted to the new. Cover the face with 1/8 in. foam using contact cement. (Note: careful when gluing foam you don't soak it with cement, it'll dimple when pressed.) Stretch and glue fabric over the panel (Don't glue to foam!) by gluing on the back, then staple with 1/4 in. staples from behind. (Speedsters don't have pockets or foam for that matter, but do have the tubular pieces around the bottom and sides. The pockets have 14 pleats 2 1/4 in. apart. Dissect an original carefully and note its construction. I allow 2 3/4 in. per

pleat with 1/2 in. allowed for each hem (1/4 in. per side). On vinyl, draw lines on the back with magic marker 2 3/4 in. apart. On leather, here's a nice trade secret; don't draw lines. Instead, with a razor, cut the leather clean through with broken 1 in. cuts .like the dashed lines on a highway, using your straight edge for reference. This allows the leather to fold "clean" without a chance of puckering.

Draw 2 1/4 in. reference lines on the foam you've backed with burlap or vinyl. Practice a few before you try for a finished product. Use your top stitching foot for the fold over the elastic cord so you don't damage the leather.

Rear panels and quarter panels are self-explanatory if you've read the previous paragraph. A helpful hint on the rear panel (under the rear panel of coupes); the rods that protrude through the firewall and secured in the engine by clamps are snipped flush at the factory. To maintain my sanity, I discovered the only way to fabricate a new panel is to weld 6 in. rods (out of 1/8 in. welding rod) to the discs, make the panel and install as they did in the factory by sliding the clips on the rod and snipping flush with the firewall. If you've removed one of these gems, you'll know just what I'm talking about.

We're now well along with our interior, but since putting it down on paper takes more than I expected, I can see I'll have to go for a third article on seats, jump seats, dash, installing glass and rubber seals.

Vol. 16, No. 2 Cole Scrogham

Carpet Kit Installation

The first step is to actually acquire a carpet kit. Bravo, you say, easily accomplished. But wait, and I do mean that literally. Since these kits are getting more and more expensive ($425 + in most cases), fewer and fewer wholesalers stock the several varieties necessary to satisfy all 356s. Some require 4 - 6 weeks or more to "custom" make a kit (Read – We are not going to have it made unless you promise to buy it beforehand). Other Porsche upholstery shops can cut down on the wait if you catch them with a fresh delivery of square weave and do not request a terra-cotta or olive match. Generally, tan and charcoal are readily available, and you may get lucky on other colors.

The mention of square weave brings up another topic, what type of carpet to use. "Look, Homer, we can save a coupla hunnert dollars if we buy this here domestic loop stuff." This is the casual mistake usually made over the phone with somebody who wants to sell off a lower grade carpet that nobody else wants. The classic rub is right there. If anybody offers you a deal for a Porsche 356, rub your eyes and look a little closer – don't be a Homer. Insist on German square weave, don't cry, pay the price gladly.

As soon as the kit arrives, open the kit and figure out if you have all of the necessary pieces; 19 if by Roadster and 12 if by T-6 Cabriolet, and so on. Refer to Brett Johnson's book in that section that looks like a Rohrshach test or one of those mazes on the back of a Pizza Hut place mat. Find your car and get a general idea of where each piece fits and how many there are. Take each piece out of the garbage bag (smart shops send them out boxed up in Hefty bags in case water gets through the box), and lay them out one at a time on a flat surface, because they will not be flat right out of the box. Do this even if you plan to procrastinate a few months or so, should I say especially if you plan to procrastinate.

Before you actually begin, *surprise*, you will have to remove all of the old carpet and vacuum out the interior. You should also remove upholstered back panel on coupes from the rear area and both sets of seats, if applicable. Find a good set of your son's kneepads from football practice, at least three cans of good spray adhesive (3M Super Trim Adhesive or Roger's Spray Adhesive are excellent. Non-aerosol may also be used, and tends to have greater adhesion), a supply of razor blades, a good pair of scissors preferably not from the wife's sewing basket, a hair dryer using the same caveat, some carpet nails and some carpet padding if you can get these locally.

Now, to begin, you should lay each piece inside the car in its approximate location. Use the picture book if you get confused. This will help orient you as to which pieces must go on top and which below, based on the bound edges which will give a finished look when completed. Use this time, don't be in a hurry, note which pieces don't fit just right and how you can compensate for this *before* you cut a single thread. Take care to see how you can make the binding look uniform around the car. Generally Speedsters and Roadsters have vinyl edges and later cars have cloth binding, but this is not *always* correct.

For the sake of your health, begin with the map pocket pieces just forward of the left and right door openings (refer to illustrations if possible). These pieces have vinyl sewn onto the edges which must be cut and stretched around the door seal channel. The door seal can then be installed over them for a finished look. Don't cut the vinyl too short, it does not grow back. Glue the larger section of the map pocket flat on the inner wall, taking care to glue both surfaces and let dry at least 30 seconds unless patience dictates other wise (time varies with type of glue used). It is helpful in some cases to glue a portion of the carpet, then get that portion to look right and go a little further. A hair dryer is also helpful when stretching the carpet around corners.

Tack the map pocket backing into place after gluing, with carpet nails, then stretch the lower portion of the map pocket into place and tack this as well. Next come the golf club pieces, which resemble a slightly oversized club face on its back. These pieces finish off the front area and are bound on all edges except the rearmost edge. You will have to cut V-shaped indentions in the map pocket pieces where the club will hide them in order to make the map pocket fit better. It is also a good idea to cut away carpeting that will be hidden and covered over to get rid of bulges and to give the carpet a solid mounting place. Where the golf club pieces overlap the front edge of the map pocket, there are two carpet nails about five inches vertical distance apart with trim escutcheons under them for a neat look.

Continue to the door sill, which is made simpler on As and T-5 cars because there is a separate piece for the door sill area only. Later cars have door sill pieces that continue on to the rear panel area and are more difficult to install. The door sill piece is rounded to the front and must be trimmed for the door step rail and the heater duct (if you like heat). Continue to the rear where the trick is to cut the side carpeting so that the vertical wall behind the front seats does not interfere with the gluing process. Generally, there are three carpet nails in this area with escutcheons on each side.

After both rear sides are completed, you should cover the hump for the transmission. Cars with no rear seats (i.e., Roadster), have the indent for the rear seat mounts covered flush with horsehair or fabric. Most also have a buffer at the front of the hump. You may pad underneath the carpeting in this area for a smooth finish, but it is difficult to get the wrinkles out of the hump area without some sort of heat. Now, you can continue on with the rear shelf in open cars (cabriolets usually have a thick fabric mat here for

sound insulation), and with the vertical wall behind the front seats in coupes and cabriolets. In Speedsters/roadsters there is a trim piece under the top shelf that must be nailed and glued or it will fall down, especially when it gets wet (don't kid yourself that it will not get wet). The last piece, the tunnel cover, should be notched out for the seat rail screws to go through but do not, I repeat, do not drill any holes through the carpeting. The bit will snag the thread and before you can stop, you will have a foot of carpet wound around the drill and a naked line on your nice carpet job. If things like that scare you, give the job to a professional because he knows how to cover such mistakes better than you do. I do hope somebody will give this a try. It is not difficult and many 356 owners have a more meticulous eye than most upholsterers. Just remember the key word, patience, and don't cut before you have to.

Door Panels

Vol. 11, No. 6 Peter Geiger

Window Crank Washers
   I don't think that many people remember is that there was a plastic disc-type washer under the window crank which kept the escutcheon from turning and ripping up the door upholstery. I used the plastic type washers obtained from old Volkswagens and they work just fine.
   There is a spring under the uphol-

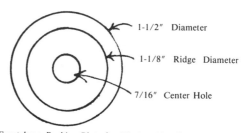

1-1/2" Diameter

1-1/8" Ridge Diameter

7/16" Center Hole

Escutcheon Backing Plate for Window Handle (crank).

251

stery that puts pressure on the escutcheon and with the washer, if the escutcheon turns at all, it turns on this washer. If you can get new ones, the VW number is 111.837.595A. They have a raised ridge near the edge so that it stays centered.

Headliner

Vol. 13, No. 4 Shep Adkins

Stained Vinyl Headliner Fix
I suggest that you spray the headliner with Krylon #1059 eggshell... as close to original finish as you can get... inexpensive, too!

Seat Belts

Vol. 13, No. 4 David Seeland

Seat Belt Installation
Von Frankenberg walked away after falling out of the flying Spyder and landing in a bush at Avus. Amazing, but don't count on miracles (he was later killed in an automobile crash). You don't have accidents so why install or use seat belts? Well, I didn't have accidents either until a few years ago. Then, in short order, I totalled one 356 and nearly totalled another. In spite of a certain reluctance to "fess-up", my experiences may contain some useful lessons on what equipment will make your 356 safer in an accident.

During the accident, I was wearing a three-point seat belt from a 1969 Alfa GTV. The three-point belt that had been in the coupe was attached to the original floor mounts and a large sheet-metal screw "attached" (and I use the word loosely) the shoulder belt to the left rear wheel well area. The belt was apparently too short to reach the stock shoulder belt mount. I removed the screwed in (up?) belt arrangement and bolted the Alfa belt to the stock mounts a couple of years before the accident. I would not have walked away from the accident if I had been using the screw-mounted shoulder belt or only a lap belt.

Installation of seat belts is easy. Please don't drive your 356 without belts because you don't want to drill holes in your new floor pan or because the concours judges will object. I have holes for a five-point racing harness and a roll bar in our 1958 Speedster. For concours I remove the belts and roll bar and use small squares of black electrical tape over the holes. We have won concours trophies with the Speedster and no judge has ever mentioned the holes (or probably even seen them). The shoulder belts in our Speedster bolt through the firewall with the roll bar rear mounts. Just roll up the fire-wall carpet from the forward edge if you don't want holes in the carpet. The main hoop of this bar is bolted down near the outboard edges of the seat recesses which makes it a bit narrow and less protective than the roll bars illustrated here. Your life and health are worth more than possible concours points lost on a few tiny purposeful imperfections. Install the best belt system you can afford and use it.

In a T-6 B or C coupe three-point belts can be used with the stock mounting points. However, see Fig. 1 for some comments about the stock mounting points.

If you are putting belts in a "mountless" car, place the belts so that the lap belt slopes down at about 45° from your hips. Eye bolts must have the eyes welded shut. I use a $1/4$ in. x 4 in. x 12 in. aluminum plate under the floor of the Speedster with 2 in. washers on the top of the floor. Also use lock washers and/or Locktite on the nuts. I have a set of rear mats with bolt-holes that I use with this setup. These are replaced with new mats for concours use. With some racing belts, each belt plugs individually into the

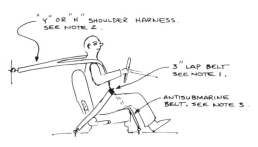

"Y" OR "H" SHOULDER HARNESS.
SEE NOTE 2.

3" LAP BELT.
SEE NOTE 1.

ANTISUBMARINE
BELT. SEE NOTE 3.

main buckle, making them more convenient, and expensive.

Full racing belts (5 or 6 point), carefully installed, are safest (Fig. 1). Racing belt use requires a certain dedication because they are more difficult to put on, so if you think you will not use them all the time, consider installing or sticking with 3-point belts. Keep the shoulder belt mount(s) at shoulder height, although I suffered no ill effects from my vigorous test of the stock mount height. Provide strong mounts and overdo the mounts if in doubt.

The object of the anti-submarine belt is to hold the lap belt in place on your pelvis, resisting the upward force applied at the buckle by the shoulder belts. Do not ever use a racing-type shoulder belt and a lap belt without an anti-submarine belt. Use of racing lap belt and shoulder harnesses alone is not the same as a diagonal shoulder belt and lap belt. The racing shoulder harness is attached to a central lap belt buckle rather than the side buckle of a 3-point set-up and will pull the racing lap belt up onto your abdomen in a crash if not used with an anti-submarine belt. It could give you the worst tummy ache you ever had, or kill you! Got the picture, I hope? Mount the anti-submarine belt far enough forward so it can counteract the upward shoulder harness force. Do not mount it under the seat as is sometimes done, because in a crash, the seat cushion will compress at the front allowing the anti-submarine belt to effectively lengthen and the lap belt to

pull up off your pelvis. An under-seat mount is okay, if you have a race seat with hole for the anti-submarine belt in the cushion or if you make such a hole in your seat.

Instruments

Vol. 7, No. 4 Richard Miller

Beck Pneumatic Fuel Gauge

I wanted to pass on some information which is probably only of interest to owners of 1954 and early 1955 cars about the fuel gauge. Most owners of these cars probably don't know how the gauge works or why it doesn't work. And the factory manual for the 1954 doesn't explain it. The key to the whole thing is item 1 in the illustration, that little chrome push button with a hole in it which never seems to do anything. It is actually an air pump and the fuel gauge is a pressure gauge.

Right now you probably think I've been drinking too much 91 octane, but let me explain. The "sender" in the tank of a 1954 is not the float actuated lever type, which moves a rheostat, but is a small inverted brass cup at the end of a metal tube. There are actually two tubes, one inside the other. At the other end one tube connects to the pump, the other to the gauge. By pressing the button (if the pump works) you squirt air into the tank and the air vents into the inverted cup. To actuate the pump more than once you must take your finger off each time to permit more air to enter the pump. After you do this a few times (if you listen closely without the engine running you can hear the bubbles) the cup is full of air and any additional air bubbles to the top and out the vent. At this point the pressure on the air trapped in the cup is proportional to the height of the gasoline above it and the fuel gauge is calibrated to send this pressure as gallons since the size of the tank is known. The diagram

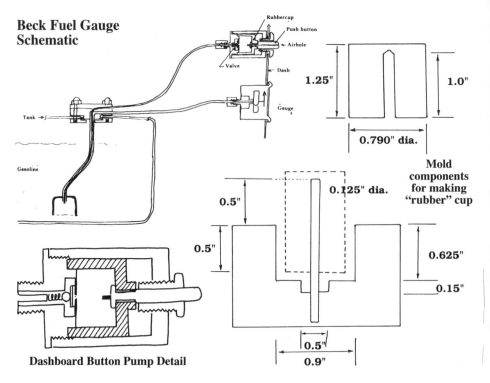

Beck Fuel Gauge Schematic

Rubbercup
Push button
Airhole
Valve
Dash
Gauge
Tank
Gasoline

1.25"   1.0"

0.790" dia.

Mold components for making "rubber" cup

0.125" dia.

0.5"

0.5"

0.625"

0.15"

0.5"

0.9"

Dashboard Button Pump Detail

illustrates the arrangement of this wonderful feat of German engineering, which was so great they only used it for about one year.

In my experience the things that go wrong with the system aside from the air sloshing out on high-G turns is the tubes get clogged up and the pump refuses to work. I have some very fine, very hard tungsten wire which I've used to unclog tubes and will send a piece free to anyone needing any. Usually if a car sits long enough for the gasoline to evaporate the gummy residue plugs up everything. The pump is shown in cross section and consists of a plunger attached to a rubber cup which is closed off by a valve assembly. The plunger has a small hole down its center so that the cup is open to atmosphere or whatever is in your car. When you push the button you close the hole and compress the rubber cup. At the end of its travel, a pin on the end of the plunger pushes a small valve open and lets the air flow

into the tube to the tank.

Aside from loose connections and obvious leaks the biggest problem here is the rubber cup which by now has turned to goo. I've made replacements out of Dow Corning type J silastic which works well. The small drawing is for a mold; if any one is ambitious. The remaining problem area is the valve. This is a spring loaded steel ball pressing on a small rubber sealing disc. Here parts are retained by a brass disc pressed into the valve body which can be unscrewed from the aluminum can holding the rubber. You can disassemble this for repair by gently prying out the brass disc, replacing the rubber piece, cleaning the ball and renewing the spring. If you didn't destroy it – the brass disc can be pressed back in and the valve should now work , otherwise make a new disc or send it to me for complete overhaul.

Since the gauge works on pressures of at about 1 PSI don't blow into it

254

with compressed air – it may develop an aneurism or bend the needle.

Vol. 5, No. 5 Vic Skirmants

Recommended Repair Facilities
In response to Dale Lucas' request for a source to repair his temperature gauge, two readers have sent in sources. Lew Larkin, Hockessin DE, recommends:

VDO
188 Brooke Road
PO Box 2897
Winchester, VA 22601
(703) 665-1700

Frank Nicholson, East Whittier CA recommends:

North-Hollywood Speedometer & Clock Co.
6111 Lankersheim Blvd.
North Hollywood, CA 91606
(818) 761-5136

Vol. 14, No. 4 Paul James

Restoring the Störk Oil Temperature Gauge
Okay, all you guys with 1954 Speedsters that have been calling me trying to get my Störk dipstick thermostat; you still can't have it but I've got a solution to your problem! Instrument Service Company, 1218 South Boyle Ave., Los Angeles, CA 90023, phone number (213) 261-4154 can rebuild your gauge and dipstick. If you have the original Störk gauge without the dipstick and capillary tube, they can graft a new dipstick and tube to your instrument. The cost on my gauge was $226.95 with shipping. The dipstick tube is of a slightly smaller diameter and does not have the grooved marks of the original brass units. The capillary tube has the same braided copper shielding, but is slightly larger in diameter (not an obvious difference).

The only other problem to overcome is making the dipstick handle. I am including dimensioned drawings of my handle which came from a 1954 coupe. The screw appears cad plated. The handle and sleeve sections look like chrome plating on rough unpolished metal. Please note that the sleeve section below the handle is hollowed out on the inside where the slotted section slips over the dipstick receiver on the engine. This appears to have been done to relieve stress and improve the clamping effect. The sleeve sections are brass and the handle is sheet metal.

Security

Vol. 11, No. 1 Dan Pelecovich

Cheap Security
Use a Sears 2 in. padlock (with extra long neck) No. 58435 for $9.95 to lock the parking brake handle so it can't be turned. The padlock goes through the hole in the support bracket and keeps the release cam from turning.

Roll Bars

Vol. 13, No. 4 David Seeland

Roll Your Own?
Are you sure you are going to keep the shiny side up? I mounted a roll bar in my 1960 Super 90 coupe with welded-in blind nuts. The car was used for autocrosses, time trials, and daily driving. Because of the design of the roll bar, it was within range of my unhelmeted head and rather than use a helmet on the street, I removed the roll bar – and left it out for a PCA drivers school at the Aspen, Colorado race track. This was not a good idea. The car had a primer finish so it wasn't shiny, but you might say that I definitely did not keep the primer-side

up. The only place the roof was high enough to allow a normal-sized human to sit in the car was right were my head was – pure luck!

My wife was working the preceding corner and was watching cars leaving her corner, so she saw me upside down about six feet in the air and had to decide what to do; flag down following cars or go to my aid. She did some of both.

How did I get into this undesirable attitude? At about 5000 RPM in second gear or about 50 miles per hour I got off the proper line into the marbles and started to spin. The car had rotated until it was at right angles to the track. The two rear wheels were sliding sideways about a foot off the track and the spin would have caused them to slide back onto the track but for the four inch drop-off at the edge of the asphalt. The outside steel wheel dug into the asphalt edge and suddenly stopped the spin which launched the car into the air. I didn't feel scared, just dumb. From the noise, it was obvious that I was doing some major damage as I alternately saw sky, then track, then sky. When the commotion stopped, the coupe was balanced on two wheels and the corner of an open door. I got out rapidly to let people

know I was still in one piece and I was, thanks to luck, a good helmet, and a five point racing harness. The coupe was determined to be unfixable; I traded the stripped shell for a leather steering wheel.

Although even a Speedster windshield frame can sometimes provide adequate protection in a light roll (ask ex-driving instructor Bill Randle), I wouldn't count on it. Unaided coupe roofs aren't enough either as can easily be inferred from the state of my Super-90 coupe's roof.

I am now nearly done with a 1959 A coupe that will replace the Super-90. It will have a roll bar installed at all times. George Wilkie gave me a roll bar a long time ago thinking it would fit my 912. It didn't. I sectioned the horizontal tube to narrow it. The butt joint is reinforced with a 10 in. length of tubing that just slid into the roll bar tubing. Diagonal braces were removed as were the original four-inch square mounts on the uprights. New diagonal braces were fabricated using 1.75 in., 0.125 in. wall, steel tubing (the same as the tubing in the main hoop).

Attachment of the front legs of the bar is to $\frac{1}{8}$ in. reinforcement plates welded to the chassis. Two "ears" of

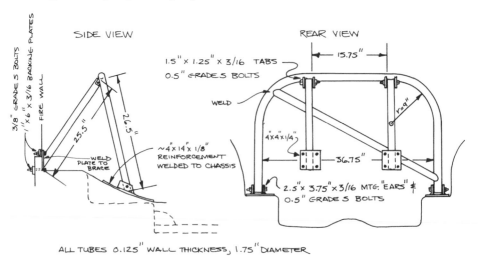

Figure 1 – 356 coupe roll bar

1/8 in. plate are welded to each plate. One-half inch bolts through the "ears" anchor the roll bar's front legs. The rearward sloping braces have 4 in. square 1/4 in. plates at the firewall end. Four bolts and two one by six inch backing plates secure each brace to the firewall (Fig. 1). I will attach my "Y" type racing shoulder belts at shoulder height on each of these braces. I am going to use a Speedster inside rearview mirror on a cab windshield rod in order to lower the mirror for rearward vision under the roll bar rather than through it.

I am using Scheel seats with headrests so there is no possibility of head contact with the diagonal brace. If non-headrest seats are used be sure to pad the tubes. Pipe insulation can be used or J.C. Whitney sells a roll-bar-padding kit.

For those of you who dislike the jungle-gym look, the factory Carrera GT roll bar is a possible alternative. Jones Autowerkes in San Antonio

made one for Jim Smith if you want to buy one ready made. If you prefer to do-it-yourself, I've included some measurements (Fig. 2) taken from the factory bar in the 1959 Carrera GS/GT Speedster number 84948 that used to be stored in a local back yard. The bar slips over solid stubs with a bar-diameter shoulder at the base. Bolts, at 45 ° to the car's longitudinal axis, secure the main hoop to the stubs. The rear braces are welded to the main hoop and are flattened at the rear where they are drilled to slip over the rear seat back pivots. The braces are held in place over the pivots with washers and bolts.

According to Norm Miller, removing the body-color roll bar from his GT coupe involves raising it and pushing it into the headliner to gain enough room to get it off the stubs. He also recollects having to drop an erected Speedster top vertically on to a Speedster with a factory roll bar because of clearance problems.

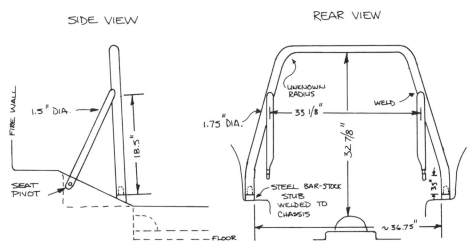

Figure 2 – Factory GS/GT roll bar

257

Chapter 14

Linkage & Cables

Heater Operation

Vol. 3, No. 5 Ed Mayo

Adjusting Heater Controls

An often overlooked detail after removal and replacement of engines in 356's is the proper adjustment of the heater controls. 356 heaters weren't notorious for putting out too much heat at their best. Improper adjustment and operation can lead to severe frost-bite.

You must start with perfect control cables. If the ends are broken off, as is usually the case. they should be replaced since it will make adjustment much easier (the longer cable goes to passenger side of car.)

Next, check the lower air channels for ease of movement and complete opening and closing of air flaps. If not, you must correct them before going any further.

The most overlooked part of the heating system is the muffler valve. It serves to muffle out valve noise and also has a flap valve to control the air supply to the front of the car. It is operated by a control rod from the lower air channel.

The tricky part of making all this

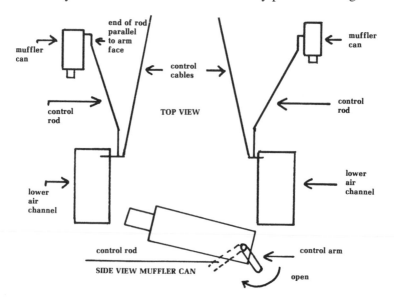

258

work smoothly is that the control arms on the muffler cans must be straight to allow the control rods to pull freely and in a straight arc. If there is any bind, rust, or bent arms, you won't get full travel at the flap valves. The control rods themselves must be bent at the ends so that they are parallel with the face of the control arm.

The control arm on the muffler can must also travel in such an arc so as to allow the flap to be pulled open by the control rod.

With the cables hooked to the lower air channels, operate the heater control to full on and check to see if the flaps close all the way. Now open the flaps and hook up the control rods and make sure the valves are all the way closed before tightening the rod clamps. Now, turn the heater all the way on. The flaps should be shut and the muffler valves open.

Vol. 6, No. 2 Vic Skirmants

356B Heater Cable Repair

For those with 1960 - 1963 "B" models. If you turn off the heater control a little too hard, a small clip is forced off the threaded shaft that the heater cable guide rides on. Rather than keep replacing the clip and having it come off again, there is a more permanent fix. Very carefully drill and tap the end of the threaded shaft for a 6 mm or similar-size American screw, and a drop of Loctite to keep it in place, and that problem should not recur.

Tach Cable

Vol. 10, No. 5 Vic Skirmants

Tach Cable Replacement

Tachometer cable installation: I may have covered this in the past, but it's worth repeating. One thing I learned in engineering school was "You can't push on a rope". You also can't push a Porsche tach cable through the tunnel; too many unseen obstructions in the way. The way to install the new cable is to attach one end of it to the old cable and then pull it through. I use a simple pipe threaded connector; I think it's a $3/8$ in., but take your new tach cable with you to the hardware store and see what fits.

Be sure to remove all the clamps and grommets around the old cable; the older cars seemed to have more clamps in the tunnel area; be sure these are undone. I attach the new cable at the engine end and pull forward. As the large part of your double cable winds through the tunnel, it will encounter obstructions. As soon as there's resistance, stop pulling! You can work the cable back and forth by pulling at the gearshift linkage access plate and the forward open end of the tunnel. With the right touch of back-and-forth, wiggling and cussing, it will eventually pull through. If someone has already pulled out the old cable, run some wire through the tunnel and attach it to the new cable, then proceed.

Clutch Cable

Vol. 6, No. 2 Vic Skirmants

1956 - 1962 Clutch Cable Failure

Have you ever had your clutch cable break at the threads at the forward end? You then put in a new cable and very shortly it broke also? Check the pivot through which the cable passes. If it is very stiff or frozen, it will not pivot as the pedal goes through its motion. The cable end will then have a bending load put on it with each application. Pull out the cable, remove the pivot (that might be difficult), clean it up, grease it, and put it back together. This applies mainly to the 1956 to 1962 cars. Later ones had a more open design, making it almost impossible for the pivot to seize up.

259

Speedometer Cable

Vol. 5, No. 5 Vic Skirmants

Speedometer Cable Installation

As you are all aware, Porsche put their speedometer cable through the left front wheel spindle. In order to seal the cable housing at the back of the spindle, they installed a small rubber grommet, pushed in place by a split bushing. When replacing the speedo cable, it is a good idea to pull out the bushing so the grommet can come out with the cable for inspection. If you don't pull the bushing, you can usually remove the cable without difficulty, but it is sometimes very hard to push the cable back in. If your grommet is gone or just bad, and you can't get another, seal the area around the cable with silicone rubber, or else water will get into your wheel bearings. It's also a good idea to put a little silicone rubber on the square end of the cable where it sticks through the grease cap.

Shift Linkage

Vol. 4, No. 4 Richard Miller

Bent Floor Interference

If you have difficulty shifting after the car has been jacked up, check to see if the sheet metal floor at the end of the shift tunnel has been pressed up against the external shift selector mechanism. To do this, remove the curved cover in front of the jump seats and watch for interference between shift linkage and floor. If there is interference, take a piece of wood, like 12 in. of broom handle, and a big hammer, and using the wood as a punch, hammer the floor back in shape. While you are at it, also hammer the jerk who jacked on the sheet metal.

Vol. 14, No. 3 Phil Planck

Popping Out of First Gear – Transaxle or Shift Linkage?

Occasionally my 1955 356 would pop out of first gear. This occurred only when starting from stop, when shifting from neutral into first. If I shifted into first before stopping and held the clutch in without shifting out of gear, then it would never pop out when I let out the clutch. After participating in the 356 drivers school following the 1988 East Coast Holiday, which amounted to about two hours of track time, this symptom was no longer occasional.

Since the transaxle already leaked and howled, and now always popped out of gear, it was rebuild time. I removed it for an overhaul. After reinstalling the transaxle, the howling and leaking disappeared, but not the gear popping.

By the way, I discovered a neat way to fill the transaxle with gear lube without access to a pump. Buy the plastic one-quart bottles of gear lube with the cut off nozzles on the caps. Remove the battery cable and other electrical wires from the starter solenoid. Now you can just fit one of these bottles into the filler opening and manage to have the bottle angled downward. Squeezing the bottle speeds up the process.

It was fairly simple to confirm that my gear popping was a linkage problem. First I adjusted the shift mechanisms fore and aft per the manual. Illustrations A and B are the left and right halves of page 17 from the exploded view parts diagram for the Pre-A. Illustration A is the hand lever assembly and B is the hinged relay assembly. After shifting the transmission into first gear, I loosened the set screw (#30 in Illustration B) in the hinged relay assembly. This mechanism is referred to as a hinged relay assembly by Elfrink and a hinged shift link in the factory manual. I believe the shaft coming out of the transaxle that the set screw sets into is called the inner shift lever. Anyhow that's what I will call it. Next I tapped gently on the end of the inner shift lever with a drift and a plastic hammer. The inner shift lever moved further rearward. Now I started the engine and let out the clutch. This time the transaxle did not pop out of gear.

Determining the cause of the shift system problem was a lengthy process. These kind of problems are fun for me if I have the time and patience to work on them. I was on vacation for a week of home and car keeping chores so the environment was right. I will tell you now that the root cause of my problem was in the hinged relay assembly, but this was the last place I suspected. That was because this assembly is not supposed to be adjustable other than clamp #32 in Illustration B. This clamp locks part #18 into position. Part #18 slides inside of the shaft.

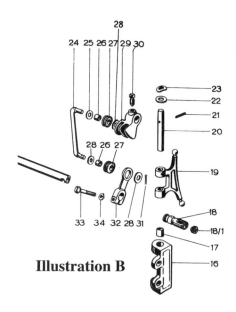

Illustration B

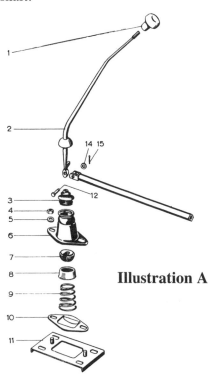

Illustration A

As your problem may not be in the hinged relay assembly, I will outline the steps I went through. First, some part of the shift lever (#2 in Illustration A) is supposed to be vertical when the hand lever assembly is properly adjusted. I have concluded that the vertical part is supposed to be the bottom part of the three straight parts of this lever. No matter whether I slid part #11 or #10 fore and aft, it was impossible to get shift lever #2 vertical. This car not being a show car, I filed the slots out longer on part #10 and #11. This allowed a little more fore aft adjustment but still not enough to make the shift lever vertical. However, all of these efforts did allow the shift lever to start approaching vertical. At this point I started the engine, shifted into first and let out the clutch. As you probably guessed, it still popped out of first gear.

I had exhausted my efforts on the hand lever assembly. The next culprit on my list was shift rod #19. Somehow it must have gotten shorter with age just like people do. I removed the rod to find a clever way to temporarily lengthen it. It turned out that part #18 is an assembly (more than one part).

For some unknown reason the front end of the back part of this assembly is drilled and tapped. I assume this part was borrowed from the VW and that threaded hole means something on the VW. Anyhow I found a suitable spacer that was about 1/2 in. thick.

After disassembling part #18, I inserted my spacer and reassembled it by using a bolt that fit the threaded, previously unused hole. This had to be done to recreate a longer part #18, since the split pin formerly used to hold the assembly together would no longer work. Now I had a modified shift rod #19 that was 1/2 in. longer.

After reinstalling the longer shift rod I could not get the bottom of shift lever #2 vertical. I was sure this extra length and properly adjusted shifting system would eliminate the gear popping problem. Of course it did not, and after two days of effort without a solution, this was no longer fun. I decided to stop for a while and do some house projects while I could think this out.

The next day I removed the hinged relay assembly shown in Illustration B. Upon inspection, it was clear that this assembly had been worked on before because washers #25 and #28 were not correct. Fortunately the rubber bushings #27 were in good shape, as I assume they are NLA, as the catalogs say. I can see why later versions of the 356 eliminated this whole contraption. I would not call this a very elegant solution for shifting a transmission. Even after installing correct washers, there is a fair amount of slop in the assembly due to need for rod #24.

As the hinged relay assembly now appeared to be in order, it was reinstalled and adjusted. It still popped out of gear. Something was still preventing part #29 from moving far enough to the rear to force the inner shift lever completely into first gear. This was still easy to check by tapping on the lever which could go farther after

loosening set screw #30. I noticed that when this set screw was loose that a metallic clunk could be heard as I slid the front shift lever into first gear position. This noise was a result of the root cause of the problem. Lever #19 was hitting the mounting base #16. This prevented the ball end at the top of #19 from moving #29 far enough to the rear.

Out came the hinged relay assembly again. The balls on each end of lever #19 were not in the same vertical plane. The bottom ball was about 1/2 in. further rearward in its installed position. Was it supposed to be this way? I do not know, but since this is not a show car I decided to "modify" this lever by bending the lower end towards the front of the car. I actually bent it beyond lining up in a vertical plane with the upper ball. Illustration C shows the before and after shapes of lever

After reinstalling the hinged relay assembly for the umpteenth time, it

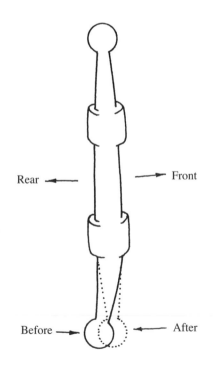

Rear ← → Front

Before → ← After

Illustration C

262

now allowed part #29 to slide about 1/2 in. further back on the inner shift lever. This test was done with the set screw removed. This fixed the gear popping problem. So, to make a long story short, I would suggest this procedure if your 1955 356 pops out of first gear. Note the location of part #29 with respect to the inner shift lever. Remove set screw #30 in Illustration B. Unclamp the shift rod by loosening bolt #33. If part #29 cannot be pushed further rearward, listen for a metallic clunk in the hinged relay assembly as you rotate it fore and aft. If you hear this clunk, your 356 probably has the dreaded bent lever #19 aging disease.

Choke

Vol. 12, No. 3 Dave K.

Repairing the Choke Cable
I'm not sure anyone out there in 356 land cares or to what 356s these cables are common to, but after 6-7

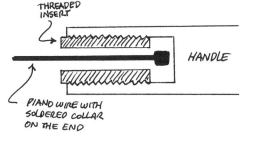

THREADED INSERT

HANDLE

PIANO WIRE WITH SOLDERED COLLAR ON THE END

months of trying to get another choke cable for my 1954 coupe, I gave up getting a replacement and fixed the one I had. When I got the car, it took quite some time to figure out what the knob with the broken wire even went to and the flex cable was broken off about an inch past the firewall (in 1954 the cable goes all the way back to the carbs).

Anyway to make a long story much shorter, to renew/replace the piano wire, what you need to do is drill out the "dimple" on the flat side of the handle. Use a 3/32 in. bit to a depth of 1/16 in. or so. The insert then screws out. The broken piece of wire comes out with the insert. All you have to do is then take off the collar and put it on the new piece of wire.

That should suffice for most people with later cables where only the wires break. However, I also had to fix the flex cable. This originally looked to be the hardest part as it was a compression fit between the hose and the other "thingee" (a technical term for what the handle slides in and out of).

Anyway, the magic trick turned out to be cutting the old flex hose off about 1/4 in. from the end and sort of "unscrewing" it with some Vise-Grips. It comes right out (sort of). The new cable, which I got from the lawn mower repair place, went in in the same manner. That is by twisting the thingee while holding the cable near the end with Vise-Grips.

Chapter 15

Luggage Compartment

Battery Cover

Vol. 9, No. 5 David Seeland

Flat black paint over racer's tape on my battery cover on my Speedster offended my sensibilities. Stoddard now has a plastic replacement for the A and T-5 B's pressed-board battery cover (which I haven't seen) but I'd rather have the real thing. International Mercantile had them a long time ago, made by an elf somewhere in California but the elf is out of the battery cover business and there are no more. Solution: make my own (Fig. 4).

*The elf is back in business, but the covers are **expensive**, so you still may want to make your own – September 1994*

First problem: how to obtain the "cardboard". Actually, it is pressed-board available at auto trim suppliers and is used for door panels and such. The stuff I bought is a couple of thousandths of an inch too thin. Or right on if the yellow enamel, black enamel and flat black paint on my cover were disregarded. Next problem: how to bend pressed-board properly. Solution: a pressed-board bender. This consists of two parallel pieces of $1/8$ in. thick metal spaced about $1/4$ in. Line up the proposed bend in the pressed-board on the gap, lay a quarter inch diameter rod on the fold line and tap lightly with a hammer forming a rounded groove in one side of the pressed-board and a corresponding ridge on the other side. Do not make the groove so deep that the skin of the board splits on the ridge side. Lay out so that the "ridge side" is at the inside of the bend. Even breakfast cereal boxes seem to be bent in a similar fashion.

If the metal part of your old box is in good condition or fixable, just trace, cut and bend new "cardboard". For those of you with less, or nothing to work from, the dimension of the cover should allow you to start from scratch on a new battery box. A wooden block one inch square by 8 $1/2$ in. long is attached to the lower front of the cover with staples and two small round-head screws. Pop rivets with backing washers are used to assemble the box. Cut the round hole in the sides with a one inch hole saw.

Another tip if you're interested in originality, don't throw away that old "tar top" external bar cell connector 6 v. battery – they are no longer available and can be rebuilt with new plates for about $40.00 here in Denver, or at an unknown price by Silver State Batteries in Phoenix.

German or Mexican tar-tops are now available – September 1994

Hood Seal

Vol. 15, No. 5 Cole Scrogham

The 356 front hood seal is a common rubber part generally stocked by most parts shops. The seal usually arrives performing some sort of contortion, wrapped with tape or a tie-wrap. This seal is a tricky ordeal from the start, and unwrapping and surveying the rubber quickly proves the point.

Once the seal is unwrapped, you should leave it alone in a straightened position for a few hours. Some opt for soaking the seal in warm water, but this is not necessary. It is particularly helpful if a warm sunny day is at hand to leave the seal outside, throw it across the clothes line or whatever. Then summon all the self-control you have as a Porsche owner and leave it alone. Go back inside and read a parts manual or something more enlightening like the *Registry*.

Once the rubber snake has cured into some semblance of a hood seal, take it over to the car and lay it in the water drain of the front hood. This will give you an idea of the length you have, some are cut shorter than others and you may have to gently stretch the seal as you install it. If you have a seal already in the car, look to see if the break in the seal is at the upper right (driver's perspective) corner of the trunk opening. If it is, you likely have an original seal or a relatively knowledgeable past owner/restorer. Also look for two curved corner plates in each corner of the trunk opening. These plates help the seal make the abrupt bend at the upper corners while forcing the rubber to lay flat. If you are missing the plates, order them and a seal kit consisting of small sheet metal screws. The plates and screws are readily available. If you are in a hurry, pick a small phillips screw with an escutcheon similar to an upholstery or carpet escutcheon (early 1955 and earlier cars had slotted screws). Be very careful not to use too large of a screw – when the screw breaks off and you have to drill it out, it will be your own fault.

If the seal is intact, you must remove it before beginning, carefully cleaning excess glue out of the way. This is also the time to locate the small holes in the car, and clean them with a small drill bit if necessary. Ideally, the seal is being installed on a freshly painted car, but this of course is not always the case. When you are ready to begin, you should enlist the aid of a friend (not a spouse), and have some sort of adhesive at hand. 3M Weatherstrip Adhesive or a silicone product will do nicely.

If it is possible, your life will be much easier with the hood off of the car before beginning. If not possible, have your helper raise the hood to its highest point without hearing any suspicious cracking in the metalwork. You will need every inch of space.

Begin in the upper right corner, right where the body is welded together. Install the seal with the lip of the seal at the top edge, so that when the hood is closed, the seal will compress the lip downward. The open edge of the seal should be toward the outside of the car. The last hole of the right corner plate is about where you will start, measure the look of the seal by eye to ensure it is in the center of the channel and poke a hole in the seal with a punch or pick right over the hole in the body. Carefully screw the trim screw through the seal and into the body, tighten only until the rubber begins to compress – you do not have to crush it. Continue to move counterclockwise around the trunk edge, keeping slight pressure on the seal to maintain a consistent look. The seal will tend to aggravate you around the bottom. Leave it until you are finished, then you can add some adhesive and stick the seal in place. When you get to the top again, you will need to have a very short or 90 degree bend screwdriver. Take care not to scratch the hood, and remember the corner plates.

It is a real trick to get the hole punched in the seal in tight quarters with the corner plate in the way, hence an easier job when the hood is off. Once the dirty deed is done and you are back to the beginning, loosen your very first screw in the end of the corner plate and slide the seal under the plate. Use a razor blade to trim the ends to meet, and finish the holes through the corner plate.

The hood seal is a tricky part to install correctly, but is a rewarding job if you have a bit of patience. Very few owners do this correctly on the cars that I have judged, so it is well worth your while to get it done right. It is also an important point to check on an "original, unrestored" car.

Detailing

Vol. 2, No. 3 Paul Allen

T-6 Plastic Front Mat Detailing
A paint brush and some DuPont tire black make the molded plastic front compartment mat of a 1962-65 look factory fresh. DuPont has given the best results.

356C Tool Kit

Vol. 15, No. 6 Jim Perrin

356C Tool Kits, I
The purpose of this article is to provide detailed information on 1964-1965 356C tool kits. The motivation for this article is the lack of detailed published information about 356C tool kits, and the incorrect information I've heard at recent events. This article documents the actual contents of several 356C tool kits for cars produced during the production run for the 1964 and 1965 models. The information in this article is based on recent detailed examination of four 1964 - 1965 tool kits which other long-time owners and I have had for many years. These tool kits include the ones for my 1964 SC GT coupe which was built in late 1963 and which I purchased used in 1965, a 1965 Dolphin Grey 356C coupe I purchased in 1967, a 1965 Dolphin Grey 356SC coupe purchased by a friend in 1971, and a Ruby Red 356C coupe purchased by another friend in about 1973. I realize that there may be variations not included in this article.

The 356C tool kit cases are held closed by two metal clasps. In contrast, the cases for earlier model push rod cars were all held closed by either leather straps or tied cloth straps. When the 356C cases are opened up, it is seen that there are seven tool pockets on one side and three pockets plus a lug wrench pouch with a snap on the opposite side. The inner material is the same material as the outside of the tool kit case (as opposed to the exposed cloth backing on a 356A tool kit or early 356B case); this is because a double thickness of vinyl is used. When the material for an inner pocket is bent back, the underside is a cloth backing material. One 356C case has a smooth black case; there is not the usual grain found, for example, on the light green 356A tool cases or early 356B tool cases. When looked at very closely, you can see a series of very small, roughly round depressions in the material. The color of the stitching is black. There are two metal clasps, each with an attached small vinyl pull tab. Two other tool kit cases are light grey with off-white thread. They have a grain pattern similar to (but not identical to) a 356A or early 356B tool kit case. The inner surface also is the same light grey vinyl. Another one of the cases is dark grey with dark grey thread. The dark grey case has a grain texture which is the same as the two light grey ones.

The tool kits each have four open end wrenches. The sizes are 8 - 9, 10 - 11, 12 - 14, and 17 - 19 mm. One side of each wrench has "DROP FORGED STEEL GERMANY" and the wrench sizes. The letters are all capital. All letters and numbers stick up from the background metal (that is, none are stamped into the wrench as is done for the numbers on a Hazet 356A or early 356B open end wrench). The size numbers are not in individual recessed areas as found in some of the wrenches which have been used as replacement wrenches. The back side of the wrenches have nothing on them. All four of the wrenches are satin silver in color, and are not highly polished. Perhaps they were grit blasted before being plated. In addition, the flats around the opening at each end of the wrenches have a series of parallel lines such as would be produced by a belt sander. Although the four original kits described for this article all have four open end wrenches, I know of original-owner late 1965 cars with five open wrenches. In these cases, the 12 - 14 mm wrench was replaced with a 12 - 13 and a 13 - 14 mm wrench. The wrenches all say "DROP FORGED STEEL GERMANY".

356C pliers are silver with no black paint. Three have "KLEIN" stamped into them, and one has no name stamped into it. Among the four pliers, the two tips of the handles for one of the pliers are thicker than the handles of the other pliers. There is a diamond cross hatch pattern on the gripping surface of the two handles.

The 356C spark plug wrenches have "KLEIN" over "21" stamped in them. This stamped information is in the end towards the spark plug socket end. The spark plug wrench is plated with a satin silver-colored plating. The wrench appears to have been grit blasted with a fine grit before plating. There are two sets of holes in the end opposite the socket end for insertion of a rod for turning the wrench. The overall length of the four spark plug wrenches is 8 $^7/_8$ to 9 $^1/_4$ in. Note that two of the four kits discussed here are from 356Cs and two are from 356SCs, and that there is no basic difference in the spark plug wrenches used for the two different engines. The spark plug wrench rods are smooth on the surface and appear to be chrome plated. The rods have no words or numbers stamped in them. One rod does have one row of marks approx. 1 to 1 $^1/_4$ in. long that looks like vise marks. However, there are no marks on the opposite side. The two rod ends on all four rods have a rough appearance as though they have been cut off by a metal saw, and the edges of the ends have been slightly chamfered to remove burrs.

The fan belt wrenches are all silver, instead of being painted black as in earlier cars. The wrenches all appear to have been stamped out of a blank of metal. The edge on one of the two sides is slightly rounded all the way around the circumference, presumably a result of the stamping process. The sides of the wrench are rough (as opposed to being smoothly machined.) One of the wrenches has a line of surface depressions along the length in a slightly diagonal line; these appear to be the result of surface flaws in the parent blank of metal.

The 356C tool kits have two screwdrivers. One of the screw drivers is a conventional one for slotted screws and the other one is a phillips. On each of the four tool kits being discussed, the two screwdrivers each have red plastic transparent handles, and each have "KLEIN" printed on them in all capital letters which are in gold. At 180 degrees around the handle they each have "GERMANY" in raised letters (not in gold); these letters are narrower and slightly shorter than the letters in KLEIN. I have seen screwdrivers in other tool kits with the gold in the KLEIN letters mostly worn off. The plastic handle on screw driver for slotted screws is larger in diameter than the one for the phillips screwdriver. (I have also seen original 356C kits with screwdrivers that, instead of "KLEIN" and "GERMANY", have "10000 VOLT W-GERMANY" embossed in them.) The tip of the screwdriver for slotted screws is flattened to produce a rectangular cross-section for a length of approximately 11/2 inches. The purpose of this is for use in holding the generator pulley when removing the nut to replace the fan belt.

The fan belt from one tool kit has Porsche in black letters on a rectangular yellow background. Additional writing on the belt is in black letters on a blue background. The additional writing says "9.25 x 825", "PHOENIX" "made in Germany", "7/12", and "DA". There is a small geometric symbol between the size designation and "PHOENIX".

The tire pressure gauges for 356Cs have plastic cases. In the case of the four tool kits being discussed, three of the cases are maroon. The tire pressure gauges have both "Lbs p. sq. i." and "kg/cm2" markings on the dial. (The 2 is an exponent.) The lb. markings of 10, 20, 30, 40 and 50 are in black. The kg. markings of 0.5, 1, 1.5, 2, 2.5, 3 and 3.5 are in red. The center of the dial has a red solid circle with "MESSKO" in white letters. Two of the gauges are in a light grey plastic case with "Messko" and "Hauser" on it. One is in a leather case (which is very uncommon for a 356C tool kit). The fourth tire gauge is similar to the other three except that it has a very light blue plastic body instead of a maroon body. Also, the gauge is graduated in "Lbs. per sq. inch" only.

The jack handles in the four tool kits either have "19 m/m" or "19 mm" stamped in the socket end of them. Two of the tool kits have a set of fuses in a small clear plastic container. I would like to express my apprecia-

tion to Alex Bivens of West Coast Haus with whom I have had numerous helpful discussions of tool kits. Ken Ito, Don Marks, Denny Frick, and Bob Raucher are others who have been generous in sharing their knowledge of 356C tool kits with me.

Vol. 16, No. 1 Jim Perrin

356C Tool Kits, II

In the 356C tool kit article I described the name Klein that appears in gold letters on many of the red plastic-handle screw drivers. Following my article, one reader called and told me his Klein screw drivers appeared to be the same as I described, except that the word Klein was the same red color as the handle. What I did not mention in the original article is that when the screw drivers are used, the gold lettering tends to wear off leaving only the name which is stamped into the plastic.

I stated that the red plastic handles of the slotted screw driver and the phillips screw driver are different sizes: I should have stated that they are the same size.

Since the article appeared, I have received calls asking me why the 356C hubcap puller listed in the owner's manual was not mentioned. The reason is that I do not believe there ever was a hubcap puller in a 356C tool kit. There was one, however, in the 356B T-6 tool kit – it was needed because Porsche had dropped the Hazet lug wrench used in the 356A and T-5 356B, which incorporated a hubcap puller in the handle. Thus a puller was needed for the T-6 356B, which had the same wheel and moon hubcaps as did the earlier cars. Note, however, the 356C hubcap is much flatter and the 356C wheel has a recess for a flat-bladed screw driver – no special tool is needed. Although the 356 C owner's manual lists a hubcap puller, it is not shown in the adjacent photograph. Also note that there is no hubcap puller listed with the other tools in the 356C parts catalog.

As I mentioned in the article, a majority of 356C tool kits have four open end wrenches, but some of the later 1965 tool kits have five open end wrenches with the 12 - 14 mm one being replaced by two other open end wrenches. I incorrectly stated the sizes for the two "replacement" wrenches; the correct sizes are 12 - 13 mm and 14 - 15 mm.

Reproduction Tools. Some of the most difficult items to find for 356A and early 356B tool kits are the red-colored wood-handle screw drivers. There are currently two efforts to reproduce these screw drivers. Jim Shuh has had a set of prototypes made which he showed at the 1991 West Coast Holiday. I have asked Jim to send me information and photographs when he starts to have them produced. The other effort to reproduce these screw drivers is by Glenn Clevenger, who has produced a small number of sets and is now selling them. Clevenger had earlier reproduced the three blue-handle Hazet screw drivers for the round Hazet spare tire tool kits. Most of these tool kits are in VWs, and Glenn's screw drivers for these kits have been very well received by VW enthusiasts. He got involved in the Porsche screw driver project when he got requests for them from people who saw his ads for the reproduction blue-handle Hazet screw drivers.

The Clevenger set includes both a long and short screw driver for slotted screws and also a phillips screw driver. I have purchased a set from him, and am quite pleased with them. Over the last 12 years there have been several other efforts to reproduce these screw drivers, and these are definitely the best of any others that have been available. One unusual feature of the Clevenger screw drivers is that the long screw driver for slotted screws includes the stamped or etched writing that is on the metal shank of the origi-nal screw drivers. The current price of the set of three screw drivers is approximately $150 a set. Clevenger can be reached at 1456 E. Brentrup Drive, Tempi, AZ 85283, (602) 730-9625.

The original-type Hazet lug nut wrenches used in 356, 356A, and early 356B tool kits have not been available for many years. A later version produced by Hazet with a plastic handle instead of a metal handle was available in the late 1980s, but I have heard that this later version is also no longer available. Clevenger has considered reproducing the metal handle version.

Vol. 16, No. 2 Jim Perrin

356C Tool Kits, III

One letter I received following my 356C tool kit article asked why I didn't describe the hubcap removal tool that is included in the 356C owner's manual in the list of tools for the tool kit. I explained to him that I was sure that 356C tool kits never had such a tool, because with the new flat hubcap design and the recesses for a screwdriver in the 356C disk brake wheels, the hubcaps can easily be removed with the screw driver in the tool kit. Therefore a special tool, such as was included in the 356B T6 tool kit, simply isn't needed. I also pointed out to him that there is no hubcap removal tool included in listing tools in the 356C parts book.

Although I was sure that I was correct, I still didn't understand how such a tool got listed in the owner's manual. However, I recently figured out the answer. When Porsche went from the late 356B to the C, they changed owner's manual photographs by putting a photo of a 356C tool kit in the new C manual. However, they failed to change the caption, and the old caption for the late B ended up being carried over into the C manual. In addition to the hub cap removal tool, the B manual caption also refers to the jack and jack handle at the top of the photograph of the tool kit, and the fan belt coiled at the bottom. This caption matches the late B photograph perfectly. However, the 356C photograph shows the jack at the side, the jack handle in the tool kit itself, and the 356C fan belt is not coiled. Perhaps in the haste to get the new 356C owner's manual done, the writers failed to prepare a new caption.

At the recent L.A. area events, an unusually nice 356C tool kit appeared for sale that looked like it had hardly ever even been opened. It was unusual in that it had a fawn-colored 356C tool kit case, which is not a very common color. It was sold to someone who is having a serious restoration done on a 356C. I have seen 356C tool cases in black, light grey, dark grey, red, green, brown, and probably some other colors I have forgotten about. I talked to someone recently who told me he thought that for the 356C model, Porsche tried to put a tool kit case with a color that complemented the color of the car. I thought this was pretty funny, as we're talking about the company that made 356 As, Bs, and Cs painted blue with red interiors.

Summary of 356 Series Tool Kits. There are basically five types of tool kits for the pushrod 356s. They correspond to the Porsche 356 types, namely, 356, 356A, 356B T5, 356B T6, and 356C. The least of these kits as far as quality and quantity of the tools is the tool kit used in most of the 356B T6 cars in 1962 and 1963. It has the fewest tools, the cheapest tool kit case (which was tied together with a flimsy cloth tie like many VW tool kits), and doesn't even have a tire pressure gauge. The nicest tool kit was the 356C tool kit. Although the 356C tools are similar in quality and number to the 356A and early 356B tool kits, the tool kit case is especially nice. It has two metal snaps to hold it closed as opposed to a leather strap. It also has double sided vinyl as contrasted with most other 356 series tool kits. As a result, there is no exposed cloth backing to get dirty or stained by rust. The most difficult tool kits to figure out are the pre-A 356s. There appear to have been several distinct versions of the Pre-A tool kit cases, and there are relatively few complete original ones around to study.

Chapter 16

Parts

Vol. 2, No. 3 Bruce Hall

The Definitive List

There has traditionally been a certain amount of pride that goes along with owning and driving a Porsche. For 356 owners there is nothing that dampens the pride more than for someone to say, "What kind of Volkswagen is this?" The truth is, the 356 is more of a Volkswagen than many of us want to admit. The front end of the 356 is almost identical to that of the VW 36 hp. Porsche beefed up their brakes and stub axles and installed grease fitting on the tie rod ends. The drive train is the same in design, only built stronger and with greater precision for increased longevity.

With the wide spread interest in preserving the vintage Porsche, authentic parts are becoming an increasing problem with a great demand and a limited supply. Your Porsche dealer can still get most of the parts that you would need to restore a "B" or "C" model, but we have no way of knowing how long this supply will last. If Porsche decides in favor of restocking the most-needed 356 parts, the problem will be alleviated. Until this hope becomes reality, we must utilize all available sources to preserve in the purist sense of the word, "a true sports car."

Through my restoration and maintenance experiences during the past few years, I have compiled a list of VW parts that are interchangeable with those of the Porsche 356. I have used almost all the parts contained in this list that are identical to those of the 356. The reason I have used this source instead of ordering the parts from Porsche is simply due to accessibility. Parts ordered through the Volkswagen dealer have been easier and quicker to get. Below is a list of parts that have been most useful to me in maintaining and restoring the 356.

In reference to VW from 1954 - 1965

Front Suspension

1. Rubber steering cookie that fits between steering shaft and steering box.
2. Tie rods.
3. Tie rod clamps, nuts, bolts, and washers.
4. Tie rod ends – VW tie rod ends do not have grease fittings (check size of tapered stud – Porsche went to larger one with "A" types).
5. Rubber grease cups that fit under tie rod ends.
6. Steering knuckle (spindle) (only up to about 1955; maybe some

1956).

7. King pins and bushings.
8. Link pins, bushing & shims. The only part that does not come in the VW link pin kit that you'll need in rebuilding your Porsche front end is the specially shaped retainer bushings that fit in the eye of the suspension arm. They serve to hold the rubber O-ring in place to keep grease in and dirt and water out. You may be able to reuse your old retainer bushings, but if not, they are still available through the dealer.
9. Bolt, nut & washer used to adjust link pins.
10. Steering damper – VW Bus.
11. Rubber bumper between front trailing arms for 1950 - 1955 Porsches.
12. Front wheel ball bearings for 1950 - 1958 Porsches.
13. Steering gear box for pre-1958 Porsches.
14. Front drum seals 1950 - 1963.
15. Front trailing arms and link pin carriers 1950 - 1955.
16. Some front torsion bars.

Rear Suspension

1. Large and small rear axle O-rings.
2. Rear axle seal and outer bearing (and bearing inner and outer spacers, bearing retainer for 1950 - 1963. 356C uses only the bearing, and inner spacer).
3. Rear axle tubes (not ends) and axle shafts.
4. Axle boot.
5. 36 mm rear axle retaining nut
6. Some torsion bars and trailing arms.

Brakes

1. Master Cylinder Reservoir for all 356s through 1963 – VW Bus through 1967. This is a plastic reservoir and fits the Porsche master cylinder with no alterations. I am a purist, but this is definitely an improvement over the Porsche aluminum reservoir that has a tendency to sprout holes after several years of use. The cost is about $5.75 opposed to $10.45 for the original Porsche replacement part.
2. Backing plate retaining bolts.
3. 19 mm wheel cylinder overhaul kits ($3/4$ in. cups available at auto supply stores; that's usually all you need).
4. Almost all nuts, bolts and washers used on the VW front suspension are interchangeable with Porsche.

Interior

1. Hella interior lights mounted in roof are the same as those used. on early model Karmann Ghia.
2. Interior door handles are VW parts.
3. Window crank will fit, but they have white knobs which would be fine for most "A" models and earlier.
4. The accelerator pedal rubber is an Opel part.
5. Clutch and brake pedal rubber 914 and 911 parts.
6. Light bulbs.
7. Speedometer cable (VW Sedan) (Check length; some VW cables a bit short when suspension is fully extended).
8. Some windshield wiper motors for early 356s.
9. Rear window latch knobs on 911s are the same as those used on the 356s.
10. The shifting lever boot on the 914.

Exterior

1. Head light assembly early VW – If you specify that you want the lens that says Hella instead of

VW, it is still available, and is the original and authentic Porsche lens.

2. The front directional signal lens and lens gaskets on 1960 - 1965 are available through Mercedes Benz. They were used on the 190 and 220 series.

3. The rubber window washer spraying units on 356C, late B mounted by the windshield wipers are 914 parts.

4. Windshield wiper blades.

5. The license plate light assemblies for 1960 - 1965 are the same as those used on the early Mercedes 190 and 220 series.

6. The back-up light assembly for 1960 - 1965 is the same as those used on the 1967 - 1972 VW Bus. (Change bulb to 6 v.).

7. The rear reflectors are the same as those used on the Mercedes 190 series.

8. In case you are short a spare tire wheel the VW 5 lug wheel will fit until a Porsche wheel can be located.

9. Fuel tank cap (early B & A).

10. Older VW jack.

Engine (36 hp VW only)

1. Generator brushes and bearings (cooling fan, generator and pulley can be used (40 hp VW also, bus generator same).

2. Starter (6v) (40 hp VW also) (Solenoid slightly higher on starter) .

3. Distributor cap, points, rotor and drive mechanism.

4. Oil pressure relief valves and spring (only for Porsches pre-1958).

5. Oil pressure sending unit (all air-cooled VW).

6. Flywheel seal.

7. Crank shaft end play spacers.

8. Dowel pins for main bearing location.

9. Some oil pumps and gears (only for pre-1960 Porsches, some oil pump housings pre-1958).

10. Crankshaft timing gear, key, spacer, distributor drive gear and clip.

11. Camshaft timing gear (will have to drill dowel pin holes).

12. Some gaskets on 1500 Porsche except valve covers.

13. Some fuel pumps on early model Porsche.

14. Throw out bearing (Ball bearing type) (Any air-cooled VW).

15. Clutch disc and pressure plate assembly (VW transporter) (Rigid-center and spring-center discs available for 180 mm and 200 mm. Coil spring pressure plates available for 180. 200 mm pressure plate not useable.

16. Dipstick (2-piece case).

17. Spark plug connector.

18. Oil temperature sending unit NLA from Porsche is available from V.D.O.

19. O-ring on distributor shaft.

20. Valve adjusting nut.

21. Oil cooler seals pre-1958.

22. Camshaft end-plug.

23. Oil drain screw.

24. Lock washer for flywheel bolt.

25. Spring washer for crankshaft pulley bolt.

26. Pushrod tubes and seals (Porsche now uses pushrod tubes with extended bottom to cut down amount of oil sloshing up to the valve covers when cornering. VW tubes are not extended; use only in emergency – recommend using Porsche, if possible).

27. Reinforcement flange (cooling - fan cover).

28. Cooling fan hub.

29. Gasket for oil pump cover (small oil pump).

30. Drive pinion for distributor.

31. Washer for pinion.

32. Spacer spring for pinion.

33. Camshaft for 2-piece case "normal" engines.

34. Flywheel and crankcase for 2-piece case engines only with modifications.

Transaxle

1. Spring for gear lock (reverse gear) Also detent balls, maybe interlock plungers.
2. Shaft for differential pinion.
3. Lock pin for differential pinion shaft.
4. Differential carrier.
5. Differential side gears & spider gears.
6. Differential bearing opposite ring gear – also available at local bearing supply houses.
7. Transmission input shaft rear bearing – also available local supply houses.
8. Differential fulcrum plates.
9. Transmission rear rubber mounts for 1950 - 1955 Porsche.

By now I'm sure you have asked yourself how authentic these parts are in relation to the original Porsche parts. If you have been involved in 356 restoration or maintenance, you have noticed the number of original parts that are stamped VW. Using these parts will not affect the restored value of your Porsche as they were originally acquired from Volkswagen.

Vol. 2, No. 4 Vic Skirmants/Stan Stanton

Addendum
Further "other car" items useable on 356s: The wear sleeve on the spindle of a 356C, part #695.341.661.01 costs approximately $11, when available. This sleeve acts as a spacer for the inner wheel bearing, as well as providing a replaceable surface for the grease seal to wear out. This sleeve is a high-mortality item because it is exposed to the elements, unlike a drum brake sleeve which is fairly well protected. I have found that a 911

wear sleeve, part #901.341.623.00, approximately $5.50, has the same outer and inner diameter, but is about 1 mm thinner. Because the sleeve is also a bearing spacer, the 911 sleeve should not be used as is. I made a shim from the oil slinger-washer, part # 616.102.163.01. This washer is located between the #4 main bearing and the crank pulley seal, and came on the later 356B/C engines. It should also be installed on all 3-piece case engines, because it deflects the oil squirting out of the #4 bearing and keeps it from striking the pulley seal directly, thus hopefully decreasing the chances of leakage. The washer is within 2 or 3 thousandths of an inch of being the correct thickness. The outer diameter can be left alone, while the inner diameter has to be hacked out to clear the spindle; I used a pair of tin snips for this, then reflattened the shim. Install the shim, then the sleeve, and you're in business. Having a special shim made would of course be the ideal solution, short of using the "C" sleeve, but this method works, and is cheap. I have installed 911 sleeves on three "C" types so far, and have no problem areas to report.

Capt. Stan Stanton, Goldsboro NC, adds the following to the list:
1) VW used a rubber gasket (Porsche is cork) for the fuel gage sender. The gasket is VW part no. 113 919 133. This would apply to the 1963 - 1965 flat gas tank Porsches with the sender in the top of the tank, as well as the 1962 bottom-of-the-tank sender.
2) The overhead courtesy light in the BMW 2002 appears to be the same as the dash courtesy light in the "C" model Porsches.
3) A standard VW spark plug wire harness will work on a 356, but the #1 wire is a tight fit. While on this subject, I would like to remind everyone to check their spark plug connectors every now and then, and especially when misfiring occurs and the plugs and points look fine. There is a resis-

tor inside the connectors for radio interference suppression. The resistance should be about two thousand ohms, but sometimes they break down and the resistance goes sky high. The VW plug connectors are shorter and smaller diameter than Porsche, so you need the VW round rubber air seal as well. You can get either a resistance-type VW connector or one with no resistor. They are also much cheaper than Porsche. While still on electrical topics, the distributor rotor also has a resistor. If this goes completely, you stop, completely. The rotor is the same as some older VW's.

Keys

Vol. 13, No. 6 Dave Grant

Dismantling Lock Cylinders

The lock cylinders used by Porsche in the 1950s and 1960s were all easily taken apart. If one needs to match a new door handle or ignition switch to the keys used on the rest of the car, it is only a matter of applying basic logic and some small screwdrivers. In the case of the shifter lock used in 356B and 356C models, only with difficulty can one take apart the cylinder without the key. With the key in the lock, it is quite easy to remove one 2 mm diameter retaining bolt, and withdraw the key and cylinder together. *Do not do this unless you have a good reason, unless you appreciate the following procedure!!*

If any of our members has been foolish enough to stumble into this trap, I have a simple, effective solution. If deliberately withdrawing the cylinder, first put the key into a position exactly halfway between locked and unlocked. With the recessed flathead bolt removed, turn the key exactly 180 degrees. If you skip this step, it is likely that you will shred the 12 tiny coil springs hiding inside, as they fall halfway into the groove, in which this

recessed bolt normally resides.

If one is just changing the key pattern, one need not remove the 12 springs. In this case, carefully push the lock cylinder out with the following tool:

The tool is a piece of 10 mm diameter metal rod, between 5 and 8 inches long. (I used the arm from a discarded motorcycle mirror.) Grind one end flat and square. Grind a notch about 5 mm by 5 mm into one side of this prepared end. Use a die grinder, or the corner of a larger grindstone. Very little accuracy is needed. Remove all burrs, with a file or wire wheel. About 2 to 3 inches from this prepared end, drill a $3/32$ in. hole, accurately, through a diameter of the rod. Remove any burrs, and clean out the hole.

The brass eccentric pin, on the end of the lock cylinder, fits into the notch you have put in the end of the tool. Press the tool and the cylinder firmly together as you remove the cylinder. When the lock cylinder is withdrawn, leave the tool in place while you work on the lock cylinder, the key, or the pins which contact the key.

Vol. 15, No. 4 Cole Scrogham

Keys, I

For years, 356 owners have been hampered by the lack of original keys. Unlike Mercedes or even common American cars, Porsche keys mysteriously disappear and it takes an act of Congress to replace them. But, once or twice a year, the Key Man can be found at a few selected swap meets. It was always a mystery who he was and how he came upon these keys, but now he has been identified and all 356 people can share in what he has to offer. The Key Man is Tony Euganeo (just call him Tony), at 1470 Elmwood Avenue in Sharon Hill, PA, 19079. You can call him at (610) 461-0519. Not only did I purchase a sample of each of his keys, but he gives out one of the more interesting sample

356 Keys

Key Blank	Profile	Part Number	Description
	B	NPN	Ignition – 356, used with starter button (Bosch)
	C / D	NPN	
	F	644.613.901.00	Ignition – 356A, combined with starter (Bosch) 644.613.101.00
		NPN	Door – 356, 356A, square style door handle
	K 1 0 0	644.613.901.09	Ignition & door – 356A, 356B, up to chassis coupe 117600, cabriolet 155600, Roadster 89600, Hardtop 61 201600
	K 3 0 0	644.613.901.10	Ignition & door – 356B, 356C, from coupe 117601, cabriolet 155601, Roadster 89601, Hardtop 61 201601
	F L	901.722.314.09	Ignition & door – early 911/912
	C	644.613.901.11	Glove box – 356A, 356B for lock 644.552.550.04
	. H K	644.613.901.12	Glove box – 356B for lock 644.552.550.05
	G Z	644.552.901.10	Glove box – 356C from chassis coupe (R) 126001, (K) 215001, cabrio 159001 for lock 644.552.550.06
	F P	901.722.313.29	Glove box – 911 to Jan. 1965
	C C	901.722.313.19	Glove box – 911/912 from Feb. 1965
	S G	644.511.791.11	Luggage compartment – 356B, 356C
	K 2 0 0	644.424.952.10	Shift lock – 356B coupe 108918 - 117600, cab 152476 - 155600, Roadster 86831 - 89600, Hardtop 61 to 201600 , chrome lock
	F E	644.424.952.11	Shift lock – 356B, 356C from coupe 117601, cabriolet 155601, Roadster 89601, Hardtop 61 201601, black body lock

276

sheets I have seen in a while.

The sheet must originate from a Porsche bulletin or some such publication, for it contains very valuable information indeed. It is very difficult to read, but the key shapes are recognizable and we can get through the small print. The first key is blank #644-613-901-00 and fits the ignition switch and door locks of early 356As. What appears to be a Hella logo is imprinted on the face.

The second and third keys are also combined starter/door lock keys. The first version has a slightly larger channel and fits As and Bs up to coupe #117600, cabriolet #155600 and Roadster #89600. The second version fits Bs and Cs after the numbers listed above. The next key is blank #644-613-901-11, which fits 356A and B gloveboxes, probably up to the IDs consistent with the ignition keys. The later 356B glovebox lock is next, blank #644-613-901-12 has a unique "GHE" logo on the face. The next, and most common according to my key drawer, is the 356C glovebox lock. This blank, #644-552-901-10, fits Reutter coupes from #126001, Karmann coupes from #215001 and cabs from #159001. The next key unlocks the front trunk on 356B and C cabriolets. Apparently the As have a mystery key although a smaller version of the key shown has been found in an original 356A cabriolet. The last two keys are NLA, and they fit the transmission lock and have a unique shape. There are a few still around, but they will probably wait for the right concours car. The smaller key fits the earlier cars up to the mid-356B range, and the larger key blank fits the later cars.

Vol. 15, No. 6 Cole Scrogham

Keys, II
I am very happy to be able to give the *356 Registry* readers an updated version of the key chart. It was impressive to say the least to note the comments that came in concerning the key chart, and hopefully this updated one is of a better design. A point to note concerns the second key which features a Bosch (not Hella) logo on the face. This was a mistake that I made all by myself and was corrected by a *356 Registry* reader, it is important to get good information out there; thank you.

The first two keys are ignition keys, the next a door handle key followed by three more ignition keys. The next five are all glove box keys, followed by a hood lock key and the very difficult to find shift lock keys. This is necessary to point out because the chart can be vague if you do not digest it all in sequence. Once again, let me know if you have anything to add or have some wild key permutation that you *know* came on your car from the factory (this only counts if you were taking key notes at the factory on June 23, 1957 when your car was completed).

Fitted Luggage

Vol. 16, No. 5 Brad Ripley

What the Original Owner Kept
Specially designed or "fitted" luggage has been available in many luxury and high performance cars over the years. Mercedes was perhaps first to provide fitted luggage in the 1930s for their 540K and later for 300SL. Often trunk space was small and odd-shaped, so special luggage pieces were created to utilize all possible space. Usually, these pieces were expensively made leather items intended to match and complement interior upholstery materials. In the last few years, it seems no Gullwing or Ferrari has been seen at Pebble Beach without fitted luggage!

Since the mid-1950s, Porsche offered a variety of luggage pieces, some to fit over and around the gas tank up front and several to go in the rear "seating" area. Leather, vinyl and canvas materials were used to produce nice but rather expensive (at the time) luggage. And frankly, the luggage wasn't a great seller which probably explains the scarcity of pieces on the market today. Now, of course, as collectors seek out optional accessories for their show cars, demand is going up especially for the rare leather pieces still in good condition. Here's a summary of the luggage pieces that were available for 356s.

Front Trunk

Both a diamond-shaped leather suitcase and a plaid canvas bag were offered to fit between the spare tire and the gas tank. The leather case was a very heavy "elephant skin" grain with matching strap, while the plaid bag came in both green and red plaid on the outside. All three pieces had a light tan plaid on the inside which was customary for luggage at the time. Of the two versions, the plaid soft-sided piece was probably the most practical as it could be stuffed to capacity and still fit around the spare tire. Of course, the usual vapors and over flow from the nearby gas cap probably made for smelly clothes and a quick demise of the canvas bag!

With the redesign of the gas tank for the T-6, new suitcases were developed in three materials: leather (black or brown), vinyl (black or "bronze") and plaid canvas (red/black combination).

The leather suitcases were done in a scotch grain hide and the vinyl versions were in "Skai Dur", the same vinyl as used in the later 911 seats. While the leather and vinyl suitcases were large and flat, the plaid canvas bags came in three sizes: (1) large and flat, the same size as the leather and vinyl versions, i.e., 27 x 20 x 6 in., (2) a smaller piece described as a "suitcase" dimensioned 20 x 17 x 5 in., and

(3) a "bag" dimensioned 21 x 12 x 6 in. It appears that the latter two were sized to fit under the hood together, although the literature doesn't indicate such use. In any event, all these pieces were specially sized to fit where commercially available luggage would not.

Rear Seating Area

Luggage pieces were made to fit the rear area both with the seat back(s) down or with the seat back(s) up, perhaps to accommodate very small rear passengers and their luggage?

The photos here show early rear seat area luggage available in brown leather only. The 356A' versions were fashioned in the same "elephant skin" as the front trunk piece described above and came in both 3-piece and 2-piece configurations. However, in early 1959, the suitcases were changed to a more modern design with rounded corners and heavy pebble grain finish, identified as 356B at right. Colors and piece sets were the same as the 356A versions.

Also offered during 356A times was a single piece to fit behind the folding seat back as illustrated below. Note how this suitcase is curved to allow full view through the rear window. These cases came in black or brown "elephant skin".

For the T-6 body change, suitcase design again changed to a flush-fit lid and more modern hardware. These large pieces were constructed in rather fine grain leather (black and brown) but not in the plaid canvas or vinyl of the pieces for the front of the car.

However, one small bag for the rear was in plaid canvas and sized to fit behind the seat backs; shown at far right. Finally, there was a suitcase for the rear of the Roadster. This was intended to fit over the transmission hump in the rear seat area since Roadsters usually didn't have a fold-down seat back. This piece is first described in a Feb. 1961 brochure but is mentioned in a parts document as early as Dec. 1958.

Best of luck in your search for old abandoned pieces of luggage likely to be found in a local "junque" shop or even at the next Porsche swap meet.

Date Codes

Vol. 17, No. 1 Brad Ripley

Determining the Age of Parts

You may have already participated in the "Dating Game" – not the TV show, but finding parts for your 356 with the "correct" date codes. The dating game is all in the attempt to prove your car is original or in making it more original.

If you know the assembly date of your car, then you can expect all components to be date-coded prior to that date. For instance, the easiest parts to check are the wheels; the date (month/ year) is stamped next to a lug bolt hole. On some wheels, you'll also find a date on the rim (tire side) which may differ by up to several months. Other easy to read codes can be found on VDO instruments and related parts (see photo above right). Many instruments prior to 1961 will have month\year stamped into the back of the case and also a blue ink inspection stamp containing the date.

Later units had only the blue ink stamp with the date. Check the stamp on the back of the clock in the photo. Many manufacturers use other meth-

ods of coding. On castings, a "date clock" insert is often used such as the symbol shown below, which reads as the fifth month (May) of 1964.

You'll find an example of this dating method on engine cases (remove the timing cover, look to the lower left). Those are the easy ones. Other suppliers, such as Bosch and Hella, make dating very difficult by using a letter for the year and two digits for the week (1 through 52),or an arbitrary assignment of three numerics. In both cases, a key is needed to decipher the codes. Perhaps some readers have figured out the codes based on parts from very original cars. After 1970, Bosch used the following numeric combinations (abbreviated from published matrices):

1970 = 0	January = 21
through	through
1979 = 9	December = 32
1980 = 0	January = 41
through	through
1989 = 9	December = 52
1990 = 0	January - 61
through	through
1999 = 9	December = 72

Incidently, the number "020" below the date code is a factory location code (German factory locations start with a zero, rest of world locations start with a nine). So, at the next swap meet, check those codes when the seller says, "It's NOS."

Chapter 17

Restoration

Restoration Basics

Vol. 2, No. 3 Brett Johnson

What You Need

In choosing a suitable subject it is usually best to select one with a good body and floor pan. This may be possible in warm and dry places like California, however, those of us who must suffer the abuses of road salting and the like will probably find only a very few examples which meet these criteria. Those that do tend to have very high prices attached to them as well. In any event, vehicles with extreme rust should be avoided if for nothing else they are not economically sound to rebuild. Accident damaged cars are a possibility. A structurally sound, damaged car can many times be a much simpler rebuild than a rusty one. In addition, a complete car is preferable to a partially stripped car (which is something that anyone who has bought such things as bumpers, lights, and engines can surely attest to).

The next problem is location. Ideally a large, cement floored, heated garage is the solution to this. In practice this is often not the case. All you can do is make the best of what you have. If you have no garage it is advisable to invest in a waterproof car cover. Fresh body work is very susceptible to water damage since most primers do little to ward off rust demons.

Adequate tools can vary considerably depending on the extent and amount of work you intend to do. Welding equipment is helpful but not really necessary. However, an air compressor and spray equipment is in my opinion mandatory. Don't rush out and buy a $200 - $300 outfit. It doesn't take much pressure (25 - 35 PSI) to spray a coat of primer and most small compressors can do the job. Other helpful tools are a slide hammer type dent puller, something called a flex-file, a sanding block, electric drill with sanding disc, a set of metric wrenches, several pairs of Vise-Grips and c-clamps, tin snips and, of course, a hammer. I am not a believer in orbital sanders as they often lull you into a false sense of security and produce very disappointing results. Besides, hand sanding is good for the soul. Some other useful items are a nut cracker, and an impact screwdriver (J.C. Whitney) which really works (the phillips head ends on mine have lasted for five years with no sign of rounded edges). A floor jack is nice but if too expensive an investment, a scissors jack is adequate. I would also recommend a set of good jack stands, or ramps. It may be wise, particularly if you are somewhat short of funds to look into used tools, especially when mulling over a compressor or floor jack.

Now that you've spent most of your money on tools, you no doubt are inspired to go out and do it all in three weeks. Unfortunately, the most time consuming part of a restoration is bodywork. To do the best job, I strongly advise an all-out effort. By this I mean substantial disassembly which, if the car is to provide transportation, will cause enormous complications. It is much better to abandon driving it for six months or so, to rebuild the body rather than doing it a bit at a time. Body work can take more time than most people expect. If it is to be done in spare time, I don't feel three to four months is an unjust estimate and, in many cases, during this time the enthusiasm begins to lessen significantly. But don't worry, it comes back about the week before painting is done. It is during this interim period that things often become discouraging. If you press on though, it usually works out in the end and the finished product can be quite rewarding from a personal standpoint.

Vol. 4, No. 6 Anonymous

Rustoration: a few hints on what not to bother doing

Don't be fooled by the title. This article is not a compromising type solution or short cut, although it may save the dedicated Porsche restorer some time, effort and/or money. The. writer has learned numerous restoration lessons the hard way and now hopes to share his experiences, disappointments, frustrations etc. The basic theme is, *Do it only once... The right way.*

A bit of background might be useful to put things in perspective. My attraction (fixation) for Porsche started at the tender age of twelve when the big kid up the street convinced me to trade my light blue 356A type Dinky Toy for a much larger (better?)

1961 DeSoto. After the trade was completed, I had a nagging feeling that maybe there was something special about "that little Porsche." For the next twelve years of Bugs, Karmann Ghias, microbuses etc; along with the normal poverty stricken years of higher (lower?) education, I somehow restrained my curiosity.

After graduation I blindly pursued my repressed fetish, sold my reliable custom VW and blindly purchased my first 356 Porsche, an extremely sexy looking silver 356B Roadster. This would be a good spot to drop some of the testimonial stuff and repeat the old warning of "buyer beware". Too many people have lost their initial and perhaps naive interest in the marque by unknowingly purchasing a poor specimen which drained both their enthusiasm and pocket book. If you start out with the wrong car, you will have neither a real winner nor a viable investment (and this doesn't include any consideration for all the "labor of love" you will put into restoring it).

Learn the lingo

First of all, it's "Por-sha" not Porsh; Roadster, Speedster. Karmann Coupe, Cabriolet, Convertible D and Coupe not: rag top, '62 convertible, two door. hardtop etc. For that matter be precise and try; 356A coupe, 356B Roadster, 356SC Cabriolet and Carrera Speedster. It is important to know the different models and engines since some are more highly prized than others. For example, Speedsters will almost always sell for at least $1,000 more than an "identical" coupe or cabriolet. To set the record straight, A bodied Speedsters are not considered to be 356A type Porsches: the factory calls them "type 540."

Meet the people

Meet the people through... what else... the Porsche Clubs, such as PCA and the 356 Registry. They will often be able to assist you in finding realistically priced Porsches (if there are any left?). Canadians should consider buying in the U.S. by checking the New York Times and the Los Angeles Times at the local library. In any single issue you will not only find the body style you want but even the color and options. When buying an older Porsche in the U.S. it must be at least fifteen (15) years old in order to be imported into Canada and then you will be charged a 12% plus 17% duty. The best selection of Porsches in North America is in California but, depending on where you live, transportation costs may eliminate the advantages of buying on the West Coast.

The writer recommends the above approach than the more common practice of buying a car and then considering its potential-more on this latter. An integral part of this procedure involves the reality of your financial constraints, which will also be referenced frequently. At current prices it could cost in the area of $10,000.00 to buy and professionally restore a "rust-free" car to national concours condition and $5,000.00 + $2,000.00 to buy and restore an old Porsche with "typical rust" to a clean, pretty and road worthy condition.

Don't let the advertised prices shown in national car magazines influence you. These adds serve a purpose but are almost always seeking top dollar. These advertisers may be looking for the proverbial New York Stock Broker who is seeking an investment to fight off inflation and often ends up buying a "classic" of questionable value at an exorbitant price. The writer realizes these situations are the exceptions but we should try to protect our own and our clubs' good names. Incidentally, you can pick out these investor types by such questions as: "How many cylinders? Is it a Vee Eight? Is it a rare model year? How many cubic inches? or Does it have cruise control?" etc. My hang up with this new breed of car collector (investor?) is that they often do not improve or even maintain the condition of their investment which simply sits in a garage and gathers dust. As Dr. Porsche has said, "Porsches are meant to be driven." Although older Porsches may only be driven occasionally, they should not be left in long term dormant storage awaiting possible profits caused by inflated prices.

Getting it Together

If you have only one other car, if at all possible do not; I repeat, do not sell no matter how much you hate it. I learned this lesson trying to get the interior fixed up and having to R & R the seat rails, etc., three nights in a row, so that I could get to work in the morning. Other examples involve being forced to drive a car with tacky paint or rushing to a parts dealer on Saturday afternoon only to arrive ten minutes after closing time due to a slow bus or tardy taxi driver. It is also almost mandatory to have a warm enclosed area to work in and to keep the car out of the elements. If you cannot be selective about when you drive your Porsche or have to park it outside, it will be a long uphill battle to reach and preserve your chosen level of restoration. The "big three" all make basic transportation vehicles so that you can save your precious Porsche from the abuses of salty winter roads and supermarket parking lots.

If you have not already done so, the next important step is to set yourself a budget and decide on the extent to which you wish to restore the car. The correct decisions at this point will save you countless heartaches and frustrations. The above factors will or should for the large part be determined by the condition or should I say the state of deterioration of the vehicle you have so carefully selected. Again, dedicated Porsche nuts can always be found to help you in this evaluation. If your car has a badly ventilated floor pan, "holey" longitudinals, body rust, high mileage. etc., there is really no way you should consider or dream of restoring the car to a level where it could compete successfully in a national type concours competition. I am personally aware of numerous exceptions to the above recommendation but then some amongst us are gluttons for punishment or are looking for the impossible challenge.

Beware of the temptation to give your new baby a nice shiny coat of paint before you have repaired the underside. Although "normal people" never see the underside of your car, imagine watching your nice new paint job bubble up and burn as even the most experienced welder carefully welds in new longitudinals. Similarly, contemplate sandblasting the underside and demolishing the finish on the body (no matter how carefully you have tried to protect the exterior paint). If there is any sign of body rust, strip the paint liberally, cut out any rusted areas and replace with metal (*not* fiberglass or Bondo).

After removing and replacing all rusty panels you would be in a position to consider a cheap paint job. Only after waiting one or two years for any undetected rust to make its unwanted appearance should you consider the $2,000.00 non-orange peel paint job.

The first time around you should spend your time and your money on rust removal and save the lacquer paint job until you have eliminated and inhibited *all* rust. For a complete restoration, totally dismantle the car and rebuild it from the ground up leaving the paint job, trim and interior until last.

Some or all of the above. may conflict with your burning desire to get the car looking good but it is your choice; do it once the right way, or at least twice the wrong way. Although the exterior paint and the car's interior are the most visible, don't rush into

these areas hoping to convince your non-Porsche friends of your sanity. They likely will never understand. As far as sanity goes, the previously mentioned advertisements in national magazines may be used to reinforce your commitment (fetish) in front of your colleagues, budget minded wives, girlfriends and the like. The fanatics that are always present at national concours also serve to assure yourself that you are relatively normal when compared to these enthusiasts.

Keeping Records

There are at least two good reasons for keeping accurate records of your expenses. Number one, a running total of all expenses will help you keep a handle on your costs. It is really surprising how those nickel and dime purchases add up. By recording your expenditures you will hopefully avoid unknowingly spending more on your car than you can ever hope to recoup and exceeding your previously mentioned budget. Have we not all seen the heartbreaking ads which read; "over $10,000 and countless hours invested, sacrifice for $6,000, transferred to Iceland, growing family etc.

The second reason for keeping records and saving receipts is a bit negative perhaps even morbid. Should your baby ever be stolen, vandalized or, heaven forbid crashed; you will find this type of documentation invaluable when dealing with your friendly insurance agent.

It may seem that I have been dwelling a lot on the financial side of Porsche restoration, but, believe me, I have not been practicing what I preach. Sometimes, in spite of all warnings, intelligent people still seem to ignore all logic, fall in love with a Porsche and throw all caution to the wind. Perhaps this is one of the stronger bonds between Porsche owners especially those in the habit of restoring and maintaining the older models.

Now it's done

The writer is aware that we have literally jumped over the actual mechanics of Porsche restoration but there are already numerous excellent articles on this topic. It is a pleasure to report that with the increased interest in restoring older Porsches a great number of high quality original and reproduction parts are now available on the market. Publication such as PCA's *Panorama* and the *356 Registry* magazine are the primary source for contacting suppliers of these items. In fact the author shares a commonly expressed opinion that these publications alone justify the modest membership fees.

One word of caution which is felt appropriate to avoid the pitfalls of over restoration. Many Porsche enthusiasts have slowly found themselves more and more restricted in the use of their vehicles due to concern about possible damage from usages that were considered perfectly safe prior to the car's restoration. A typical example would be no longer daring to park the vehicle unattended because of fear that someone might carelessly damage the $2000 paint job. Such concerns recently forced the writer to purchase a clunky Convertible D for uses where his Speedster is no longer suitable.

Another word from the voice of experience suggests that your second attempt at restoring a Porsche will be at least 50% easier than the initial effort. The limiting factor here is that many people have trouble preserving the first restoration and, if a second restoration is attempted, their energy and possibly their wives' understanding reach a low ebb. The above would suggest following the theme of setting out to *do it once the right way* rather than going through a progression of restorations to achieve your initial objective. One final word in regard to the possibility of one day selling your pride and joy. If you have "over invested" in your vehicle, the only way you may break even or come out ahead would be to sell it to a naive unsuspecting Porsche enthusiast. This could destroy you socially with the local club, but, more importantly, really provides little benefit to anyone.

If by chance you find anything worthwhile in this article, pass it on to a budding Porsche nut who might otherwise have to learn some of these lessons the hard way. Good luck and may your jack spurs withstand the forces of 100 consecutive tire rotations!

Vol. 5, No. 2 Bruce Baker

Bruce's Basics

I am impressed with the amount of information provided by the *Registry* on the restoration of 356s. Since my first issue several years ago, I have felt that I was in good company. As a bit of background on myself to lend credence to any information I may try to pass off as "expertise", I have been involved with the restoration and maintenance of 356s since I traded my "Bugeye" Sprite for a Speedster in 1965 and it has been evolving since. My shop mainly does the now well known "East Coast Restorations" but we have done some show winning cars and exotica as well. All this brings about the main concern I have about owning a 356 that needs major structural and cosmetic restoration.

Few people can afford to have it done professionally from the ground up, even a less "picky", but solid, "street" restoration. Therefore, this column in the *Registry* is for the "do-it-yourselfers". So many considerations must be taken into account other than the financial one; such as personal talent, availability of tools, a place to work and the proper information to back up the project. It is not so much my feeling that one should "do it right or not at all," as much as some mis-or-uninformed people actually have done more to harm the car than restore it, over a long period of time.

There are so few of these cars left that I feel that you should proceed armed with the basics of "do it right" and not experiment with a 356 body as your first project. Be realistic. Everyone knows by now the three main priorities in Porsche body restoration are 1) structural, 2) body (since it is also structural) and 3) paint and trim. I personally have been involved in developing our own techniques so intensely that I haven't read as much as I should from all the sources there are to see what has been said about setting up the project of restoration. If I repeat a premise already put forth, bear with me.

Keep in mind that it is just as much drudgery and plain, boring hard work, as any special talent and technique that will give you that "new 356". We have also been asked to save and rebuild cars in far worse condition than ones we cut up for parts and threw away 10 years ago. Ironically, parts are easier to find now. Anything is possible to reconstruct, but recognize the intangibles; like the "frustration factor" the "Peter Principle" and "Murphy's Law", and the tangibles; your job, your neighbors and another member of your family that could inhibit the progress of the project. As an example, one of my former employers is doing an 812 Cord. He's been at it for over 22 years, with another 15 to go if all goes well. He's a talented guy, has money, a nice shop in his carriage house, understanding family, but he constantly goes back to something and does it again, better; and says that it will be the best he can do, eventually, and it's more therapy than goal. A 356, though, can hardly be treated this way. It should be driven! Any owner of any 356 can appreciate near perfect show cars that are around, but the conflict arises that puts you between balancing the risk of driving one that is "nice" or potentially restorable and the anti-purpose of

making it a large, pampered, restored object d'art, that is rationalized as an investment. You must strike your own compromise and recognize your own limits.

In this admittedly negative vein, let me continue with a list of "don'ts" (amazing how many people don't know.)

Don't jack or support the car anywhere other than the suspension points. Always keep the doors on when doing any welding or cutting, especially on open cars. Rust removes enough strength, but removing what's left of a panel could mean a major misalignment. I have done cars that people just learning to braze have put on large threshold patches (on coupes) and noticeably torqued the whole unit, so that it becomes more expensive to fix and wasteful of their time, therefore –

Don't use any more heat than necessary for strength. It is very hard to achieve the strength of a factory spot weld in the repair process, but do try, if only for alignment of panels and aesthetics. MIG (metal inert gas) welding is then the logical follow-up. This electric wire feed system generates minimal local heat and is extremely controllable for the restorer's needs, as it can also be used as a "filler" spot, with even one-handed operation.

Don't believe that there is such a thing as a "rust-free" 356, but the more you acknowledge that "cleanliness = ease of restoration" the better your results will be."Pop" riveting has it's place, and so does wire mesh and bondo, but nothing should be done with any rust (or cancer) present- because it will only get worse later on. Cut out and/or clean the area before any type of work is done. And a word of caution. Even if it looks good to you now- expect the worst and investigate, i.e., it is far easier to uncrimp a door's bottom edge now and clean it, than to have to weld a skin on later.

And don't expect to pour some "miracle goo" into your already rusted blind areas to make it go away.

Don't undercoat to hide your problems. Undercoating is only valid if the metal is fresh, primed correctly and secure. These "protectants" can be deadly when you finally get around tofixing it right later on.

Many things have been said about sandblasting and dipping. All I can say is that we use both, with phosphating, beading, zinc chromate primers and epoxy sealers. Remember that in both processes, the cleanest areas will be the exposed ones. The blind areas only fill up with sand which is messy and for either process, you must open up the crimped seams and blind panels to get the most of these messy procedures or you're wasting your time.

A word about the fitting of the repro panels available to the restorer. They are excellent starting points, but few fit exactly as you get them. This can throw you off in the beginning and be very discouraging. Be forewarned that much work needs to be done on the areas adjacent to and on the repro panels that will make or break a job in final finish, both structurally and aesthetically. As if you need reminding, a panel on a Porsche body is only as strong as the panel next to it, especially on the underside.

Vol. 9, No. 6 David Seeland

Restoration Rationale

I'm about to paint my C Coupe and finish painting the 1968 911 (I hope) this fall, so I thought I'd run a series on amateur painting of 356s. My car painting experience started with a 1965 Corvair, followed by a 1967 Alfa, a 1964 VW, a 1959 356A coupe, a 1957 Speedster, a 1958 Speedster, a 1963 VW sunroof bus, and a 1973 VW Super Beetle. The 1958 Speedster has placed third twice in Porsche Parade concours competition and the bus has lived in the driveway for many years and is still shiny. A "specially treated" car cover removed the clear top coat from the silver Corvair, so I've had both winners and losers. Hopefully, I don't have too little or too much experience to convince you that you should paint your own 356.

The following ramblings seemed a bit incoherent when I read them. To summarize: painting your 356 takes time, some kind of shelter, the desire to do-it-yourself, perhaps prompted by finances or personal satisfaction. For you to survive and complete a paint job or restoration, be very careful choosing the 356; body condition is most important. The rarer and more desirable the 356, the more time and/ or money you can justify spending.

The major ingredient of a perfect paint job is not skill or equipment or material, it is time. If you have little time to invest in painting your 356 then all the skill and Imron and Binks 7's in the world will be of little help. If you have the time, do you have a place to paint your car? A spray booth would be heaven, a garage is nice, a home-built plastic shelter is about as good in the summer, the shade of a large tree is possible (unless it's a cottonwood in the spring!) and forget it if you live in an apartment and park on the street.

You might say why bother, I don't have the equipment, my garage is dark and dusty and Joe said he'd paint my coupe for $400 and it would look just like new. After all, he does all the cars for Slippery Sam's Used Car Sales. If a shop says they will do a perfect paint job for $400, subtract the cost of materials, about $150 (primer, paint, plastic, wet-or-dry paper, thinner, respirator cartridges), getting $250 for labor, then divide that by their $20-$30 per hour rate to see how much time they expect to spend on your car. I wouldn't put an eight hour paint job on anything better than a 1963 Rambler.

Of course, this doesn't include any

body work. A body-shop rule of thumb is that a hand-sized dent is one hour of work. Classic Auto Restoration in Farmington Hills, Michigan charges $38 per hour. Rust-repair is another matter, and an expensive matter. If done correctly it can add thousands of dollars to a paint job. The only proper way is to fusion-weld in new metal, anything else is a makeshift and shouldn't be considered unless it is acknowledged as a temporary expedient. I would estimate that a hundred hours would barely do a good paint job. I'd rather spend the money on other necessary things like engine parts and tires and carpet kits and floor mats and hubcaps and the 101 things most 356s need.

If you are considering painting a 356, then in most cases you are really contemplating some sort of restoration. It probably needs new carpets and a headliner or top, the seats redone and depending on where you live, some sort of rust repair. Then, if a 356 is to remain rust-free, the bottom should be detailed and painted and rustproofing material applied in the internal cavities of the chassis. I once stripped and painted a Speedster without doing anything to the cracking paint on the lockposts and door edges or dash. I traded it for another Porsche and the new owners had to strip and paint the parts that I neglected to do, and it was much more difficult that way. Plan your restoration carefully and you will end up with the best car for the least effort and the fewest dollars.

If you decide to restore a 356, it probably is not a rational decision. It's probably not necessary to provide transportation, it's probably not an investment. It's a fantasy, an attempt to capture a vision of what your 356 could be, even should be. But then, if you succeed and you're afraid of rock chips, door dings, ultraviolet fading, thieves, dirt, water, salt, dust, driving it, the rust coming back, in fact afraid of most everything – have you really succeeded or have you failed? Some people don't like to worry, to upset their nicely organized lives and for them, a restored car can be a disaster. Many of them come to this conclusion and really never do drive the car, selling them after the first concours they enter.

Of course, the basis for many of these worries is financial. Did that first stone chip decrease the value by $100 - $500? It may be that one of the major advantages of do-it-yourself painting and restoration is that most damage is easily fixed and if you've done the work yourself, you will know how – and worry a lot less. In fact, you may even be able to drive the car after it is restored. For example, see page 50 of the December 1983 *VW & Porsche* for a picture of our Speedster on the way to a second place in the Parade autocross. Half of the cloud of dust behind the Speedster is in reality flying rocks.

Those of you who are contemplating having a 356 professionally restored should consider the following statement made by Daniel Charles Ross in the January 18, 1982 issue of *Autoweek*: "If you can afford the time and money to have the car of your dreams restored, you can probably afford to buy it restored and avoid all the headaches." In fact, maybe even spend less money. Ross gave as an example a dirt-cheap reasonable quality, authentic restoration of a Model A Ford Roadster costing twenty grand. The kicker is that's for a car you could buy already restored for ten grand!

Another aspect of the planning process involves choosing a 356 to restore. I think the most important factor is buying a good car to start with. I recently heard of a rusty 356C bought for $4000. The proud owner then spent $6500 on a new pan and paint job. Now he probably has to do the interior and the engine and transaxle and the brakes and ... a $20,000 dollar

C coupe! The bargain C coupe looks like it might become a bottomless sinkhole swallowing up every spare dollar the owner can come up with. Body condition is paramount; severe rust and heavy accident damage (front or rear clips, a roof) are financial catastrophes. Spend some money on airline tickets if all the local cars are rusty – you'll be glad you did.

The rarer the car, the less fussy you have to be. I'd buy an Abarth Carrera in a flash even if I couldn't see the floor pan, but there is no need to buy a rusty 356A, B or C pushrod coupe to restore. If you have either the money or the time and skill and are somehow personally attached to a rusty car, go ahead, realizing that it's an emotional decision rather than a rational, financially sound restoration project.

Vol. 10, No. 1 David Seeland

What You Need

Well, I had one letter in response to my question on restoration costs. I suspected restorations cost a lot, but I had no idea how much. The car: a Convertible D, many small dents, no major collision damage, almost no rust. The restoration costs: top and interior, $6,500; body work and paint, $7,400; miscellaneous trim, $1,400; disassembly, $1,200; reassembly, $3,000; mechanical rebuild (engine, transaxle, front end), $6,100. The grand total for a complete mechanical and cosmetic restoration: $26,000 and "the car needs extensive detailing to make the *concours circuit*". This of course did not include the initial investment of about $6,000 in the 356.

Comments from the owner included: "Obviously I had more money than time or restoration skills; I would never again have a restoration done - disregarding the financial end, it is a severe emotional hassle; I like the car a lot and in many ways it is probably as good or better than when it was new; I appreciate more than ever the

not-so-perfect, do-it-yourself restorations seen often at *Registry* events".

This example should be near the upper end of the restoration cost spectrum. It was first-class work, with no shortcuts, done by recognized professionals. These are very interesting numbers and should help you decide how to proceed should you be contemplating either the purchase or restoration of a 356. If you contemplate doing it yourself, be prepared to spend far more time than the approximately 530 hours represented by this restoration. I wouldn't be surprised if twice as many hours would be necessary by an amateur who would do far more parts chasing, learning, redoing, and teeth gnashing. As was mentioned, the above example needs 'detailing' to be concours material. I'd guess at least another hundred hours or so for detailing for a total of 1160 amateur hours, and at 2.5 hours per night, that is 464 consecutive nights of work (14.5 months!). This is probably why I'm often asked "what have you taken apart lately". Disregarding the time spent "taking apart" (how many hours would you expect it took me to use up 11 gallons of paint remover on one car?), I could spend 3,480 hours on the three cars I'm presently working on – not counting the non-car (a 1968 911) that I'm about two-thirds done with. That's 2.5 hours every night for nearly 4 years! No wonder restorations seem to take forever – they do. Maybe you really should go buy a Rabbit GTI and spend some time driving instead of lying on a cold concrete floor, with an eye full of dirt that fell off the exhaust stud just before it broke off. Maybe I should buy a Rabbit too, but I won't.

O.K., now that you have a pretty good idea of which 356s are most desirable, and of the desirability of minimally rusty cars, and if the time investment detailed above hasn't sold you on that Rabbit, let's get down to the nuts and bolts–or wrenches–of

288

Porsche painting.

First, you definitely should plan to buy a gas (oxyacetylene) welder or you'll be tempted to take shortcuts like using fiberglass or pushing the panel in and filling it with plastic instead of shrinking the metal. Solidox welding outfits are no substitute. If you buy a welder, you'll be glad you did because you'll be able to "glue" pieces of metal together which immensely widens your ability to repair most mechanical devices. (Weld up the handle on your neighbor's lawn mower and he'll look more kindly on the "body-shop" next door.)

Then, you'll need an air compressor. I have a 3 HP 220 volt Sears (7.4 SCFM @ 40 PSI, 6.0 SCFM @ 90 PSI). I couldn't live without it. It's great for blasting the dust out from under the strings on our piano, clearing the sink drain, inflating tires, blowing out oil passages in cranks, and painting. The compressor is a little oversized for my $10 Sears air brush, but a bit undersized for the Binks 7. You should have a gauge at the gun because of the pressure drop in the hose. This is quite substantial – I can't maintain 60 PSI at the gun even if I set the regulator at 120 PSI (although I can with my old Sears gun). I think the problem is too much hose of too small a diameter.

You should use pipe for part of your air distribution system as it helps condense moisture out of the air supply. This is more important in areas with high humidity. The only other major air-tool that I use is a Rodac straight-line sander. You could shape plastic filler without this but at $75 I doubt if you could justify not buying one; it saves me many, many tedious hours of work.

A grinder/polisher is one of the electrical tools that you can't do without. It has two speeds, fast for grinding, slower for polishing. I use the polishing function most, but the grinder comes in handy for paint and rust removal. Not pictured, but equally useful, is a variable speed 2500 rpm 3/8 inch electric drill with either a 3M "Roloc" grinding disc (24, 36 or 50 grit) holder or 3M "Stikit" disc holder. Both have $1/4$ in. shanks and are three inches in diameter. They are excellent for removing plastic from "bag-of-walnut" panels – and for removing the inevitable paint that occupies all the low spots in such panels. I use mine much more frequently than my big grinder.

To apply plastic you need a plastic spreader. For rough shaping of the plastic before it is completely dry, use a half-round Stanley surform blade without a handle. I use three sanding blocks on plastic. One is a rounded block which holds the sandpaper along its sides with spring-loaded rods. Next is a foam padded flat block. To insure (or to check for) absolute flatness, I use the homemade plywood block with no padding. The handle clamps the paper in place. Buy a box of 100, 36 grit, 2 $3/4$ in. by 17 $1/2$ in., paper sheets and throw it away when it gets dull. A worn out piece of paper is like a dull knife. It's hard to do good work with either.

If your car doesn't need plastic filler, fine – but why are you painting a new car? Well, anyway, much finer paper than 36 exists and is necessary when sanding primer and top coats. Al West Paint Co. here in Denver has Japanese 1000, 1200, 1500 and 2000 wet-or-dry paper for color sanding. This is much liner than 3M's new ultra-fine, about 800 grit. Use as long a block as possible to eliminate or minimize ripples. I usually use the block which takes strips cut lengthwise from a sheet of wet-or-dry paper. For color-sanding use a 3M sponge pad with a half sheet of paper wrapped around it.

I should mention safety equipment. Wear goggles when grinding or wire brushing. I have a friend who even welds without goggles and for some reason his eyes are bad enough to require $1/4$ in. thick glasses. Body work and painting generates lots of different dusts and fumes. First, try to have adequate ventilation. Use paint remover outside on a breezy day. If you have an attached garage put in an exhaust fan so you can draw warmed fresh air out of your house and exhaust the noxious stuff outside. Don't try to paint with this setup though; all the dust in the house will be attracted by the paint and I doubt if you want to flock your 356. I speak from experience – a bad experience.

For dust protection use a non-toxic particle mask. For *less toxic* fumes a chemical mechanical filter using charcoal cartridges is appropriate. I use it when applying primer and lacquer finish coats. I also use this when applying plastic filler with the garage doors closed (styrene fumes).

Urethanes, hardened enamels, Imron and epoxy primers are significantly more toxic and for these I use a DeVilbiss hood-type respirator with an air supply. One of our neighbors walked by one night after dark when I was painting some bumpers with acrylic enamel and hardener in the driveway. "David??? what are you doing?" I should have told her I was playing deep-sea diver and if she didn't look out, that octopus behind the petunias would get her! – but I didn't. Mostly because my brain doesn't work that fast. Isocyanates are present in many of these products and can cause lung irritation and asthma-like allergic-respiratory reactions. If you are alone you could die. A friend passed out while spraying a Model A frame with Imron. Luckily he had someone else in the garage at the same time who was less sensitive to isocyanates. It is also smart to wear rubber gloves when painting both to avoid spray mists and so you don't have to wash your hands in reducer or thinner to remove the purple paint. Some of these organic liquids go right through your skin into your body so keep your hands out of the stuff.

Disassembly

Vol. 2, No. 4 Brett Johnson

How to Take Your 356 Apart

Before plunging into disassembly it is wise to invest in a copy of the good book, *The Official Factory Workshop Manual*. If you are foolish enough to buy a non-official version, you will never know whether or not your windshield wipers are at the right angle or how long your doors are, and a myriad of other essential details. Seriously, however, a shop manual is very helpful to the restorer. Most are relatively complete but lacking in detail, especially concerning the body work. The official Porsche manual can never be accused of not having enough detail. Unfortunately, they tend to be expensive and if beyond your means, manuals like *Clymer's* or *Autobooks* are adequate.

The first step in any restoration consists of disassembly. Depending on what you are planning this could be a minor or a major task. A thorough restoration consists of complete disassembly – all lights, trim, interior, suspension as well as engine and gearbox. While apart, these components may be reconditioned or replaced.

When taking the car apart, it is surprising how many things there are, how much room they take up, and how easy it is to forget over a period of months how to put it all back together again. It is helpful to be organized and put things in boxes, label parts and also to make drawings of potentially troublesome aspects (especially wiring).

An annoying problem encountered when disassembling a 356 is that things no longer come off as easily as they went on at the factory. Characteristically, small bolts break, large ones round off and intermediate-sized ones do a combination of the two. In an attempt to avoid this, generous applications of penetrating oil may be tried. However, don't expect miracles.

Bumper strips, rocker moldings, turnsignal units and horn grills are held on by the famous "Porsche one time studs". With the exception of a well maintained car, these will invariable break nine times out of ten. The large screw which holds on the headlight unit is also a prime candidate for breakage. Other problem areas include door sill and carpet edge strips. An impact screwdriver comes in handy, but some of those philips screws are bound to be stubborn. When all else fails, drill. When removing dual mount transaxles, you inevitably run across another Porsche feature, "the rotating stud". The rubber mount which secures the transaxle to the body has four studs within it and a combination of rust and de-vulcanization with old age results in studs which turn but don't loosen. The manner in which they are mounted makes breaking the nuts impossible.

The cure is drilling them out or using a cutting torch. Either way, new mounts will be required for re-assembly. There are other troublesome spots (removal of glass, door mechanisms, suspension) but these are well detailed in most shop manuals. All cars age differently and each car has certain unique features. I have a 356A which has a non-removable rear brake drum.

Spot Weld Removal

Vol. 4, No. 4 Rip Patterson and Wayne Potter

How to do it

Peeling spot welds saves the good panel and eliminates the swiss cheese effect. Saving time is what it's all about.

Tools: Pneumatic hammer with flat chisel, grinder with resinoid semi-ridged wheel, pliers, side cutters

Example: Longitudinal member at side box member floor pan junction. Since the Longitudinal member is to be replaced this can be sacrificed. Cut: tin snip, saber saw, air hammer chisel, nibbler, or parting blade; the longitudinal member at the outboard edge of the side member. This will leave about 20 mm ($^3/_4$ in.) along the side member lower lip still spot welded together. *Note:* If you use a saber saw, be careful. There are two bulkheads that support the heater duct. These can be damaged *plus* sawing up the longitudinal member can damage the fibre muffler duct running forward of the jacking post. Using the chisel, separate the strip from the side frame. It is usually solid enough to stay when the chisel is used to peel the strip along the lip. Crosswise you'll deform the lip you're trying to save. If the side frame gives, it is probably rusted through and will have to be replaced or patched. Using the grinder to thin the metal of the strip will allow the spots to be peeled like perforations using the pliers. The thinned metal fractures much easier and saves damage to the "good" metal. The small spot projections can be ground for a smooth lip ready for the new Longitudinal member. Of course some areas will need new metal at the front and rear. Similarly at the upper junction of the longitudinal member sill, and threshold the sill must be removed to make a good joint. Besides it probably has holes at the front and rear door posts.

Cut the sill as close to the upper bend as possible. Next clamp a heavy angle iron on top of the threshold. Trim and carpet are removed to put the bar directly on steel threshold. You now have provided a backing plate to prevent the parting chisel from bending and cutting the good metal. Spot welds here are generally light. The air chisel easily peels the metal strip without the need to grind first. If the peeling pulls holes or deforms the good metal *stop* and thin the strip with the grinder. Cut away the remaining longitudinal member and proceed to grind and/or peel as needed. Be sure the backing bar is well clamped, and you'll save the good threshold edge.

We have used these methods to successfully peel floor pan to side frame welds, battery box floors, floor pan to center section welds, inner fender panels to cowl sides, and others without creating the myriad of holes, which result from drilling out spot welds.

Sometimes it is necessary to sacrifice a good panel to get to the problem area. If it saves time and makes the job easier and neater, *do it!* If you restore as a hobby there are only so many hours available to play after you take care of the necessary duties at home.

Rust

Vol. 2, No. 5 Brett Johnson

Definition

Rust is from oxidized iron and there is no chemical process that will turn it back into sound metal without using a smelting furnace. There are a bewildering number of rust killers, rust eaters and other antirust potions in accessory shops. They all act by changing rust into a chemical compound which no longer attacks the metal but they will not put strength back.

Vol. 5, No. 4 Nancy and David Jones

What is Rust?

Rust is simply the reddish-brown residue from oxidation of iron. Any unprotected steel is quickly attacked by air and moisture and begins to rust in less than thirty minutes. The formula is:

Exposed Steel + Air + Moisture = Rust

Add in the corrosive catalyst of salt and the results can be devastating in a very short time. Given the steel body of a Porsche, the best way to try and prevent rust lies in protecting all steel surfaces from air, moisture, and possibly salt. The most common prophylaxis is a combination of paint and undercoating.

Rust and Porsches

The following analysis of that peculiar relationship between rust and Porsches is rather subjective, but seems fair, based on our personal experience. We believe the nature of the problem lies in two separate, but closely related areas: design of the vehicle and idiosyncrasies of the typical Porsche owner.

We cannot do much about the basic design of the vehicle. Without a doubt, there are inherent design deficiencies that encourage the development of rust and once incubated in these spots - the rust spreads with a vengeance. Later on, we will try to isolate some of these potential trouble spots in a section on "The Dirty Dozen".

On the other side of the coin, something can be done about the apparent idiosyncrasies of the typical Porsche owner. It seems to us that the usual Porsche-Pusher wants a car that looks sharp and performs well. Thus, the average Porsche has excellent paint, good interior, and well tuned engine, but the out-of-sight areas are also out-of-mind. Thus the undercoating is probably original and hasn't been looked at, much less worked on since the car was purchased. The rusted out battery box is forgotten since "they are all that way". For every article and hour spent on timing or valve adjustment, how much has been spent on rust prevention or detection? Let's all be more vigilant and increase our collective awareness of the rust problem.

That is the basic hope of this article.

Where Does Rust Start?

Rust will begin wherever the steel is not protected and exposed to the elements. This can range from a stone chip or door ding in the paint to an accident where the exterior was made to look like new but the undercoating was not repaired. The original or even replacement undercoating can dry and shrink leaving a pocket where condensation can nurture rust from the inside while all external surfaces look "good". Leaky rubber gaskets around any glass and/or a porous soft top will permit water to seep under the carpeting or behind the soundproofing to silently eat away at the body. The point is simply that rust will start anywhere a steel surface is not protected.

The deterioration following a paint chip is easy to observe. Since the latest 356s are now nearly 15 years old, and given the typical Porsche driver's desire for a good looking car, most have been repainted at least once. But many carry only what is left of the original factory undercoating to protect the underside. Deterioration in the non-painted areas is less easy to observe but more vital to the health of your car. Thus, it seems most useful to concentrate on the undercarriage. Do you even have any undercoating in the wheel wells where it may have been sandblasted off by 100,000 miles of road grit? Probe around under the car with a screwdriver or awl and you may well be shocked at what is or isn't there!

The Dirty Dozen

The surest way to see what is going on beneath any undercoating is to remove everything down to bare metal. This may be frowned upon if you are contemplating the purchase of a car in someone's driveway or merely want to check the condition of the car in your driveway. But with just your eyes and bare hands, you can examine closely some areas of the 356 that seem particularly susceptible to rust. The condition of these spots – which we affectionately refer to as "The Dirty Dozen" – should provide a reliable indication of the overall health of the undercarriage: .

(1) Battery Box Floor – this low spot collects all the water that gets past the hood gasket and the problem is compounded by corrosion from the battery and sloppy servicing of the battery;

(2) Headlight Buckets –the bottom will rust when the drain tube is clogged by a paint or rust flake; dirt and moisture thrown up by the wheels accumulate on top of the bucket where it abuts the fender and starts both of them rusting;

(3) Front Fender Brackets – "u" shape (in cross section) provides strength but also a place for moisture and debris to collect as rust eats back along the bracket and into the front bulkhead;

(4) Door Joint Closing Panels – in an incredible design defect, the top portion is curved back providing an ideal storage shelf for everything thrown up by the wheels (why not clean this area right now!);

(5) Longitudinal Or Strut Reinforcing Member – water just lies in bottom of the channel;

(6) Diagonal Member – that critical "v" shaped support in the center of the car has those strength-giving indentations – enough said...;

(7) Longitudinal Member – rusts from the inside-out and outside-in;

(8) Jack Receivers – especially where attached to longitudinal member;

(9) Floor Pan – particularly either side of pedal cluster where water and salt drip off shoes and remain behind the pedal boards where there is no air circulation;

(10) Running Boards – water drips from drain holes in the door onto the rubber mat covering the running

board, gravitates to the rear and attacks both the running board and base of the lockpost;

(11) Lock Posts – base is worst place, but also the flanged edge with fender and area where door latch is attached to the lock post; and finally,

(12) Doors – especially the bottom after the rubber window seal has deteriorated and the drain holes have been plugged.

Paint/Rust Removal

Vol. 2, No. 4 Brett Johnson

Chemical Paint Removal

Dipping the entire car is an efficient and rapid means of stripping and derusting. Of course, it is best if the car can be almost totally disassembled although the solvents will not harm wood, rubber or fiberglass – just the paint, undercoat and rust. After the car is stripped it is sprayed with a rust-inhibiting treatment. Cost will vary with the particular establishment.

A less drastic form of the same procedure involves stripping of removable panels. It is much easier to find a place which can accommodate doors and hoods than one with facilities for dipping a complete car. Prices are variable but generally quite high. This was a paint and rust removing chemical similar to the type described above. Because these panels were oddly enough rust free, I took them to a furniture stripper. His chemical solution was not strong enough to affect rust but removed the paint quite well.

Paint stripper is chemically corrosive and generally unpleasant to work with. According to the instructions it is applied by brush, the paint loosens, and you wash it away with a stream of water. If only it worked like that. By the time you work through three coats of paint, you have applied three to four coats of paint stripper and your stream of water had best be assisted

by a putty knife. Cleaning up the resultant mess is no fun either. Considering the cost of paint stripper versus my commercial furniture stripper, I know I saved time and labor. This is not to say that paint stripping should never be attempted. If you can't afford or rationalize dipping, it's about the only way to remove paint aside from sanding.

Undercoating which covers the bottom of your floor and tar which covers the top present new problems. When they were originally applied they were not intended to come off and thus they don't, or at least not very well. The two no-cost methods are scraping and heating and scraping. Both are a lot of work and hardly fun. However, they are successful and a follow-up sand-blasting makes quite a nice job of it. Of course, if the car was dipped you don't have to worry about undercoating.

Now that the paint and undercoat are gone, the metal will quickly begin to oxidize if paint is not applied. Thus, before you do any patching, you might consider applying metal conditioner and a light coat of primer as an interim measure. Metal conditioner, primer and thinner are available at your local auto body supply house. You need very little metal conditioner as it goes a long way.

Vol. 2, No. 4 Brett Johnson

Sand Blasting

Sand blasting is an excellent rust remover. It also removes dirt and loose under coat. It is cheap and available almost everywhere. Unfortunately, the heat and pressure have harmful effects on sheet metal contours (warping) and under no circumstances (except for rust removal) should exterior body panels be sandblasted. In addition, due to the resilient nature of both tar and undercoating, sandblasting alone has negligible effect and should not be used specifically for this

294

purpose. Another drawback with sandblasting is the damaging overspray. It pits glass and paintwork even remotely close to the area being blasted and infiltrates oil seals, air filters, and wheel bearings. It is important that all potentially damageable components are covered with a combination of heavy non-porous material and silver duct tape. Prices vary widely from place to place and depending on the amount of work done but generally are reasonable.

Glass beading is a variety of sandblasting using larger grains. Many machine shops use it for cleaning heads. The main problem is most of these units are small and can only cope with small items such as bumper brackets. The cautions are essentially the same as with sandblasting.

Vol. 4, No. 3 Rip Patterson and Wayne Potter

Sand Blasting Horror Stories

How many times have you heard of the Porsche Nut that had his car completely sand blasted for a good paint base? Only to end up with wavy sheet metal and sand in every crevice forevermore. The sheet metal waves created by the high pressure you say. *Not so!* Heat caused the metal to warp. The high velocity sand hitting the metal in a localized spot heats the metal red hot. As the nozzle is moved this hot spot warps the panel just like a welding torch. Try your Sears Sandblast gun on a piece of 18 gauge some night and see the hot spot. As Jim O'Neil said at Indianapolis 356 Registry Holiday, sandblasting is good for cleaning local areas of rusted metal for repairing or on heavy members. Body panels, hoods, and deck lids should not be sandblasted. Sometime you can get away with it; most of the time it means trouble.

Vol. 4, No. 3 Mike Woodham

Undercoating Removal

I am currently getting relatively close to the completion of a ground-up restoration on a 1963 B coupe. I had gone through the long and hard task of undercoating removal on several other previous 356s, and believe me, I was willing to try almost anything to make it an easier, faster, and better process.

About this time, a friend (who once owned several new 356s and now restores antique cars) gave me information on a sandblasting unit manufactured by Truman Industrial Products in Canfield, Ohio. They usually run a full page ad in *Hemmings Motor News* and do a lot of business with antique restoration people.

Well, I'm sure the word sandblast puts some people into instant fear and skepticism, but let me say right now that this Truman sand blaster is without a doubt the best money I ever spent for restoration related equipment. The company offers several model blasters. The smaller ones are primarily intended for home/hobby use of very rugged construction, as well as larger models for commercial use. The smallest is the TIP-30, but probably the most popular model is the TIP-50 (numerical figures denote sand capacity in lbs.) There are several factors which make these blasters so good. First of all, by design, the sand is placed in a "pot", which is pressurized by the air supply. This puts the sand under pressure before it ever enters the hose, which is also supplied with direct air. By using this type setup, a smaller air supply with less output is required, as compared to large commercial blasters, or even comparable size conventional blasters. By "conventional" I mean that old design sand blasters, even small units, worked strictly on the siphon-feed principle. Simply, large amounts of air had to be available to "suck" the sand from its container up a hose, with no additional "help". Truman says their equipment will do twice the work, using half the sand and half the air. I have a Sears 3 hp twin cylinder compressor with a 20 gal. tank, rated at 9.2 scfm @ 40 PSI, and have found that it keeps up with the blaster quite well. It will never pump up and stop during blasting operations, however, but will manage to maintain 70 - 75 lbs. at the pot, which provides enough force for most operations. At this point, please, don't misunderstand me, I'm no salesman for this company. It's just that they have a fine product worth telling about, and I know that many people restoring Porsches could use such equipment. All the models are shown and described, along with a section on paint equipment and other shop goodies in their free catalog: TIP Sandblast Equipment, 7075 Rte. 446, PO Box 649, Canfield, OH 44406, (800) 321-9260.

So, on to our main topic. By using this sand blaster, (I have the model TIP-50, which now costs $200) not only is undercoating easy to deal with, but so is the largest of problems – *rust*.

Some people may say that not every Porsche needs its undercoating removed, especially if it appears to be in good shape with a good base metal. This may be basically true. On my 1963, I had areas that still contained good, *live* factory undercoating. However, even though these areas did look good, only a few scrapes would sometimes reveal thin layers of surface rust which had developed just under the coating. So, the question is, why leave areas which may be in doubt? True, only thin minor surface rust may present no problem in certain areas of California and the South West, but in the rest of the Country, especially places with high moisture levels and temperature changes, a seemingly insignificant amount of rust can really spread.

With sand blasting all fender well areas, the pan (inside and out), engine compartment, transaxle area (with the transaxle removed!), headlight buckets, battery compartment, etc. can be cleaned of everything, including rust. And I do mean everything. Believe me, its a beautiful sight to see a fender well with that clean, slightly dull look of freshly blasted metal. Of course, it's very important to prime this bare metal with a good quality, rust-resistant paint. I use Rustoleum Damp-Proof Red Primer, #769 (available in spray cans or cans for brushing) which contains fish oil. I'm sure a lot of folks are acquainted with the Rustoleum products. This stuff really does prevent rust, especially if the metal is like new and clean when its applied. This priming should be done as soon as possible after an area is blasted, because just the moisture in the air can start a thin film of "brown" on the metal in a relatively short period of time. The nice part is that you can do a fender well in 10 - 15 minutes, and when you're finished, you know its right. Most old and original undercoating comes off almost as if it were dirt; no problem. My 1962 was in original condition, and of course had some rust. Surface rust was removed with ease, while bad areas took a little longer. Now, if you get to an area where the sand starts to eat through the metal, so what, let it go. You want to get rid of every trace of rust. Remember, rust is like a cancer; you want to get every trace. If a metal section is thin and weak enough to break through anyway, you will probably want to replace it.

Another nice feature about sandblasting is that you can get into all those cracks, seams and areas where it is impossible to get a wire brush or even your hand. Naturally, the more stripped-down the Porsche is, the better, especially if you're after a full restoration. I had everything out of my car that could be taken out or removed, except torsion bars, trailing arms, etc. The car was practically a bare shell.

A very special piece of equipment was next rigged up for supporting this shell. I took an old four-wheeled warehouse dolly, approximately 3 x 6 ft., and welded an angle iron frame to it that was about the same dimensions as the pan of a 356. After putting the Porsche on this dolly and frame assembly, the wheels, brakes, and transaxle could then be removed without immobilizing the whole thing. Also, the car can be rolled outside for blasting and then back in the shop for other work and storage. This set-up also places the rocker panels of the car approximately one meter off the ground, which is a good height for working on various areas.

On a final note, I also removed the paint via sand blasting. This may also cause some people to grimace. Yes, this can cause warping of the body metal due to heat build-up at the point of sand impact. However, as I have stated, this blaster uses minimal air pressure, and a significant build-up of heat never takes place.

Now is a good time to mention sand, which is an all important factor. I use the finest grade commercial blasting sand available. I'm fortunate to live only a few minutes from a silica mining company, which has no less than eight grades of blasting sand. They actually grade the sand according to a grit number, similar to sand paper. By using the finer grades of sand and relatively low air pressure, metal damage is all but impossible, and metal pitting is held to a minimum. Actually, slight metal pitting caused by blasting is a good thing. This creates a good, slightly grain-like surface which offers excellent adhesion for paint films. I did, however, go over the body lightly with dry 180 grit sand paper after the blasting to smooth any slight burns. Usually one good coat of primer surfacer will fill all these blasting pits.

In closing, I'd like to say that every process has some "drawbacks". Sand blasting makes one hell of a mess. Sand goes everywhere, so its imperative to have an area in your back yard or behind your shop so the sand can go where ever it wants. If you decide to do any blasting with any trim pieces or glass in the body, they must be covered and protected and be as careful as possible not to get too close. Even if the body is stripped, you will do good to tape all holes, cracks, and areas, especially inside the car and around the instrument panel, where you don't want sand to get. Then, after all blasting is completed, take an air hose and start blowing, everywhere, from all directions. It'll take a while to get it all out, and some places will have to be vacuumed, but when its all done, you'll have a perfectly clean, rust free Porsche body ready for paint, interior, and mechanical installation, almost like it was back at Zuffenhausen!

Vol. 4, No. 3 Robert Gummow

Undercoat Removal
My 1959 coupe is absolutely devoid of any undercoating anywhere! It can be done. Back in the winter of 1966, when I began my project. I removed a loose flake of undercoating and went to visit a friend at Smith Oil Chemical Division. After experimenting with several potions there, we found that a substance made by L&A Products, called Formula 60, really ate the undercoating. Harold told me that this was an industrial paint remover. It is purple in color, jelly-like in consistency and has good clinging ability. I recommended it to Chuck Shank who later informed me that it is NLA. He did find a few cans by scouring Chicago. Therefore, I would try any heavy-duty paint remover, the thicker the better, so that it doesn't drip too excessively.

If you do your own panel beating, painting, etc. this is better, as you can put the car on stands and remove the engine, transaxle and all suspension front and rear. Also, steering box, damper, tie-rods, master brake cylinder – in other words, anything that can be unbolted. With all these items removed, you will be surprised how easy it is to get into those comers and other difficult places.

Do one area at a time, like a fender well. Spread newspapers under the work area, pour your favorite potion into a bowl and paint it on generously with a 2 in. brush. Allow it to penetrate for a half-hour or longer, depending on how dense the undercoating is. The basic tool will be a good steel putty knife or scraper with a blade 1 $1/2$ in. wide, sharpened. Make a test scrape.

If the remover has soaked in, the scraper will reach the metal and the undercoating will peel off in strips. This stuff is gooey and sticky and the Frau will become alarmed when you track it in on the carpets.

After most of the undercoating is scraped off, the tar-like residue left can be wiped off with a turpentine soaked rag.

Open and clean the drain areas in the body; one under each of the rear windows; the two small pipes from the fuel tank area which exit at the inside of the front fender wells; the opening at the bottom of the V-structure where it is welded to the front of the bellypan; and of course, the battery box.

After the necessary sheet metal repairs are completed, the underside may be cleaned further by wire brushing, hand sanding rough spots, and filing off sharp comers.

In my case I did not do the finish work on the underside of my 356 until the entire exterior was painted, in order to avoid the dust and overspray on the newly painted underside.

Is this the end of the undercoating removal saga? Not really. I found that the factory had rewarded me further by spraying another 14 lbs. in each

door, impeding the drainage process and thereby causing that horizontal line of rust that was beginning to appear at the bottom of the door. The doors are easy to clean. After everything is removed they can be placed flat on the bench for easy access. Use the same removal procedure as with the bottom. The seam at the bottom must be thoroughly cleaned of rust. A thin-edged blade, such as a knife from Frau's Kuche will do here. After the door is repaired it is again cleaned and the seam blown out with compressed air.

After cleaning and preparing the metal, various finishes may be used. With a brush, I applied Rustoleum Damp-proof Red Primer, followed by two coats of medium gloss black. Rustoleum paint, primer and thinner all contain a fish oil base. Do not use or mix with any other type paint. In seam areas, such as the bottoms of the doors, it should be thinned so that it will penetrate the seam generously.

By now, all the suspension parts, backing plates, axle tubes, etc. which you have left at the platers are ready! (a little satire there). Anyway, after all of these pieces are refinished and properly installed, brake drums polished, etc., there is your old 356 still on the jack stands. You haven't put the wheels on yet because you are still admiring the net result of a good investment in time and labor. After much scraping, wire brushing, filing, sanding and finally a careful painting, the bottom of your 356 looks better then the top side of many.

Vol. 4, No. 5 Bob Frank

More Sand Blasting
First off, Body preparation for undercoating or painting. To blast or not to blast – that is the question. I tend to agree with most of Mike Woodham's findings and it's surely from experience he speaks. One thing he did not stress was the absolute

298

necessity of having a proper hood and mask for spraying sand; besides all the sand on the floor, the driveway and wherever else you'll end up with an equal share in your ears, eyes, mouth and shorts so proper protection is a must. Even with low pressure (75# or so) there is such a cloud of sand everywhere I'm sure I saw Lawrence of Arabia galloping through the ensuing haze.

Sandblasting is elective yes, but it will not always completely rid the metal of rust unless you follow up with a chemical rust neutralizer. The metal will appear to be clean but microscopic particles of oxide will still be present and will come back to haunt you some day. The best follow-on treatment would be a zinc paint coating, at least on the underbody, but an 8 oz. can of pure zinc (95% zinc, 5% epoxy binder) costs over $10 and will do about two fenders. Rustoleum is a fine substitute and besides the colors are lovely.

Has anyone tried the "dip and strip" method of paint removal? I did on my still incomplete 1956 Speedster. The commercial stripping vats are what I am referring to where the whole process consists of paint removal, derusting and a final dip in a phosphate solution and the car comes out squeaky clean, But, it ain't cheap. Mine cost $230 for all three processes (you can have any one or all) and there are some pitfalls. You had better unbolt every part that is not welded on, aside from the obvious removal of your favorite leather seats and the "Bra", you best remove even the torsion bars and all suspension and steering parts too. It seems the steering gear box cover was made of aluminum and now it looks like a wormwood antique. Just recently I got around to checking the trailing arm setting and figured I might as well renew the grease on the torsion bars at the same time. They were nicely embalmed in some of the dipping solution but luckily not cor-

roded! There are some other little hazards too; carting the body to the stripper requires a trailer or truck and the underside of the body ends up with little dings and nicks all over some of which are nearly impossible to remove. Would I do it again? I doubt it, besides the smell of paint remover turns me on and I get to play "Body-man" with my $99 body grinder. As they say in the bodyshop trade, "you can have it good, you can have it fast and you can have it cheap – but you can't have all three at the same time."

Vol. 4, No. 6 Dave Russell

Chemical Paint Removal
    The following article concerning removal of paint and rust was supplied by Dave Russell, General Manager of Resto-strip Chemical Paint and Rust Removal in Westlake Village. California.

The 356 Porsche with its frequent problems of paint and undercoat build-up over rusted sheet and structural steel deserves special attention to insure the future of the remaining cars. The various degrees to which the 356 owner can aspire in a restoration should each include attention to the rust problem, and when there is the opportunity for a complete treatment of the integral body, the restorer should take advantage of the time and effort-saving processes available. The choice of paint and rust removal methods cannot be made lightly, however, in that the stripping of a Porsche car is a fairly complex affair, and experience indicates serious consequences for a wrong approach. For what may have seemed to have been a thoroughly paint-stripped and de-rusted body later becomes a nightmare of rejected paint.

The restorer who has gone to great lengths to prepare the metal surfaces will probably never again consider the expedient approach, and will be satisfied to return to his hand-scraping and grinding methods.

So there is a matter for argument among the restorers concerning the merits and pitfalls of the two best-known industrial methods of coating and corrosion removal from steel: sandblasting and chemical stripping. The utilities of each are discussed at length but it is chemical stripping which likely emerges as the most practical and thorough method. But as the dangers of sandblasting are easily recognized (pitting through thin sheet metal, deforming and loss of temper, and residual sand particles), the drawbacks to chemical stripping have been of subtle sorts and are just now being understood and corrected in an industry which is really less than ten years old.

As the demand has increased considerably for chemical treatment facilities capable of accepting automobile bodies, so also in recent years has there been a demand for stock chemical formulations and procedures for use in the stripping business. A number of chemical systems have been made available to the industry and have been somewhat casually accepted for their apparent effectiveness. It is not surprising then that there are also some casual problems that have appeared in various forms. From bleeding and staining of purple cyanic compounds to paint attack from residual alkalines, the complications can become evident a week, a month, or even years later.

The general feeling here is that when the stripping process is complete that the metal surfaces and mating-metal seams be as chemically clean as possible. Such chemically clean metal has had all paint and undercoat removed in a hot alkaline solution, rust removed in an acidic solution, and has been water washed and rinse neutralized. In addition the metal has not been returned to the alkaline tank after acid treatment, nor has it been treated with a rust-preventitive reducing agent or other chemicals which serve to give the metal a "new look".

Even as the "new look" of post-acid treated sheet metal can be easily appreciated by the customer, the proprietor's parenthetical instructions to be sure to wipe off the metal before priming are understating a serious consideration: that paint will not be compatible if these various chemicals are present, and the unlikelihood of being able to remove them by mere wiping.

It is for the most part that the proprietor will give these instructions with honest intention and near confidence. But come a humid day months later when mating metal-trapped alkaline capillaries out to attack the fresh paint, then it becomes apparent that the understating of instructions becomes an understatement in itself.

Again it should be emphasized that the important consideration with all stripping operations is the final chemical and particulate cleanness of the metal sheet. Here it is recommended that the sheet, having been paint-stripped, de-rusted and acid neutralized, be allowed to flash oxidize as it air dries. For appearances' sake this would indicate that the metal is rusting again and it certainly is, but in a controlled manner that actually protects the sheet. It is an oxidation that is spread evenly over the metal and is easily removed by the metal conditioner (dilute phosphoric acid) that is recommended before most priming operations. And from experience this flashed sheet can be stored as is for quite a long time (at least in the drier climates) but ideally should be primed soon afterwards.

The allowing of flash to occur is the simplest case under the general principle that at the point where the sheet metal is chemically clean it should not be exposed to any agents which will interfere with the primer and paint adhesion processes. This leaves open the options for treatment with pre-priming intermediates like the so-called hot phosphating process, though it must be cautioned here that phosphating need be a precisely controlled process requiring a degree of sophistication. Equally critical would be maintenance and use of anti-oxidants like BHTA in solution which may be used to check flash in the interim before priming. It would then be on the safe side to prefer nothing after the neutralization rinse to something questionable.

So it becomes apparent that the claim of a "rust-free" 356 Porsche may be as dubiously offered as a claim for an "original" car. But attention to the rust problem is energy well-spent as it becomes more clear that the integrity of the bodies is the first concern in perpetuating the vintage 356.

Vol. 10, No. 3 David Seeland

Chemical Paint Removal at Home
Should you remove all the paint? Probably, particularly if the car has had multiple repaints. It is possible to remove a single repaint without damage to the underlying original paint (if the original was enamel) by working on small sections at a time, then as soon as the repaint softens, remove it with a stiff rubber squeegee. The two inch square blocks that 3M sells for spot putty should work well. Do not use a metal scraper because you'll get scratches that are hard to remove.

If the car was in excellent condition – very few dents, scratches, chips and so forth, then it might be easier to leave the original paint in place. However, it will be much harder to block-sand scratches and orange-peel out of the original paint than out of primer-surfacer. I usually remove all the paint.

It helps to use various brands of paint remover as they seem to vary in their effectiveness on different types of paint. The more expensive viscous types are the only kinds to buy. The watery less expensive kind don't stay put long enough to soften the paint.

Before removing the paint, take your 2500 rpm drill and a 3M 36 grit Roloc disc and grind on all the door dings and other small imperfections. This is to mark them so when you get the paint off you can tell where the dents were – they are much easier to see when the car is still shiny.

Remove most of the paint with the windows in place. This keeps the paint remover off the dash top and seats. Carefully complete the paint removal with the windows out, and please don't paint your car without removing all the windows. The most noticeable indication that a car has been repainted is paint on the window seals. Furthermore, the area under the seals is a favorite breeding place for rust and if you don't take care of it (grinding, naval jelly or metal prep), the rust will crawl out of its hiding place and lift off your shiny new paint.

If you want to save the seals, take a blunt screwdriver and with adjacent repetitive pushes, push the inside rubber lip outside the body lip (which has the headliner glued and clipped to it). Then push the windshield, seal, and aluminum trim loose as a unit. *Do not* remove the aluminum trim first, or you will bend the trim and not be able to straighten it. Cut the lip off the rubber if you are going to replace the seal.

To reinstall, put the rubber seal on, reinsert the aluminum trim, and place a drapery-pull sized cord in the body-lip groove. Overlap the ends of this cord. Lubricate everything with talc or slightly diluted detergent or glycerine or silicone spray or whatever. Have someone push down from the outside while you use the cord to pull the rubber lip over the body lip. I use a $1/8$ in. piece of heavy wire bent into a $5/8$ in. by 6 in. "L" to help coax the rubber over the body lip. I fastened the "L" to a handle after filing the $5/8$ in. tip smooth and round.

301

Don't consider dipping the car. I don't feel that all the chemicals can be removed from all the cracks and crevices. Besides, you will be removing paint from places that are next to impossible to get at to repaint. A final objection – it has been said that paint adhesion is poor on leaded area that have been dipped. This could be a problem with do-it-yourself paint removers too, but I haven't seen it happen. Just in case, I'd sand the leaded areas after using paint remover.

If you want to do the best job possible, it is best to strip all the paint including door edges, hinge area, lockposts, undersides of lids, etc. Unless you carefully mask off all the areas where the original paint is to remain, you'll likely get dribbles of remover onto the paint resulting in a "dribble-mark" under the paint. You could carefully fill each one, but they'll probably still show. The underside of most rear decks on repainted cars is peeling because they have a tendency to get oily. Painting oily surfaces doesn't work well. Stripping the paint makes sure you get the oil off.

Be sure to remove all stripper residue or the subsequent paint will not dry. If you get areas of primer that do not dry, beware, there are still traces of remover on the surface and you'll have sticky top-coats too. Remove the primer and remover residue and reprime. To avoid this problem, scrub thoroughly with steel wool and water rinse, wipe with lacquer thinner and finally, sand lightly.

Paint can also be ground off with a coarse grit (16, 24, 36) on a body grinder but you are very likely to grind flats on crowned panels. I have found it better to use a 36 grit Roloc disc in an electric drill although it takes more time. It is often very difficult to get all the factory primer off with paint remover and this is where I often resort to grinding. Thick plastic should also be removed with a grinder. Plastic filler can also be removed

by heating with a torch and then scraping with a putty knife.

One final thought on complete paint removal: you will also be removing all the plastic that was ever applied to the body and it will all have to be redone. One positive aspect is that you should be able to use much less of it with a bit of hammer and dolly work.

Vol. 16, No 6 Brett Johnson

Paint Removal Methods Comparison
Virtually everyone has heard all sorts of horror stories about things that are ruined by one or another form of stripping.

There are five basic types of paint stripping:

1. Chemical strippers that come in a can, like Zip-Strip
2. Chemical strippers that come in a great big vat, like Redi-Strip
3. Sand blasting
4. Media blasting
5. Sanding or grinding

The first variety of paint removers generally have a couple of associated complaints. They don't work as well as you think they should and you have to do coat after coat and spend hours and hours doing it. You also have to wear protective clothing and most importantly, it makes a mess. When you're done, you still end up having to sand the remaining paint off of the car. It also has no effect on rust.

On the plus side, it is reasonably inexpensive, and can be done in the confines of your driveway or garage. This last feature can be a real plus for the hobbyist restorer, who doesn't plan to totally dismantle the car and put it on a rotisserie.

I've got to admit, I didn't really know a great deal about chemical stripping, except the horror stories. Most of the stories have to do with parts that do not get all traces of metal eating chemical removed and involve ruined multi-thousand dollar paint

302

jobs or worse.

When Bruce Baker at Auto Research recommended that it should be done on #10712, he put me in touch with Marc Albanese at Redi-Strip of Allentown, Allentown, PA. I asked Marc to do a brief scenario of the process.

"After receiving the completely disassembled car which included body shell (sans floor), doors, trunk, deck lid, and various repair panels, we inspected the items and determined the best way to process them."

"The doors and body had a good amount of undercoating, caulk and sound deadening (although much less than the A, B and Cs). We put them into our refractory brick-lined kiln and baked it off at around 650° for four hours. We placed the deck lid, hood and miscellaneous sheet metal that didn't have undercoating into our hot strip tank."

"We removed the car body and doors the next morning, after they had cooled to room temperature (to prevent warping). They were then rinsed with high pressure hot water where most of the solvent based chemicals which were turned to ash from baking blew off. They were then put into the hot strip tank to finish the job. After 24 hours, they were removed and rinsed with high pressure hot water."

"They were then put into our derusting tank for approximately 36 hours, then rinsed again (each rinse up to this point was approximately one hour). The car and parts then went into a neutralizing bath for 24 hours. They were then rinsed with a special water based solution to prevent flash rusting for approximately two hours. Finally everything was allowed to air dry and was ready for Bruce to pick up."

"We usually then advise how to prepare the parts for paint. We recommend heating all seams with a heat gun or propane torch. This is the most important step. It insures no chemical bleed through. (The seams are where metal is joined to metal). The body should then be washed with "prep sol" (available at body shop supply businesses) to remove any impurities from handling and transporting. It is then ready for priming and sealing."

"I would like to stress that we do R & D on the best ways to prepare our parts for paint. I currently am restoring a 1959 365A sunroof coupe, which we dipped. I pass along any helpful hints to Bruce and other customers restoring Porsches."

Bruce pointed out that in areas where problems have occurred in the past, such as door bottoms, it is a good idea to open up the seam prior to dipping so that proper neutralization can occur. Other drawbacks to this process include the total disassembly part, unsuitability for certain non-ferrous metal parts and relatively high cost:

Marc supplied the following prices for 356s:

Body $1200
Door $85
Front lid $100
Rear lid $45
Gas tank $100
Engine sheet metal $175

On the positive side, it is the most thorough way to remove both paint and rust. If done properly, no body panel distortion occurs.

He also pointed out that while their particular Redi-Strip location did not do aluminum or magnesium, other locations have that capability. They are set up to do stripping of small zinc and pot-metal castings.

Sandblasting does a nice job on large thick things like bridges. It can be used on thick 356 parts, such as wheels and iron/steel-based suspension components with reasonable success and it is generally less expensive than other methods. Use on thin metal items such as body panels often leads to warping or distortion due to the heat generated by the process. The resulting surface of stripped metal is noticeably rough textured.

If the surfaces are covered with the road filth of the ages, the sand will likely be unable to penetrate (Sand also "bounces off" flexible surfaces like rubber), so you must clean parts prior to blasting.

For removal of structural rust, sandblasting is second only to dipping. The risk of distortion of the remaining good metal is still a significant problem, though. It is also generally not possible to get all of the sand swept out of all of those nooks and crannies that make 356s the endearing vehicles they are. So you get anything from the beach movie effect to, the ruined mechanical parts from stray grit, to the grains of sand in your paint problem. Careful masking and cleanup will help reduce this, but nothing eliminates it.

"Media" blasting is the new kid on the paint removal block. It is similar to sandblasting in that particles are sprayed at reasonably high velocity to physically remove paint. The particles are made of plastic (recyclable for those who care) and their size varies with the material under the paint. It can be used on steel, aluminum, fiberglass or even wood. Because of the low amount of heat generated by this process, a skilled operator (key words) can effectively remove the paint from a soda can without distortion. To keep the paint, metal and other residue particles from contaminating the media, sophisticated filtration systems have been developed, so that the media may be reused.

It still has the "mess factor" and does not have the rust removing capabilities of sand or chemical stripping, but definitely has a significant place in the restoration scenario. It may be difficult to find shops with this capability (or competency), due to comparative recency to the scene. Prices in this area seem to be a little high.

The final method of sanding or

grinding works; I've done it several times. It makes a mess and you need to have a grinder that lasts longer than an hour and doesn't heat up to the point that it glows in the dark, i.e. not one from K-mart. I bought a used electric one at Sears for less than $70. Air powered ones make a niftier sound and generally spin faster and weigh less. You also need a respirator and protective eyewear, even if you plan to do it outside.

It is inexpensive, fairly time consuming requiring total dismantling of your car.

So what's best? It depends on you and your situation; all have good and bad points. The situation with my car #10712, was that media blasting was done first, but the amount of structural rust required additional action. The media did a nice job of paint removal without distortion. It left the traces of chrome plating on the side window frames in place and revealed nasty nose and tail repair of restorations past.

Vol. 16, No. 6 Ron LaDow

Sandblasting vs. Plastic Bead Blasting
Since the Speedster was to undergo pretty serious modification, that car was sandblasted in 1971.

The car had been thoroughly disassembled, in that anything which didn't need a cutting torch or a cold chisel had been removed. The removed panels were also hit by the blaster. It worked, and unlike the chemical strips, there have never been funny bubbles creeping up under the paint near the various body seams. The process also removed the hardened undercoating from the bottom of the car, and we all know how pleased I was with that result.

On the other hand, the process is sufficiently violent that removal of old bondo would have damaged the underlying panels from heat generated; that stuff got removed by scraping/sanding/etc. The sand also got into every-thing. Everything!

What looked to be completely closed areas got sand in them. The clutch and emergency brake conduits through the tunnel were packed with sand (giant "Q-tips" made of welding rod and paper towel wads worked, but slowly. The first wads were soaked in solvent, the later ones dry, and finally the vacuum cleaner and air compressor completed the process. Then, you get to re-pack the conduits with grease. Oh, boy!). During the entire fabrication/reconstruction, which lasted a further ten years, the sand continued to rain down and leak out of unknown sources, and this wasn't from a lack of cleaning effort. Even now, while cleaning the car, I'll come upon small piles of sand.

Plastic-bead-blasting was done on my non-Porsche vintage racer. While the same caveats apply to the mess involved, I'm told that the media is available in various hardnesses, and so can be "tuned" to the job at hand. My aluminum tub came back completely bereft of paint, with the aluminum untouched and unwarped. The fiber-glass parts came back with the paint gone, and most of the gel-coat still in place. If this stuff got into 356 cable conduits it probably wouldn't make the grinding compound that the sand does (in mixture with grease), and depending on the grit of the sandpaper you select, may leave deep grooves in your sheet metal, definitely in the leaded areas. It also is one of the methods not as likely to eat the cables.

It seems that the plastic-bead-blast has sort of made the sand-blast tech-nique obsolete for our purposes. This is the process I'll use on the next effort, but a couple of cautions still apply:

A) Use either of the above only if you plan complete disassembly (and restoration). Cleaning up the mess will require it.

B) This applies to other services as well: Talk to various vendors and their customers. Don't allow your car to become the practice piece for some on-the-job-training effort. Why do I have to keep relearning this?

Ron's last bit of sage advice is true for chemical stripping, as well. Know what type of metal you are putting in the tank. I remember hearing about a Gmünd coupe that was having its steel doors dipped. When the shell was removed the aluminum inner structure had dissolved...

Vol. 17, No. 1 Brett Johnson

More Information on Dipping

A letter also poured in from John Mueller of Barrington, IL. concerning the discussion of chemical dipping described in my last column. He included a reprint from Midwest Rod & Machine which described the pro-cess used by International Metal Strip-ping (IMS) in St. Paul, MN. I phoned there and received some additional information and then spoke to Marc at Redi-Strip of Allentown, who did my car. I am now much better educated about chemical stripping and will attempt to explain the variations in an understandable manner...

In the last issue Marc described the process used by his company, Redi-Strip of Allentown (RSA) which con-sisted of:

1. Baking the shell and other parts to remove undercoat, plastic body fill-er and most of the paint. This proce-dure takes four hours.

2. Rinse with high pressure hot water.

3. Dip in hot strip tank (also called caustic or alkaline tank) for 24 hours to finish remaining paint and body fill-er removal.

4. Rinse with high pressure hot water.

5. Dip in derusting tank (also called acid tank) for approximately 36 hours.

6. Rinse with high pressure hot water.

7. Dip in neutralizing tank for two hours.

8. Rinse with water based solution that inhibits surface rust.

Marc recommended that all seams be heated with a propane torch or heat gun to insure that no chemical bleed through takes place.

The procedure at IMS is different. It consists of the following steps:

1. Parts and body shell dipped in hot caustic tank for removal of paint, body filler, dirt and grease.

2. Rinse with high pressure hot water.

3. Dip in electrolytic rust removal tank. Time in this tank is dependent on amount and extent of rust.

4. Rinse with water based solution that inhibits surface rust.

It is perhaps worth mentioning first that "Redi-Strip" is not a process, but rather a company that sells equipment. It is up to the end user, if they wish to use the name in association with their business. Depending on the location, different processes may be used, including media-blasting and various methods of chemical stripping. Indeed, both methods listed above have been used by Marc in Allentown. The main drawback in his case for the latter method was the local water supply which has high mineral content, making it difficult and time consuming.

Comparing the two methods, the omission of the oven baking phase at IMS is, again, just one of personal preference. Ignoring it, they both start exactly the same way, with a hot caustic dip, followed by rinsing. They also end the same way with a rust inhibiting rinse.

The steps in the middle are how they differ. At IMS the car becomes part of an electrochemical reaction. The chemical balance of the tank is alkaline rather than acidic. Current is applied to graphite electrodes immersed in the solution. Negative current causes release of oxygen from Fe_2O_3 (rust), causing the iron molecules to go into the solution. Periodically the current is reversed which causes release of hydrogen gas which repels negatively charged particles of soil. In this method only rusty metal is attacked because only rusty metal has oxygen in it.

At RSA instead of the electrochemical reaction there is just a chemical reaction. Inhibitors in the acidic solution prohibit attack on the solid metal. In order to have a substantial "lightening" of non-rusted metal, pieces would need to remain in the tank for months. Rinsing and neutralizing are necessary though to stop the reaction from continuing to progress from rust to good metal in the years following.

Another potential problem during rust removal concerns metal becoming brittle in the process. While this seems to be mostly associated with acid dipping, it also occurs with caustic dipping and sand blasting, as well. The knowledge and care of the facility operator and staff has a major impact on the final results.

The take home message here is to find out as much as you can about the options in your area before doing anything. Ask for the names of shops and/ or individuals that have had work done in the past. Talk with the people at the stripper to find out what procedures are used. People who take pride in their work generally are more than happy to tell you about what they do. If you find that they are "car people", you've probably found a place that will understand what you want.

If this discussion has not been thorough enough, you might want to contact Marc Albanese at (215) 432-2324. He has put together a 20 minute video that takes you through the entire procedure, using a 356A coupe. Putting "pictures" with words certainly helped me understand it better.

Bodywork, Rust Repair

Vol. 2, No. 5 Brett Johnson

Rust and Chemicals

There are two types of rust which the 356 owner is likely to encounter, surface rust and structural rust. Though outwardly a lesser problem, surface rust may be the start of a nice new hole and must be dealt with accordingly.

First, prepare yourself with a drill and sanding disc or disc-sander. The paper I use is 3M 20 grit. It is relatively cheap, has a strong backing, is very coarse, and thus is very efficient. (The appearance of such a low grit paper is more like a rock garden than sand paper and may startle you at first.) Assuming there is no resultant hole, a rust preventative is in order. Before deciding which one to use, perhaps a little knowledge of what they are and how they work is advisable.

All the rust killers are acid based. Some, almost all the old established ones, use phosphoric acid. A few, which are popular because they work faster, use hydrochloric acid as well. You can see them bubbling away, but they don't work any better, just faster. And it has the disadvantage that you have to neutralize the hydrochloric by washing it down with plenty of water. If you don't, it will start on the good metal as soon as it has finished on the rust. It will also bite unmercifully into any paint you put on.

The other disadvantage is that when you wash it off, you have to dry the metal, especially the seams, almost immediately to stop it rusting again. Without some form of heat this is almost impossible except in a heat wave. All in all, I regard hydrochloric acid as nasty corrosive stuff and prefer to steer clear of rust killers which need washing off.

Compounds with phosphoric acid don't need washing off. The acid attacks good metal, but nothing like hydrochloric. Even if swabbed on neatly, it would only etch the surface to a matte grey before it spent itself. In rust killers it is used at less than 50% strength, and even then there are often inhibitors to stop it etching the metal too much.

Some potions use tannic acid instead of phosphoric. These turn the rust into a blue-black compound, but straight tannic acid is not as good a rust killer as phosphoric. Later developments of these rust killers use the more sophisticated pyrogallic tannic acid which, the makers claim, puts back the power and has better inhibiting properties to stop further rusting. Like those with phosphoric acid, the tannic acid killers do not need washing off. I'm inclined to be neutral about the relative merits of pyrogallic tannic and phosphoric acid rust killers. The reason I use phosphoric is that it's under half the price.

You can buy paints which have a rust killing action, usually because they contain phosphoric acid. The acid converts the rust, then the paint dries and seals the metal off from further attack. Where there is no rust, the paint won't dry and has to be cleaned off, usually with methylated spirit.

Some paints contain finely powdered zinc dust. This in itself won't kill rust, but if there is enough zinc it helps to stop further rusting. There has to be enough zinc for the particles to be in electrical contact with each other and the metal. If any water gets in, the zinc and iron act like a battery with the car body as the cathode and the zinc as the anode. The zinc corrodes, and the body doesn't, which is why these paints are sometimes called sacrificial anode paints. The zinc corrodes to zinc oxide, which has the big advantage that it doesn't bubble and swell like iron oxide. It stays the same size as metallic zinc and clogs up the pores of the paint to stop more moisture getting to the body.

Well, now its up to you to decide

which to use. I have used DuPont metal conditioner with complete satisfaction but would be interested to hear of anyone who has positive or negative remarks about current products on the market. Once again I'd like to mention that a car in primer is not protected from rust. The porous nature of primer allows water to penetrate so it is essential to have your vehicle under cover until the first waxing.

Vol. 2, No. 5 Brett Johnson

Repairing Structural Rust

Concerning structural rust, as anyone who has read the rust articles of recent months will know, you cut out the bad metal and weld in new. There are no substitutes. The local discount auto parts stores have all types of hole patching kits which require no welding. Providing that you enjoy patching the same holes each year there is nothing wrong with them. Filling a hole with plastic or aluminum foil can have disastrous effects when a piece falls out of your car at the concours.

The most common structural weaknesses are underneath the car – the front struts, the rear torsion bar mounts and the floor in general. They are the most serious because of their intimate involvement with the suspension and the unit body construction. In addition, they are the most expensive areas to repair because of the necessity of new or fabricated panels that must be welded into place. There are of course other areas on the body which are commonly involved – around the headlights, in front and behind doors, the rocker panels and along the rear roof seam just to name a few.

Professional welders in my area recommend to save them time and you money to have all pieces fitted and the metal bright and shiny. Neighborhood welders rarely charge much per hour and might even let you off with cost of materials and a six-pack. Though

quality often is not professional, the price is certainly right.

Not being an expert welder myself, I went to my neighborhood welder and asked him what was needed in the way of tools and how the non-welder can save himself some money by doing preparation work for the welder.

The tools recommended are the oxy-acetylene unit (no arc-welders), a small aircraft torch with tips, 1, 3 and 5. A small light torch is much easier to use for awkward places and usually easier to control. Vise-Grips, C-clamps, and hammers are all essential. He suggests a body hammer and dollies but crude-types like myself can manage with two conventional hammers, one backing up the other. Rounding out the tool collection are tin snips and a jig saw.

Concerning materials he states that cold rolled steel 16 - 20 gauge, approximates the original. In addition, to those reasons supplied in the April issue by Peter Thompson, galvanized steel is a potential health hazard and loses the zinc coating around the weld. You'll also need welding rod which can be supplied by a welding supply house.

Patching holes or replacing panels is the next decision. Depending on the number, the cost, or the availability of the panels involved, this can be a difficult decision. When replacing complete panels the amount of work is reduced substantially. Cut around the edge of the body where you plan to fit the panel with a saw or snips, fit the piece, clamp, screw or rivet it in place and then weld.

Patching is essentially the same process but on a smaller scale. If making your own pieces, there is the problem of shaping the piece. This can be done by first making a cardboard template, then cutting the piece with snips or saw and bending it to general shape. Keep in mind that original appearance is important, but that the strength is more important than appearance, at least underneath. I recommend welding as opposed to brazing for any highly stressed surface and, of course, continuous bead welding is better than spot welding. Providing the finished patch looks similar to what was there originally, you'd be surprised how much you can cover up with a thick undercoat.

After welding in the piece, again clean the surface occasionally covered with carbon residues and then paint immediately both sides if possible with a rust preventative paint, (such as Rustoleum red primer). Use it generously and leave no bare metal uncovered. With the floor pan repaired and ready for the undercoat, it is now appropriate to start considering body work and rust removal on the "shiny side".

Vol. 2, No. 6 Brett Johnson

Body Rust Repair

Body rust, although the same phenomenon as underbody rust, must be approached in a slightly different manner. The obvious reason being that more people are likely to notice the top of the car and the underbody technique of covering up repairs with undercoat is not generally applicable.

With rust repair on upper body surfaces, warping of the metal due to heat is an important consideration. To avoid warping, using hammers and dollies, while welding will be necessary. This is where experience comes in, so if in doubt consult a good body man or welder.

To minimize warping several techniques are used. Most can be explored in greater detail in a welding textbook but I will discuss a relatively simple and highly successful method.

First remove the rust and some of the surrounding solid metal. The resultant hole will allow you to protect the back of the remaining metal by spraying some anti-rust primer on it before patching. A cardboard template can

then be made. When cutting the actual metal patch, it should be made $1/16$ - $1/8$ in. smaller than the hole to be filled. This piece should be clamped into place and tacked with welds 1 - 2 in. apart. Then using welding rod to fill the gaps, join the metal between the tacks. To reduce warping it is advisable to work to opposite corners thus not overheating any particular spot. The surrounding gap allows a screwdriver to be inserted for lining up the metal before welding, While welding, warping will occur, but use of hammer and dolly should be employed to keep the patch and surrounding metal as flat as possible. When finished the welds may be ground with a grinder or sander and the result should be slightly below the normal contours of the bodywork.

The spots usually needing attention are those in front and behind the doors, If the rust in front of the doors is extensive, the repair is not nearly as simple. The main complication of this type of repair is trying to maintain the original appearance of the fender edge at the door. Large sloppy welds or blobs of bondo were not what the men in Zuffenhausen envisaged. If the fender edge remains, it is possible to patch just the hole. However, typically the fender edge is damaged and in this situation it is necessary to rebuild it if you are trying to achieve original appearance. Here you need a skilled metal worker or a replacement panel (a factory fender is no good as it does not contain the finished edge.). Because the area is curved, the rolled edge is not a simple task but conceivably you could do it yourself if money is of prime concern.

Vol. 12, No. 5 David Seeland

Rust Repair on the ex-Ruff Rusty Roadster

About a year ago Alan Ruff told me he was selling his Roadster. I'd seen it a couple of times over the years. It was awaiting restoration in the mega-garage of the new house Alan was planning. After developing a very smooth handle on his hammer and a depleted money supply (but a beautifully crafted house and the mega-garage), Alan decided to sell the Roadster and I bought it. The drainage holes that the original owner had shot in the floor (this may still be the Wild West after all) had merged with the rust holes developed from the years of topless outdoor storage. All-in-all a most unsavory looking car to the casual observer: cracked and peeling paint, bare cracked wood instrument cowl, shreds of vinyl on the dash, tattered and shredded carpet, dents front and rear. The sun had fried all the plastic dash knobs. Even the oil pressure and ammeter warning light plastic lenses had disintegrated. It was also partially disassembled with the top, windshield frame, and doors off the car. But more important, as Mark Eskuche has pointed out, was the desirable lack of "high rust." (The highest rust I've ever seen was in the sheet metal above the windshield on an east coast Carrera 2 cabriolet.)

The Roadster is probably one of the rustiest 356s I've owned, yet with it's perfect door fit, unkinked hood, and basically straight body, it has the potential to be a concours winner. A step-by-step recounting of what I did and why will probably bore Arizonans and those of you who have done a thoroughly rusted 356 from the rust belt, but should prove interesting to those who own or are planning to purchase and restore a less than perfect moderately rusty 356.

Ron Roland's article (originally in Vol. 7, No. 3) is the definitive floor pan article and I see no need to try to replace it. Nevertheless, since rust is undoubtedly the 356s "Achilles Heel", it is impossible to say too much about it and some of my roadster's rust problems just weren't covered by Ron: inside the rear cowl area, the front

struts and the front diagonal member. The outer and inner longitudinals and torsion bar areas on this Roadster are not noticeably rusty. I also used a MIG welder in addition to an oxy-acetylene welder.

I have a repair estimate made for another prospective buyer of the Roadster by a local body shop. Since I have kept careful track of time spent, the comparison will probably be useful for those deciding between the "do-it-yourself" and "write-another-check" methods of restoration.

So, where to start? Floor removal is probably the hardest part of the job. I began by using a variable speed sabre-saw to cut out as much of the floor as possible. This leaves the area under the tunnel and a strip around the floor's perimeter (Fig. 1). The inner longitudinals and rear bulkhead are of heavy gauge metal and if not thinned by rust deform less than the flange at the tunnel. An air chisel can be used without tearing up the flanges. A spot weld removal bit didn't really seem to work. The spot welds on the Roadster nearly overlap so there are plenty to remove. Some hand chiseling with a sharp, thin chisel may help. The final removal has to be with a grinder. I used the edge of a $1/4$ x 5 in. wheel on a grinder/polisher. A smaller grinder might be handier.

The tunnel is light gauge sheet metal and the edge must be removed from underneath. Patience and care with a sharp chisel are necessary. The air chisel is useless here. Repairs will have to be made to the edge unless you are more successful than I was.

Fig. 1

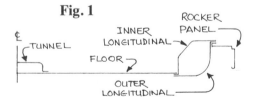

Cross section of one-half of the tunnel floor - longitudinal area. Floor is spot-welded to the flanges at the base of the tunnel and inner longitudinal.

Floor removal took me 25 hours. More hours than estimated for removal and installation of the floor by a local shop. I could see some "quickie" repairs that could be made by not removing the area beneath the tunnel and laying the floor in two pieces between tunnel sides and longitudinals or a double bottom under the tunnel. In either scenario, a quickie job's preparation work would stop with the sabre-sawing. Forewarned is forearmed for those who pay someone else to do the floor.

Vol. 14, No. 2 Phil Planck

Battery Pan Replacement

The first repair that was 356 specific (removing 11-year-old fuel deposits from the fuel tank is not 356 specific so I won't bore you with that) was replacing a rusted out battery pan. I used the spot weld removal tool (available from Eastwood) that fits an electric drill. This is a time consuming task that required getting on knees and leaning into the trunk or front compartment. As there are many, many welds you will have many aches and pains. Laying a throw rug over the nose of the car provided some relief from bruising my chest. Additionally, cutting out most of the remaining rusted out battery pan provided easier access to the spot welds. Once the welds had been cut around with the Eastman tool, the remaining nuggets then had to be ground down or cut off. I used a Dremel high speed tool finding success with both the cutoff blades or grinding bits.

Since my hometown is near Indianapolis it was easy to personally inspect a reproduction battery pan. The interesting parts of my pan were disintegrated so I used the parts manual pictures as a reference. The pan appeared to look appropriate for my model. I purchased same and proceeded to the next step.

This 356 body is not exactly square in the battery pan area. The rear edge on the right (drivers side) of the tunnel is not perpendicular to the centerline of the car. I made a cardboard template (from a large cardboard box) that exactly fit in the pan opening, including the nonsquare rear edge. Not having welded in years, I drove the car to an expert sheet metal fabricator in our area to have the pan cut to the template and installed. This guy makes fenders for and builds up street rods. He thought the car was cute, but also understood my desire to fool the car's next buyer by making the installation look original. He made excellent fake spot welds and even applied seam sealer. The total cost for his efforts was around $80. I will not describe how I drove the car without a battery pan but with a battery as this type of making do is not specific to 356s.

The next step was to acquire the two triangular pieces that help enclose the battery. Illustration A is from page 27 of the exploded view part diagrams for the Pre-A. Parts #29 are the triangular pieces I am referring to. They also hold one end of the springs that hold down the battery cover. These triangular pieces are welded to the battery pan and the vertical walls of the tunnel. Although I did not make an exhaustive search, I could not find these parts. Fortunately for me Ted Stanek, who owns a concours 1955 Speedster and lives near me, allowed me to measure his Speedster's triangu-

Illustration A

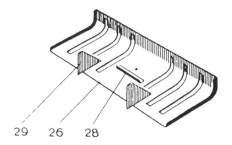

29   26   28

311

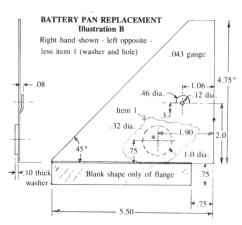

BATTERY PAN REPLACEMENT
Illustration B
Right hand shown - left opposite -
less item 1 (washer and hole)

.043 gauge

4.75"

.08

1.06
.46 dia.
.12 dia.

Item 1
.3

.32 dia.

1.90
2.0

45°
.75
1.0 dia.

.10 thick
washer
Blank shape only of flange
.75

.75

5.50

lar parts. Illustration B gives the dimensions for the driver's side part. The passenger side is symmetrically opposite. These parts are not hard to make, except for the spring attaching tabs. I had these welded in at a local weld shop for $10 and they did a decent job, even leaving the gas tank in the car.

The final step was to prime, paint, and apply undercoating. I have not actually applied the undercoat, but am considering Eastwood's battery tray coating for the whole battery pan. As this was the only rust on this 356, my next article won't bore you with another, "How I Replaced Every Piece of Sheet Metal on My Porsche."

Floor Replacement

Vol. 7, No. 3 Ron Roland

The Definitive Article

Spurred on by the continuing number of incorrectly/poorly installed floor pans, in this age of enlightenment, I decided to reply to your appeal for a floor installation article. Hopefully this article will dispel, once and for all, the myths about "installing a new floor pan" in a 356 Porsche.

The goal in this article is to show how a floor may be installed to look exactly as original. Never mind all the short cuts and "it's OK for a driver"

excuses. Anybody can throw in a floor pan; doing it right takes a little knowledge and a lot of care and patience. So you will find no brazing, or license plates pop riveted in, here. On the other hand, it is equally unnecessary to have a $1200 MIG welder and some cosmic jig. In fact these two tools, if used without understanding, can do more harm than good; especially the rotisserie. I also do not believe in doing extra damage by welding and drilling holes for braces which will later have to be removed and repaired.

If you have not obtained your dream car yet, and have never done a job like this before, start on a car that is not "too" rusty. Cars which are "first stage rusty" (have not been repaired before) are best because there will still be some structure from which to take measurements and alignment. And you don't have to undo someone else's hack job. Also, if you are inexperienced, don't learn on some priceless museum piece like a Gmünd coupe or an original Carrera GT Speedster. Pick up something more Normal to practice on.

Now the preliminaries: this is not a weekend job, so plan your time and space. Next start reading, photographing and looking at all the *original* literature and cars possible; including yours if it has never been worked on before. At the same time disregard all the "repaired cars" and helpful hints from their owners. Also realize that the details of Porsche body construction varied from model to model. The early 356 is somewhat different from the late 356 which is different from As and early Bs, and the T-6 Bs and Cs are different again. Nothing major but you will need Brett Johnson's Restoration articles as the factory service manuals do not go into body detail like they do mechanical detail. You will also need a knowledge of sheet metal welding, so pick up a good book on auto body repair like *Automobile Sheet Metal Repair* by Robert L. Sar-

gent, Chilton Book Co.; then spend some time practicing small, neat welds. Time to check your tool supply. In addition to the usual mechanical tools the following body tools are essential:
* Oxy-acetylene torch - light weight with #1 tip
* $1/16$ welding rods - 5 lbs (no brazing rods)
* Pick hammer - about 10 oz., blunt tip
* Toe dolly
* Metal shears - compound action, right
hand cut and left hand cut
* Scribe - to mark the metal, not to keep your records.
* Chisel - long, thin, and sharp; can be made from an old, large screwdriver
* Vise-Grip clamps - welding clamps, sheet metal bending clamps, c-clamps
* Body jack - push/pull type; this is nice but really not necessary

You will also need:
* Floor jack – any type – hydraulic, mechanical or scissor;
* Jack stands – 4; adjustable to 18 in. 3,000 lb capacity
* 2 x 4s – no, we are not going to build an English Porsche
* Angle Iron - 2 pieces, 2 in. x 2 in. x 3 ft. and 3 c-clamps to hold them
* Sheet metal - 20 gauge, mild steel; 2 sheets about 2 x 4 ft.

This is probably a good time to start on the car before your impatience causes you to chuck this article and do something foolish. First, what not to do: this is not the time to strip the car of every last nut and bolt and have it sandblasted (hopefully never) or dipped. That will come much later. Nor is this the time to cut off every piece of rusty metal. We will cut only as we need to and progress in steps.

With this in mind, put the car up on jack stands. Put the stands under the suspension next to the brakes. Do not put the stands under solid parts of the chassis as this encourages warping the body. The suspension will help absorb the stresses the body undergoes as it is heated,reinforced and cooled, etc.

Make sure the car is approximately level and the stands are square on the floor and suspension so the car is not teetering. To this end shake both the stands and the car and do not crawl under until you are sure. Also, *put the tires under the engine and front suspension*, so if the thing does fall, it's not on your head. Now carefully remove the carpet and all sound deadening pads. You will need these for replacement, patterns or matching carpet vinyl edges, etc. later. If you are not double jointed, also remove the steering wheel.

If you had not previously assessed the situation, do so now. The first thing you will notice is that the floor is not the only thing that needs replacing (Murphy's Porsche Law). If it is the only thing rusted, then you live in Southern California, do not have a real Porsche, or are lying. The rest of you will find the inner and outer longitudinals, tunnel, and a whole bunch of other stuff underneath, rusted. So you have nothing to attach that nice new floor pan to. Now order all parts you were sure you wouldn't need.

Next is body alignment, especially critical on convertibles (here this means: Cabriolet/Speedster/Roadster) but you can warp a coupe body. Latch the top up securely on convertibles; then be sure the doors open and close freely and check the gap around the edge. You may have to repair the lower hinge area on the doors if they are rusty or weak. The techniques described later for butt welding, etc. should also be employed here. On convertibles you can fit wooden wedges between the door jamb and the top end of the door. Also long 2 x 4s wedged from under the dash to the firewall (in front of the engine) will keep the body from collapsing. If someone has previously welded in a "boiler plate" for the floor and bent the body, one way or the other, you will now have to cut it loose. At this point you may need a jack under the transmission cradle, to force the body back together, or the above mentioned 2 x 4s, to force the body back apart.

Caution: the preload on your jacks and braces must be checked and adjusted constantly throughout this whole operation. Remove half of the floor up to about two inches from the tunnel; do not cut into the tunnel, or the edges, yet.

Now a word on welding. Your new welding book should show butt welds, spot welds and lap welds. We will use a butt weld wherever we have cut a rusty piece off an original panel. Properly finished this is the closest approximation of the original piece. Most of the original pieces in a Porsche chassis were lapped over before welding. In very early cars many of these areas have a gas welded bead (lap weld), while in later cars these panels are mostly electrically spot welded to facilitate "high production". Be sure to practice butt welding and lap welding before starting on your precious Porsche. A spot weld can be approximated by the following "buttonhole" weld process: clamp the two pieces of metal together; with the torch burn through the top piece then weld the bottom piece to the top piece through the hole and then fill the hole with weld. These "spot welds" are placed about one inch apart and hammered flat against a dolly while still hot (Fig. 1).

In our first actual "act of restoration," we will start on the inner longitudinal (either side). Measure the

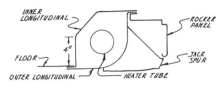

Figure 2

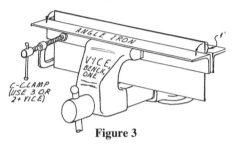

Figure 3

height of the vertical wall, from a remaining piece of the base flange to the first bend: about four inches (Fig. 2).

Use a pre-fab inner longitudinal repair panel or make one as follows. Take a 5 x 28 in. piece of 20 ga. sheet metal: clamp it between the two pieces of angle iron with C-clamps and/or in a vise, leave one inch sticking out. Hammer the one inch end over 90° onto the angle iron (Fig. 3).

Cut away all rusty metal from the inner longitudinal until you hit metal that is like new. Clamp the above piece behind the remaining inner longitudinal using the same vertical distance that you measured above. Clamp the two pieces with Vise-Grips and scribe the new piece along the cut edge of the old longitudinal (Fig. 4).

Note: before welding; if you have a NOS Porsche part (ha, ha, ha!), or a reproduction part with the green "protective" coating, remove the coating with lacquer thinner. This coating is

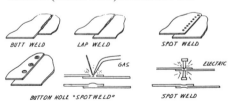

Figure 1

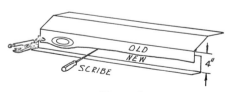

Figure 4

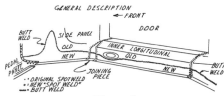

Figure 5

not primer, nor is the surface properly prepared to hold paint. This coating is guaranteed to chip, peel or crack off in short order taking whatever you put on top of it along with it. Now you can clamp the new inner longitudinal edge to the old inner longitudinal: leave about $1/16$ in. gap, tack weld every five or six inches, then butt weld-them together stopping every couple of inches to hammer the weld flat with hammer and dolly. Next follow the same procedure on the side panel (Fig. 5). Use a long straight edge (angle iron or whatever) across the bottom of your new inner longitudinal and, if possible, a remaining chunk of the pedal panel (front bulkhead). This whole edge must be straight and level; remember this is what the floor sits on. Now fabricate the little joining piece between the inner longitudinal and the side panel and weld in place (Fig. 5). Check body alignment and make sure doors open and close freely.

This side should start to look like something now, but the fun is just beginning. At the rear of the longitudinal there are multiple inner panels holding the heater tube and rear torsion bar tube. It is impractical to go into precise detail here, as models differ; so observe closely and repair each of these pieces in "logical" order. You will need the long thin chisel to reach

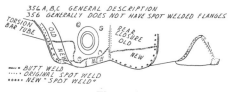

Figure 6

and cut away rusted areas, and patience to form and weld in the required pieces. Repairing the area under the rear torsion bar tube may cause some difficulty (ha). In addition to the Porsche parts and shop manual information for your year car (Brett Johnson restoration articles), you may do well to take a side trip to the library. Look for a book on sheet metal layout and forming and also something on weldments (which is what the Porsche body/chassis really is). Armed with this information, you will probably find it easier to form the area under the torsion bar tube from several small pieces rather than one large one. If the pieces are all butt welded and hammered out, this area will amaze your friends by looking like new. Remember, when you weld the newly formed piece to the solid, neatly cut edges of the once rusty body, you will not be able to work this final weld out with hammer and dolly; so take care. (Fig. 6)

Heater tubes will have to be repaired as you go here. "Prebent" and straight exhaust tubing can be obtained from J.C. Whitney or sometimes your local hot rod shop; then cut and weld together as needed. Also, thin wall electrical conduit makes a good corrosion resistant heater tube. On Bs and Cs, remove the cardboard insulator/muffler before welding. The rusty clamps will probably fall off in your hand; then just compress slightly, as in accordion, and slip out. Don't forget to reinstall it before you put the outer longitudinal on – I don't need any obscene phone calls in the middle of the night.

Assuming that you have now repaired the heater tubes, the bulkheads holding them in and the cups which hold the cardboard tube (Fig. 7), we are ready to do the longitudinal and closures. Small repairs are easily fabricated as above but for *rusty* Porsches you may do well to get the store bought pieces. The deep depressions

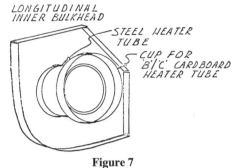

LONGITUDINAL
INNER BULKHEAD
STEEL HEATER
TUBE
CUP FOR
'B'/'C' CARDBOARD
HEATER TUBE

Figure 7

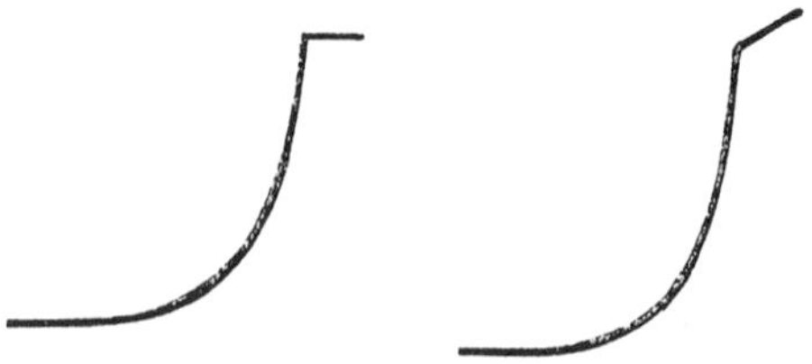

Figure 9

on the front closing panel and the T-6 rear panel are especially difficult to form. Now, align, cut rust, realign, scribe new panel, final cut, etc. Use the bottom of the new longitudinal, remains of the old longitudinal, fender and imagination to properly fit these pieces. And just because you bought a piece measuring 2 x 2 ft. doesn't mean you have to use it all. Many of the front closure repro parts are made in two pieces and spot welded together to simulate the original; these parts are easier to handle if obtained not welded. Don't forget to remove the green "protective" coating; then use extreme care in fitting and butt welding the closures in place. The inner half of the front closure is fitted first, then the outer half is lapped over it (this is the piece that folds back against the front fender and helps form the edge next to the door) Fig. 8. The lap is secured with "spot welds" and everything is hammer and dolly finished. Finally, dress the welds with a body grinder or DA sander (do not grind excessively as this will weaken the welds). Remember, when all is said and done, these are the only panels, except the

ones under the rear torsion bar tube, where the welds are really visible.

Ah, the "longitudinals." Remember when the guy said "all it needs are longitudinals and a floor pan"? Everybody says this is easy because almost nobody does the complete job. Look at Fig. 1, note how the outer longitudinal is located at the door sill between inner longitudinal and the rocker panel. Don't panic. By now you are no longer a novice body man and *anything* is possible. Take your long thin chisel, split the spot welds and cut around or through the flange weld beads. Work the panels apart enough to pull the old rusty outer longitudinal out. Unfortunately, the new outer longitudinal is not going to fit perfectly. So, flatten the upper flange slightly from 90 to 45 (Fig. 9) and force it up into place between the rocker and inner longitudinal; scribe, remove, cut and reinstall until the fit is right.

Clamp in place, then roll tightly under car and clamp against new lower edge of inner longitudinal, scribe lower edge from inside car. Remove once more for final trim.

Reinstall cardboard heater tube in Bs and Cs. Check door and body alignment.

Remove green "protective" coating; install outer longitudinal and clamp securely at top, between rocker panel and inner longitudinal, with Vise-Grip welding clamps. Three panel sandwich "spot welds" are a little more tricky than two panel, but by now you

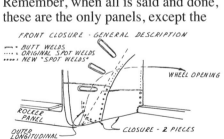

FRONT CLOSURE - GENERAL DESCRIPTION
— • BUTT WELDS
···· • ORIGINAL SPOT WELDS
••••• NEW "SPOT WELDS"
WHEEL OPENING
ROCKER
PANEL
OUTER
LONGITUDINAL
CLOSURE - 2 PIECES

Figure 8

can handle it. Make the "spot welds" between the "fingers" of the Vise-Grip welding clamps and about one inch apart, hammer and dolly each one flat as you go. Don't forget to weld the edge of the flange in a few places the way the factory did. You can dress these "spot welds", also, if you wish.

Check door and body alignment here frequently.

Don't go so fast you warp things. If something does become badly warped and the doors won't open and close, *Stop.* You will have to cut things loose, readjust the preload with the jacks and braces and start over. Now wrap the other longitudinal tightly around the heater tube bulkheads and clamp against the bottom flange of the inner longitudinal – tapping lightly with a large rubber mallet helps sometimes – do not dent! Start "spot welds" at the center and alternate toward front and rear of car. The "spot welds" will appear neatest if performed through the inner longitudinal down into the outer longitudinal.

Check body alignment, you are at a critical point.

"Spot weld" outer longitudinal to end closures. The rear closure on 356 models is a corner, or half of a 'T', joint and is welded solid. On very early 356 models don't forget the additional reinforcement at the back of the outer longitudinal! Position the jack spur housing $1/2$ in. below the rocker panel with fore and aft measurement taken off a good original car. Be sure you have the right type jack spur for your model car. No, I don't recommend buying the outer longitudinal with the jack spur already attached because occasionally the jack spur will be improperly located. Anyway it makes it just that much harder to fit the outer longitudinal. If your rocker panels need repairing, you can leave the jack spurs off for now.

You did it! You have one side like new. Piece-of-cake, right?

Now do the same to the other side!

Once both sides are done, carefully checking body alignment as you go, you can breathe easier, because 75% of the structure is back in your car and you will really have to work at it to screw it up, from here. Screw up the alignment, that is, because we have now reached the tunnel (through which the light is just visible). If your car wasn't real rusty, you may be able to just break the spot welds, remove the old floor and press on to the section on floor installation. But you would do well to read this anyway.

Assuming you will have to repair the edge of the tunnel the same way you repaired the inner longitudinal, consider what's inside that tunnel.

The wiring harness (bad for the car if you burn); the fuel line (bad for you if you burn); etc. If you, especially as still an apprentice, do much, if any, welding on the right side of the tunnel, it is guaranteed you will burn the wires up and have to remove them anyway. So remove them to start with, unless you like bleeding.

Don't forget the big battery cable. To remove the wiring harness disconnect everything at the back of the car. Use wife's hair dryer to make everything pliable, if necessary. Wrap tightly with masking tape to streamline, and pull through. If it goes that easy don't tell me, I don't want to know.

Disconnect the fuel line at both ends and blow out. On T-5 and earlier (1961) models, remove the gas tank (unless you like real bleeding) so it doesn't drip on your weld and put out the flame.

Now, simply make the new tunnel edge like you made the new inner longitudinal edge – it looks the same, just shorter. The pedal panel (front bulkhead) is next (Fig. 10). Note depression which floor sits on. Fabricating and welding this piece is the same hammer and dolly, vise/brake, and butt weld/"spot weld" process you have been using. The rear bulkhead, in front of the rear torsion bar tube, may

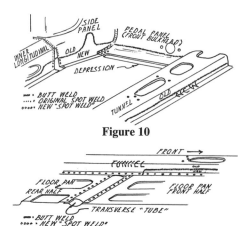

Figure 10

Figure 11

also need repairing, although it is much heavier steel and often will not be rusty. All done? Finally you have that mythical Porsche that "just needs a floor".

Clever as you are by now, the first thing you will notice is that the floor is much wider than the hole it must pass through, especially since the repro floors give you extra material. So, using your jack and a 2 x 4, position the floor up against the bottom of the hole, overlapping the two pieces in the center (Fig. 11) to form a transverse, structural tube. Scribe along inner longitudinals, pedal panel (front bulkhead), and rear bulkhead. Make your marks very carefully and recheck; then cut about 3/4+ in. outside this line to leave an overlap. Remember, the floor sits on top of the inner

Figure 12

Figure 13

longitudinal (Fig. 12). So how do you get a square floor into a round hole? Simple (ha). Bow the floor pans slightly (Fig. 13) and slip in allowing a greater overlap in the middle. Slide the pans fore and aft until the proper overlap is obtained in the center and the floor sits on the pedal panel ledge and the rear bulkhead ledge. Take care not to bend the floor permanently! Now reflatten the floor as much as possible, use the jack and 2 x 4 under the bow. Carefully perform the final alignment and hold the bottom of the floor tightly against the tunnel. Begin the "spot welds" at the center, working fore and aft, side to side to minimize warpage.

Check body alignment occasionally whenever welding.

When the tunnel is finished, force the outer floor edges against the inner longitudinal and tack weld near the floor center "tube". "Spot weld" floor center tube together (Fig. 11) starting at the tunnel and working toward the longitundinals. Alternate side to side, top to bottom to minimize warpage. Hammer welds as you go and try to keep floor pan halves pressed tightly together; difficult because you can't clamp. Now lap (bead) weld the floor solidly to the longitudinal, top and bottom, at the "tube".

Finish "spot welding" the floor edges as in Fig. 14. Essentially you have four small pans to weld now. If you start in the far corners next to a weld and work toward the unwelded corner, alternating "pans", you allow for expansion and minimize warpage. Use the long thin chisel to hold the pan

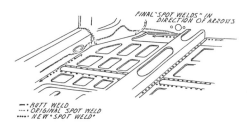

Figure 14

318

Figure 15

against the longitudinal while starting several "spot welds", then go back and finish welding them and finally, hammer flat. This is not easy and takes patience.

Install pedal assembly, mark and drill holes, remove pedal assembly and weld nut plate in from the bottom (Fig. 15). Bolt seat rails to the tunnel and seat rail supports to the new floor mounts. If you have a late "B" or "C" (T-6), be sure to get the proper style seat mounts; the type with capture nuts rather than studs. Early 356s just have a single bolt through the floor in the front, welded underneath, and a similar single bolt in the rear mount. Anyway, install seat as normal and align new mounts, tack weld in place, remove seat rails. "Spot weld" T-6 rear mounts and 'A' and T-5 front mounts. 356, "A" and T-5 are bead welded on the rear mounts.

Voilà! New Porsche. Piece-of-cake, right? But let's paint it before you have to do it all over again. Remove all loose and burned paint and undercoating, etc. Sand, wire brush, etc. then scrub with metal-prep (phosphoric acid solution) per instructions. *Use eye protection and rubber gloves.*

After flushing with water and wiping, use torch to assure that all seams are dry. A little heat is fine. the metal doesn't have to glow back at you. Let everything dry for a few hours if you are in doubt – everything must be bone dry. Primer: the best is DuPont Corlar (epoxy), although Rustoleum Damp Proof Red is still very acceptable; and may be better on original sheet metal still showing traces of sur-

face rust. When primer is dry, cover all seams with fibrous roofing tar, working well back into the cracks and crevices. This is critical as it prevents water from being siphoned into the seams and starting the rust process all over. Those of you fortunate enough to own Carrera GTs will now be ready to apply a coat of black DuPont Imron. The rest of us proles must first apply a couple of layers of 3M Body Schutz to the bottom, then the black urethane. Inside should be body color, except black around the seat mounts;

The Carrera GT owners are now finished. Everyone else will have to start working on sound deadening pads. Since locating the material, cutting the patterns and form fitting the stuff is a subject in itself, suffice it to say that you can use the roofing tar to glue your original pads in if you are fortunate enough to still have them. Just apply tar to pad and body (only where pad goes), allow to become tacky, then stick pad to body. Use tape to hold until dry, if necessary.

Your Porsche bottom is now as close as possible to the way it came from the factory.

Vol. 7, No. 6 Bruce Baker

A Professional, Tells All

"Floor Installation" is a euphemism for undercarriage repair of which the floor is the easiest and least important aspect. The car as a whole is a unibody and therefore is like a chain, no link of which should be overlooked.

A. Preparation

1. Assessment of Damage – Ascertain where the underside repair coincides with the external body work.

2. Accumulation of Parts – Assume you need everything until proven otherwise!

3. Cleaning – The better the prepara-

tion, the easier the installation and the better the final results. If a "turn-over device" is available, it will make the process cleaner, easier and faster. Convenient tools to use for the following procedures are:

(a) Chipping – Air hammer
(b) Scraping – Putty knives
(c) Grinding – Small electric or air tools
(d) Sandblasting – Can be commercially done or with small home unit which is very slow and messy, requiring:

    (1) Dismantling
    (2) Masking

A word to the wise – sand gets everywhere, from handbrake levers to instruments, shifters, heater system, not to mention engine, brake and transmission.

4. Equipment and Tools – These often require a power source and/or air supply. Plus you will need:

(a) Eye protection – Either full face shield, safety glasses, welding helmet and/or goggles.
(b) Ear protection – External earphones, plugs or cotton.
(c) Hand protection – Sturdy leather gloves and long sleeves.
(d) Respirator for dust and fumes.
(e) For undercoat removal – Power air chipper or electric wire brush. Hand scraping with putty knives and gasket scrapers, screwdrivers, etc. Heat is optional and not recommended.
(f) For rusty metal removal/trimming - Use tin snips, air craft shears, small carbide cut-off wheel or saber saw.
(g) For surface rust/old paint removal Use chemicals such as: paint remover, Naval Jelly, Phosphoric Acid. Sandblasting is preferable if feasible.
(h) For welding – Oxy-Acetylene torch and/or electric (preferably wire-feed) machine with resistance spot-welding capabilities if available.

(i) For final finish rust proofing – Spray painting facilities, brushes (of varying sizes), 3-M Body Schutz Sound Deadener spray gun will be needed.

B. Trimming and Measuring

After cleaning, it will become obvious where the weak sections are that need to be explored. Remember that the more you take away the weaker the car. Open cars especially need constant measurement and door gap correction. Always support the car as if it were on its wheels. A simple brace may be fabricated to insure a more stable alignment of body halves, using existing body holes on dash-top and rear seat swivels.

1. Cutting away of thin metal until an area of original thickness is reached should be done regardless of whether it is for the replacement of a whole panel or a small patch.

2. Paper templates and patterns for patches are best made before or during trimming to keep the function and spacing clear in the mind. Don't trust your memory!

3. The cutting of 20 gauge metal sheets into appropriate patches (from #2 above) is accomplished via snips, band saw or power shears.

4. The fitting of reproduction stampings & panels to existing original metal for acceptable fit must be done before welding. (It should be noted that there is no guarantee that non-original pieces will fit directly to an existing area with no modification. There also should be as little overlap as possible as this is where rust starts.)

5. Subrepair
(a) Domestic exhaust tubing is adaptable for heater ducting.
(b) Suspension points which are not currently available as reproduction

320

items must be fabricated.

(c) Tunnel functions are best serviced when exposed, i.e.:

(1) Wiring

(2) Brake lines and cables

(3) Shift components

(d) The pedal assembly must be removed anyway and should be checked and serviced off the car.

(e) Shocks, suspension components and brakes are usually an interference and their removal makes for efficient rebuilding or replacement.

(f) Paint inside all areas to be closed before welding (as the factory did not).

C. Installation of Repair Panels

1. Alignment, spot or tack welding and checking are very important.

2. After total assembly, join welds, being careful not to concentrate heat in one area.

3. Grind welds only where necessary for maximum strength.

4. Saturate all joints with rust proofing primer (apply liberally).

5. Seal any seam prone to leak with good grade exterior caulk.

D. Finish Operations

1. Paint inside and (optional) outside with durable black enamel.

2. Spray sound deadening material, i.e. "3-M Body Schutz".

3. Reinstall adroplass or substitute sound proofing or waterproof material where usually found, especially inside under carpets, if desired.

4. Refit any applicable trim (i.e. carpets, etc.) assuming external body work is completed.

E. Optional Points to Consider

1. Dismantle suspension to be rebuilt and detailed off of the car.

2. Overspray on undercarriage from external bodywork may be painted over with black enamel as originally done at factory.

3. Clean all contacts for electrical components for improved function i.e. horns, starter motor, brake switch, lights, ground straps, etc.

4. Engine and transmission, i.e. unit work, may be rebuilt, cleaned and painted if removed to facilitate undercarriage repair.

F. Considerations

1. An experienced person with proper equipment may take as long as 150 hours for this procedure.

2. The bought pieces may cost nearly $1,000 plus any simultaneous subrepair.

3. Trim items may be postponed but are inevitable.

4. And again – alignment is of utmost importance!

Conclusions:

After all this is taken into consideration – here is the answer to the direct request for "the installation of a floor":

1. Place car in normal upright position at working height of generally 15 - 20 in.

2. Assuming there is a perimeter and no longitudinal ducting interfering, join floor halves and center side-to-side and fore-and-aft by eye, trim, and locate with whatever means available to you, i.e. floor jacks, scissor jacks, milk crates and boards, special low

horses, etc. An additional helper is recommended.

3. Fabricate the forward edge and tack in first to bottom of bulk-head (not sold by after-market suppliers).

4. Tack into place starting at tunnel center and proceed as if torquing head bolts or tightening a wheel or stretching a canvas to avoid oil can effect.

5. Following the tacking of the floor to the perimeter of inside longitudinals and tunnel, the external longitudinals may be attached followed by outer rocker panels and front and rear suspension points.

6. Remember, it is easier to install wiring, brake lines or shifter components before sealing bottom of tunnel.

7. Position seat mount pads using an actual seat bottom and toe-board supports with pedals in place.

8. Finish welding. Grind only where necessary. Clean welds and paint.

Vol. 8, No. 1 Bob Heimann

Another Man's View
I have replaced two floors to date, both on very rusty cars. I'll try to explain the second, and most recent installation touching on the differences between the two.

Tools needed for this job are expensive, however, they last forever, with care and I imagine floor replacement at a body shop is also expensive. Two professional floor jobs would probably pay for parts and tools and you'll always have the tools. Another route is for you to remove the floor, fit and pop rivet in the parts, then tow it to a body shop or weld shop for welding. Removing the old floor is super easy with an air hammer ($30 - $40), however, you need an air compressor $300 - $400. Aviation snips for fitting floor

and sidewalls are needed ($8 - $10 each). Electric drill for drilling spot welds $30 - $40. Pot riveter $10. Acetylene torches have many different uses welding, cutting, brazing are just a few. However, heat creates warpage, although with floor replacement, a small amount of warpage will not be noticeable. You can get by with a torch with help to hold parts down and having them well clamped ($200 - $250 plus gas and tank rental). My latest acquisition, a Millermatic 35 with spot weld attachment, is the way to go. It is a MIG welder and the spot weld feature is fantastic. Just clean the two metals, put the gun where you want the spot weld, pull the trigger, and it's done. Minimum heat, distortion is eliminated. Complete outfit at $1,300 is expensive, but if you are going to do more than one car or do a lot of replacing on one car, it is well worth the price.

Both cars were stripped down, bare, so if yours is not, that's the first step. How far you go will depend on how much metal you are going to replace at this time. If only the floor is to be replaced, you will need to remove the seats, floor mats, toeboard, pedal assembly, carpeting, and sound proofing (tar paper). Now you will be able to see how far the rust has gone. Test the sidewalls with a pick. If they're bad, they will also need to be replaced. If you have rust through the floor-side wall angle, but the upper sidewall is good, some 20 gauge angles will do. Small angles are available from suppliers.

Floor removal is next. Measure for height and seat mount locations. The fastest way is with an air hammer. If your sidewalls and angle are good, cut around the inside of the angle. Peeling off the remainder of the floor from the top of the angle and the bottom of the tunnel will probably be the hardest part of the job. If you can see the spot welds, use either a spot weld remover or drill trying not to drill through the angle. Once this is done remaining strip of floor will peel off easily.

Caution: Trying to chisel this strip with air hammer or cold chisel will lead to tears in the angle.

If you are going to replace the angle or sidewall with angle, cut above the angle, saving as much good metal as possible. When cutting the tunnel try to cut right in the angle. The tunnel contains some small braces, so watch so as not to cut these. In both of my cars, the angle at the rear and underneath the tunnel was good. It seems to be a thicker metal than the rest of the angles.

If you're just replacing the angle at the bottom of the sidewall and tunnel, just use your measurements to set depth, clamp or pop rivet in place, then weld, braze, or spot weld in place.

If you're going to replace the sidewall also, you'll have to fit several pieces, especially the pieces below the radio speaker housings. However, with a little snipping and bending, these will fit very nicely. After filling, secure with clamps or pop rivets and weld, braze or spot weld in place depending on your equipment. A word of caution: for either sidewalls with angle or just angles, the struts are part of the angle for the floor. If yours need replacing, do it now and if they don't, be sure not to cut them off when removing the floor. Don't forget to cut the hole for the heater outlet with sidewall and angle installation.

Both of my cars had part of the toe board area rusted out. You are best off to get some 20 or 22 gauge steel and form your own.

Once all the sidewalls with angles or angles are in place, it's time to fit the floor. I place the back half on a floor jack, roll it under the car and jack it up loosely, then center it in the opening and scribe around the inside of the angle. Also mark on the sidewall where the front of the rear section ends. This is necessary as the front

and rear sections overlap. As soon as you've scribed the rear section, remove it and scribe new line to the outside of the ones you just put on. These should be just a little less than the width of the angle i.e. angle 1 in. scribe $7/8$ in. Trim off the excess material as the floor panels are wider and longer than the opening.

Now go to the mark on the sidewall where the floor ended and measure about 3 in. on either side and cut the angle, then bend this 6 in. piece straight down. You can now slide the rear half of the floor in place. It will rest on top of the sidewall angles and below the tunnel angles. If you haven't noticed before, you will now, that the floor bellies down as the tunnel is lower than the sidewalls. It may be necessary to jack the area under the tunnel up before riveting or welding in place. Use a piece of wood, 2 x 4, under the jack as this will spread the force over the whole panel and not just in one place which could lead to kinking the floor.

The front half is a repeat of the rear. Be sure you have enough lap where the rear and front sections meet. The rear section should go in first and be on top where the floors (front and rear sections) lap.

If you're welding or brazing, I would suggest pop-riveting about every 3 in. or else have a helper hold the floor down in front of your torch as you go along, as the heat will cause the floor to pull from the angle. Locate the seat and toe board mounts and weld or braze in place. Install pedal assembly, drill holes and put your old bracket on from below. You did remove it from the old floor and save it, didn't you?

If you're replacing a floor on anything but a coupe, special care must be taken or your door may not close, or be higher at the back than the front. I did a Roadster, and by using small hydraulic jacks (1 $1/2$ ton $8.00 each) and leaving the doors on with latches

323

removed (no binding) was able to get a perfect fit on doors that were sagging due to rusted floor and sidewalls. Just go slow with the welding and make frequent checks and raise and lower the jacks as need.

I know this may not be the perfect way to do the job, but it has worked for me twice.

Bodywork Basics

Vol. 5, No. 4 Nancy & David Jones

DIY Restoration

Assuming you have found at least one spot needing work, there are two obvious alternatives for repair; commercial and do-it-yourself. Paying someone else to do the work is xtremely expensive (e.g. $20/hour labor plus materials) – especially if it is done properly. Doing it yourself is laborious, dirty, potentially expensive (if you need to buy much in the way of tools and/or equipment), but ultimately rewarding. This latter satisfaction can come from a job well-done in "saving" a 356. No matter who does the work, there is no easy way to properly repair rust damage. There are quick and dirty short cuts for a temporary cosmetic cover-up, but certainly this cannot be called restoration. To do it right is very time consuming (and therefore money consuming if someone else does the work). Forget body filler, fiberglass, brazing, etc. – butt welding (or hammer welding where both sides are visible like a fender well) and lead are the only way to go.

Many excellent tomes have been written on the technical side of metal working, but here are some personal comments on the basic steps involved:

(1) Preparation – The first problem is access to the affected area. There are many commercial and shade-tree options available depending on the magnitude of the restoration and loca-tion of the problem area(s). Once you have clear and easy access, remove the bad metal and an additional ring of undercoating or paint to assure containment of the rust.

(2) Welding – Weld in new metal .032" or 20 gauge seems to match well) or a new part using a butt weld where only one side will be exposed, hammer weld for strength and best finished appearance where both sides will be visible as in a fender well.

(3) Metal Shaping – Rough and bump with a dinging hammer and dolly to approximate original contour(s) in newly welded areas. Use body file to locate high and low spots (raise low spots with a pick hammer if possible rather than lead everything). A good job here saves lots of time later on.

(4) Metal Straightening – The repaired area can have the proper contour and be absolutely smooth, but not straight. We have all seen such "waves" looking down the side of many "restored" cars. Metal filling with lead should be followed by the body file (or #24 grit open coat paper on a disc sander). This will eliminate the minor indentations and waves left during the metal shaping.

(5) Metal Smoothing – This step is nothing more than the use of a sanding board (or #80 grit on a disc sander) to get rid of the file marks and make an extremely smooth base for the primer (s) and paint.

(6) Metal Preparation – Do not forget to etch the bare metal with a conditioner so the primer(s) hold better.

(7) Priming – Spot prime with a zinc chromate primer since this is the best rust inhibitor, then think about using a primer-surfacer (instead of a straight primer) for a smoother base which can't hurt and probably will help the appearance of your final coat.

(8) Painting – I hesitate to recommend brand names, but DuPont's Imron seems to be the best choice available at this time.

(9) Undercoating – Undercoat what-

ever is not painted. Without some protective film, the rust will just start all over again. Here again are three brand names: Ziebart, if you go the commercial route or 3M's Body Schutz, if you undercoat yourself; use Imron if you prefer paint to undercoating.

(10) Weatherproofing – Check and replace all imperfect rubber gaskets and window weatherstripping to keep water out of the car; then check and periodically recheck door drain holes to make sure the passages are open.

Bodywork, Lead

Vol. 3, No. 2 Brett Johnson

Fixing Dents the Olde Worlde Way

Well, all you anti-plastic, old school, do-it-in lead types, here goes... lead work for the layman. And for those of you with open minds, after you've read this I'm sure you'll understand the advantages of using plastic. The tools you need for leadwork are not extensive or costly. More than enough heat is provided by blowtorch or propane torch. Also required are a paddle to apply the lead, and a coarse file or rasp to remove it. All these tools should be readily available from your local hardware or auto body supply store. While there, you might as well pick up your lead and tinning solution. Lead comes in several different grades varying in percentage of lead and tin. The cheaper grades available contain a higher proportion of lead and are less workable due to their responses to very small differences in temperature. A good 70 - 30 lead, while slightly more expensive, will prove much easier to work.

Just as with plastic, the first step is to clean the metal. Again a disk sander with very coarse paper is the best way. Any residual paint or rust are definite no-no's. The next step is tinning the metal. If tinning is not correctly performed the lead will not adhere. Tin-

ning may be approached from several directions. The old school method is to acquire a roll of acid core solder (Rosin core is not very useful unless you wish to install transistors to your fender). With your torch heat the metal that the lead is to be applied to and melt small amounts of solder on to this area. Taking a rag, vigorously rub the area coating it with a thin layer of solder. The resultant metal should have a shiny appearance. If not, it is improperly tinned and this procedure should be repeated.

A slightly easier method of tinning is to apply a tinning solution (available at auto body supply stores) to the fresh metal and apply a very thin layer of lead on top. Again, only shiny surfaces are properly tinned.

After tinning, lead should be applied by heating metal and lead and depositing blobs of lead on the surface. I feel it necessary to again stress that when filling a dent, a rule of thumb is to use as little filler as possible and dent removal is the real art. Attempt to keep the metal at a uniform temperature and spread the molten lead with your paddle soaked in oil. There is no need to worry about this oil becoming incorporated into the lead as it rises to the surface where it can be wiped off after the lead solidifies. As with plastic, it is wise to slightly overfill the dent so that the surface may be filed down to match the original contours.

Now the bad news. When you heat the metal with your torch it warps. Thus, the area you are working on may grow until it engulfs the entire car and you will be the proud owner of a 6000 lb. Speedster. Another problem is applying lead to a vertical surface or even worse an overhang. Obviously it drips. I've got no solution aside from turning the car over or not using lead.

Now where do you use your new found skill? If you have illusions of being Dr. Porsche, you are permitted to cover welded joints, the fronts of doors, and door jambs. If you're wise, that's where you stop. If you're GM, Ford, or Chrysler, you don't go that far. In fact, you use no lead at all. Seriously though, covering welded joints is the best use of lead I can think of. It is not perfect as it can be observed to change appearance over the years. Using lead for other purposes such as accident damage is quite time consuming and I wouldn't advise it. Plastic is superior in this type of work.

Bodywork, Misc.

Vol. 2, No. 6 Brett Johnson

Dent Repair With Plastic
With all patching done, body work at a simpler level emerges unless of course you think it must be done in lead. I encourage you to talk to body men and professional restorers and get their opinions. I think you'll find that most if not all will tell you that though there are places where lead is necessary, the overwhelming amount of work may be and indeed should be done with plastic.

Plastic is easy to apply and easy to work. Anyone with a little patience and a few inexpensive tools can do body work at the same level or higher than the professional shop. Be prepared for a long haul as body work can be very frustrating, especially the first time. Lead on the other hand is difficult to work. On top of that it is relatively expensive. Aside from the fact that lead is metal (and offers the psychological advantage of being what the factory used to cover welds) it has no true advantage over plastic.

Vol. 3, No. 1 Brett Johnson

Dent Repair With Plastic, Again
Assuming that all the rust is now in the past the next item on the agenda is

other body imperfections such as ill fitting panels and dented ones. Dent removal may be approached from several different ways and the type and position of the damage will dictate how. In the simple case, it is possible to get behind the dent and using hammers and dollies remove as much of the dent as possible. Attempt to keep the area at or below the original contours. In other places, it is impossible to get behind the dent or to swing a hammer. Here it is necessary to cut out metal, rework or replace it and then weld back in place.

With most of the dings flattened, its back to the old what to fill with problem. Again let's start with plastic. First of all, the number of different types of body fillers is staggering and they range in size from a pint to five gallons. Generally, a gallon will be more than enough. My choice is DuPont Polyester Auto Body Filler. It does not dry as hard as some others and thus is more easily worked.

Before applying plastic it is necessary to prepare the surface. This consists of removal of all paint and roughing up the surface to freshen the metal, best achieved with a disc-sander and low grit paper.

Use of metal conditioner before applying plastic is in theory an excellent idea, but in practice, residues are left on the metal causing the plastic to adhere to it instead of the metal, resulting later in cracks. In this case, leave your metal conditioner in the bottle. Before going any further I should probably describe the tools which I use for body work – putty knives, sanding block, a wood rasp, and flex file. The occasional use of power tools, disc sander and orbital sander can be helpful. The sand paper I use for initial sanding is a 20 grit disc and 40 grit sheet for use on the block, flex file, and orbital sander. Use of a less coarse paper will result in slower and less satisfactory work. Using your putty knife, mix the plastic on a piece of cardboard or something similar, making sure to get enough hardener in. Mixing directions are very vague and it is usually a case of trial and error to determine correct mixture. Too much hardener and it dries before it gets to the car. Too little and it never dries. The latter of these two is to be avoided at all costs as it will cause cracking and other defects in the finish.

The only other major concern in respect to application of plastic is thickness. A rule of thumb is to put on as little as necessary and as thin a coat as possible. Filling a deep dent is just like any other dent except plastic should be built up gradually in thin layers. This will enable the thorough drying of each layer and assure no future surprises in the finish.

As the plastic dries, there is a stage when the texture is semi-solid and it is possible to work the surface with the wood rasp before complete hardening takes place. This only lasts for a few minutes – roughly 5 - 10 minutes after initial hardening occurs. But taking advantage of this will save a considerable amount of future labor.

From my experience I have found that hand sanding gives better, smoother results. Obviously, power sanding has its place which I consider the initial work of removing high places. When this is accomplished, I find it easier to feel the surface by block sanding. I'm sure this is not the universal method employed in body shops or in books on body work, but most examples of body shop work I've encountered have the distinct wavy appearance brought on by power sanding.

To determine if body work is good there are two methods which I use. One which is obvious is feeling the area. If the difference between plastic and metal proves a problem, a light coat of primer may help. The scratches in the surface may be detracting but major flaws should be detectable. I should note with this method don't trust your eyes. Everything looks good in primer and if you plan on finishing the car in crushed velour or flat black for that racy appearance, no more body work is necessary. Most of us prefer a shiny finish and this requires nearly flawless bodywork. If your hands are not trustworthy or uneducated, a simple method is to wet the surface and look for dents. Obviously, if you haven't primed the area, wetting it a faux pas. Not only does your metal rust but your plastic absorbs water which brings about future disasters.

For the poor at heart who staunchly refuse to buy a compressor priming is apt to be a very costly procedure. Spray cans are unsatisfactory due to both cost and lack of coverage while brushing primer tends to leave brush marks, no matter what it says on the can. You don't need a very powerful compressor or a very good spray gun to shoot an adequate coat of primer. The primer I use is DuPont dark gray (a light gray, red, and black). Any cheap lacquer thinner can be used with primer. This type primer is mixed between 1:1 and 1:2 with thinner depending on temperature and use. When attempting to fill scratches, paint should be quite thick while final coats should be much thinner.

Now that the primer covers all the nastiness one must decide if the area needs additional work. If it does, the primer must be sanded off. Plastic must never be applied on top of paint (*except polyester primer, which did not exist when this was written*). If, however, the area seems to be adequate (remembering that only perfection is adequate), some of the remaining small imperfections may be remedied by judicious use of lacquer putty (which is essentially thick paint in a tube). This should be used to fill paint chips and scratches and should only be applied on top of paint and in very thin layers.

Problem: Dents and Creases

Cure: Bumping – done with a hammer and dolly (a fist-sized hunk of steel). Plastic body filler is easy to use and cheap, but use minimum amounts. For example, the 1968 911 that I've been working on had a crease front to back along one side. There were places that had an inch of unnecessary plastic. A few minutes of work and I had to use less than an eighth of an inch of plastic. Metal stretches when dented or creased so if you try to take a crease out of a door, you end up with too much metal. Either the panel has to be pushed in too much or pulled out too far. It also may "oil-can", pop in if pushed on lightly.

The cure is to shrink the metal as described earlier in this article. But it may be necessary to do it at dozens of spots, depending on the degree of stretch. If you have doubts, practice on the floor of the battery box or on an old Chevy door. Never leave any metal higher than the general contour or it will have to be hammered down later. Small high areas are best lowered by careful tapping with a pick-type hammer. I find filing lightly with an ordinary fine file is one of the best ways to find high spots – file and they become shiny. In fact, if you have the patience and have excellent access to both sides of a panel, a file, a hammer and a dolly can be used to do *fillerless* body work.

Problem: General signs of old age

Cure: Look at the contours carefully from many angles. Are both front wheel openings the same? If not some kneeing and pulling by hand can do wonders; ditto with the rear wheel openings. How does the hood fit? A wooden block and some leaning on the hood can help a lot. Check the bottom edges of the body and carefully use your hammer and dolly on them.

Bodywork generally decreases in quality from the roof downward. If you did any welding on cracked sheet metal around the door hinges, reinstall the door and check the fit. Add or remove door shims if necessary. Doors can be twisted to fit better if you break the appropriate welds on the inner panel. Do it now, not after all the paint is on! I know!

Problem: Major body damage

Cure: The "Kruger technique". Even Satch Carlson uses it! Attach a chain at the point of impact with welded shut eye-bolt and a 4 in. diameter, $1/4$ in. thick washer or a two by four or whatever. Put the chain around a telephone pole, leave a few feet of slack in it, and back up (or pull forward). Briskly if it's severe damage or more slowly if it's only moderate damage. If the side of the car is damaged, you may have to use a borrowed pick-em-up instead of the pole. Chuck Kruger once made a "C" shaped 911 relatively straight again using this technique.

Fitting Removable Panels

One area in particular that is difficult to deal with on any car is the fit of panels. How the doors close, how the hood fits; this is all critical to a fresh restoration or a car to be sold. It is extremely difficult to replicate the fit of original, undamaged panels, but not impossible. The easiest way to ruin a door gap is to use reproduction rubber seals that are thicker and less pliable than the original. One seal by itself is difficult to work around, but when all of them are replaced in a complete restoration, gap problems are compounded to the point that the panel won't even close!

I was reminded of the fact when Dennis Strauss called about replacing the top-to-window seals on his Roadster. He went to great lengths to come up with some different samples, and the differences were indeed amazing.

328

The sample that we settled on came from International Mercantile, and was very soft and thin compared to the others. It was obvious that the door with the window up would have been very difficult to close with the other seals. I have been using the same source for years, and have had very few problems since then, so I guess I never really thought about the pitfalls of lesser quality rubber seals. The advice here is, unless you can secure an original seal that is not dry rotted from age or save your original, you should talk to Terry at International Mercantile.

The next step in getting good fit from your car is to try all the new seals *before* the car is painted. This allows the panel to be fitted to the body without paint flying and the car returned to the body shop. This does involve some extra work for the body shop and their attitude is sometimes, "It fit fine before it left," but truly conscientious shops will ask for the seals you plan to use to get it right. This is most important for the door fit, where there are four or five sealing surfaces to deal with, any one of which can ruin the gap. The hood is also difficult to deal with, the seal offered by some suppliers is drastically different from the original product and the hood will never fit right with these seals. Again, the hood should be fitted with the proper seal in place, then painted and reassembled. The hood seal gap is always located in the upper right (passenger) corner on all 356s, right at the body weld. But even after you have done all of this correctly, how do you get the hood to sit just right against the contour of the body?

The first step to adjusting the hood (after paint and fitting is complete) is to remove the right (passenger) cover in the luggage compartment. This will allow you access to the latch when you get the hood stuck. Then you should take the upper latch, loosen the retaining nut and make sure the

"pointer" moves freely within the latch frame. Next, you must cover the lower latch opening with some sort of tape and lightly grease the end of the upper latch. Lower the hood just until the two surfaces touch, then raise the hood again. The grease mark on the tape will tell you what to do. If the mark is in the center, you can proceed. If not, you will have to turn or bend (off the car) the upper latch "pointer" until it hits the lower latch dead center. Note that all bolts, springs and latch surfaces are painted body color, as are the hood handle nuts. Note also that the area that the safety latch drags on is taped as well to prevent you from scratching it during the adjustment. On a concours car, you would have to take care to release the safety latch each time you lower the hood to prevent the scratch, as well as having an accomplice pull the drawstring while you push the hood into place to avoid the latches and fresh paint from damaging each other, but enough of that nonsense. Once the pointer hits the tape dead center, you are ready to go on.

Now that we know the latches are in synch, you need a helper to pull the drawstring while you press the hood down. You should feel only the resistance of the latch spring as you compress it. Any other motion or resistance is not healthy, and will hang the hood up if you release the string. Move the pointer accordingly until there is no obstruction. This step should not be necessary if you hit the tape mark just right, but should never be left out. If the hood does hang up, the first resort is to have your friend pull the string while you gently move the hood from side to side with the hood handle. If you are dealing with a GT, be careful. The next resort is to reach through the access cover under the car and pop the latch with a paint paddle or the like. You can also remove the small plug under the left front fender and thread a wire rod with a rounded end through the hole in the body to pull on the latch. Contrary to popular belief, on all A's and T5 B's, there is no safety string tied to the latch, only the hole for you to reach through. As a side note, the jack must be installed with the jacking mechanism to the right side of the trunk or it will interfere with this procedure. The last resort is to try the paint stick from the outside, striking the latch pointer from the front. Of course, the true last resort is a Sears Model 120A pry bar, but we are trying to avoid this.

Once everything is in position, you can lower the hood until it latches. The hood should give off a slight ping as it latches. The height of the hood where it is closest to the front edge of the body can now be adjusted by turning the pointer to raise or lower the hood. As the pointer threads up, the gap gets smaller. Remember, if you had to bend the pointer, you must mark the front and turn the pointer in full turn adjustments or it will turn from center. With this last adjustment, the hood can be dialed in to sit perfectly against the body contour, and all of the Reutter elves will feel a flutter of happiness.

Paint

Vol. 3, No. 5 Brett Johnson

Masking Materials
Newspaper as Tom Oerther pointed out in the April 1977 issue tends to break down and allows small particles to fly around when hit by the air pressure is true. Newspaper is also very porous and lets the paint soak through (even quick drying lacquers - remember your final "flow-out" wet coats) the paper and will eventually stick to the surface which you've masked. When wet sanding lacquer (or acrylic lacquers) in between coats, the newspaper can be easily torn by air pressure when blowing off water in the crevices and through normal handling.

A better material for masking is simply – the commercial automotive masking paper which can be purchased at any well stocked automotive paint supply store. It comes in various widths; it does not have the properties that newspaper has when used as masking paper described above. One drawback is you've got to buy it, where as newspaper costs next to nothing, if not free. It is well worth the extra few dollars for the commercial masking paper and not worth the problems newspaper can cause. Let's not practice false economy here, since you probably are going to have a few thousand dollars invested in your Porsche.

Also, on the same subject, beware of the cheap masking tape sold commonly at discount paint stores. They tend not to adhere very well and allow the lacquer thinner to bleed through. I must agree with the final remarks concerning masking tape and add a warning of my own. Don't leave any masking tape in place more than a few days. It will refuse to come off. Removal can be achieved using lacquer thinner but it is no fun when you try this on a freshly painted car.

Vol. 6, No. 4 John Paterek

Custom-Mixed Nitrocellulose Lacquer
There are a number of alternatives. Usually one sits down with a color book at the old body and paint supply store and pick one that looks about right. John Paterek of Chatham, N.J., sent me an alternative to this. You can send off a piece of your car if it has original paint to:

Bill Hirsch, Inc.
396 Littleton Ave.
Newark, New Jersey 07103
(201) 642-2404

They will match it in nitrocellulose lacquer for $55 per gallon, minimum purchase 3 gallons. Red, Maroon and metallic colors cost more. Color match is done on a spectrograph so it should be exact.

Price checked prior to publication – September 1994

Vol. 10, No. 3 David Seeland

Pre-Paint Prep Work

Plastic body filler? Bondo? I'm sure you thought real restorations were only done with lead. Styrene fumes are bad enough. Lead fumes are exceedingly toxic causing brain damage and other problems. I'd just as soon retain what limited mental faculties I now possess. Lead is bad stuff, besides heat is necessary for its application. Heat causes warps, more lead, more warps, more lead... and whee! a 4,500 pound lead coated low-rider Speedster.

I have been using plastic with glass microsphere filler instead of talc filler. Ditzler aluma-lead uses aluminum powder for filler and is waterproof and tough. Paul Orkild used it over Porsche-like rust at the rear of a Datsun's front fender after denting in the rusted area and now, several years later, it hasn't fallen out or bulged or anything. Quite amazing, but use metal for rust repair on your 356. Ask your automotive paint store for their recommendation.

Another point that should be made here is that it is always better to use plastic filler than lacquer based spot putties or glazes. Spot or glazing putty is essentially thick lacquer-based primer in a tube and if applied thickly will continue to shrink for a very long time. Polyester glazing putty is far superior and eliminates the need to use the lacquer-based spot putties (Evercoat #400 is excellent). Plastic filler sets up chemically and does not continue to shrink although it seems to absorb solvents from primer or finish coats and swell slightly and then shrink slightly as the solvents are lost.

Before applying plastic filler roughen the sheet metal with a 36 grit Roloc disc. Do not apply metal-prep or other metal-etching acid solutions. Although metal-prep helps primer to adhere, it inhibits proper plastic-filler adhesion.

An alternative to roughened bare metal that Ditzler recommends is the use of DP-40 epoxy primer before plastic-filler application for maximum adhesion. Mark Eskuche uses this technique and says that he has seen cars that were restored using DP-40 under filler and then involved in an accident and the plastic cracks but does not come off. However, Ditzler's product information sheet says the epoxy primer should not dry more than one week before applying other undercoatings and/or top-coats. I don't work fast enough for this kind of timetable.

Plastic should be applied over a larger area than you think is necessary. If, after sanding, the plastic/metal margin looks sharp it is probably low. It is right if the plastic gets almost transparent on the edge when sanded.

"Tin" the area with a thin coat of plastic by wiping a thin coat on with lots of pressure using a plastic spreader (*Registry* Fig. 3, p. 14, vol. 10, no. 1). Immediately, build up with a more liberal application of plastic. Wait until the plastic starts to set up (cheese-like consistency) and rough-shape with a half-round Stanley Surform (Fig. 3, p. 14, vol. 10, no. 1).

Add more filler to any low spots found by the filing and file again. File from the edges of the repair toward the center or the filled area will be too flat (if the area is convex, outward). Let it dry thoroughly (24 hours is best) and sand the plastic with a 17 1/2 in. long piece of 36 grit paper either in an air-operated sander or on a sanding board. Be sure to use a fresh piece of sandpaper so the sanding can be done without using a lot of vertical force. If you have to use a lot of vertical force the edges of the filled area will be low. Always use the longest sanding block possible when sanding plastic (or primer or paint) in order to minimize waves.

The ultimate goal of body work is, of course, to restore your 356 to a condition that is not detectably different from factory new. This means that feeling the underside of a fender should not reveal the presence of overlying filler. Also, 356 sheet metal is not $1/8$ in. thick and if it appears this thick at the bumper bracket holes, then it is obviously different than factory new. The cure is to do careful metalwork on the bracket holes so that essentially no filler is necessary at the holes.

You will probably find it necessary, even on a relatively straight car, to cover large areas with a very thin layer of body filler. This is not something you should worry about, the plastic will last a lot longer than the paint. Body-work novices commonly use too great a thickness of filler over too small an area.

Here are some ways to check body contours before the primer stage. Use your hands with a rapid brushing motion. Block sand both bare metal and plastic. Careful examination of the sanding marks will reveal highs and lows. Try directing a floodlight parallel to body surfaces.

Before going on to primer, it might be best to explain sand scratches and how to avoid them. I have seen original equipment sand scratches but if this is what it takes to reproduce a factory original finish, then I'd rather over-restore. Sand scratches are the sanding marks that can be seen in lacquer or enamel top coats. They may not have been there a day or week after the painting was completed. But in a few weeks they will become noticeable and will continue to develop and deepen as long as the paint continues to shrink which may be as long as two years.

The reason sand scratches form is simple: assuming a perfectly smooth paint surface upon completion of the topcoats, there is a greater paint plus primer thickness over any underlying scratch than in an adjacent unscratched area. If the paint over both shrink the same percentage, then the paint over the scratch will shrink a greater amount in absolute terms (because it is thicker) and the once smooth surface will now have a sand scratch. If the paint shrinks 10 percent, the depth of the newly formed sand scratch will be 10 percent of the depth of the underlying scratch. It therefore behooves you, the painter, to get the substrate quite smooth before applying primer-surfacer.

You might think it is possible to avoid the problem by applying the primer, waiting a year with the car out in the hot sun, and then block sanding the entire surface after the primer has shrunk as much as it ever will and then applying the topcoats. This could help to some extent, but what actually happens is that your year-old primer absorbs solvent from the topcoats and then what you get is sand scratch swelling. The primer swells the same percentage everywhere, but in absolute terms it swells more where it is thicker (over the scratches in the plastic or metal beneath the primer).

Now, if you would wait another year these raised areas would slowly shrink until the topcoat surface was again parallel to the primer surface. But if you become impatient and decide to wet sand and buff the paint to remove the ridges before the year is up, then sand scratches will later develop where you once had ridges. Sounds hopeless, doesn't it?

Tune in two months from now and see if our hero, the do-it-yourself painter, can escape or if he has painted himself into a sand scratched corner.

Paint Selection and Application

I went to look at a C cabriolet at a small body shop today and talked to the owner about paint. He showed me a C coupe with shiny but crazed lacquer and said that lacquer-like, but more durable, results could be obtained with acrylic enamel with isocyanate hardener. *Cough*. Every time I've painted a car with hardened acrylic enamel I've coughed for several weeks even with a hood respirator. You will have to decide if the health problems are significant.

Choosing the paint

Enough of that, time to apply some paint to that soon-to-be-concours 356. If it seemed that this series was at least 90 percent preparation and 10 percent painting, that is the way to get perfect paint. Paint only magnifies blemishes in the body; it does not conceal them.

There are only two basic choices in automotive paint: lacquer and enamel. Most lacquer now available is acrylic lacquer but the original nitrocellulose lacquer is still available and although less durable is reputed to be the ultimate for show-quality paint. I haven't tried it and probably won't. The second major choice is acrylic enamel with or without a hardener. Non-acrylic enamel is also available but it is not suitable for a 356.

What should you use? If you are painting a race car or a beater, then straight acrylic enamel is a good choice. The bugs and dust in the paint won't matter and it will look shiny enough. I've just completed painting a 1968 911 with acrylic enamel with hardener and I don't think it was worth the hassle for some possible extra long-term durability. Without hardener acrylic enamel can't be sanded and buffed but with hardener it can be wet-sanded just like lacquer. Wet-sanding lacquer always seems to cause

a paint buildup on the paper, but this doesn't happen with hardened acrylic enamel. The two disadvantages of hardened enamel are: 1) isocyanate fumes, and 2) a visible margin around any areas spotted in later (even after sanding) and the same visible margin problem if you sand through a complete recoat.

If acrylic enamel is applied in a paint booth so dust is not a problem and if you have enough skill to apply the paint with no runs or orange peel, then you can get a spectacular glossy completely flat finish with no additional work, but even a pro doesn't manage this 100 percent of the time. There are other enamel-like urethane paints available: Imron, Deltron, Durethane, Sunfire and others. These paints have many of the same problems as hardened acrylic enamel– toxicity, repairability–and to these are added: high price. I have tried Imron and it is a very tough glossy paint but I still prefer lacquer.

Lacquer is the amateur painter's friend. It is easy to apply and with lots of elbow grease can be brought to a brilliant gloss. I think it is much less toxic than most other paint, but still be careful.

Paint application–lacquer

If you are at the stage where you can't find any more blemishes in any of the panels, then it's time to get out the Binks and put some color on. How many coats? I really don't know. A complete Speedster – inside the doors, undersides of lids – should have about six to eight quarts of unthinned lacquer applied. Thinned for spraying it's a lot more. A coupe should take about two gallons. I tried one gallon on just the exterior of an A coupe and had buff-through problems, although I did some wet-sanding between coats. I have found that there is little reason to put on $1/4$ of the paint, let it sit, wet sand, the next $1/4$ of the paint, und so weiter. It's going to take more paint if you work this way, and I have had no cracking or other durability problems putting all the paint on at once. Paint stores will estimate a lot less paint but most of their customers don't wet-sand and buff the paint.

The undersides of lids, water shield on the engine lid, door edges and hinge areas should be painted with ultra high gloss thinner. This gives an enamel-like finish that is easily hand rubbed. If you get pebbly dry lacquer on these areas, it won't be easy to get them shiny. You'll sand through on edges and generally have a difficult time getting them nice. Don't use this

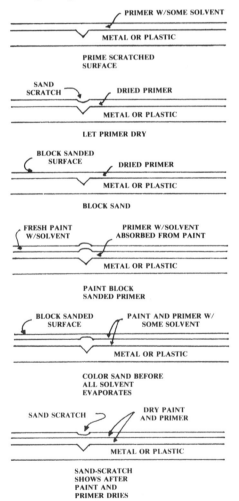

Fig. 1 – How sand scratches result from scratches in a metal, plastic or primer substrate

thinner on the exterior though. It will take longer to evaporate from the paint film and you should be wet-sanding and buffing anyway so initial gloss is of no consequence.

Try for uniform paint thickness from rocker panels to roof. Avoid the natural tendency to skimp on the lower portions of the body and load the paint on the fender tops. Each pass of the gun should be at a uniform speed overlapping the previous pass by one-half. The spraying distance should remain constant too.

Silver or any other metallic paint presents difficulties because it changes brightness depending on how wet it is applied. It is brighter where applied dryer and darker where applied wetter. The end result is a striped car if you change speed or distance between strokes.

Color sanding

Color sanding is done with 600 and finer wet-or-dry paper prior to buffing. Its purpose is to produce a perfectly planar surface. Then the surface is power buffed and hand rubbed to a mirror-like shine. Simple? Not really. The most critical point here is deciding when to sand, not if you should sand. It is possible to paint a car with lacquer and just buff it or hand rub it, but if the paint has the normal complement of bugs, dust and sand-scratches, you won't be happy unless the car is white.

What causes sand scratches? The cause is differential shrinkage of paint or primer, the thicker paint over a scratch in a metal, plastic, or original paint substrate shrinks more in absolute terms (though not proportionally more) than adjacent thinner paint (Fig. 1).

It appears as though the proper procedure is to wait until the primer is dry (Fig. 1, step 2), then sand (step 3), apply the paint (step 4), wait until the paint and primer are dry (step 6), and then color sand and buff. Right? Yes, but... do you know how long it takes lacquer to dry here in hot and dry Denver? About two years! You probably will buff after step 5, before all the solvent evaporates unless you are exceedingly patient. So how do you ever get a lacquer paint job without sand scratches (step 6)? Be patient and let the paint dry as long as possible before color sanding the first time, then buff it and expect to color sand and buff the car again when the sand scratches that will continue forming begin to offend your sensibilities. If this is less time than two years for a garaged car, expect to color sand and buff a third time about two years after first applying the color.

There is one more caveat: the car must have a sufficient paint film thickness so that you don't sand and/or buff through the paint to the primer. Each time the paint is color sanded, less paint will have to be removed because the sand scratches that do develop are shallower and less extensive. Don't scrimp, put six quarts on a Speedster and eight on a coupe. However, excess paint film thickness is bad too, and can cause cracking of the paint.

Wet-or-dry paper appropriate for color sanding is available in 600 and ultra-fine 1200 from 3M and 1000 and 1200 from Nikken. I use a little detergent in the water and start with 600 and work up to 1200. Before sanding, be sure the car is surgically clean or you will put in more scratches than you take out (a positive scratch flow). Use a clean new sponge to dribble water onto the surface as you sand. If you have the patience it probably would be better to start with ultrafine because sanding not only levels the surface but puts in fine scratches which must be buffed out. The finer grits put in smaller scratches which buff out more easily.

The sanding progression should remove all the less than 1200 scratches but you'll probably miss some. Always use a foam pad – 3M has one

that a $1/2$ sheet of wet-or-dry wraps around. If you sand with longitudinal strokes in the concave areas along the sides of the hood and the tops of the rear fenders, you may get grooves so attempt a crosshatch sanding pattern in these places. Be as careful on the lower edges of the body as along the fender tops even though the lower parts are hard to see and difficult to get at. This is one of the things that separates so-so paint from real concours paint.

A window squeegee is great for drying an area to check how the sanding is going. It isn't possible to tell if the sanding is complete when the surface is wet.

Be very careful not to sand through on the edges of panels. If you do, touch up the paint with a brush and unthinned paint and resand when dry. Touch up any other imperfections in a similar fashion.

Buffing
Buffing is fun. It will transform the paint and suddenly the car that seemed to be perpetually scruffy will turn into a gleaming gem.

Why all this sanding and buffing? Let's look at what happens when light glances off a smooth finish and a rough finish (Fig. 2, next page). From a rough finish, Fig. 2A, the light scatters and since less light arrives at the observers eye, the paint appears dull. From a smooth flat finish, Fig. 2B, the reflected light rays are parallel and the surface appears bright and "shiny".

Power-buff where possible and finish up by hand rubbing areas that are impossible to buff with the buffer. I use a Sears two-speed buffer-grinder on low speed with contoured pads. Do not use the tie-on type of pad. If this is all you have, buy a contoured pad and throw the tie-on pad away. It would be better to hand-rub the whole car than scar up the paint with a tie-on pad. In fact, some people will not use a power buffer at all, saying that you won't be able to get rid of the swirl marks.

Make sure the pad is moving from the body toward the edge when approaching a fender opening or any other edge. If the wheel is moving toward the body it will grab the edge and is likely to remove the paint at this point. The buffer is not reversible, just use the opposite side of the pad. Don't let the rotating pad touch the cord either. I used to rent buffers and they all had very short cords. The pad will grab the cord faster than you can imagine and instantly wrap it around the shaft. When it runs out of slack it tears the cord off. It can jerk the buffer right out of your hands. I know. If you want to test your vocabulary just see what you say when the buffer whacks a dent in that fender that you've been trying to make perfect for six months. Be very careful and you won't have this problem. Practice on something else (like a 1962 Ford) before trying to buff your SC cabriolet.

I use two grades of 3M buffing compound, coarser first then finer. Then I use dry cornstarch. ACHOO! But it really works. Next I buff with 3M Fill-n-Glaze or Liquid Ebony.

The trick on hand rubbing (and power buffing) is to apply friction until the compound begins to dry. At this point the gloss really begins to come up. Hand rubbing usually uses coarser abrasives than power buffing compounds. I have a can of Classic Finish Restorer that is the best hand rubbing compound I've ever used, but I've never seen it in a store again. Pat

Scanlan, who does perfect concours paint in his home garage, said he used some kind of stove polish! Try a bunch of different "cleaners" and you'll soon have a favorite hand rubbing compound. Just remember to rub until it dries.

After power buffing and hand rubbing you will probably find some blemishes. Sand them out with 1000- or 1200-grit paper and repeat the buffing or rubbing process.

The final step is waxing. I like Meguiars because it seems to deepen the color. Johnsons Sprint is nice for just-before-the-concours re-wax because it leaves no chalky residue.

That's it. Take your 356 outside in the early evening, put it on the lawn, lean back against a tree and savor the reflections and color changes in the warm light of the setting sun. When it is too dark to see, roll your masterpiece back into the garage and install the carpeting and headliner and lights and bumpers and... In a month you may be done, but your 356 will never be more satisfying and appealing than it was those first moments outside in the warm evening light. All the compliments and concours trophies will never be the equal of the satisfaction of realizing that the gleaming 356 on the lawn was wrested from the clutches of rust and disrepair by your own hands.

Vol. 13, No. 6 David Seeland

"...did you paint it with a spray can?"
No, I didn't. But I must admit, my out-of-the gun first-time Deltron job on our 1959 356A sunroof coupe did look like it could have been. This was in spite of painting with epoxy primer (PPG DP-40), catalyzed primer (PPG-K-200) and Deltron polyurethane paint.

Painting is actually a 3-step process: 1) bodywork and filler application, 2) application of primer and paint, and 3) color-sanding and polish-

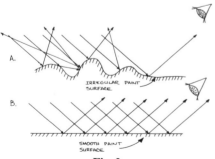

A.

IRREGULAR PAINT
SURFACE

B.

SMOOTH PAINT
SURFACE

Fig. 2

ing. In a previous *Registry* series "Paint your Porsche", I emphasized steps 1 and 2. In this issue of the *Registry* I'll talk about color sanding and some background painting information. And by the way, no one will ever ask again if the sunroof coupe was painted with a spray can. It is one of the shiniest cars I've ever done. The orange peel, runs and sags, and grainy surface are gone.

Before paint can be polished it must first be made flat. If it can be color-sanded flat it even could have been applied with a brush. If the paint is not made flat before polishing, the result will probably look like a shiny pebble-surfaced basketball. The flattening is followed by buffing to increase the smoothness and reflectively of the surface. The process is gradational because after wet sanding with 2000 grit paper the paint is already glossy.

Reflectively or "shine" depends on the surface being smooth on a microscopic scale. A sheet of glass and a concrete driveway are both flat, but only the glass is reflective because light from an object is reflected in the same direction (toward the observer) from adjacent parts of the surface. The granular material in the concrete causes the light from an object to be reflected in many different directions and the concrete is non-reflective. Enamels, because they are slow drying and consequently self leveling, due to surface tension of the wet paint film, usually have a higher initial gloss than fast-drying lacquers. The initial gloss of lacquer is nearly always less than that of enamel, but can be increased by using a slower drying thinner or the same thinner with a "retarder" to slow the evaporation rate.

You might wonder why many concours cars are painted with lacquer. It is because the slightly granular, as painted, surface has been flattened by wet-sanding with fine-grit waterproof silicon carbide paper and polished

with a liquid abrasive compound. Ordinary acrylic enamel, unless very old (years) cannot be sanded and polished.

Polyurethane paints such as Imron (Dupont) and Deltron (PPG) and catalyzed acrylic enamel (enamel with hardener) harden all the way through and can be wet sanded and polished.

If the painter is skillful and a bit lucky, an out-of-the-gun paint job can be near-perfect and as good as a factory paint job. Factory painting is done mostly with acrylic enamel under controlled conditions and is good, but not perfect. Look at the orange peel on the vertical surfaces of a 911 or 944 where the paint is not applied as heavily in order to avoid runs. Perfection requires hand sanding and buffing and not many manufacturers want to put $6000 paint-jobs on their cars. The best factory paint I've ever seen was on a black replica Cobra – "factory", but not mass-produced.

Enough of generalities, what sanding techniques and products are available? The most significant recent development is the availability of very fine grades of waterproof paper.

About 15 years ago, a friend painted Al Lager's T-5 coupe with catalyzed acrylic enamel, wet-sanded with 600 grade waterproof paper (the finest then available) and power buffed the sanded finish. The result never did look like much even though he tried hard. Today, with 3M ultra-fine (1000) and micro-fine 1200) paper, Tom Conway, owner of Karossirie Fabrik, a Boulder shop, obtains impressive results based on a black C coupe and a couple of 911s that I've seen. His painter sands and power buffs Deltron the day after it is painted because it is softer and buffs easier then.

Even finer waterproof Nikken paper is available from Nikken or Meguiar's. Nikken paper is available in grades as fine as 1500 or 2000. According to the owner of a local paint store who got some a few years ago and took it home for his own use, Nikken apparently makes or made 4200 grade paper (smoother than a baby's skin).

Use of these papers and other Meguiar's products is detailed by a Meguiar's video tape and a couple of their technical data sheets (vol. 1, no. 3 and no. 5). The advantage of using the finest possible paper for sanding is that the sanding marks are more easily minimized by buffing. The disadvantage is that it takes longer to sand out imperfections with the finer papers.

I used 400 paper to sand out the runs in the Deltron on my 1959 sunroof A coupe. Even though you plan to sand and buff, don't use this as an excuse to be sloppy while painting. Smoothly applied paint can be sanded more quickly with finer paper and then the buffing will be quicker and the final result more satisfactory. Use of progressive paper grades will allow larger defects to be removed more quickly, but some deeper paper scratches almost always remain. Mequiar's says: "most defects can be removed with 2000 grade sanding paper" and "always use the least abrasive product to remove paint defects". Before starting to sand, thoroughly wash all dirt from the car to avoid dirt scratches. Soak the sanding paper overnight for best results. While sanding, continuously dribble water from a sponge or hose onto the surface. Detergent added to the water will help prevent paint buildup on the paper and the paper lasts longer. Fairly large quantities of detergent may be necessary.

Use a foam sanding block. Mequiar's makes a hard one good for flat surfaces and 3M makes a softer one good for curved surfaces. Slotted hard rubber sanding blocks can be used to remove minor waviness from doors and fenders if the paint film is thick enough. It is best to remove waves at the substrate stages, however. The hard rubber blocks are also best for removing runs. Two block lengths are available, one takes strips cut from the length of a sheet of sanding paper, the other from the width of a sheet. Mequiar's makes tiny little abrasive blocksfor the removal of small high areas.

The paint-film thickness must be great enough to remove lows such as orange peel, incipient fish eyes, or scratches, without sanding through to the primer. Put extra paint over runs and the surrounding area or you might sand through next to the run before the run is gone. I put second and third coats of hardened acrylic enamel on a red 911 once because of dirt problems (each coat dried overnight). Sanding through the last coat left irregular edges. These were not easily seen being only just a color change or hardness difference but I would rather not have had them. The better the body work under the paint the less likely there will be unexpected highs to increase chances of sanding through the paint.

Clear coating is necessary on metallic colors such as silver and popular on solid colors. It is nearly as bad to sand through the clear coat as through the color into the primer. I've only clear coated one car so I'm no expert. Be sure to use enough so that you don't sand through the clear – I'd guess about 1.5 gallons on a coupe. I prefer not to use clear on solid colors, it's just one more step to worry about.

My advice is to use lots of paint if you are going to sand and buff. I was told that two quarts of Deltron would be enough for an A coupe – not true. I sanded through in a couple of places using one gallon. I'll use one and one-half to two gallons next time. I used 6 quarts of lacquer on our speedster and had no sand-through problems. Thicker paint films are said to be more fragile, but I'll take my chances. A digital meter for measuring total thickness of paint plus primer plus plastic over ferrous metal is available. However, measurements of plastic plus primer thickness would have to be made at known locations to be able to keep track of paint thickness as sanding progresses. Lots of paint is easier.

Two schools of thought regarding the pattern of sanding strokes exist. One says to sand in one direction only. The other says that a crisscross pattern at 60 to 90 degrees is better. I think it depends on the surface contour because if the area is concave as along the sides of the hood parallel strokes will form slight groves from the edges of the sanding block. I crisscross the pattern in concave areas and use a parallel pattern on convex fender tops or nearly flat doors.

To summarize, put on plenty of paint, clean the finish thoroughly before sanding, use a pad with the finest grade paper you can manage, put detergent in the water and use lots of it as you sand. Sand carefully along edges because of reduced paint film thickness. *Don't sand through the paint!*

Vol. 17, No. 5 Brett Johnson

Having Glasurit Paint Mixed

I was aware that Stoddard had obtained a number of mixing codes for early colors, but had heard that they couldn't ship paint due to our friends at the EPA. They told me that Glasurit has a toll free number that has people on the other end who can give out color information (800) 825-5000.

I called them and requested Adriatic Blue Metallic (the color of my still unfinished 1955 coupe). They said, "Our Porsche colors only go back to 1956. Try tech services at (800) 825-3000."

What it boils down to is that any paint store that sells Glasurit (BASF) paint can call the second number and get the information required to mix most 1950 - 1955 paint colors. Adriatic Blue Metallic is not one of them. If the Adriatic Blue is of interest you can call Bruce Baker at (610) 454-1055. He can tell you what color was actually used on my car.

Both of the toll free numbers listed above are for your reference, so that you can supply them to your paint seller. If you call them you will not be able to order paint. They can supply the formulas so your dealer can mix the colors. The first number 1956 and later. The second number 1950 through 1955. Paint can only be mixed in single stage urethane. If you want the original lacquer (1950 - 1955 coupes and cabriolets), a couple of firms that advertise in *Hemmings* can accommodate you, but unless you have a sample of the color you'll probably have to have a small quantity of the Glasurit mixed. Below are the colors that are available:

I would suspect that #501 Black (5401) can also be obtained, although they didn't specifically mention it. They recognize these early colors by either name or the Reutter numbers.

1950 - 1953	Reutter #	Porsche #
Ivory	504 Lacquer	-
Fish Sliver-Grey	505 Lacquer	-
Radium Green	510 Lacquer	-
Azure Blue	522 Lacquer	-
Pascha Red	523 Lacquer	-
Strawberry Red	524 Lacquer	-
Palm Green	526 Lacquer	-
Sand Grey	527 Lacquer	-
Medium Grey	531 Lacquer	-
1954 - 1955		
Turkish Red	538 Lacquer	5402
Graphite Metallic	537 Lacquer	5403
Ivory	504 Lacquer	5404
Jade Green Metallic	536 Lacquer	5405
Silver Metallic	535 Lacquer	5406
Pearl Grey	534 Lacquer	5407
Azure Blue	522 Lacquer	5408
Terra Cotta	533 Lacquer	5409
Signal (Fire) Red	601 Enamel	
White	603 Enamel	

Rustproofing

Vol. 3, No. 6 Marty Muszak

Using STP

To prevent rust formation on interior chambers (caused by condensation) such as doors, inside longitudinal members, hidden compartments on fenders etc., apply a thinned solution of "STP" and non-lacquer paint thinner using a spray gun or "pump" oil can. The thinner allows the gooey oil to leach into sheetmetal crevices. Apply on a hot day when it is certain the areas are dry.

Vol. 9, No. 1 David Seeland

Rustproofing, the Long Version

Why rustproof? Porsches *rust*, mostly a lot more than the C coupe from Arizona. So for those of us who don't live in Arizona, it's either don't drive them much in the wet, and never drive them when it's wet and salty, or plan on multiple sieges of rust-fixing. The alternative is rustproofing and careful cleaning and maintenance of the barriers between the body steel and water. If this is done properly, there is no reason not to drive your 356 all year in all kinds of weather.

Chuck Stoddard, in an excellent article on rustproofing 911s and 914s (*Porsche Panorama*, v. 20, no. 1, p. 10 - 16, also in *Up-Fixin*, v. 4, p. 198) said that a Porsche body that has been rustproofed should last at least twice as long as an untreated one. all other factors being the same. I hope that this estimate is on the low side because I owned a terminally rusty five year old 1968 911L from Minnesota in 1973.

Materials

Barrier type and placement are the the crux of the rustproofing process. Rust is partially hydrated iron oxide (*College Chemistry* by Linus Pauling) and can be cured by three 500 mg. vitamin C tablets a day. Well, vitamin C cures everything else, doesn't it? More seriously, unchipped paint is an excellent barrier, but underbody seams expand and contract and soon the paint cracks. Something more is necessary here. Flexible sealers and calks such as 3M no. 8500 autobody sealant or 3M no. 8578 strip caulk are best here. Asphalt based undercoating is primarily a sound deadening material and it is usually applied to the broad surfaces least likely to rust. Chuck Stoddard recommends the use of a wax-like rustproofing compound instead, Lubrizol 2043. I personally like to use 3M no. 8864, a flexible rubber based undercoating (Body Schutz), followed by black Ditzler acrylic enamel applied with a brush. – *More recently (1994) I have begun to use Würth black underbody seal, # 0893 075-U. The Würth undercoating seems to more closely approximate the very coarse orange peel of the original, because of its greater viscosity –* Bare rusty metal should be primed with Rustoleum rusty metal primer after wire brushing.

The interiors of box members, such as the longitudinals, present another problem since the factory did not apply any coatings in these areas. They are all rusted and some people argue that before anything else is done the rust should be "killed". Chemically I'm not sure what this entails. Phosphoric acid changes rust to a water soluble iron compound that can be washed away and etches the steel for better paint adhesion. DuPont metal prep and Rustop #3 (Centerline Products, Box 1466, Boulder, CO 80306) are two of these acidic compounds. This can create problems because the next step involves spraying the interior of these cavities with a solvent-based wax compound containing rust inhibiting phosphates and if crevices and seams are still wet, capillary action won't pull the wax compound into the seams. Of course, if you are patient enough, the acid solution will

340

eventually dry. Stoddard mentions one of the wax-base products (Lubrizol 785J and Centerline sells a similar material which I am using, Rustop No. 40, for about $18/gallon. Note: Application of Body Schutz and paint must precede application of any of the wax-base rustproofing materials.

Procedures

Let's first look at rust in front of the doors, typically one of the first places to rust. A friend of mine did a rustoration of a C coupe from Wisconsin (rust country). The car had lots of rust, but where there was still an intact fillet of factory caulk in the "V" at the rear of the front wheel well, the fender had not rusted through – but above and below the remnant of caulk it had rusted through. I don't think the 356As had appreciable caulking here.

By the time the factory realized what a problem they had designed into this area, they were already building 356Bs and Cs. The same progression is apparent again in 911s. Early 911s had inadequate or no caulking here, but a friend's 1977 911 has a very substantial fillet of caulk at the rear of the front wheel well. You would think they would have learned something from the 356s.

My procedure for rustproofing this area is first to remove the old caulk if it has pulled away, clean out all the dirt, spray in rusty metal Rustoleum primer (with a WD-40 type wand and spray tip on the can of primer), let it dry a day or so, paint with black acrylic enamel (use a 2 in. "sash brush"), put in a fillet of 3M strip caulk (no. 8578). Warm it in the sun first and make a $1/2$ in. diameter strip by squeezing together 5 or 6 of the thin strips, next cover the whole works with about $1/16$ of an inch of 3M auto-body sealant (no. 8500). Painting before the caulk is necessary to get the best adhesion (caulking does not adhere well if the surface has any dirt) and to provide an additional barrier if

the caulk fails. Be sure to do a good job all the way to the very top where there is a large amount of factory caulk that usually pulls away from the fender leaving a dam, and a perfect water reservoir, which usually causes rust to go through the top of the fender.

Repeat this process at the back of the door at the joint between the lock post and door, inside the rear wheel well. Here you are trying to seal the lap joint between the fender and the lock post on the inside front of the wheel well. The gap shouldn't be larger than about $1/16$ of an inch so just use the 3M auto-body sealant (no. 8500).

Four more areas under the front fenders warrant extra attention, behind the fog-light bracket, the rolled edge on the wheel opening, the lap joint in the center of the ridged closing panel at the rear of the wheel well, and the joint between the fender and the vertical inner panel.

Clean out behind the fog light bracket with a wire and air blast, then squirt in Rustoleum primer with the wand nozzle. Scrape and wire-brush along the top inside of the rolled edge of the fender opening, dribble Rustoleum along the seam trying to get it to run down around the wire. For more protection, seal the joint with 3M no. 8500 sealant after priming. The closing panel rust always occurs first in the area of overlap between the two panels and is the result of capillary action pulling salty water up from the bottom edge, although if the undercoating is really bad, water can get in anywhere along the seam. The cure is Rustoleum and a thin coat of 3M sealant.

The next step is undercoating with 3M Body Schutz (no. 8864); it is expensive, about $10 per quart can and you can figure on about one can per wheel well plus two or three more for the pan and battery box. You also need a $25 3M Body Schutz gun and an air compressor. If you are worried about original appearance, use a scraper to partially feather the edges of areas where the undercoating has broken off and then use a bit of body sealant as a filler. If you don't, then even after undercoating you will see the chipped area. In the front wheel wells, concentrate undercoat application on the rock spray area of the tire, particularly over and behind the tire.

The last step is the most important. Paint absolutely everywhere with black, unthinned, acrylic automotive enamel and a sash brush. You might consider using a plasticizer in the paint which should make it more resistant to rock chipping. Ditzler makes a plasticizer for use in painting plastic bumpers and such but it contains isocyanates which are very toxic. I'd rather repaint once in a while. I did use DuPont Imron (which contains isocyanates) on my Carrera 2 and it is tougher than acrylic enamel, but I wouldn't do it again after hearing some isocyanate stories.

There are places that are very difficult to reach with a brush and I have used black Rustoleum and the WD-40 wand. A rechargeable spray can with a wand and a regular spray head is available if you want to use all acrylic enamel. Be sure to get extra paint on the problem areas previously mentioned. The battery box is another problem area. Be sure the drains at the front of the hood and in the floor of the box are open. Use baking soda to neutralize any acid, dry, scrape, apply Rustoleum primer, Body Schutz (inside and out) and a couple of coats of acrylic enamel. Be sure the drains in the headlight buckets are open and that the light assembly is well sealed. It might help to caulk around the wires where they enter the tube in the floor of the buckets as done in 911s and remove the caulking where the tube enters the battery box.

Bolt holes through any exterior sheet metal – side trim, bumper trim, hood ornament name plates, rear bumper tip attachment – are places where rust is likely to start. When installing trim (except Speedster side trim) wrap the bolt threads with a layer of masking tape so the paint doesn't get chipped. Rustop no. 40 can be applied to the body and trim strip before attaching the strip. Try to keep the bolt threads from rusting by painting, molding on caulk, or using Rustop no. 40.

Rear bumper tips should be kept clean on Bs and Cs and painted on the inside – a squirt of Rustop 40 might be a good idea. Remove the rubber mounting grommets and brush Rustop 40 on the body and grommets and reassembly. Spray Rustop 40 inside the bumper bracket mounts on both front and rear bumpers.

Longitudinals should be sprayed inside with Rustop 40 or another good solvent-based wax compound. A Body Schutz gun can be rigged with a four foot long $3/32$ of an inch in diameter plastic wand (air shock tubing) and a homemade radial pattern tip or use the rechargeable spray can available from several sources, one of which is Miners Incorporated, P.O. Box 1301, Riggins, Idaho 83549 (Aero-can, AX 300, $21.95 plus shipping). Access to this area can either be through the fender well or from inside the car after lifting the carpets. In either case use a $1/2$ in. hole saw and plastic plugs. T-6 cars have drain holes in the longitudinals; earlier cars don't and they may or may not be worth having in the earlier cars. I am of the opinion that if the longitudinals are well sealed and internally rustproofed, then the drain holes are a liability. Use of the jack receiver seems to open up the inner seam and the rocker panel seam in its vicinity.

Careful sealing along both the pan and rocker panel edges of the longitudinal is wise. Use of the jack receiver should then be avoided. Clean and straighten the jack receivers, then spray the interior with Rustop 40. If they aren't straight they won't drain and they'll collect water and rust.

The box members (front strut reinforcement) under the tie rod holes can be treated like the longitudinals and access holes will have to be cut with a hole saw unless you are completely redoing the battery box - if so they are accessible and open to the front. While working in this vicinity, be sure to clean out the dirt inside the channel-shaped diagonal member and either prime with Rustoleum and paint, or coat with Rustop 40, depending on whether you lean toward concours or practicality. Be sure the drain channel at the rear, where they come together and join the pan, is open. Work in this area is facilitated by removal of the gas tank on T-6 cars.

The interior of the box member under the rear torsion bar tubes should be sprayed with Rustop 40 as should the interior of the torsion bar tubes. 1 haven't heard of a torsion bar tube on a 356 failing because of rust., but I know they do on 911s. While you're at it, replace the spring plate grommets - both for better sealing and better handling. Paint and regrease the torsion bars if necessary.

Door rust is most common in the joint between the door bottom and the outer skin. Remove the interior panels, carefully clean, and vacuum out the debris, then work Rustop 40 into the joint. Be sure the horizontal rubber glass seal is in good condition and the drain holes are open. The factory paint on the outside bottom of the door is somewhat thin and repainting of that area is probably worth while.

Even if your windshield and rear window gaskets don't leak, water from melting snow from your shoes can rust the floor. The asphalt saturated fell mat (on T-6 bodies) under the rubber mat must be removed. Scrape and wire brush or carefully use a needle scaler, an air operated device for removing rust scale (or loose undercoating - but not on the back side of finished surfaces). Caulk any places where you have removed the factory caulk, prime with Rustoleum and brush on black acrylic enamel. I suggest leaving out both the felt mat and the rubber mat during the winter and just using sisal mats. This allows the water to evaporate and will substantially cut down on the likelihood that your floor pan will rust through from the inside as it did in my "new" C coupe from Arizona. A concours freak might object to removing the felt, but I don't expect a concours car would be driven in the snow anyway.

I also am suspicious of the sound deadening material in the engine compartment. I think it makes a good water trap and your car would be less likely to rust without it. You could remove it, paint or spray the side panels with Rustop 40 and reinstall the sound deadening. If this is beginning to sound as though you should remove the engine, you're right. The most common place for rust to occur in the engine compartment is at the rear of the engine compartment pan, where it joins the vertical inner body panel. Rustop 40 should be sprayed into the rather complex recesses on the underside of the horizontal body panels and the only way to do this is to remove the engine. If you live in the fringes of rust country, you might be able to skip this step.

Summary

1) Look at cars in various stages of disintegration so you can prioritize and plan your rust proofing.

2) Assemble the equipment and material.

3) Clean the underside of the car with a high pressure washer.

4) Let dry thoroughly.

5) Be sure all body and window seals are in perfect condition.

6) Apply material in proper sequence-wax base rustproofing last.

7) Keep the underside of your car clean, particularly in the known areas of rust susceptibility. Check the integ-

343

rity of the caulking, sealing, under-coating and paint regularly. Spend more time cleaning the underside than the top side (remove the wheels or you're not doing a good job). Use soapy water and a "fender brush". Heavy duty rubber gloves are a must in the winter.

8) Put on four studded snow tires, install a gas heater, and go out and have fun in the snow!

Vol. 10, No. 1 Richard Miller

Extend

Have also included ad on new product which should seem like the holy grail to old Porsche pushers – Extend – just got some to test – will let you know in 20 years if it works. Test samples are impressive – coating is like black vinyl. Maybe I'll paint an entire car with it and dunk it in the Pacific Ocean.

The following description of Extend is from a Loctite Corporation newsletter called *Shop Talk*. Extend . . . What It Is, And Isn't "Rust conversion" technology has been on the market for several years in one form or another. Its chief benefit is to minimize surface preparation, which is labor-intensive. A slightly rusted surface actually aids the conversion process.

Loctite Corporation's contribution to this technology is to combine conversion chemistry with a tough latex polymer base to produce a rust-free surface that is protected by a tough coating. Unlike previous conversion formulas, it cannot be easily removed or damaged.

Extend One Step Rust Treatment is a surface interacting material. It is not a coating which simply acts as a barrier to oxygen, as do most of the fish-oil anti-rust paints now used. Nor is it an etchant. The new formula is best described as a "rust converting latex coating".

Vol. 10, No. 2 Pat Ertel

Extend, II

I used some Extend about 18 months ago when doing some body repair on my DOLT (DodgecOLT). The car had some fairly extensive surface rust on the outer body. In some places I attempted to grind away all the rust and in others I chipped away the worst stuff and glopped on some Extend. When finishing the car some of the areas were covered with bondo and some with primer surfacer. The car was painted in acrylic enamel with urethane hardener. Both the primer surfacer and the bondo stuck to the Extend just fine and the Extend treated area look great now 18 months later. The areas that got only grinding, etching, primer and finish are a different story. The paint is beginning to bubble up in a few places and I suspect it is because I left pinhead size specks of rust in the steel. These things are impossible to see because the rust spots are smaller than the grinding marks. I believe a good system would be to grind a little and treat the area with Extend. You should be warned that Extend is a rather thick coating and any surface it is used on will have to be slightly dented or ground away if the area is to be smooth when the job is finished.

I've been getting in to corrosion lately and I've learned some useless but interesting things. Did you know that both magnesium and aluminum corrode (oxidize) more readily than steel? Why, you ask do my 'tudes rust through when my engine doesn't?

Because the products of oxidation, "oxides", (iron oxide, or *rust*, is the product of the oxidation of steel) attach themselves firmly to the parent material in aluminum and magnesium and protect the parent material from further electron transfer (another name for oxidation). Iron oxide, on the other hand, runs away from home and leaves the parent material exposed so that it can corrode some more. And that's why our cars fall apart. The lesson here is that we can prevent our cars from rusting if we attach magnesium rods to the body. By keeping the rods moist and polished, we can cause all of the electron transfer to take place on the Mg and not on the steel. The rods could be kept moist by running booms out the side of the car in front of the Mg rods with little nozzles that spray water onto the rods. This isn't done a whole lot because most people feel a little self conscious driving porcupine, but Porsche owners *have* done some strange things.

Vol. 12, No. 3 Richard Miller

Extend, III

I would like to add to Bob Malley's comments on the subject of "Rust Killers". They work! A number of products similar to Neutra Rust are on the market. These are basically latex resin-phosphoric acid coating systems which passivate a rusty surface and seal it against further corrosion. They are different from zinc rich paints which like cadmium plating, are electrochemical attrition coverings which "corrode" instead of preserve the steel.

The system which Bob describes sounds very effective and quite like the one I use which is called Extend. This product is made by the Loctite Corp. and is distributed by many industrial chemical, supply and paint stores. It costs about $15 per quart, a bit less than 661. I have used it extensively for about 5 years and the only failure was where it was applied to an oily surface. The best example of protection was a rusty roadster in the backyard with red scaly floorpans where water collected. A liberal coating turned them a vinyl-like black and the rust *stopped*. Two years later I scraped them a bit, replaced some sections, recoated with Extend, primed, Tremco'ed (Tremco auto underbody

coat is better than Schutz; more build, less porous, better texture and paintable, if you want) and painted with polyurethane paint – that fixed it. Extend can be brushed, rolled, sprayed, dipped or sloshed. For spraying small areas some paint shops sell small do-it-yourself spray units made by Preval. These have a "power unit" screwed on a bottle. One unit filled with Extend will do an old rusty Speedster seat. Stripped doors, trunks and deck lids can be sloshed by putting Extend into channels and corners and tilting to flow it into seams and cracks. Try not to be too sloppy. What you get on your hands takes weeks to wear off and I don't recommend it under cosmetic surfaces. It swells when top coated.

I have also sprayed it into compartments with the home-made applicator shown in the sketch. The nozzle works as an aspirator with the air flow at about 30 to 40 PSI sucking the Extend out of the bottle and atomizing it. The flexible plastic tubing is about five feet long and half an inch in diameter so you can stuff it through a small hole, turn it on and coat everything as you pull it out slowly. The stuff even comes out the seams sometimes. I drill holes about $3/4$ in. diameter and plug them with the flat rubber plugs used to cover hinge access holes in early Porsches and VWs. Just try to keep the spray where you want it and don't breathe the mist, use mask and glasses.

On cosmetic surfaces I use a paint system which seems to be the best anti-rust treatment short of galvanizing. Strip to bare metal with paint remover – don't grind good metal, just rusted areas. Next scrub with Dupont 5717S Metal Conditioner using steel wool pads and wearing rubber gloves. This stuff eats rust and leaves bright bare metal. Next use Dupont 224S Steel Conversion coating. After this step you can leave the metal laying around and it won't rust but you should go to the next step before it gets dirty again. Next use Dupont Corlar Epoxy and then you're ready to prime and paint with a good polyurethane paint. Guaranteed not to rust. As with all chemical products, follow manufacturer's instructions and especially safety precautions. According to the label Glasso 21 series polyurethane can cause brain damage. Some of the milder chemicals can make you itch and burn for days, so be safe.

Vol. 12, No. 4 Bill Vaughan

Methylene Chloride Paint Removal
On the subject of rust control and paint, during the latter half of 1985 and early 1986 *Hot Rod* magazine ran a series of articles titled "How to Paint Your Car – Start to Finish." One article on preparation mentioned an efficient technique using starch thickened methylene chloride paint remover.

Don't stand in a cloud of methylene chloride fumes over a surface that is to be stripped, globbing it every five or ten minutes with a fresh brush of stripper. Instead, keep the methylene chloride concentration high at the painted surface and low in the surrounding air by covering the freshly globbed surface with a layer of plastic food wrap. Using plastic food wrap the methylene chloride can be confined against a painted surface for hours, after which time even thick coatings of paint can easily be removed with a dull chisel or a Red Devil wallpaper scraper in one pass.

As the *Hot Rod* article indicates, this technique will even permit the convenient removal of the baked on factory primer (for example, prior to welding). Something you might want to do.

During a low budget engine rebuild the methylene chloride/Saran Wrap technique can be used to remove thick greasy muck and oil stains from the crank case halves, heads and timing cover. Just swizzle it with the tooth-

brush and blast it off with a garden hose.

The plastic wrap sufficiently confines the methylene chloride vapors and reduces the volume of remover used to the point that it is bearable to use the stuff indoors.

Vol. 12, No. 5 James Cunningham

Rust Neutralizers, the High-Tech Way
I also got a letter from James Cunningham of Austin, TX regarding rust conversion. He included an article from *Materials Performance* magazine. It was a little on the technical side but it was written about the use of rust converters on automotive steel. It speaks to the fact that there are two general types of tannin-based rust converters on the market, those with a waterborne polymer and those without. The ones containing polymers (resins) have higher viscosities and due to this produce a thicker covering. The non-polymer compounds, however, have better penetration and can be applied directly to rusted surfaces without surface preparation. The conclusions of the article are as follows:

1. The inherent limitations of rust-converting products include their dependency on the barrier properties of the applied primer or incorporated resin and their limited application to surfaces with only marginal amounts of rust. The use of these products on surfaces that have been exposed to very aggressive environments appears inappropriate.

2. The reaction of tannin with rusted surfaces does not produce a completely inert, water impermeable, or insoluble coating.

3. Because of the formation of soluble iron-tannates, rusted surfaces treated with resin-free, tannin-based solutions, rinsed and subsequently primed will provide better topcoat integrity than surfaces treated with resin-based conversion coatings.

4. Although the use of rust convert-

ing products may be adequate, the use of other direct-to-rust types of products, such as inorganic solutions, sealants, etc. may provide a more technically sound approach.

As you gathered, this is a research paper rather than advertising literature. Due to this, they didn't name names; however, one of the resin-free products available is called Chesterton Rust Transformer and is available from A.W. Chesterton of Stoneham, MA.

Plating

Vol. 4 No 5 Brett Johnson

Chrome Plating

I'm sure most of you are aware from your high school chemistry that plating is basically an electrochemical process. Whereby the part to be plated is made the cathode in the electrical circuit. It is placed in a solution such as chromic acid. This solution is the source of chromium ions which are attracted to the cathode via the flow of electricity through the circuit. These ions accumulate on the object to be plated.

Chromium used for decorative purposed is generally applied over a layer of another type of plating such as nickel or copper plating. The first layer serves to seal the base metal from oxidation. Chromium, usually applied .00001 to .00002 inches in thickness, is quite porous. This would allow oxidation to readily occur. Acid solutions are used for cleaning prior to plating in tanks where pH and temperature must be maintained within specific limits for the desired results.

This is the basic theory as I understand it. If any of you are platers or chemists, please come forward and fill in appropriate information.

On the practical side plating can be a series of problems, monetary and

otherwise. First, a glance through the yellow pages in a reasonably large city reveals a myriad of plating shops. It is probably a good rule of thumb to stay away from shops specializing in bumper straightening. Most don't get the hang of intricate or non-steel parts and usually can't understand why you would want that engraved "Hella" on the license light to remain intact.

I have had the most luck with platers specializing in custom motorcycle work. The prices have been competitive and the work impressive.Some specifics to watch out for come from personal experience and related stories from others:

1. Plating Non-Steel Parts – Specify to your plater what metal you need plated. For example 356A bumperettes are chrome plated aluminum. These have been known to disappear in stripping tanks. Other metals frequently used are pot metal and brass. Very few chrome parts on 356 series Porsches are steel parts. A number of platers will shy away from these metals and very few will plate aluminum.

2. Condition of the Part – Deeply pitted or damaged parts are often uneconomical to replate. Check into the price of new parts before having marginal parts plated. 356A horn grilles are a good example, deeply pitted ones are quite common. Replating them is not always satisfactory due to the amount of metal which must be removed in order to reach a level that will produce a good finish.

3. Loss of Detail – The process of chrome plating requires buffing at various times. Due to this fine detail, such as manufacture's, marks are often partially or completely removed. It is best to point these out to your plater prior to having the job done.

4. Loss of Function – Replating of the door handles on my car was particularly satisfying. Not only was it relatively inexpensive but the plating was good and has weathered quite well. Plating of the lock cylinders, although

cosmetically very attractive, caused sufficient deposition of metal to make it impossible to lock or unlock the door from the outside.

5. Plating Originally Non-Plated Items – This can lead to problems. The only handy example I've got is a 356A hood handle which lost about 50% of its plating over the winter months. The plater had complained about the extremely porous base metal and advised something of this nature could take place.

6. Poor Weathering of Replated Parts (along similar lines to the example above) – I have noted numerous examples of replated parts which pit or rust within months following exposure to the elements. Choosing which will and which won't is impossible as far as finish goes, so the soundest advice that I can give is to heavily wax all newly plated parts and continue to do so on a regular basis.

Vol. 14 No 4 Pat Ertel

Cadmium Plating

Pellow's is the only mention of replating that I can recall reading in any Porsche repair references. I had read over and over The Maestro's enthusiasm over "Cadmium" plating. Personally, I always thought it looked stupid. It's just my own personal preference, but I never liked yellow nuts and bolts. Since I had the facilities of a rather large aerospace laboratory at hand, I took the opportunity to investigate the replating problem in depth and learned some rather interesting things. First of all, the original plating on the Porsche's nuts and bolts was probably zinc and not cadmium anyway. Almost all car manufacturers bought zinc plated parts. I had the opportunity to learn for free exactly what the original plating was, but I must confess that for some reason I turned it down. It was one of those mental lapses that take place now and then and allow you to say things like

"I do." I don't know what I was thinking of, the guy was standing there in the lab holding up one of my KMAX 10 mm case bolts and he said, "You want me to test it for you?" and like an idiot I was a nice guy and said "No, that's alright, you've been enough help already." Some investigative reporter, huh? Anyway, here is what I learned about cadmium plating:

Pellow's "Cad 11" apparently refers to part of military specification MIL-S-5002 "Surface Treatments and Inorganic Coatings For Metal Surfaces of Weapons Systems." (The version of this specification that I used for this article is Fed Spec QQ-P-416E which is approved for public release, so don't anybody get all excited and send this to your cousin in Iran, he's probably already got it). To get something plated, you really want more of a specification than just "CAD II". QQ-P-416E also specifies plating thicknesses and recommends certain post-plating coatings and processes to be used. The spec is 16 pages long, so I'll give you a real condensed version. The thickness specification is called the "Class", and "Class 3" (0.0002 in. thick) is specified for fasteners. The spec for all other hardware is "Class 1" (0.0005 in. thick). The reason behind the thinner coating of cadmium On fasteners is to avoid thread interference on nuts and bolts.

Military specifications for nuts and bolts require a much tighter fit between the threads than is usually found on automobile parts, so we car guys can get by with a thicker layer of plating. I chose "Class 2" (0.0003 in.) and had no interference problems. If you're brave you might try "Class 1" on all your hardware.

QQ-P-416E also addresses post plating coatings, which are designated by "Type". "Type 1" has no coating on the cadmium layer. It comes out looking dull and white. A quick swipe with 0000 steel wool dipped in light oil cleans it up nicely so that it looks something like unpolished aluminum. You can also have the plater give the parts a chromic or nitric acid "bright dip" which will give them a shiny bright appearance. It is not quite as shiny as zinc plating, but in my opinion it is the most visually pleasing of all the coatings and it gives the best corrosion protection you can expect.

"CAD II" is an occasionally used industry term which refers to the "Type II" coating. This is a chromate conversion coating which increases the corrosion preventive properties of the plating in some applications and usually (but not always) colors the parts yellow. "Type II" is recommended by QQP-416E for "... surfaces exposed to stagnant water, high humidity atmospheres, salt water, marine atmospheres, or cyclic condensation and drying." It is *not* recommended on parts which will be exposed to temperatures in excess of 150 degrees F because the anti-corrosion properties of the coating are degraded at that temperature. This coating is normally used on parts that are not expected to get hot and that are expected to be exposed to unusually corrosive environments, like salt water, so it's pretty much useless on an engine. The bottom line is that the only reason to use Cad II is if you *like* your engine to look stupid (or great, depending on your sense of esthetics) or if you never expect to run your engine and you intend to expose it to a corrosive environment, say like you're rebuilding it to use as an anchor for your yacht.

Your engine parts do exceed 150°F by the way, I checked by taping a thermocouple to the oil filter bracket and driving around for an hour on a 90 degree Ohio day. The peak temperature reached was 185 degrees. Interestingly, if your plater follows the Mil Spec exactly there is no guarantee your parts will come out yellow. The Spec calls for a color that is "... distinctly iridescent bronze to brown including olive drab and yellow." The plater can control the color with the processing though, so if you tell him you want it yellow, he can make it yellow.

So there you are walking into the plating shop holding your parts in your hand, as scared and confused as a newborn fawn alone in the woods, now what? If your experience is like mine, you'll probably get thrown out of the first half dozen places you visit. This can be frustrating and embarrassing. It's not that I'm any stranger to rejection, I've been thrown out of some of the best bars and restaurants in the Dayton area and I would consider it a personal privilege to be turned down for almost anything by the likes of, say, Deborah Norville. But to be rejected by some cigar chomping, round little greasewad because, "... yer parts ain't clean enough for me, buddy!" is more than even I can accept with dignity. Most plating shops don't like to do small jobs, they're set up for production work, so anything you can do to make the job easy for them will help you convince them that they really do want to do your job.

First of all, clean all the dirt, grease, and rust off the parts. There are dozens of ways to accomplish this, but I soaked everything in grease remover for about a week, then rinsed them off real good with soap and hot water and gave them a final cleaning with a wire brush. If you are using any new hardware, have it plated along with the old stuff so it all matches. String any parts that have any dimension smaller than about $1/2$ in. onto a loop of 18 gauge steel wire, this is so they won't get lost in the plating vat. Most of the parts can be "barrel plated" which means they get tossed in a barrel and dunked in the plating solution. Long pieces, like the A and B fuel lines and the throttle shaft that goes across the back of the fan housing may have to be "rack plated" which means they are hung on a rack and dunked. Smaller shops (the kind that might accept a small job) may not have the facilities to do rack plating. I found it very difficult to find someone to do the long parts. Everything you get plated must be completely disassembled. If you show up at the plater's door with parts that are totally clean and ready to go, so he can treat them just like the brand new parts he regularly receives from machine shops, you've a good chance of getting the job done. Expect to pay anywhere between $30 and $50 to have an engine's worth of parts done. Since the guy spends more time taking in the job and writing up the invoice than he does actually working with your parts, I found it cost no more to have two engines' worth done, so if you've got any extra stuff lying around, you might as well have them done too. I got over two engines' worth of hardware plus some stuff for the house done for the minimum charge of $35 here in Dayton, Ohio.

So what do you say to the plating guy when you walk in? If you say, "Cadmium plating Type 1 Class II, please." you'll probably get thrown out whether your parts are clean or not. In industry they usually go by thickness in mils and coatings by color, i.e. , "half mil clear cad" will get you Mil Spec "Type 1, Class 1" and "half mil yellow cad" or "half mil cad II" will get you Mil Spec "Type 1, Class II". Maybe you could take this handy little chart along.

One last word on plating is that you *never* want to have the connecting rod nuts, or the connecting rods, any internal engine parts, transmission gears, or any parts that are made of high strength steel (over Rockwell C40) cadmium plated. Any springs that you have plated must be baked at 375 degrees F for three hours within four hours of being plated. There is a phenomenon known as hydrogen embrittlement which can be induced by the cadmium plating process. A part subject to hydrogen embrittlement will

fail at much less than its design load if the baking process is not carried out.

This means that at some inconvenient moment our throttle return springs could suddenly no longer return and send you off into the weeds somewhere. There is some controversy concerning hydrogen embrittlement, some people just don't believe it exists, saying things like "I've had springs plated years ago and they haven't broken yet, why worry about it?" There is no guarantee that the phenomenon will occur in any given part, just as there is no guarantee that if you drive around the block without your seat belt on you will be thrown through the windshield and run over by a cement truck. There are, however, statistical chances for each phenomenon and the consequences of coming out on the short end, statistically speaking, are severe. This is not a problem with low alloy steels or steels of less than Rockwell C40, so normal nuts and bolts aren't a problem, but it is foolhardy to have internal engine parts plated, it can only do them harm.

Sound Deadening

Vol. 4, No. 5 Bob Frank

Rubberized Undercoating
The undercoating project is another bear if you brush it on and about as pleasant as a three hour soak in a tub of used 90W oil. A rubberized undercoat made by 3M and called "Body Schutz" is the same as the German original, but it costs about $4 a quart and takes about 5 - 6 cans to do the job, and there is another slight catch; the stuff requires a special spray head that costs $23 and fits right on the can - but the finished job is superior. Besides, you can always use the spray head again when you set up your own shop for the other Registry members. (Anyone want to rent a spray head?) Schutz can also be painted over with-

out bleed-through which is a definite advantage if you like your convertible D with an overall ripple finish.

Vol. 4, No. 5 Steve Cox

Materials
Three types of soundproofing were installed in the car:
1. Adroplass – sheet tar with a paper backing, approx. 4 mm. in thickness
2. Felt – tar impregnated fiber matting, available from Mercedes approx. 4 mm. in thickness
3. Insulation – Vinyl backed jute matting with a tar center layer. Mercedes number 2 and 3 are the closest approximation to the material in the car and must he altered as follows:
a. When using the felt under the gas tank and rear seat area, use two layers to match the original material thickness of 8 mm.
b. The insulation should be used vinyl face out in the engine compartment as it is installed on Mercedes cars. Some black vinyl dye will give a more original appearance to the surface exposed. In the rear seat area, the vinyl surface scruffed and glued to the metal or adroplass. This insulation material most closely matches the original jute material which had a layer of lead laminated in the center.
I cut all of the material with an Exacto-knife. The tar adroplass must be heated with a torch until the liquid tar starts sweating through the paper and then pressed to stick.

Material – Supplier – Part #
Adroplass – Porsche – 644.556.990.00
(no longer available, September 1994)
Insulation – Mercedes-Benz – 000.983.42.91
Felt – Mercedes-Benz – 000.983.29.94

(no longer available, September 1994)

Vol. 7, No. 2 Vernon Crotts

Engine Compartment Insulation.
An excellent substitute for the sound deadening insulation in the engine compartment is Mercedes part number 000.983.42.91. It comes in a one meter square piece, enough to do one car. You will need to spray one side with vinyl spray.

Vol. 12, No. 4 Lynn Baker

Using Building Materials on Your 356
Regarding the problem of the sound deadening material breaking, drooping and fall off in the engine compartment, I have a solution that may be of interest.
I had some #15 building paper left over from building my house. This is not thick enough, so I glued three layers together using Atco, (American Tar Co.) wet surface roof patch #1823, coating both sides of the paper and pressing together to remove any air. Being it was a warm sunny August, I left it out in the sun for a week until it could be cut with shears without the tar oozing out.
I carefully removed the usable material from engine compartment with a putty knife and scraped the old hard tar from the back of the sections that could be reused.
Using the Atco #1823 I glued the usable sections back in and cut the built up #15 building paper into shapes to replace the missing sections. I tried to get the waffle pattern in the sections I made by using a piece of 3/8" wire screen but it didn't look right. Maybe someone has an answer to this. It remains to be seen if this will hold up to engine heat.

Chapter 18

Storage

General

Vol. 3, No. 2 D. A. Bartlett

Long Term Storage

Having just taken my 1957 Speedster out of seven years storage, I'd like to comment on the folly or wisdom of certain actions to preserve a 356. The fact that mine survived reasonably well after so many high-humidity Florida years is as much a tribute to the basic soundness of the car as to my actions or the garage,

The garage was a two-car, decrepit wooden structure with dirt floor which contributed great gobs of dirt, wooden bits, and a dark haven for all sorts of animal life which visited and dwelt in the car. Six months previous to storing the car it had been completely stripped, minor body work done and completely repainted. The car went into storage with the leatherette upholstery intact but the carpeting was removed. I had a carpet kit to install when it came out of storage. All instruments, radio, speakers etc. were removed for cleaning and more secure storage. All chrome as well as many other sheet metal areas where Factory undercoating, still almost totally intact, was absent were slathered with Texaco Compound L undercoating compound. The paint was waxed. Tires were inflated and the car was set on jack stands with tires off the ground. Gas was drained from the tank. Suspension greased and fresh engine oil installed, plugs removed and generous quantities of oil squirted into the cylinders and the engine turned over by hand a number of revs. Plugs loosely installed. Carbs drained, oil squirted into their throats, and the tops covered with Saran wrap. The soft top was removed and stored elsewhere. A Glaspar hardtop remained on the car.

Seven years later the paint had retained its gloss despite the dirt and salt air – two blocks from Tampa bay. I had missed a couple of spots on the chrome and of course had rust. The leatherette had its share of green mildew "fur" but that was removed easily with soap and water plus the addition of several Armor All treatments.

Although I was prepared for problems in the braking system and with dried carb gaskets, I had none of these. My problems were a terribly rusty gas tank and sender unit. I overcame the rust by having a radiator shop steam clean and soak the tank as best they could. But, that didn't rid the tank of all the rust. Additional scraping, brushing and vacuuming helped, but to insure I wouldn't have a steady supply of rust throughout the fuel system for the next ten years, I gave the interior of the tank two coatings of aircraft "Sloshing Compound"/sealer which effectively sealed the remaining rust particles in place. A 450 mile drive confirmed that solution worked.

The second and most puzzling problem was the disintegration of the plastic bushings and guides in the shift linkage (a 1961 trans axle with all shift linkage is installed). The two bushings in the yoke at the front of the transmission crumbled, the guide ring and spherical cup didn't exist! Lots of miles and telephoning found the needed parts. The only other problem to date, i.e. 450 miles later, was the unannounced failure of the starter solenoid. Fortunately, a VW part is the needed replacement.

For those so rash or brave to contemplate a long term storage, mine was not planned to be so long. It just turned out that way. I'd do much the same as before but be more thorough in coating all plated metal and any other sheet metal which didn't have a fairly fresh coat of paint or undercoating. I'd probably give the painted surface a coat of Armor All in addition to doing the leather/leatherette. If there was a chance of dampness I'd remove the carpeting. I'd remove the fuel tank and at a minimum, coat the interior with light-weight oil or even better, the aircraft sealing compound for indefinite future protection. Tires too would get several coats of Armor All which wasn't available when mine went into hiding. But, the Goodyear G-800s didn't seem to suffer without it. Thus far, there has been no sign of shock absorber leakage or malperformance, which probably can be attributed to the overall superiority of Konis which were new when the car went into storage.

The real answer is, of course, don't store it but enjoy it and give it lots of TLC. But, if you must put it away, give it the extra bit of time and preparation and it will pay off someday in the future.

Vol. 6, No. 3 W. Noroski

Long and Short Term Storage

There have been a number of requests for "How To" Store or Winterize your Porsche. The following are my recommendations.

Follow the step by step procedure in the order given for storing a car for extended periods. For shorter periods such as four to five months, follow the steps marked with a *.

You will need a suitable garage, one that is above ground and dry. Heat is not essential, but will help. Refrain from washing other cars in adjacent stalls. Remember, any form of moisture should be kept to an absolute minimum.

*1. Cleaning – Inside, outside and underside. The greatest advantage of participating in our annual concours is that it gives you a head start on your winterizing program. Be sure carpets and floor beneath carpets are dry. Polish, touchup, and wax are recommended but not necessary.

*2. Lubrication – All points - grease fittings, connections, hinges, latches. cables, etc.

*3. Tire Pressure – Use 45 - 50 PSI.

4. Additives to fuel – Your tank should contain only a few gallons at most. Treat what is there with Drygas and other additives such as Stor-X. Use prescribed amounts.

*5. change oil and oil filter – Use your favorite top-grade oil and filter. Be sure to run engine until hot before draining the oil. Don't forget the sump. Fill with fresh oil and run engine up to normal operating temperature to recirculate oil.

6. Stall out engine – With remaining fuel and car in its final resting place {at least for the duration}, remove the air cleaners

and hold the engine at a fast idle. Pour approximately one cup of clean fresh engine oil into each carb. Force the engine to stall but not until it has digested a good portion of the oil. Replace the air cleaners. For extended storage, I seal all openings with oiled rags or Saran Wrap stretched and held by rubber bands. Openings include the carb intakes, oil filler tube, tail pipe, etc.

7. Drain fuel – Disconnect at connection beneath the car (at lowest point) and drain remaining fuel from tank and lines. Use the usual precautions when handling gasoline. In the 356 and 356A tanks, you can wipe out all traces of fuel and sediment with clean dry rags. Cap and seal the tank.

*8. Remove battery – Remove battery from car and store in basement. Top up water level. Begin a maintenance program such that you can discharge and recharge the battery about once each month. Discharge by energizing a small bulb for an hour or so, then recharge slowly. Battery will tend to sulfate if kept in fully charged condition without occasional discharge. Never store the battery on a concrete floor. Always use a 2x6 or piece of plywood.

*9. Tires – Situate car on small plaques of plywood in order to separate tires from concrete surface. Tires should be pumped up, rotated and marked about once each month to prevent flat spots from forming.

*10. Release hood and engine cover latch – Do not latch doors securely. Roll windows down about one inch for air circulation. Remove windshield wiper blades. This keeps the weather stripping and rubber parts from taking a set.

11. Check antifreeze – Be sure you're protected to about -25 to -30°F. This instruction is for water-cooled models only, but don't forget your windshield washer lines and reservoir.

*12. Cover the car – Use a proper cover. The common green drill cover is best. It is not waterproof and therefore breathes. It is best to put a clean smooth (no seams) bed sheet between car finish and cover on flat, horizontal surfaces. Never use a plastic cover.
Finally – light a green or red votive candle and kiss your darling goodnight!

Some people will recommend variations to these procedures. I have found these to be adequate and/or essential as the case may be. I don't believe in starting the engine periodically. This is dangerous if you do not get temperature up to normal operating condition. I do on occasion turn the engine over by hand after injecting a small amount of oil mist, WD-40 or equivalent into the spark plug holes.

Some say to relieve the tension on valve springs. This, of course, means an adjustment before operating in the Spring. I prefer turning the engine over by hand occasionally to change positions and compress other springs. It is important to stress the need for a dry garage. The obvious dangers exist to body rusting, etc. Brakes can deteriorate and freeze up if dampness is excessive. Remove the wheels and spray CRC-5-56 on discs or drums to prevent seizure. It cleans, penetrates and lubricates and will readily burn off during the first few applications of the brake in the spring. *Good luck!*

Vol. 17, No. 4 Bill Rohrer

Long and Short Term Storage, II
A lot of people "store" their favorite vehicles for all but July and

August; we 356 folks never really store ours, we just park them during the really nasty months. There is a pretty simple "how to" that will help your baby to come out of the garage in as good a condition as when it went in.

I am making the assumption here that you do thorough regular maintenance, that you have had a fairly recent tune-up/carburetor cleaning and that your windshield washer antifreeze is good to the temperatures you experience in your area. If these are (like so many assumptions) not true, you should put this article away for a few days and make them happen.

When To Do It

Pick a dry, sunny day, as warm as possible. Temperature is not as big a concern as humidity- cold is OK, damp is bad. On this sunny, dry day, open the garage and let it dry out.

While you're waiting for it to dry, clean it. Sweep the floor, remove any oil or grease spots, pick up bits of wood, cardboard or other debris - these can attract moisture, insects and rodents which may later end up in your car.

Where to Start

The first thing to do is to drive over to the best car wash in town – the one that uses only fresh water and has an undercarriage wash. Spend the extra three bucks and get the deluxe job. Take along some Windex, Armor All, paper towels, a bath towel and a chamois. Stop at the high power vacuum cleaner and do the best vacuum job you've ever done (again, spend the extra dollar and the time to do it right). Towel or chamois dry the car exterior, including the door wells, door bottoms and fuel filler door; wax the car if you have a nice enough day. Clean the windows, interior and seats. Bottom line here is that everything; body, seats, carpet, windows, etc. should be as clean as you can get

them. Any dirt left in or on the car now will be twice as hard to get off next spring, and may do damage to the paint or upholstery.

Nice and Clean - Now What?

Well, now the errands. In order. First Stop: the local auto parts emporium. Purchase enough oil for an oil change, a new filter, one can of 'dry gas', one can of Stabil or other fuel stabilizer, one spray can of WD-40, some belt dressing and a tire pressure gauge (if you don't have a good one). You can get engine fogging oil too, if you want to. I don't bother to fog mine for three or four month storage periods. If you can, open your hood in the parking lot and put the belt dressing on the belt (note: some people don't like belt dressings -do what you think is best).

Second Stop: Home, after a nice 20 or 50 minute cruise (longer is fine – remember, all you'll be doing for a while is wishing you could drive it, and it is a nice sunny day). Now is the time to change the oil. Remove the drain plug (preferably the sump cover plate too if you have gaskets handy) and let the oil drain. While waiting, grease the car, check the brake fluid and just generally hang around to be sure everything is clean and in good order. Two things of import here: One, drive on the highway for at least ten minutes to get everything good and warmed up. Two, let the oil drain for at least twenty to thirty minutes. You'll be surprised at how much more dirty oil comes out. This is my major complaint about "quick" oil change places.

Third Stop: The gas station nearest your storage garage. Pull up to the alcohol-free Super Premium pump or the race gas pump, if you can find it and afford it.) Get out the "dry gas" and the Stabil and put them in the tank. Fill the car full, but not to over-flowing. The idea here is to minimize air, and thus water vapor, in the tank.

Make sure you put the gas cap back on tightly. Now pull over to the air pump and inflate your tires to 55 psi. This keeps your tires from developing a flat spot from being parked for a long time.

When do I Actually Get to Put the Car Away?

Now. At last, you can drive over to the storage garage. On the way, run the heater for a few minutes to dry the air in the car. Park the car where you can get at the engine compartment. Before you get out, take the paper goods and other things out of the glovebox, door pockets, kick panel pockets, etc. These items and any tools should be stored inside your house. Close all windows, vents (floor, cowl, etc.), glovebox, ashtray - in short, make sure the vehicle is closed up as tightly as possible. This prevents unpleasant spring surprises like finding a new family of mice or spiders. Close the floor heater slides - critters can crawl into your heater channels through some remarkably small holes in heater hoses or mufflers! I put a small glass bowl with two or three mothballs on the floor (and in the trunk) as a further deterrent to potential tenants.

This is important: *Do not set the parking brake!*

Open the hood (which should be as clean as the interior) and the deck lid. These should be dry by now, but if not, wipe up any stray water from the car wash. Remove your tool kit and leather tire strap and close the hood. Get out your WD-40 and spray the carb linkage lightly. Close the fuel-cock and run the gas out of the carbs. If you are going to fog the engine, do it now and drain the gas out of the carbs.

After things cool down for a half hour or so, cover the engine air intakes (air cleaner "horns", mesh cans or ....) I use a piece of plastic film and a rubber band on each horn.

Use whatever works – the idea is to seal out moisture and critters. If you have a fan housing without the mesh screen, cover the air intake opening. I also seal my tailpipes since a neighborhood mouse decided my muffler was a good place to store seeds one year.

You're almost done now. Undo the battery cables (both of them, negative-first). Move them aside and secure them so they won't flip back up and touch the battery terminals. If you have a safe place to store it (cool, dry, up off the floor, away from the kids), take one last loving look, close the hood, put the car cover on and lock the garage door.

Last step: put this article someplace where you will be able to find it in the Spring. Reading it again will help you remember what you have to undo, uncover and reconnect.

Brakes

Vol. 3, No 6. Mike Robbins

Frozen Brake Shoes

A friend and I recently encountered the same problem – we couldn't move our 356s due to brake shoes "freezing" to the drums. His is a restoration project that is sitting in the garage while mine is a parts car that is sitting out doors. I finally broke my rear drums loose and decided to remove the brake shoes to prevent recurrence of the problem. The moral of this story is to at least back off your brake shoes if you have a car sitting for a while.

Engine

Vol. 16, No. 5 Mike Robbins

Is Your Engine Mouseproof?

We all know that assembled engines will deteriorate if just sitting around but lots of us are guilty of having such. I recently encountered a couple of situations that point to the need for taking special steps if an engine is sitting idle for a long period. The worst situation involves an engine I put together about three years ago. At that time I ran the engine on the test stand to balance carbs, check for leaks, etc. and then set the engine aside until it would be needed. Occasionally I would turn it through a couple of revolutions. I recently put the engine in my Speedster and then found a problem – it would not turn over. I pulled the engine and proceeded with disassembly. Upon removal of the right engine head, I found the no.1 cylinder contained a significant amount of D-CON mouse poison granules. (I keep several open D-CON dispensers in the garage.) A little furry devil had crawled through the J-pipe (no muffler attached) and apparently found the exhaust valve open and deposited the granules in the combustion chamber. I was fortunate in not bending a valve or rod and the engine is now running fine in the Speedster.

This brought to mind a previous experience that involved a similar set of circumstances - rebuilt engine set aside until needed. Sometime later I decided to remove the fan housing and generator to use on another engine. Upon lifting the fan housing off the engine, I found a mouse nest adjacent to the oil cooler. Bits of fiberglass insulation, paper, string, and other miscellany not the kind of stuff you want in the fins of the oil cooler. I was sure glad I hadn't put that engine in a car before making this discovery.

Should I get a cat?

Vol. 17, No. 1 Vic Skirmants

Is Your Engine Bugproof?

Most of our beloved 356s spend the majority of their time sitting around. Also, many of them spend time sitting around dismantled; especially engines. And in particular, fuel lines. Fuel lines are the insect world's preferred size for nest or cocoon building. Spiders and wasps spend most of their lives inside 356 fuel lines. Mud-wasps are especially fond of oil passages in exposed engine cases. So, before using anything that could harbor a critter, blow it out, flush it out, pound it out.

Chapter 19

Suspension

Alignment

Vol. 4, No. 1 Vic Skirmants

Front Wheel Alignment

Beginning at the front; the only actual adjustment at the front end is the toe-in. Factory spec is 1 to 3 mm; I shoot for $1/16$ in. to $1/8$ in. This is adjusted by shortening or lengthening the tie-rods. On the older models with VW steering box, the left tie-rod is unadjustable. After setting the toe-in to specs, what if the steering wheel is at an angle? Remove it and reposition on the steering column. Don't do that on a 1958 or later with the ZF steering box!! Assuming the steering wheel is straight in relation to the center-point of the ZF box, don't change it! The ZF steering box is designed for zero freeplay at the straight-ahead position, with increasing "sloppiness" the further you go from center. First, measure the toe-in. If it needs readjusting, drive the car to see if the steering wheel is level when the car is going straight. If it is, adjust both tie-rods an equal amount until your toe-in is at the required measurement. If the wheel is at an angle while the car is going straight. proceed as follows after stopping; turn the wheel to the level position and mentally picture what happens to the front wheels. For instance, if the wheel was turned left while driving and the front end had too much toe-in, turning the wheel right to the level position would result in the left wheel toeing in more and the right wheel in toeing out. Therefore you would shorten the left tie-rod to toe out the left wheel. Measure toe-in, drive the car again, and repeat if necessary. Sounds tedious, and sometimes it is, but if you don't have a multi-thousand dollar alignment machine handy, this works pretty well. Excessive toe-in will cause accelerated front tire wear, while any toe-out will cause a wandering of the front end.

While on the front suspension, when doing the link pins, don't just count the old shims and put in the new ones in the same order. Who says the old ones are correct? Measure the offset of the trailing arms and shim according to the factory set-up. I use a straight-edge held against the face of the lower trailing arm and a common 6 in. scale to measure the offset of the upper arm. The whole idea of the shims is to position the link pin carrier against the trailing arms so that the link pins are parallel to their bushings. Any angularity and there will be binding and accelerated wear of the pins and bushings. That's also a good reason not to jockey the shims to get a little more negative camber for better handling in autocrossing or racing.

358

You're not going to get enough of a change to notice, you'll just get a sloppy front end and not pass tech inspection to begin with. If you want negative camber, you can get the remachined link pin carriers from aftermarket suppliers.

Vol. 4, No. 3 Vic Skirmants

Rear Wheel Alignment

Two issues ago I discussed the 356 front suspension with a promise to also cover the rear suspension. I didn't have room last time, so here it is now. There are two basic adjustments that can be made on the rear suspension; camber and toe-in. If you change one, you'll affect the other. As you decamber, the trailing arm moves upward; swinging in an arc, the end of the arm also moves forward, thus producing more toe-in. Too much toe-in and the rear wheels will drag slightly sideways when going forward, thereby moving themselves toward positive camber; when backing up, they will decamber. With the right toe-in, they won't change forward or backward.

Factory specs for camber range from plus 3 degrees to minus $1 \frac{1}{2}$ degrees depending on the year, the engine, and the type of torsion bars. No one should willingly be running positive camber; the factory specs for the Carrera-engined cars of minus $\frac{1}{2}$ to minus $1 \frac{1}{2}$ degrees should do nicely for all types. For general street driving use minus $\frac{1}{2}$ degree, for occasional spirited driving use minus $1 \frac{1}{2}$ degrees. Factory toe-in is 0 plus or minus 10'; I use a toe-in of $\frac{1}{16}$ in., *never* any toe-out.

If you decamber your car, be sure to check the rear toe-in. Also, if the transmission has been changed, it is a good idea to check the toe-in. To change toe-in, note that there are three large bolts holding the axle tube to the trailing arm. There is a fourth equally large bolt that holds a large washer to the trailing arm. The axle tube flange should be tight against the large washer. If you have too much toe-in, loosen the three bolts, tap the axle tube rearward a little and retighten. Put the car on the ground, roll it back and forth and check toe-in again. If still off, repeat above procedure. When it's finally right, loosen the fourth bolt, slide the fat washer against the axle tube and retighten. Don't forget to tighten the three bolts also. Now if you have to ever pull the transmission, you can pop it back in again, shove the axle tubes against the washers and not have to worry about the toe-in; that is if you put the front transmission mount spacers in correctly. If you misplace a spacer, you move the transmission; if you move the trans, you've changed your suspension location point.

Why fuss with toe in? If you have too much, your car will understeer; great just what you were looking for? Wrong way to do it; you'll also use more power pushing those toed-in wheels sideways down the road. If you have toe-out you'll really appreciate the meaning of "dreaded oversteer".

You say your car oversteers in one direction but understeers in the other? Your wheels could be toed-out on one side and toed-in on the other. Or, your front sway bar mount is broken on one side.

Vol. 9, No. 2 David Seeland

Rear Camber Measurment

Here is how to measure rear camber with no fancy equipment. Use a large carpenters square on the garage floor pushed up against the sidewalls of a 40 PSI tire, if the upper wall is "in" $\frac{1}{4}$ in., that is 1° negative camber, $\frac{1}{2}$ in. 2° negative camber... Just be sure your garage floor is flat. Camber should be the same side to side and this is insured by measuring from equivalent reference points down to the end of the spring plates on both sides. I do use an inclinometer to get close to factory specs, but all fine fiddling is done with a tape measure.

Vol. 12, No. 2 Dan Pelecovich

Adjusting ZF Steering Box

Adjusting ZF-Ross type steering to high point and tie rods to straight ahead

For years, I have suspected that the steering wheel of my 1958 1600S Coupe with GT gasoline tank was not positioned for straight ahead on the steering high point. On two previous attempts to assure the high point on the steering box, the gasoline tank was removed and the steering shaft and steering box carefully inspected for factory match marks. No matter how hard I tried, the mark on the steering shaft could not be confirmed due to corrosion. It is very important that the steering be placed on the high point for mesh adjustment and also before the tie rods are adjusted for straight ahead driving and proper toe-in.

My curiosity could not be contained and another attempt was made to locate the mark on the steering shaft by adjusting light, etc., etc. to no avail. I did discover that by loosening the GT tank straps, the tank could be raised in the front sufficiently to remove the large access plate and permit inspection of the steering shaft. Care must be observed here, otherwise, you may stress the gas valve against the cowl.

The thought occurred to me that the most precise method of finding the high point would be to turn left full lock and right full lock and that the center point is the high point – wrong!!. Fortunately, I have a spare front end with installed steering box and detached tie rods and steering damper to go to school on. With the tie rods and steering damper disconnected, the steering shaft could be rotated left and right to positive lock. The match marks are clearly visible

and are stamped both on the shaft and box by indented lines approximately $3/16$ in. long by $1/16$ in. deep. The mark on the box being slightly offset from the mould parting line. The match marks line up approximately 20 degrees from center of the lock to lock position.

Because I could not feel positive lock in both directions on my coupe, tie rod ends were broken loose and steering damper disconnected. With the front end raised, both locks could now be positively felt. It occurred to me that there must be a way of determining the high point by rotating the steering wheel and feeling the resistance when it's going through high point by varying the adjustment. With the front of the car off the ground and the mesh adjusted a little tighter than normal, give the steering wheel a swing to the left towards the high point, and noting where a referenced steering spoke stops and then swing the wheel in the opposite direction and noting the stopping positions, the steering high point is the center between these stopping points. A little practice will be required to get your confidence up.

In my case, the stop points were about 20 degrees apart and high point was determined to be at the center between these stop points. At this time, place the steering wheel on the steering shaft in the exact straight ahead position and with a center punch, mark the steering shaft on the steering wheel end at 12 o'clock so that it will never be lost again. After the steering mesh was properly adjusted on high point and the tie rods and steering damper reconnected, a road test revealed that the steering wheel was about 40 degrees off straight ahead position. No wonder there was so much more thread showing on one tie rod with respect to the other side. By eyeballing head on, front tires to rear tires while adjusting, you will be surprised how quickly you can adjust the tie rods for straight ahead driving. In my case, only one slight adjustment was required. Of course, toe-in should be adjusted to $1/16$ to $1/8$ in. at the front.

Simple and very accurate method for checking toe-in front and rear wheels

Over the years, I have made several tools for checking the toe-in of Porsche front and rear wheels. All subsequent tools were improvements over the earlier versions, but I never reached the point of development that gave me that good warm feeling after a toe adjustment. The problem is because the Porsche carriage drops below the horizontal center line of the wheels and a plain telescoping tool will not work.

A simple and accurate method is to use a plumb bob. I can hear the laughter from here. The method is as follows: With the Porsche in a straight ahead mode, on a smooth floor in a relaxed attitude, with a piece of chalk, mark tire at 3 o'clock on the outside of the tires on both sides. Drop a plumb bob from the outside edge of the rim at this point and using necessary precautions, mark an "X" on the floor at this point. In order that the plumb string does not rub against the tires, I found it necessary to hold a $1/2$ in. socket against the rim and drop the plumb bob from the socket. Do the same thing on the other side of the car and mark an "X." Push the car straight ahead so that the tire marks are now at 9 o'clock. Get your two additional marks the same way. Using a good steel tape, simply measure distances between the two sets of marks. It's a good idea to start at 1 inch on the tape. The difference in lengths is your toe-in (toe-out). Since this method is so simple, you probably will want to do the same to your rear wheels and finally find out if you're toeing-in or out back there. While you're at it, have you ever wondered if your wheel base is the same on driver/passenger sides?

I found out my car was out 0.20 in. which was put right in a jiffy.

The adjustments are straight-forward but be sure steering is on high point, steering wheel in straight ahead position and to remain there after adjustment. By the way, with respect to the front wheels, you can not have too much toe-in on one side and not enough on the other side. This can not be so because the toe-in (toe-out) equalizes when you drive down the road. This is why your steering wheel goes off straight-ahead position if the two tie rods are not properly adjusted.

I have made several repeat measurements using the plumb method of toe measurement and the results are extremely accurate. I think you'll like this method if you try it.

Incidentally, when measuring the toe-in at the rims, by simple mathematics, $1/8$ in. at the rims equals approximately 0.20 inch at the tread face. You may want to keep this in mind when setting the toe-in and shoot for $1/16$ to 0.10 inch at the rim.

Anti-Sway Bar

Vol. 4, No. 2 Vern Lyle

Use of a 19 mm Front Bar

Front sway bar: A 19 mm bar (in place of factory 16 or smaller) will reduce lateral weight transfer in the front by a great deal. In so doing, the entire chassis is kept more upright on the wheels and the tendency to oversteer and/or tuck the rear wheel is markedly reduced. The addition of a 19 and Konis set to full soft in front and full stiff in the rear gave an improvement in the ride and handling of my C coupe that was hard to believe.

The shock setting doesn't seem to be very critical and something completely different may work better for others, but for my driving style this works. Forget about oversteer unless

361

you do something really dumb, like lifting in a corner or tightening the line in a jerky manner.

Vol. 4, No. 5 Vic Skirmants

Sway Bar Bushings
I'll leave this column with one more hard-earned tip. If your car feels like its going to spin when you first turn the steering wheel, check your sway-bar bushings for excess play and replace if necessary.

Vol. 9, No. 2 David Seeland

Sway Bar Theory
Anti-sway bars are relatively simple. Don't ever use one on the rear of a swing axle car unless you would like more oversteer. Original fronts are available in 15 and 16 mm, H and H makes a 19 mm adjustable bar and Weltmeister makes 19 and 22 mm front bars. To compare relative stiffness the 4th power of the radius is used as for torsion bars. If the 15 mm bar has a stiffness of one then the 16 mm bar has a stiffness of 1.29 and the 19 mm bar has a stiffness of 1.98 – if all have the same lever arm length. The rule here is that a larger front bar increases understeer. Larger front bars also compromise ride quality by decreasing the independence of the front wheels.

King & Link Pins

Vol. 1, No. 4 Brett Johnson

VW vs. Porsche Parts
I recommend using VW king and linkpins for the front suspension instead of the Porsche items. The VW kits usually are four to eight flat shims short for the Porsche, so save your better old ones; also, VW doesn't use the same type offset spacer that carries the rubber seal, so save the old ones or buy new ones. You can take the

assemblies to a VW dealer or specialist to have them rebuilt. (The kingpin bushings have to be reamed to size after installation.) Tell them they are VW spindles. It costs less to have it done.

Vol. 4, No. 5 Vic Skirmants

Installing Link Pin Shims
A while back the front suspension was discussed, including the importance of measuring correctly the trailing arm offset and setting up the shims properly. If you have no way to measure the offset of the trailing arms, there is another way. Place the link pins in their bushings in the link pin carrier and install into the ends of the trailing arms without any shims. If both link pin bushing ends contact the trailing arm ends equally you have the regular spacing and need five shims inside and outside, top and bottom. If there is a gap at one location, either top or bottom, when the other end is contacting, just add however many shims are needed to fill the gap. Keep in mind that there should be a total of ten shims at the top and at the bottom, counting inside and outside, and the outer shims have nothing to do with the offset.

Vol. 3, No. 1 Vic Skirmants

Maintenance, King and Link Pins
One last important item, grease the link pins. These should be done every 1500 miles or less; more often in the winter or rainy season. I usually neglect mine until the 3000 mile interval and have been lucky so far. Only the link pins need that frequent a service. The torsion bars and tie rod ends can be done every other time. The best way to grease the link pins is to loosen the clamp bolt, back-off the link pin, grease, tighten the link pin as hard as possible, grease again. This sometimes helps to get the grease first to the link pin and then to one end of the

king-pin, since one fitting serves both. Then back off very slightly on the link pin and retighten the clamp bolt. On the C models, slide a piece of cardboard between the mushroom end of the link pin and the dust shield to keep grease off the brake rotors.

Rear Wheel Bearings

Vol. 7, No. 3 Vic Skirmants

Chronic Rear Bearing Failure
Michael Hudick, Los Gatos CA, wrote in about a 1963 S-90 coupe he had a few years back that would regularly chew up its left rear wheel bearing every 10,000 miles. Changing the bearing cap improved the life to 20,000 miles. Mike didn't mention any other checks that were made, since he sold the car. My own guess would be that the axle tube and/or axle shaft were slightly bent to keep causing failure of the bearing. The rear wheel bearings should be good for 100,000 miles and more; early failure indicates some strange load being put on them. In SCCA racing, most people I know have not experienced rear wheel bearing failures; they replace them every season or two just to be on the safe side. However, the Porsches that regularly run our local track at Waterford Hills will chew up a left rear wheel bearing in about five or six race weekends! The track is very tight, most of the turns are right-handers, and everyone gets a lot of track time during a club race weekend.

Rear Wheel Seal

Vol. 16, No. 6 Vic Skirmants

Rear Seal Kits
The currently available rear wheel seal kit for the drum-brake cars is an excellent buy. You get everything you need for a very reasonable cost. You

also get more than you need! The kit was made for Volkswagens, so it includes a paper gasket you don't need and shouldn't use. Throw it away. I don't care if you found a gasket when disassembling your old setup; that just means someone else put it in there previously. Porsche never used the paper gasket. One other item you don't want to use is the supplied shim that goes between the bearing and the drum spacer. It looks great, but it's a very mild steel and very squashable; the proper shim is a spring steel and quite tough. You can probably reuse your old one. This shim is what you're basically compressing when torquing down the axle nut. All your rear cornering loads are also put into this shim. If you put in the soft shim and it squashes even more after tightening, then you will lose torque on the axle nut. If the nut gets loose, the cotter pin will not hold it. The nut will simply slice off the cotter pin.

Shocks

Vol. 9, No. 3 Vic Skirmants

Replacing Shock Bushings
When removing the shock absorbers, sometimes the bushing is frozen to the stud and you end up pulling the shock and rubber off the bushing. After getting the bushing off, either with penetrating oil or by heating, how do you get it back in the rubber? It usually won't slip in or push in. The solution is to push it back in using a bolt, nut and two large washers. Put a washer on the bolt, slip through the bushing, put the bushing against the shock rubber, then put on the other washer and nut. Now tighten the nut and bolt and the bushing will be forced in.
While on the subject of pressing things, the rear wheel seals for the 356-356B can be pressed in by using

an old #3 356-356B (non-S-90) main bearing. It's just the right diameter to push the seal in from the back by putting everything in a vise and tightening. If you try to install the seal from the outside, the sharp edge of the bearing retainer will usually cut the outside rubber on the seal. Pressing in from the inside will eliminate the problem. The 356C seal is a different size; the inner race of a differential carrier thrust bearing works well for that one.

Vol. 15, No. 3 Don Fowler

Koni Shock Specifications

Don Fowler of Fairfax Station, VA sent additional information about Koni shocks in the form of a letter dated June 1, 1964 from Kensington Products Corporation, the US Koni importer. This letter states that there were actually four types. All of these are stamped with the month and year stamp in this form 6.58 (June 1958). The date is stamped on the top part of the shock.

Two measurements on shock absorbers that define their feel are bump and rebound. The bump is the resistance to compression and the rebound is the resistance to expansion. On Koni shocks the rebound is adjustable by compressing the uninstalled shock absorber and turning it. With the exception of the blue shocks, all were originally supplied at the minimum amount of rebound. Bump was not adjustable.

1. The first type is the 80A-1044/80A-1191 listed above as the "red" shocks. They were indeed the red/orange color that most replacement Koni shocks were and still are today. Front rebound 100 kg. Bump 45 kg. at minimum adjustment. Rear rebound 120 kg. Bump 30 kg. at minimum adjustment. These were the original Koni shock absorbers fitted by Porsche starting in 1958 on Carreras only, then becoming standard on Supers and optional on Normals. Early versions were stamped 01 and 02 rather than the complete part number. Porsche stopped using these in May of 1960 although Kensington continued to supply them until late 1962.

2. The second type 80A-1044SP/80A-1191SP were "red" when supplied on the aftermarket, but initially light grey and later darker grey when installed at the factory. The Porsche part numbers were 644.343.501.11 and 644.333.501.11.

Front rebound 75 kg. Bump 45 kg. at minimum adjustment. Rear rebound 75 kg. Bump 45 kg. at minimum adjustment. These were designed to give a smoother ride and were fitted to Supers and Super 90s from the time that the others were phased out in 1960.

3. The third were numbered the same as the first, 80A-1044/80A-1191, but have date stamps of 1.63 or later. This variety does not have a Porsche part number and were never fitted by Porsche. They were also red.

Front rebound 70 kg. Bump 20 kg. at minimum adjustment. Rear rebound 60 kg. Bump 20 kg. at minimum adjustment. These were even softer than the preceding type. It notes that many owners would want to adjust them. It also states that when fully adjusted, they are softer than any of the others and as such are unsuitable for racing.

SHOCK ABSORBERS

DESCRIPTION	FRONT	356A, 356B, 356C
Boge, brown	644.41.501.2	356A 1600 Normal 356B 1600 Normal, 1600 S, S-90 356 1600 C
Koni, red	644.343.501.10 80A-1044	356A 1600 S and Carrera 356B optional 356C optional
Koni, blue	644.343.501.12 80A-1044SP20	356B Carrera 1600 and 2 litre 356C 1600 SC and Carrera 2

DESCRIPTION	REAR	356A, 356B, 356C
Boge, brown	644.34.501.2	356A 1600 Normal 356B 1600 Normal, 1600 S, S-90 356C 1600 C
Koni, red	644.333.501.10 80A-1191	356A 1600 S and Carrera 356B optional 356C optional
Koni, blue	644.333.501.12 80A-1191SP20	356B Carrera 1600 and 2 litre 356C 1600 SC and Carrera 2

4. The final type 80A-1044SP20/80A-1191SP20 is the "blue" shock listed on the chart. It does not state when they were first introduced. The Koni information states standard on SC optional on C, while the Porsche information says that they were used on some 356B as well.

Front rebound 80 kg. Bump 20 kg. at minimum adjustment. Rear rebound 60 kg. Bump 20 kg. at minimum adjustment. These were fitted by Porsche and supplied by Koni adjusted with one turn resulting with the following:

Front rebound 140 kg. Bump 20 kg. at minimum adjustment. Rear rebound 80 kg. Bump 20 kg at minimum adjustment. Further comments state that the adjustment of this particular shock was more sensitive and for racing applications at least two full turns should be used. It goes on to say that their existence was due to a six year cooperative development between Porsche and Koni.

Steering

Vol. 5, No. 5 Floyd Hollandbeck

Low Cost Late Steering Coupler Fix

An annoying amount of unpredictability developed in the steering mechanism of my 1965 356C recently. Quick inspection, based upon years of skillful and cunning troubleshooting, revealed that the lower end of the steering coupler universal joint, part number 644.347.203.00, had loosened and worn the internal splined surface of the coupler away leaving only the clamp bolt to transfer steering inputs to the gear box. (Fortunately, the splined shaft of the steering box is tougher than the coupler.) Since the cost of a new replacement part was considered to be excessive, a low-cost alternative was found by cannibalizing an apparently identical coupler out of a wrecked 1970 VW Sedan.

Vol. 9, No. 4 Richard Miller

Early Steering Coupler Replacement

I'd also like to pass on an unsettling observation which I made the other day while checking brake fluid level (just because it's hard to get at doesn't mean forget it until the pedal goes all soft). The first thing you see after prying up the panel under all that junk in the trunk is the steering shaft. Attaching it (and you) to the steering box are some parts from an early VW. If this area hasn't been exposed to the light of day for 20 years or more, chances are that the little round flex coupling, (which looks like it was cut out of an old tire casing) may look like it has parasites. Replace it. Now look at the bolts which pinch the two clamps on either side of the rubber coupler, one to the steering shaft, the other to the box input shaft and imagine what happens if they fall out. These should be marked 10K on the head and should be tightened with a torque wrench to the recommended spec. If you tighten them till they squeak they may crack and it may not happen right away.

Also, notice the lockplate keeping them from vibrating loose. This originally is held at both ends under the bolt head and nut and bent up against the hex flats. To make me feel secure I replace the bolts with new hardware and make my own lock tab, the ends of which extend up and over the bolt head and the nut as well to keep them in place should fatigue set in and they come apart (I intend to drive this car another 30 years).

Vol. 9, No. 6 Vic Skirmants

Replacing VW Steering Box With the Later (1958 -) ZF Style

Larry Dickinson, Glen Falls NY, asked about putting a ZF steering box into his 1956 Porsche. The installation is very simple. The only problem is in getting the steering box into position. When putting the box through the access hole, it will be necessary to slightly bend up the forward lip, which can later be bent back down.

The locating dowel in the ZF steering box fits right into the old locating hole in the upper torsion bar tube. The steering arm of the ZF is located further to one side than on the old box. This will require readjusting the right tie-rod and replacing the left tie-rod assembly. On the pre-1958s the left tie-rod is a one-piece assembly and non-adjustable. Simply replace this with a 1958 - 1965 unit and adjust as needed.

Vol. 10, No. 4 Vic Skirmants

Rebuilding Steering Boxes
Dan also asks about rebuilding the VW steering box. I don't know of any rebuild parts for the old VW-style boxes or the ZF box. You're better off getting a good, used ZF steering box and installing it; you will also need the adjustable left tie rod.

Vol. 11, No. 5 Rick Veneski

Use of a VW Bus Damper
We know that a cure for front end shake caused by potholes and railroad crossings is replacement of the steering damper. Replace it with a VW bus damper (part #211.425.021 A). Unfortunately, the bus damper is a little short, so it takes away about half of a right steering wheel turn. To fix this, loosen the two castle nuts securing the damper bracket to the torsion bar tube. Slide the bracket toward the driver's side. This allows full expansion of the damper on a right turn. But be careful: moving the bracket too far will cause excessive damper compression on a left turn. A $1/2$ in. movement of the bracket to the left should result in equal turns of the steering wheel left or right.

Tires

Vol. 7, No. 4 David Seeland

Mounting/Dismounting Tires
You may not believe this but I have 77 wheels and even more tires. In spite of this lifetime supply of rubber, I'm forever having to switch tires from one set of wheels to another. I've had wheels bent, scratched and chipped by people that said they knew what they were doing. If you have had similar experiences, then you should consider mounting and dismounting your own tires.

This of course is predicated on the ability to dismount them yourself. Several years ago I built a lever-type bead breaker modified from a picture in a J.C. Whitney "This may be your last" catalog. This worked fine on non-safety bead 4 $1/2$ in. rims, barely worked on 5 $1/2$ in. safety rims, and wouldn't break an XWX bead from anything.

So, last week, after having spent $35 and two hours of hard work helping the tire shop man mount four XWXs and dismount four Semperits and two XWXs I decided I'd rather not worry about someone else scratching my 5 $1/2$ in. chrome wheels, or worse, bending them. A note of caution here: XWXs cannot be removed from A or B wheels with a tire machine unless a "VW adapter" is used. They will bend if only the conical hold-down device is used.

The solution to my problem was a never-fail, no-grunt bead breaker. It consists of a slightly curved $3/16$ in. blade about 9 in. wide arc-welded to a 6 in. long $5/8$ in. bolt. The bolt slips into the base of a Porsche jack. Lay the tire and wheel under your VW bus and place the blade of the bead breaker against the tire. A few strokes of the jack handle and presto!, off comes the bead. Flop the tire/wheel over and repeat and you are ready for the tire irons. If you don't have a bus, put a 4 x 4 under a front and rear wheel of your Porsche to gain enough ground clearance.

Now for a few words on tire dismounting/mounting in case you've never tried. You will need a thin, flat tire iron wrapped with filament tape, a couple of big screwdrivers, and a can of dishwashing detergent mixed with water. Three basic rules apply to tire removal (and mounting). One, the bead on the opposite side of the tire from where you are prying with the tire iron must be in the deepest groove in the rim, two, place the valve near the initial point of removal, and, three, always take the tire off the front (outside) of the rim. Lubricate the beads and rim with the detergent solution.

After removing the bead on the outside of the wheel remove the tube and then the backside bead using the screwdrivers. Practice on a Michelin XZX on a 4 1/2 in. rim to get the hang of things. Put air in the tire and then deflate it to straighten out any wrinkles in the tube. Reverse the process to mount a tire. I use a metal valve-stem extender with a loop of wire in it to pull tubeless valve stems into place.

Wheel Covers

Vol. 10, No. 1 Richard Miller

Turbo Discs
One final bit of information to add to the "Turbo Disc" beauty rim controversy, "which way do the louvers face" – The "Qualitest" accessory catalog shows 356A cars, but with the absence of a publication date one can only guess. However, some pre-A cars are shown and the wheel rings are only available for 16 inch wheels, so my guess is 1955 or 1956. The picture shows a right hand front with the louver's angled to scoop up air as the wheel turns despite what is said by people who have theirs fitted the other way.

Wheels

Vol. 15, No. 3 Dick Koenig/David Seeland

Factory Fitted Lightweight Wheels
We have had some interesting calls and correspondence regarding wheels. For example, Harry Bytzek knows an ex employee of a German Wheel manufacturer who said that Kronprinz (KPZ) went to race tracks and offered to trade new reinforced alloy-rim wheels with thicker 3.3 mm centers for old wheels with 2.9 mm centers. Just about all the old wheels eventually failed and KPZ wanted to quietly get them off as many cars as possible to head off bad publicity. They broke around the mounting bolts leaving five "washers" attached to the drum. The following service bulletin pictures the reinforced wheel and the identifying "incision" (pimple at arrow). Don't drive hard with early "no-pimple" 2.9 mm-center wheels!

Some relatively random bits of information about alloy-rim wheels follow. Six or seven (?) inch drum-brake wheels were seen on a flared-fender 356B S-90 GT (?). Bruce Jennings had 6 inch alloy-rim drum-brake wheels near the end of his four-cam racing career. Alloy-rim wheels, both 15 and 16 in., were made in offsets for both 40 mm and 60 mm brakes. The 16 in. wheels for 40 mm drums (early 550 Spyders) had a 93 mm inside offset and the 16 inch wheels for later Spyders with 60 mm drums (S597A) had enough offset so the outer part of the center is outboard of the rim. The 15 in. wheels for 40 mm drums have a 97 mm inside offset and those for 60 mm drums had 10 mm of inside offset.

Paul Allen in Ohio points out that 904 disc brake wheels have 19 rivets (we said 20 on 906 wheels) and have 3.7 mm centers in 5 1/2 and 6 in. widths, thinner than the wider (7 and 9 in.) 906 wheels we listed that have 3.9

and 3.8 mm centers, but much thicker than the 2.9 and 3.3 mm centers on 3.5 in. and 4.5 in. drum-brake wheels.

Südrad made both 16 and 15 in. drum-brake steel wheels. Jim Saunders, Sydney, Australia mentions his interest in different types of GT/ Spyder brakes, backing plates, and even spacers.

Tim Herman has solved the problem of the curious 1/8 in. holes drilled in both steel and aluminum wheels in the bead area. He has a 16 in. Spyder wheel with a lead wheel-weight having a brass pin that goes through the rim and weight and is "bradded over" on the bead side of the rim. In addition, the weight is also held to the rim with a steel clip in a sort of belt and suspenders effort to keep the weight in place.

Finally, a graduate of Porsche's February, 1957, Carrera School has surfaced. Gerry McCarthy of KAM Motorsport, does Porsche service and restoration and specializes in four-cam engines and cars. He can be found in Waterbury, CT at 203/754-1547.

With respect to wheels and brakes, Gerry's class notes state: "(550A-1500) RS brakes are the same as GT Carrera and 550 after chassis 056 except for drums which had larger fins and a flange in the air stream. Before chassis 056, the 550 had normal (but milled and drilled 40 mm, ed.) brakes. 550 wheels will not fit RS drums."

Al Zim took the time to write that the German vehicle inspection agency (TUV) insisted on tubes in non-safety bead tires.

Vol. 14, No. 5 Ed Hyman

Brazilian Chrome Wheels
Wheels for the drum brake 356's. Two days ago, I finished the full front end rebuild of my 1957 Speedster, with a little (a lot of) help from my friends. When I bought the car, the previous owner had just bought "new" wheels from a well-known purveyor

of parts for Porsche with a well-deserved reputation for quality. The wheels sure looked pretty – 5.5 in. chrome rims with their new, narrow 165/15 tires. They have been on and off of the car quite a few times over the years, and I have put many miles on the car.

This fall, when we disassembled the front end for king pins and link pins (which ultimately included, new trailing arms, spindles, etc...)

I noticed a scary symptom. One of the A drums (I believe it to be an original) was gouged out on the surface facing the wheel. This region, along with the studs, is always treated to an application of "Never-Seize" when the wheels are removed.

Of course, I thoroughly cleaned and repainted the affected areas on the drums – not having access to a lathe or being a concours freak, this was the extent of repair. I assume the wheels are the famous (infamous) Brazilian chrome 5.5s, I can find no identification marks. As I started to mount them back on the drums, it occurred to me to check the back (non-polished) side of the wheels, to see if they were smooth. *They were not!*

Around each bolt hole and each brake inspection hole there were fine burrs. This hard, ferrous metal would dig into the soft, old alloy surface of the drum. Probably the burrs were from the drilling process. As I had already started to dab Never-Seize on, I decided to use it with a fine grit "emery" type cloth and gently rubbed each and every hole. Then, after cleaning, I treated the wheels again with Never-Seize, mounted them and torqued the nuts. If you have these, or any aftermarket wheels, please check them, as good A brake drums seem to be made of unobtainium and the list price type drums seems to be in the region of $500.00 + each. A pretty tough region for those of us that still drive the 356 on a regular basis.

What Color to Paint Steel Wheels

In reference to a letter sent by George Duval of Venice, FL, I spoke to Bruce Baker at Auto Research in Pennsylvania, keeper of my still unfinished 1955 sunroof coupe. The question was about what silver to use on 356 wheels. He said that this is a frequently asked question among people in his profession and that the answer is "Well I've tried this and I've tried that." His two suggestions were:

1. Long standing suggestion: PPG Non-Smudge Aluminum Enamel for street use. Lacquer for show only, chips badly. It is a one step process product. A quart does two sets of wheels.

2. Convenient, but expensive suggestion: Würth aerosol spray paint, made in Germany. Good comparison to original color, but hard to find and really pricey.

He also said that most "aluminum" spray paints are actually fairly close, but have to be continually renewed to look right.

Note: Later wheels are clear coated. 1985 Corvette silver is another alternative, that can be applied with a spray gun and then, they may be clear coated – September 1994

High Performance Handling

Vol. 8, No. 6 David Seeland

Trailing Arms, Transmission Mounts, and Torsion Bars

First, let's look at some of the sources of unwanted suspension movement. At the front, the trailing arms will flex under high lateral cornering loads allowing positive camber to increase. Why did I say increase? Because, with a trailing-arm front suspension set at 0 degrees of camber (wheels perpendicular to the ground), 3 degrees of body roll means 3

degrees of positive camber on the heavily loaded outside wheel and 3 degrees of negative camber on the inside wheels. This decreases the size of the tire patches and produces understeer (plowing). Of course, there are three cures for positive camber induced by cornering; first, static negative camber, second, decrease the roll, and third, decrease trailing arm flex.

I'll deal with a trailing arm flex cure first, which Vic Skirmants says is more effective than initial negative camber. The obvious solution is to box the trailing arms. German Precision in Sunnyvale, CA, (408) 747-0728, does this using a jig. The jig is important both to check the arms before welding begins and to check them as the welding progresses.

I boxed my own arms, but then I had some extras so if they didn't turn out I was in no trouble. I used an AC arc welder and carefully tack-welded the three parts of the box into place and then welded short sections allowing cooling time between welds. I also welded on alternate seams to try to minimize warpage. Two of the pieces, top and bottom, were cut from 2 x $\frac{1}{8}$ in. mild steel from the hardware store, the front pieces are 1 $\frac{1}{4}$ x $\frac{3}{16}$ in. telephone pole crossarm braces. (Ma Bell would prefer that you got them from the hardware store too) I wrapped the bearing surfaces with masking tape to protect them from weld splatter.

An easy straightness check of the arms after you're done welding is to replace them and measure the offset at the eyes; it should be between 5 and 9 mm if you haven't warped them. Better yet is a before and after check.

The "link" connecting the trailing arm can be reinforced. Sway-A-Way and the Wright Place both sell reinforced links. I haven't tried to do my own because almost all the links I have laid my hands on have been bent – and these were not from wrecked cars! They are VW parts and cost about $50 each so the $110 for a reinforced set is quite reasonable. Vic Skirmants had an unreinforced one break on his race car and strongly suggests that they be beefed up for safety. They also stiffen the front suspension slightly. Also available are chrome-moly kingpins in standard and oversizes as well as chrome-moly linkpins.

At the rear, solid transaxle mounts can be used to good advantage. One of the causes of the dreaded trailing-throttle oversteer is the rubber transmission mounts. If the throttle is closed abruptly, especially in a lower gear, the wheels pull back forcing the transaxle forward against its mounts, since they are rubber and do move. This allows the rear wheels to toe out – a very unstable situation that results in instant oversteer, especially if you are turning. I found out about trailing throttle oversteer in my dune buggy when it had a 911 engine. I backed off in second gear at about 50 mph after passing a couple of cars on a curve – because the speed limit was 45 and it was time for the cops to be out hunting homeward-bound skiers. I felt a little foolish going sideways down the highway, but at least it wasn't backwards! Alignment changes are only part of the problem. If the rear tires are using all their adhesion to keep the car from sliding sideways, then decreased vertical load from weight transfer under braking and being required to provide braking force (either engine braking or brakes) or being required to provide acceleration cause them to start sliding – oversteer! Thus replacing the transaxle mounts with solid mounts is only a partial cure (and a noisy one at that). The front circular mounts can be replaced with aluminum blocks appropriately drilled with long bolts all the way through from transaxle to body mounts.

At the rear solid mounts can be made from the original rubber mounts by welding in scraps of steel after hack-sawing off the rubber.

The last item I'll discuss is front and rear torsion bars. Stiffening these is another method of decreasing suspension movement and therefore camber changes. The relationship of front and rear spring rates also affects oversteer/understeer. Stiffer springs at either end of the car cause that end to take more of the cornering force. Theoretically anyway, because in the real world camber changes also affect balance. An oversteering 356 with larger rear torsion bars will sometimes oversteer less because camber changes at the rear wheels are decreased, when theory says increased rear spring rate (roll stiffness) should increase oversteer.

Let's assume that to a certain degree stiffer is better. The choice in front is easy. 20 percent stiffer laminated torsion bars are available for VW link-pin front ends. These require drilling a recess for the Porsche front end height adjustment screw at the rear center because VW's have their set screws on the front of the torsion bar tube.

At the rear, things are more complicated. Two lengths of torsion bar were used. 21 $13/16$ in. on the 356C and 24 $11/16$ in. on the 356A and B. These can be interchanged by swapping spring plates. A short 28 mm bar has approximately the same spring rate as a long 29 mm bar.

I found a torsion bar spring rate graph from Russ Harmon of Sway-A-Way in *Dune Buggies and Hot VW's* magazine. (October. 1974) I couldn't use it here because it had some probable errors. Torsional rigidity is directly proportional to the length of the bar and varies as the fourth power of the radius. I tried using the formula for torsional spring rate with a middling modulus of elasticity for steel and came up with a number that meant a 24 mm torsion bar should be stiffer than it actually is. In disgust, I used an empirical approach: 1959 Carrera

DeLuxe coupe, 2100 pounds, 58.6 percent, on rear wheels, about 15 degree setting of spring plate for $1/2$ degree positive camber of the rear wheels. This is 41 pounds per degree of twist because 41 x 15 x 2 equals 58.6 percent of 2100 pounds. I then constructed Fig. 6 by comparing the fourth power of each bar radius to the 24 mm bar (12 mm radius).

But what's the graph good for? It can save a lot of time if you are changing bars. For example, if you had the spring plate inclination at 15 degrees in your 1959 1600 GS coupe (a little less than stock for near-vertical rear wheels) and now decide that you'll be the terror of your local autocrosses if you install 29 mm bars, then what spring plate inclination should you use? Simple, referring to the dotted line on Fig. 1, follow it from your 15 degree original adjustment to the 24 mm bar line then horizontally to the 29 mm line. Drop vertically to the horizontal axis at about 8 $1/2$ degrees, your new setting. You probably won't get it exactly right the first time, but if you've ever adjusted your car's rear camber, you know that getting even close is tough and being able to get close on the first try will save lots of time.

Here is another example of chart use: the trailing arm setting for factory 23 mm bars in a 356A 1500 GT coupe with transverse spring is 10 degrees or about 340 pounds per side, so we can infer that the transverse springs share of the 1200 pounds on the rear axle is about 500 pounds.

Another possible use is torsion bar selection. Say for example, that you like the way your car handles now but you'd like to stiffen it slightly and have added 20 percent stiffer VW front bars. What rear torsion bar is 20 percent stiffer? A 24 mm bar with a 18 degree twist will support 750 pounds, 20 percent more is 900 pounds, so continue up the 18 degree line and you will see that a 25 mm bar will support about 875 pounds with an 18 degree twist. Not bad, a 26 mm bar would be too stiff at 1000 pounds for a 18 degree twist.

And, a reminder, Fig. 1 is for long torsion bars (24 $11/16$ in.) and you'll have to make your own graph for the shorter 21 $13/16$ in. bars found on 356Cs. Just remember that they are stiffer by the percentage that the unsplined working length is shorter than the unsplined working length of an A or B bar.

There is one more point in the 356 rear suspension that can provide unwanted toe changes and that is the

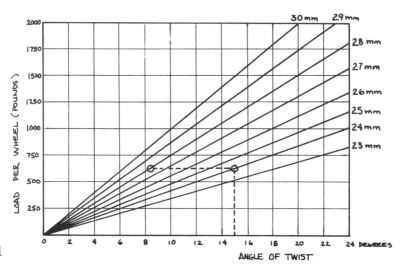

Fig.1

371

spring plate grommets – the doughnut shaped rubber rings at the spring plate pivots. If yours have never been changed and have 100,000 miles they are loose and sloppy and should be replaced. Sway-A-Way makes urethane grommets with a 1 7/8 inch inside diameter for VW's. The outside diameter is a bit large and will have to be cut down using a lathe or a homemade arbor (big washers and a bolt) for your electric drill and a Stanley sur-form.

Vol. 9, No. 2 David Seeland

Suspension Tuning

When considering handling modification, you should realize that as it came from the factory the late 356 was an excellent handling car; Ludvigsen reports 0.81 to 0.83g skid-pad figures for the 356C at Weissach, depending on the pad diameter. Of the 77 cars listed in the January *Road and Track* road test summary, only four cars had better skid pad numbers than the 356: the BMW M1, the Ferrari Berlinetta Boxer, the Lamborghini Countach, and the Lamborghini Jalpa. The 356 equalled the 930 Turbo and was better than the 911 SC, the 944, and the 928. Not too shabby at all! And, most likely, the 356s 0.83 was with 4 1/2 in. wheels and 165 tires. I'd love to see some skid pad figures on a 356 with 6 in. wheels and sticky 195/60 Yokahamas.

If you plan to drive your 356 mainly on the street, start making modifications after making sure everything is factory new or meets new specs. Then align to factory specifications. You might be pleasantly surprised. Most 356s are badly out of alignment. Has the rear ever been aligned? Is the rear camber and toe-in equal from side to side?

How are its tie rod ends, link and king pins? Is there any oil in the steering box? Is it properly adjusted? Are the front torsion bars the same on both

ends? Check for a body list while supporting the rear at the center of the transmission hoop. Check the front trailing arm bushings, inner and outer.

Are your "C" links bent? I think most of them are, even on no-accident cars. Are the grommets at the spring plate pivots worn out? They probably are if they've never been changed, and they probably haven't. Replace with stock rubber or urethane grommets before aligning.

If you plan to do any competitive driving with your 356 be sure to have a copy of the pertinent rules and read them very carefully. Development of a well-handling 356 will do you no good if it is illegal.

Relatively minor modifications when done intelligently can make major differences in handling. Ruben Romero and John Samson in an article in the *Alfa Owner* in the early seventies attained 0.956 g's on a skid pad with a 1750 GTV on street tires. Although the 356 suspension is much different than an Alfa GTV (front A-arms and solid rear axle) use of carefully controlled conditions and measurements to evaluate suspension and tire changes can and should be applied to a 356.

Romero and Samson said with reference to a slalom course, "I 'felt' the car with the 5/8 in. bar was faster and by the end of the course the car was just about out of control. One or two more gates and I would have been off the course. With the 3/4 in. bar control was easier to maintain and I could have gone through any number of gates more without loosing control. I believe this shows the importance of making objective measurements on which to base modifications. I am sure I would have subjectively decided on the 5/8 in. bar because it 'felt' faster.

Obviously I felt faster because I was in less control. Unless the driver is very experienced and possible even then 'seat-of-the-pants' suspension tuning is inadequate."

They began by subjectively evaluating understeer with progressively increasing front tire pressures – least at 42 PSI more severe with lower and higher pressures. Next, using a slalom course they evaluated 165 HR, 185 SR and E 60 (bias belted) tires at many combinations of front and rear pressures (5 runs at each combination). The best time with 165 tires was 15.2 sec., the best time with 185 tires was not much better at 14.8 sec., but the best time with E60 x 14 tires was substantially better at 13.0 sec. Tires and tire pressure are important handling variables. Following this, testing at Willow Springs Road Course was done to check handling at lower slip angles but higher speeds. Next was more skid-pad testing varying rear bar sizes and tire pressures. Maximum g rate was up to 0.91. Using the skid-pad information the slalom course was tried again and the best time was reduced from 13.0 to 11.9 secs. The old E6O tires were replaced with new E6O tires with $^{10}/_{32}$ tread. This produced 0.944 g's on the skid pad, but I always thought those near-bald XWXs were better.....Next 1 $^3/_4$° negative front camber was tried producing 0.956 g's!

I hope I didn't belabor the Alfa example but I do believe that quantification of the results of performance modifications (handling, acceleration, and braking) is the only way to approach the performance limits of your 356.

In summary, for a street car, be sure everything in the suspension and steering is up to stock specifications, then decide if you really want to change anything. Making all the possible modifications is neither necessary or even possible. If you put 30 mm rear bars in a car that is to be driven only on the street you'll wish you had something softer, like an MG TC. A super-stiff front sway bar will snap your head back and forth on minor one-wheel bumps.

An excellent street setup, tried on our Carrera 2, was 5 $^1/_2$ in. wheels, 165 x 15 tires, 19 mm H and H front sway bar set on soft Koni shocks set on soft, 27 mm long rear torsion bars, and a factory rear transverse spring (camber compensator). For auto crossing with this set up I would suggest 6 in. wheels with 195/60 Yokahamas or race tires, with the rear shocks set at full hard. I would also run a little more negative camber at the rear. Slackening off on the transverse spring is the easy way to reduce the rear camber with this set up and to me is one of the major advantages of the transverse spring. Stiffer torsion bars with the camber compensator is the reverse of what the factory had in mind but I liked the results.

For a competition car read the rules to find out what changes can he made. Make planned changes one at a time and record the quantitative effects on a skid pad, slalom course, or race track.

Vol. 12, No 3. Vic Skirmants

356C Suspension Settings
Tom McGuckin, Las Cruces, NM, asks how to improve the handling of his 1964 SC coupe. He's been told to go softer on the rear torsion bars, stiffer on the rear torsion bars, add a camber compensator, don't add a camber compensator. I'm going to tell him to do something completely different. The 1964 - 1965 cars had a 16 mm front sway bar and softer rear torsion bars than the earlier cars. This made them the best-handling stock 356s. If tire pressures and everything else is OK, the main thing to check is the rear toe-in. Factory specs call for practically no toe-in at the rear. Actually, rear toe-in is more important than front toe-in. I would set the rear toe-in to $^1/_{16}$ or $^1/_8$ in. Absolutely no toe-out! And be sure both sides are equal in relation to the centerline of the car. Many cars get their handling messed

up when the transmission is removed and replaced without proper consideration for the shims at the front trans mounts. Don't assume they're identical on both sides! Be sure the shift finger is aimed down the middle of the hole in the chassis; if not, shim accordingly.

Some more negative camber in the rear would help also. Two degrees would be max for a regularly street-driven car. My race car is set at 3 1/2 to 4 in. camber with 3/16 in. toe-in, with coil-over springs that would make a Mack Truck harsh riding. It also has a 19 mm Z-bar to keep the nine-inch wide racing slicks from jacking up in corners.

It all works pretty well; especially since a swing-axle is the worst suspension imaginable for high-performance driving.

Vol. 10, No. 6 Vic Skirmants

Fat Tires and Suspension Mods.
Suspension modifications to make the best use of modern wide footprint tires. This basically means limited camber changes in order to keep the tire tread on the road. Our suspension is the worst type for limited camber change. As the front suspension leans in a corner, the trailing arms translate every degree of body roll into camber change, adding additional degrees due to trailing arm flex. On our race cars we reinforce the trailing arms for less flex; practical for the street. We remachine the link pin carriers for negative camber; still possible for street use – maybe not too desirable. With the coil-spring shock absorbers we also stiffen up the suspension to practically eliminate body roll; not practical for the street. The rear suspension can use a Z-bar to decrease the effect of jacking due to the high center of gravity inherent with swing axles. Here also we use monster coil springs to keep suspension travel to a minimum. Suspension travel at the rear translates to

camber and toe-in change.
Actually, if I understand radial tires, they shouldn't be as sensitive to camber as bias ply, so I really wouldn't worry too much about it. After all, there's only so wide a tire one can stuff under a stock 356 body.

Vol. 10, No. 5 Vic Skirmants

Teflon Suspension Bushings
Chuck would like me to comment on teflon suspension bushings. For the front suspension, the only bushings available are for the sway bar. Not a bad idea, but if your rubber bushings are in good shape, the teflon ones aren't going to make that big a difference on a stock suspension. The rear suspension is the place for teflon bushings to do some good. First, however, the transmission mounts have to be in good condition. If the rear mounts are too soft, separating, etc., then during cornering the car body is free to move slightly in relation to the transmission. So what, you say. So the transmission is the center pivot for your swing axles. The rear of the car can be glued to the road by the stickiest tires you can find, but if the body moves sideways, you feel it and it translates to your brain as "unstable". That's why on our race cars the rear rubber mount gets replaced by angle iron, and the front mounts are replaced by solid blocks. For a street Porsche this would transmit more noise into the car and would probably be unacceptable – to most people.

The teflon bushings for the rear end replace the rubber ones at the ends of the torsion bars. Since the outer end of the torsion bar is a suspension pivot for the trailing arm, teflon bushings at this location are a good way to limit movement of the trailing arm. Under acceleration the rubber bushings compress, causing more toe-in, while under braking, you get less toe-in, or even toe-out; definitely not wanted at the rear wheels.

Vol. 9, No. 2 David Seeland

Coil-Over Shock Absorbers

Coil-over shock absorbers are the hot setup perhaps because they make it easier to change spring rates front and rear and camber at the rear. Fronts are essentially bolt-on but rears require a groove be made in the inner wall of the wheel well below the upper shock mount. Not difficult, but you might not want to chop up a con-cours car to add coil-overs. Mighty stiff 30 mm rear bars are available and to balance their stiffness might take more than the 20 percent stiffer front bars, so coil-overs in front could be necessary. Another reason for using coil-overs is to make small adjust-ments to balance the car side to side.

If you lower your car too much you may need shorter shocks than stock because if you use your shocks for bump stops, they won't work long.

Vol. 8, No. 1 Pat Ertel

Tires & Wheels

I have been an avid autocrosser since I got my first 356 and I have explored many ways to make the cars handle better without compromising street driveability. Because the second most important element in a car's han-dling is the connection between the tire and the road (the first is the driv-er) I have done quite a bit of research on the subject of wheels and tires. All of my findings are applicable to street driven cars.

The best handling wheels I have found have been a combination of 4 1/2 in. on front and 5 1/2 in. on the rear. Wheels in 6 in. and 7 in. widths have been used without positive results. The 356's swing axle suspen-sion is not able to take full advantage of wheels wider than 5 1/2 in. unless modifications such as severe decam-bering or a spring over-shock conver-sion is used. These modifications aren't recommended; they can make driving a 356 on the street difficult and unpleasant. The 5 1/2 in. wheels now being used are the Brazilian type available from *Registry* advertisers. I do not recommend their use on the front. The extra 1/2 in. of width on the inside of the wheel causes it to rub against the front suspension stops dur-ing even moderate parking maneuver-ing. My test car, an early "A", experi-enced a decrease in its turning circle of 6 feet. Wider than stock wheels at the front do not improve handling enough to offset the disadvantages. One inch wider wheels at the rear improve handling.

The question of the best tires is far more difficult to answer and requires a short discussion of the 356's suspen-sion. The front suspension works very well. The whole problem of 356 han-dling centers around bringing the back of the car up to the level of cornering ability of the front. The nature of the 356's swing axle rear suspension is such that the tire is almost never flat on the ground. When traveling in a straight line, the tire rides on its inside edge and when cornering, the outside edge is doing all the work. Therefore, the popular wide flat tires with square shoulders are the worst thing a driver can put on a 356. The perfect rear tire for a 356 would be rounded, like a huge motorcycle tire. The best way to approach this ideal using automotive tires is to choose a tire with rounded shoulders, put it on a rim that is at least as wide as the tread, and fill it with lots and lots of air.

So what tire to choose? A radial, of course, but what size and grade? There are two sizes commonly found on 356s, 165 x 15 in. and 185/70 x 15 in. The first number indicates the width of the carcass measured (very roughly) in millimeters. The second number refers to the wheel diameter and will always be 15 in. on 356s. The 165 tire is fine on 4 1/2 in. or 5 1/2 in. rims. The 185 on 4 1/2 in. rims is a ludicrous waste of rubber. On 5 $\frac{1}{2}$ in. rims they are better but still too heavy and too big around, and expensive besides. There is a tire seldom seen on 356s which is the perfect compromise for 5 $\frac{1}{2}$ in. rims. A 175-70 x 15 in. has approximately 5 $\frac{1}{2}$ in. of tread width, is the same diameter and weighs about the same as a 165. The recommended tire size is 165 x 15 for 4 $\frac{1}{2}$ in. or 5 $\frac{1}{2}$ in. rims and 175 x 15 for 5 $\frac{1}{2}$ in. rims.

There are three grades of performance radials available. Anything without one of these three grade letters should not be used on a sports car. The types are SR, HR, and VR. SR indicates a tire that is safe at sustained speeds of 113 mph. These tires usually have fabric belts under the tread but are not available with high performance tread patterns. They are good for 356s that are not going to be driven hard. The HR tires are safe at speeds of up to 130 mph, but for 356 drivers their most important attribute is that they have treads designed for hard cornering and braking. Some of them have fabric belts and some have steel belts.

Fabric belts are better for achieving the curved tread profile 356s need because they flex more easily. VR tires are good for speeds over 130 mph. They offer no advantages over HR tires for the 356 owner. The recommended grade of tire is HR. Of the dozens of brands and models available, the ones tested are Continental TS772, Michelin XVS and XWS (a VR grade), Semperit M401, and Pirelli CN36. The Pirelli is slightly favored over the rest.

Of the various combinations of wheels and tires used in several years of testing, the favorite is: Pirelli CN36 165HR15 in. tires on 4 $\frac{1}{2}$ in. Brazilian wheels for the front and Pirelli CN36 175/70HR15 in. on 5 $\frac{1}{2}$ in. Brazilian wheels on the rear. This combination provides the best compromise between original appearance

and increased performance. The wider wheels in the rear help fill up the vacant-looking rear wheel wells of the stock 356.

Tire pressure is critical to getting the maximum out of wheels and tires. For comfortable street riding use 22 - 24 PSI in front and 26 - 28 in the rear. On the autocross course use (depending on the course) 31 - 35 in front and 40 - 42 in the rear. On a tight course where oversteer is useful use 35 front 40 rear. On a course with sweeping turns where more neutral steering is needed use 31 front 42 rear. These recommendations are for cold tires that are expected to make one lap around a course. For very long tracks or other sustained high speed use where the tire can be expected to become hot use lower pressures.

Vol. 8, No. 2 Pat Ertel

Addendum

One paragraph of the article on wheels and tires got badly scrambled someplace between the first draft and the finished copy. In the paragraph that begins, *Of the various combinations...* I did not mean to imply that 4 $\frac{1}{2}$ in. Brazilian wheels are any better than 4 $\frac{1}{2}$ in. stock wheels. From a performance standpoint I have found no difference between them. Also, I did NOT mean to recommend 165X15 Pirelli CN36 tires. This model of tire does not exist in that size. I know of no manufacturer that makes both a 165 and a 175/70 tire in the same model. So, if you want to maximize handling *and* have front tires that match the appearance of the rears, you must use 175/70 tires on 4 $\frac{1}{2}$ in. rims at the front and 175/70 tires on 5 $\frac{1}{2}$ in. rims at the rear. However, if you want performance and don't care about looks, a 165 tire works as well as a 175/70 on the narrow front rims. Moral: wider rims under stock-sized tires improve handling more than wider tires on stock-sized rims.

A More Radical Approach

This is a further extrapolation of the tire/wheel article by Pat Ertel in the last issue. His article was a good place to start, but what about us lower, wider, steamroller, gumball freaks? I have been campaigning (autocross, driver's school/time trial, general sick dog speed events) a 1964 Coupe that has been lowered in the front as far as the adjusters allow, with the rear transaxle hoop redrilled 5/8 in. for lowering, plus 1 1/2 degrees negative camber screwed in. H&H adjustable 16 mm sway bar in front (full soft setting) and H&H 13 mm Z-bar in back. All this was done as "the quest" was started.

"The quest" is defined as the most rubber stuffable under the rear fenders without body modifications. The fronts rub at full lock now, but they did with the stock skinnies, too. First step (for mankind, giant leap toward sick dog) about seven years ago, I replaced the original 165 Michelin X-stop cast-iron tires and 4 1/2 in. rims with four 185/70VR15 Pirelli CN36s mounted on 5 1/2 in. 911 rims. They were phenomenal in the rain, especially at Summit Point where it rained every weekend I was there. The only problem experienced was on an unexpectedly dry Saturday (it rained Sunday for timed runs which was great since I didn't know my way around without wipers keeping time). Under hard cornering I could hear clicking from the rear end of the car. I'd listen intently for the impending death rattle on the straights, but the noise only appeared in the corners. Removal of the rear wheels showed something scraping away the inside wheel weights.

The upper bump stop hat section was assumed to be the offending party so about 1/2 in. of the stop's outside horizontal surface was removed. For insurance a set of early 911 spacers, about 1/4 in., was installed. Problem

"fixed" with no rubbing, anywhere. Three years ago the Pirellis became autocross, Baldini specials and replacements were sought. Michelin XWX's were recommended as "the" Porsche tire so a set of 185/70VR15s were purchased and installed on another set of 5 1/2 in. 911 rims. Again no clearance problem but I had exactly the opposite of the "ideal" combination - bald XWXs for dry and "new" CN36s for wet. With a name like mine what can you expect. Last Fall the XWXs were re-installed with early style (deep) 6 in. 911 factory alloys for a 1000% appearance improvement over painted rims (Ugh!). The rear spacers were removed with no clearance problems. The only problem came from the fact that those early alloys require tubes installed under the tubeless tires (heavy).

I'd like to add a comment here – I believe Charlie means that the hole for the valve stem is not the proper type for a tubeless tire valve stem. I have these same wheels on the front of my race car. I merely installed the valve stem as usual; it looks a little strange, but works just fine. VS.

The last step, so far, in my quest was the purchase this past Spring of the "thick rubber bands" now installed. Four Fulda Y-2000 tires (German Goodyear branch is supplying this optional tire for European Golf (Rabbit) GTIs and Scirocco) were wrapped around Stoddard's 6 1/2 x 15 in. Minilite Sports (cast aluminum). These were initially installed without spacers. After a few hard events an inspection revealed very slight scraping on the ejector pad locations where wheel weights would have been hammered on (tape-ons were used). The "scraper" was diagnosed as point contact with the lower shock hex head mounting bolt. It could probably have been ground away but cheap, thick hardware store washers were installed resulting in no rubbing anywhere, except full lock. This last change results in a kind of roller skate, low-rider look since they lower the car about 1 $1/4$ in. The biggest "disadvantage" with this grossly reduced overall diameter is that, combined with the 6:31 ring & pinion, the tub gets very busy at high-way speeds, 4100 RPM at 60 mph! Top speed is also reduced to about 90 mph, but Boy, what a hole shot at the autocross. They are cheaper than CN36s and felt better than my XWXs at the Mid-Ohio driver's school. Also, a recent, semi-official Northern Ohio Region PCA tire test rates them barely behind P7s and equal to or better than NCTs (European), 3011s and bald XWXs on the skid pad slalom. Plus they've still got $3/4$ of the tread left.

Regarding Pat's recommendation for tire pressures: Since I've been autocrossing, etc., I've found that equal tire pressure at all four corners generally works best, range 35-37 PSI, depending on tires, track, etc. The past couple years for very tight autocrosses (Triumph club, of course) I've actually used 2 PSI higher pressure in front! I've felt somewhat like a leper because of this, especially in the Porsche Club. But it works, despite all the "experts" claiming it should be vice versa. Imagine my relief while attending an autocross seminar at this year's Parade given by Dick Turner, co-author of *Winning Autocross Solo II Competition*, when he shocked many by recommending this same pressure differential I've "discovered". I've been healed! He even convinced a few of them to try this to solve their slow speed turn plowing. Thank you Dr. Turner. Maybe you should try it too.

Vol. 8, No. 3 Bob Napier

Bob Napier's Autocross Setup

The combination below has worked well enough on my 1959 356A Cabriolet for me to win both of the last two Porsche Parade autocrosses I've entered; the 1973 Parade Autocross at Laguna Seca (against the onslaught of "California Stock" 356s) and the 1975 Parade Autocross (which I co-chaired) at Seattle International Raceway. Both times I competed in Class I (stock Normals and Supers, sans Speedsters).

I had a Portland, OR racing wheel manufacturer weld Porsche centers into Porsche-appearing 6 in. rims. The rear wheel's centers have a $3/8$ in. difference in offset from one side to the other to allow for my particular car's idiosyncratic relationship between body and under-carriage.

Following Chuck Stoddard's lead I mounted 165 HR 15 Michelin XASs on the 6 in. rims – they stretch nicely. Chuck had found this setup safe in racing situations and I've never encountered a problem in the nine years I've used them (always with tubes). I did run one set of 185 VR 70 XWX Michelins, and they are definitely better handling tires, but the XASs with tubes will run around $95 each list, and the XWXs a little over $200. Its pretty difficult to give a head-to-head evaluation between the two, but you might expect to lower your time 7 to 8/10ths of a second in a 40 to 50 second duration run with the XWXs, and I've been in many autocrosses where this might be enough to move you from fifth to first place. My personal recommendation though would be to go with the XASs and make your driving just a tweek smoother all the way around to offset the other guys XWXs. It worked for me.

The wheel offset on the rears is such that with the XWXs there was enough space between the fender and the tire to pass a credit card through (+ .045 in.) and the tires never touched the body in competition. The 6 in. wheels decamber the rear end by virtue of their increased offset to the outside.

These are run in conjunction with a 19 mm H&H Sway Bar in front and Konis all around, with the front set on full soft and the rears on full hard to minimize understeer at low speed. And, believe me,, with this setup it does plow at speeds under about 35 mph (a Z-28 Camaro driver had to teach me how to get around slow auto-cross corners). But as the speed increases I can get away with all kinds of things I couldn't with a stock set-up. Things like getting off the gas and gently onto the brakes while in a four wheel drift at 85 mph. With a stock configuration, this action is guaranteed to get you a 360°panorama of the world real quickly.

And, lastly, with this setup, I usually run 36 PSI in the front and 34 in the rear. The higher front pressure partially offsets the low speed understeer tendency, and, on a real tight course. I might drop to 33 or 32 in the rear in an attempt to get the rear end to come around. On the street I run 30 PSI front and 28 rear, and, except for a firm ride, this setup serves me very nicely.

When you remember that all other things being equal, the bigger the footprint the faster you can corner I see no justification for using 4 $1/2$ in. wheels in the front just to try to arrive at neutral steer. Go with 5 $1/2$ in. or 6 in. all around and drive accordingly.

Vol. 8, No. 4 Vic Skirmants

Comparison of Z-Bar and Camber Compensator
Now for some words of wisdom about one of my favorite 356-related myths. "Bolt on a camber-compensator and corner twice as fast." Bull! This misconception has been around for quite some time and seems to have gained fresh converts with the influx of new people to our hobby.

"Well, gee, an S-90 handles better than a stock B, and it has a compensator, therefore, the compensator makes the car handle better." Bull, bull! The S-90 handled better (less oversteer) due to the fact that the factory installed softer rear torsion bars; the rear end then rolled more in a corner, forcing the front end to handle more of the total cornering forces. A stiffer front sway bar would have had approximately the same result. The factory did just that with the C model. A 16 mm sway bar replaced the 15 mm bar, and the rear torsion bars were slightly softer than an S-90. The compensator was an option. The only official factory reason for the compensator was to "compensate" for the softer rear bars. The compensator brought the load carrying capability of the softened rear end back up to the stock specs. The compensator does nothing when cornering. It does not prevent nor decrease wheel jacking when cornering. With its original mounting hardware it is impossible for the compensator to prevent jacking. It can only pull the axles down, it cannot push them which is what you need to prevent jacking.

Now, for those who have bolted on an after-market compensator for a VW and did notice an improvement in handling, yes, it is possible. First you have to understand that the mounting of the VW compensator is different than the Porsche compensator. The VW uses short, rubberized straps that go around the axle tube. These are cheap and simple, and have the advantage in that the rubber between the compensator and the axle tube can permit the compensator spring to push the axles upward. That's not all! The compensating spring has a bolt or large rivet attaching it to the cradle that bolts to the bottom of the transmission housing. This bolt prevents the spring from dropping when the axles try to droop. The factory spring has support bolts at each end that are not set up to transmit loads in both directions; they only transmit one way – the wrong way for handling improvement. You could modify the connecting bolts so they could work in both directions, but then the spring

379

would just drop free of its trans cradle. You would have to attach it to the cradle or the transmission, then it would work.

One final *however*! Bolt on either the VW or modified Porsche compensator incorrectly, and you're worse off than without it. The compensator should not pull downward excessively on the axle tubes, or it will cause a decrease in your negative camber, which will also hurt your cornering. The ideal modification is a Z-bar, which is just a sway bar with the ends pointing in opposite directions. A Z-bar also must be attached and adjusted correctly. There is an after-market Z-bar for our cars. The attaching hardware is a bit strange, but for a bolt-on modification, this is the only way to go. For all out racing, we take a 911 front sway bar, switch one end around, add heim-jointed adjustable links, hang everything in place, and then weld bars all over the bottom of the car to hold the whole mess in place. It works.

Now to confuse the whole matter and make most of you turn to the classifieds. The factory put in softer rear torsion bars and the car handled better; *true*. If you really want to go fast, go stiffer; *true*. What?!? Earlier I explained why the softer torsion bars worked; now to explain why, for all out racing, you go as stiff as your kidneys can stand, then go another step.

The Porsche 356 suspension system is just about the worst imaginable type for good handling!

Put down the noose, purists, and look at the ridiculous way our wheels are controlled. At the rear, a swing axle permits horrendous camber changes with suspension movement. The trailing arm or spring plate off the torsion bar forces large toe-in changes with suspension movement. At the front, the wheels move up and down parallel to the chassis; beautiful; as the chassis rolls in a turn, every single degree of body roll is translated to that many degrees of positive camber of the outside tire. On top of that, the spindly front trailing arms flex, and that much more positive camber is forced into that outside tire. The car is perfectly balanced.

One of the worst front suspensions to compensate for the worst rear suspension imaginable. Why? Back in the early 1930s when it was designed for the VW, it seemed like a good, cheap, practical, cheap, logical and cheap method of providing independent suspension in an era when many cars still had solid front axles, let alone rear axles.

So, for a street car, the softer rear bars worked fine. Now set that car up for serious racing. Bolt the transmission rigidly to the chassis; if it moves your suspension moves. Now put solid plastic or teflon bushings in place of the rubber ones at the torsion bar end of the trailing arm. Better yet, throw away the torsion bars, bolt on coil-over shock absorbers, and put heim-joints in the end of the trailing arms and move them up a couple of inches. At the front, reinforce the trailing arms to decrease flex and mount the sway bar with solid bushings and heim-jointed links. Now that all the rubber is out of the suspension, you can feel what the wheels are doing in a turn. The stiffer you make it, the less the suspension will move, the less unwanted and unasked for camber, toe and self-steering effects will take place.

Vol. 9, No. 2 David Seeland

Z-bars and Camber Compensators, II
So what is a Z-bar? It functions nearly, but not exactly like a transverse compensating spring in that it increases bump resistance, but not roll resistance. All the latest VW swing axle sedans (1967) had them as standard equipment, so if you would like

to see one, go find a 1967 Bug in your local supermarket parking lot, or go look at an E-production 356. Fig. 3 is a sketch of a Z-bar. The bar itself is usually a 911 front anti-roll bar. The arms are also from a 911, but one is reversed. The bar in a VW crosses above the transaxle, but all the home-made Z-bars pass beneath the transaxle. In Don Erickson's ex-E Production time trial car the sway bar is enclosed in a piece of pipe to which are welded two mounting arms that bolt to the body box section behind and above the outer ends of the torsion bar tube. The Z-bar tube also has a wooden

block at its center that bears against the bottom of the transaxle. The H and H Specialties Z-bar has two box-like arrangements that surround the axle tubes at each end and bolt to the bottom of the body at the top.

However it is located, the Z-bar's torsion bar must be fixed so that it can't move either up or down. Look at the photos of E production 356s in the December/January 1978/1979 issue of the *Registry*; the cars with Z-bars are obvious – the rear wheels don't droop when the cars are jacked up. This should help eliminate jacking of the rear end while cornering.

Camber Compensator

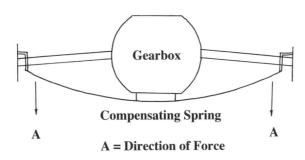

A = Direction of Force

Z-Bar

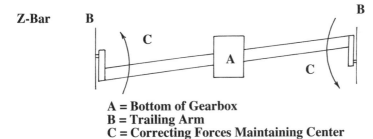

A = Bottom of Gearbox
B = Trailing Arm
C = Correcting Forces Maintaining Center

Chapter 20

Tools

Rotisseries

Vol. 6, No. 3 Jim Puckett

Home-Built Rotisserie, I

My home-style *porscherotisserie* was born out of a statement by my friend, a fire sprinkler contractor, that his shop could do anything with steel. Well, 15 minutes on the drawing board and the following sketch was produced-and two weeks later my rotator was ready for delivery. My eyes being bigger than my back – a sturdy structure was produced per the attached sketch. Evolution being what it is, my rotator is mounted on casters (8 in.) and verrrry sturdy.

The ascension of my cabriolet occurred late in October. My lifting process follows:
  Place a hoist at the front and back.
  Lift the front, crib;
  Lift the back, crib;
  Lift the front, crib;
  Lift the back, crib;
  Run out of cribbing!
  Tie the front car brackets to the hoist with rope (or whatever);
  Lift the back, lift the front.
  Lift, lift, lift.
  All this is going on with one person, me, and one floor jack.
  Damn! It's falling. Whew! The ropes caught it.

Lift, lift, lift.
  Anyway – my lifting process boils down to: do it carefully – use two people – have adequate cribbing to support the car front and back – and be careful. My lift was in excess of three feet – with only a floor jack? – and I was not really adequately prepared. However, I succeeded regardless.

My hoist works great! I have rotated the car 90° both ways, but have hesitated to do a 360.

My "bumper brackets" are out of $1/2$ x 2 in. bars and include a "saddle" that goes down from the bumper attachment point on the car and spans from one side to the other. I have wood wedges between the body metal and the saddle steel and this adds a great deal of strength to the assembly and reduces the stress on the body metal.

The car turns easily and it is fantastic to be able to turn the body virtually upside down to make the angle of attack proper on the "Old devil rust hisself"!

By the way, my "design" was without the aid of the good picture of the Hansen Roto-Hoist in the *Registry*. I was impressed with theirs being so similar to mine. I do not have bearings at the pivot, just one pipe inside the other, and it turns just fine. The whole assembly rolls easily out of my garage to allow cleanup and picture sessions.

Jim Puckett's Rotisserie

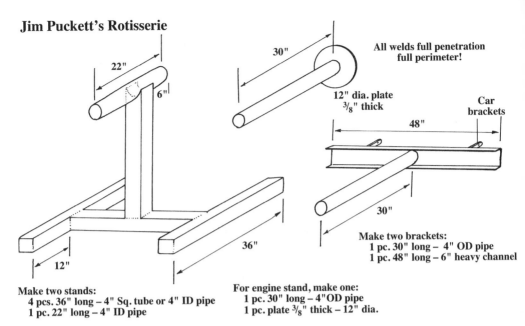

22"

6"

30"

All welds full penetration
full perimeter!

12" dia. plate
3/8" thick

Car
brackets

48"

36"

30"

12"

Make two brackets:
  1 pc. 30" long – 4" OD pipe
  1 pc. 48" long – 6" heavy channel

Make two stands:
  4 pcs. 36" long – 4" Sq. tube or 4" ID pipe
  1 pc. 22" long – 4" ID pipe

For engine stand, make one:
  1 pc. 30" long – 4"OD pipe
  1 pc. plate 3/8" thick – 12" dia.

Vol. 6, No. 3 Jacques Brownson

Home-Built Rotisserie, II

Vic Skirmants *356 Registry* tech editor, prefers not to use a rotisserie to put in a new pan because he feels that it is easier to use jack stands and a floor jack to straighten out the sag in rusty open cars (by adjusting door gaps). I have only had the experience of putting one not very rusty car on my rotisserie and observing Jacques Brownson of Denver used his on a Convertible D. Jacques did replace the pan and found his homemade rotisserie useful in many ways. For example, he drilled access holes, appropriately sized for plastic plugs, into his new longitudinals, poured in several quarts of Rustoleum, then rotated the car through 360 degrees to coat everything then rotated the car farther to drain out the excess paint. Try that with your floor jack, Vic! A sketch of Jacques very simple device follows. The circular, one-half inch thick, steel pieces are called "cut-outs" at the local used-metal yard. These are the leftovers from the construction of

some kind of steel storage tanks.

Another advantage of inverting a slightly rusty car, or one that you plan to concours, is that your repairs, cleaning and painting will be done faster and better, and more completely. I did all the straightening and welding and undercoat removal on my car lying on my creeper. The bottom of the car. except for painting was done, or so I

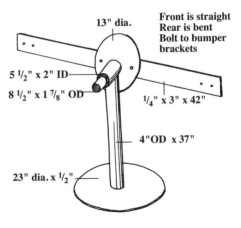

13" dia.

Front is straight
Rear is bent
Bolt to bumper
brackets

5 1/2" x 2" ID

8 1/2" x 1 7/8" OD

1/4" x 3" x 42"

4"OD x 37"

23" dia. x 1/2"

Jacques Browson's Rotisserie

thought, until I put the car on the rotisserie. Then I spent one whole Saturday heat shrinking and otherwise making the battery box perfect. Upside-down perfect and right-side-up perfect are an order of magnitude removed from each other. Molten metal up your sleeve hurts now, and paint remover hurts in a while, but with a rotisserie you can avoid most of the pain – if you can avoid splitting open the skin on your forehand with the back of your hand when your home-made dent pulling hook slips. "Well, doctor, I was removing a dent from the bottom of my Porsche and..."

"Well, you probably shouldn't have mentioned his questionable ancestry!"

"But I was removing . . ."

"Sure you were, hold still while I take a couple of stitches."

Tools You Can Buy

Vol. 1, No. 3 Jim Lamb

Cylinder Head Removing Socket

Snap-On makes a $3/8$ in. drive 10 mm Allen wrench, 4 $1/2$ in. long, that is well worth the money if you change heads a lot.

Vol. 1, No. 5 Vic Skirmants

Tools Required For Engine Rebuilds

In response to a request for a list of tools and micrometers needed when rebuilding a Porsche engine: I will assume everyone has a decent selection of open and box-end metric wrenches, sockets, and ratchet. In addition you will need a torque wrench with a range of 0-50 lb-ft; a 10 mm Allen-head socket for the cylinder head bolts; a clutch-aligning tool, which will also double nicely as a piston-pin driver; a piston-ring compressor that can be disassembled after the cylinder is slid over the piston; a valve spring compressor (any "C"-clamp type will do nicely); a valve spring

height gage or some other means of measuring the valve spring installed height; a 1 $7/16$ in. (36 mm) socket, $3/4$ in. drive, for the flywheel bolt; a $13/16$ in. (32 mm) socket for the crank pulley bolt; a 3 - 3 $1/2$ in. micrometer for measuring the pistons, as well as a dial bore-gauge in the same range to measure the cylinders; a 50 - 75 mm micrometer for checking the crankshaft. These are most of the basic tools that will be required.

Vol. 3, No. 6 Robert Frank

One Man Starter Removal Tool

Has anyone come up with some neat little trick to make that starter/ engine bolt a true one-man-removable operation? Yes, there is a cute little magnetic wrench with two short arms on it. You simply place it on the bolt head by the starter, then go and pull the nut in the engine compartment. The magnet holds the wrench on the bolt head, while the arms keep it from turning while you're taking off the nut. Of course you use the wrench on the other top bolt also. It used to be a standard VW tool and is still listed by Performance Products; tool #T-7, $11.95.

Vol. 13, No. 4 Tim Walls

Lifts

Over sixty-two years ago the first automotive lift was invented and mechanics' lives were made a lot easier. The following fifty years, lifts stayed basically the same in design. An inground, one or two piston, air operated, frame contact, full-hydraulic or semi-hydraulic lift.

These early lifts had advantages and disadvantages. The disadvantages ... these lifts had to be installed inground. This meant two days to saw and break out the cement floor, excavating a hole and installing the piston/tank/ piping, then backfilling with clean sand. You then added forty gallons of oil, cemented the hole and waited for two days for the cement to cure. There the lift stayed for the rest of its useful life.

How long was its useful life? Anywhere from ten to twenty years. Acids and electrolysis, both present in the ground, erode holes in the cylinder casing, tank and piping. This is what makes finding a good used lift from an old gas station or dealership as hard to find as a 356 with an original floor pan.

But we have entered the new age of above ground or surface mount lifts. These lifts come in two column, frame contact or a four-post drive-on design. Installation is a quick six hours using normal hand tools & a large hammer drill (for the sixteen 3/4" holes for anchor bolts). Only two requirements... a 5 in. concrete floor and a 220 v. electrical outlet. This will run the lift power unit, which holds 24 quarts of ATF and puts out 3,000 PSI.

The advantages to above ground lifts are numerous. Although most home garages are too small, a pole barn is ideal. The bay size needed is 12 ft. wide x 24 ft. long x 12.5 ft. high. These lifts can be moved anytime. They do not require compressed air and no maintenance is required.

The best two column lift is the asymmetrical which repositions the vehicles's center of gravity behind the center line of the lift. This lets you open the car doors without hitting the column and has an overhead equalization system for unobstructed floor surface.

But the perfect lift in my opinion, for working on a 356 would be a four-post, drive-on lift.

This lift gives easy access to the floor pan, longitudinal members and the battery box. But remember, when replacing these, the car must be supported by the wheels and suspension to help absorb the stress the body undergoes as it is heated, reinforced and cooled.

These lifts can be raised or lowered to any height to weld inside or under the car. With the addition of a rolling bridge or center jack, all services can be performed, even on vehicles whose pictures you don't carry in your wallet.

Like any piece of equipment you purchase, be sure to look for a quality brand with a good warranty. Also important, is ease of service and availability of parts. Some of the leading brands of lifts are Rotary, Weaver and Globe. Prices range from $3,500 to $5,000 depending on model and does not include installation.

Tools You Can Make

Vol. 1, No. 2 Vic Skirmants

Flywheel Holding Tool
Take a 2 1/2 or 3 ft. length of angle iron, drill two holes for bolting to your flywheel as shown: Take a 3/4 in. drive 1 7/16 in. socket and slide bar handle (available at Sears) slip a 4 ft. length of pipe over it, and lean on it hard. For tightening, reverse the angle iron, and lean hard again. Don't be afraid of overtightening. I apply my complete weight (175 lbs.) at the end of the pipe and have no problems.

You do have to watch the bolts holding the angle to the flywheel. Use a couple of extras, because they tend to get deformed and don't work too well on the pressure plate.

If the gland nut starts to strip, stop! It wasn't any good anyway. Remove it in time, and you won't have any problem with having to remove the stripped threads from the crank shaft.

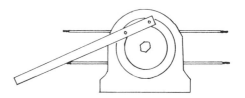

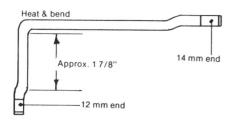

Heat & bend

Approx. 1 7/8"

14 mm end

12 mm end

Vol. 3, No. 3 Mike Robbins

Carburetor Wrenches

How many times have you sworn at the front (car direction) nuts holding Zenith carbs to the manifolds: With the engine in the car, these are awkward to reach; even with the side opening open-end wrench P 23. I've seen instances where the wrench slipped in the hands of ham-handed "mechanics" and the result was breakage or bending of the idle bleed screws and/or breaking of the accelerator pump link. Removal and replacement of these nuts can be simplified through the use of a special box end wrench that can easily be made from a standard double box wrench. Sears 12-14 mm wrench #9H42956 works fine for this. Merely heat the wrench (an acetylene torch is necessary) and bend it as shown. A screwdriver shank, handle for the Porsche spark plug wrench or other appropriate rod can be used through the 14 mm box end to turn the wrench.

Vol. 5, No. 3 Capt. Charlie Cutshaw

Crank Pulley Removal Spanner

Last weekend I was trying to get the center nut off the crankshaft pulley in order to relace one of the tin screws behind it which had fallen out and to check the tolerances in the oil pump, but was meeting with little success after having tried a strap wrench (the pulley just slipped), a rope wrapped through the pulley holes and anchored to the generator upright, and various and sundry curses on the cretin who

had apparently used a six-foot cheater to tighten the nut I was at my wits' end when the final solution to the problem dawned. It looks like this:

In use, one simply inserts the bolts into two of the pulley holes, holds one end of the homemade "spanner" and turns the nut off. It falls within the category of one of those tools you seldom need, but can't do without when you do. Mine has become a permanent part of my toolbox.

Vol. 8, No. 3 Dick Pike

Motor Dolly

Once you have experienced this four-wheeled wonder, you'll puzzle on how you managed to get alone, without it for so long (I did!). The motor dolly is great for trundling your powerplant around the shop, for use with the test rig I'll describe next time, and most of all – for really slick removal and refit of the Porsche motor. The dolly consists of a 3/4 in. plywood base, a 1/2 in. or 3/4 in. plywood top piece of similar size but cut out and notched to match protuberances on the bottom of the 356-912 motor case, and a 3/8 in. or 1/2 in. circular plywood disc on the bottom to fit into the round cup of your 1.5 ton hydraulic service jack (or whatever creative device you may have for lifting the motor). Nail and glue the three pieces together as in the picture. All this is spiked and glued to two 2 x 4 in. side

Crank Pulley Removal Spanner

aluminum bar stock
bar is 1/4" thick

file to clear nut and allow wrench to fit snugly.

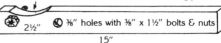

2½"   3/8" holes with 3/8" x 1½" bolts & nuts

15"

Motor Dolly

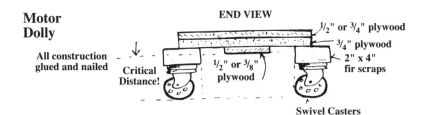

END VIEW

1/2" or 3/4" plywood

3/4" plywood

2" x 4" fir scraps

All construction glued and nailed

Critical Distance!

1/2" or 3/8" plywood

Swivel Casters

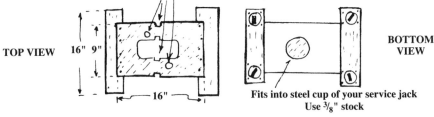

Top piece only: Cut-outs for sump plate and drain plug, etc.

TOP VIEW   16" 9"

16"

BOTTOM VIEW

Fits into steel cup of your service jack
Use 3/8" stock

pieces of cheap fir scrap, to which you have added some reasonably decent casters. The only annoying bit is getting the cutouts in the top piece to the motor case; lots of trial and error if you're in a hurry. The critical point, though, is that when on the ground, the dolly should be just tall enough and wide enough so your fully collapsed service jack fits under it. Let the glue dry and fully set.

To pull your 356 motor in just minutes, (1) jack up rear of the car and place jack stands under rear torsion bar tube, (2) remove rear engine plate and disconnect all those cables and lines, etc., (3) raise dolly on the service jack to motor, (4) loosen the four retaining bolts, release the motor and lower it to the floor, (5) pull out jack, leaving motor under car but still on the dolly, (6) raise rear of car further with service jack (and a 4" x 4" x 4' timber placed just forward of the rear torsion bar tube) until lower edge of rear body just clears the top of your motor, (7) wheel out motor on dolly, (8) lower car to any convenient height, on jack stands (or car dolly to be described here in a future column). Boy, was that quick! Make a second dolly for your spare motor(s).

P.S. I always remove the front

engine plate (and the fuel line to the pump) before dropping the motor, and reinstall it only when the motor is back in place. This makes removal and refit much easier; it is a lot easier to refit the front plate with the motor in place than you might think. Trust me. Try it and see.

Bushing puller

One corollary to Murphy's Law reminds us that the more rarely an automotive procedure must be performed, the more expensive and specialized (and hard-to-find) is the requisite tool. It is always deeply satisfying to short-circuit this truism; the following tool costs virtually nothing and is simplicity itself.

The bushings in the front torsion bar tubes of your 356 (or old VW) don't have to be replaced every day, it is true, but if for some reason one or all eight must come out well, they gotta come out, period. The set up illustrated here will do the job as well as Factory Tool VW272. The basic principle, for both the inner, smaller, plastic bushing and for the outer, larger, caged rollers, is to get behind the object to be pulled with an oval washer on a piece of threaded rod. Get three flat washers, one for 5/8 in. bolts

387

Bushing Puller Front Torsion Bar Tubes

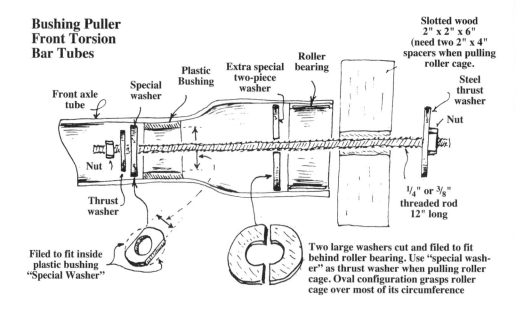

Front axle tube

Nut

Thrust washer

Special washer

Plastic Bushing

Extra special two-piece washer

Roller bearing

Slotted wood 2" x 2" x 6" (need two 2" x 4" spacers when pulling roller cage.

Steel thrust washer

Nut

$1/4$" or $3/8$" threaded rod 12" long

Filed to fit inside plastic bushing "Special Washer"

Two large washers cut and filed to fit behind roller bearing. Use "special washer" as thrust washer when pulling roller cage. Oval configuration grasps roller cage over most of its circumference

and two for $3/4$ in. bolts (respective overall diameters: $1 \, 3/4$ in. and $– 2$ in.), at the hardware store and cut and file them to shape. The larger diameter of the oval washer should be no more than 1 mm less than the inner diameter of the axle tube at the location of the bushing. The smaller diameter of the oval disc(s) should be small enough so that you can poke it through the bushing (on the threaded rod) it is designed to pull. I thought it prudent to make the larger of the two puller discs in two pieces, using both $3/4$ in. flat washers, so that the maximum possible area on the outer perimeter of this take-apart disc contacts the relatively thin-walled and hence fragile bearing cage. If welded together, the two pieces would no longer fit through the cage. To do the pulling I used a $1/4$ in. piece of all-thread 12 in. long, but a $3/8$ in. size would be sturdier. Place at least one flat washer (small hole) behind the special oval discs. A couple of wooden 2 x 4 in. scraps under the slotted wood frame will give the caged roller room to get out of the tube; this isn't needed for the inner bushing. Set up the tool, crank on the nut with a wrench, and out pop your

bushings. Cha, cha, cha!

Vol. 8, No. 4 Dick Pike

Welcome to the second installment of your Original Amateur 356 Tool Hour. This time, we look at a couple of homely devices that just might tip the odds in your favor when you venture to play that ever-alluring game; purchasing used Porsche parts.

Motor Test-Rig
The next time someone offers you a "bargain" 356 or VW motor that "ran when we took it out of the car last week (or month, or year, or whenever)," spring this one on him and make sure it really does, and how well. This setup will enable you to run a motor out of the car, virtually anywhere, to trace leaks more effectively, to take compression readings, to test electrical accessories, and to tune carburetors. All this rig involves is a Porsche voltage regulator, an on-off switch, starter button, and warning lights for oil pressure and generator installed in a U-shaped panel of 16 gauge steel (about 6 x 18 in. overall) that is bolted to an old VW (or Porsche) transaxle case

via the side-plate studs, plus the starter motor.

The components are wired such that they comprise a mini-electrical system, complete with the requisite wires that go to the engine bolted to your test rig: three leads to the generator, one to the coil, and one to the oil-pressure indicator. I'm too lazy to make up a wiring diagram for this, but honest, it's not that esoteric! If I can do it anyone can. You also need a battery (take one out of a running car so it will be fresh) and a fuel source. My favorite fuel container is a spare Porsche tank, complete with fuel cock, but a nicely-soldered outlet spigot on a gallon container with a convenient handle or hook for hanging on the garage wall above the test-rig is okay too. Just be careful with gasoline. Get fancy and add a tach and oil pressure and temperature gauges to an enlarged panel, if you like.

To use the rig, first set the motor on a stable and handy resting place (like the motor dolly I described last time),

and bolt the test rig to the motor. Attach battery leads, low-tension wiring, and fuel line. Fire it up. Don't worry about the torque from your mighty mill twisting the assembly off the stand onto the floor and starting a conflagration. If the test-stand or dolly is stable, you have nothing to fear. In fact, the Porsche four-banger somehow seems a little impotent and naked, out there all by itself! Run it up to 4 or 5 grand: it still doesn't intimidate. I used the setup to locate a pinhole leak in a case by running the motor without the shrouding, and to check various swap-meet purchases, such as fuel pumps, generators, and voltage regulators. Believe me, this is the way to set carburetor float levels! Just be careful where you point those tail pipes: this setup is to be run in the great out-of-doors, not in your basement or apartment.

Axle-Checking Jig

Ever pick up a Porsche or VW half-shaft (to replace what you bent that

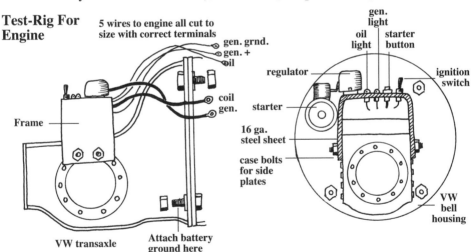

Test-Rig For Engine

5 wires to engine all cut to size with correct terminals

gen. grnd.
gen. +
oil
coil
gen.

Frame

VW transaxle

Attach battery ground here

gen. light
oil light
starter button
regulator
ignition switch
starter
16 ga. steel sheet
case bolts for side plates
VW bell housing

Wire all components using Porsche or VW wiring diagram and common sense. Battery hot lead goes to starter. Set engine on dolly – no need to brace against torque when starting or running. Best fuel supply setup is extra Porsche gas tank and fuel cock, hose. Don't forget to allow for lots of ventilation! Tach and oil temperature and pressure gauges may be added if desired.

Axle Miking Jig

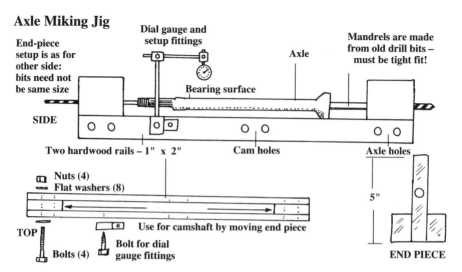

End-piece setup is as for other side: bits need not be same size

Dial gauge and setup fittings

Axle

Mandrels are made from old drill bits – must be tight fit!

Bearing surface

SIDE

Two hardwood rails – 1" x 2"   **Cam holes**   **Axle holes**

Nuts (4)
Flat washers (8)

5"

Use for camshaft by moving end piece

TOP

Bolt for dial gauge fittings

Bolts (4)

END PIECE

night in the rain you sideswiped a curb at speed in a strange neighborhood), only to find after a visit to the machine shop, or much worse – from a ruined wheel bearing and yet another R&R of the same parts, that the used axle has 0.005" or so of whip in it? Hey, you can't eyeball even 0.010" whip in a shaft, let alone the 0.0015" urged upon us by the Factory. So how do you get an instant verdict on a candidate halfshaft right on the spot? I've found one solution. Take your dial gauge (with its accompanying setup hardware) and this wooden jig to the junk yard or swap meet and never get burned again. I went through a dozen supposedly "*okay*" shafts at a reputable local salvage yard before turning up two that were within spec (the gents behind the counter were very accommodating). Make the frame from hardwood; use old drill bits as the mandrels, which must be an interference fit in the drilled holes in the end pieces. The bolted joints must be snug as well. Drill the hole for the dial gauge accessories wherever it is convenient for getting your gauge to bear on the wheel-bearing surface of the axle.   Hardly professional, but it works just fine, is cheap and very easy to lug around with you. Use a hammer or whatever to get the mandrels snug

into the dimples at each end of the shaft. Whip this out and people will know you as one serious seeker-after-straight-axles (or camshafts).

Vol. 8, No. 5 Dick Pike

Hello again, seekers! We are gathered together here for yet another session on shade-tree tool technology. Do you lack flexibility in your garage space? Do you want to overhaul your pet 356s front end all by yourself? Are you otherwise up-against-the-wall over some pressing (or pulling) problem? Fear not and read on.

Car Dolly
   If you've ever had to play "musical shells" (that old shell game) with two or three non-running 356s in a typical suburban two-car garage, then you know what this thing is good for. Mobility for an immobile 356. It nicely complements the ingenious and more permanent (and more involved) storage tips presented by Dave Seeland and Mark Turczyn last year (V. 7, No. 6). This is a cheapo 4-wheel edition of the Factory's 3-wheeler; there must be a dozen variants of this one by now. All you need are four four-foot 4 x 4 in. lumbers, a 2 x 4 in. diagonal brace, and four industrial-

quality heavy-duty swivel casters, plus the necessary carriage and lag bolts to get it together. This is so uncomplicated that it makes a very nice family project. Now you can roll those 356 shells around the garage, carport, and/or driveway all by yourself. Getting a 356 up onto one of these things is a snap: jack one end of the car up and slide the dolly underneath. Remember that the car's center of gravity will change if you remove say, the motor and transaxle, so plan accordingly. If you want the car way up off the ground for ease of work underneath (or storage!), simply add more 4 x 4s. Then you will probably have to use jack stands to get the car high enough to fit all this cribbing underneath. Happy rolling!

Bushing Press Plus

If you've thought that one of these heavy-duty Springfield No. 500 Universal Hub and Gear pullers is good for little other than recalcitrant brake drums, guess again. Aside from a micrometer, a power drill, and a large profane vocabulary, I can't think of many more useful or versatile tools. I've yet to pull a drum with this thing, but I have R&R'd link and king pins, axle-tube flanges, transmission shafts (seriously), and once managed to draw an impossibly-rusted spring plate from a rear torsion bar. It also, in a pinch, removes tight rear-axle bearings that need not be reused. The trick, of course, lies in made-up accessories you use with the frame and its big forcing screw. Essential are an 8 x 8 x $3/4$ in., steel plate drilled for three $7/8$ in. diameter holes (two will do quite well) in the right places (lay out puller frame on plate to see where these are; refer to diagram for the general idea), and a pair of $5/8$ in. threaded rods about 20 in. long, plus a handful of $5/8$ in. bolts, nuts, and washers. The plate plus the three puller arms (two holes each) supplied with the tool will do your link-pin bushings. The plate and the long threaded rods will do king pins and some work on gearbox shafts. The frame, screw, and a metal (or hardwood) 3-hole anvil will do more gear shafts and the axle flange. The two "gear puller" arms that come

Car Dolly

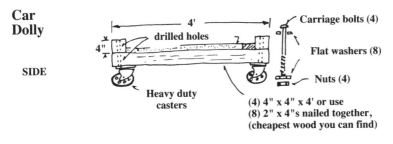

SIDE

4'

drilled holes

4"

Carriage bolts (4)

Flat washers (8)

Nuts (4)

Heavy duty casters

(4) 4" x 4" x 4' or use
(8) 2" x 4"s nailed together,
(cheapest wood you can find)

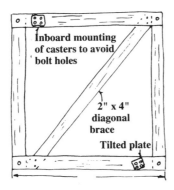

BOTTOM

Inboard mounting
of casters to avoid
bolt holes

2" x 4"
diagonal
brace

Tilted plate

I used lag bolts to fasten casters, two for each caster. Use big ones.

Casters must swivel freely. If you use four bolts, tilt mounting plate to avoid splitting wood

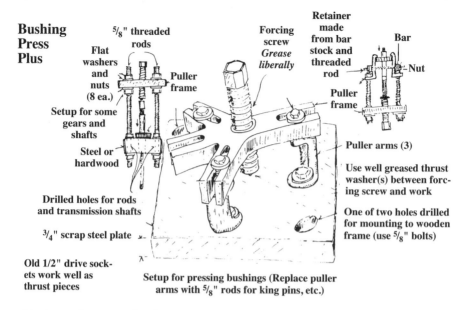

Bushing Press Plus

⅝" threaded rods

Flat washers and nuts (8 ea.)

Setup for some gears and shafts

Steel or hardwood

Drilled holes for rods and transmission shafts

¾" scrap steel plate

Old 1/2" drive sockets work well as thrust pieces

Puller frame

Forcing screw *Grease liberally*

Retainer made from bar stock and threaded rod

Bar

Nut

Puller frame

Puller arms (3)

Use well greased thrust washer(s) between forcing screw and work

One of two holes drilled for mounting to wooden frame (use ⅝" bolts)

Setup for pressing bushings (Replace puller arms with ⅝" rods for king pins, etc.)

with the tool are good, when combined with the threaded rods, for the balance of the gearbox work. The threaded rod extends the puller's capacity considerably, but for most applications you will need to make up a jury-rigged device to keep the puller jaws from spreading and losing their grip on the gear or whatever. I've made up mine from steel bar stock and some 12 x ¼ in. threaded rod, and it has worked well. I'd be very interested to learn of any other ways you folks have learned to use this type of puller. Surely a proper hydraulic floor press is the way to go for The Serious Enthusiast, but many seemingly "impossible" jobs can be handled easily with the relatively inexpensive rig described here.

Vol. 9, No. 5 David Seeland

Valve Spring Compressor

There are many reasons for having a valve spring compressor. Valve springs on late 356s and 912s are progressively wound and should be installed with the widely spaced coils near the valve keeper end of the valve. Based on a small sample, a lot of people that do Porsche head work don't

know this! While the spring is out replace it with a soft thin spring out of your junk box (or the hardware store), install the retainer and keepers, cut a piece of wire to the proper length and use it to check the installed spring length. Add or remove shims to get it right or your valves may float at 4000 rpm. Be sure the top shim is the special thick one (another often neglected point).

I have always borrowed a "C" type valve spring compressor. I decided it would be much more convenient to have my own so I built one (Figs. 1 next page) of two by fours, plywood and some mega-nails (steel rod will do). The real thing (P7) may be a bit more esthetic but it is also much more difficult to fabricate. The only hang-up you might have on the two by four P7 is the metal keeper extracting device that attaches to the lever arm. I used a scrap piece of chrome plated steel tube left over from a plumbing project and two strap-iron scraps. (To use a "C" valve spring compressor you must have a similar device so you can get at the exhaust valve – but it should have a section of tube at both ends).

356 Valve Spring Compressor

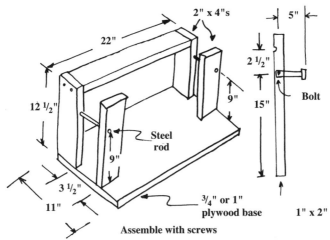

2" x 4"s
22"
5"
2 1/2"
9"
15"
Bolt
12 1/2"
Steel rod
9"
9"
3 1/2"
11"
3/4" or 1" plywood base
1" x 2"
Assemble with screws

Vol. 11, No. 4 Richard Miller

Generator Spring Inserting Tool

I recently had an unusual generator problem and in the process of fixing it, I made a trick tool you might find handy. The generator light had come on and an output voltage measurement read zero volts, so I pulled the brush cover. The lower brush spring had lost its tension and was not pushing the brush against the armature commutator. If I held the brush down with my finger, the red light would go out with the engine running. The brush length was above the holder so I assumed the spring was somehow defective. I didn't want to pull the generator and fan shroud so I designed the tool

shown in the sketch to insert a new spring. The spring is wound with a flat tang which slips over a post next to the brush, and while it is easy to slide off with a small screwdriver, getting a new one on is a problem. If you wind the spring onto the tool and offer it up against the post, it's easy to push it the rest of the way on with a screwdriver. This is a little awkward done upside down in a mirror but I practiced on the top one until I could do it in about 30 seconds. Try it without the tool for comparison.

Vol. 15, No. 1 John Fabac

Hello, Dolly

Aw, come on, admit it. How many

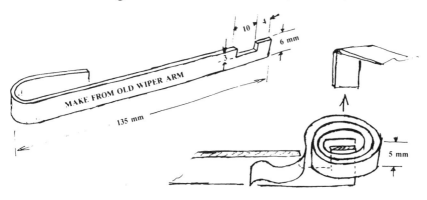

MAKE FROM OLD WIPER ARM
10
6 mm
135 mm
5 mm

393

of you have put your relationships with the opposite sex on the line because of your long-term commitment to the restoration of a Zuffenhausen Beastie? You paid too much for it in the first place; the cost of parts is skyrocketing and it's taking much more time than you ever thought possible. So much so, it seems to be permanently fused to the garage floor; right through the jack stands. As a result, you have neither the room to work around it, nor can your beloved park the room-wagon in the space you said she would always have for her own.

Cry no more, I have just what you need, a roll-about dolly. With a few lengths of low-grade two-by-six (1 $1/2$ x 5 $1/2$ in.) lumber, four salvaged ball-bearings casters and an infinite variety of screws, nails, construction adhesive, nuts and bolts, you can gain a little breathing room and re-join the ranks of the loved. The accompanying drawings (courtesy of my friend, Tommy Gilbreath) will help a lot.

Begin by cutting all of the pieces of two-by-six according to specifications. Assemble as shown. Remove the engine and heater cans. Raise the 356 way up in the air. My technique began by permanently fastening four jack stands to creosoted railroad tie end-pieces. Under the advice of my attorney, I'll let you use your own creativity from this point on.

Lower the car so the notches in the rear uprights cradle the torsion bar tubes. The tallest front upright carries no weight. It protrudes up through the triangular opening formed by the diagonal member and the pan. This piece serves only to position the scabbed short front upright so that it can support the pan from below. Caution! This dolly has only been checked out with C coupes and cabs.

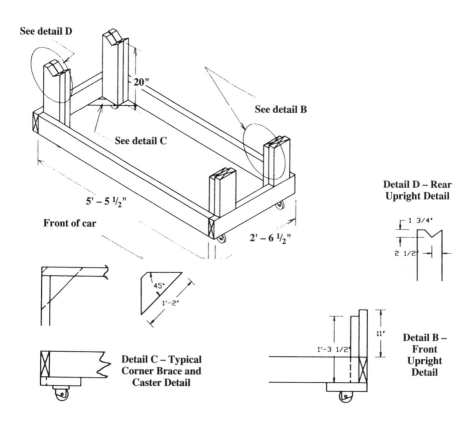

See detail D

20"

See detail B

See detail C

5' – 5 $1/2$"

Front of car

2' – 6 $1/2$"

Detail D – Rear Upright Detail

1 3/4"

2 1/2"

45°

1'–2'

Detail C – Typical Corner Brace and Caster Detail

1'–3 1/2"

11"

Detail B – Front Upright Detail

394

Chapter

Trim

Doors

Vol. 7, No. 2 Micheal Hudick

Installing Furry Strips

I recently installed the furry strips for the roll up windows in my 1960 Roadster, and found the easiest way differs substantially from the technique described in the shop manual. As always, the second door was far easier than the first.

Unfortunately for us, Porsche did not design the windows to roll down far enough for access to all of the fasteners which hold the furry strip and chrome trim to the door. So the window must be moved out of the way. To begin, remove the trim from the door, being careful not to crack the black escutcheons surrounding the two handles. Then, with the window rolled down, remove the 10 mm (head-size) bolts which secure the regulator and carefully lower the assembly enough to clear the phillips head screws holding the furry strip. Detach the chrome trim with old strip and separate. Clean any components which will be reused, then measure and cut the length of furry strip to be installed.

At this time, it is necessary to properly position the strip and pre-punch the holes so that everything fits during installation. I found it easiest to run all the screws through the strip and into the chrome trim (prior to installation) to pre-size the holes and insure that they lined up. Glue the out-side rubber trim to the chrome strip, then remove all screws but the end ones. Run two nails through the next two holes in from the edges to align all the trim holes with the holes in the door, and last, carefully turn in the end screws until bottomed. When screwing, one must be careful to hit the holes, otherwise a perceptible bend in the trim will occur. Also, if any screws were broken during removal of the assembly, it is best to clean out the remnants so that the original screw holes can be used. This is because the original positions cause the bottomed screw heads to become invisibly buried in the fur.

Continue by greasing the window rails (Roadster remember), and the regulator, and then reinstall the window assembly. Insert the rubber wiper into the chrome piece. Run the window up with the top on and the door closed to check the fit. Adjust the rails in or out to get that comfortable interference between glass and rubber; that is, without air gaps and not so much compression that the rubber seals distort (this leads to rapid cracking). At this time, the door handle can most easily be removed for key making or oiling simply by running a long screw driver through the inspection hole (window up) and removing the one attachment screw. Otherwise, continue by reinstalling the door trim, observing that the holes in the door were usually covered (with the same vinyl as Porsche used on the interior) to keep out the rain (for those of you that engage in such driving). Also notice that on the inside of the large panel, just forward of center, there exists a large flat spring steel component which is used to catch the inside of the door. This forms the concave pocket on the forward part of the door.

The rest of the procedure is fairly straight forward and even if a mistake is made, quite easy to undo. About the only precaution I take is to check the positions of the window crank and the door lever to make sure they do not interfere with my knees (window full up full down).

Vol. 7, No. 6 Rich Williams

Installing Side Window Seal
Side window seal gasket material comes in a single piece which must be cut into four fitting dissimilar pieces before installation. Each piece is enough, with about four inches to spare, for one side of the car. If your old seals are factory originals, or fit well, you are in luck. Just use the old pieces for patterns. An electric knife makes very nice clean, accurate cuts.

The old seals on my car fit badly, so I decided to start from scratch. The first thing I found was that none of the corners of the window opening are square. A carpenter's T-bevel, sometimes called a "devil square" is a real lifesaver for transferring the proper angles from the opening to the rubber. Your local hardware store should have one for about two dollars. This nifty little item looks like a small carpenter's square, but has a hinge and a setscrew so that it can be set to any angle desired. Just take off the old rubber, set the T-bevel's arms and apex snugly into the corner, tighten the setscrew, and voila!, you have the angle

you need.

Next, lay the thick arm of the T-bevel along the edge of a writing tablet and draw a line on the top sheet along the thin arm. Immediately, draw a small mark on the side of the angle you will be working with. You will be bisecting this angle for the pieces fitting into the two top corners of the window. If you accidentally bisect the wrong side, you probably won't find out until you notice that the two pieces of rubber don't fit together, and by then you'll have wasted a whole big piece of rubber.

The angle you have just traced can be transferred as-is to the rubber for fitting into the bottom corners of the window. At the top, however, you must fit two pieces of rubber into one corner at a mirrored angle. Leaving the sheet of paper on which you drew the angle attached to the tablet, fold the edge over so that it lies along the line you made with the T-bevel. Be sure you have the right side of the line. That should give you the same angle you took from the window opening. Then, fold that angle in half and you will have the angle at which you will be cutting the rubber for the top corners.

Now you are ready to mark the rubber for cutting. It will help to remember that all cuts will be made so that the longest part of the rubber is along the spine. The piece of molding will probably be quite curly from shipping and storage. It will be easier to work with at this point if you run a rod through it to straighten it out. First, take a carpenter's square and mark the length across the spine of the molding. This is very important in getting a good fit. Then, use the folded piece of paper to mark the angle for cutting or transfer the angle to the T-bevel and use that. When making the cuts, use both the perpendicular line on the spine and the angle on the tubular surface as guides.

If you do make a mistake and cut a

piece too short, the easiest place to add length is in the middle. That way, you won't have to contend with the odd angles you have at the ends. Make all your cuts square, and the metal track should hold the pieces together in a clean, tight joint. You might want to use a flexible adhesive, but this probably isn't necessary.

Bumper

Vol. 4, No. 1 D. L. Oughterson

Bumper Deco Insert Installation
This is not to imply that you people didn't come through. D. L. Oughterson from Marshfield, MA, got a letter to me shortly before the holiday stating that rubber bumper deco inserts should be allowed to swim in very hot water. The results should be that this softens the little fellas making them more agreeable. He closed with the warning that when the rubber cools, it shrinks. I will attempt this if I ever get the bumpers painted.

Vol. 8, No. 1 Richard Miller

1954 Bumper Guard Restoration
Brief restoration note: original bumper uprights in 1954 were anodized aluminum, but with a slightly hazy surface – almost iridescent. Mine had suffered on many curbs and from doing what they were obviously not intended to do – like stop marauding Cadillacs. I removed them from bumpers, removed studs, (a trick in itself, helps to have a steady hand and curbside drill bit and helicoil set) and stripped the anodize by a brief dunk in a hot caustic at the local platers. This is necessary as the anodize is very hard and makes refinishing difficult. Next, I annsal the aluminum to make it softer for straightening. Light up your oxy-acetylene and make soot by burning straight acetylene. Deposit a medium coating of soot on the

uprights (and everything else within 50 feet), then turn on the oxygen. Adjust a neutral, gentle flame and gradually heat the uprights until they get just hot enough to evaporate the soot. Be *very* careful because this temperature is near the melting point of some alloys. Let them cool and then, using various body working tools (hammer, dolly, block of wood, clamps, etc.) reshape them until they all look alike and fit the bumpers, then file, sand and polish. Don't put studs, or helicoils in until after the next step which is: find a plating shop which will do a type 2 clear anodize with *no etch* as per *mil spec 8625* ($2/10$ mil thick). Make sure uprights are well polished as any scratches are going to stay there after anodize. The local shop was reluctant to guarantee results (some alloys turn black or disintegrate) but since this has been done before to these particular pieces of aluminum it worked. The result cannot be duplicated by chrome plating or by polishing and lacquering – just the right original touch.

Vol. 16, No. 4 Del Johnston

Bumper Guard Restoration Revisited
Those of you who strive for originality in restoration on some of the early 356As and pre-As have probably been having difficulty renewing and/or replacing bumper overriders. Even if you find these parts in so-called "NOS" inventory, they are generally scratched beyond minimally acceptable concours condition.
After a thoroughly frustrating search for acceptable parts, I did what I always do when all else fails – call Dick Miller in San Diego. Dick reminded me of his earlier article relevant to reconditioning these parts; but felt because of the California EPA and other *well-meaning* local agencies, some of the processes had been discontinued. Upon initial investigation I found Dick to be correct, as usual and

I then set about to find a way to get the job done.

Fortunately my previous company had a factory in Germany, and I was able to enlist the aid of my friends there to run down the original supplier of these parts to Porsche and determine their manufacturing process. It turns out there were two suppliers but their process was the same, i.e. thin-walled castings of three-nine (99.9%) aluminum with a polished, anodized surface.

Borrowing from my German and San Diego connections, I was able to produce parts which duplicate the original article to a very high degree of acceptability.

The best way to start is to have parts that need as little straightening and welding as possible. If yours are really bad, I suggest you visit your local used parts supplier and buy some old originals that need the least amount of straightening and no welding. Beware of reproduction parts – they do not turn out the same. The process after this has to be done sequentially or the end product will not be satisfactory and the cost can get quite high. Also, you should keep all of the parts together since there are minimum batch charges which are the same for 1 or 20 pieces. Here's how:

1. Remove the studs and lock nuts from the parts as anything but pure aluminum will react disastrously to the process.

2. Have the batch of parts *stripped* of the existing surface anodize. Your plater can do this in their hot caustic tank but they should avoid leaving the parts immersed for more time than it takes to just remove the anodize, exposing the softer, pure aluminum surface beneath.

3. If you are an expert in working and forming aluminum, you are well prepared for the next step. If not, you need to search for someone who can *renew* these parts to their original shape. I tried several shops before I found my artist. Yes – this really is an art and the cost is entirely dependent on the condition. The renewed parts should be free from dents, weld beads, and deep scratches. It really helps if you have a part that is not bent and torn for a sample.

4. After you are happy with the renewal and have your parts together in a batch, take them to your plater for the *bright dip* step of the procedure. This is an electro-polish process which etches the surface both inside and outside. This step is essential to clean the inside of the parts from the effects of stripping/renewing and leaves that shiny, bright finish as supplied by the factory.

5. The next step is to *buff* the outside surface to a high polish with special attention to removing all scratches and blemishes. Anything that you see on the parts now is going to be there when they are completed. Also, the time between finishing this step and starting the next one should be kept to a minimum as the unprotected aluminum starts to oxidize. Caution, metal polishers vary in competence and quality.

6. Now is when all of your effort in finding a good plater will pay off. I searched the Southern California area and out of about 50 platers contacted, only one would commit to doing the anodize process on small batches of vintage auto parts. The environmental protectionists have stopped this process in Orange and San Diego counties and made it very difficult to perform in Los Angeles county. However, I did find one individual who was interested in the program and was willing to try to duplicate the factory finish. That person is Jesse Fairless; he tried numerous variations of the anodize process before finally duplicating the original finish.

Without intruding on the proprietary aspects of their process, here are the steps they perform:

6.1 Vapor degrease and rinse.

6.2 Rack properly to expose the parts to the process and prevent damage from contact.

6.3 Alkaline clean and rinse.

6.4 Deoxidize and rinse.

6.5 Sulfuric acid anodized in accordance with mil-spec MIL-A-8625 TYPE II, Class 1 Clear. The time, temperature and voltage applied during this step is critical to the appearance of the final product. If left in the process too long, the parts will appear dull and cloudy. If too short, they will not receive the proper thickness (.0001 to .0004 inches) of anodize. This is where Jesse was very patient and experimented with the variables to finally produce the correct finish.

6.6 SEAL with a Nickel Acetate wash (Duralox B) to preserve the finish and seal any micro-voids on the surface.

6.7 Final rinse and dry.

6.8 Unrack and package to avoid transit damage.

7. During the time to accomplish the above, you should have sent your studs and nuts out to be Cadmium plated (Type 1) to complement your like new overriders. Now is the time to carefully insert the studs and lock them with the nuts. If they do not screw in easily, run an 8 x 1.25 tap into the holes to clean the threads. A small amount of Never-Seez will facilitate removal if you have to remove them in the future.

8. That's all there is to it. Now, just be careful putting these on the bumper. One scratch or dent and you have to start all over. The last time I had a batch of these restored (mid-1991), it cost about $500 for 9 pieces. That's a little over $50 each, plus your time, for originality. As you can see by the photos, the difference in before and after is really astonishing. It surely beats the chrome-plate or buff and lacquer restoration done by some so-called experts.

Finally, you can restore your 1954 - 1959 (crested) aluminium front hood handle in exactly the same way the overriders are done. As a matter of fact, I did mine all in the same batch.

Aluminum Restoration

Vol. 1, No. 3 Jim Lamb

The Easy Way

To clean the engine deck grilles, remove and put them in an automatic dishwasher, badges and all. They usually come out looking like new if not badly corroded.

Vol. 4, No. 1 Don Fowler

The Hard Way

All Porsches have aluminum trim pieces such as bumper trim, side trim, rocker panel trim, window trim, deck lid grilles and door sill trim. These aluminum parts are pretty when new, but very easily damaged as you have probably already discovered. Some of the parts are no longer available and all are pretty expensive. The ideas suggested below will help you restore many of these items, thus avoiding the cost of replacement.

The 356 and 356A Porsches have raw aluminum trim and trim from these cars are most easily restored. Most 356B through 911 Porsche aluminum trim is protected by a process called "bright dipping." This coating must be removed prior to restoring. Your local plating shop should be able to remove this protective coating although my one experience with this left me with a heavily etched part and the plating shop foreman grumbling about "those Germans." Another simple and less expensive way to remove the coating is by sanding it off with 320 or 400 grit sandpaper as described in step "A" below. A simple test to determine if a part has been bright anodized is to try to polish it with some Simichrome polish. If the rag turns black and the part becomes more shiny, then it has not been anodized.

The polish will have little or no effect on a protected part.

The problems most often encountered with aluminum trim items are pitting (corrosion), stone nicks and scratches. Parts that are heavily pitted are almost impossible to save since often times the pitting goes very deeply into the metal. If that is your problem a new part may very well be the only acceptable solution. However, if you have stone nicks or scratches try the following:

A) Sand the part with 400 grit sandpaper using a mixture of water and lots of liquid detergent. Sand until all traces of pits and scratches are removed and the part has a smooth, satin finish. (Note: Many times small dents can be removed by prying or tapping from the backside and then filing smooth with a fine toothed flat file followed by sanding).

B) Polish the part vigorously with a wet Brillo pad using long, lengthwise strokes. This will remove the sand scratches and leave the part with a smooth, fairly shiny finish.

C) Obtain a hard felt buffing wheel for use in an electric drill. Also purchase some buffing wheel compound (Sears sells a set of four compounds 112896 that is ideal). Put your drill in a vise if possible. Start buffing the part with Tripoli (brown compounds] applied to the buffing wheel and be careful! The aluminum parts are very soft and bend easily, and are almost impossible to straighten perfectly. After buffing with Tripoli, buff the part with red rouge and white rouge in that order. Each grade of compound is a little finer than the preceding one and as you use them in sequence the part will become more smooth and glossy. If the buffing wheel loads up with aluminum while buffing, clean it with a screwdriver or other sharp object while the buffing wheel is rotating. Finish the process by polishing the part by hand with Simichrome polish which will impart a near chrome-like shine. Caution: Wear safety glasses while buffing – you can't drive your Porsche with the shiny aluminum trim if you're blind!

If the aluminum part in question is only slightly scratched and it has not been anodized the finish can be restored by merely buffing with Brillo and then polishing with Simichrome. Your newly repaired/polished part will be un-protected and will require occasional polishing with Simichrome. This gives you the advantage of having a part with more shine than it did if it was previously anodized and also future repairs will be easier. Parts not subject to much wear/abuse such as the aluminum beading on the dash and doors of 356 A and B cars can be protected if you wish by spraying them with a coat of clear metal protector sold under many brand names. I recommend the polyurethane type sprays rather than clear lacquer sprays.

Coachbuilder Badges

Vol. 9, No. 5 Richard Miller

1954 - 1955, Which Badge is Right?
Comments on coachbuilder badges remind me that I wanted to put one of those nifty cloisonne badges on my 1954 coupe, but it wouldn't fit. The holes in the fender were too far apart but they did match the later style aluminum version. You can tell which badge belongs by measuring the hole spacing, if the rust termites didn't get there first. The cloisonne badge hole, are 32 mm apart, the aluminum badges are 37 mm. My 1955 Speedster #80799, has this style.

By the way, the term cloisonne is not correct for the various Porsche badges, emblems, etc. – they are really "Champleve" – look it up.

Windshield Trim

Vol. 9, No. 5 Richard Miller

Restoring Windshield Trim

A helpful hint on aluminum window trim - the small clips which bridge the ends of the two halves are still available – PN 644.541.921.00 – except that these, if you are doing an early car, are too long (40 mm). The solution is to cut them in half with a fine saw and you then have two 20 mm clips. The trim is only available second hand (*availble September 1994*) – I found some and by annealing (read heat softening) and straightening, heliarcing holes, filing smooth, I was ready to feed them to my buffer. After making pretzels a few times, I got the technique worked out and they now look like new. Just remember to put them in the rubber before installing the windshield.

Luggage Racks

Vol. 17, No. 3 Brad Ripley

Original vs. Period Accessory Racks

For any long distance traveling in small sports cars of the 1950s, a good luggage rack was a necessity. The car manufacturers filled the need with "official" racks delivered with the new car or through dealer parts departments. Aftermarket accessory makers also produced racks, usually of lesser quality and certainly at lower cost. Probably from the earliest days racks were available for Porsches from both sources.

Probably as early as 1952 Reutter offered their first rack. This rack is described in an undated Reutter brochure which lists "silver-bronze" and "color of the car" (no chrome) versions. Also, metal ski brackets are offered in a coupe and a Cabriolet version. Holes were to be drilled in the engine lid and the brackets were rein-forcement pieces.

In October, 1956, threaded brackets were provided in the four corners of the grille opening to make it far easier to mount the rack. The design of this rack had squared off ends and other design differences. This rack is first mentioned in the earliest 356A accessories brochure (Order No. QA 38). In a later brochure (Feb., 1959) the rack is listed as available either with silver (paint), in the color of the car or chrome. However, most, if not all, Reutter racks were supplied in a hammer-tone silver paint.

These later Reutter racks differed slightly in construction, although at first glance they all appear to be the same. Since the Reutter racks remained in the accessory program through the 356C, they were drilled for both single and twin grille engine lid mounting points.

At least one aftermarket manufacturer, American Carry Products Co. (AMCO), made a simple tubular rack for 356s. Some early single grille versions were made but mostly the twin grille versions are now found at swap meets.

A new and larger luggage rack was announced in *Christophorus*, May, 1960 (No. 27 English) as an addition to Porsche's accessory program. This was for the now well known Leitz "butterfly" rack which the announcement said "will again be available as an accessory".

One has to conclude that the chrome-plated version of the Reutter rack had been discontinued or never was produced. In any event, this new rack, at about $31 was about twice as expensive as the painted Reutter rack. It was larger and came with eight leather straps to hold four pairs of skis. Longer and wider leather strap assemblies were available separately to hold suitcases to the racks which were also listed in the various accessory catalogs.

Leitz continued on producing racks

for 911 models and to this day a luggage/ski rack is offered by Porsche for all models.

License Light

Vol. 16, No. 5 Brett Johnson

Fixing What The Plater Ruined

About a year ago, I took my totally disassembled non-dented shine-down license light housing (from my 1955 sunroof coupe restoration project) to the best local plater. I pointed to the lovely Hella logo and told them to be very careful when buffing because it was very important that it remain in its pristine original condition.

When I went back to collect it several months later, I noted with some distress that they had apparently let one of their trained bears do the buffing and had screwed up the left side of the logo. Of course, they said it was not possible to avoid this type of damage, which is *not* true. I filed my disagreement with the complaint department and left.

I conferred with my local fine metal plater, who does not do chrome and other such common metals. He suggested that I contact a gun engraver. $50 later I had a very nicely restored logo that looked just like it used to. It wasn't even necessary to replate the housing!

Side Trim

Vol. 17, No. 6 Cole Scrogham

Fitting Beltline Side Trim

One of the most unusual and typically elegant exterior additions to a 356 is the "Speedster" side trim, offered on Speedsters, Roadsters and Conv. D's as normal practice and as an option on all other body styles.

This trim is essentially a hollow aluminum strip about a half inch wide that clips and bolts to each side of the car in four pieces. The trim is especially attractive on an A coupe for some reason, it follows the rounded lines of the car well and adds just a spark of reflection to the side. Many owners are confused about this trim, thinking it to be an "only" Speedster option, but this is not true. While all Speedsters have the trim (yes, except for GTs – put your pen down), the option was offered on standard production 356s all the way through 1965.

The addition of this trim to a car that did not originally have it proves to be a difficult undertaking. The original holes were about $1/4$ in. diameter and aligned along the car in as straight a line as the 356 body would allow. Replicating this is extremely difficult, to the point I would not advise updating unless you have a car ready for paint (because it will need to be if you mess up). But for cars that do have the holes, clean out that bondo (or "leveler" if you are offended by that term) and find them. There are six holes in each fender and door, do not be fooled by extra holes or ones not $1/4$ in. in diameter.

Once you have located the holes, you are ready to begin. Buy a reproduction side trim set from Stoddard, or search for an original at a swap meet if you have time and money. The reproductions are very good. Take the set and polish the daylights out of it until you are happy with the finish. You will not be able to polish the trim very well once it is installed because of the proximity to the paint. Once the finish is to your liking, lay out all eight pieces and study them. The fender pieces are easy because they have the rounded ends that taper into the body for a finished look. The door pieces have a straight cut on one end and a 45 degree cut on the other end.

What's this? – two of the fender pieces have this angle too. They are the front fender trim. The front fender trim and door trim are designed to mesh together so that they look like one continuous strip with the door closed, they neatly tuck into the door opening when the door opens. Otherwise, the trim would run into the leading door edge each time the door opens. Also notice two small pieces designed to fit just behind the door handles. Do not lose them in the shuffle, make sure you have all eight pieces.

Start with the side of your choice. It is probably better to give the right side the first shot though, practice on the side you don't see as much. Fill in the center holes with side trim clips, and leave the first and last holes in the fender (i.e. outermost) open for "T" bolts to secure the ends. The clips install by pushing the squared off end through the hole first, then sliding the rounded off end through the same hole to lock the clip in place. This is best done with a sharpened paint paddle (not a screwdriver) to avoid paint damage when you slip. Once the clips are in, you can slide the T-bolt into place using the channel in the trim. If the T-bolt does not allow you to move the trim piece to the edge of the door opening, cut it off a little shorter (the T-bolt, not the door) until it fits just to the edge of the door opening. The door trim and handle piece may give you trouble here because of fitted aluminum plugs in the ends of the trim to finish off the edges. These plugs can be carefully removed with a flat punch and hammer, then reinstalled after the T-bolts are in place. The procedure is the same for the rest of the pieces except for the door handle piece. This short trim is held in place with a single T-bolt.

Be careful when installing to lightly push the front and rear T-bolt studs through the body at the same time so that one or the other does not gouge the paint, then push the trim into place over the clips to snap in place. The T-bolt nuts should be tightened snugly,

but not over tightened, or you risk a slight dimple in the body around the trim. You may have to slightly bend the trim around the radius of the fender for a consistent look (do it off the car!) with no gaps between the car and the fender. Also be careful that the door piece is tightened prior to any attempt to open the door, or it will take a chunk of fender with it when it goes. Hopefully, all these caveats will come in handy, for each one has a story (or scratch) to tell.

It should be noted that Speedsters did not originally use T-bolts at all and that Roadsters had them only on the front hole of the front fender trim and the rear hole of the rear fender trim. All other areas were held in place by clips mounted to the body.

Also before attempting to fit new strips, they should be carefully bent to fit the body, by making small bends, a little bit at a time and offering them up to the car until an acceptable approximation to the cars contours is acheived – September 1994

Rubber

Vol. 4, No. 4 Brett Johnson

Rubber Preservatives

I had an inquiry concerning rubber preservation for items such as door seals and rear 1/4 window seals. The two methods I am familiar with are Armor-all and glycerine. Glycerine is by far the least expensive.

Vol. 5, No. 3 Charlie White

Blackening Rubber

For years I have tried a variety of products and preparations to restore and "blacken" the rubber parts on my 356 Porsches, including the tires and trim. One product that you see a lot in auto parts stores is something called tire black which is painted on. The problem with this product is that it tends to visibly streak, and it leaves the surface of the rubber with an unnatural shine. It's also not too good for paint.

My approach has been to find something to make the rubber look "new". This "new" look is very black and with a minimum of shine. Soap and water are a good start, at least for getting the dirt and grease off. But as rubber ages, it tends to crack and turn grey. You can imagine what the heat does to rubber here in Arizona. One problem we have is that the water in Arizona contains a lot of minerals and when the water evaporates, after washing the car, the minerals are left. Over a period of time this mineral residue tends to turn the color of the rubber from black to grey, looks terrible! Maybe you have the same problem.

I've tried shoe polish, but that doesn't work too well and doesn't last. Some of the highly advertised products, and you all know the ones I'm talking about, don't last much longer either. One very effective material is brake fluid which both softens the rubber and makes it very black. I've found this very effective on tires, provided you take care to wipe away all excess. You guessed it though, brake fluid does pose some problems around paint – it ruins it! Because of this, it has to be eliminated for a lot of jobs.

An old friend and fellow Porsche-Pusher recently recommended a product called Dow Corning #4, which comes in a toothpaste-like tube and looks like clear hair grease. Technically it is a "silicone dielectric". What this is I don't know, and I don't know what this product was originally intended to do. Maybe some of your engineer-types have heard of it! But it does wonders on black auto rubber! Rub some of this stuff into the rubber with a soft cloth, taking care to wipe away any excess. You'll notice immediately that it blackens the rubber giving it a "new" appearance with only a minimum of shine (excess shine means you didn't wipe off all the excess). Then let the car sit in the sun for a while to let it "soak in" and then wipe again. I think you all will be pleased with the results.

According to the package label, this stuff will withstand temperature extremes from 20 degrees below zero to 400 degrees above. It does a great job and it lasts a long time (so far it hasn't eaten away my hands!). Seriously, I did the rubber bumpers on my 914 which really looked bad, about eight weeks ago, and they still look fantastic. We had a PCA Zone 8 Concours here several weeks ago (which by the way included in excess of 50% 356 Porsches), and tried this stuff on a number of the 356 entries. The stuff works. Try it, and I think the five bucks you'll spend for a 5.3 oz. tube will be an excellent investment – particularly if you are a concours enthusiast.